Praise for

SUMMER OF FIRE AND BLOOD

"This is a riveting account of a seismic event in German history that conveys a real sense of why so many ordinary people thought they could change the world. Lyndal Roper writes beautifully and displays a compassionate understanding for the protagonists on both sides of this complex and bloody struggle."

—Peter Wilson, author of *The Thirty Years War*

"*Summer of Fire and Blood* is an extraordinary and brilliant book. In Roper's evocatively beautiful, crystal-clear prose, the complex landscapes of early sixteenth-century Germany—physical, psychological, spiritual, social, and political—unfold before our eyes. She shows us the dreams and deeds that shaped the Peasants' War, the greatest popular revolt in western Europe before the French Revolution, and the ways in which that war shaped the future that followed. This is a profound account of an attempt to change the world, a sensational narrative that is both human and humane, illuminating, resonant, and unsettling."   —Helen Castor, author of *She-Wolves*

"*Summer of Fire and Blood* brings the drama, violence, and contingency of the German Peasants' War to vivid life thanks to the unparalleled scholarly and writing skills of historian Roper. There is simply no more compelling or insightful account of this tumultuous mass uprising."

—Joel F. Harrington, author of *The Faithful Executioner*

"Beautifully and sensitively written, *Summer of Fire and Blood* tells the forgotten trauma of the sixteenth century—when thousands of ordinary people risked all they had in the hope of ushering in a new world. It takes the stories of our unlettered, peasant ancestors from the sidelines of history and, recentering them, restores their full humanity. And it warns us that the questions they posed are the very urgent questions that confront us again now."

—Suzannah Lipscomb, author of *Journey Through Tudor England*

"Roper is a breathtaking storyteller. Her explosive reassessment of the Peasants' War is a theological, ecological, and social epic. She shows why the chaotic violence, symbolic arsenal of brotherhood, and maze of dreams and visions should matter to us in the twenty-first century."

—Joanna Bourke, author of *Fear*

SUMMER OF FIRE AND BLOOD

SUMMER OF FIRE AND BLOOD

THE GERMAN PEASANTS' WAR

LYNDAL ROPER

BASIC BOOKS

NEW YORK

Basic Books
Hachette Book Group
1290 Avenue of the Americas, New York, NY 10104
www.basicbooks.com

Printed in the United States of America

First Edition: February 2025

Published by Basic Books, an imprint of Hachette Book Group, Inc. The Basic
Books name and logo is a registered trademark of the Hachette Book Group.

The Hachette Speakers Bureau provides a wide range of authors for speaking
events. To find out more, go to hachettespeakersbureau.com or email
HachetteSpeakers@hbgusa.com.

Basic books may be purchased in bulk for business, educational, or promotional
use. For more information, please contact your local bookseller or the Hachette
Book Group Special Markets Department at special.markets@hbgusa.com.

The publisher is not responsible for websites (or their content) that are not owned
by the publisher.

Print book interior design by Sheryl Kober

Library of Congress Cataloging-in-Publication Data
Names: Roper, Lyndal, author.
Title: Summer of fire and blood : the German peasants' war / Lyndal Roper.
Other titles: German peasants' war
Description: First edition. | New York, NY : Basic Books, [2025] | Includes
bibliographical references and index.
Identifiers: LCCN 2024016050 | ISBN 9781541647053 (hardcover) | ISBN
9781541647039 (ebook)
Subjects: LCSH: Peasants' War, 1524–1525. | Peasants—Germany—Social
conditions—16th century. | Social movements—Germany—History—
16th century. | Germany—Politics and government—1517–1648. |
Reformation—Germany.
Classification: LCC DD182 .R674 2025 | DDC 943/.031—dc23/eng/20240925
LC record available at https://lccn.loc.gov/2024016050

ISBNs: 9781541647053 (hardcover), 9781541647039 (ebook)

LSC-C

Printing 1, 2024

For Martin

CONTENTS

Map: The German Peasants' War, 1524–1526   *x*

Introduction   1

PART ONE: AUTUMN

Chapter 1: Stirrings   9
Chapter 2: Land   37
Chapter 3: Freedom   67

PART TWO: WINTER

Chapter 4: Winter   99
Chapter 5: Lordship   123
Chapter 6: Dreams   147

PART THREE: SPRING

Chapter 7: Early Spring   179
Chapter 8: Movement   213
Chapter 9: High Spring   243
Chapter 10: Brothers   279

PART FOUR: SUMMER

Chapter 11: Summer   319
Chapter 12: Aftermath   343
Conclusion   367

Contents

Acknowledgements   *391*

Abbreviations   *399*

Notes   *401*

Bibliography   *481*

Index   *509*

For Christ redeemed and bought us all with his precious blood,
the lowliest shepherd as well as the greatest lord, with no exceptions.
Thus the Bible proves that we are free and want to be free.

—The Twelve Articles

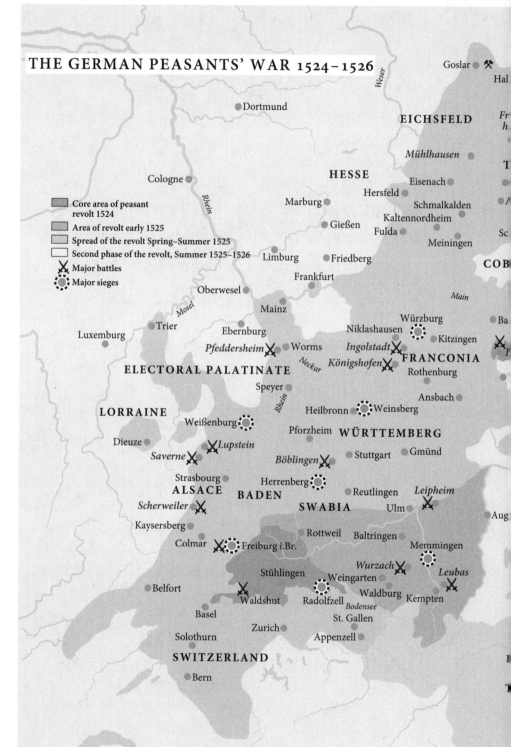

THE GERMAN PEASANTS' WAR 1524–1526

Goslar

Hal

Dortmund

EICHSFELD

Fr
h

Mühlhausen

T

Cologne

HESSE

Eisenach

Hersfeld

Marburg

Schmalkalden

Kaltennordheim

Gießen

Fulda

Sc

Meiningen

Rhein

Core area of peasant
revolt 1524

Area of revolt early 1525

Spread of the revolt Spring–Summer 1525

Second phase of the revolt, Summer 1525–1526

Major battles

Major sieges

Limburg

Friedberg

COB

Frankfurt

Oberwesel

Main

Mosel

Mainz

Würzburg

Ba

Trier

Ebernburg

Niklashausen

Kitzingen

Luxemburg

Pfeddersheim

Worms

Ingolstadt

Königshofen

FRANCONIA

ELECTORAL PALATINATE

Neckar

Rothenburg

Speyer

Ansbach

Rhein

Heilbronn

Weinsberg

LORRAINE

Weißenburg

Pforzheim

WÜRTTEMBERG

Dieuze

Lupstein

Böblingen

Stuttgart

Gmünd

Saverne

Herrenberg

Strasbourg

ALSACE

BADEN

Reutlingen

Leipheim

Scherweiler

SWABIA

Ulm

Aug

Kaysersberg

Rottweil

Baltringen

Colmar

Freiburg i.Br.

Memmingen

Wurzach

Stühlingen

Weingarten

Leubas

Belfort

Waldshut

Radolfzell

Waldburg

Kempten

Basel

Bodensee

St. Gallen

Zurich

SWITZERLAND

Solothurn

Appenzell

Bern

I

T

The German Peasants' War, 1524–1526. Map drawn by Peter Palm.

INTRODUCTION

The German Peasants' War was the greatest popular uprising in western Europe before the French Revolution. Like a vast contagion it spread from southwest Germany through Württemberg, Swabia, the Allgäu, Franconia, Thuringia, and Saxony to Alsace in what is now France, Austria, and Switzerland. Peasants massed in armed bands in one region, then another, and rebellion would break out even in areas far away. At its height it involved well over a hundred thousand people, perhaps many more, who joined with the rebels to bring about a new world of Christian brotherhood. And for several months, they won. Authority and rulership collapsed, and the familiar structures of the Holy Roman Empire were overturned, exposing the fragility of the existing social and religious hierarchies. People even began to dream of a new order.

But this moment did not last. In spring 1525, the 'Aufruhr', or 'turbulence', as contemporaries called it, had reached its height, rolling all before it. By May the tide had turned. The forces of the lords put down the revolt by slaying somewhere between seventy thousand and a hundred thousand peasants. That summer of blood, maybe 1 per cent of the population of the area of the war was killed, an enormous loss of life in just over two months.[1]

1

Despite its enormity, the Peasants' War and its bloody defeat have been forgotten in recent years. People remember the era for Martin Luther and his Reformation, which split Western Christendom forever between Catholics and those who would eventually be known as Protestants. The Peasants' War has come to be seen as a diversion, an interlude important mainly for what it tells us about Luther, for this was the moment when Luther came out in support of the princes and against the 'mad dogs', the rebelling peasants. From then on, the Reformation in Germany would be conservative. Mainstream reformers would go on to ally with rulers to advance the goals of the Reformation, and when the new church was set up after the war, it would have the backing of those in power.

The Reformation's possibilities, as well as its limits, cannot be grasped without an understanding of the Peasants' War as the giant trauma at its centre. Equally, the ideas, dreams, and hopes unleashed by the Reformation shaped the Peasants' War. And the war, in turn, cannot be understood if it has been severed from the heady atmosphere of religious excitement in which it took place.

To understand why such a massive movement mushroomed from such small, apparently isolated beginnings in a distant corner of the empire, we need to listen to what drove the peasants. It is no accident that just three years after Luther defied the emperor and the estates of the empire, the peasants of first one or two lords and abbots decided to down tools and gather in bands. In 1520 Luther himself had written a short but powerful tract, one of the three great Reformation writings from that year setting out his theology, titled *The Freedom of a Christian*. The cover of the German edition was emblazoned with the incendiary word 'freedom'. It was all very well for Luther's supporters to argue later that he had meant spiritual freedom, but the fact was that many peasants in the southwest, particularly those ruled by the Catholic monasteries, convents, and abbots Luther was attacking, were serfs, owned by their masters. For them, freedom meant ending serfdom too.

Despite Luther's later condemnation, the Peasants' War is unthinkable without the ideas he unleashed.[2]

By standing up to the emperor, Charles V, at Worms in 1521, Luther had provided an unforgettable example of resistance. A lone monk in a borrowed cassock before an audience of dignitaries arrayed in all their finery, he had confronted the mightiest power in the land and had said his piece, refusing to recant unless convinced by 'Holy Scripture'. Small wonder that the peasants drew on his ideas for their cause. Small wonder they assumed he would support them.[3]

But he did not. By late March of 1525, the peasant revolt had become a mass movement whose demands found shape in the Twelve Articles. These were probably composed by Sebastian Lotzer, a townsman and furrier, on the basis of hundreds of complaints that different groups of peasants had been formulating for weeks beforehand. Influenced by Martin Luther; the preacher Christoph Schappeler, himself a follower of the Swiss reformer Huldrych Zwingli; and a strain of radical evangelicalism, Lotzer helped transform a set of specific, apparently random grievances against particular lords into a wide-ranging theological vision that chimed with radical Reformation ideas. Local spats could now feed into a mass movement that spread far beyond individual disputes between a peasant and a particularly nasty abbot or lord. Yet Lotzer did not invent this theology, nor was he the first to apply it to agricultural relations—that had already been done by the peasants themselves as they formulated their complaints. The Twelve Articles then became a document that the movement everywhere acknowledged, even when the rebels did not know exactly what the articles contained, and even though many areas revised them to suit local circumstances. Soon they were printed using the new technology made possible by the invention of movable type, and they spread all over Germany. You could pick them up and hold them in your hand, point to each demand and the biblical passages that proved their godliness.[4]

The key thing about the Peasants' War was that it was a mass movement. For too long, histories of the war have emphasised its leaders, men like Thomas Müntzer in Thuringia, adopted by Friedrich Engels and then by the East German regime as a revolutionary hero to rival the reactionary colossus Luther. There are indeed a series of outsize characters who populated the war: Götz von Berlichingen, the knight with the iron fist, who became a peasant leader after his mother-in-law failed to hand him his liege-lord's summons to fight against them, or so he later claimed in his mendacious autobiography, written in his nineties. Or Florian Geyer, a noble who also led peasant armies and was finally knifed by an assassin. Or the Black Hofmännin, a peasant woman who claimed she urged on the peasant troops and rubbed the fat of the slaughtered nobles onto her shoes. Or the 'Bauernjörg', Truchsess Georg von Waldburg, who led the lords' army of the Swabian League and mercilessly torched rebel villages.[5]

But this was a movement, not a drama of Great Men. The peasants' side of the story has been forgotten because they did not write it down, either because they were illiterate or because they were slain or executed in the war. The winners—the lords and mainstream theologians who were the peasants' enemies—instead wrote the history.

The passions and dreams that drove the movement can seem inchoate, naïve, and contradictory. Though historians have tried to distil the movement's ideology from the programmatic writings of some of its leaders, this was not a revolt driven by the literate few. It was a mass struggle by individuals who risked and lost their lives to try to bring about a new world. To reconstruct what they did, what they said, and what they wanted to achieve, this book ranges widely to follow the turbulent flows of vast numbers of people.

The vision that drove them was about humans' relationship to creation. They were angry that lords claimed ownership of natural resources—the water, the common land, the woods and forests—when these were God's creation, given to all. They were enraged that the lords had stolen their freedom and claimed to own them when, as Luther showed, Christ had bought us all with his precious blood, 'thus the Bible proves that we are free and want to be free'. They were incensed by the growing inequality they saw around them, as individuals like the Fuggers, the richest merchants in the world, amassed wealth on scales never seen before. They wanted men to live as brothers, in mutual obligation, and not as lords and serfs. Theirs was an unabashedly male ideal, nourished by bonding amongst the peasant fighters, though this does not mean that women did not support it too. They wanted decisions to be made collectively and to manage natural resources in a way that would respect the environment, which God had created.[6]

To understand their revolt, we need to recall a world where animals such as oxen, horses, cows, pigs, sheep, and poultry lived closely with people, and where the vagaries of the weather mattered in a way that modern generations have often forgotten. The relationship between labour, harvest, and food was obvious, rather than mediated by powerful firms and complex industrial processes. The energy to drive machines came from water, from wood, and from charcoal, and it was clear who owned these resources and evident when they restricted access to them.

Despite the forces ranged against them, for most of the war the peasants were nonviolent; they humiliated but did not kill their lords. They questioned the established order at just the moment when capitalism was expanding and when Europeans were encountering new worlds, but they did not necessarily want to destroy authority of all kinds. Yet the authorities destroyed them, obliterated their movement, and built the structures of the current world on its ashes.

The peasants' story matters. It can help us see new answers to questions that confront us today. It also discloses a radical Reformation, whose theological, social, and political vision could have taken history in a very different direction. This is the Reformation we have lost sight of, and this is why we need to understand what drove the peasants. For what mattered to them also matters to us.

PART ONE

AUTUMN

Hans Wertinger, *September* (Landshut, 1525–1526). Germanisches Nationalmuseum Nuremberg.

CHAPTER 1

STIRRINGS

Hans Behem, with his pipe and drum, tending sheep as the Virgin appears to him. The woodcut image is surprisingly positive, as if advertising a pilgrimage. ART Collection/Alamy Stock Photo.

The Peasants' War did not come out of nowhere. From the later fifteenth century on, there had been revolts and traditions of formulating grievances and bringing lords to court, though none of them approached the Peasants' War in size, scale, or vision. The most dramatic of these was a religious movement that culminated in a mass revolt outside the huge castle of the bishop at Würzburg.

It began in 1476 with a vision. In the small Franconian hamlet of Niklashausen, a shepherd named Hans Behem claimed to have received orders from the Virgin Mary. She commanded him, 'Say to all the people that my son wishes and orders that all tolls, levies, forced labour, exactions, payments and aids required of the prelates, princes and nobles be abolished completely and at once. They shall oppress the poor no more'. Besides being a shepherd, Behem was a drummer, but Mary demanded he give up his 'vanities', burn his pipe and drum, and preach. He called on audiences to repent and destroy their own vanities as well: their shoes, fine clothes, and jewellery. Shortly after Walpurgisnacht, 30 April, in the Tauber Valley, crowds of people with candles and offerings began to gather around Niklashausen to see the visionary. A great pilgrimage movement had begun with the Drummer of Niklashausen at its centre.[1]

Alarmed, the local bishop soon alerted the Archbishop of Mainz. Behem's visions were beginning to criticise the church. They contained revolutionary calls for a world without taxes, dues, and tithes. The Virgin told him that fields and woods must be held in common. In early July, after crowds of pilgrims entered the town of Eichstätt with Behem, the bishop of Würzburg acted. On 13 July, while pilgrims thronged in Niklashausen, Bishop Rudolph had the drummer arrested and taken to his castle above Würzburg. The appalled pilgrims now formed a mass pilgrimage to the Marienberg to rescue the drummer, led by Conrad von Thunfeld, a local knight. Perhaps sixteen thousand people marched through the night. They reached the bridge over the Main in the early morning and shouted, 'Return the Youth to us,

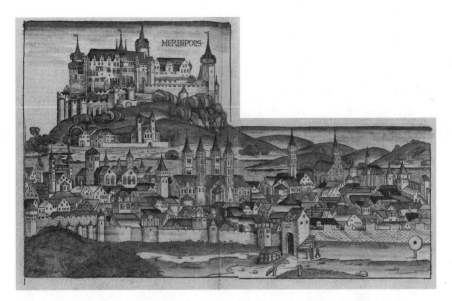

This woodcut from Hartmann Schedel's famous *Chronicle of the World* illustrates how the Marienberg dominates the town of Würzburg below. Würzburg, Schedelsche Weltchronik, 1493.

return the holy and innocent man, or else we will destroy the fortress and the city'.[2]

The crowd must have believed that Mary herself would appear and restore the drummer to them. But after a long standoff, Mary did not materialise. Once part of the crowd surrendered, the castle doors opened and the bishop's men shot their weapons into the masses who had refused to move. The bottleneck at the bridge made them easy targets. Many were killed and hundreds more taken prisoner. Peasant blood stained the path that led to the fortress, where the bishop quietly burnt the Drummer of Niklashausen as a heretic. It would be the very place where the Peasants' War would stall almost fifty years later.[3]

But though the drummer was defeated, he was not forgotten, and his revolt would not be the only one. In the Black Forest and Württemberg, peasants were accustomed to challenging authority. They took their lords to court, performed rent strikes, and refused labour. They resisted giving the small symbols of fealty—the Lenten hen, for example—that cost little but symbolised servitude. In 1493, near Schlettstadt in Alsace, revolt broke out calling for the Jews to be expelled (they were blamed for charging usurious rates of interest), for priests' incomes to be limited, and for justice to be reformed. The peasants formed secret leagues held together by oaths, which met at landmarks such as the hill of Ungersberg. Reputedly they would swear with three fingers and draw a circle in the ground with a spade; those who would enter the circle had joined the league.[4]

Boots were the symbol of these revolts, which came to be called the Bundschuh rebellions. A play on words, the name referred to a 'Bund', a union of people 'tied' together, as well as a 'Bundschuh', a boot made from cheap leather that peasants typically wore, tied to the legs by long leather strings. The footwear of disorderly, rough folk, they were the most basic sort; they did not require the cordwainer's skill and had nothing to do with the fabulous leather objects worn by nobles. A woodcut illustrator had only to present the peasant boot on a flag to warn his audience that dangerous people were on the march.

The uprisings continued through the turn of the century. They broke out in 1491 in the Kempten area and in several places ruled by monastic institutions, and in 1493 around Schlettstadt in Alsace. In 1502, in the region of Speyer, there was a far more significant uprising, led by the redoubtable peasant revolutionary Joss Fritz. This revolt had a religious dimension, too, for those who joined had to kneel and recite five paternosters and five Ave Marias. Its password was 'God greet you, fellow. How fares the world?' The answer: 'We cannot rid ourselves of the plague of priests'. Religious devotion went hand in hand with deep-seated anticlericalism.[5]

A decade later, the same Joss Fritz was involved in a major revolt that centred on the Breisgau region near Freiburg, planned for autumn 1513. Its participants flew a blue and white flag adorned with Christ on the cross, Mary, and John the Baptist, the papal and imperial insignia, and a kneeling peasant; on the other side was the Bundschuh. The rebels called for the woods, forests, water, birds, fishing, and hunting to be free to rich and poor alike, for the incomes of convents and monasteries to be restricted, for interest payments on loans to be limited, for the imperial court at Rottweil and the church courts to be removed from jurisdiction over them, and to have no lords but pope and emperor. The plans were betrayed, and the revolt never materialised, but Fritz continued to forge a network of insurgency linking villages and small towns across the region.[6]

That same year, peasants in neighbouring Württemberg organised against their ruler Duke Ulrich, who, in a year of bad harvest, had tried to increase taxes and then adopted the expedient of reducing weights while prices remained fixed. They held a 'trial' of the new weight by throwing it in the river, and when it sank, they concluded it was illegitimate. The rebels called themselves the 'Poor Conrads', the condescending term used towards poor folk by the nobility, which they repurposed as a badge of honour. The Marbach doctor Alexander Seitz supported them but was condemned to death in 1514, although he managed to survive by fleeing to Switzerland. Authorities suppressed the revolt by taking as many as seventeen hundred peasants prisoner, forcing them to swelter for many hours in the heat at the very place where they had first assembled illegally before their show trial. Once the princes arrived, the peasants, on their knees, begged for mercy and received their freedom on condition they surrender their weapons, though four 'leaders' were beheaded on the spot. In the days that followed, several more rebels were executed in towns including Schorndorf, where one man's head was stuck on the city tower, and Stuttgart, where the beheadings were carried out in the marketplace. And yet the rebellion was successful in some respects: Duke Ulrich had to withdraw his weights. Just five years later he would be deposed by the troops of the Swabian League, the military and political organisation of princes, towns, and bishops in the southwest.[7]

The tireless Joss Fritz apparently tried to revolt yet again in 1517, but the uprising was once more foiled before it could begin. Unable to round up all the conspirators, authorities apparently believed the rebels continued to command support in the Black Forest, Württemberg, and Alsace, though this may have been more a reflection of the authorities' edginess than a material threat. The rebels continued their clandestine work and reputedly had a secret sign, with the thumb in the right fist and the code words 'That is good'—'Das ist gut'—a cheery and apparently innocuous-seeming phrase. Though the revolts that followed the burning of the Drummer of Niklashausen never got very far, they may have given the rebels practice establishing networks of organisation, information, and support that would prove important later on.[8]

To critics, the Drummer of Niklashausen revolt of 1476 came to stand as a symbol of all that was wrong with the uprisings. As early as 1494, Sebastian Brant, who was by this time living in Würzburg, published his humanist classic *The Ship of Fools*, which included a section on 'fools of scripture'. It derided none other than the 'Piper' of Niklashausen, with his own 'chapels and hermitages', who according to Brant was the kind of fool who ignored scripture, thought you could ask the dead for news of the afterlife, and set himself up as an authority on Hell and Heaven. Brant thus linked 'fools', misusers of scripture, and rural revolt not only to Niklashausen but also to the agrarian revolts of his own time.[9]

It was a potent connection. In 1506 and again in 1514 the Würzburg abbot and historian Johannes Trithemius wrote a history of the Niklashausen movement, demoting Behem the shepherd drummer to a mere keeper of swine. He, too, called Behem's followers 'fools' and mocked them for seeking the tufts of the drummer's cap to use as cures like holy relics. The dates of these writings were not accidental, as 1506 had witnessed revolt in the Black Forest, while in 1513–1514, the Poor Conrad revolt had shaken Württemberg.

Patterns that would emerge twelve years later were already evident in these revolts and in the responses to them. Though ostensibly geared towards the plight of the peasant, the revolts managed to create a

In 1514, a rhyming pamphlet on the Ship of Bundschuh Fools featured
a woodcut of a fantastical ship that sported two pairs of boots, heading
in opposite directions. Johannes Adelphus, *Narrenschiff vom buntschuch*
(Augsburg), 1514, title page, Staatsbibliothek München.

coalition between townsfolk and countryfolk and made use of leagues
to grow membership. Religious ideas about fairness were important,
but so was antisemitism. The banners were often religious, featuring
Mary in particular, but also Christ, John the Baptist, and St George.
The Black Forest, Württemberg, and Alsace had harboured such rebellious sentiments. The rebels of 1525 would flourish there as well.

What distinguished the earlier revolts from those of 1524 and
1525 was the scale of their ambition. The earlier rebels targeted specific abuses and taxes rather than the system itself. Many of the revolts
were easily snuffed out before they even began—there were turncoats
aplenty who betrayed their plans to the authorities, and it is unclear

how widespread their support truly was. Indeed, the fear of revolt may have been more powerful than the revolts themselves. Though religion was important, the revolts were not primarily anticlerical; in Württemberg, the Poor Conrad revolt was directed against Duke Ulrich, not the church or even the nobility more broadly, and did not have an overall theological rationale. The early revolts were much more limited in scope geographically. In the comparatively peaceful decade that followed, an observer might have thought that the rebels were exhausted and their campaigns finished, as peasants once again took rulers to court rather than risking revolt. But they would have been wrong.

The Peasants' War of 1524–1525 was both far more serious and more widespread than the earlier Bundschuh revolts because of the influence of Martin Luther, the beginning of the Reformation, and the religious fervour that followed. From the outset, Luther's ideas were incendiary. His Ninety-Five Theses, which sparked the Reformation in 1517, were printed on a single piece of paper about twelve by sixteen and a half inches and could be stuck up on walls as well as on the door of the Castle Church in Wittenberg. A call to repentance, they attacked a church and a papacy that sold salvation and fleeced the poor. The Theses spread everywhere within a few weeks, and, translated from Latin into German, they were soon on the streets in Nuremberg, where those who had no Latin could read them. Luther's was an unsettling as well as an emancipatory message. He insisted that Christ had come to bring not peace, but a sword, as Matthew's gospel put it. 'Away then with all those prophets who say to the people of Christ, "Peace, peace", and there is no peace!' (Jer. 6:14), he wrote, praising those who preached the cross.[10]

The Ninety-Five Theses were just the beginning. In 1520 Luther wrote *To the Christian Nobility*, a powerful polemic in which he spelt out what his ideas would mean for secular society and what layfolk should now do. In a bonfire of regulations and long-held verities, he made short work of pilgrimages, saints' cults, and monasticism, even suggesting that clergy should be able to marry. *On the Babylonian Captivity*, published in Latin in the same year, was perhaps even more earth-shattering, for it attacked the pope directly as the Antichrist and condemned the papal court of 'courtesans'. Luther announced that Christ himself insisted layfolk should have communion in both kinds—wafer and wine. The wine of the mass should not be reserved to the clergy alone. As if conversing with the reader, he explained, 'But what carries most weight with me, however, and is quite decisive for me is that Christ says: "This is my blood, which is poured out for you and for many for the forgiveness of sins". Here you see very clearly that the blood is given to all those for whose sins it was poured out. But who will dare to say that it was not poured out for the laity? And do you not see whom he addresses when he gives the cup? Does he not give it to all?'[11]

Luther adopted and developed ideas of social and political criticism that had been articulated at the Imperial Diets, the so-called Gravamina or complaints of the German nation, and made sure he addressed ordinary people in German. Another 1520 pamphlet, *The Freedom of a Christian*, circulated widely in German and was deliberately intended, as Luther put it, for 'the unlearned—for only them do I serve'. It starts with the paradox that 'a Christian is a free lord of all [things], subject to no-one. A Christian is a perfectly dutiful servant of all [things], subject to everyone'. The terms in which he posed this contradiction were themselves striking—a Christian is not only free, but a *Herr*, a lord of all things, using the word for feudal overlord, and yet a Christian also has the duty of service to everyone, a formulation that undercut the pomp of the church. But the most incendiary word was 'Freiheit', or freedom. Luther wrote, 'One thing, and only one thing, is necessary for Christian life, righteousness, and freedom. That one thing is the most holy Word of God, the gospel of Christ, as Christ says'. Luther of course meant 'freedom' in the religious sense, but even this claim was inflammatory, and rebels took the emphasis on freedom to heart. When the peasants drew up their programme, the Twelve Articles, it would be known as the 'Articles of Christian Freedom', and 'gospel, gospel, gospel' became their mantra.[12]

Even more powerful was Luther's notion that the church was withholding something precious from the people. Christ had bought us with his precious blood, and yet it was the wine of the mass that had been kept from the laity and reserved to the clergy alone. Evangelical preachers were just then beginning to be appointed in parishes and communities all over Germany, and layfolk were receiving communion wine for the first time. This unexpected and novel experience must have cemented their feeling of having been cheated of the very thing which had bought their freedom. Once the religious foundations that had been funded with indulgence monies or used to found masses were dissolved, new money was suddenly made available. Here was wealth that could be used to support the poor or to build schools. Social and religious reform therefore went hand in hand.

In 1521 one pamphleteer even compared Luther's journey to defend his works before the emperor and the assembled estates of the empire at the Diet of Worms to that of Christ himself. Another pamphlet, describing the 'Passion' of Martin, was illustrated with a woodcut of a doughty friar on the cover. Luther became a hero, and on another pamphlet cover he was shown taking on pope, cardinals, and emperor. Like the evangelical peasant, he was depicted as a fighter. News of these events spread to taverns, council chambers, and bathhouses, reaching the literate and illiterate alike. So when Luther wrote of freedom, the peasants could hardly be accused of having wilfully misunderstood him. At this early date, it seemed as if the world could be made anew in accord with evangelical principles. The pamphlets that featured the evangelical peasant sold alongside Luther's works, intended for the same market. Freedom was a secular as well as a religious issue.[13]

By the early 1520s, as the implications of Luther's ideas were beginning to be worked out in a host of towns and villages across the empire, the peasant, so recently regarded as threatening, came to be seen as virtuous, as a spirited fighter for the gospel. In a text advocating for the scripture's primacy over the bulls of the pope or the councils of the bishops, reformer Andreas Karlstadt insisted, 'I say...that biblical scripture is superior to a General Council, and if a peasant at the plough could show a verse of scripture to the Council...the Council should give way to the peasant, and give him honour, for the sake of biblical scripture'. Luther's followers encouraged ordinary folk to read the Bible in German with the implication that they were as wise as, if not wiser than, university-trained theologians with their hair-splitting irrelevancies. Karlstadt himself dropped his academic titles and started to dress like a peasant. Layfolk began to publish pamphlets calling for religious change, and 'dialogues' in which the peasant outwitted monks, priests, or academics became popular. The Waldshut preacher Balthasar Hubmaier asserted, 'Whoever does not seek his bread by the sweat of his brow is to be banned, unworthy of the food he eats'. In 1521 Luther himself even discovered his rural roots, stopping at the village of Möhra on his way to the Wartburg after the Diet of Worms to meet his country relations. Everyone, it seemed, wanted to be a peasant.[14]

In 1522 an illiterate peasant from the village of Wöhrd named Diepold Peringer began to preach the gospel, drawing huge crowds. His sermons were printed, and he became something of a sensation, only to be unmasked as a renegade cleric who could certainly read and write. His story reveals a great deal about the febrile climate of the early 1520s, for the times required a miraculous preaching peasant. Peringer's pamphlets were usually illustrated with a picture of a man in a strong standing pose wearing a peasant hat and boots. But these were not Bundschuh, tied to the leg. Rather, they were boots of better quality and hence less threatening, and even the dagger he carried at his side was not menacing. He looked straight at the reader, as

Title page, Diepold Peringer, *Ain Sermon
geprediget vom Pawren zu Werdt*, 1524.
Bayerische Staatsbibliothek Munich.

if to engage as one Christian to another. The 'evangelical peasant' was so widespread that his presence even rivalled that of Luther himself, whose face was depicted on the cover of many of his works in those early years. The figure of 'Hans the Hoe' ('Karsthans' the preaching peasant), who could take on bishops and popes, began to appear in Reformation woodcuts. Soon he had a real-life counterpart when in 1523, in Alsace, an itinerant preacher known as Karsthans was said to be preaching 'Lutheran opinion'. For this brief period, then, peasants were fashionable, individuals with points of view, not a faceless, animalistic mob. In woodcuts propagandising for the Reformation, they were shown as true defenders of the gospel, holding books and arguing with monks and priests.[15]

One of Luther's ideas in particular influenced the course of the Peasants' War: his understanding of the priesthood. He insisted that priests were not a separate caste of people, consecrated by the sacrament

Diepold Peringer, *Des Christlichen Pawern
getrewer Rath*, Nuremberg, 1524.
Bayerische Staatsbibliothek Munich.

of ordination and set apart from layfolk. He argued instead that every believer was a priest and that the community—the word for 'political community' and 'congregation' is the same in German—was to appoint its preacher. Such ideas were explosive because the German church in the 1520s was run through a complex system of property rights. A local priest might be appointed by a distant authority who happened to own the benefice rights and revenues and might never even have seen the place.

This became critical in the autumn of 1524, when the people wanted to hear the gospel preached. Priests who did not support the new ideas were reviled, and congregations looked for 'godly' preachers to replace them. Luther had originally called for communities to have the right to call their own pastors, but he soon argued that they could enjoy this privilege only if they provided the funds to support the pastor. Tithes could not simply be claimed and diverted for this purpose since the property rights of the owners had to be respected. In making this suggestion,

Peter Vischer, *Allegory of the Reformation*, 1524. Luther is shown as a naked Hercules leading the heroic peasant; other female figures represent the virtues and key Lutheran ideas. The Roman church lies as a shattered colossus. The sketch, from the collection of Johann Wolfgang von Goethe, is displayed in his house in Weimar. By kind permission of the Goethe-Nationalmuseum Weimar.

Luther knew he was being unrealistic. Rural communities lacked the money to pay double for a preacher, so they had to put up with what they had. Indeed, if towns and rural communities had followed Luther's advice, it would have effectively stopped the Reformation in its tracks unless the ruler himself expropriated the revenues and created a territorial church. At that moment, such a solution was not on the agenda—not even Luther's own ruler had declared for the Reformation. When a monastery owned the local pastorship, it had no intention of allowing an evangelical preacher, and so conflict with a congregation inspired by the new ideas was unavoidable. In the meantime, local communities who wanted to hear the Word and have the gospel preached had no solution.

In October 1524, just after the first revolts of the Peasants' War, a pamphlet appeared purporting to be the contract for the new pastor of Wendelstein near Schwabach. It was written in the informal 'you', a disrespectful form of address, and told him roundly, 'So we will not recognise you as a master, but only as a servant of the community, so that you do not command us, but we command you'. Printed at Nuremberg, it provided a template for a new kind of contract between pastor and parish. The pamphlet claimed to reproduce the conditions of employment for the new pastor that the village commune and headman had presented to the officials at Schwabach. In defiance of the rules of ownership of benefices, or indeed of any political authority, the commune itself had drawn up a contract. The pamphlet was almost certainly the work of a local Reformation pamphleteer, locked in bitter conflict with his brother, a Catholic priest. But it showed what was possible if a community decided to act on its own account. As the commune of Seewen near Solothurn would later put it, 'We want our people's priest to have an appropriate, honourable income for two, not have him begging off us like before'. They wanted him to have enough money to support a wife, not live with a concubine, and they were willing to pay for it.[16]

Another of Luther's ideas, his insistence that 'monkery' was not a good work, proved to be potent for the rebels as well. He made no distinction between friars and monks but rather liked to poke fun at the sheer variety of different orders. Praying and meditation, saying the hours, were no longer valued as services that monks performed for the whole of society. Monastic vocations collapsed, and over the next years many former monks, nuns, and friars simply left their monasteries. In Wittenberg, when Luther returned from the Wartburg, he found a monastery empty except for himself and one other monk, and though he remained a monk for a time, many others did not. All over the empire, monasteries were being deserted.[17]

The collapse in monasteries' standing had huge social and economic consequences, both in towns and in the country, where monasteries controlled vast tracts of land. Many monasteries were rich and powerful landowners. They had impressive buildings, stores of grain, cellars of wine, ponds stocked with the fish needed for Lent and Fridays, libraries of books, and stores of documents. They lent money, increased their landholdings, and owned property in towns, often in central locations.[18] Some monasteries acted as local landlords, and they had their own system of ecclesiastical courts. Many ruled tiny local territories and were incorporated into the political systems of the empire as independent entities. Some, like the Teutonic Knights, were military orders which had both priestly and knightly members. Founded during the crusades, they continued to act as colonising powers, subduing 'heathen' local populations. And all had their own structures of authority that went from local to regional, superregional, and beyond the borders of countries.

Monasteries' collapse meant that the peasants, many of whom were serfs of bishops, abbots, monasteries, and convents, confronted an unprecedented situation where their old complaints about lordship might suddenly succeed. There was a power vacuum as straggling groups of monks who had remained despite the Reformation in buildings with empty cells lost much of their social status. If there was no point to a life of prayer and contemplation, if begging and vows of poverty were to be rejected, what social function did monks serve? The collapse unleashed a visceral hatred of the monks and nuns who lived in these rich institutions, dotted about the countryside and reliant on the labour of local peasants. They were visual reminders of the agglomerations of wealth and power that could be put to other purposes. They stood for inequality and exploitation, and now their devotions had been unmasked as religious fraud. Antimonasticism was further fuelled by the angry polemics of ex-monks and the occasional nuns who now rejected their former lives and former selves. When a monastery owned the patronage rights of a local church and refused to appoint an evangelical priest or introduce 'preaching of the gospel', hatred of monasteries fused with evangelical fervour. And in towns where there were active

Reformation preachers, it was easy to whip up anger against Catholic monks who preached the old doctrine.

Religious and economic grievances grew indistinguishable. Monasteries occupied valuable land in towns, where their barns, often prominently situated, stored their tithes in grain while corn prices rose. They had churches and 'town houses', accumulations of wealth that were conspicuous in the crowded urban landscapes. They were exempt from taxes, were not citizens, and did not have to do guard duty—and their products, like beer, were often tax exempt too, giving them another economic advantage. In Zwickau, for instance, the Cistercian abbey of Grünhain brewed beer that was sold in competition with that of locals, and its massive town buildings became the focus of violent attacks. In Heilbronn the Teutonic Knights owned a huge property in town with additional outposts nearby, while in Mühlhausen they controlled the two largest parish churches and had a fine house in the centre of town and another in the lower town. In December 1523 furious Mühlhausen women armed with knives chased the hapless priest Johannes Textor of the Teutonic Knights into the church. Demands for evangelical preachers could thus easily turn into attacks on monks and monasteries, and their wealth, temptingly standing there, could be used to fund new projects that would benefit the community. A sense of possibility could lead to radical action, propelled by bitter anger against accumulated monastic riches.[19]

All these grievances and the feelings they aroused were coming to a head in 1524. There had long been predictions of impending disaster that year, when the planets would be in the sign of Pisces, the fish. The astrologer Johann Virdung of Hassfurt had foretold in pamphlets which went into multiple editions that there would be floods and poor harvests; the grapes would not grow; there would be battles, illnesses, and divisions amongst Christians; the clergy would 'drink the cup of bitterness'; and political disasters would ensue.

Title page, Leonhard Reynmann, *Practica vber
die grossen vnd mannigfeltigen Coniunction der
Planeten... 1524*, Landshut, 1523. Saxon State and
University Library, Dresden.

Such anxieties might soon circle around the possible resurgence
of peasant unrest, especially in a time of religious flux. In 1520 the
medical doctor Alexander Seitz, who had supported the Poor Conrad
movement back in 1514, wrote a pamphlet about the feared conjunction of the planets. A graduate of the universities of Padua and Tübingen, a humanist who wrote popular medical tracts, he also had a strong
line in antinoble rhetoric. Just as 'the drum or pipe of man moves the
mood, and incites anger to war or lust to dance according to its tune/
type', he wrote, so also the planets affect people's emotional states. Recent signs like a cross in a wheel and a rainbow that had appeared in
the sky above Vienna presaged disaster. Then, the 'poor man' will take
the cross on himself, though he already carried the greatest burdens,
for 'what the lords lose the peasants have to endure'. Seitz's pamphlet
was a barely disguised attack on the existing rulers. And he was not the
only one to link portents of disaster not just to the natural world but

also to the social order. Something terrible was about to happen, the soothsayers agreed, but what? The mood of foreboding freighted events with greater significance.[20]

It took a year for Seitz's prognostication about the cross in the wheel to be fulfilled, but as Lorenz Fries, the chronicler of the Peasants' War, noted, the astronomers had got one thing wrong. It was not a flood of water, but 'a flood of blood, for in German lands alone more than a hundred thousand people drowned in the space of ten weeks in this flood'. That autumn, the feared catastrophe took shape.[21]

Autumn is the season when the sun has turned away from the earth on its journey and the long summer days of labour grow shorter. As the agricultural year ends, it serves as a time for reckoning. The harvest is brought in, and for once there is enough to eat. Fields must be ploughed and winter crops sown. Produce is stored and preserved; hay stacked; the grain cut, winnowed, and put into barns; oil pressed from seeds; vegetables pickled or salted; fruits dried, salted, or put in sand or ashes; and nuts stored. Beer is brewed, and grapes must be trampled in barrels to make wine in October, 'wine month'. In late autumn the animals who cannot be kept over winter for lack of food must be slaughtered, the meat sold or cured. Mushrooms and berries are collected from the forest, and the pigs are let loose on the acorn mast. Autumn requires a weather eye. Peasants must judge when the last rays of sun can warm the grapes before harvest, when to avoid the rain that could ruin a crop, when the snows are about to arrive and work has to stop.

Harvest also meant delivering the tithes and rents to the lords. As their barns filled, peasants' stores dwindled. The tithe, a tenth of all grain, was theoretically devoted to supporting the priest, though in practice it sometimes went into the pockets of investors, who bought up tithes speculatively, or into the hands of ecclesiastical institutions out of whose incomes the priest's stipend was paid. Another small tithe was levied on all other agricultural produce, including fruit, oil, cheese, wax, and small animals. Peasants almost universally objected to these demands because paying them did not have an obvious purpose. Nevertheless, they had to be paid in autumn, sometimes on St Michael's, sometimes St Martin's Day. There were labour services, help with harvest and sowing, cartage, and a host of minor obligations that were onerous at a time when all hands were needed. And in autumn, as in Lent, the hen that symbolised the serf's bodily ownership by the lord had to be paid.[22]

Autumn was the season when peasants felt the extractions of the church and the lords most keenly, and when they were well fed and optimistic enough to challenge the authorities. Once harvest was in, they had the time to articulate their grievances and the money to pay for them to be written down.

It all began with snails, or so contemporaries agreed. In Stühlingen in southern Germany, near the border with the Swiss cantons, the Countess of Lupfen ordered her serfs to collect snail shells for the women of the court to wind their thread around. The sheer idiocy of the demand spoke volumes about the lords' indifference to peasant life. On 23 June 1524, the peasants rose up at midsummer, when the sun changed direction (*Sonnwende*) and lighted straw wheels were rolled downhill in the old heathen custom to persuade the sun to stay. That May, the peasants of the nearby monastery of St Blasien had also revolted against their lords, and unrest continued through the autumn, when the rebels were soon joined by peasants of the Hegau in southern Baden down towards Lake Constance. By autumn they had stopped work, entered into legal dispute with their lord, formed a band, and made a flag. The Peasants' War had begun.

The snails became part of the folklore of the Peasants' War, emblematic of the collapse of reasonable relations between lords and peasants. But when the Stühlingen peasants later listed their grievances, snails did not feature, though we know about them from at least three separate sources. They had enough else: sixty-two complaints, covering just about every other detail of peasant life, from picking and crushing wild berries, to searching for morel mushrooms, to keeping hunting dogs for the lords, to sowing, binding, picking, and drying hemp for spinning. It was an indictment of an entire system.[23]

They chose Hans Müller of Bulgenbach, a subject of the Abbey of St Blasien, as their spokesperson. A brilliant orator and a shrewd tactician, Hans Müller had military experience, having fought as a mercenary in France. Probably aged about thirty-five during the Peasants' War, he was articulate, willing to take risks, a man at the peak of his physical prowess, and young for a commander in a society that valued the experience of age. He could also be ruthless: later, when the army discovered a spy, he reputedly confiscated the spy's money, beat him severely, and personally hanged the man from a branch and left him for dead. (An executioner's work was dishonouring, and the story became well known since the man escaped to tell the tale.)[24]

The revolt began in the extreme southwest, a place that had long been riven by unrest and where tense relations between lord and peasant often resulted in legal challenge. In its earliest days it does not seem to have been directly religious. But it is difficult to tell how the rebels really felt because their complaints were written in language for a court case, not the inspirational religious rhetoric that would come later on. Soon enough, Hans Müller and others in his band would be invoking 'Christian Love' and calling others 'to stand by godly justice and support the Holy Gospel'.

Anticlericalism and hatred of monks certainly propelled the revolt, especially at the neighbouring rich Benedictine Abbey of St Blasius near Waldshut, whose peasants refused to pay tithes and dues that autumn, demanding freedom. The abbey had large landholdings in different regions and extensive local power, and many of the peasants who became involved in 1524 were its subjects. They made connections with towns and with reformers, though not necessarily at first for religious reasons. The nearby Stühlingers, led by Hans Müller, formed a band, and by late July no fewer than six hundred of them arrived in the tiny town of Waldshut and stayed for three days. By October the Hegau peasants were also in revolt, and soon the nearby Klettgau area—which stood under the protection of Zurich, where the Reformation was in full swing—asked Zurich for help.[25]

Why Waldshut? In Waldshut, the preacher and intellectual Dr Balthasar Hubmaier was developing a congregation-centred Reformation, inspired by Andreas Karlstadt at Orlamünde, Luther's former ally who had by then broken with him. Now religious complaints joined grievances about feudalism, an explosive combination in an area where many peasants lived on monastic land. Waldshut had a long history of conflict with the Abbey of St Blasien: the abbey claimed rights in the town, was an economic competitor, and kept a watchful eye on peasants tempted to move there. Hubmaier had been a student of none other than Luther's Catholic opponent Johannes Eck, and likely with Eck's patronage he had gained the important position of cathedral preacher at Regensburg. He had helped whip up antisemitism there, and in 1516 attacks began on the local Jewish community, based on accusations of usury. The synagogue was burnt to the ground, and on its site a chapel to 'the beautiful Mary' was built. Miracles were reported, and Hubmaier himself kept a record of them. Pilgrims thronged to Regensburg.[26]

And then for some reason the well-known preacher left town for Waldshut, ostensibly because of an outbreak of plague in late 1520. In place of a bustling, large, and wealthy imperial city where Hubmaier could move in elite circles, he was now in a small town, albeit one that lay on important routes between Basel, the Black Forest, and Zurich. At first he seems to have remained an orthodox Catholic and even to have returned to Regensburg to preach in the chapel to the 'beautiful Mary'. But by April 1523 he came under the Swiss reformer Huldrych Zwingli's influence, and soon he was preaching against 'Satan's clergy, the soul eaters'—that is, the Catholic priests who were leading the people to Hell by not preaching the gospel. Inspired by Hubmaier, people in Waldshut were smashing images, even hurling the crucifix from the pulpit, while the Bishop of Constance claimed that Hubmaier preached 'that no-one should be compelled to give interest, tithes, rents or dues anymore, not to be obedient or subservient to his rulers'. Hubmaier consistently denied that he had ever preached against the tithe or had advocated disobedience, but he did condemn usury. By May 1523 the former Marian was preaching on the proper way of understanding the Annunciation, and he was no longer inside a church but preaching outdoors, as other radical evangelicals had done, on a mountain. Because the area was ruled by the Catholic Austrian Habsburgs, his preaching immediately pitted the power of the local council against that of the territorial ruler.[27]

By May 1524 the Catholic clergy had been forced to leave Waldshut. Hubmaier himself departed for a time when the town was threatened with Austrian military intervention. Even though the interests of townsfolk and peasants did not always align, and despite their mutual suspicion, the town now began to ally with the peasants in opposition to their Habsburg rulers and strengthened its defences. In late August or early September, eight hundred peasants entered town again. On 6 October they began a well-organised march through the area to gain support, and when Hubmaier returned to Waldshut he was received as if God himself had come down to them from heaven. He introduced the German mass and had images, altar lights, altar clothes, and flags removed from the Waldshut churches. The religious radical Thomas Müntzer—of whom more later—was also in the Klettgau area late that year for perhaps as long as eight weeks, including in Griessen, ruled by the abbot of St Blasien, and he may well have been in contact with Hubmaier.[28]

Women especially were drawn to Hubmaier, and even participated along with the community when decisions were taken, much to the horror of a later chronicler; they also reputedly appeared armed at the town hall when the Austrians ordered Hubmaier to leave. Hubmaier apparently respected women: though he conceded that women should be silent in assemblies and learn from their men at home, he added, 'If men are shocked by fear and become women, then women should speak and be men, just like Debora, Olda, Anna the prophetess, the four daughters of Philip the evangelist and Argula in our own times'. (Argula von Grumbach was a Lutheran noblewoman who had roundly attacked the academics of Ingolstadt University for punishing Lutheran students, and whose pamphlets were extremely popular—the title pages showed her dressed as a respectable married woman, book in hand, castigating the fusty professoriate.) Hubmaier's remarks were amongst the most positive statements about women's roles in the early Reformation, and he was unusual in explicitly addressing sisters as well as brothers in his printed work.[29]

Talks continued as the authorities assembled troops to quell the peasants, but by early December the peasant leader Hans Müller of Bulgenbach mounted a march through the Black Forest. Wherever they went, the peasants 'had their complaints read aloud and said they would not harm anyone and would pay for what they drank and ate, and they admonished all the peasants to help them get justice'. The marches through the difficult terrain of the Black Forest displayed grit and determination and allowed them to reach isolated villages and create alliances that would last until the following autumn. Three hundred years later, during the Revolution of 1848, the revolutionary hero Friedrich 'Carl' Hecker would mount a similar march through the Black Forest, probably inspired by Müller's campaign. Even one hostile chronicler who knew Müller described him as clever, of good height, experienced in fighting in France, and a gifted speaker with no equal. He and his supporters succeeded in taking the town of Bräunlingen and widening the scale of the revolt; he would eventually help form the three peasant armies of the Allgäu, Lake Constance, and Baltringen bands.[30]

The Hauensteiners occupied the St Blasius monastery of their over-lord, moving into the institution which had dominated and exploited them and making it their own. Then on 1 December the peasants plundered the Benedictine monastery of St Trudpert, 'purifying' it and creating a new religious space; one of the rebels exclaimed 'he no longer wanted to have the perjured traitorous rascal the Abbot as his lord', adding further insults for good measure. Meanwhile the Waldshuters melted down monstrances that were used to house and exhibit the host, and cut up the silk of the ecclesiastical vestments to use as trouser belts. They then instituted a mass in German, which ordinary folk could un-derstand. Religion was not about the exhibition of magical objects or the performance of priestly power but about hearing the Word.[31]

The Stühlingers proceeded on two fronts, marching, refusing to pay dues, and mounting a legal case against their ruler, the count, which proceeded very slowly over the next months and was passed up to the Reichskammergericht, the imperial court of appeal at Esslingen. Meanwhile the Hegau peasants in the south of Baden, who had also risen against their lords, also tried to resolve their dispute through le-gal means but were granted only a non–legally binding agreement. In a departure from custom, only nobles were represented amongst the judges. Such experiences must have undermined the attractiveness of legal routes for the peasants while keeping grievances alive. Religious issues did not yet loom so large, and the second visit of the peasants to Waldshut happened when Hubmaier was not even in town. But the fact that the Stühlingers chose to march there shows how the conflu-ence of peasant and town concerns, both in revolt against their Aus-trian rulers that autumn, may have worked to radicalise both sides while exposing the peasants yet further to 'Lutheran' ideas.[32]

Andreas Lettsch, a chronicler who was a monk and worked for the Abbey of St Blasius, had no doubt that Hubmaier was 'a beginner and provoker of the entire peasant war'. Johann Fabri, writing in 1528 af-ter Hubmaier's death, blamed Hubmaier too and saw his preaching as following a familiar script. First he preached that the time had come for the sword to be taken away from secular authorities; then that the people should gather and vow to keep their word and elect leaders for the whole district; next, that the ban should be used to exclude the ungodly; and finally, that nobles and clergy should leave all castles, monasteries, and priests' houses to live in 'common' houses. The man, Fabri insinuated, was a rabble-rouser with a programme—but this is to read later events back into a revolt that had not yet even formulated its demands. Nor is it clear how much support Hubmaier had amongst the peasants at this point; his published works include little that addressed their concerns. He did, however, inspire courageous loyalty amongst the Waldshuters, who recalled how their representatives had been bullied at a meeting with the Austrians, who threatened the Waldshuters: 'By God's wounds, we will beat your wives to death when we come in, we want to rip out the weeds by the roots, we want to box your ears with the gospel so that you will clap hands above your heads, and punish you so that you will be an example to all people who join the Lutheran sect'.[33]

By 13 October the lords were offering the Stühlingers and other peasant groups arbitration and mediation, though discontent continued to rumble. It was spreading, but it centred in an isolated corner of southwest Germany and regions near Switzerland and did not include Franconia or reach to the region around Würzburg where the Drummer of Niklashausen had started his pilgrimage in 1476. It still mainly focused on specific rural grievances, and the peasants used negotiation and pursued their claims through courts. Religion was important, but nascent; Waldshut was pursuing various defensive options and stood aloof from Müller's marches through the Black Forest, while not all the peasant rebels saw their grievances in religious terms.[34]

As the weather cooled it seemed unlikely the peasants would want to fight. Matters did not seem to warrant an urgent response from the authorities, and the Swabian League, judging that the revolt could be easily suppressed as others had been before, had other priorities. Even so, in Swabia the Baltringen band formed on 24 December. By January, the Klettgau peasants, who had sought help against the rebels from Zurich, had been drawn into their evangelical orbit: as a price of their aid the Zurichers had demanded to know whether they would support 'the right, true Word of God'. Zwingli himself, reformer of Zurich and the son of a well-off peasant, understood peasant complaints and so was not temperamentally inclined to dismiss them as mere disobedience, though his position would later become more complex. On 29 January the Klettgauers marched to Waldshut, just as the Stühlingers had done before them, and were welcomed with open arms. It seemed that winter had not frozen the fires of revolt after all.[35]

CHAPTER 2

LAND

When Johannes Cochlaeus penned his *Brief Description of Germany* in 1512, he envisaged a land divided by mountains—the Alps to the south, the Carpathians to the east, Kahlenberg around Vienna, the Fichtelgebirge stretching towards Bohemia, and the Mittelgebirge between Hesse and Westphalia—and crossed by rivers, Rhein, Danube, and Elbe. In the middle was Nuremberg, 'not just the middle of Germany but of the whole of Europe'. This might seem like patriotic exaggeration by a man who was after all rector of its Latin school and had grown up nearby. But Nuremberg truly was, along with Augsburg and Strasbourg, one of the most important of Germany's cities, a centre of communications and wealth, and home to many of Germany's finest craftsmen. His description was necessary because Germany was still an idea, a humanist pipe dream, and certainly not yet a territorial unit on its own, aside from being part of the Holy Roman Empire. He was one of the first to describe it as a geographic whole.[1]

Cochlaeus, later a bitter antagonist of Luther, was fascinated by the distinct landscapes and economies of the place he imagined as a coherent whole. Upper Germany, Cochlaeus's 'south', included Swabia, 'famed not so much for the fertility of its clods as for the industry of its people'. It comprised lands of different kinds: the Ries plain, 'once filled with forests and bogs and now brought under cultivation'; 'Vindelicien' around Augsburg, full of towns and not so fruitful; the mountainous Allgäu, and the Hegau, full of castles. Beyond the extensive Black Forest and the fertile Breisgau lay Württemberg, rich in grain and wine, while westwards beyond Mainz and down the Rhine lay Alsace, so blessed by Ceres and Bacchus that 'Alsatian wine can keep for up to sixty years'. Franconia comprised the small towns around Würzburg, situated on 'very fertile soil' and a major wine-growing region, with three major forests, the Spessart, the Steigerwald, and the Odenwald. Eastwards lay Meissen, rich in metals, whose terrain produced 'much fine beer' but no wine, while Thuringia possessed a large forest, 'a very fertile soil, rich sowing, white bread and it speaks Saxon'. Saxony itself, he observed, 'is poor in wine, has a lot of fruit, [and is] rich in beer', but though he conceded that 'no area of Germany can equal Saxony for the number and size of its cities', he had nothing whatsoever to say about the wider region's rich mining and metals industries, which would go on to play a role in the Peasants' War.[2]

Artists, too, were just beginning to discover the landscape of Germany. Albrecht Dürer and Albrecht Altdorfer produced perhaps the first 'real' landscapes, using watercolours, paint, and the newer medium of engravings. Altdorfer's landscape of a castle near Donauwörth (c. 1520) shows the rolling hills of this region near the Danube, but it is the forest that takes centre stage, with its giant spruces and smaller mixed trees. Altdorfer was the poet of the spruce, whose tall trunk produced the fine wood for buildings, with its mournful-seeming, downward-turned branches and needles. Dürer painted scenes from the Franconian landscape around Nuremberg and from his travels through the Alps towards Italy. In his *Pond in a Wood* of 1496, he hints at the menacing darkness of the closely wooded part of the spruce forest. Lukas Cranach the Elder's workshop painted hunting scenes in a nod to the favourite pastime of his patrons, paying careful attention to the silver rivers and dark forests. In other works, the Cranach workshop even mixed elements of birch, fir, and spruce trees into one ideal composite tree, the essence of the German forest.[3]

This land of rivers, towns, mountains, and forests would have looked and felt much different for peasants than artists. Where Cochlaeus abstracted a bird's-eye view of Germany and the artists pursued the landscape's ineffable essence, the peasants' world was close-up and local. Lordship and labour were written into the land around them, in the fences made of woven saplings that surrounded the village, in the field patterns, the paths between the fields, and the way-crosses by the road that led to town. This carefully managed environment was the outcome of generations of interaction between people, animals, and soil. When the relationships of lordship and hierarchy came to be disturbed by the Reformation and its ideas of freedom, a whole agrarian ecology was put into question.

Even peasants' conception of distance was shaped by status and whether they owned a horse. Mostly they used oxen as draught animals to pull the plough and transport carts; the nobles' horses, by contrast, were bred for speed and flexibility. While peasants saw the land in relation to the boundaries of their own fields, the woods, and the complex patterns of ownership and crop rotation, for nobles, fences, ditches, and hedges were obstacles to leap across in the chase.

Lordship and power were represented by height: the fine steeples of rich monasteries dotted the Franconian and Swabian plains, literally making their wealth visible, while the castles of the lower nobility mostly stood high up on hills and peaks above the towns and settlements. Not all of them were still working castles—some were more like administrative outposts, with little in the way of defence, and some were virtually deserted or were crumbling to pieces. Yet others were well fortified and provisioned, like the castle of Heldrungen in

Thuringia, newly rebuilt by Ernst of Mansfeld with moats and protruding fortifications to make it one of the most defensible of the day. A ruler like Luther's prince, the Elector of Saxony, would progress from castle to castle in a cycle over the year, controlling his territory through face-to-face encounters with locals. In his absence, the castellan and a bureaucracy of officials would be responsible. But while some castles embodied government and order, others owned by lesser nobles might be little more than fortified houses. Some of these were not integrated into the system of rule but were potential threats to it, lairs for knights who still engaged in feuds and who used their remaining military power to hold rich merchants to ransom, or who hired themselves out as mercenaries in the service of others. As recently as 1523 one Thomas Absberger had preyed on merchants travelling between the major cities of Nuremberg and Augsburg, holding them captive until they paid— and he had a network of supporters so large that it took the army of the Swabian League to put them down.[4]

Germany in 1524 was a colder and darker world than ours. The little ice age had not yet fully taken hold, but temperatures were still lower and winters harsher than we know today. Weather was a major determinant of survival for townsfolk and peasants alike, for if the summer was cold and wet, crops would not ripen. Many chroniclers note the weather, not day by day but looking back over the year as its effects became clear. Hail in spring could ruin a whole fruit crop. Light was at a premium, and candles made of tallow had to be hoarded to produce evening light in winter; spinning bees in village groups saved on light and heating, while gigantic, tall candles would even be brought as pilgrimage offerings and are depicted in contemporary woodcuts as towering over church roofs. Winter was a time of shorter working hours and indoor crafts, while in spring, as the days lengthened, the pace of work speeded up.[5]

In such a landscape it made sense to grow crops that were not risky, and whose return was reliable even if not large. Peasants grew rye, spelt (an early form of wheat), barley, and oats, and they mostly seem to have rotated crops in a three-field pattern, keeping a field fallow every third year. They kept cows, pigs, and poultry and maintained gardens. Some had horses, though others did not. Some had the right to free tenure; others, even prosperous farmers, were serfs. Cottagers with little more than small gardens insufficient to feed a household had to engage in paid labour on other people's farms. Those without horses or oxen to plough the fields depended on the help of the richer peasants, who in turn hired poorer peasants for labour when all hands were needed. Everyone's work had to be coordinated since fields lay next to one another, and so the village organisation administered common land and determined which crops should be sown and when. The village's animals grazed in single herds, and sheep, cows, oxen, pigs, and horses were moved in a regular cycle by herdsmen employed by the whole community or *Gemeinde*.[6]

True, the rich peasants could benefit most from the common land because they had more animals to graze on it. They also cared more about rents, for tenant farmers had to pay them.[7] But this also meant that they had a real stake in the village's collective possessions and could identify with communal interests as against those of the lords. After all, the social gap between lord and peasant was still far wider than that between rich and poor peasant. This social divide also cemented the bonds of equality between peasants, who might think of each other as brothers.[8]

Most peasants lived in fenced villages, a form of social organisation that fostered community. Settlements clustered around a parish church, and there might be a smithy, an inn, a bathhouse, a communal oven, and, on the rivers outside the village where the stream flowed fast enough, a mill. It appears that the larger villages with such amenities were especially likely to support the Peasants' War. The Gemeinde, the village community organisation, employed not only shepherds but guards to protect the fields at harvest time and undertook a series of

collective duties, including responsibilities for the church. Village organisations were largely independent, with their own elected heads,
though in some areas, such as Saxony, they were by this time increasingly coming under the financial oversight of the territorial princes.
A *Schultheiss* or *Vogt* appointed by the ruler represented the villagers'
interests to the ruler and carried out some functions of rule on his behalf. Richer peasants dominated these assemblies, and in some areas
not even the cottagers (*Seldner*), let alone day labourers and servants,
had the right to participate. Women do not appear to have had a voice
at all. Many areas practised equal division of inheritance amongst all
the heirs, which led to fragmented holdings. As population increased,
pressure grew to restrict inheritance of the farms to one heir only, thus
forcing the siblings who did not inherit to become labourers and creating inequalities amongst kin. How far this would have been evident in
1525 remains unclear, nor would the Gemeinde yet have seemed to be
an organisation of the rich, since kin connections would have undercut
wealth consciousness. In any case, inheritance practices varied widely
from region to region: in Hohenlohe, for example, there was no established custom, and each family was vulnerable to a potentially vicious
struggle over who would inherit the farm.[9]

The strength of these village organisations meant that the peasant
bands would have an address to which to write—the Gemeinde—and
it was these communities that provided the administrative bedrock of
the armed bands which were now starting to form. By writing to a
neighbouring village's Gemeinde and persuading them to join a band,
they knew that their letter not only would be delivered but would be
discussed. By contrast, when they wrote to towns, they deliberately addressed their missives not only to the mayor and council but to the
Gemeinde of the town as well. A village Gemeinde was a corporation
of all its members that met as a group, typically under the village tree
in the open air, and it had financial responsibilities and duties. But a
town Gemeinde, in the sense of all its citizens, did not have a voice

that was independent of the council, because in town constitutional theory, the town citizenry as a whole delegated its power to a council. These councils, sometimes called Small Councils, or Inner Councils, or even just named by the number of their members, crystallised out of 'Large Councils' of perhaps a hundred or more people. By the sixteenth century they were often oligarchies, dominated by the interests of patricians, merchants, and craft elites, while the Large Councils, still only a subset of the total number of citizens, were too unwieldy to make decisions on a day-to-day basis. Indeed, a far more select subgroup of the Small Council undertook the actual business of government. In writing to a town Gemeinde, peasants thereby attempted to create a democratic partner organisation in towns whose citizens lacked this experience. Though city air proverbially made one free, it was peasants whose organisations provoked town democracy.

Just as sixteenth-century artists begin to depict landscape, so they began to depict the peasant. This art can tell us something about the elusive peasants who are the heroes of this book, even if their depictions are framed by artistic conventions and changing fashions.

Though it is difficult to find images of working peasants, it is revealing that many popular woodcuts of the period portray peasants without the landscape in which they worked and with symbolic rather than real animals. By contrast, Sebastian Brant's edition of Virgil's *Georgics* from early in the sixteenth century, apparently a more exalted form of literature than popular pamphlets or woodcuts, illustrates the classical poems with realistic scenes from contemporary rural life. Women tie the grain in bales; oxen and occasionally horses pull ploughs. Peasants wield scythes, dig, sow seed, plant trees, graft fruit trees, pollard trees to use their flexible shoots for fencing, repair machinery, and get the animals to mate. They tend hives of bees (a major area of focus in Virgil's poem), and watch pigs eating acorns. The simple scenes convey the sheer variety of agricultural tasks and the numbers of people engaged in tilling the land. In the background stands the village fence, made of branches plaited together and held between posts, which kept domestic animals in and wild ones out; it also had legal significance denoting the bounds of the village.[10]

Other depictions tell us less than we might wish. Albrecht Dürer made several etchings of peasants. His *Three Peasants in Conversation*, from 1497, shows a figure wearing a turban, another the typical felt hat; one leans on a long sword highly inappropriate for a peasant, while the felt-hatted peasant wears spurs more suited to a knight. Whoever these subjects might be—and debate rages about the incongruous turban, sword, and spurs—they are confident, armed men with none of the disfigurements often associated with 'peasants'. A Dürer etching from

Albrecht Dürer, *Three Peasants in Conversation*. Engraving, 11 x 7.9 cm. Metropolitan Museum of Art, New York, Fletcher Fund 1919.

Albrecht Dürer, *The Peasant Couple at Market*. Eggs, often shown with male peasants as items for sale, also represent 'balls', the subject of many jokes. The woman holds a dead cock. Engraving, 11.5 x 7.3 cm. Metropolitan Museum of Art, Fletcher Fund 1919.

1514 shows a peasant couple dancing; though it represents a wonderful study of movement, the faces are generic, and the woman holds the purse and keys that represent her power over the household. A third, from 1519, shows a peasant with a torn smock, monumental boots, and an open mouth. He is selling eggs and chickens with his wife; both have boorish features.

Dürer's is an urbanite's view of peasants. His portraits are clearly not representations of reality, and yet they may be more complex than they seem: it has been suggested that some of the poses of his peasants are based on the famous antique statue of Laocoön, whose discovery in the Renaissance made such a stir. By presenting not antique heroes but contemporary peasants in the same poses, he subverted classical values while nevertheless caricaturing them as rustics. But there were other, more positive images. The artist Lukas Cranach produced one remarkable watercolour portrait of a peasant, a finely realised study that shows a thoughtful man with a weathered face in a felt hat whose gaze is directed away from the viewer into the middle distance. His mouth is shut—often lower-class people were depicted with open mouths and visible teeth—and his features are not deformed. This is an image of an individual, not a stock character. Tellingly, it is usually taken to date from between 1520 and 1525, the years just before the war, when peasants enjoyed a vogue.[11]

But this was not the dominant way of picturing peasants. A large number of woodcuts and etchings of peasants in the 1530s and 1540s resolutely associate them with sexuality and licentiousness. Popular subjects included the church ale (the annual festival of a church's foundation) and its related genre, the dancing peasants. It might seem that such caricatures have nothing to tell us. They were comic variations on another popular theme, that of the wedding dancers, which showed patrician couples in their finest attire. These urban worthies even have long, etiolated limbs, which are associated with high social status. By contrast, the peasants are squat figures, men and women alike. Yet even though these images are not realistic, they may well reflect the reality of peasant bodies, for peasants probably ate less protein and were likely shorter and more muscular, while their posture would have been shaped by years of hard physical labour. While the burghers, patricians, and nobles are straight-backed and stand somewhat stiffly with both feet on the ground, peasants have a stronger horizontal axis, with only one foot on the ground, arms and legs curved outwards and away from the body in movement. The extensive clothing of the elite literally made them look bigger and slowed them down, forcing them into an erect position, while the peasants' simpler dress allowed their bodies to bend as agricultural labour required. Peasant men wore simple hose and jerkin; women's skirts were shorter than those of elite women.

Hans Sebald Beham's comic woodcut the *Nose Dance*, 1534, reverted to linking peasants with sex. Male peasants with gigantic phallic noses cavort around a pole capped with the sexual symbols of the breeches, the nose, and a wreath. Others dance exuberantly to the bagpipes— another sexual symbol—and if this were not clear enough, there is a cock on a pole in the background. Interestingly they are shown without their actual animals, and there is no landscape of fields or farms. The Trustees, the British Museum.

The ubiquitous daggers the men carry, and which the artists linked to their sexuality, were items they were in reality permitted to wear at church ales.[12]

These ales were moments of release from everyday drudgery when people feasted, danced, and drank instead of hoarding. As a result, they were often the occasions on which rebel peasants met. For the towns-folk who bought these prints in the 1530s—some of them in long, extravagant multiblock series that would reach most of the way around the wall of a room—rustics were quaint creatures, people who were not their equals and who had been defeated, their disorderly rebelliousness curbed. Even so, the woodcuts convey the sheer energy and uproariousness of such events, as well as the pleasures of eating and drinking

Barthel Beham, *Peasants' Fair* (it is in fact a wedding), 1535–1540? On the left, peasants dance around the pole with bride and groom wearing wreaths; note the village fence, made of sapling branches. On the right, peasants play various games, including the maidens' race for the codpiece, wreath, purse, and sword; the sword race; and a form of skittles. Engraving, 38.5 x 107.5 cm. Ashmolean Museum, WA1863.3074, bequeathed by Frances Douce.

to excess. They reveal why peasant gatherings like church ales played such a key part in the revolt—and why townsfolk were both intrigued and alarmed by them.[13]

The 1500s were a period of economic upswing, as population levels recovered from the Black Death and agricultural products began to rise in price. This may seem a puzzling backdrop for an uprising as

momentous as the Peasants' War. Changes in agrarian relations were about to take off, and differences between serfdom in the regions east and west of the Elbe were starting to take shape. In the regions roughly east of the Elbe, a 'second serfdom' would later tie peasants into lordship through increasing labour services, so that the lords employed only a small workforce and most farmwork was done by tenants who paid rent in the form of labour dues on the lords' large estates. In the west, however, most farmers paid rents in money or kind, and while they also might be obliged to perform labour services, their burdens were generally lighter than they had been, although some lords were increasing a wide range of dues as they sought to profit from a more commercialised agriculture. Aside from miscellaneous taxes to support armies and campaigns against the Turks, the state had not yet started imposing taxes at the levels which, in the coming centuries, would become the major burden on peasants. Though political inequality was apparently growing throughout many regions at this time—with village offices becoming increasingly monopolised by a small group of rich tenant farmer families, half a dozen or so in each village, who had more land, draft oxen, horses, and animals—this process, too, did not really get underway until the generation after the Peasants' War.[14]

The context of the revolt was therefore not desperation but relative prosperity, albeit with some poorer harvests and intermittent bad years. The Peasants' War seems to stand at a golden moment of communitarian values and peasant egalitarianism, certainly compared with much of what came later, especially in the east. And yet the war was paradoxically most severe in the southwest, Franconia, Thuringia, and Alsace, regions that included most commercialisation, powerful peasant organisations, numerous towns with close economic ties to the land, and lower impositions. By contrast, the regions east of the Elbe, the duchies of Bavaria and northern Germany, were the least touched by the Peasants' War, but these were not areas where landlord and noble power was weaker, far from it.

People at the time believed that the revolt was the product of unbearable burdens imposed by selfish and grasping landlords. Yet for Thuringia, historian Uwe Schirmer finds that peasants were well-off and their legal situation was secure; they were certainly not suffering from poverty. Indeed, throughout Germany grain prices were broadly stable in the twenty years leading up to the revolt, and harvests generally good, though there are also indications of poorer harvests in many areas in the years immediately before the war, especially of wine grapes.[15]

The war was driven by different issues in the different landscapes; no one explanation applies everywhere despite the uniformity of the rebels' slogans. Conditions probably worsened, but even more importantly, peasants *felt* they were worse because they were becoming less submissive: as ecclesiastical landlords exploited their lands more, or insisted that all their peasants were serfs, peasants sensed their depredations more keenly. Their grievances then gained force because the Reformation was attacking monasticism and church hierarchies, putting their legitimacy into question. Revolts very often began in areas ruled by abbeys and bishops. A confident peasantry, fuelled by Reformation ideas, felt able to refuse to pay the tithe or do the labour services bishops or abbots demanded, and to imagine a world without the ecclesiastical lords they knew. The strength of peasant organisations then meant that it was possible to organise and communicate with the Gemeinde of the next village.

Most farming was subsistence, but growing commercialisation meant that peasants increasingly reared livestock, grew vegetables, took eggs and dairy products to market in towns, and grew cash crops, just as the lords did. In many areas peasants had secure tenancies which were passed on through inheritance and did not revert to the landlord at death. Landlord-peasant relations were a matter of negotiation. Lords imposed rents and labour services and might collect taxes; in return, peasants were supposed to receive protection, 'Schutz und Schirm', from the lord. In many areas the lords had also obtained legal jurisdiction, giving them control over the courts—sometimes the lower courts, sometimes the higher, criminal justice courts as well. As the peasants of Öpfingen and Griesingen in Württemberg put it, if a poor man complained, the noble would grab him by the neck and say, ' "I'll give you justice" and clapped him in the tower'. Other peasant grievances ranged from being forced to use the lords' mills, bakeries, and bathhouses to being required to pay death taxes and dues on a dizzying array of produce; in the southwest they included the host of issues that followed from personal serfdom. Labour services, required whether peasants were serfs or not, were a source of tension—many complained that they were being increased or involved unreasonable demands. Nearly all mentioned control of the key natural resources: wood, water, and meadows.[16]

These complaints and their variety suggest that 'feudalism' was never the monolithic system that Enlightenment thinkers liked to imagine. It was in flux: 'seigneurialism was still dynamic and flexible, changing and adapting to new economic and social circumstances, and often provoking peasant resistance', as historian Tom Robisheaux has characterised it. Peasants may well have experienced it as both protean and bewildering.[17]

Landlord and peasant relations were in flux, but they informed peasants' experiences and lives in crucial ways. The system known as *Leibeigenschaft* or personal serfdom had been abolished in many parts of Germany, persisting chiefly in the southwest, and even there, historians have argued, being an unfree serf had become more a matter of status than a serious problem. The dues that serfs had to pay and the symbols of their bodily subjection—the best hen, some eggs, a coin—may have been humiliating, but they were scarcely oppressive taken singly. Leibeigenschaft also required the payment of certain taxes, such as the best ox upon the death of a man, or the best dress upon the death of a woman, which were more serious but hardly worth risking revolt over. Even the marriage fines seem irksome rather than unbearable. But there can be no mistaking peasants' anger at the system.

As the revolt unfolded, the sharpest condemnations were heaped on the 'grewel' (abomination) of Leibeigenschaft, in which the lord technically owned the serf's body. This was viewed as against God and an affront to Christ, who has bought us all with his precious blood; it denied our shared baptism. Peasants presented it as contrary to the gospel, rejecting it root and branch rather than seeking to negotiate its burdens.[18]

In practice, Leibeigenschaft affected women especially. The symbolic dues of hens and eggs and small livestock all came from women's working sphere. As is the case in many African societies today, women were the ones tasked with travelling to nearby markets, which afforded them more experience with market culture than their menfolk. The requirement of ceding a capon to the lord was a reminder that, no matter how far they travelled or how much they earned, they were still owned by a lord. Eggs and cocks represented fertility and potency: eggs were associated with female love magic; 'eggs' also meant balls, male generative capacity. This was not just a symbolic association; in 1414, a year for which we happen to have the figures, the Teutonic Knights house of Beuggen received the astonishing total of 1,250 hens: 642 of them were tithe hens, 458 were autumn hens, and 150 were carnival hens. Even with large numbers of monks to feed, this was a lot of poultry. The serfs of the monastery of Salem all had to provide a Shrovetide chicken. All those hens could not be slaughtered at once—they had to be fed, kept, and tended and their eggs collected. A flock on this scale may well also have constituted competition to market the women's eggs.[19]

From at least the Black Death onwards, lords had needed labour, and so they had sought to insist on limiting the power of their peasants to marry 'out' of their domains. This practice came to be extended by many monasteries and convents even to those formerly classed as 'free', especially from the fifteenth century onwards. If a woman were to marry out of the lordship to someone from another lord, she had to either pay a fine or else agree that all her offspring would be owned 'leibeigen' by her lord. From his point of view, her reproductive powers belonged to him, and if she did not confer her children to him, it would constitute a denial of his right to future labourers. If a man married out, his wife might be forced to become Leibeigen even if she were of free status. There are examples of women with citizenship in towns becoming servile through marriage, a strategy that secured the lord's labour in the next generation. The peasants reviled these practices. For servile status to be transmitted through marriage was humiliating. The costly marriage fines for 'marrying out' ruined the hopes of the next generation, the peasants of Bronnen said, preventing access to enough land to make a living 'which is bestowed and allowed by God, so that they don't get the happiness and salvation from God, just for the sake of money'. Moreover, as furious peasants pointed out, the wide-ranging rules of what counted as incest devised by the church meant that it was virtually impossible to find someone owned by the same lord who was not related and was of marriageable age.[20]

A booklet from the abbey of Kempten recounts exactly how 335 peasants reported that the abbot had stolen their freedom. Each of the entries is a life story of the misery that efficient lordship could create. Hainrich Dorn, for example, told how he and his five brothers and sisters had been 'captured in our childhood' and forced to swear an oath to the abbey that bound them to remain there. Hainrich Schmaltznapff described how his wife had been imprisoned by the abbot in a castle, bound in irons for five weeks, and how in order to get her back he had to promise to give up his freedom to the abbey. Ursula Necker had been imprisoned, her goods impounded so that she could not sell them, forcing her into starvation, all because her sister had married a townsman and she was compelled to pay the dues in her stead.[21] These peasants were incensed by the loss of 'mein freyhait', my freedom, which the lord took, over and over again, by force.[22]

Even in areas without personal serfdom, such as the Sundgau in Alsace, lords could levy marriage fines, leading free peasants to object that they were being fined for marrying outsiders. The Habsburg subjects of Rheinfelden were free, but though marriages to subjects of a different lord were permitted, their lord insisted that if a free woman married a serf, her children must 'follow the mother' and remain free, acknowledging Rheinfelden's overlordship by supplying the castle with a hen at autumn and carnival. This provision did not protect these women's freedom, however, because Rheinfelden's territory overlapped with that of the Teutonic Knights of Beuggen, who charged such high fines for 'marrying out' that Rheinfelden women had to become subject to the Teutonic Knights to avoid paying. Rheinfelden responded by forbidding such marriages, ending the subjects' freedom to marry whom they chose. Such cases proliferated.[23]

As tenants of a lord, peasants incurred a host of obligations and dues, which might mean payment of money, giving up a proportion of the crop or 'fruit', and days of labour. How onerous these were varied widely, sometimes even within the same village on neighbouring pieces of land, contributing to a sense of unfairness. The same land or piece of property might also be encumbered with other dues to other 'lords' over time—rents and payments that had passed from one person or institution to another, and whose origins might be lost in the mists of time. On top of these were rents owed to landlords and debt repayments that peasants might have taken on during difficult years. The years just before the Peasants' War had seen poor harvests in some areas, and monastic and ecclesiastical institutions, along with towns, burghers, and Jews, were major moneylenders. Taken together, the dues owed the lord could be crippling: on some monastic estates in the southwest, it has been estimated that the monastery got between 20 and even up to 40 per cent of the crop.[24]

Judging from the peasant articles, it was widely agreed that the 'big tithe' was more or less acceptable and should be paid to the church for the upkeep of the local pastor. However, peasants were beginning to demand that the community should have the right to administer it, cutting out the whole system of ownership of tithes that gave clerical institutions power of patronage, and giving the community power to hire and fire their pastor plus manage the surplus once he had been paid. Indeed, the demand was also directed against the system of investments in which tithe ownership was an asset that could be bought and sold, with the owner keeping the profits after the pastor had been paid. The small tithe was deemed unacceptable by almost all groups. It amounted to a tenth of everything else, including garden produce, small animals, orchard fruits, berries, and the like, and it went to the lord (unless, as often happened, it had been sold to someone or something else). All these miscellaneous crops and produce came from the peasants themselves on the land they tilled, much of it by women.[25]

All peasants, not only Leibeigenen or serfs, had to provide labour or *Frondienste*. Nearly all peasant articles mention labour services, days during which the peasants had to work for the lord, demanding that they be reduced but generally not abolished. It is difficult to find out just how many days' labour was required and how onerous this was. The peasants of the Teutonic Knights at Beuggen complained bitterly that the knights oppressed them 'with hard and difficult labour and obligations without rest and peace, they insist and compel us by force, so that to our great disadvantage and to the ruinous harm of us and our young children we have to neglect our own and let them rot' while the knight acts 'as if he had bought us from death out of the sea'. These services could include ploughing and other agricultural tasks that were often precisely specified, but also cartage, such as transporting provisions for the lord's house, work that could be time-consuming and burdened their animals. It could include repair work such as fixing outbuildings, and it could extend to new construction. Given the shortage of labour and the high wage costs, historians have reasoned that lords in this period were probably converting paid labour performed by their servants into compulsory services provided by serfs for nothing—a gradual transformation that was hard to spot and resist. Haulage, for example, might be a labour service that peasants always had to give—but when building was going on, when crops were starting to be sold commercially, when goods were being imported in a more complex economy, haulage could suddenly expand into a major burden requiring peasants to work overnight and travel long distances.[26]

The structures of lordship, however, varied across the German-speaking lands. In eastern Europe and in Austria, as the long-distance grain trade became more lucrative, the later part of the sixteenth century saw the beginnings of the 'second serfdom', when lords increased labour dues dramatically and tied serfs to the land so that richer peasants, who could afford to employ others to work the lords' lands, effectively became labour organisers for the lords. And yet it was precisely in these areas that the peasant revolt was weakest or came with a delay. The Salzburg region did not revolt until May, and Michael Gaismair's revolt did not take place until the following year; in Prussia, the revolt was short-lived and seems to have involved richer peasants. Interestingly, the Twelve Articles did not prohibit labour services but demanded an inquiry into their extent in line with scripture, and other articles of complaint offered to do labour services willingly and obediently if the work was done at reasonable times and paid for fairly. Timing was important because lords and peasants alike needed labour most at the busiest times, especially at harvest.[27]

Many of the original detailed sets of peasant grievances comprise such a torrent of impositions and dues that it is exhausting even to imagine ever fulfilling them all. There were rents (*Gülten*) and tithe rights, legal rights, 'entrance fines' on taking over a farm, imposts of various kinds (*Ungelt*), water and wood rights, the right to drive one's animal along a field corridor (*Vertreib*), tavern rights, death dues— and in lordships that were feeling the pinch as prices for agricultural products fell, these might be pawned or sold off, adding yet further to the complexities of lordship, which was rapidly becoming a commercial rather than a personal relationship. Money itself was often of poor quality; locally minted, its metal content varied, and there were complex rates of exchange that could catch out the unwary. The levels of dues and rents also varied greatly: death dues might consist of the best dress in the case of a woman, or the best animal in the case of a man. But in the southwest they might be as much as a sizeable portion of land, even a third or half of the farm, and yet more apparently unjust, neighbouring villages might pay different amounts. One gets the impression that each right was being exploited, each due increased and extended, labour services expanded so that there was not one single grievance but a flood of ever-increasing burdens. Things that had once been done 'out of good will' transformed into obligations that were now written down and codified in law. Several articles went on to complain that whereas 'before', they were respected and meals were provided in the castle when the peasants gave their labour service, now peasants were expected to bring their own food and were not even allowed to sit indoors. 'Before', when peasants carted wood and produce to the lord, the draught animals were given feed and the peasants refreshment when they arrived, but now they were expected to manage without either.[28]

The sense of exploitation is unmistakable in these grievances, as is the sheer drudgery of agricultural labour. And yet the precise cause of the misery remains intangible, a fact that may well have increased the peasants' anger while also making it harder to negotiate in the time-honoured way, because more than just specific practices were at stake. Though they doubtless idealised a golden age that had never existed, peasants were complaining that relationships which had formerly been based on mutual respect had become matters of compulsion. The entire system had become more complex because of its growing entanglement in an economy where many owned rural rights. With whom should they negotiate? The local 'lord' was one authority, but other lords might also be owed tithes, and taxes might be owed to a ruler. Because of the vagaries by which land was acquired, leading to far-flung territories, and because of the widespread practice of 'pawning'—transferring lordship to another lord for a time in return for payment—the 'lord', and often the monastic or clerical 'lord', might be very far away from the peasant. One individual peasant might owe dues to a host of different individuals, some distant and faceless. As abbacies became more lucrative posts for the scions of noble families, monastic abbots, for instance, often lived outside monasteries in castles or in towns, where they were removed from the realities of farming. When monasteries or nobles in the southwest, for example, tried to rationalise this system by consolidating their estates, they often proceeded by simply swapping large numbers of serfs with other lords, so that while people could not be bought and sold, they could effectively be transferred as if they were chattels that went with the holding. Clergy, the church, and monastic institutions owned substantial amounts of agricultural land, while territorial lords had bureaucrats who did the administration for them, and they, not the lord, were the face of lordship.

Peasant grievances centred on ecology, creation itself. As the lords began to exploit the forests, moving peasants off woods or blocking their access, wood became an increasingly contested resource. Wood was the main fuel for heating and cooking, and so it was vital for all to have access to it. The peasants at Ludwigstadt were furious when they were banned from their nearby forest and had to travel miles to get wood. They were no longer told when the wood was properly dried, and they maintained that it was divided unfairly and that they were 'given it with curses and unfriendly words'. The peasants of Obhausen complained that the lords had taken their collective oven—an important communal resource because of the amount of wood required for baking. Even hay was an issue as lords began to charge for it. Wood for building was at a premium as towns expanded; the half-timbered houses required not only high-quality timber frames from big trees but sticks for the wattle and daub that formed the walls. Sawn timber would be sent down the rivers on barges as the lords began to grow and manage their woods for income. Peasants complained that their access to building wood was being restricted—and it must have been galling to see the forest trees and be unable to chop them down for routine building. Instead, peasants had to pay because wood was valuable. Packaging of all kinds—the barrels that transported wine, beer, and herring—was made of wood. Crockery, also, was often wooden, while wooden stakes were needed for vines and sapling branches for fences. Charcoal made from processed wood drove the smelters for the ore of the mines, and as production of copper increased, so did the need for charcoal. Salt panning in towns like Frankenhausen relied on

evaporating water from brine and hence required kindling for fuel—
they had so little wood that they had earlier been reduced to burning
hay. By mid-century over 260 waggons of charcoal arrived every day to
fuel the smelting furnaces of Hettstedt, Mansfeld, and Eisleben, power
produced in the wooded Harz Mountains.[29]

Woods also played a part in the delicate ecology of farming. On
the forest floor were the nuts and acorns that fattened the pigs in autumn, the 'Köß' as it was known in Swabian dialect. Restricting access
to woods made it harder to get that source of animal protein. For peasants the plants and berries of the forest, the kindling and timber were
resources that were part of creation and should be available to all. Even
local woods that were common land were being encroached upon.
From the lords' point of view, beech and oak supplied food and shelter
for boar and deer, which they liked to hunt. As wood became more
valuable, the forests needed policing, and so the lords began to develop
a bureaucracy of forest officials. These men had to protect the forest,
stop the felling of trees, prevent poaching, ensure that the forest was
husbanded and that the peasants' pigs, for example, did not take all the
nourishment from the soil, destroy the mushrooms, or ruin the forest
floor by rootling. The peasants' interests were thus at odds with those
of the lords, and the forest officials were resented. Some peasant articles
demanded that the community have the right to appoint forest officials, not the lords, for they saw the forests as their domain. And as
the war unfolded, woods enabled peasants to hide from the mounted
knights, who would get stuck in the thickets. Peasant armies often deliberately lined up their forces with an escape route into the forest.[30]

Meadows and commons posed another thorny issue as peasants
complained that the lords were encroaching on the areas the Gemeinde
owned collectively. In Hausen, the village complained that 'although
according to long custom and practice no-one is allowed to drive their
animals through our autumn meadows', the lord and his employees
were doing just that, through 'the best autumn meadows, so that we

can't use them any more'; his actions were destroying their careful husbanding of the land. In Alsace, peasants objected to their local lord driving his animals onto a *Matte* (meadow) they considered to be theirs, and they tried to make him swear brotherhood with them—though this probably would not have given them access to the meadow. But it was not just that lords were taking common land that had previously been available to all villagers for grazing. Peasants resented their takeover of wet, boggy land and reed beds, along with their seizure of waste 'corridor land', because this made it difficult for animals to be moved from one area to another. In Alleshausen, the peasants of the abbot of Marchtal still fumed about the loss of a meadow which had been sold years before to the abbot of St Blasien—he had turned it into a pond, promising to provide a replacement for livestock, but had not done so. At the height of the fighting, Jäcklein Rohrbach found time to intervene in a dispute to get the return of a water-logged meadow to the commune. The bogs (*Moos*) around Leipheim and Gaisbeuren featured in the war, as the peasants positioned their forces on the other side of bogs to prevent the enemy's horses from reaching them.[31]

Nearly all articles raised the question of water. Streams drove the flour mills, the subject of much resentment because peasants were often prevented from using mills other than the lord's. Rivers powered the wire-drawing mills that Dürer admired on the River Pegnitz outside Nuremberg, and they provided the energy for the timber saws. Some articles demanded access to that power, so that peasants, too, could drive mills. One reason Wendel Hipler—a leader of the rebels whom we shall meet later—may have alienated his noble neighbours was because he attempted to run a glass smelter that would have taken both wood and water. In mining areas, rivers were being polluted as production increased. Rivers were also a major transport system for heavy, bulky items. Logs from the forests passed through Wittenberg along the Elbe; produce from the market gardens outside Bamberg was sent down the Regnitz River.[32]

Dogs enraged the peasants. As the hunt grew in popularity, a sport that only nobles could pursue, the nobles required local villagers to feed their hunting dogs with meat. Villagers in Bußmannshausen near Biberach in Upper Swabia complained that that they were terrorised into feeding their lord's dogs, even if it meant letting their children go short, 'and if the dog is not fat enough, he [the lord] hates those people… when he comes to them'—in other words, those who failed to feed the dog adequately felt the lord's displeasure. Keeping dogs to protect the peasants' own crops from the hunt was not permitted, or it was allowed only against payment to the forest official.[33]

By contrast, the lords were able to trample fields of corn, grasslands, and meadows with impunity as they pursued their quarry on horseback in the excitement of the chase, ruining months of work. Often the hunts entailed large numbers of people on foot using ropes to pen all the wild animals into an ever smaller area so that they could be slaughtered en masse. Peasants could not hunt deer or eat venison; this coveted meat could only be provided by lords. It was a status marker, and so when the Lutheran reformers all married in the 1520s, the dukes of Saxony regularly provided venison for their wedding feasts. Lords could hunt boar, deer, and hares, while peasants could hunt hares only in certain areas or not at all. It was when the local official in the region around Mühlberg allowed the hare hunt in a place traditionally off-limits that peasants began to think revolution was on the way and 'perhaps everything would become free'. The following Monday they threw caution to the winds, chopped wood, and went hare hunting. In the skies, the lords could use their trained hawks to hunt birds; peasants and townsfolk caught birds with sticky nets or used special whistles to lure them with cunning. For the peasants, the land was a working environment; for the lords it was a locale of pleasure—and a resource to be exploited for profit.[34]

Above all else, the peasants' anger focused on fishing. In the southern Tyrol, the bishop of Brixen sparked a revolt when he threatened to execute Peter Pässler for repeated illegal fishing. A crowd gathered on the cathedral square and summarily freed him. Often owned by monasteries, fish ponds encapsulated all that irritated relations between layfolk and monastic clergy. Fish was the food for fasting, but ordinary people had to pay for salted herring from the North Sea, while monks had a larder of fresh, delicious fish, there for the taking. Peasants knew how to catch fish with their hands—the clergy did not. River fishing was far more difficult, uncertain, and time-consuming, and as the lords claimed more rights over water, they even banned fishing there. When peasants attacked monasteries, one of the first things they did was to plunder the fish, taking them out with nets and then breaking the dams so that any remaining fish were let back into the streams. At Eichstätt the bishop had erected a bridge over a stretch of common water, for which people were willing to pay, but then he claimed full rights over it, preventing them from fishing. So the local peasants all went fishing, catching bucketloads of fish, and they fined those who did not join in. Fishing out the ponds was fun: in Henneberg, the women persuaded the entire village to drink beer and go fishing, while in Neustadt they fished in the lord's waters to the sound of pipes and drums. A witness who just happened to be in the woods at the time joined in, saying to his wife, 'I'm bored, I want to have a look at how they're fishing'—when unfortunately for him, the lord's official (*Vogt*) rode up.[35]

Some grievances centred on commercial crops. In the region of Swabia around Ulm, Augsburg, Ravensburg, and Memmingen, for example, flax had become important for producing *Barchent*, a mixture of linen and cotton cloth. One local lord described his tenants putting manure on the flax crop, not the garden, because flax was worth more—the lord followed their example. Preparing, washing, bleaching, and combing flax was hard work, mainly performed by rural women. By the sixteenth century, Barchent production had massive economic importance, and the weavers of Augsburg were a powerful force—it was through the weaving industry that the fabulously rich moneylending Fugger family first became wealthy. The putting-out system of weaving was beginning to develop in a whole series of villages in Upper Swabia. These changes meant not only that lords who exploited it became richer, but that peasants who engaged in flax agriculture prospered too. It is striking that some of the areas most actively engaged in the Peasants' War included these flax-growing regions.[36]

As towns grew larger and richer, wine also became a commercial crop. The work was intensive yet seasonal, so many who worked in wine making lived in towns, providing a reservoir of independent-spirited townsfolk with strong rural connections but not subject to lords. Vintners frequently played a role in the Peasants' War. Peasant armies only had to threaten that they would dig up the vines for villages to fall into line—such a threat was credible enough for town and village communes to present it to the authorities as their excuse for joining the rebels. In towns, where water was not always safe to drink, wine and beer were essential. Monasteries were famed for their cellars, huge storage areas that not all peasant households possessed, and this gave them an advantage in selling wine—along with their freedom from civic taxes. For those peasants with enough land to grow wine for sale and export, their interests were furthered by the possibilities of transport and trade; like lords and monasteries, they too prospered, and they complained of unfair competition.[37]

Over the course of the fifteenth century, many lords moved out of less profitable grain and into livestock, which required less labour—though it did require shepherds, including night shepherds, to guard flocks. Many took up sheep farming. Grown for their wool, sheep decimate vegetation, taking land out of cultivation and preventing forests from regrowing; they produce less dung, and it is less rich than the manure of horses or cattle. In Franconia, especially around the Franconian Alps, nobles and monasteries were increasing their sheep holdings dramatically, often at the expense of common land. The wool was not for local but commercial use, and for the lords' profit, not their own. Time and again peasants complained about the lords' shepherds and the encroachment of sheep onto communal lands. Manure was another major issue, for there were no commercial manures and fertility had to be husbanded in the land itself, using the three-field rotation system. Some complained that the lords simply took their good manure without paying.[38]

Taken together, the peasants' grievances were as pluriform and protean as rural lordship itself, and they frequently justified their demands as traditions 'from time past', 'from ancient custom and practice', appealing to an era when relations had been more generous and there was more give-and-take. Of course, such an idyllic past may never have existed, and in a predominantly oral culture it was hard for peasants to prove claims about custom. Their lords, by contrast, had frequently moved to formalising customs in writing, to the peasants' disadvantage, as they believed, convinced that the lords just exploited their mastery of documents to increase dues and trick them. For their part, lords wanted to create coherent estates that were not geographically scattered, and some wanted to get rid of the multiplicity of different local arrangements, creating a single body of subjects who all had the same rights and personal status. This meant breaking with tradition and putting things on paper. Peasants hated the tools of administration, and during the war they frequently burnt the registers and land books that formalised relationships in writing. A peasant of the monastery of Zwiefalten even slashed them with a sword. But the peasants were right that economic growth was changing the countryside and putting pressure on resources.[39]

The coming war therefore had no single cause, but arose from a buildup of smouldering resentments, some petty, some large. There was a pervasive sense that rights had been eroded while dues had increased, amenities had been lost, village independence undermined, and people persecuted through abuses of justice. Every feature of daily life, from acorns in the forest to legal courts, seemed to have been distorted by lordship and its demands, so that issues which were trivial on their own formed part of a whole system of exploitation and unfairness. Often these pitted villages against each other: one village might be exempt from providing the carnival-tide hen, another under the same lord might be giving double; one might be required to provide six days' service to the lord, another, eight—arrangements that came out of the long history of how estates had gradually been put together. Formulating their grievances in discussion with other villages meant people reflected on the specific things they wanted to change, which created political possibilities. The sheer range and variety of complaints reflected a whole economy and set of working relationships that peasants felt to be unjust and unbrotherly. The Reformation exploded in this landscape because it provided a set of ideas showing that such arrangements were 'not Christian'. They had to be transformed.[40]

CHAPTER 3

FREEDOM

The tale of three men, Martin Luther, Andreas Karlstadt, and Thomas Müntzer, is essential for understanding what happened in the German Peasants' War, but their story comprises just a small part of the greater epic. They were far from the only religious leaders on the ground. In south Germany alone well over two hundred preachers were involved in the war, some of whose names we do not even know. Though their ideas and decisions played essential roles in events, it is a mistake to reduce the movement to battles between the radicalism of Thomas Müntzer and the conservatism of Martin Luther. To do so misses how militant, even revolutionary, Luther's ideas could be. In 1520 he was the first to introduce the word 'freedom' and its powerful resonances into evangelical theology. Even more, the course of the Peasants' War was determined not by three theologians, but by many lesser-known pastors, layfolk, and peasants who developed existing ideas and took them in new directions. They did not care to differentiate cleanly between the ideas of Luther, Karlstadt, and Müntzer—all were good gospel folk. Those battle lines did not begin to be drawn until after the Peasants' War was underway, and they did not become clear until after it was over.

The theologian and Wittenberg professor Andreas Karlstadt had once been Luther's right-hand man, but their friendship, which had at first powered the Reformation, began to fall apart by 1522. After Worms, Luther had gone into hiding in the Wartburg, leaving his followers in Wittenberg to implement a Reformation in line with his ideas. At Christmas in 1521 the evangelicals distributed communion in both kinds, with layfolk receiving the chalice. The liturgy was said in German, not Latin, so that ordinary folk could understand, and plans were made to close the now largely deserted monasteries and use the money to establish a poor relief fund for craftsfolk to borrow money cheaply and to give dowries to poor girls. Images were removed from the churches, and clergy who insisted on collecting alms for St Anthony became targets for mockery. Andreas Karlstadt carefully worked on reform proposals influenced by the new religious ideas, and the council was on the brink of instituting a new poor law. Meanwhile in the nearby town of Erfurt, a major ecclesiastical centre with many churches, monasteries, a university, and the cathedral where Luther had been ordained, people had taken matters into their own hands by attacking the hated clergy's houses and property. The Reformation's potential to cause disorder was becoming apparent.[1]

Even Wittenberg's cautious Reformation proved too extreme for Luther. Shortly before Easter 1522 Luther dramatically returned to his university town and set about reversing the reforms that had taken place. In a series of eight sermons he denounced the changes, insisting that 'I was first on the Plan', meaning the field of battle. This was his Reformation, not Karlstadt's. Services would again be held in Latin, communion was to be given in one kind only, the removal of images was halted.[2]

Reform, Luther now argued, had to be gradual and could be introduced only after people had been prepared for it by the preaching of the Word. 'Freedom' ceased to feature in his theology, and though he wrote a preface to a pamphlet that described the founding of a common chest for poor relief in Leisnig in 1523, he grew more circumspect about the social implications of his teachings. Through his close friend and confidante Georg Spalatin, secretary to his ruler Friedrich the Wise, Elector of Saxony, Luther knew the consequences of overt defiance of imperial law. He may also have been alarmed by the following his erstwhile supporter Andreas Karlstadt had gained in the town since his departure, as their friendship was now strained.

Though few outside humanist circles would have known that these two Reformation theologians no longer saw eye to eye, Karlstadt's trajectory diverged from Luther's more and more. Gradually forced out of the university, Karlstadt increasingly doubted the value of academic work altogether. Unable to publish, he moved to Orlamünde, the rural parish he had once paid a lowly priest to administer. All the while he continued to develop his ideas further, arguing that images should be removed from churches in line with the Ten Commandments. He married and started a family, and at Orlamünde he tried to forge a popular Reformation where ordinary people would learn to discuss the Bible themselves.

Two years after returning to Wittenberg, in August 1524, Martin Luther himself arrived in a waggon at Orlamünde, fresh from a debate against his erstwhile friend in Jena. Karlstadt now dressed as a peasant, and Luther had not recognised him under his peasant felt hat. In his sermon at Jena, Luther had implied that Karlstadt had become a rebel, a fomenter of revolt, and a fellow traveller of Thomas Müntzer. Karlstadt had denied having anything to do with sedition, maintaining that his theology could not be lumped together with Müntzer's, and had insisted on a face-to-face meeting with Luther after the service was over. The two men met in the Black Bear Inn, and the discussion, with Luther and the electoral Saxon officials in their livery on one side of the table and Karlstadt and his friend Martin Reinhard on the other, had escalated into the formal declaration of a feud. 'Write against me publicly and not in secret', Luther had shouted, giving Karlstadt a gold coin in earnest of the promise. 'Take it, and attack me roundly, hit me!' Karlstadt had taken and bent the coin. The rift between the two was official.[3]

But Luther had nonetheless undertaken to visit Karlstadt's parish, Orlamünde, and, as good as his word, he arrived two days later to find no one there to welcome him: the peasants were all out in the fields. Irritated by the discourtesy, he was yet more annoyed when the locals appeared and, dispensing with his doctoral title, addressed him by the informal 'you'. They explained that they had removed the images and crucifixes from the church because their presence went against the commandment that you shall have no graven images, quoting scriptural texts at the professor of the Bible. Nothing could better represent the Reformation Karlstadt had created in Orlamünde than the audacity of ordinary parishioners arguing with a university-educated Bible scholar, who was forced to sit with them on their level rather than haranguing them from a pulpit.

By this time Karlstadt no longer used his hard-won doctoral titles in theology and law. Signing his pamphlets as 'a new layperson', he insisted that there should no longer be any division between the laity and the clergy. The 'new layperson' could interpret the scriptures for themselves, and simple folk could experience the grace of God in mystical union with the divine. He trusted that his parishioners were good enough Bible students to defend their views to anyone, even a world-famous theologian like Luther. The sacraments were merely outer signs and were not essential to salvation; the job of the priest should not be merely to administer the sacraments, but rather, along with layfolk, to expound the scriptures. The Reformation was about true freedom, spiritual freedom, but it had social consequences too. The meek, not the academically educated, would inherit the earth.

Luther was not impressed. He scoffed at the ignorance of the countryfolk and set off in his waggon to return to Wittenberg. He sniggered at the peasants' use of the text 'the bride must take off her nightgown and be naked if she is to sleep with the bridegroom' to prove that images must be destroyed: such literalism was the consequence when a village cobbler was let loose on scripture. For his part, Karlstadt rang the bells for half an hour after Luther had left, as one did to warn of storms or scare away witches. Karlstadt had succeeded in humiliating Luther, even more so when he made the story public in a pamphlet written by his ally Martin Reinhard. These disruptions would not go unanswered, however, and soon enough the electoral authorities banished the troublemaker from Saxony. By the end of September, despite his congregation's pleas, Karlstadt had to leave his rural home.[4]

Theologically, Karlstadt was departing from Luther ever more radically, and now, since Luther had validated their feud with the gold token and had enjoined him to 'attack me roundly', Karlstadt was able to publish, free at last of Wittenberg censorship. He began to question the Catholic doctrine that Christ was truly present in the bread and wine of the Eucharist. Surely Christ had died just once, and it diminished the enormity of that sacrifice to insist otherwise. For the Host to become just another relic was symptomatic of the religion preoccupied with objects and money. What was important, he argued, was the spirit, and union with the divine.

Karlstadt was not alone in his view of the Eucharist. In Zurich at much the same time, the Swiss reformer Huldrych Zwingli was starting to develop similar views using different arguments; others agreed, and many reformers in southern Germany also began to share this view, which came to be called Sacramentarian, arguing that Christ was not literally present in the elements of the bread and wine of communion.

It would become a very important rift amongst the reformers, developing in tandem with the Peasants' War. Its legacy, which became evident after the war was over, divided the Reformation forever between Lutherans and Zwinglians, and later Calvinists.

Meanwhile, though freedom receded in Luther's theology, it remained significant in Karlstadt's. In 1525, Karlstadt insisted, 'My understanding of Christian freedom is as true, sound, and certain as Dr Luther's ever was', averring that 'the greatest freedom and true salvation is in the knowledge of the truth which is the Son of God'. When he came to set out the chief ideas of his doctrine, four of his fifteen points concerned it. But he immediately linked 'the fruits of true freedom' to good works that 'bear witness to the inner nature of the tree'. This allowed him to preserve the socially critical dimensions of the word 'freedom': 'But when we do not sense such fruit in our rulers or see the very opposite, such as when a ruler accepts gifts, and favors one person ahead of another, barks at the poor, scares them and such like, we know him to be a false judge, captive to the devil, and of a perverse nature'. Freedom, which, back in 1522, Karlstadt had termed 'the wonderful evangelical light of Christian freedom', retained its radical political potential in his work.[5]

Some months before his enforced departure, Karlstadt had received a letter from his friend Thomas Müntzer. When he read it, Karlstadt's 'blood ran cold', and he was so 'shocked' that 'without reflecting I ripped the said letter in pieces from top to bottom'. But he then had second thoughts and leapt on a horse to ride four kilometres away to enlist the help of his friend Bonifacius von Roda in Heilingen. Roda was as appalled as Karlstadt, but the two men pieced the letter back together on Roda's table and read what Müntzer had to say.[6]

The original letter does not survive, but from Karlstadt's reply it seems to have been an invitation to insurrection. Müntzer seems to have proposed that Karlstadt should join Müntzer's Allstedt league and should write to the mining town of Schneeberg and its surrounding villages to encourage them to join a league designed to resist the authorities. Müntzer had also written to Karlstadt's congregation at Orlamünde, and so first, Karlstadt rushed back to warn them in the strongest possible terms to reject Müntzer's proposal. Then he wrote Müntzer directly, refusing to have anything to do with the scheme, which replaced 'blessed trust in the living God with accursed trust in a man, that is, a hollow staff'.[7]

Who was this man who could reduce Karlstadt to a quivering wreck?[8] Luther named him the 'Satan of Allstedt' and would blame him for the entire Peasants' War. A former supporter described him as 'born for schisms and heresies'; others condemned him as bent on 'murder and bloodshed'. Not one to hold back, Müntzer reportedly spat at another former ally, 'I shit on you and your God, prophets and Bible'. Locals in Mühlhausen and even the officials from the surrounding territory referred to him as the 'Allstedter', the man from Allstedt, as if to emphasise that he was not one of them. And yet the enduring loyalty Müntzer inspired suggests that this ill-tempered outsider must have possessed extraordinary charisma.[9]

Müntzer's theology was and remains hard to grasp. It was at once majestic in its apocalypticism and modest in scope. He preached a radical unworldly mysticism, rejecting the fleshly constraints which held people back from God—but he was a shrewd political tactician, binding village and town to his cause with oaths. He was drawn not to the New Testament but to the Old and its prophets, and knew his Bible so well that he sounded biblical himself. Like no other Reformation theologian he understood and conveyed the Bible's message of social justice, but freedom was not a central theological concept in his thought, and he did not often use the word. Most of what we know about Müntzer is refracted through the lenses of his opponents or of those who desperately tried later to distance themselves from him. It is almost impossible to disentangle the man from the myth—which presents him as someone who acted alone, a convenient fiction that allowed others to deny blame. Yet Müntzer's modus operandi was always to work with others. Even the letter he had written that had so shocked Karlstadt followed a relationship between the two men that Müntzer had built over some years. Given Karlstadt's strained relationship with Luther, he had every reason to expect Müntzer's support.[10]

Müntzer's background was remarkably similar to Luther's. Both were born in mining areas barely forty kilometres apart, Luther in Eisleben, Müntzer in Stolberg in the Harz. Luther was born in 1483, Muentzer no more than six or seven years later, and since we do not know the year of Müntzer's birth, it is possible that the two men were even closer in age. We know very little about his early years, not even the names of his parents. He may conceivably have been the son of a Müntzmeister or money minter (hence perhaps the name), and like Luther, he likely belonged to the handful of families who faced both ways, at once part of the local elite and yet just below the noble rulers with whom they also dealt.[11]

Stolberg was a small town of about fifteen hundred inhabitants whose economy was dominated by the rough work of mining. Miners worked lying down in the tunnels using handheld pickaxes, intimately coming to know a world those aboveground would never see. The ore they unearthed had to be picked over and washed, a task women often undertook. Smelting the ore required charcoal, and slag heaps dotted the landscape. Within the town itself, next to the city wall, the tower of a smelting works is still visible today—the smell of burning wood and ore must have been overwhelming. Müntzer therefore grew up in a double world: one whose depths he probably did not know, and the hilly world above, where even the favoured, clever son of a rich citizen could not escape the hierarchy of the counts in the castle above town.[12]

Unlike the craft-dominated prosperous imperial cities, places like Augsburg, Strasbourg, and Nuremberg, or big markets like nearby Leipzig, with their affluent streets and inward-facing courtyards, mining towns employed large numbers of people who lived in their own households, not those of their employers. In the urban craft workshops, the social relations of inequality between master and servant were masked by one's place in a 'natural' household order. Apprentices, servants, and journeymen were fed, housed, and cleaned for by their mistress and her servants, and they lived above the shop with their fellow workers. And whereas the apprentice would expect to become a journeyman and then a master, by the sixteenth century a miner could only dream of becoming a smelter, running his own shafts, and dealing with merchants in faraway Leipzig or Nuremberg.[13]

Though Müntzer's social world connected him to this rich elite, he also grew up with an understanding of the lot of the miners and their back-breaking work. Unusually, amongst the leaders of the Peasants' War, he saw that the miners would be important to the struggle. He knew how to preach to them, and they responded: in 1525, miners from Stolberg and from Mansfeld were amongst the rebel troops. Luther, by contrast, drew his friends from amongst the mine owners and the bureaucrats who worked for the counts of Mansfeld. Elites, not miners, were his audience.

At some point the young Müntzer moved to Quedlinburg, a larger town not far away, nestled in a valley north of the Harz Mountains. The town, which boasted two Latin schools, was dominated by the castle and by the abbey, a large women's foundation built on the castle hill with a male companion house lower in the town. The abbey dwarfed the town buildings, and the abbess played a crucial political role. The abbey's founder was St Mathilda, the first abbess her granddaughter Mathilda, daughter of Emperor Otto I. The town had a proud history, too, and had been part of the Hanseatic League, only to be expelled through the machinations of the abbess in 1477. Müntzer likely experienced the secular power of the church firsthand, and also observed the political prestige that noble ecclesiastical women could enjoy. Listed as 'from Quedlinburg', he enrolled at the University of Leipzig in 1506.[14]

Alliances and leagues or groups were central to Müntzer's conception of politics. Remarkably for a theologian, he had a gift for creating political momentum, and oath-swearing was key to it, for leagues bound by oaths created lasting alliances. In Zwickau he seems to have formed a group of 'twelve disciples and 72 followers'; in Allstedt, he created a league and got people to swear brotherhood; in Mühlhausen, he called on people to swear an oath to be on God's side—only to be overruled by the local captain, who pointed out that everyone supported God and so there was no need to swear. Müntzer secured both emotional and legal commitment through the ceremony of swearing, and the names of those who made the oath were written down in a book. Perhaps Quedlinburg's history shaped Müntzer's philosophy too, for when its abbess secured the town's expulsion from the Hanseatic League, she stifled its prosperity. The league remained his ideal political form, probably inspired by the Old Testament leagues of the Israelites; in his final confession he admitted that when young he had even formed a league against the bishop of Magdeburg.[15]

Everywhere Müntzer went, from his first post in Braunschweig onwards, he seems to have engineered the same situation. Arriving in a new town, he would join forces with a sympathetic local. The friendship would be compelling and creative, and together the pair would gain adherents, including people from the elite. Worship would be reformed, congregations were fired with evangelical fervour, and it seemed that everything could be transformed. And then, Müntzer would provoke a clash with authority. Blazing with rage, he would force the authorities to hold a hearing in which they would either support or banish him. The process was exhilarating, but the result was always the same: Müntzer's departure. Müntzer was apparently 'driven' from Braunschweig if not formally expelled; in Jüterbog, he became embroiled in a controversy with the local Franciscans that eventually involved both the Catholic Johann Eck and Luther. He was expelled from Zwickau, perhaps forced to leave Prague; he left Allstedt of his own accord and was banished once from Mühlhausen.[16]

His preaching postings were reliably fraught. During his second sermon in Zwickau, panic ensued when one of the beams of the church collapsed, threatening to fall into the nave, perhaps a sign of what was to come. He then moved to another parish, where he gained support amongst the clothworkers. When the Catholic pastor Nikolaus Hofer from Marienthal happened to be present in the congregation, Müntzer attacked him from the pulpit; soon, a crowd was throwing dung and stones at Hofer, and he was chased out of town. Summoned to appear before the bishop's court, Müntzer refused to recognise its authority, calling instead on the bishop's representative to come to Zwickau and 'get into the pulpit and proclaim the word of God'. Next he fell out with a former ally, another evangelical preacher. He wrote to Luther, appealing for his support, and asked him, somewhat grandiosely, 'not to lend your ears to those who criticize me. Do not believe those who have said I was inconstant and biting and who have cursed me with many other titles, I care not a penny for them.... I face difficult struggles.... My cross is not yet complete'. His erstwhile friend Johannes Agricola, a supporter of Luther, found his behaviour impossible; people were saying, Agricola wrote, that 'you are bent on nothing but murder and bloodshed'. Alienating authorities and former friends, Müntzer had settled on an embattled style that fused anger about social inequality with religious fervour.[17]

Banished from Zwickau, Müntzer departed for Prague, leaving his followers in Zwickau bereft. Prague was the centre of the Hussite movement, which had attacked the papacy and called for communion in both kinds a century earlier. We know little about Müntzer's stay except that he produced his Prague Manifesto there, one version of which is a document closely written on one side of a large piece of paper, as if it were designed to imitate the format of Luther's single-sheet Ninety-Five Theses. Deeply anticlerical, it set out Müntzer's theology and reveals his penchant for drawing vivid imagery from the natural world. He begins with himself, in the style of a testament—'I Thomas Müntzer born in Stolberg now in Prague'—and boasts of his ability to understand faith better than any 'pitch-anointed' priest or 'spiritual seeming monk'. Müntzer insists that we are living in the last days and concludes with a demand for a 'reckoning' of faith with God on the part of every believer, himself included, and if he cannot provide it, then 'may I be subject to temporal and eternal death, I can offer no higher pledge'.[18]

Müntzer saw himself as a new kind of preacher, one who explained the text to whoever wanted to listen and whose authentic role was to strengthen the elect by leading them to true faith, which comes through suffering and 'Anfechtungen', temptations or trials, a word that was important to Luther too. Remarkably, centuries later, the East German regime presented the Czech original of the Prague Manifesto (there were also versions in Latin and German) as a birthday gift to Joseph Stalin, and it remains in Moscow to this day.

Müntzer's next sojourn, at Allstedt, repeated the Zwickau experience. He joined the local preacher Simon Haferitz, and the two worked together cleansing the churches of all images, crucifixes, and the like. He commandeered a printing press in Eilenburg to produce a complete liturgy, with music, and began translating the mass into German. He finally opened a printing press in Allstedt itself—as legend has it, in the ducal sheep shed. He seems to have inspired a profound and enduring religious commitment amongst his parishioners, who must have been transfixed not only by Müntzer's rhetoric but by the singing of the mass in German and the ability to follow music and word in print. The whole congregation could now hear and understand the words that transformed the bread and wine. And Müntzer's liturgy allowed the congregation to see at last what the priest was doing at the altar, when before it had been hidden behind curtains as the priest stood with his back to the congregation.[19]

Allstedt was administered by Duke Johann, the future Saxon elector, and was subject to Elector Friedrich, Luther's ruler and also Johann's brother, so that while Johann dealt with the local officials, major decisions were made in concert with Friedrich. Nearby lay the territory of the Catholic duke Georg and the lands of the Catholic count Ernst of Mansfeld, who could draw on Georg's support. When Ernst forbade his subjects to travel to nearby Allstedt to attend sermons, Müntzer and the Allstedters reacted angrily. Hearing that Müntzer was insulting him from the pulpit as a 'heretical rascal and knave' (the English does not fully convey the derogatory tone of the German), Ernst called on the Allstedters to arrest him.[20] However, Duke Johann more openly supported the Reformation at this point than his brother the elector. The region was short of evangelical preachers, Müntzer was educated and inspirational, and his following included town notables, so Johann steered a careful course, reporting to his brother while counselling tolerance. This situation created just the kind of confused authority in which Müntzer could thrive, and which also fostered the early success of the peasants as they began their revolt.

Müntzer had secured powerful support. Hans Reichart, one of the seven richest men in town, along with another of the wealthiest, Schultheiss Nicolaus Rückert, were apparently on his side. Farther afield, the wealthy Christoph Meinhard, a leading personage in the mining world and a councillor at Eisleben, corresponded with Müntzer; Meinhard's cousin may have been Hans Zeiß, the local ducal official in Allstedt. Once again, Müntzer and Haferitz created a faction in the form of a league bound by oaths. As one of the members put it later, they vowed 'to stand by the gospel, not to give monks and nuns any dues, and to help destroy them and drive them out'. The league was not confined to Allstedt citizens; at least five hundred, including miners from Mansfeld, joined on a single day. Luther had grown up with these miners, but Luther was a mine-owner's son, and it was Müntzer's message, not Luther's, that appealed to them.[21]

Although only men could swear oaths, Müntzer urged the unmarried and married women to fight with pitchforks against those suppressing the gospel—and of their own volition some of them rioted in June 1524, while another group of women was so keen to act that they could barely be prevented from ringing the storm bell. In March, after Müntzer preached against it, the Allstedters attacked the pilgrimage chapel at Mallerbach, burning it to the ground. It belonged to the Cistercian convent at Naundorf, and the town now found itself at odds with the abbess, who resolutely insisted that the culprits be punished, just as she had earlier managed to block the Allstedters' attempt to refuse to pay the convent dues. The chapel had a miraculous icon of the Virgin Mary, so the attack also represented an assault on Marianism. Müntzer's rhetoric did not spare the authorities either, not even the elector himself. He reportedly said in public that the elector, 'the old grey beard, has as much wisdom in his head as I have in my backside', while Haferitz preached that the lords were the ones who had founded 'the convents and churches, or you might say whore houses and murder shafts'.[22]

Haferitz and Müntzer were apparently summoned to the castle in Allstedt for private 'admonitions' from Johannes Lang of Erfurt and Justus Jonas, both close to Luther. The local electoral official Hans Zeiß at first tried to downplay the Mallerbach incident and then dragged his heels, helping the culprits to escape. But when Elector Friedrich pressured Zeiß to punish the guilty, he tried to summon the town councillors to the castle to secure their support for the elector's policies—which precipitated a riot. By mid-June 1524, Luther was writing to the electoral prince Johann Friedrich that Müntzer just 'sits on our dung heap and barks at us', and that since the 'Satan of Alstedt' had not come to Wittenberg as he had offered but was fuming in his 'corner', he should be brought to Wittenberg by force to justify himself. By August, Müntzer, together with the town councillors, mayor, and local official, had been summoned to Weimar to meet with the duke's officials.[23]

Once again, Müntzer had precipitated a confrontation where the ruler was forced to choose between him and the opposition. But though the interrogations at Weimar apparently remained polite, Müntzer knew which way the wind was blowing. A week later, back in Allstedt, he climbed over the city wall at night, never to return. A week after that, he wrote a letter to the Allstedt council, explaining that he had to attend to business out of town and promising to return. This letter would come in handy when the local official, Zeiß, had to write to Duke Johann and to Elector Friedrich explaining why he and the council had not informed them of their preacher's departure. The official seems to have been giving Müntzer time to get away—while pretending to the duke that the Allstedters thought he was only temporarily absent.[24]

But if Zeiß was hoping to control the flow of information to the duke and conceal the council's connivance with the preacher, he was out of luck. Duke Johann already knew that Müntzer had left town for good because he had heard it from Georg of Ebeleben, a nobleman who happened to be passing through Eisenach at the same time as the duke. It was old news. Indeed, on 21 August, Luther himself wrote to the town of Mühlhausen warning them against Müntzer; he knew that was where Müntzer was headed. His letter, however, reached the town only after the preacher was already installed. The town would become infamous for serving as the epicenter of Müntzer's Peasants' War.[25]

Mühlhausen was a very different place from tiny Allstedt. A self-confident imperial city of between seven thousand and eight thousand inhabitants, it was not subject to the Saxon rulers and thus was able to formulate its own policies. It boasted fifteen churches, three monastic institutions, six chapels, and several hospitals as well as a powerful establishment of the Teutonic Knights, which had patronage over the main church of St Mary's in the upper town and the second church, St Blasius, in the lower. It had an important cloth-making industry, both in wool and linen, a sizeable tanning industry, and it traded beer, wheat, and the dyestuff woad. But it was also an agricultural centre with an unusually large territory of forest and villages surrounding it.

Mühlhausen had recently experienced an uprising of its own: in 1523 the citizens had formulated a series of political demands calling for constitutional and other reforms, and demanding that the Teutonic Knights ensure that the parish churches were staffed with 'good evangelical preachers'. There were several evangelical preachers in the town, including Heinrich Pfeiffer, Simon Hildebrandt, and Matthäus Hisolidus. When a travelling Augustinian monk preached in St Mary's and called the evangelicals 'martyr thieving', a pun on Martin Luther's name, the itinerant was nearly lynched and had to be escorted from town. It seems likely that some of the Mühlhausen evangelical clergy, knowing of Müntzer's difficulties in Allstedt, seized the chance to bring the powerful preacher to the town. Certainly, he must have had considerable local support from the other preachers, because in a short space of time he was already playing a leading role in civic politics.[26]

Matters came to a head at a wedding in the Star Inn on 19 September 1524; the simmering religious and political tensions boiled over. During the celebrations, the civic court secretary vomited over the mayor, Sebastian Rodemann. Disgusted by this affront to his honour, Rodemann summoned the civic watch to deal with the secretary, whom they clapped into prison in the town hall cellar, a humiliating punishment. But soon other members of the guard released the secretary and escorted him back to the wedding party, laying hands instead not only on Sebastian Rodemann but also his ally, Mayor Johannes Wettich, whom they summoned from his house. Both men were required to appear the next day before the council. Wettich and

Rodemann promptly left Mühlhausen and headed towards the town of Langensalza, putting themselves under the protection of the Catholic duke Georg. They took with them Mühlhausen's flag of black silk, which bore the town's coat of arms, one of the keys to the town gate, and the town's silver civic seal, which was used to validate all documents, depositing all three in a little cupboard with a cathedral canon in Erfurt. These acts effectively destroyed Mühlhausen's civic legal standing. About a third of the town council left as well, creating a power vacuum. The departure of the conservatives created exactly the conditions in which a charismatic preacher like Müntzer could build a faction.[27]

Mühlhausen now began to split between supporters of Pfeiffer and Müntzer, who were based around the Felchta gate in the suburb near Pfeiffer's church of St Nikolaus, and the rest. Trying to gain control of the situation, the council—or what remained of it—locked all the town gates, but the supporters of the two preachers kept the Felchta gate open. They held a procession led by a crucifix through the city, calling on those who wanted to support the Bible to come armed to the Felchta gate, and the group, about two hundred strong, marched from there with a red cross and a sword to the 'Klause' outside town, where they spent the night. It may have been at this point that the 'Eternal League' of the godly was formed. Its members were 219 craftspeople from Mühlhausen, most from the inner city, some from the suburbs, most poor. The next day, however, they reached a compromise with the council and returned to the city. But there was a price: Müntzer and Pfeiffer were banished from town.[28]

In Zwickau it had taken nearly three years for matters to reach a climax; in Allstedt, over a year; this time, in Mühlhausen, less than two months. In Mühlhausen, there had previously been unrest, and Müntzer stepped into an already radicalised situation. Here the tempo had undoubtedly accelerated, perhaps because of Müntzer's presence, perhaps because of his apocalyptic rhetoric.[29]

But matters were moving faster everywhere, not just in Mühlhausen. In Waldshut that same summer, an evangelical faction around the radical preacher Balthasar Hubmaier had gained power, and their vision of a future had joined with that of the peasants. In the much larger and richer merchant city of Augsburg in 1524, there had been an uprising when the council attempted to eject the radical preacher Heinz Schilling and the weavers had tried to prevent it. Long-standing political issues and social tensions had fused with support for the preacher and the gospel. In Nuremberg, peasants from the surrounding villages had met and were refusing to pay tithes, and in early June 1524 a crowd had gathered outside the town hall to show support and demand change, alarming the council there.[30]

Lutheranism could be a radical creed. In Eisenach, Jakob Strauss, a conventional Lutheran, was preaching against usury, attracting crowds. For him, preaching the gospel was inseparable from attacking the injustice of charging interest and fleecing the poor, and since monastic institutions were implicated in lending money, his message fuelled hatred of monasteries and convents. Strauss had formerly been preacher at the mining town of Schwaz and at Hall, a salt-mining town which also was a base of the rich Fugger merchants, so his antagonism to monopoly capitalism and financial practices had deep roots. In 1523 he argued that usury was a mortal sin which had arisen from the Jews and was now a major cause of the 'insatiable greed of the priests and monks'. He went a step further, claiming that those who paid the interest on usurious loans were guilty as well. This earned him a rebuke from Luther, who insisted that he was going too far—that it was not the common man's business to abolish usury but the authorities'. Strauss continued agitating against usury, especially since many owed interest to the Eisenach cathedral chapter. Debtors, he argued, should pay only when interest payments were specifically requested because clerical personnel changed so often that these days no one knew who should receive the interest, an ingenious anticlerical argument that the Eisenach town council then also deployed against the cathedral. In 1524 Strauss published another pamphlet which pointedly asserted that charging usury was against the Christian faith and against brotherly love, 'brüderlicher lieb', the concept that would become central to the peasant rebels.[31]

Antisemitism played a rule in these disturbances. As in Waldshut, Balthasar Hubmaier also voiced concern at 'the huge burdening' of his parishioners from the 'great excessive usury' of the Jews, and he preached publicly 'that one should neither suffer nor endure it'. In his case, concern with usury had led him to preach antisemitic views and then sermons potentially critical of the authorities. After all, Luther himself had condemned usury in sermons of 1519 and 1520, and in 1524 the reformer published his own treatise on usury, which also dealt with financial practices of all kinds. Though he condemned usury and advocated that Christians should lend without hoping for any reward in the form of interest, he also insisted that interest, when charged, had to be paid.[32]

Others attacked the tithe, arguing that it should only be used to support the local priest, and whatever was left over should go to the support of the poor. And in Alsace, usury was an urgent issue because a series of alternating good and meagre wine harvests had forced many into debt and so into the hands of usurers. There, antisemitism and anticlericalism went hand in hand because monastic institutions, ecclesiastical institutions like cathedrals, and Jews were major moneylenders.[33]

Back in 1522, Karlstadt had written that 'God demands of us more freedom than servitude', adding, 'Though a free person in God is God's servant, he, nonetheless, dominates all creatures in the air, in the water, and on the earth'—an argument that peasants later used to argue that they should be able to hunt, catch birds, and fish, and that these rights should not be restricted to nobles. In 1525 he argued that good works follow from 'the nature of the tree', and so 'anyone who knows Christ has been set free by the knowledge of Christ, he walks in good works', whereas the lack of such works proved that a person 'is still held captive in his heart...and has not yet become free in the truth'. Karlstadt, too, was writing about spiritual freedom, but whereas Luther distinguished it completely from secular freedom, Karlstadt's insistence that works flow from freedom allowed him to criticise those in power.[34]

By late 1524, those in Lutheran circles knew of the breach between Luther and Karlstadt, but it would not yet have been evident to those without links to Wittenberg. There were inklings that Zurich and other Swiss and south German theologians were also inclining towards Sacramentarianism, the doctrine that denied the real presence of Christ in the sacrament. Someone like the humanist Otto Brunfels could still hope for a reconciliation: 'I am very upset by the dissension between Karlstadt and yourself, for I favour you both, and I do not love you in such a way that I cannot also embrace Karlstadt most sincerely', he wrote. Zwingli did not arrive at his final view of the sacrament until November 1524 and did not celebrate communion in the new fashion until just before Easter 1525. Luther's attack on Müntzer and Karlstadt, *Against the Heavenly Prophets*, appeared in late December 1524, while its second part, which set out his eucharistic theology, was published in early 1525; the treatise did not yet include the Sacramentarian Swiss or Zwingli amongst its targets. Indeed, the contemporary chronicler Heinrich Hug of Villingen consistently described evangelicals as 'Lutheran' even though many of those he mentioned were in fact Zwinglian or Sacramentarian. For him, as for most observers, they were all the same. Karlstadt's own defence of his positions could not be published until late 1524 because Wittenberg had censored his works, so most people would have been unaware of his position on the Eucharist. Even then, Karlstadt used such tortuous language that it would have been hard to see where he diverged from Luther. Karlstadt forbore from attacking his former friend explicitly or systematically until publication of his *Several Main Points of Christian Teaching* in 1525. In this work, since Luther refused to debate with him, he ventriloquised the reformer, putting words into Luther's mouth that Karlstadt then refuted.[35]

Müntzer was less interested in adumbrating a systematic theology than in promoting the mystical, intensely emotional religiosity that could transform the believer, and for this he needed singing. When he had had access to a printing press at Allstedt, he had chosen to use it to produce his gigantic liturgical works. Music, therefore, and the spirituality it released, came before doctrine. His views were spread in part orally by others and through his own preaching, and this meant that the influence of his ideas was perforce circumscribed. For this reason alone, he cannot be blamed for the Peasants' War because his was not the theology that inspired most of it. Freedom was not one of his major theological concepts, and he had little to say about humdrum rural life, though he railed like a prophet against the 'tyrants', the unjust, unchristian rulers.[36]

Evangelical ideas were evolving quickly, often with dramatic variation from place to place. The hundreds of evangelical preachers, each with their own way of conveying the message and applying it to their own situation, cannot be easily pigeonholed as followers of Luther, Karlstadt, or Müntzer. Many of them would participate in the war, some supporting the peasants, some the authorities; in southern Germany alone we know of at least 220 individual preachers, and over the whole region of the war there were many more. No territory had yet adopted the Reformation, and there was as yet no common liturgy because every local community developed its own.[37]

Even the reformer's attempts to rebuke those who took the Reformation too far had little hope of bringing upstarts into line. Local townsfolk knew their own preachers, not Luther, Zwingli, or Müntzer, and they encountered evangelical theology through their sermons, an oral and emotional medium. In 1524, it might not have been clear to everyone that Strauss's position was more extreme on usury than Luther countenanced. Nor would it have been obvious to all that

Karlstadt was not 'evangelical' in the Lutheran sense. As late as 1526, Balthasar Hubmaier imagined his enemies taunting that 'I was the most wicked Lutheran arch heretic that one could find'—he still assumed they would think him a Lutheran.[38]

Through all the tumult, freedom remained a powerful idea and one that the orthodox preachers could not monopolise. For peasants in southwest Germany, freedom encompassed the abolition of serfdom and the reduction of unfair dues; for others it meant no more unreasonable labour services, rents, and dues. It explained why the lords were behaving in an unchristian manner, and it linked Reformation ideas to agrarian reform. These calls for change proved to be too much for many Reformation thinkers. Facing the spectre of revolt, orthodox reformers backtracked. In March 1525, Johannes Brenz, Lutheran preacher of the town of Schwäbisch Hall, glossed freedom as 'consisting in salvation from sins, temptation, death and hell, and such things'—a definition that had nothing to do with serfdom. Even then, others were becoming still more radical as peasants also began to develop these ideas, turning them into slogans and actions.[39]

The peasants' theology was not the same as Luther's nor any single reformer's. Since the peasants mostly did not write and were not interrogated about what they believed, we must piece their theology together from their actions, the grievances they formulated, and what they were reported as having said. Simply put, they said they wanted the pure word of God to be preached without human additions, they wanted their communities to have the right to appoint their own pastors, they wanted Christian brotherhood, and they wanted freedom. These elements were present in their grievances even before the Twelve Articles were written down, as we can see, for instance, in the articles of the Baltringen peasants of Upper Swabia that have survived and in many others. This shared theology became part of a worldview, enabling them to join with others from different lordships in supporting 'the godly Word'.[40]

For their opponents, these ideas were nothing more than opportunism. One critic condemned this theology as religion 'under the appearance of true piety, as if one were only seeking God's glory, and that the truth of the gospel had been hidden hitherto...and then, everything that leads to disobedience and suppression of the authorities is prettily drawn in'. But even this hostile Alsatian observer recognised that a genuine peasant movement was afoot.[41]

At first, religion played little part in the grievances that peasants articulated. Many lists of grievances from Swiss areas, for instance, did not include theological demands, even after the Twelve Articles had been published. Sometimes demands were limited only to controlling the big tithe on grain and how it was used, or insisting that the community have the power to appoint the pastor just as it had the authority to appoint the local shepherd. These complaints nevertheless owed something to Reformation ideas and were now applied to the situations in which people found themselves.

Soon religion would turn the Peasants' War from a series of specific grievances and complaints addressed to individual lords into an assault on the social order. It was not that previous revolts had lacked religious ideas—religion had often been important—but the sheer scale, coherence, and range of the Reformation's attacks on the church encouraged very diverse groups to join in and helped make the Peasants' War a mass movement. Its theology was remarkably consistent across a very wide area, and its slogans—brotherhood, standing with the gospel, freedom—made sense for a wide variety of people, even though all the areas had different terrains, different property systems, and different legal systems.

They built upon the idea of freedom, the word Luther had used in his *Freedom of a Christian* and which was now linked to the demand for communion in both kinds. 'Freedom' in a legal context could mean 'exemption', a privilege that freed one from a particular due or burden, but now its meaning became wider. Peasant articles used the word 'free' repeatedly; just two years before, when Luther's Catholic opponent Thomas Murner wanted to point out the link to Luther's ideas, he showed a Lutheran peasant carrying a banner with the word. Freedom meant that serfdom was wrong, for people should not be sold 'like the cows and the calves', as one group of peasants said. As the peasants of Äpfingen put it in Swabian dialect, nowhere in scripture can you find 'that one lord should own a human being[;] we all belong to one Lord, that is Christ, he made us and bought us with his sufferings, we want to be his'.[42]

Freedom was about creation itself. As the peasants of Attenweiler said, 'On serfdom, think they [should] have no lord, except God, who created us and made people like himself'—that is, in his own image. Luther, too, had turned to Old Testament creation theology when he based his theory of marriage on the idea that God had created man and woman with natural physical differences so that they were designed for one another. Now the peasants applied it not just to people but to the environment. Woods must be free, water must be free, the animals of the forest and the birds must be free for people to hunt. Here 'free' meant not sovereign, but free for people to use. These demands were not new, but now they formed part of a religious vision.[43]

Creation was familiar to peasants from its common depictions in churches, showing God creating the earth, animals, and Adam and Eve. God made the woods, the water, the earth, and the air, resources given to all humans. As the Baltringen peasants put it, 'God the Almighty let the wood grow and it should serve the poor as the rich'. It was implicit, too, in the symbols rebels chose: in Schmalkalden, the banner had a crucifix on which was written 'Those on the side of the word of God, join this banner!' Fish, birds, and woods were painted on it to show that they should be free.[44]

Yet the peasant theology of creation was not conservationist in the modern sense because it held that the environment was there for human beings to use, not for its own sake. Martin Cronthal, the syndic of Würzburg, reported that peasants themselves said, 'God created the earth and the waters for the help and use of men'. This is a version of the idea that God had given human beings dominion over nature, which is often associated with disregard for the natural world and ruthless exploitation of resources. But as a *collective* dominion, shared by all, it could foster respect for creation, for forests, water, meadows, and animals. Because these were owned by the community, they must not be exploited for individual gain.[45]

This understanding of creation drew on an old distinction between resources that were the result of human labour and resources that God had created for everyone. Peasant theology therefore did not generally demand equal shares of wealth or insist on land ownership or redistribution but concentrated primarily upon dues and obligations and upon how resources should be used. To this extent it was limited in its ambitions. The inhabitants of a group of villages around Bamberg complained that they were very heavily burdened with the hay tithe, the dues on *Schmalz* (lard), and house tithes, which they thought were not in accord with the 'Word of God which has been kept from us for so long'—as if the unscriptural nature of these excessive demands, like scripture itself, had been hidden from them.[46]

Though labour dues should be reduced to a level that was fair, the peasants did not always reject them outright. This, too, followed from their creationist theology, because just as people could not be owned, they did not see labour as a straightforward commodity to be bought and sold. Everyone should labour as Adam and Moses had done, insisted Ulrich Schmid, leader of the Baltringen band. Because Christians owed each other neighbourliness and service, labour dues were not wrong in principle. While the lords should pay peasants fairly for their labour instead of compelling them to provide more services, and should only demand services at 'proper times', the peasant should also 'willingly serve his own lord before others'.[47]

We can see how distinctive this vision was if we contrast it with that of the rebels of the English Civil War a little over a century later, who were inspired by neorepublican ideals of liberty that derived from Roman history. They grasped 'liberty' as the absence of constraint by any higher power, and linked it to independence, not being dependent on anyone else. So long as the king, however, could limit that freedom, even if he did not make use of that power or oppress people, liberty did not exist. The peasants a century earlier thought of freedom as relational, connected to the environment and to each other. In a world of complex interlocking rights where even what crops were planted had to be agreed on, no one decided things on their own but only in concert with others. Agricultural labour could not be performed alone, and land was generally not owned by an individual but was leased from a lord in a contract that extended beyond an individual's lifespan to that of the eldest or even the youngest child. Indeed, in areas of partible inheritance, this resulted in complex shares of land—a half of three-fifths, a quarter of a third, and so on—a gigantic jigsaw of ownership that had to be rearranged whenever someone died or married and formed a new household.[48]

In this society it would have made no sense to talk of 'liberty' of the republican kind that would drive revolutions in later centuries, because freedom was not individual but rather enmeshed in obligations to others. Dependence of various kinds was inevitable and was part of social life. Liberty by contrast fitted a nascent capitalist society with individual property rights, which would soon also include the income derived from the labour of distant slaves, just as the original Roman ideal suited a slave-owning, male-dominated society.

Indeed, the English neorepublican adulation of the free individual 'vir' hid the costs of liberty to others and to the environment; by contrast, the German peasants' claim that Christ had bought us all with his precious blood condemned slavery. Though 'slavery' was not a word the peasants used to describe their situation, their marriages could be restricted or even banned, their children owned by a lord as serfs and pawned to other lords, they could be required to work a fixed number of days on the lords' estates, and they might be subject to the lords' arbitrary justice. In short, many features of serfdom were akin to slavery, so their articulation of freedom was truly radical. What ensured that freedom was the collective, the Gemeinde. For all its limitations, this is why the peasant conception of freedom remains worth pondering today. It encompassed the environment and the obligations of care we owe to others, our mutual dependence, and did not begin by imagining the individual—originally a property-owning male—in isolation.

Creation theology thus elevated brotherhood as a key moral and religious value linked to creation. We are all brothers, rich and poor alike. When a lord arrogated water or the forest to himself, this was unbrotherly. Feudal dues and the small tithe were not to be found in the gospel, and they were 'against brotherly love'. Brotherliness should regulate relations between people under feudalism, a principle that was greater than specific legal demands and expanded the vision of the movement. The Bible should govern behaviour, not 'Eigennutz' or 'Geitz'—self-interest or greed—and in these years the vice of 'Geitz' was widely castigated because it put the individual above the community and conveyed how individuals sought to appropriate resources and wealth for themselves. It meant changing language; every peasant writing is saturated with the language of brotherhood. And it meant changing behaviour, too, refusing all the customary signs of deference towards the lords, such as doffing the hat or using the formal 'you', and forcing the lords to get off their horses.[49]

In practical terms it followed that the true Word of God must be preached and the community must have the right to call their own pastor. As the villages of Erolzheim, Waltershofen, and Binnrot put it, 'As the very first article we want to be able to employ preachers ourselves, who will proclaim the holy godly word to us purely [*lauter und rain*] without any human additions'. The authority of pure scripture took on a totemic quality, for the details of the message of the Word of God were less important than adherence to it. Peasant bands called on villagers to decide not whether they would join the rebels but whether they were on Christ's side. Like the simple dualistic depictions of Reformation visual propaganda, which typically contrasted Christ's life with that of the wicked papists, you were either on the side of the Word of God or you were opposed to the peasants.[50]

Associated with this, especially in southwest German iterations of the articles, was 'godly right', 'Göttlich recht', a term that could be understood as godly 'law' but encompassed far more, meaning 'right' in the sense of true, just, or correct. Peasant complaints mentioned the arbitrary punishment meted out by the lords' courts, but godly justice or right was a larger concept. The Swabian grievances in February of 1525 were formulated at the invitation of the Swabian League for the league's judges to consider; and the autumn's revolts had been initially expressed by bringing a case against a lord. But though this shaped the nature of the league's complaints, they soon moved beyond that framework, leaving it behind in March as they engaged in revolt instead. The peasants wanted to rid the world of 'human teaching' and institutions, that is, of more than 'law' in the narrow sense of human justice systems. Indeed, they were trying to articulate a moral value that would escape the system of courts and adjudication in which they were enmeshed, and which offered no way out of the feudal system. Godly law and the Word of God were understood as self-evident; God's Word as it emerged in their nascent theology was not a complex narrative but a sole, simple truth. It was a badge of belonging.[51]

Fraternalism went hand in hand with a profound and aggressive antimonasticism, an old tradition within anticlericalism that gained new life with Luther's rejection of monasticism. But though Luther criticised monasticism while remaining a friar, his attack unleashed a visceral hatred of monks and friars that shocked contemporaries. Even Lutheran writers like Eberlin von Günzburg were soon backpedaling, warning that not all monasteries should be closed or all monks forced to leave. But it was too late. No peasant articles defended monasticism. Even while pro-peasant pamphleteers castigated 'fleshly lusts', the monastic values of thrift, asceticism, and sexual renunciation were also discarded when the peasants began to march. The peasant movement focused on sharing, enjoying, and consuming together, and rejected the idea that a spiritual elite could ever do the work of renunciation for others.

Theirs was also a vision of the church as local, not universal, and based in the parish alone. This accorded with Luther's early theology: he had questioned the need for bishops and had rejected the pope, the papal curia, and the papacy as the Antichrist. As late as 1523 he had argued that a 'christian assembly or commune' should have the right to call and to dismiss its pastor. He too had dreamt of returning the church to its original purity under the apostles, before bishops and monks were invented. Indeed, in its early years, the Reformation was a congregational event because each preacher devised their own new liturgy to celebrate the Eucharist. For the peasants, the church's place as a relevant spiritual institution was in the familiar landscape, not in the unseen and often unknown world beyond the village. Reorganising the tithe meant abolishing the claims of financial markets and investment vehicles based on tithes. It also meant rejecting the control that the local church's patrons claimed to have over the appointment of clergy as well as the role of the wider church itself. Peasants saw no reason to fund the church beyond their own local parish; they did not see why they should pay for bishops, still less St Peter's in Rome. The church they had in mind had no superstructure, no hierarchy, and no pope; it made good on Luther's early promise to return the church to its state under the apostles, where all were equal and every Christian a priest. That community was to be held together by the fundamental moral value of brotherhood.[52]

The revolt gathered pace through a ritual that was the same everywhere, and through which people lived out this invigorating theology. A peasant band would form and would send an ultimatum to the next village, addressing them as brothers and offering hospitable fellowship. 'We have formed a band of brothers to support the gospel and we invite you to come to us', they would write. This would precipitate the summoning of the community, the Gemeinde, to determine what to do, and the whole village would decide either to join or else to stand aside.

The Gemeinde was both the parish congregation and the body of men who laboured as farmers or as rural craftsfolk and headed the households that produced the next generation of peasants. In a strip-field farming system, where plots of land adjoined so closely, the Gemeinde and not the individual decided when to plant, plough, or harvest, and it paid for communal shepherds, maintained fences, and regulated commons—in short, the Gemeinde was the group of those who husbanded fertility in its widest sense. It was at once religious, political, and economic, which was why the issues the Gemeinden faced in the Peasants' War when they had to 'choose' were also inseparably religious, political, and economic.

It was not an easy choice. If the Gemeinde chose to join, it was rebelling. If the Gemeinde chose not to join, it risked exclusion from its fellow villages and worse. Some later claimed they were bullied into joining, a handy excuse afterwards, though the pressures on those communities were intense. As the slightly menacing second half of the invitation put it, 'and if you will not come to us, we will come to you'. What brotherhood meant, and how it fired the movement, would become clear as the nights drew in and winter advanced.

PART TWO

WINTER

Hans Wertinger, *December* (Landshut, 1525–1526). Germanisches Nationalmuseum Nuremberg.

CHAPTER 4

WINTER

Winter was no time to take on the lords. As the snows fell, pigs were butchered and the animals that had not been slaughtered were brought indoors, into the barn or the lower storey of the house. The granaries were full, the tithe had been delivered, and wood was stacked for winter fires. Animals still had to be fed and watered, cheese made, poultry tended, and eggs collected (though fewer in the winter). In the growing darkness women turned to spinning and men to rural crafts, such as woodworking. This work was often done in groups indoors to save on heat and light, in the so-called spinning parlours, where it was rumoured that courtship and worse went on. Travel became more difficult if heavy rains raised river levels or flooded them, or if there was snow or ice on the roads. Mud slowed carts and made some routes impassable. For once, being on foot had advantages over travelling by horse-drawn cart, and locals knew the right paths. The ground was cold, and when it froze, no tool could pierce it. There were fewer birds to catch with limed nets, but the stags in the forest were tempting targets even though poaching was strictly forbidden.

The slower pace of life and the shorter days made winter a time to think, gossip, organise, and prepare, to travel to nearby villages, and to build coalitions by getting peasants to swear oaths of loyalty to one another. Over the cold months of indoor meetings, grievance hardened into true revolt. Acts of disrespect against authority proliferated, and rumours and provocations led to reactions ranging from the downing of tools to the first truly revolutionary acts. These included receiving communion in both kinds and swearing brotherhood, after which there was no turning back. People began to link their grievances with each other's, connecting the clergy's insistence on communion in one kind alone with their upholding of serfdom. They learnt from neighbours and from tales of past uprisings, and they started to believe that change was possible.

What happened in Waldshut or Heilbronn in the winter of 1524–1525 was soon repeated in many other places. Here is a sketch of events and how they unfolded locally as individuals and communities became convinced that God wanted them to be free. Their intransigence solidified as thousands of people changed their beliefs, emotions, loyalty, and theology so profoundly that they became willing to take up arms.

By December, the revolt that had begun in Stühlingen and the Hegau had definitively spread beyond the Black Forest. On 24 December, peasants met in an inn at Baltringen near Ulm and Biberach, and by early February they had chosen Ulrich Schmid, a blacksmith from the village of Sulmingen, as their leader. They went from house to house, using carnival as an excuse to travel, and when asked what was afoot they innocently replied, 'We are fetching the carnival cakes from one another'. A nun's story suggests how local banter took an ominous turn. A town councillor from Ulm happened to be in the local tavern and asked them what they were doing. 'We want to have a dance', they said. But there are no women here, the councillor responded. The peasants pointed meaningfully at the convent. Scandalised, the councillor warned the nuns at once.[1]

In villages around Memmingen, the peasants had 'sworn together' and promised they would help each other. Church ales, the annual festive celebrations of a church's foundation, offered a pretext for peasants to travel to neighbouring villages, to drink together, and to organise. These had traditionally been held in the summer, when the weather was warm, but such gatherings had been so vital to the outbreak of the Bundschuh revolts that the authorities had been trying to move them to the winter. Weapons could traditionally be worn at these events, making it easier for peasant villages to size up each other's preparedness. In February at Steinhaim the peasants wanted their preacher to preach the word of God and give the sacraments in both kinds, and they wanted the local official to give them wood. They had told him that if he did not join them and help, 'one day they would come and have breakfast with him', a scarcely veiled threat. Marriages, they insisted, should be free, inheritance dues abolished. Clemens Volckamer, on business from Nuremberg at Ulm in early February, was delayed because peasants were assembling everywhere. Others were threatening to join the peasant army if their demands were not met. At Wettenhausen, an Augustinian monk noticed that the local peasants were in a rebellious mood, and when they sent a delegation of twenty-two men to the monastery provost, they refused his proposals. Soon after, they formed a brotherhood and ordered all the pastors in the district to preach 'nothing... but the gospel' or be sacked.[2]

Peasants formulated articles in language inflected by their dialect, demanding that the 'clear word of God' should be preached without human additions. They demanded the right to hire and fire their preacher. They wanted no lord, by which they meant lords who own people, 'but God alone'. The peasants of Mittelbiberach wanted 'no other lord but God for only God the Almighty is a lord of all people'. This was a critique of lordship itself and of its religious sanction. They accused the lords of behaving in an unchristian manner, taking rights over pasturelands, restricting access to woods, chipping away at the reed meadows, the bogs, and the lands that were part woodland, refusing them permission to hunt, forcing payment of dues, and running courts unfairly, demanding unreasonable labour services. These grievances, they explained, had obliged them to gather together, to 'erect the holy gospel and the word of God'. At Baltringen they took to meeting on the moor every Thursday and 'discussing with each other'.[3]

Assembling together, first in hundreds and then in ever larger numbers, they created a group with a collective, Christian identity. They had become a brotherhood, a word they now began to use explicitly. It deeply alarmed the authorities.[4]

And then suddenly in February, as criticism of monasteries and abbeys mounted, Albrecht, the head of the Prussian main province of the order of the Teutonic Knights, declared for the Reformation. The first ruler of a territory to do so, he secularised the main order in Prussia and swore allegiance to King Sigismund of Poland. It was a massive coup for Luther, who had advised him to take this course of action, and it galvanised the Peasants' War, too, because it undermined one of the most powerful of the religious orders, whose monasteries were also major landlords.[5]

In effectively founding Prussia, Albrecht's decision had long-lasting consequences. A brilliant power grab, it turned the Hohenzollern Albrecht from a monk and grand master of an order into a duke, a weighty figure in the empire who could at last found his own dynasty and bequeath his lands to his progeny. The third son of Friedrich of Brandenburg-Ansbach, Albrecht had been destined for a career in the church, and his connections through his mother to the Jagiellonians, the Polish dynasty, meant that he had been chosen as grand master of the Teutonic Knights in 1510. But he had refused to recognise the

Polish crown as his overlord and had involved the order in a costly war with the Jagiellonians between 1519 and 1521. Albrecht's dramatic step in 1525 meant capitulation to Sigismund, but it was a price worth paying. Having secularised the duchy, the following year he married the daughter of the king of Denmark, who also supported Luther, creating an important alliance for the evangelicals. The Hohenzollerns were greatly strengthened, and their manoeuvres showed what determined dynastic strategies could accomplish.[6]

The Prussian commandery (*Komtur*) was the heart of the Teutonic Order, the region of their greatest and most complete dominion.[7] Losing it meant that the order outside Prussia was suddenly and dramatically weakened. Albrecht's example showed how a whole territory could be secularised when a monastic ruler chose to side with the Reformation. At a stroke, Albrecht's step removed the confusion between secular and religious authority that Luther and others had been questioning in the case of the pope. It took yet a further brick out of the edifice of secular monastic power, already threatened by revolts attacking the legitimacy of the wealth and power of the peasants' monastic overlords.

It also was a major stroke against military monasticism, against knights who had been effectively brutal colonisers living in fortified square-shaped castles in a hostile land. They were at once knights and monks, celibate warriors blending different kinds of manhood, housed alongside priestly members of the order. Not so easy to mock as effeminate, nor were they properly knights either.

On the eve of the Reformation, the Teutonic Knights held about 120 monasteries in the empire, some of which were amongst the richest monastic institutions in German lands, populated by 160 knights and 348 priests. On the sunny island of Mainau near Constance, they had a rich, powerful fortress and large incomes from wine growing. In Heilbronn they had an impressive foundation in the centre of town as well as a base in nearby Neckarsulm, where they also stored gunpowder and weapons. In Mühlhausen two separate Teutonic Knights monasteries had the patronage rights over appointments to the two main churches, St Blasius's and St Mary's, as well as a huge stone house in the centre of the upper, richer part of town near St Mary's and another in the lower town. At Beuggen, in the southwest near Switzerland, they had an extensive territory and many serfs in what was otherwise a region of free peasants, and they had patronage rights over fifteen churches, 'with huge, innumerable goods, possessions, woods, fields, meadows and fields. Bigger and richer than three or four villages', as the angry peasants wrote, complaining that it paid no taxes.[8]

So when Albrecht shocked the empire by secularising the Prussian territory, he put into question the future of all monastic rulers and leaders of imperial abbeys, precisely the groups the peasants were attacking. And he undercut the prestige and internal cohesion of one of the richest orders. The furious chronicler of the order concluded, 'May the devil give him luck'. In southern and central Germany, the Teutonic Knights suddenly looked like a realistic target for the peasants and no longer an invincible bastion of military power.[9]

Albrecht's action changed the political imagination of the future and dreams of the Reformation's possibilities. If Duke Albrecht of Prussia, why not Cardinal Albrecht of Mainz? In the same year, Luther wrote to Cardinal Albrecht, the man against whom the Ninety-Five Theses had been directed, cheekily suggesting that the cardinal marry his mistress. If the churchman had done so and secularised his lands, the Reformation would have been vastly strengthened and the cardinal's family's power hugely increased. Wolfgang Capito, who was at the court, seems to have thought earlier that the cardinal was on the verge of turning Lutheran. We know with hindsight that Capito was mistaken, but in the summer of 1525 the cardinal even sent Luther a wedding present of twenty Gulden, as if he approved the marriage of a former monk. Monasticism, it seemed, was on the way out. In Beuggen, the Teutonic Knight Komtur Ludwig von Reischach saw the writing on the wall: he joined the Reformation, married, and was pushed out of his post, so he tried instead to get his hands on some of Beuggen's incomes.[10]

Half a century later, by 1577, there were only fifty-three priests left in the entire Teutonic Knights order, mostly in the Catholic Habsburg territories; in Franconia there were just two priests to thirty-six knights, who were obviously unable to meet the needs of parishioners. The monasteries of Saxony and Thuringia, which had formerly been full of the order's priests, disappeared. In Franconia the peasants caused 9,000 Gulden worth of damage to the order's commandery at Mergentheim and burnt down its German headquarters at castle Horneck above Gundelsheim. In all the regions where the war raged, the peasants, especially the order's own subjects, attacked it bitterly. In Prussia that August, the bishop of Samland transferred all his secular authority to Albrecht, on the grounds that 'it is not fitting for a prelate and bishop, whose first duty is to preach and proclaim the Word of God, to rule over lands and people, or to occupy castles, territory and cities, but rather to adhere to the true and undiluted Word and render it obedience'. This statement repudiated a system that allowed bishops to be secular rulers, using Luther's radical distinction between worldly and religious power. Though the order ultimately survived, partly because it remained attractive to noble families, for a while its peculiar combination of wealth, secular power, knightly values, and racial superiority seemed to have finally had its day.[11]

The winter's events in Heilbronn displayed how religion was becoming everybody's business. That February, in his nearby village of Zimmern, the knight Götz von Berlichingen was trying to stage his own Reformation showdown. A Franciscan from Heilbronn had been preaching in the area, attacking the Lutherans, amongst them Götz's own preacher at Zimmern. The wily Götz noted that a local lord like himself was obliged to protect his subjects from false belief. But since a lord was not expert in matters of faith, he had decided to stage a disputation between the Franciscan and his own preacher. As judge, Götz nominated Johann Lachmann, the Lutheran preacher of Heilbronn and a leading light of the Reformation in the district—a master stroke that embroiled the town of Heilbronn in what would otherwise have been a minor local spat. He not only wrote to Heilbronn of his plan but had placards posted announcing his intention, thus placing Heilbronn on a collision course with the empire because Lutheran preaching was technically banned. The Franciscan wisely refused to take part and appealed to the emperor. Lachmann, who should have been keen to trounce Catholics in debate, found himself in an uncomfortable position because the council did not want him to be drawn into this dispute. Götz, however, had brilliantly displayed his evangelical credentials, and he had created a cause cèlébre in Heilbronn: posting the placards had all the hallmarks of declaring a feud. It also stoked evangelical fervour.[12]

By March at the Heilbronn Carmelite monastery, people were mocking the mass on Marian feast days and toasting the Host at the elevation, and an evangelical bathkeeper had tricked his way into the monastery, where he tried to convert the monks. One monk retorted, using the informal 'you', 'Dear fellow, I will not dispute with you, you are not on my level, I'm a priest, you're a peasant'. He clearly could not tell the difference between a peasant and a town bathkeeper. The bathkeeper had been accompanied by a prominent noblewoman whom the monk had also failed to recognise, and she lost no time in putting their side of the story to the council. The Carmelites fumed, but their abbot had just made the mayor's daughter pregnant. By 9 March, the council was ordering the monasteries to preach the gospel and was making an inventory of their valuables, another intimidating gesture.[13]

Pressure to introduce the gospel was also mounting from outside Heilbronn. In Lent, the peasant leader Jäcklein Rohrbach wrote to citizens in the town, asking them 'to help...bring the children of Israel into the promised land'. When Lachmann, the town preacher, was shown these letters he warned them not to join. Jäcklein Rohrbach may have seen himself as a latter-day Moses, leading a pilgrimage to a land flowing with milk and honey. But such words were more than just a call to religious reawakening. In the Old Testament, Moses leads the people into the land that was to be theirs to possess, a dream of a landscape which the common people, not the lords, would own. Old Testament visions were yoked to calls for ending serfdom and owning the land.[14]

The ripples that had started the previous year in Waldshut with Balthasar Hubmaier's Reformation continued to spread that January and February. His motto, used on many of his printed works, became 'The truth cannot be killed', a saying that implicitly evoked martyrdom and struggle. Hubmaier was profoundly influenced by Zwingli and the Swiss Reformation, but soon he questioned the baptism of infants since Christ had called for believers to be baptised, not babies. This mattered hugely, because the practice of infant baptism meant that everyone was a member of the church, and if believers alone should be baptised, only a minority, those with true faith, would be members. Such a doctrine would mean that the church congregation and the secular community would no longer be the same thing; the church would not include everyone. Hubmaier had sounded out other leading Swiss theologians for their views on whether infant baptism was scriptural, and they had agreed with him. But by January 1525, Zwingli in Zurich finally made it clear that he disagreed with Hubmaier. Soon Zwingli and Hubmaier, once allies, became bitter enemies, like Karlstadt and Luther, who had also fallen out.[15]

By supporting their preacher Hubmaier, the townspeople of Waldshut were disobeying their Habsburg overlord in Austria, and so they were soon threatened by the Habsburgs, who had the military capacity to defeat them. They would soon be isolated from Zurich as well, which did not agree with their stance on baptism. Hubmaier himself married in January. Because of Waldshut's political isolation, the town was sucked into the conflict that had now moved to southern Germany, and it came out in support of the peasants.[16]

Meanwhile the peasant revolt was spreading. In February a Lake Constance band formed at Rappertsweiler near Lindau, led by the nobleman Dietrich Hurlewagen. And in January up in the Tyrolean Alps, the miners rebelled, marching by the thousands towards Innsbruck. Archduke Ferdinand was not going to risk a revolt in the mines as well as of the peasants, and so they were soon bought off with concessions.[17]

Meanwhile, banished from Mühlhausen, Thomas Müntzer and his co-worker Heinrich Pfeiffer went to Nuremberg. We know that Pfeiffer was exiled from Nuremberg in late October as a 'disciple' of Müntzer. Nuremberg had just been embroiled in the case of the 'godless painters', the brothers Barthel and Hans Sebald Beham and Georg Pencz, who were members of the artist Albrecht Dürer's workshop and had apparently belonged to a radical circle involving Hans Denck, a schoolmaster and proto-Anabaptist. Its town council was therefore alive to the potential for sedition and unorthodox belief amongst its own citizens.[18]

In September 1524 the later Anabaptist Hans Hut had taken Müntzer's *A Manifest Exposé of False Faith* (*Ausgedrückte Entblössung*), the reply to Luther which he had attempted to print at Allstedt, to Nuremberg, a far larger printing centre with a greater market. He had it printed by Hans Hergot, who by a fine irony had also printed Luther's two attacks on Müntzer. When Hergot's workshop was called to account by the council in late October, his journeymen claimed that they had printed it without his knowledge—a not entirely convincing assertion, since Hergot himself would later be involved in distributing, printing, and possibly even writing the radical anonymous tract *On the New Transformation of the Christian Life* (*Von der newen Wandlung eynes christlichen Lebens*). This later tract would cost Hergot his life:

arrested in Leipzig in 1527, he was beheaded on the town marketplace for printing it. In Nuremberg, Müntzer now had his pamphlet *Vindication and Refutation* (*Hoch verursachte Schutzrede*) printed by Hieronymus Höltzel, who had also printed a work of Karlstadt's.[19]

From the Nuremberg area, Müntzer next went to Basel, where he met with the Swiss theologian Oecolampadius. This humanist scholar had adopted a Sacramentarian position on the Eucharist that Karlstadt also held, denying that the body and blood of Christ truly were present in the elements of bread and wine. Two excruciating versions of a letter to the Catholic patrician Willibald Pirckheimer of Nuremberg survive in which Oecolampadius, desperately minimising the extent of his contact with Müntzer, attempted to exculpate himself from accusations of being a peasant sympathiser. As we saw, Müntzer may have contacted Hubmaier or even have been in Waldshut and in the Black Forest region in late 1524 or early 1525. We know that he was in Schweinfurt in early February, and the surrounding area would soon play a central role in the Peasants' War. Meanwhile Müntzer's coworker Pfeiffer had already managed to return to Mühlhausen, possibly by gaining support from the surrounding villages, and on 13 December he was back preaching at St Nikolaus in the suburbs. In early January, in Mülverstedt near Mühlhausen, a group of women, including Ottilie von Gersen, Müntzer's wife, interrupted vespers at the Wilhelmite monastery, also the parish church, and they were held under house arrest with guarantors for some time before finally being interrogated by the local official Sittich von Berlepsch. These intersecting itineraries reveal how radical ideas were finding new audiences. It seemed that by banishing Müntzer and Pfeiffer, the town council had merely succeeded in spreading their radicalism.[20]

Pfeiffer's church was St Nikolaus, just outside the city wall, and when Pfeiffer's supporters gathered there, the council locked the gates and tried to exclude them. Unable to reenter, they had to spend the night encamped outside. But they soon insisted on having their own lock and key, and when they returned their movement grew more powerful.

By mid-February, Müntzer began his return journey—but not without a brief period of imprisonment in Fulda, where the authorities failed to recognise who he was.[21] Nevertheless, on 28 February, riding the crest of the populist wave, he was installed as town preacher in the most prestigious church in the centre of Mühlhausen, St Mary's. At last, patronage over appointment to the main civic church had been wrested from the hands of the hated Teutonic Knights, who, as the council chronicle noted, had consistently failed to provide the people with evangelical preachers. The man who had been forced to leave town just months before could now move into a massive house opposite St Mary's, with a large, well-appointed kitchen and fine rooms. This impressive residence, which belonged to the embattled Teutonic Knights, symbolised his new power—Müntzer had installed himself in the best house in town.[22]

The situation in Mühlhausen had changed. Once again, control of the city became territorial—though St Nikolaus's is outside town, it is close to St Mary's, and this axis gave the evangelical faction a real base. Mühlhausen became radicalised, and events moved fast. Peasants from the surrounding villages were flocking to Mühlhausen to hear Müntzer preach, and soon the reviled Ernst, one of the counts of Mansfeld, was threatening his subjects with punishment if they dared attend the preacher's sermons, even attacking them physically when he caught them. Müntzer condemned Ernst as a bloodthirsty tyrant, later accusing him of having 'attempted to obliterate the Christians'. The preacher took to walking about the streets with a Bible, stopping to give extempore scriptural exegesis to passersby, and the demands of eschatological time overtook the lives of ordinary townsfolk. Though he did not speculate on what exactly the Last Days would be like, Müntzer was certain that a final battle was approaching. He trusted that when it came, the Lord would protect his people.[23]

*   *   *

The local bands of peasants began to flow like streams into a river as the revolt spread. Bands that had started with scores of men now swelled to groups of hundreds, and then thousands. They chose leaders. Soon the subjects of the bishop of Augsburg joined the Allgäuers after thousands of peasants had assembled at Oberndorf in a 'ring'—a formation that underscored equality in brotherhood—to insist that the bishop come in person. He did, telling them in a friendly manner 'not to be rebellious', but matters had already gone too far for such appeals. The peasants refused to speak to him and formulated articles of grievance instead. And when he would not give them the keys to the church at Oberndorf, they simply battered the door open with a plank, rang the storm bell, and plundered the parsonage. The Kempteners decided to take the abbot to court at the Swabian League and sent their representative to Ulm, but soon they called him back, sensing they were strong enough to engage in direct action.[24]

By February eight thousand peasants had formed what they soon termed the Christian Union, bringing together various bands in the region. The Lake Constance army wanted the Word to be preached 'with its fruits', by which they meant its implications for ethical human behaviour, a word that also evoked the fertility of the earth. By the beginning of Lent, the Baltringen band from the Christian Union was writing to towns explaining that a 'Christian Assembly' had met to act 'according to the word and content of the godly word, which one should discover and learn through learned, Christian men', and asking whether the town would be 'helpful and advise' if our 'Christian offer' were to be 'attacked'.[25]

The letter reveals how the peasants' mood was shifting. Although written by a scribe using all the customary formulae of politeness, the missive contains important twists. In place of the normal salutation, it wishes 'much salvation, grace, peace and a strong belief in Christ', and appeals to them not only, as was usual, as 'Wise, gracious dear lords' but as 'brothers in Christ'. Addressed not only to the council, but to the 'whole community as well', it reminds the council that, unlike a lord, its power was not its own but derived from the whole 'community'. The rebels would advance this idea throughout the war as peasant armies repeatedly refused to deal only with town councils, preferring popular assemblies that would take a different line from the old, conservative oligarchies. Since the 'community' was included in the salutation, locals could claim that the council had withheld a letter that was addressed to them as well. It was these popular assemblies that would prove vital in subverting the power of the old town councils and forcing them to admit the peasants.

Behind the courtesy, the letter's menace is unmistakable. If the town will not be 'helpful' to the 'Christian band' against its 'many enemies…who plan to resist the godly word', then—what will happen is not specified. The entire document is a religious statement, not a demand. Instead of saying that the peasants have grievances, it says only that they have joined 'to act according to the letter and content of the godly word alone'. By repurposing letter-writing conventions of address, which always began by restating and acknowledging relationships of power, the peasants' scribe had composed a revolutionary document.[26]

Conventional Lutherans could also become more radical, as is clear in the case of the town of Memmingen. Little more than a year before, in 1523, their town preacher Christoph Schappeler had attracted the bishop's notice for preaching that it was not true that failing to pay the tithe was a mortal sin; the spy who reported him added that Schappeler had said that priests would soon be confessing to layfolk, both men and women. Schappeler was excommunicated by the bishop of Augsburg, but the town council refused to banish him.[27]

Though they outraged the bishop, the ideas circling in Memmingen at this point looked like orthodox evangelicalism. When the local lay pamphleteer and furrier Sebastian Lotzer published his pro-Reformation *Thirty-One Points of Christian Doctrine* in 1524, he spelt out standard Lutheran doctrine, stressing the importance of brotherly love and true works, condemning monks, and explaining that those who preach the gospel are truly 'bishops'. Lotzer dedicated his pamphlet to 'Bishop' Schappeler, a dig against the local bishop, who had excommunicated him. Lotzer made the sharp distinction between flesh and spirit that would later become important to south German evangelicalism, urging his readers to 'gird your body so that it does not become too lusty but remains subject to the spirit'. He did not mention Zwingli or Luther and avoided most thorny theological issues, such as images or the real presence in the sacrament, insisting that he was a layperson. But he concluded by praising those brothers in Christ 'who have put their hand to the plough' and who are called 'Lutherisch': 'they are the ones of whom Christ speaks'. Clearly in Lotzer's mind, south German evangelicalism was not distinct from Lutheranism.[28]

About the turn of the year, this serious Christian layperson, concerned with good morals and upright behaviour, suddenly became much more radical, perhaps because of a powerful religious experience that has left no trace in the records. At Christmas 1524 he probably took part in the Reformation disturbances in Memmingen, for he then wrote a pamphlet in their defence. There were true evangelicals, he wrote, and then there were hypocrites, those who were steeped 'in greed [*geytz* or *Geitz*] and fleshly desires thinking that the heavens will fall on them at every moment'—and yet these people want to be thought good evangelicals. They 'buy many books, talk a lot about the subject, but their wealth suppresses the Word'. He defended those who had recently caused a disturbance in Our Lady's Church in Memmingen, likening the uproar to Christ clearing the temple of the moneylenders.[29]

Christ's clearing of the temple had featured in the popular Lutheran *Passion of Christ and Antichrist*, a set of thirteen pairs of images satirically contrasting the deeds of the papal church with Christ's actions to point out how far the church had wandered from the Christian ideal. Written by Luther's coworker Philipp Melanchthon and published in 1521, it was a brilliant piece of propaganda and one of the best-known works of the Lutheran cause. It included an image of the pope and his indulgence sellers greedily gazing at piles of money opposite an image of Christ scattering the moneylenders. The contrast between the papal church and Christ could not have been starker, and perhaps this was the image Lotzer recalled. Perhaps he saw himself in its light.[30]

On 2 January 1525 the town council held a 'disputation' to decide on true religion, and 'Bishop' Schappeler (who had spent time in Zurich, where he was influenced by Zwingli and had chaired the Second Zurich Disputation, which confirmed the Reformation there) formulated a set of demands that mixed religious reform with condemnation of the tithe. He now disputed the legitimacy of tithes altogether, insisting that the idea that divine law obliged people to pay the tithe did not appear in the gospel. The two men were working in concert, and Sebastian Lotzer, who had begun as a stalwart citizen craftsman, gradually ceased to care for the views of the rich and powerful, the hypocrites who were guilty of greed.

As winter drew to a close, peasants began arriving in Memmingen in numbers. They had already formed armed bands and elected captains. On 6 and 7 March a peasant parliament of representatives from the bands met at Memmingen and formed a much-expanded Christian Union of Upper Swabia, which brought together all the various groups of the wider region. Three hundred lists of local grievances that the communities had formulated were submitted to the Swabian League. Just getting a scribe to put down on paper that, for example, 'they want to have no [over]lord but God alone' was radicalising, and hundreds of tiny villages did it. Even individuals had their say: Christian Reyter wrote that he wanted 'no [over]lord, for he had God, who is a lord of his body and of the soul'.[31]

Religious language and ideas were intrinsic to the ways in which many of these articles constructed their arguments. It might be objected that they could have been written by priests, some of the few literate people, and that their religious phraseology was imported, not authentically 'peasant'. But the references to God, creation, and Christ were not added by Lotzer when he formulated the Twelve Articles; they were already part of peasant discussion. The ideas and demands of the grievances were similar, but they were phrased in different words and applied in varied ways; they were being 'thought with'. In simple words that were close to dialect, they connected religious ideas to the specific requests in such concrete terms that it seems almost comic: 'for we think also, that the divine scriptures does not prove this, that no lord should have ownership [serfdom], for God is the true lord. But we are heavily burdened with paying the carnival hens'—and they went on to list other dues to which they objected. This is not high-flown religious rhetoric. Priests in small communities were often also farmers, so there was little division between the worlds of the church and of the peasant. The sheer range and specificity of the other demands (which vary greatly from place to place) reveal how close these articles were to local experience.[32]

The town of Memmingen had also asked its peasants to formulate grievances in an attempt to head off revolt. They ultimately presented not individual complaints but a programme of ten articles. We know that the Christian Union's members were by then divided into three clear groups, the Baltringen, Allgäu, and Lake Constance bands, and it seems they disagreed about whether to resort to force, with the Allgäuers refusing to rule it out and preacher Schappeler insisting on nonviolence.[33]

Each group consisted of local armies, a total of twenty-nine at least, and up to 5 representatives per army were present. A surviving list names all 110 representatives, grouped under the areas from which they came, and it covers the entire region surprisingly evenly. The bands were clearly in flux as they grew larger, encompassing more groups: the Wettenhausen peasants, for instance, whose 22 delegates we saw earlier refusing to negotiate with their abbot, had now disappeared as a group, subsumed into the Leipheim band. Simply meeting together must have been an overwhelming experience, as the assembly covered most of southwestern Germany. They would have spoken with slightly

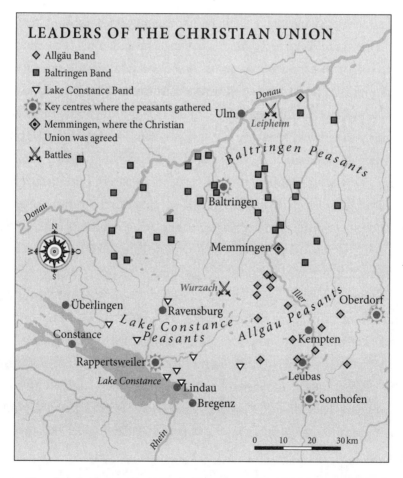

Source: Cornelius, *Studien zur Geschichte des Bauernkriegs*, 191–196. Map compiled by Aaron Larsen; drawn by Peter Palm.

different dialects—and indeed, the Allgäu ordinance insists that no one should mock anyone else for their dress or their speech.[34]

Peasants from monasteries and with overlords far from one another could now share information and experiences beyond their local community. They seemed to have elite supporters too. When asked by the Swabian League to nominate judges, they could list half a dozen preachers and the mayors of twelve different towns amongst others whom they thought would be sympathetic; originally they had proposed Luther, Melanchthon (Luther's coworker at Wittenberg), and others but soon realised their mistake.[35]

With the peasants massing in the town of Memmingen, Lotzer the furrier retired to the pedlars' guild house, now the peasant headquarters, to organise the hundreds of local complaints into a set of clear articles. The Kramerzunft was that of the small retailers, not the rich merchants, and its members probably sympathised with the peasants. Brilliantly reducing hundreds of detailed points of complaint to twelve key demands, Lotzer's articles allowed everyone to recognise their own concerns: peasants free and unfree, townsfolk, and, as we shall see, miners.[36] Written in rhythmic, memorable prose, the demands sounded biblical, and there were twelve of them, like the Twelve Apostles; indeed the document reads at points almost like a devotional creed. Providing scriptural texts for each claim, a technique Lotzer had used in earlier pamphlets, it gives chapter and verse from the New Testament (which Luther had translated into German in 1522) to prove that the peasants were on Christ's side.[37]

The articles began by addressing the 'Christian reader', vigorously rebutting their opponents' standard charges that the peasants were disobedient or rebellious by arguing that 'the gospel does not cause rebellions and uproars, because it tells of Christ…whose words and life teach nothing but love peace, patience and unity. And all who believe in this Christ become loving, peaceful, patient, and one in spirit'. Rather it was their antagonists, the 'antichristians' (*Widerchristen*), ranged against them who were calling the gospel 'a cause of rebellion and disobedience'. However, it continued, 'it is not the gospel that drives some antichristians and foes of the gospel to resist and reject these demands and requirements, but the devil, the deadliest foe of the gospel, who arouses through unbelief such opposition in his own followers'. Lotzer here neatly turned the tables on the peasants' enemies, arguing that it was they, not the peasants, who were led by the devil. Satan wished to 'suppress and abolish the word of God', but that Word, which the peasants were defending, 'teaches love, peace, and unity'. Indeed, 'it surely follows that the peasants, whose articles demand this gospel as their doctrine and rule of life, cannot be called "disobedient" or "rebellious"'. Since all they wanted was to 'be permitted to live according to his word', to resist their plea was to oppose God himself. The preamble constantly invoked nonviolence, using words like 'love', 'peace', 'patience', and 'unity' to build a picture of peasant piety while attributing aggression and diabolic inspiration to the other side, an emotional template they would employ repeatedly during the war. But it was also a carefully constructed demolition of their opponents' claim that the peasants misunderstood 'freedom' and the 'gospel' and were nothing more than fiendishly inspired rebels.[38]

The articles themselves began with the request that 'henceforth we ought to have the authority and power for the whole community to elect and appoint its own pastor. We also want authority to depose a pastor who behaves improperly', the principle first set out by the Schwabach contract of employment for its priest. A theological document as well as a charter of revolution, it stated in unforgettable terms in the third article that 'it has until now been the custom for the lords to own us as their property. This is deplorable, for Christ redeemed and bought us all with his precious blood, the lowliest shepherd as well as the greatest lord, with no exceptions'. Therefore, it continued, 'the Bible proves that we are free and want to be free'. This ringing statement echoed Luther's invocation in his *Freedom of a Christian* and Zwingli's idea of godly justice, as well as the articles many peasant bands had already drawn up, insisting that God was their only lord and that we are all serfs of Christ. Lotzer made the link to communion in both kinds explicit: the blood redeemed us and secured our freedom, and therefore the clergy had done wrong by keeping it from the laity.[39]

The articles then addressed all the grievances of agricultural life, grouping the plethora of specific complaints by resource and deriving the demands from the theology of creation. Peasants should be able to hunt, because 'when the Lord God created man, he gave him dominion over all animals, over the birds of the air, and the fish in the waters'. They should have access to the forest, and it was wrong that 'our lords have seized the woods for themselves alone'. The 'small tithe' levied on animals should not be paid because it was unscriptural since 'the Lord God created cattle for man's free use; and it is an unjust tithe invented by men alone'. Labour services should not be excessive, rents and laws should be fair, common meadows and fields expropriated by the lords should be 'restore[d]' 'to the community', and the death tax should be abolished because it treated orphans and widows 'shamefully'. Similar demands had also been made by the Bundschuh and Poor Conrad movements years before, but now they formed part of a comprehensive religious vision. The articles concluded that if any article were shown to contradict God's word, they would rescind it 'when this is proved by the Bible', echoing Luther's statement at Worms that he would recant only if he could be proved wrong with scripture.[40]

When Ulrich Schmid, a smith from a village of the convent of Heggbach and leader of the Baltringen band, formed the peasant army, Lotzer was asked to be its secretary. At first he refused because, as he recalled saying, 'Dear Ulrich, it is not unknown to you that you are the leader of a great army, which is why you need especially talented, learned men. But I am a simple, common tradesman; I have never practised in any court or in any chancellery, or even substituted for any notary, so considering the seriousness of your business you won't be well served with me'. But he finally agreed to do so, 'so far as they should be satisfied with his industry and seriousness'. Lotzer refused to take any pay. In the space of barely three months, the pair of ortho-dox evangelicals, Lotzer and Schappeler, had become revolutionaries, prepared to risk everything to support the peasant cause. They were not the only ones to undergo such a transformation. The peasants had already experienced it.[41]

The Twelve Articles did not invent the theology of the movement but synthesised ideas that peasant groups had already formulated during that autumn and winter; many had already called for the com-munity to be allowed to hire and fire its preacher and for the true gos-pel to be preached. Those ideas came out of the experience of talking, holding meetings, and joining in bands to take on the lords. Nor were they adding a religious veneer to demands that were economic. By this time the attack on monasticism and monastic lords had become a driv-ing force of the movement, while calls for Christian brotherhood had been part of its appeal from the outset. Neither townsfolk nor those who could write had a monopoly on deep religious experience, and the peasants were clear that they felt compelled to call for godly justice and the word of God.

Admittedly, compression brought losses: written by a townsman journeyman furrier with the help of a preacher, the articles did not in-clude all complaints—women's about midwives, for instance—or al-ways convey the detail of the rural economy. Many peasant articles had demanded total abolition of service dues, and some had questioned the tithe altogether. But the articles accomplished a clear programme with a biblical justification that all could accept.

In a sign of the times, the Twelve Articles were printed: twenty-five printings appeared within two months, a total of perhaps twenty-five thousand copies. They could be distributed and held, pointed at or stuck on a nail on the wall, and their materiality was perhaps even more important than their contents. Time and again, peasants would call for their lords to accept the Twelve Articles, even when they did not know what the articles contained, and when other peasant bands drew up their own local version of 'articles', they frequently devised 'twelve' as well.[42]

A Memminger Bundesordnung (Ordinance of the Memmingen league, also known as the Allgäuer Bundesordnung) was agreed for all three groups, founding a Christian Union, and it was to be proclaimed from all pulpits. It, too, was printed. Though the ordinance proclaimed that all dues would be paid, order and peace maintained, and all debts repaid, it also stated that disputed dues like tithes, rents, and *Gülten* should be withheld until matters had been resolved. The occupants of all castles and monasteries were called upon 'in a friendly manner' not to provision, arm, or place guards on their property, unless these were members of the union. All 'servants' of the princes and lords were to break their oaths, and then they might enter the Christian Union—or else they should leave with wife and child. Pastors should be admonished 'in a friendly manner' to preach 'the holy Gospel', for which they would be paid fittingly, or sacked and replaced if they refused.[43]

The ordinance envisaged a new order for the region: each army should elect a superior and four councillors to make decisions so that the whole Gemeinde did not constantly have to be summoned. And while they might have forsworn violence for the moment, the ordinance would have undermined the nobles' administrative power by requiring their officials—their 'servants'—to swear to the union and preventing them from arming and provisioning their castles. The title page of the Augsburg printing shows armed mercenaries and peasants in a thicket of lances, pikes, pitchforks, and clubs, with a final image of two peasants about to shake hands. It was hard not to view the ordinance as a declaration of war, or at least of resistance with military threat. Schappeler seems to have been advising the peasants too, and the Swabian League soon wrote to Memmingen complaining that the pastor's interventions made it harder to reach agreement. The council should either instruct him to distance himself from the peasants, it warned, or else admonish them to be obedient to the authorities.[44]

By early March, something much wider than local revolt was afoot. As the days lengthened, the soil warmed, supplies from last year's harvest thinned, and Lent began, it seemed that the whole of Germany might rise. But no one could have predicted what would happen next.

CHAPTER 5

LORDSHIP

'We want to have no lords', the peasants demanded—or so the authorities said. But what they meant by lordship, which lords they wanted no more, and even whether they said this at all cannot be taken for granted.

As a part of the Holy Roman Empire, Germany in 1525 was ruled by Charles V, who also ruled Spain, Austria, the Low Countries, and parts of Italy and the New World. The vastness of Charles's international empire affected the course of the German Peasants' War. When the war broke out, Charles's troops were too busy in Italy fighting the French during the Italian Wars to deploy against the peasants. Even when Charles's German mercenaries gradually returned after late February, the feudal levy system of raising military forces failed to function properly, and authorities struggled to recruit men willing to fight against the peasants. This military vacuum allowed the peasants to make considerable advances initially, bringing many areas under their control between March and June. But it cannot explain why, during the Peasants' War, an entire edifice of rule collapsed, at least for a time, like a house of cards. Lords who had never known having their right to exercise authority questioned now found that their subjects simply ceased to obey. Families split, and hundreds of knights, town councillors, and local bureaucrats who had run what seemed to be a stable political system went over to the peasants.

One cause for this collapse of authority was the empire's confusing patchwork of different rights and claims. What prevailed was not what we today understand by 'rule'. Rather, it was a kind of negotiated governing that depended on cooperation and, ultimately, comparative strength. Rights and jurisdictions could be bought and sold or even swapped. The buyer of a castle might gain judicial rights associated with it; the tithe of a village could be bought as an investment. This system of scattered authority gave many a stake in power, strengthening its hold. But because sovereignty was frequently fragmented and not unitary, subjects could sometimes pick their fights and play one authority against another. When the system came under pressure in the war, and the seemingly unshakeable grip on power of individual lords suddenly loosened, the allegiance of those below them faltered too. And since so many people exercised power in such a multitude of ways, as landlords, tithe owners, judges, administrators, abbots, or abbesses, there were more potential points of attack.[1]

The word 'Herren' referred to the landlords, but also to social superiors and governmental authorities in general. God himself was the 'Herr', the Lord. And yet rule constantly had to be shored up in the face of threats. Duke Ulrich, for example, stepped into the revolt in Württemberg, allying with the peasants to try to recover his duchy from the Austrian Habsburgs after the Swabian League had deposed him in 1519. Though he did not succeed, he gave legitimacy to the peasant cause, and he undermined the power of the remote Austrians. After all, the Habsburgs were not the 'natural' rulers of the area, and so peasants and townsfolk felt they could legitimately support Ulrich. In 1534, his persistence paid off when he finally got his lands back. Hubmaier in

Waldshut could also thumb his nose at the Austrians, whose authority he did not accept, remaining the town's preacher because he had the town council's support. Conversely, for the chronicler Heinrich Hug, from the same region, the Austrians were the rulers of his town, Villingen, and for him, Catholicism was inseparable from loyalty to the Habsburgs. Villingen did not join the peasants' revolt when much of the area around it did, even when the troops of the Swabian League delayed coming to its aid for so long that the town risked being taken by the peasants.

Within these units, sovereignty was frequently shared, not monopolised by an individual. For example, the counts of Mansfeld governed their territory as a group until 1501, and all five of them, brothers and cousins, even collectively administered the mines they owned until they finally split the mine revenues between themselves in 1536. Similarly, the knightly Schwarzburg family jointly owned the salt dues of their lands, and in Saxony, Duke Georg ruled the separate ducal territories, while his cousin Elector Friedrich governed Electoral Saxony, giving his brother responsibility for administering parts of it.[2]

A narrow ruling class joined people in the church, monasteries, and states through kinship and marriage; lords thereby exercised their power through their family relationships. Rulers were constantly writing to kin. When Wilhelm of Henneberg wrote to the coadjutor bishop of Fulda, he could address him as 'Dear Son'; he had the family features too. Count Hermann of Henneberg wrote to his son Albrecht advising him to inform his 'cousin' ('Vetter') Count Wilhelm of the peasants' movements. In this intimate world, relationships were publicly manifest in an elaborate language of coats of arms. Family ties kept this ruling class together, conferring both secular and ecclesiastical power on its members.[3]

A younger son of a noble family who went into the church, or a daughter who became a nun, could still enjoy the trappings of their status, and since abbots, abbesses, and bishops might also be territorial rulers, they exercised similar forms of power. The Benedictine abbot of St Georg in Stein am Rhein, David of Winkelsheim, had his own private lodgings in the monastery with a bedroom overlooking the Rhine, and as the war broke out he had just finished decorating his fine parlours with gorgeous frescoes of classical figures in the latest style, including a shapely Lucretia, all of which he funded by pursuing the monastery's debts. These churchmen memorialised themselves too. The bishop of Strasbourg featured in an elaborate monument in the church of Saverne, the town that was his episcopal residence. He is shown in three-quarter relief with his pudding-bowl haircut, kneeling before Mary, John, and the crucified Christ in front of a fine Renaissance double archway that shows off his taste. Albrecht of Mainz, son of the elector of Brandenburg and a member of the Hohenzollern family, commissioned no fewer than three funeral monuments, including one massive stone sculpture in the cathedral of himself in bejewelled mitre. Both men were secular rulers heading extensive administrations as well as men of the church, and they embellished their memorials with family coats of arms.[4]

Everywhere, blood was thicker than water. The young Philip of Hesse had just married the daughter of Duke Georg of Saxony, cousin to Friedrich the Wise, who ruled the electoral half of Saxony; and so it was to Georg and Friedrich that Philip turned when he determined to put down rebellious subjects in Fulda and near Hesse. Meanwhile, Duke Johann of Saxony took a much more aggressive line than his brother the elector, and he could do so because he had long been responsible for the Thuringian region. The five counts of Mansfeld, subject in turn to Electoral Saxony, would each build their own perfect Renaissance castle on a shared site. Ernst of Mansfeld, who remained Catholic, was deeply hated by Thomas Müntzer and his supporters because he persecuted those who travelled to Müntzer's sermons. At Heldrungen he had built the latest in castle design, a grim, squat redoubt with thick walls that also housed a dungeon, which Thomas Müntzer itched to attack. Ernst provoked conflict, while his cousin Albrecht of Mansfeld, sympathetic to Luther, initially took a more conciliatory line. Though other members of the family would eventually join Luther, leading to bitter arguments and splits within the family, they were united in opposing the peasants.[5]

But such intimate bonds of blood and kinship fomented family dramas, too, which likewise affected how the rulers responded to the revolt. The elector Friedrich the Wise wrote moving letters to his brother Johann in which he confided his weakness, while treating his cousin Georg with more distant respect; he could trust his brother but not his cousin, who must have envied Friedrich's electoral status. Wilhelm of Henneberg walked a tightrope between cajoling and bullying a son who was not up to the task of resisting the peasants. The young Ulrich of Rappoltstein worried that if he was not able to prevent the peasants entering town, he would be 'shamed' before his father, brother, and entire kinship—though he was also careful to point out that his father had left him in the lurch when he failed to provide any assistance. (He recorded how one of the peasants claimed that the gospel said, 'The father will have to be against the son and the son against the father'. He mocked the man's ignorance of the Bible, but he had remembered the words, which described his situation exactly.) Father-son relations were indeed strained by the war, and the legacies of filial ruthlessness from before the war affected it too. Casimir, Margrave of Brandenburg-Kulmbach, who proved one of the most vicious avengers against the peasants, had deposed his own father in 1515 and locked him in a castle.[6]

The peasant uprising jolted this ruling elite. At first it seemed that Electoral Saxony, sympathetic to Luther, might escape the revolt altogether, leaving Duke Georg of Saxony, a Catholic, to bear the brunt. Elector Friedrich, Luther's ruler, was seriously ill, and he did not believe in fighting the peasants. He preferred always to wait, manoeuvre, and take a middle course; politics for him was the art of compromise. As the revolt spread, he became resigned, writing to his brother Johann on 14 April 1525, 'Perhaps the poor folk had reason for this disturbance and especially with the forbidding the preaching of the Word of God. Thus the poor are burdened by us secular and spiritual authorities'. He went on, 'If God wants it so, the result will be that the common man will rule. But if this is not his divine will,…matters will soon change', revealing a surprising passivity on the part of one of the most powerful princes of the empire. His brother seemed to agree, worrying that 'your grace and I are now destroyed princes. It is without doubt the will of God', though he was not prepared to stand idly by. Friedrich's fatalism was not unique: the coadjutor bishop of Fulda wrote that the revolt was 'perhaps God's judgement and punishment'. A deep-seated crisis of legitimacy seems to have overtaken some leading rulers during the Peasants' War, as if they feared that God might punish rather than support them.[7]

The crisis extended to lordship itself. Feudal relations were not always sanctified by the patina of age. Lordships were pawned or sold, and nakedly monetary relationships displaced ones built on hoary precedent. The Lord of Rothberg sold the villages of Rottersdorf, Hofstetten, Metzerlen, Wytterswyl, Bettwyl, and others to Solothurn, turning them into serfs of a town. The town of Kenzingen came under the overlordship of the Austrian Habsburgs, but they regularly pawned it to Strasbourg in the fifteenth century, and then in 1515 to the noble Wolf von Hürnheim. When the Austrians insisted on expelling Kenzingen's Lutheran preacher, von Hürnheim had to find a course between the town and the Austrians, now at loggerheads. Wendel Hipler, later a peasant leader, had followed the usual career path of social ascent for a commoner official. Through canny purchases he built up a small estate for himself at 'in der Fischbach' and accumulated local tithes, while developing a river-transport business of wood he had cut down. In 1507 he called himself 'von Fischbach' and devised a coat of arms featuring two fish above some waves. His business ventures and career as an official helped him become a 'knight'.[8]

Lordships had always been bought and sold. But the greater the market in land, and the more knights, lords, and religious institutions exchanged territory or pawned the odd castle as they tried to unify their territories, the less certain the dues and feudal relations attached to land appeared to be. More than one lord might have claims on the same farm, and a single individual might have to deal with several of them. A neighbouring farm with similar land might have different seigneurial dues to pay merely because of its ownership history, and this could nurture a sense of grievance. A single village might have more than one 'lord': the peasants of Oberholzheim were subject both to the nuns of Gutenzell and to the town of Biberach; the district of Hilzingen had no fewer than three local overlords. Lords were equally ensnared in the system because they owed allegiance to a ruler above them. Caught in the middle were many small-scale knights, like Georg of Werdenstein, who owned a castle or fortified house but lacked the wherewithal to defend himself from bands of peasants. The 'lords' you could see were the most hated. With misplaced optimism, the peasants in the territory of Bregenz, who were ruled by the distant Austrian Archduke Ferdinand, told the local officials that the archduke himself was supporting them 'in part' and would not like the measures being taken against them.[9]

The law was meant to mediate feudal and monetary relations, yet it was also multiple and complex, lacking even a single legal code applicable to all. The Swabian League functioned as a judicial authority as well as a league of mutual support and military force for those in its region, and there were imperial courts of appeal as well as local ones. Higher courts could simply override other courts' decisions. Land lordship did not always bring judicial lordship, and judicial rights could be sold or divided. Justice was sometimes meted out by courts of local nobles, and villages might have to purchase their judicial sovereignty. On top of that, clergy could insist on being tried by church courts, a completely separate justice system with its own law. Appeals often took years, even decades, to settle. But justice nonetheless offered a forum for peasants to try to regulate the lords' behaviour, or at least slow it down, to insist on customary rights of use and access, and to defend common lands—in short, to test serfdom. Courts generally imposed a moratorium while a case was being heard. Argument, legal cases, rent strikes, and even uprisings had thus become part of the tissue of relations between lords and peasants where the revolt began in southern Germany, Switzerland, and the Black Forest.

The weakness of overarching structures was glaring. The Swabian League was a relatively recent creation from 1488 that covered parts of southwest Germany and included many free cities, knights, and rulers. It relied on the assessed contributions of its members, which had to be agreed by all. It was therefore not in the league's interest to pay mercenaries for long periods, and it was hesitant to commit to fighting the peasants. It had, however, succeeded in suppressing the disruptive Franconian knights in 1522 and 1523, and when it expelled Duke Ulrich from his lands in 1519, it proved it could be a powerful force once it had decided to act. Because the league valued consensus, it took time to decide to give up on negotiations with the peasants, which many still thought the better course.

So when, during the early weeks of the war, the authorities suddenly lacked the military power to shore up their position, lordship was exposed as a bond not of affection but of domination. Many lords were shocked to find their subjects had turned on them. Georg of Werdenstein was at mass when the peasants arrived, and with his wife and daughter standing by, he asked them, 'Dear chaps, what are you accusing me of, what have I done to you?' Soon he found that even his own servants had 'fallen to the peasants' and were holding their meetings in 'his' parish church, and 'no-one was allowed to speak with me, or with my folk, or have any companionship with us'. In Alsace, Ulrich of Rappoltstein expostulated, 'What was all this?...For they had gracious Lords, and it ill suited them to believe a rascal rather than me'. Georg

Truchsess, commander of the Swabian League, was incandescent when his own peasants in the lands he had inherited from his father joined the rebels, because 'I have never oppressed my poor people and others…but helped and counselled them'. The prior of Weissenau tried to persuade his peasants at Ummendorf to resolve their differences. He summoned all the local officials to meet in his house, along with his secretary and other clergy, and reminded them that the village had belonged to the monastery peacefully for 150 years; he himself had been their pastor for 23 years and had shown them 'much good', making peace between parties, advancing money and corn and other things, being godparent to their children. How could they want another lord? The Bambergers, by contrast, refused even to meet their bishop when he offered to ride out to the peasant camp.[10]

Men like Werdenstein, Truchsess, and the prior believed they were good lords, not exploiters, and that their peasants were bound to them by love and loyalty. They could not comprehend this antagonism. But the lords could choose whether to be gracious to their subjects, a luxury the peasants did not have. To its shock, the convent of Heggbach found itself threatened by its own peasants, who refused to give them the hens and eggs that symbolised serfdom and then withheld the grain they owed, saying it was theirs; the nuns these peasants hated most were the notary and the dues collector. Some of the anger towards the lords and the ruling monasteries can be heard in the words of Hans Schulte, the captain of the peasants in the bishopric of Bamberg: 'For we have decided to leave no castle or monastery in the land standing', because many an honest man had been imprisoned in them, and 'you would find more criminals' bones in [the monasteries'] prisons than Halstatt where the condemned criminals are buried'.[11]

The flip side of a system of lordship bound by oaths of loyalty and idealised mutuality was the feud. In his autobiography, the knight Götz von Berlichingen mentioned no fewer than fifteen feuds in which he had personally participated. He had attacked merchants between

Forchheim and Nuremberg in 1512, captured Philipp of Waldeck and won a handsome ransom, and been imprisoned in Heilbronn by the Swabian League. These men earned their living by threatening towns and taking hostages to ransom. During the short-lived Knights' War of 1522–1523, Franz von Sickingen had laid siege to Trier on the pretext that the town had not paid a ransom it owed him. It was therefore fully in line with past behaviour when men like Götz von Berlichingen or Florian Geyer threw in their lot with the peasantry, and they were often pursuing previous enmities through joining the rebel armies. Their idiosyncratic sense of personal honour and loyalty acted as a kind of wild card, upending the verities of feudal society, and the Peasants' War gave their aggression scope.[12]

To maintain their standing, knights had to invest in armour, horses, and military kit. They were trained in how to carry the weight of armour, how to ride a horse while wearing armour, and how to wield weapons while riding. Suits of armour were highly crafted objects sometimes decorated with filigree engraving, works of immense skill that had to be fitted to the individual, and the craftsmen of Nuremberg led the world in producing them. With the advent of gunpowder, knights were having to learn how to use handheld firearms, which were still inaccurate and unreliable. Soon the knights' power would be dwarfed by the might of massed pikemen, but this technological revolution in warfare was just beginning. With his imposing armour, war horse, and upright posture, the lord looked nothing like the peasant in his hat, boots, and jerkin. A group of no more than half a dozen mounted nobles in armour could still put a small band of peasants to flight, and even the sight of mounted lords was sometimes enough to make peasants flee.[13]

But the days when armoured knights dominated warfare were numbered. Their castles were often cold, draughty, and hard to heat, and so, not surprisingly, they liked to spend time in town. Many castles had outdated fortifications that were difficult to defend, while others had simply crumbled. To maintain his standing amongst his fellows, the knight had to give hospitality, keep a good table, dress well, and have a stable of horses, all of which was expensive. Castles—often built and maintained through the forced labour of peasants—could be seen for miles and wrote lordship into the landscape. It was not surprising, then, that peasants hated them. The articles of the Franconian peasantry called for 'harmful castles, moated houses and fortifications' to be 'pulled down or burnt', and in barely ten days in mid-May about two hundred castles were destroyed in the region of Bamberg alone.[14]

The lords' servants—their bureaucrats, some of them noble—were also related to each other, and the Peasants' War caused this group perhaps even greater anguish. The brother of Wilhelm of Henneberg's official Tham von Herda, for example, was a Saxon official. Hans von Berlepsch was castellan at the Saxon elector's castle, the Wartburg, and his brother Sittich von Berlepsch was the electoral official at Salza. These men lived in the castles dotted over the landscape and travelled from one to another, and each had his own servants and retinues. But the court of the ruler was often far distant, and help took time to arrive. They were the lords' men, who might even wear their lords' liveries, the colour and cut of their clothing making them instantly recognisable. While they might own lands themselves, they were isolated and had to get on with their local communities. They had to send reports back to their superiors, but if they were too candid they might invite intervention, undermining their local standing. They needed to gather news and gossip, and so they had to win local trust.[15]

Much of the Henneberg official Tham von Herda's correspondence is therefore taken up with reports of conversations. Von Herda described how nearly all the other officeholders and officials had gone over to the peasants' army; they could see where power now lay, and they could not afford to act differently from their local community. Even his brother had been forced to join the peasants, and some of his own men had gone to the peasant camp, becoming 'powerful' in the army. Officials might not always agree with their lord's policies either. Hans Zeiß, electoral official in Allstedt, seesawed between attraction to the emotionally powerful theology of Thomas Müntzer, who had militant local support, and alarm at some of Müntzer's views. He must have become personally close to the preacher, for when Müntzer's wife gave birth, it was Zeiß's wife who brought Müntzer the news, probably having attended her in labour. As the revolt spread, these men shared their rulers' sense of crisis and the nagging worry that their own behaviour was to blame, 'for perhaps we earned it with our own sins and how we governed', one wrote.[16]

Despite this society's deep-rooted sense of family and hierarchy, lordship did not stifle strong traditions of local decision-making or the experience of how to exercise power. Indeed, it fostered them. Village communes appointed shepherds, ran parish churches, and managed village affairs, and bureaucrats had to do business with them because the ruler was often far away. When local mayors went over to the peasants, the bureaucrats often wobbled in their allegiance as well, and they looked to village notables to see which way they inclined. Many of the representatives who met to form the Christian Union of Upper Swabia were local mayors, betraying the extent of disaffection. Their willingness to get involved also reveals their self-confidence. Such men had faith in their ability to organise an army that encompassed offices like captains, provosts, and bannermen. These largely reflected local hierarchies, so there were risks in not joining and being left out. This was a revolt of men with a lot to lose, not of the desperate. On their side, too, kinship mattered: the brother-in-law of the influential and prosperous baker Hans Müller ('Flux') of Heilbronn was a captain of the peasant army, and the two worked in concert. In Rothenburg ob der Tauber, the ex-mayor Ernfried Kumpf acted as an official in the Würzburg peasant army, while his brother was also active in the army.[17]

The new religious ideas split urban as well as rural elites. Towns might seem to have been islands of freedom in this sea of lordship, but though towns were ringed by walls that were patrolled by the citizens, and though their gates enabled them to control who could come in or go out, the myth of civic freedom was true only to a certain extent. Towns had town councils, and in imperial cities (subject directly to the emperor), they were independent. But many territorial towns, like Luther's Wittenberg, had to have their decisions approved by a local ruler, the elector in Wittenberg's case. How deeply ordinary guildsfolk were involved in government varied too. In Heilbronn and Rothenburg, guilds did not exist, only craft representatives; in Augsburg, by contrast, guilds were part of the governing structure, with a number of guaranteed seats on the council. Rich town guilds had their own guild houses, handsomely decorated and with fine silver plate and painted glass windows celebrating their members. But in small towns there was often less to separate town from country, and many townsfolk were agricultural workers, such as vintners or market gardeners. In the fifteenth century and before, many towns had experienced civic unrest and division as craftspeople and merchants sought to wrest power from local patricians and oligarchies, and in some cases they had succeeded.

As factions within towns sought to introduce the Reformation, they undermined the power of councils that opposed it. Sometimes divisions were superimposed on existing conflicts, exacerbating tensions. The demands of the rebels in Mühlhausen in 1523 did not at first seem to concern religion, but once people demanded the right to appoint preachers, the stage was set for a confrontation fired by religion. Müntzer's rise to power was enabled by these earlier struggles. In Erfurt, the town had already weathered several attacks on priests' houses and had a history of conflict with the archbishop of Mainz, to whom it was subject, while its other powerful neighbour was Electoral Saxony. When the peasants massed outside Erfurt and urged the townsfolk to join with them, they were let in, giving Erfurt the appearance of having been 'occupied' by the peasants and forced to join the revolt. In Mainz, the peasants took key ecclesiastical buildings and sites of the Mainz government, which the council had already cleared of valuables, while factions within the town exploited the situation to reform the council and introduce the Reformation.[18]

These histories played out as the war unfolded. Townsfolk and countryfolk shared enemies since the same monasteries or bishops often ruled towns or owned rich property inside town walls. Townsfolk, too, resented the power of monasteries and their big, opulent townhouses and barns, which made these institutions visible in the town and not just the countryside. The nuns of Günterstal, for instance, had a house and library in the town of Freiburg, while their substantial landholdings and main convent buildings were hidden out of sight in the valley. And yet towns might also be enemies of the peasants, because they had often amassed large territories in the countryside outside their walls. Indeed, towns, these so-called islands of freedom, were themselves frequently feudal overlords; like the local bishops, monasteries, and nobles, the towns of Basel, Solothurn, and Memmingen, for example, all found themselves negotiating with their peasantry over serfdom and its conditions.[19]

Mining areas were not immune from lordship, and the Habsburgs were well aware that miners downing their tools would threaten the chief source of their wealth and power. Because the mines were usually owned by local rulers who leased their rights to mine owners (who were generally the smelter masters), they were also tied into lordship. They depended on the lord to renew the lease, and the lord's officials were powerful figures in mining towns, supervising and regulating the mines. Not just the Habsburgs but other rulers as well were dependent on the riches of the mines. Mining contributed to the power of Saxony and made the counts of Mansfeld (subject to Saxony) wealthy, at least for a while. On the other hand, the mine owners frequently became financially dependent on large-scale financiers, like the Fugger family of Augsburg or the Baumgartners of Nuremberg, who controlled international markets. In a region like Mansfeld, the numbers of independent mine owners were beginning to shrink as the accessible seams were exhausted and more investment in equipment was required to reach the deeper seams and pump out the water. These smelter masters as well as the miners hated the 'grosse Hansen' ('fat cats'), the rich urban merchants who were profiting from their hard labour and whom they blamed for the adversities they were experiencing.

Miners had been amongst those most keen to purchase indulgences from the church's indulgence sellers, because the dangerous conditions underground made them especially aware of the risk of death and eager to buy some kind of insurance against Purgatory. The sellers knew that places like Annaberg, named for the patron saint of the miners St Anna, or Mansfeld offered rich pickings. When Luther attacked indulgences as a waste of money, miners were amongst those who felt strongly that they had been duped by the old church. They flocked eagerly to preachers who condemned the Catholic church for fleecing the faithful or who criticised usury and the sharp financial practices of merchants and capitalists like the Fuggers.[20]

A whole social structure therefore fissured under the impact of the peasants' revolt. Relationships that seemed to be built on family feeling, grateful loyalty, and hallowed tradition turned out to be nothing of the sort. Hierarchies that had appeared to be natural crumbled. Even powerful rulers wondered whether God wanted to punish their pride and let the peasants win. Devolved, shared systems of power turned out not to reinforce rule, at least in the short run; rather, they placed the officials who mediated between communities and lords, and the knights who were too weak to resist large armed bands, in an impossible position. At the same time, because of the strength of family and communal bonds, those who went over to the peasants took many of their fellows with them. We will never know just how many joined the peasant cause, at least for a time, because afterwards, when lordship was restored, everyone wanted to pretend they had been loyal.

*　　*　　*

The glue that held the edifice of lordship together was the oath: peasants swore a vow of loyalty to their lord, and he promised them protection, 'schutz und schirm'. It was a highly personal relationship, for the oath in God's presence was made to a person, not an institution. Every time a new abbot or a different lord succeeded, oaths had to be sworn anew, and the lord or his representative would have to travel to each community to receive the oath in person, a process which could take a long time.

A form of religious bond, oaths were crucial in a society that lacked a police force and had only a thin crust of officials. In towns, likewise, the citizens swore an annual oath to the council, and the mayor and councillors swore to them reciprocally. In the country, all the men of the community would gather in the village to swear the oath in the presence of God. The ritual was choreographed: with right arm raised, finger pointing heavenwards, and hats doffed, they stood outdoors under heaven as a body, looking up at the lord or his representative while he looked down on them. They were a collective, and the experience of all the men standing close together on the ground where they lived and farmed would have made that tangible—while the women, children, and outsiders who were not part of the 'community' were reminded of the fact.

The first step of revolt was therefore to break one's feudal oath and to swear a new one to each other. When the peasants did so, they sundered a solemn promise to an individual they had made as a group in the presence of God, a breach many were hesitant to make. Some resorted to equivocations later to explain why their vow of brotherhood did not invalidate their feudal oath; some recruiters for the peasants tried arguing that the new oath was compatible with the old, but everyone knew this was obfuscation. Others temporised: when the peasants turned up at their castle, the knightly von der Tann brothers told them that they were equally keen gospellers, but they could not swear unless they had their overlord's permission to do so.[21]

Swearing brotherhood, or 'swearing together', the expression commonly used, subverted the inherently hierarchical form of the oath, because it was sworn to each other. In villages around Kempten, they 'promised' instead of making an oath and reinforced the pledge by walking 'through and under' a lance held aloft by two men. Old ways died hard, however. When the peasants of the monastery of Weissenau rebelled and swore to their leader Stefan Rahl, he stood on a raised bench as they did so. All the same, they held their pole weapons upright, and they kept their hats on.[22]

Having established a band, sworn an oath, and created a corporation that was outside the existing structures of lordship, the rebels also had to make themselves accepted as interlocutors of the lords. Force of arms and the sheer size of the peasant armies compelled lords to negotiate, but the armies also had to nominate speakers and leaders, design banners and coats of arms, and find some way of writing official letters.

Above all they needed people who could read and write. Often they relied on former priests to deal with correspondence, to add the polite formulae of letter writing, and to read letters aloud. Karlstadt described his terror when militant peasants forced him to read letters for them. The group he encountered had no one who could read, and so they could not assess letters of safe conduct or test who was friend or foe. In Würzburg, the town syndic Martin Cronthal was appalled to get an answer from the Bildhausen band that was written on a mere slip of paper, the letters so poorly formed that the document looked like the work of a village tanner. In many cases, however, the mobile 'chancelleries' seem to have been reasonably organised, kept in bags, and guarded, because in enemy hands they were incriminating. It was Thomas Müntzer's cache of letters that gave him away in the end while he was pretending to be an innocent old man. The contents of a leather satchel from an army of the peasants of Württemberg has survived, and it shows how far their network of correspondence stretched and how carefully they dealt with other peasant bands, with whom they did not always agree. A priest who was captain of the Wurzach band wrote in desperation to the band at Grönenbach, asking why they had not come to help despite previous appeals: 'We see that you don't come, for what reason we do not know'. Addressing them in 'brotherly troth', he admonished them, 'Therefore, dear brothers, do the best to return good with good, and hurry, hurry, for it's an emergency'. The appeal worked and they were sent a detachment.[23]

Letters were crucial because the armies progressed by urging the next village to join. For the most part, they show mastery of all the polite forms of the letter, are written in flowing script, and generally use the correct forms of address, even when they employ the levelling informal 'you'. To deliver the letters, they relied on a system of messengers who knew the local routes. At the same time, as the peasants won control of territory, they could disrupt the lords' communications. Lorenz Fries described how 'the result was that you couldn't send any letter by land any more; they were almost all broken open by the peasants'.[24]

Lords routinely used seals to authenticate their documents and stamped sealing wax to close their letters. Likewise, the bands needed their own wax and seals, and each band needed a name with which to sign its missives. Those they chose were often temporary and geographical, describing where they happened to be; the profusion and variety in bands' names belies any simple model of six or seven overarching armies, especially since even small groups apparently had their own seals. The peasantry 'assembled outside Schmalkalden' used a seal featuring a ploughshare and the words 'Dei burschaft', 'peasantry of God'; the peasants encamped outside nearby Meiningen used a similar design, with a ploughshare and the letters 'Die bursc', the peasantry. The 'whole assembly' at Reinsdorf of the 'willing and Christian brothers' sealed their letter to Zwickau with a seal showing a cross, with the letters *V D M IE* in each of the four fields, standing for 'The Word of

God Endures Forever'—a religious, not a peasant, design. At Bamberg they chose a lion, signifying courage, and three ploughshares; the design probably also incorporated the letters *L* and *S* for 'Landschaft' (region or landscape) and 'towns', underlining the alliance between town and countryside.[25]

They needed banners too. The bannerman was an important office in mercenary armies, visibly holding men together and creating an identity, and the loss of the flag signified defeat; conversely, it was highly prized booty. Hans Foeditzsch described how 'When I came to the Haufen with others of my neighbours, as soon as he saw me the Schosser [treasurer] ordered me to fetch the flag, he would entrust it to no-one but me, because I had previously carried the "Amts" flag for more than eighteen years', his pride still evident in the telling. The flag he had carried before was that of the local administration, the Amt, and now the army, exploiting the old patterns of respect, appointed him to the same job. Distinctive banners gave their groups an identity, and they were so important that back in the early revolts of the century, Joss Fritz had even delayed the start of uprisings until the flag could be sewn and painted, risking the revolt's success.[26]

Lordship meant social distinctions, which the peasant bands deliberately tackled amongst their own members and in how they dealt with the lords. The distinctions took various forms, in particular, in how people addressed each other. From the twelfth century on, in German, a person of higher rank had to be addressed with the formal 'you', while the informal 'du' was used to address those of lower status. Indeed, as status differences increased in the sixteenth century, the formal 'you' began to be used between elite married couples, polite titles such as 'your grace' and 'your princely grace' began to proliferate for each kind of nobility, and even between nobles, forms such as 'your most dear' were employed. Town councillors began to be addressed as 'honourable and wise Lords'. 'Du' was universal amongst peasants. In their correspondence, the peasant bands mostly followed these conventions, writing with all the formulae of politeness to the lords and couching their appeals in terms of brotherly love. But they also subverted conventional forms, always writing to both the 'Rat' and the Gemeinde so that they were addressing not only the council but also the commune from whom they drew their legitimacy. Consequently, where the commune was divided, as in Würzburg, Heilbronn, Rothenburg, and other towns, the 'commune' had to know that the peasants were asking them, and not just the town councillors, to join in brotherhood. If the councillors did not tell them about the letter, they were guilty of keeping secrets from the people.[27]

Many treaties deliberately made deals with opponents of higher standing as if they were equals. The clerics Lienhart Denner and Hans Hollenpach, who led peasant bands in Franconia, joined with the nobleman Florian Geyer, hoping to win Margrave Casimir to their side. Their treaty with the local leader of the Teutonic Knights promised him protection in return for a hefty sum; they clearly envisaged lords and rulers becoming part of 'their' side. The Odenwald peasants joked to the town of Tauberbischofsheim that they did not consider its ruler to be their 'gracious lord' but their 'ungracious lord'. They intended to open all his market towns, doors, castles, and bars, to see and know all his treasures—'and we want to be lords'. In Saxony and in Thuringia, several local officials noted with alarm that the peasants had shot a stag; one group had even taken a stag back to the army camp as food. Since only nobles were allowed to hunt deer, and since they decorated their castles with the prized antlers, this was tantamount to proclaiming that now peasants were 'lords'.[28]

Some, like Thomas Müntzer, deliberately withheld courtesy titles and used the informal 'you'. In 1523, he had written to Ernst of Mansfeld as 'the noble and wellborn Count, Master Ernst of Mansfeld and Heldrungen', employing the polite 'ihr' form throughout, but by May 1525 he addressed him as 'brother Ernst', and used the 'du'. He often used emotional terms—'most beloved', 'heartily loved'—and replaced the direct salutation with an invocation of God: 'Strength and comfort in Christ Jesus, most beloved'. Those writing to him did the same: 'Christian love and brotherhood in Christ our Saviour, Dear Brothers', wrote the community of Walkenried. Graf Günther XL von Schwarzburg-Blankenburg, who had joined Müntzer's Christian Bund on 30 April together with his subjects, saluted Müntzer as his 'christian dear brother, Master Thomas Muntzer' and addressed him as 'your dear/your grace', as if Müntzer and he were of equal rank now that he had joined the Bund. He signed off as 'Gunter the Younger, representative of the Christian community', his Christian rank now replacing his noble status—though he added 'born von Swartzburg'. One can almost hear his teeth grinding as he expresses his 'christian and brotherly love' which he will earn through his devotion. But it was all a front. The letter actually explained that he would not be sending Müntzer any armed help, because he had been unable to subdue the peasants in his lordship![29]

The authorities in town and country were particularly sensitive on this issue. Michael Gross von Trockau noted that the peasants now refused to name Margrave Casimir 'gracious' or even to address him as their lord, the most basic courtesy. When the peasants of the area of Solothurn assembled in the open field at Reinach to negotiate with representatives of the towns of Bern, Lucerne, Basel, and Fribourg, Switzerland, the citizens of Solothurn took offence because their 'subjects' behaved in a 'quite unseemly and disobedient manner' by taking a banner from the church of Mariastein and using threatening words. They were so annoyed that they nearly rode away—a classic demonstration of elite status—before a compromise could be reached. Calm was only restored when the peasants 'inclined to obedience', as the scribe put it. He may have meant that the peasants literally bent the knee.[30]

Time and again, when peasants were interrogated, their questioners reported that they said they wished to have no authorities at all. In fact, the structures of authority the peasants created in their bands suggest the opposite; far from wanting no authorities, they wanted leaders and officeholders and a clear system of organisation. Their vision seems to have been of a new kind of authority in which men of respect, locally known and chosen, would have power. As the Twelve Articles had put it, the peasants wanted to be free, 'Not that we want to be utterly free and subject to no authority at all; God does not teach us that'. Rather, God's commandment is that Christians should humble themselves before everyone, not just the authorities, 'so that in this way we will gladly obey our elected and appointed rulers (whom God has ordained over us) in all reasonable and Christian matters'. This of course still allowed considerable room for disobedience. But there was at that point no explicit reference to getting rid of authorities or even of feudalism, only of serfdom.[31]

The articles of the Christian Union also carefully stated that they were directed against no one except those who were opposed to their plans, and that the peasants did not want to press anyone to swear against their lords and authority further than as specified in the articles. There is, however, another version of the oath, according to which they swore to administer 'angelic truth, godly justice and brotherly love, and to have one lord, namely his Roman Imperial Majesty and no other'. Such a declaration would have been tantamount to rejecting the system of lordship altogether, and as the revolt progressed, some began to develop these ideas further; indeed, the ambiguity of the concept of lordship made this inevitable.

The tentacles of lordship reached into every area of life, determining how one addressed people, whom one could marry, what clothes one wore, even physical comportment and how one stood. But lordship was relational, and those who were lords were also subject to those above them, while even the lowest village official was implicated in the system of rule. Lordship was collective and consultative; 'rulers' were frequently family groups or even corporations, and bishops, abbesses, and abbots had chapters from whom they took advice and were part of regional and national structures through their orders.[32]

It took imagination to conceive of a world without the lordship that the peasants knew. They probably did not want to overturn the entire system of authority, or at least not at first, but merely to change the system of landlordship. And yet their slogan, 'We want to have no lords', addressed everyone—peasants, miners, and townsfolk alike—because everyone had some experience of lordship in its different forms or could tell a story about the overbearing behaviour of some lord or other. In its place they wanted a society based on mutuality, brotherhood, and trust. As spring beckoned, they began to envision a world without the familiar semifeudal structures, with a new kind of rulership that would give them agency and the power to decide. This was the dream they now set out to make reality.

CHAPTER 6

DREAMS

Every revolution must be nourished by dreams of a new world. The revolt was not brought about by sets of ideas in books; it unfolded as people applied Reformation ideas they had heard to their own lives and experienced together what change could mean. Dreams were part of the heady atmosphere of the times: actual dreams, visions and prophecies, and utopian blueprints for a new future. Biblicism—hearing the Bible and using scripture as the measure for all things—had opened the door to dreams and visions, for both the Old and the New Testaments promised that in the Last Days, 'your sons and daughters shall prophesy, and your young men will see visions and your old men will dream dreams' (Acts 2:17; Joel 2:28; Isaiah 44:3). The utopian hopes of those who rebelled reveal the wide variety of their views of the future and the different sources from which their inspiration came. They also reveal the growing gulf between the scripture-based piety of a reformer like Luther and the revolutionary spirituality developing amongst some of those engaged in the Peasants' War.[1]

Despite their presence in scripture however, dreams subverted ecclesiastical authority because the visionary could appeal to their own experience, without the mediation of the church. A dream can order the dreamer to do something, sending a direct message that must be obeyed. In the county of Henneberg in the fifteenth century, many said they were told to go on pilgrimage 'in a dream', and they set about doing so, much to the dismay of their lords, who could not understand these vast movements of peasants—events the authorities recalled in 1525, as the peasants massed again.[2]

For the peasants' opponents, visions could also express the nightmarish disorientation of the war that could not easily be put into words. A Catholic nun from Bamberg described how, after Easter, a great roaring wind arose, so that it became dark and gloomy near the convent, though elsewhere it was light and good weather. Perhaps, she thought, the noise came from the evil spirits who had been driven out by the ringing of all the church bells. On Easter night and for the next month, the nuns heard a voice at night at the window, now sobbing and howling like a human, now laughing, now screaming like a bird.[3]

Sixteenth-century people had a rich tradition of paying attention to portents and dreams, stretching right back to antiquity. There were printed dream books to help decode the symbolism of dreams, some even with indices to make the process easier. But dreams are not simple coded messages. They required contemplation and interpretation, and their meanings could be uncomfortable, expressing views that could not be articulated directly. The remarkable Dr Alexander Seitz, whose 'prognostic' foretelling disaster in 1524 we encountered earlier, had published a tract on dreams and their interpretation back in 1515, including a hermit's dream which he said depicted the 'accursed servants', who 'unashamedly rip the bloody sweat from the poor, yes, and often rob the sustenance of the poor infant children from their mothers' breasts'. He described these exploiters as 'tyrannical wolves with terrible raging', language Lotzer, Müntzer, Hubmaier, and many others would later use of the lords. Though disguised as a 'dream interpretation', this was social criticism, and the tract does not conceal its hostility to the nobles and lords.[4]

Because they posed questions about the relationship between scripture and direct communication with God, and hence about the relationship between authority and individual revelation, dreams raised fundamental spiritual issues. They also epitomised very different devotional styles, and this soon became articulated in arguments about their status. At the very point when the Peasants' War was intensifying, in late 1524, the standing of dreams became one of the major theological fault lines of the Reformation. When Luther broke publicly with Karlstadt in *Against the Heavenly Prophets*, he ridiculed both Müntzer and Karlstadt for claiming to have direct access to God through dreams and visions. With biting sarcasm, he dubbed them the 'heavenly prophets'. He condemned Karlstadt's teaching as 'dreams', as if Karlstadt had simply dreamed up his denial of the real presence of Christ in the sacraments, and accused him of mistaking 'dreams' for the Eucharist itself. He ridiculed Karlstadt's emotionalism, too, mocking his 'splendid words' about the spiritual reception of the Eucharist, the 'ardent memory, passionate knowledge, tender taste'. All this flowery reverence, he said, was like locking the sacrament up in a monstrance again as the old church had done, 'where we can see and smell it until we're full, yes, in our dreams!' while depriving us of the real thing. 'Karlstadt's whole teaching', he concluded, 'is just dreaming of this kind'.[5]

What was so devastating about Luther's attack was his keen recognition of what was really at stake. As Karlstadt's writings became more radical, so did his understanding of the place of visions. For him the key Christian experience was of 'Gelassenheit', or 'letting go' of all one's attachments to people and to things of this world. Only through suffering and only in a state of Gelassenheit could one hear the voice of God, which God 'has transmitted...to our forebears in visions and through his living voice', as Karlstadt wrote in 1523. The 'Word' was not to be understood as the formal words of the Bible, though this is the chief way we know God. 'We must all fathom the spirit of the letter if we are to serve God readily', he wrote. All the same, Karlstadt was careful to point out that even prophets could not be sure about their visions and needed help interpreting them. He also voiced doubts about the Book of Revelation, which he grouped amongst the third, lowest level of scripture along with the Epistle of James, the two last visionary chapters of Daniel, and Daniel 3's story of the fiery furnace where Shadrach, Meshach, and Abednego were punished for their faith. These, however, were all key texts for those interested in dreams.[6]

Müntzer's approach was very different from Karlstadt's nuanced one. God communicated with the believer directly through dreams, which must be had 'while in tribulation and suffering', a state that allowed the dreamer to approach Christ's suffering and so to identify profoundly with him. This was what Müntzer termed the 'living' word as opposed to the 'dead' letter of scripture, which he repudiated along with the pettifogging theological learning he had received in Wittenberg. Luther, he argued, had a 'fleshly understanding', an empty learning of scripture that was opposed to the 'spirit' of God. This dualistic demeaning of the fleshly characterised much of Müntzer's theology and was evident early on. His opponent Johannes Sylvius Egranus had mocked him at Zwickau as 'Tommy Müntzer you holy man, when the crazy spirit comes over you', condemning his 'buzzing' or 'enthusing' ('schwärmen'). Luther himself later used this same word to ridicule Müntzer, Karlstadt, and their followers as the *Schwärmer*, the enthusiasts, swarming and buzzing like bees. The insult stuck.[7]

Yet Müntzer had put his finger on a key feature of Luther's intellectual temperament: his remarkably positive attitude towards physicality, unusual in the Western Christian tradition. It predisposed Luther to develop his distinctive consubstantionist account of the real presence, maintaining that the bread of the Eucharist was at one and the same time *both* bread *and* body of Christ. He was not satisfied with the orthodox Catholic explanation that the outward appearance of the bread remained the same while the true inner substance was transformed into Christ's body, because it relied on a rigid distinction between 'accidents' (physical appearances) and 'essences' (spiritual reality), which he rejected.

For Müntzer, Luther just substituted fleshliness for spirituality, all too typical of a well-paid university professor of scripture with friends at court. This, Müntzer believed, alienated Luther from the poor, who could draw near to God without any empty learning obstructing them. It was later said that Müntzer had encountered the mysticism of the fourteenth-century German mystic Johannes Tauler not through university lectures, but on the recommendation of a pious woman with whom he read the text. The hostile Lutheran who made this charge said the woman was a fellow student's 'cook' or mistress; whatever the truth of his remark, it suggests that Müntzer's opponents believed he took the views of women and the unlearned seriously. For him, spirituality was not the preserve of university-educated theologians; ordinary folk, even women, could show what true piety meant.[8]

Müntzer's attitude to dreams and visions underpinned much of his social radicalism. Indeed, he made dreams part of his congregation's devotional life. He himself apparently recalled few dreams and did not use them as a form of self-aggrandisement. Instead, he encouraged the dreamers in his community, creating a kind of spiritual democracy as members of his own congregations came forward with their visions. This was the sign of the 'true spirit of the apostles, the patriarchs and the prophets': 'to expect visions and to receive them while in tribulation and suffering'. He condemned Luther for not taking them seriously: 'hence it is no wonder that Brother Fatted Pig and Brother Soft Life'— Luther—'reject them'.[9]

Johannes Agricola alleged that Müntzer's secretary transcribed the dreams of an elderly man at Müntzer's Allstedt congregation so that he could base his daily sermons on them. There may have been some truth in this because the old man and the secretary were the only two people—apart from his family—whom Müntzer wished to follow him to Mühlhausen. When Müntzer was summoned for interrogation at Weimar by Duke Johann, the old man had a particularly disturbing series of dreams, including scenes such as the following:

> I was spoken to: 'You are to open the church' and I looked out the keys and went to open up. Then it seemed to me that the door was my sister, and I took the key and turned the broad side of the key upwards and looked for the key-hole but was unable to see the key-hole for blood. So I turned the broad side downwards and then the key went in and I opened and pulled out the lock with one hand and opened the door and got my sister's clothes, which were bloody, and pushed the clothes behind the door and woke up.[10]

It is hard to know what to make of this dream. The keyhole symbolism and blood might invite a sexual reading, but this is probably not how the dream was understood; evidently, the dreamer felt he had to 'open the church' in Müntzer's absence. The church had become a living person, his own kin, drenched in the suffering, blood, of the true Christian. The dreams repeatedly circled around blood, doors, keys, mills, wheat, and the church, as if eucharistic symbols had become internalised and made literal. Late medieval images showed Christ in the hopper, being literally milled into the hosts of communion; Müntzer's followers made this their own and dreamed of their local mills. As the interpreter of dreams, Müntzer, like Daniel, could arbitrate meaning, and people outside Allstedt sent him dreams to decipher.

Other dreams focused on water. Hans Puttyger, one of Müntzer's many correspondents, whose letter suggests he had little formal education, wrote to him with a dream of two ships on the water, on which hung a big linen sack. 'In the ship lay 2 dead people. And he [a speaker on the ship] said, "Dead they be but drowned they are not". And as for the other ship, it was full of blood; on it someone was washing two fleeces, and great dread encompassed him. Then he spoke, "Sir, show me your faith", and the water rose up and from it emerged a nix [water sprite] who wanted to lure me into the water. At that I woke up'. The water evokes the fearful predictions of floods for 1524, which were later taken to have foretold the disaster of the Peasants' War. The letter is undated and there is no address, suggesting that Puttyger lived locally, and it was probably written in the summer of 1524, shortly before the outbreak of the revolt. Puttyger himself did not interpret his dreams in straightforwardly apocalyptic terms but thought they were about weakness of faith; he concluded by asking Müntzer to teach him more about God.[11]

Another in Müntzer's circle dreamt that all the princes, tyrants, and those who struggled against the gospel had become cowardly and frightened, and 'he saw, that their hearts were black in their bodies, full of pure cowardice'. Heinrich Pfeiffer, Müntzer's right-hand man at Mühlhausen, was said to have had a dream in which he chased away a lot of mice in a stable. Melanchthon, who reported this, poked fun at him for believing that the dream meant he was destined to put the nobility to flight, and for marching across the Eichsfeld inspired by it. Ships, fleeces, corn, water, blood—these dream images all had powerful scriptural resonances, as if the Bible had begun to emerge from the unconscious. Perhaps the discussion of dreams, and their role in the movement, drew members of Müntzer's congregation closer together as they shared such intimate messages; perhaps, too, it helped persuade people they were living in the Last Days and made them ready to risk their lives. Müntzer's theology had apocalyptic resonances: Joachim of Fiore, the twelfth-century apocalyptic visionary, was a writer Müntzer deeply admired.[12]

Müntzer's most famous sermon concerned dreams too. Astonishingly, he was asked to preach in the castle at Allstedt to honour the visit of Duke Johann and his young son. As his text, he chose the Second Chapter of Daniel, where Daniel interprets King Nebuchadnezzar's dream, and he preached not in the tiny chapel but in the banqueting hall. Like Daniel, Müntzer expounded the scripture to the princes, and just as Daniel did not shrink from telling the king that his dream signified that his empire would end, so Müntzer boldly told the princes that if they did not 'destroy' the godless, then their own rule would be over. They must have choked on their repast as he warned them that 'if they did not carry it out'—he meant exterminate the godless—'the sword will be taken from them'.[13]

Though Müntzer rarely spoke about his dreams, he did recount a dream to the whole army at a critical juncture in the war. The men were still on their procession through the Eichsfeld while forces were gathering at Frankenhausen. Pfeiffer and the representatives of Niederorschel had earlier overruled Müntzer and persuaded the army to march through the Eichsfeld instead of proceeding to Nordhausen or Heldrungen, the castle of Count Ernst, whom Müntzer believed to be their greatest enemy. Müntzer then told the army that a dream had instructed him that he 'should march after daybreak'. This dream message may have been the only way to carry the day and initiate a new march. It worked. What was left of the army returned to Mühlhausen, rested for a day, and then began the fateful march to Frankenhausen, where they would face the forces of the lords.[14]

Müntzer's interest in dreams was closely related to his mysticism and his insistence on the spirit over the flesh. At times, Müntzer seems to have taken this emphasis to the point of advocating sexual abstinence, and yet we also know that he married Ottilie von Gersen during his time at Allstedt and had children with her. The Luther loyalist Johannes Agricola wrote of how, when Müntzer was told that his first son had just been born, he showed no reaction whatsoever, an indifference Agricola viewed as inhuman. Lutherans apparently enjoyed this anecdote, and the reformer himself told the story again in a lecture several years later. Indeed, Müntzer did evince a pronounced revulsion for the physical along with his contempt for the honours of the world. He attacked the evangelical preachers for wanting to be bailiffs and hangmen (dishonourable professions whose members could only marry others of their kind), not sufferers for the truth; and he mocked them for marrying 'old women with great wealth because they are worried they'll have to earn their own bread'. He had Johannes Lang in mind, Luther's old friend and fellow Augustinian, who had just married a rich widow. Yet this was not straightforward misogyny. Rather, it seems that his hostility to the flesh sprang from his immersion in medieval mysticism, and the German mystic Johannes Tauler in particular. Luther read and published Tauler too, but he seems to have retreated from the kind of mysticism that his beloved confessor Staupitz had also espoused, with its highly sexualised meditations on the 'sweetness' of Christ. In Müntzer's hands, mysticism nourished a revolutionary hostility to the lords of this world who trod the poor underfoot.[15]

Did Müntzer have a vision of the future after the war? He seemed to relish the immediate struggle for its own spiritual sake, rather than for a new society it might usher in. The sensitivity to others that made him such a brilliant pastor also meant that material conditions seemed insignificant in comparison to the cosmic dramas of the present. His strategy for obliterating the godless focused on individuals—like his nemesis Count Ernst of Mansfeld, or on Luther, 'Dr Liar'—not on establishing a church, still less on a practical system of poor relief with a common chest. As he put it at the very end, his followers had been to blame for the 'disaster': 'there is no doubt of its root cause', he wrote, 'that everyone was more concerned with his own self-interest than in [the justification or salvation] of the Christian people'. The word he chose, 'Rechtfertigung', deliberately invoked Luther's famous 'Reformation discovery', that we are saved by faith alone, and he probably intended his comment to apply to Luther's followers as well as his own in Mühlhausen. He also used the word 'eygennutz', self-interestedness, the sin that men like Lotzer and so many others excoriated, the opposite of brotherhood; but he meant that his followers had been too concerned with the things of this world instead of with spiritual 'Rechtfertigung'.[16]

The fundamental cleavage between Luther and Müntzer over the status of dreams and visions had far-reaching consequences for radical utopianism. When Müntzer incorporated people's dreams into his conception of the living Word, he made individual spiritual revelation part of his movement's radical egalitarianism, even if he shied away from programmes of practical social reform. This had clear consequences for each man's view of authority. Luther turned away from mysticism towards a religion centred on exegesis of the Word, which required university-educated theologians to expound it. Müntzer was not alone in prizing God's revelation through dreams, and after the war was over, spiritualists, Anabaptists, prophets, and radicals of many kinds, including women, would also have visions in which they attacked their society's injustices and questioned secular rule, some even going so far as to reject marriage and propose spiritual unions. This was the work of the 'Holy Spirit', which spoke to them in dreams, and these ideas would appear in many radical movements all over Europe in the centuries that followed.

During the Peasants' War, such radical spiritualism contrasted with less exalted dreams of the future. Some were prosaic, like that of the man who boasted that he intended to take over his lord's house, where the noble would have to 'stay in the back parlour' while he would be host 'in the front parlour'. The same man wanted an end to lords altogether: 'they wanted to drive out princes and lords and take over the land and possess it and wanted to drive them all out of the towns'. The dream of possessing the land does seem to have been widespread, though this man may have confessed it because he was tortured. Another had read in a book of the Sibylline prophecies that it would come to pass 'that the small birds will eat the big ones, when the prince has already been chopped to pieces', a crude echo of Müntzer's rhetoric.[17]

Others, however, had wider social goals in mind. The townsfolk of Münnerstadt wanted their children, both boys and girls, to be taught for free, and hoped to use the assets of the Teutonic Knights to pay for it. The burghers of Frankfurt envisaged transferring incomes from benefices no longer needed to a common chest to support the poor; while in Erfurt they wanted the university revived to its former glory. In Schleusingen, the mayor himself held meetings with town citizens in his house as they excitedly drew up articles of grievance. But for the most part, town programmes of reform concerned local, specific issues, not wider dreams. They addressed matters as lowly as whether sow owners should have to pay to rear their animals in their houses, or if a town square in Würzburg should be cleared of rubbish.[18]

Peasant rebels did not commit their dreams to paper, and when they were interrogated after their defeat, they were wary of confessing their hopes. The Taubertal peasants of Franconia swore that 'what the holy gospel ordains, should be ordained, what it rejects should be rejected and remain rejected'; meanwhile, they would not pay anything, the tithe, rent, interest included. Castles, moated houses, and fortifications should be burnt to the ground. Nobles, both layfolk and clergy, should have no legal privileges, 'and not be more, than what another common man should do'. The Black Forest band wanted all those who lived in castles, monasteries, and clerical foundations to be placed under the ban—except if they agreed to live in 'common houses' and join the 'christian union'. This vision of practical equality intended to level the towers of lordship so that differences of rank would be overcome. Beyond that, the Taubertal programme was as vague as it was idealistic; the coming 'reformation und ordnung', which was to be determined by those learned in scripture, would supply the details, a vision which gave the clergy remarkable power and reflected their prominent position in the group's leadership.[19]

The letters the peasant bands wrote one another are full of the language of 'gospel' and 'brotherhood' but were generally equally careful to respect each band's independence. They might be on the same side, but the brothers 'encamped before the castle of Sotemberg' knew they had to politely request the 'dear brothers in Christ Jesus' of the Bildhausen band to send them military help—and provisions. Still they shared a fundamentally egalitarian outlook. Part of the radical dreaming that bound the bands together was being able to laugh at authorities. We can imagine the peasants chuckling, for example, as they forced the commander of the Teutonic Knights at Mergentheim, Wolfgang von Bibra, to state in a formal contract 'that everything that the Word of God erects should be erected...and conversely what kills it and overturns it, should lie, be dead, and overturned'. After all, as an ecclesiastical dignitary he should have promulgated these ideas. Even sweeter, he had to admit that 'it is manifestly against the word of God and the love of one's neighbour, that one should have to pay *handlon* [entrance fines on taking over a farm] and *hauptrecht* [the lord's right to the best animal when a tenant died]', quoting the peasants' own words. It was a vision of what 'Christian freedom' might mean.[20]

Yet why the peasants were gathering often remained a mystery to the lords. One who 'knew some of his own peasants, asked them why they were in revolt', and they replied that 'they wanted to go to the band, what it did, they would do too'. This answer seemed to confirm the view, widely held amongst the authorities, that the peasants came together merely because others did, and not because they knew what they were fighting for.[21]

But these peasants were expressing something that their lords did not, or could not, hear. Being part of the 'band', the rebel army, was itself visionary. It meant imagining a world beyond local lordship and bonding with others outside feudal structures in a community writ large. As time went on, and bands joined together with other bands or split after disagreements, peasants began to realise that 'union' implied boundaries too. By the first week of May, Hans Müller's Black Forest peasants planned to ban those who were not prepared to join, excluding them from fellowship of all kinds.[22]

'Freedom' was part of this ideal of belonging to the 'band', even in areas where serfdom had been abolished and where the Twelve Articles were often known as the 'Articles of Christian Freedom'. It was as if the village Gemeinde could be imagined without lordship and could extend far beyond the bounds of the village. As one peasant band put it, they had joined 'in Christian assembly together' in order 'to bring forth the holy gospel and godly truth again, and to destroy the illusionary seduction, which had raged most cruelly, and the great burdens with which the poor man was unfortunately burdened by his lord'. A band of peasants at Salzungen explained that they had joined together not because they were 'rebellious or mutwillig', but because 'they very much wanted to erect a common peace and unity (as the holy gospel teaches)'.[23]

This group wrote to another nearby village that 'our Lord Christ Jesus and Saviour has and will lead his children out of Babylonian captivity and save them from the power of Pharaoh', echoing Luther's language in *On the Babylonian Captivity*, and warned the village that if they did not join, they should fear 'the future anger and harsh judgement of God'. The universal invocation of the vision of an 'assembly', 'common peace', and 'gospel unity' by peasant groups suggests that this may itself have been the dream that inspired them, a dream of union perhaps even more than a specific set of demands that could be put into words. The Salzungers signed off as 'Christ our Saviour with his brothers in the camp at Salzungen', as if Christ himself were one of their number.[24]

Some, however, did articulate ideas of what a peasant future might be like. Their writings range in scope from longer pamphlets to sketchy programmes, some of which, like Hubmaier's, we can reconstruct only from their opponents' accounts. But though these texts have often been treated as if they inspired or codified the movement's ideology, they do not represent a single credo, and they are not what the peasants believed. As idiosyncratic pieces of writing produced by the literate minority rather than the peasants themselves, they are nonetheless interesting because they reflect the ideas that may have influenced the rebels, or some of them at least. They reveal how, in those momentous months, people began to think in new ways. And they disclose how the people would learn from reverses and would harden their views as the revolution's hopes soured.

The most interesting of them is a remarkable pamphlet probably composed around the time of the Twelve Articles. Its title, *To the Assembly of the Common Peasantry*, used the resonant word 'assembly', *Versammlung*, and it also deliberately referenced Luther's *To the Christian Nobility*, which had called on secular authorities to take reform into their own hands. Addressed not to the nobles but to the *assembly* of the peasantry, which had gathered together for the first time, it is one of the fullest articulations of the new theology. It also conveys some sense of what ideas and dreams may have been inspiring peasants as they imagined new forms of collective life, of 'assembly'. Now thought to have been written by Sebastian Lotzer or perhaps Christoph Schappeler, it is a product of the energies of those extraordinary days, when thousands of peasants from all over Upper Swabia met together at Memmingen, and like the articles, it has eleven chapters, with a twelfth peroration.[25]

The author set out to justify revolt, and to refute Luther's 1523 pamphlet *On Secular Authority*, which had insisted that the realm of Christ and the realm of the secular world are distinct. In the secular world, Luther had argued, the Christian must obey the rulers even if they are unjust or tyrannical or persecute Christians. Since secular authority is instituted by God, the Christian can also be an official, even an executioner, because the world is full of sinful people who must be retrained by secular law. Using Luther's own language, particularly the notion of the 'Babylonian captivity', the term Luther had used in 1520 to describe the state of the church, the author tackled his arguments head-on. Whereas Luther had opened his *Freedom of a Christian* with the paradox that a Christian is lord of all and yet subject to all, the author of *An die Versammlung* started with the paradox that a Christian must be obedient to secular authority, although 'true Christian faith will not accept any human authority'.

He begins by describing how the peasants were being condemned as 'the disobedient ones', who refused to give the lords what they owe. 'A huge army rages against you of many storm winds'. But the greatest sin, he argues, is 'Geitz', greed, meanness, or self-interest, while the highest value is 'brotherly love', in which, as Paul says, 'there is neither servant nor lord'. Hence, Luther's distinction between the kingdom of Christ and the kingdom of this world fails, because 'political matters' (*politica*) cannot be separated from 'divine matters' (*divina*). The political authority must further the common good, that is, it must exercise brotherly love, which is essential for the soul's salvation. Agreeing with Luther that human beings are inclined to 'pride, miserliness and pleasure', he argues instead that secular authority must do more than merely punish wrongdoers. It has a positive task, to further brotherly love.

A breathtakingly crisp set of arguments follow. Those who say secular authority must always be obeyed stretch the scope of obedience too far; no one has the right to rule based on tradition or precedent. We are all equally 'serfs' ('leibeigen') of Christ, and secular authority is based on what he calls the 'dominus terre', the power of the householder over the earth. (This is of course implicitly a male vision, for the members of the Gemeinde were men, and in a revealing aside he claims that the 'Latin' word 'dominus' or 'lord' in scripture—the author probably did not have Greek and certainly not Hebrew—derives from the word 'domus', 'house'. The lord therefore ought to have the natural authority of the male head of the house.) Like Müntzer and Karlstadt, he distinguishes sharply between things of the 'flesh' and things of the 'spirit', aware that this distinction differs from Luther's between 'divine matters' and 'political matters', or as Luther would have put it, between the two realms or kingdoms, that of this world and that of Christ.

The pamphlet stands apart for how it summons a sense of peasant life, describing the backbreaking work not only of ploughing and sowing but also of combing flax. An entire chapter defends the peasants' right to hunt. And yet the author struggles to explain exactly what they are rebelling against. He describes a 'Behemoth army', a vast system of financial interests that exploit the peasantry, imposing a 'Babylonian captivity' that he links repeatedly to the devil. He condemns the 'bribers and runners, the gamers and banqueters, who are more drunk than vomiting dogs' and their 'taxes, tithes and dues', the accursed 'handlon und hauptrecht', which he mocks as 'shame payments and right to rob' ('schandlon' and 'raubrecht'), and the officials who 'trouser' the taxes and customs dues. The 'lordship' against which they are rebelling now encompasses a whole system of corrupt exploitation.[26]

Somewhat surprisingly he then supplies a potted history of the tyrants of Roman history, not what one would expect in a peasant manifesto. But he does so because the word 'tyranny'—unlike 'Aufruhr' not a German but a Latin word taken from Greek—encapsulated a nascent political theory, not yet fully articulated. Because it came from the stories of the tyrants of Rome which schoolboys learnt as they acquired their Latin, the author sets this history out for everyone, including those with no Latin. 'Tyrant' and its derivatives echo through much of the radical Peasants' War rhetoric. Müntzer inveighed repeatedly against the 'godless tyrants', the Frankenhausen army called Count Ernst the 'tyrant at Heldrungen', and in October 1524 the town council of Waldshut had complained they were 'oppressed...by some godless tyrants'—meaning the Habsburgs. Tyrants were unjust rulers, and the word implied their rule was not legitimate. Roman history was important because it proved that tyrants could be defeated by revolt. As the author put it, the peasants must act like the 'oxen and bulls, who gather faithfully in a ring and sticking their horns out, to protect themselves from the ravaging wolves'—a description that evokes the peasant armies' military tactic of placing their waggons in a circle and massing around to defend it.[27]

He concludes by imagining a cow bellowing on the Schwanenberg, a mountain near Kitzingen in Franconia. It moos so loudly that it will even be heard in Switzerland, by which he meant that the peasants' call for freedom would resonate as far away as the Swiss cantons. The Swiss, who had won their independence, were a byword for freedom—even though, he remarks, the current Swiss had let themselves be bought and sold as mercenaries. Whoever the author was, this pamphlet is the fullest attempt to provide a theology that justifies revolt and explains what is meant by 'wanting to have no lords'. It adumbrates the claim of the Twelve Articles that the peasants do not wish to have no lords at all; what they want is no tyrants, and rulership according to Christian principles of brotherly love.[28]

This remarkable pamphlet is an impassioned piece of writing, full of puns and wordplay, by a writer freeing himself from a Lutheran mindset to articulate why the peasants can and must rise up against their rulers. But it paints a terrifying picture of the future if the peasants fail to support each other. There can be no going back, for relations with the lords cannot now be repaired: 'Listen dear brothers, you have embittered the hearts of your lords so greatly with an excess of gall that they will never be sweetened again'. The lords will be merciless, and 'your children will have to pull the plough themselves'. Those who are serfs will become slaves, things to be owned and unable to own property; 'in Turkish fashion you will be sold, like the animals, horse and oxen'. Punishment will be merciless: they will be 'branded through the cheeks, their fingers chopped off, their tongues ripped out, quartered

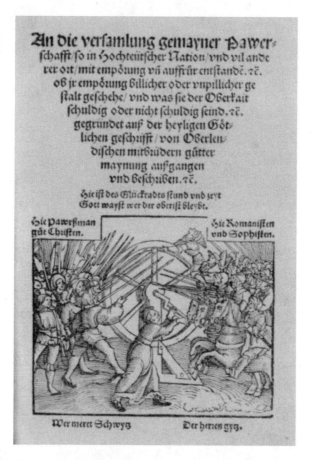

Title page, *An die Versammlung gemeiner Bauernschaft*, Nuremberg, 1525. Bayerische Staatsbibliothek, Munich.

and beheaded. There will be less pity shown you than any evildoer or murderer'. This is a nightmare vision of defeat.[29]

But perhaps *To the Assembly*'s most daring dream is its title image, which shows a wheel of fortune. The radical doctor Alexander Seitz amongst others had referred to this in 1520, with the portent of the cross floating in the wheel, and it had also recurred in Reformation visual propaganda. On *To the Assembly*'s cover, the lords and church dignitaries, 'the Romanisten und sophisten', stand to the right, while on the left are armed peasants and 'Landsknechte', the 'peasants, good

Christians'. The wheel turns and the pope moves downward while the peasants come to the top, and the motto above it reads enigmatically, 'Here is the hour and time of the wheel of fortune, God knows who will remain uppermost'. A couplet below asks, 'Who increases [the power of] the Swiss?' and answers, 'The Geitz [greed] of the lords'. The final page has another teasing couplet about somersaults: 'Do a somersault, get moving, and in brief, you must go around, no matter how bent you get'. The world, the verse seems to say, is not being turned upside down; *the lords* must turn upside down, bend—and give up their stiff superiority.[30]

We do not know how far these ideas were shared, but there are hints that others held them, and even more radical views, like Steffan Mann, the weaponsmith (Sichelschmidt) of Schmalkalden, who apparently said, 'All things must be common and a new reformation should be made'. 'Reformation' clearly meant something to him, the creation of a new, fair order in which everything would be 'common', though whether he envisaged community of goods this brief fragment does not reveal.[31]

In advance of the very first 'peasant parliament', summoned to meet at Heilbronn that May, the university-trained bureaucrat Wendel Hipler also wrote a remarkable utopian programme, at once both prolix and sketchy. Not an obvious revolutionary, the commoner Hipler had at first pursued a brilliant career working for the counts of Hohenlohe. He had purchased a small feudal estate and designed his own coat of arms but then became entangled in a dispute with his employers and their noble peers over feudal rights. The counts apparently allied against him, forcing him to sell on bad terms. He had then made a career out of defending knights against legal claims of rulers. His vision of the Peasants' War was to create an alliance of knights and peasants against local rulers.

Hipler's plan of what should be 'pondered' and 'considered' opens with this observation: 'the beginning of this undertaking, how it has proceeded up until this day, has its form'—a striking evocation of what it must have felt like to be caught up in the excitement and confusion of the war. It must have seemed chaotic and formless, and yet, Hipler reminds his fellow fighters, it 'has its shape [*Gestalt*]' or form. But first, he points out, the representatives of every army should tell each other 'in what manner'—he uses the same word here, *Gestalt*—'they have taken on the hamlets, towns, castles and villages they have conquered, and with what conditions'. They should also compare and improve their field ordinances for their armies. He tries to impose a spatial logic on the chaos by mapping where their armies were at that moment and what strategic aims each had, asking what they intended to do once the Odenwald peasants had taken Würzburg. How far did they mean to go? Who were their enemies? How could they get nobles from other areas to join their side? He even raises the possibility that they might gain some 'comfort' (*Trost*) by allying with 'foreign' rulers, such as those in Electoral Saxony, 'who have more of a mild view towards the poor man than other princes' (he might have meant that they were Lutheran, although he does not use the word). He asks whether they should proceed against the Catholic foundations of Trier and Cologne as they have against Mainz and Würzburg. Though he worries about what might happen if the emperor were to involve another 'foreign nation' or other princes, he does not mention the enemy's immediate military strategies or how their advance might endanger the peasants' position; the document was written at the high-water mark of peasant success and focused only on the peasants' own experience and hopes. He uses the word 'Ordnung' (order) and its derivatives no fewer than nine times in this short piece, and sketches an ongoing system of representatives who should propose a 'Reformation' and create a better Ordnung while dealing with all the abuses of the established order.[32]

'Reformation' was the word Steffan Mann had also used, and like Hipler he did not primarily mean a religious reformation. Though Hipler mentions God, this document is not religious, nor does the gospel feature in it, because his primary concern was how to construct a new consultative body. He seems to have imagined it as covering primarily Franconia and not 'foreign' lands such as Saxony. But his vision was conservative, firmly anchored in the existing social order, for he imagines that soon the 'common man should be sent back to his work' as the army is gradually reduced in size. He even suggests that the lords who join the union and lose their income in tithes, customs, and other such dues should be compensated through the goods of the church—a proposal which would have transferred the wealth of the church and monasteries not to benefit the whole community by funding poor relief, as most imagined, but to the ruling class.[33]

At around this time Friedrich Weigandt, an official of the elector of Mainz in Miltenberg, set out what may have been a fuller blueprint of a new order for the peasant assembly to discuss. It was based on a pamphlet of 1523, *Teutscher nation notturft* (the so-called *Reformation of Emperor Friedrich III*), and so harked back to the ferment of ideas around the failed Knights' Revolt of 1522–1523, a brief movement led by two supporters of Luther, Ulrich von Hutten and Franz von Sickingen. Its visionary elements are fewer and its plans more practical. The Word must be preached; the 'poor people' are not only held in contempt but have had new demands and impositions placed on them so that 'the devil is bound on our tail'. Like Hipler he proposed compensating princes, lords, towns, and nobles for the loss of their various taxes and impositions with wealth confiscated from the church. (Not even Philip of Hesse, when he secularised ecclesiastical foundations, envisaged using monastic wealth simply to enrich his own coffers.) His design for the Franconian peasantry was mainly concerned with legal reform, unsurprising given his own experience of the law. He had no time for university-trained lawyers, 'because the doctors are not inherited custodians of the law, but contracted servants', language similar to that being used about pastors, who were employees of their congregation, not of the lords. It should be possible to buy out land tax. No cleric should have any legal role. All secular law should be abolished across the empire and replaced by godly and natural law, with a chamber court (*Kammergericht*) in which 'communes' and 'towns' should also be represented; and there should be an overarching integrated system of courts. But though legal reform was high on his list of priorities, this does not mean it was the peasants' main goal.[34]

Balthasar Hubmaier may also have had a vision of political reformation, which we can glimpse through the account of his former student friend and later enemy Johann Fabri. Fabri, not a sympathetic witness, had been tasked by the Austrians with summarising the contents of Hubmaier's papers. His pamphlets aimed to destroy Hubmaier's reputation and justify his execution as a heretic; Fabri also slanders Hubmaier as having used the money from the sale of chalices to buy himself a black coat. But the detail he provides from Hubmaier's papers suggests that, while retailing scurrilous rumours, Fabri was also précising *something* and not just making it up. It has even been suggested that some of Müntzer's writings may have been mixed in with Hubmaier's papers, since he might have had—or made—copies of them. Indeed, Fabri clearly states that the documents were not all by Hubmaier but included works by others, with additions and amendments in Hubmaier's hand.[35]

Of all the preachers, Hubmaier was best positioned to put his ideas into practice. Waldshut was amongst the first of the revolutionary utopian communities and amongst the last to be defeated, so he had about a year, whereas most had just a few months. Many of Fabri's claims seem fantastical, such as that Hubmaier insulted the emperor, calling him a 'childish lord' who led his people astray, saying 'you see-sawing chatterbox-tongue [*wipernaterzüngl*] can't hurt me', even making up a mock song about him, but they do suggest he may have had an anti-Habsburg irreverence. Fabri alleges that Hubmaier preached 'aufrur', revolt, and insulted pope, king, and emperor, asking, 'Who said they should be princes?' and teaching 'how the common folk have the power to appoint and to dismiss the authority'; that no one was obliged to pay tithe, interest, and other dues; and that those who paid off the capital they had borrowed were not obliged to pay any more interest.

But Fabri also claims to summarise a book of the 'intentions and plans of the peasants' that included eight leaves written in Hubmaier's own hand, with the rest written by others. These eight pages offer something that resembles a worked-out political programme. According to Fabri they stated that the people of each region (Landschaft) should join together and make a league, for the time had come when God would no longer endure the 'shaming, dirtying, forcing…and other tyranny' of the lords, who were acting like Herod with the innocent children. To prevent this terrible state of affairs, the community should admonish the 'authority' to join the brotherhood and union three times. If it refused, the Landschaft should be allowed to take the sword away from the authority and give it to another, for otherwise it shared in its sins. The people should gather and vow together to keep the word, and the peasants should propose twelve individuals, one of whom (excluding nobles) should be elected. If this person should prove unsatisfactory, he too should be replaced. The Landschaft should bind themselves together in body, honour, and good, 'to shed and pour out their blood together'. If the ruler who has been deposed tries to avenge himself, he should be put under the ban (that is, excluded from communion and Christian fellowship), or if that did not work, war should be waged against him, 'so that the bloodthirsty tyrants should be rooted out'. Fabri claims that Hubmaier's own handwriting explains how one should win cities, markets, and villages and get the whole land to join in the Aufruhr. The ban, in Fabri's version of Hubmaier's thought, is to be used as an instrument of discipline but also, Fabri alleged, as a class weapon to exclude all those who live in castles, monasteries, and vicarages.[36]

It is difficult to know from this garbled version what, or even whose, this vision was, because Fabri is summarising several texts that might include works by Müntzer and others. No dates are given. We do not even know that Hubmaier was the author of the eight leaves in his hand—he may have been copying out the words of others, a common practice. Even so, Fabri seems to be describing a scheme for establishing godly rule by a single, elected, nonnoble individual who is to be subject to popular approval. In the later public 'confession' that Fabri reports, Hubmaier admitted preaching 'so that he should have a comfortable life and be a lord', and also 'that their cause and plan was to have no authorities'—the standard canard. However, Fabri completes the sentence, *'except only to select and elect one of themselves'* (emphasis added), essentially the same idea as in the papers. Like the preacher who is to be hired by the local community and sacked if he misbehaves, so also this ruler is to be replaced by the community if unsatisfactory.[37]

The concept and even some words are reminiscent of the opening demands of the Twelve Articles, which called for the 'whole community to choose and elect its own pastor. We also want authority to depose a pastor who behaves improperly'. The bond of brotherhood is essential, with the league—extended through the whole region or Landschaft—joining together in blood to reject the tyrant. It is not a universal community, but composed of those who choose to join, defined by their use of the ban to exclude others. But perhaps as a result of the experience of war, it has moved beyond the naïve idea that nobles or the rich could be brothers as well. It is both radically democratic and radically autocratic, for there is one leader only, with no structure of administration or government. Whosever vision it was, it did not transcend the simple model of the pastor chosen and removed by his congregation, and so betrays an inability to think about political structures. Instead, it idealised the league of brothers as the ultimate legitimating body without thinking through what this would mean in practical terms.[38]

But the most radical and fully thought-out programme was that of the Second Landesordnung of Michael Gaismair for Tyrol, written during his exile in 1526, when he had learned the lessons of defeat. He envisaged a government of representatives of peasants, craftspeople, and miners, but excluding nobles and clergy. He recognised the need to create alliances with miners and townsfolk, particularly urgent in Tyrol, where the development of salt, silver, and gold mining had drawn in the rich mining companies and capitalists of southern Germany. The plan demanded that all the mining companies be expelled, and the proceeds from the mines go to the government, effectively nationalising the income for the common good. Just as at Memmingen, when the peasants hoped to secure leading theologians to adjudicate their grievances, three university theologians were to be part of the government. The entire system of rule was designed 'first to seek the honour of God and after, the common good', and the tithe was to be the only due. All castles and fortifications were to be destroyed—and also all town walls. Towns were to become 'villages, so that there should be no differentiations amongst people, and thus no-one should be higher or better than another'—a dour egalitarianism that breathes a hatred of urban life and of its elites and luxury. Instead, one place was to be chosen where all trades and luxury items were to be made, and what could not be made locally must be ordered in and sold at cost. All monasteries and foundations were to be abolished and turned into hospitals, and pastors must be elected by their communities; chalices and jewels were to be taken out of churches and monasteries and melted down for the good of the state.[39]

The ordinance also had its xenophobic side: all the ' "godless" who persecute the eternal Word of God, burden the poor common man, and hinder the common good' should be driven out—a provision which would have exiled the Jews, capitalists, nobles, and feudal lords—and no one was to be allowed to commit usury. The bogs were to be dried out to prevent disease and turned into pasture for animals, more crops were to be planted, including olive trees and saffron, and vineyards should be replaced with crops; river transport should be open to all, and tolls should be abolished.[40]

These provisions betray its author's limitations. He did not really understand peasant life but was raised, like Luther, as the son of a mine owner, and so there is no mention of access to common resources like wood or water, no theology of creation, and no understanding of the importance of boggy meadows and common land for local ecology.[41] It was a defensive ideal that did not offer much scope for individuality or creativity but sought a 'total equality', a complete parity in status (and one that showed no recognition of either women or their concerns). And while it developed some of the utopian ideas that had featured earlier in the revolt, like the creation of a new system of government that would escape lordship altogether, it had the same weaknesses. No attempt was made to explain how this government should operate, how its representatives should be chosen, or how disagreements should be managed; instead, all elements of conflict were to be removed by making everyone the same. Its leaden immobility reflects the gloom of defeat.

But the hopes and dreams of the Peasants' War were not yet extinguished. In 1527, Hans Hergot was executed on the marketplace at Leipzig for printing a book that he may have written, *On the New Transformation of the Christian Life* (*Von der newen Wandlung eynes christlichen Lebens*). The book falls into two halves, which might have been composed at different times. The second half is an angry lament at the bloodshed of the Peasants' War and an indictment of those 'learned in Scripture' who think their reason so great that it exceeds God's wisdom. They, more than the peasants, are to blame for the war, but the 'peasants have eaten the leather, they have to pay for the cow, and they have paid double'. With bitter sarcasm, our author calls on those learned in scripture to 'suck quickly, and teach the nobles not to leave anything in the cow's udder, so that the little ones will find nothing there.... There is neither milk nor blood there, wife and child die of hunger, there has been enough of the cry "Kill them, slay them whoever had a hand, it is just, God will find it good"'. This powerful image evokes not only the world of the peasants but also the image of the cow on the Schwanenberg whose bellowing will be heard in Switzerland, the land of the free. By those 'educated in Scripture', he means Luther and his supporters, who called in 'against the robbing thieving Hordes' to 'smite, kill and slay' the peasants. Without naming him, the author unmistakably places the blame for the disaster at Luther's door.[42]

The first half is a visionary imagining of a perfect world. God will humble all estates, the villages, castles, foundations, and monasteries, and will institute a new 'Wandlung', or transformation, in which no one will say 'that is mine'. The common people will possess the houses of the nobles, and the four mendicant orders will no longer beg, while the other rich monasteries will lose their rents and interest dues. Everything—wood, water, and meadows—will be for the sole use of the community (*gemeyn*), and every region (*Landt*) will have no more than one lord, and the spiritual and secular lords as they are now will pass away. All will eat from one pot and drink from one vessel—there seems to be a eucharistic echo here—and obey one man as far as necessary for the honour of God and the common good. The family is to be abolished: at the age of four, boys are to be taken to church and assigned to the 'father' best fitted to raise them, while girls will be instructed by the woman of the house to which the boys have gone. There will be no need for poor relief or hospitals, and people will wear only garments that can be made from the field with local dyes—that is, white, grey, black, or blue colours only. Everyone will do work appropriate to their skills, and there will be enough land because the ground and fruits of the monasteries will be used. The entire vision is structured around the number twelve, the number, of course, of the peasants' articles and of the twelve tribes of Israel. The 'twelfth man' will be elected to serve God and the common good. The twelve rulers will elect a 'head' who will travel around with them and see that they rule properly over their twelve lands.[43]

This is an uncannily static vision, not democratic but hierarchical, even though all goods are shared. The author imagines the abolition of all dues and rents but does not pursue what this village community might be like as a social entity, and the Gemeinde apparently has less power than the leader. Hergot, if he is the author, provides for the possibility of war, and of levying military service from every third man, echoing the systems of rotation used during the Peasants' War, so this is not a pacifist ideal. And he imagines that the abolition of monasticism in its current form will be enough to restore prosperity, a belief probably shared by many in those intoxicating days of revolt. Women have little agency in this gloomy autarchic worldview; even their children do not remain with them.

It was not a serious political programme but a mystical dream of how things might have been, based on the naïve antimonasticism of the early months of revolt. It lacks the creative energy of writers like the author of *An die Versammlung*, or even of Hipler or Weigandt, leaders whose programmes hardly reflected peasant outlooks. But its advocacy of the peasant cause was enough to cost its printer his life. Once the peasants had been defeated, daring to dream of a radical future in this way—or still worse, casting blame on Luther for the war and recording the misery it caused—was simply not tolerated.

But as spring beckoned, hope was in the air, and people dared to imagine a new future. Revolutions require dreams and visions, for they inspire the conviction, however inchoate, that another life is not only possible but worth fighting for. Of all the writers discussed here, Müntzer took dreams the most seriously, but he saw himself as an interpreter of dreams rather than a dreamer. When he turned the dreams of ordinary folk into sermon material, he must have made his congregation feel that everything they did was charged with apocalyptic significance. They were truly equals, and their spirituality was as important as their preacher's. This was the priesthood of all believers in action, and it may help to explain the extraordinary affection and loyalty this man inspired, even to the death.

Yet is hard to discern any vision of an earthly future in Müntzer's writings. A mystic, he was concerned with the process of worship and encounter with the divine. This was why he put so much effort into writing the music for a German mass, translating the words, and getting them printed. He did not choose the vernacular melodies of the everyday to help people remember them and bring God into daily life; rather, he re-created a meditative religious environment that was a heightened form of religious receptivity so that ordinary folk could practise the kind of religious athleticism formerly reserved for monks and nuns. He was concerned with the last battle of the apocalypse and the defeat of the princes. And yet the field of the apocalypse was his backyard, not even the whole of the empire, and his targets were local officials, Count Ernst of Mansfeld, Duke Georg of Saxony, and Luther.

Karlstadt was not much of a dreamer, but he was a utopian and a mystic. For him, the primary goal was spiritual: attaining Gelassenheit and leaving the things of this world behind. Temperamentally he was not inclined to engage in revolutionary activity, and though he had courage and was unconventional, the pressure of the Peasants' War in the end tore him apart. He engaged seriously with peasant life and flirted with becoming a peasant, giving up his secure academic career to do so. He participated in the Reformation in Rothenburg ob der Tauber, joined with the evangelical radicals who supported the peasants, and played his part during those feverish days when the town considered swearing brotherhood with the peasants. But then he left. When he encountered the peasant armies in real life, they frightened him, and he tried to escape. His enduring respect for Luther and for secular authorities meant that the Peasants' War shocked rather than formed him. It did not foster his creativity—his later works, and there are few, mainly worked out the concepts he had developed in 1524 and before. He was not able to build a second Orlamünde.

As for Luther, he was neither a dreamer, a visionary, nor a utopian, but a realist. He had been formed in a mystical piety, but mysticism was not the wellspring of his devotional life, and he soon left the tradition of Tauler behind. He did not strive to reject the world and elevate the spiritual, and he remained a nominalist, refusing to explain meaning through abstractions or use Aristotelian distinctions: a thing was a thing, words were names, and multiplying abstract entities should be avoided. He wanted to integrate the divine and the physical, not purify the earthly away, and so he insisted that Christ really was present in the elements of bread and wine of the Eucharist. His realism armed him against the charms of utopianism, and he could see what the outcome of rebellion would be.

But there were many preachers and pious layfolk who did dream of a new world and who did all they could to bring it into being. Some of them wrote, like the author of *An die Versammlung gemeiner Bauernschaft*, but most did not have the time or opportunity to get their thoughts into print. They imagined what a new order might look like, they experienced a new way of making decisions collectively, they slept together under the stars, and they risked everything for a world in which all would be brothers on Christ's side. When spring came, they would have their chance to live out those dreams.

PART THREE

SPRING

Hans Wertinger, *March* (Landshut, 1525–1526). Germanisches Nationalmuseum Nuremberg.

CHAPTER 7

EARLY SPRING

As spring warmed the ground and Easter approached, winter's planning and pondering were over and there was work to do. There were calves to be born, lambing, sowing, planting and tending crops and vegetables, and all the building, fencing, and repair work that could not be done in freezing weather. And yet even at this peak agricultural period, the peasants found time to gather in bands. The ideas of the winter gave way to a period of action in early spring 1525 that was far more widespread and wide-ranging in its targets than anything that would be seen in western Europe before the French Revolution. It was a time of optimism and dreams as the possibility grew that, together, peasants, miners, and townsfolk could remake their world. Brotherhood was on the move.

We know with hindsight that their actions were doomed to fail, but they did not know that. They believed they were fighting for the gospel, when mainstream reformers maintained they were doing the devil's work. Their springtime action would reach from Waldshut, near the Swiss border, and the Hegau, where the rebellion had begun the previous year, through the Black Forest to hilly Upper Swabia and parts of what today is Württemberg, and up the Rhine to Alsace. Revolt spread to the valleys of the Neckar and Tauber and up into Franconia, gathering pace along the routes suggested by the landscape, not by the map of lordship. Contemporaries were overwhelmed by its speed. A vast tide, it seemed to carry everything with it. As it rolled, it transformed the varying ideals and plans of many individuals into something far greater, a collective force that could smash the world they had known, destroying monasteries, abbeys, and castles, and changing the landscape forever.[1]

Assisted by the liturgical calendar itself, peasant unrest now spilled over into towns. Lent reached its climax in the second week of April, and so did the calls to celebrate Easter with communion in both kinds, including the wine hitherto received only by the priest himself. So convinced was the peasant assembly that their calls accorded with evangelical theology that they named several Lutheran town preachers amongst those they would accept as arbiters of their cause, including Luther. The Twelve Articles were circulating widely and must have appeared to many to be a document inspired by Luther's ideas. In Nuremberg, the pro-Reformation mayor and council were impressed by the peasants' 'printed' appeal, and though they did not support the peasants, they thought their complaints were fair 'and cannot be denied'. It was easy to blame the preachers, they wrote, but the problem was actually the way the lords had behaved tyrannically, persecuting the Word of God and those who preached it.[2]

In early March, Abbot Jacob of Weissenau wrote to Abbot Gerwig of Weingarten in southwest Germany, about a hundred kilometres away. The previous day, his peasants and those of the Weingarten monastery had sworn to the peasant band of Rappertsweiler. The day before,

Weingarten's steward had informed Abbot Gerwig that everyone was joining the peasants, sticking together like birds 'in a trap'; foolishly, the local officials had summoned the peasants, and two hundred had arrived. But then fourteen hundred determined peasants had gathered, and then their numbers swelled to three thousand. The signs were not good. Still, the abbot's steward was not yet seriously alarmed, for they were not harming anyone, and they paid for all they ate. Soon peasants from further afield were joining them, ringing the storm bell at night and running to the field outside Weingarten, where the band (*Haufen*) was encamped. Hostile though these accounts are, they convey how invigorating it must have been for peasants to gather in such large numbers.[3]

Abbot Jacob of Weissenau could breathe a sigh of relief that knights from the town of Tübingen were to be sent to help him, but the Tübingen authorities were alarmed because they needed at least four hundred knights to protect the town. The size of the revolt was growing rapidly: the Rappertsweiler group that the Weissenau peasants had joined now numbered seven thousand and was nominating provosts, mayors, and a court; at Staufen there was another group of fifteen hundred, and at Sonthofen five thousand. The Rappertsweilers formulated demands similar to the Twelve Articles, omitting mention of common lands, woods, and service dues, which were not a problem in their region. By late March, the prior of the monastery of Ochsenhausen was writing to their abbot, Andreas (who was away in the town of Ulm), that the 'bright band' had demanded the monks hand over all their 'firearms, powder, pikes and all weapons'—and had already taken the firearms (*Büchse*). The peasants had given them half a day and the night to decide if they would join the peasant brotherhood; the prior hoped that the absent abbot would consent, for otherwise they were not safe. At Weingarten, the band was encamped on the field nearby, and the local peasants had made common cause with them. At Altdorf, the townspeople had a day to decide whether to break their oaths to the abbot and swear to the peasants, so they drew up an official notarial statement setting out all their attempts to avoid doing so. It would be handy to have such a document if the peasants were defeated.[4]

Southern Germany was dotted with imperial abbeys subject directly to the emperor; they ruled their own territories as if they were secular authorities. Both Weingarten and Weissenau were pilgrimage centres as well, and both possessed 'holy blood' relics, blood shed by Christ on the cross mixed with earth. Though these monastic institutions were rich and crammed with manuscripts, books, opulent silverware, and art—the cultural capital of their day—they were also extremely exposed. The legitimacy of their rule was now questioned, and they lacked troops to protect their monasteries or preserve their power over their subjects. Truchsess Georg's assurances that he was on the way with the army of the Swabian League meant little when no troops arrived. Abbot Gerwig of Weingarten might later reprimand his brothers as furiously as he liked for swearing brotherhood with the peasants 'while you were not even in physical danger', but he himself was writing from the safety of the large town of Ulm.[5]

On 10 April, after a short siege, the peasants captured the abbot of Kempten's own castle, Liebenthann, where they found 30,000 Gulden of cash, silver plate, and jewels. Not a single shot was fired against the peasants. They smashed the windows for their lead (which could be used for shot) and filled a hat with the pieces. They even took the bed 'in which his grace himself slept' and sold it to a carpenter. Undressing the abbot down to his shirt, they found another 500 Gulden in gold hidden on his body. They left him 300 Gulden, sat him on an ass, sent him packing to the town of Kempten with a single servant, and burnt the castle to the ground. So ended—at least for the moment—the reign of Sebastian von Breitenstein, the man in whose lands peasants' burdens had been raised so ruthlessly.[6]

We can get some sense of what joining a peasant band might have been like from a wonderful visual chronicle that the abbot of Weissenau commissioned when the war was over. It shows the peasants confirming their oaths to the abbot by raising their two fingers, and how, soon after, they swore perjured oaths to Stefan Rahl, the peasant commander, who stands on a stool so the peasants can see him. Its centrepiece is the peasants' assault on the monastery. Peasants, fighting and vomiting, guzzle the monastery's wines, while others make off with barrels of beer. They invade the refectory, where the peasant Johann Wetzel takes the abbot's place at table. They fish out the monastery's ponds, smashing the weir so the fish escape. The next picture shows the prior and brothers hastily fleeing to Ravensburg, taking the monastery's valuables with them.[7]

The oath-swearing takes place inside the village fence, and all the men are armed, their weapons creating a forest of poles. Their leader Stefan Rahl (labelled 'ral') stands on a stool so he can be heard. The peasants gather on the Rappertsweiler mountain, shown in the background, centre right. The prior and priest, meanwhile, having ridden out to the village and having failed to suppress the peasants (centre), flee back to the monastery (left, foreground). *Weissenauer Chronik.*

The scene is one of utter chaos. In the middle, the peasants invade the monks' refectory, expelling the monks, taking their seats, and helping themselves to their food. Underneath, they raid the cellars. In the foreground drunken peasants fight one another, and though 'Frid' (peace) is shouted, they take no notice: one has a cut to the head, another's hand is severed. Notice the depiction of the peasants' hats, boots, and doublets, just like those of the evangelical peasant. Left background: peasants fish out the monastery's pond and open the dam gates. Others ride off with barrels of beer, sacks of grain and flour, loaves of bread, and other supplies, while yet other peasants ('men and women', the text explains, though no women can be seen) loot whatever they can. On the right, peasants wield an axe and a club to smash the monastery kitchen and bakery doors. Dogs are everywhere. *Weissenauer Chronik*.

For all that Abbot Gerwig might insist to his monks in Weingarten that they should tough it out and not leave unless they were invaded or threatened with death, it was clear everywhere that the monks had no choice but to flee. For the next weeks, the Weissenau monastery was run by Wetzel—and this was no isolated incident. In nearby Schussenried, the peasants arrived between five and six in the morning and occupied the abbey for fifteen days, causing 3,225 Gulden in damage. They invaded Ochsenhausen, another rich abbey; they threatened to attack St Georg's abbey in the

The peasants swear to the abbot, raised high above them in the monastery building. Their hats are off in recognition of his authority and they are unarmed; their weapons had been confiscated as part of their punishment for revolt. We know that they were still refusing to swear and had to be forced by soldiers to do so. *Weissenauer Chronik.*

town of Isny; and at Ottobeuren the monks tried in vain to reach an accommodation with the peasants and persuade their absent abbot Leonhard to return and sign an accord in person. But the peasants would not accept an agreement and attacked the surrounding castles instead. At the abbey of Marchtal, the abbey's peasants joined the Baltringen band when the abbot said he was unable to protect them; he claimed they caused 2,000 Gulden in damage to the monastery. Right across the region, the rich monasteries were captured and plundered by peasants, libraries destroyed and papers burnt, and there was seemingly nothing to stop them. Nobles stood idly by, and no armed support arrived.[8]

It had not even required much force to overturn monastic rule and get rid of the old religion; sheer numbers had been enough. The peasants 'reformed the monks'. At the abbey of Schöntal in

Hohenlohe, they tore the monks' music and books and smashed the windows. At Anhausen near Schwäbisch Hall, they ripped the manuscripts, threw books in the well, and cut off the heads of Jesus, Mary, and the saints. They played ball with the sacrament, throwing it about the church in its pyx, and dressed up in the priest's chasuble with a mass vestment on top. This was not mindless vandalism; they intended to destroy the relics of the old religion and its reverence for holy objects, which felt like a giant fraud in light of the truth that Christ himself had bought their freedom. They entered the buildings that had once been closed to them, ate their fill in the refectories, drank the cellars dry, butchered the livestock, stole the chalices that held the wine of communion, and slashed the hated registers that proved their serfdom and the dues they had to pay. At last they could get rid of the monastic lords who had oppressed them for so long and the 'human doctrine' with which monks and priests had distorted the gospel. They were free.[9]

By mid-April, Luther had read a copy of the Twelve Articles and dispatched his withering response. *Admonition to Peace*, his first published intervention in the rapidly polarising situation, was probably written before he went on a tour to Thuringia and Mansfeld through the first week of May. Luther did not visit peasant lines, and so far as we know he did not encounter groups of peasants again after his disastrous visit to Orlamünde the year before.[10]

In *Admonition to Peace*, Luther deployed the rhetoric he had been sharpening in the sermons he had given in March. Between the copy that went to the printers and the final product, little was apparently altered, and language about the *Mordgeister*, the murderous spirits, which Luther had developed when writing *Against the Heavenly Prophets*, was integral from the start. He begins like an

Old Testament prophet by admonishing the people. Invoking the peasants' own rhetoric of 'brotherly love', he castigates the lords for their refusal to listen to the gospel, threatening them, 'The sword is on your neck, and you still sit so firmly in the saddle that you think you can't be lifted out of it'. He continues, 'For I see, that the Devil, who has not managed to kill me through the Pope, now tries to root me out and eat me up, through the bloodthirsty murder prophets and sectarian spirits amongst you [he meant Müntzer and Karlstadt], yes, let him eat me up, that will give him constipation'. Luther rewrites the peasant conflict as a divine struggle about Luther himself.[11]

When Luther finally turns to the peasants' articles themselves, he only comments on the first three: a community can indeed call its own preacher to preach the true gospel, but it must pay for it; the tithe must be paid since it belongs to the authorities, and not to do so is therefore robbery. Here Luther overlooks the question of whether tithes should be paid to religious authorities such as convents and monasteries. On the third article, Luther can scarcely hide his contempt: 'There should be no serfs, because Christ has freed us all. What is this? This means making Christian freedom completely fleshly'. This article is 'completely against the gospel and is robbery'. There were slaves in the Old Testament, he argues, and to take away serfdom would be to rob a lord of what is his. Even other Lutherans, like Urbanus Rhegius, were taking a more nuanced position here, avoiding endorsing the sale of serfs and suggesting that if a peasant wished to become a craftsman, the lord should let him go. Though in this first intervention, Luther stopped short of calling for the peasants to be slain, and appeared to be even-handed by scolding the lords, it was clear that he would take the lords' side. When one group of peasants had proposed him and other Lutheran preachers as impartial judges early that spring, it was now evident how badly mistaken they had been. But Luther was no longer in control of his Reformation.[12]

In Switzerland and southern Germany as well, where the revolt had started back in midsummer the year before, religious reform gathered pace. In Waldshut, Hubmaier, who had once drawn crowds to the miraculous Virgin of Regensburg, now wanted to get rid of the 'useless rubbish' of Catholic worship: infant baptism, vigils, masses for the dead, purgatory, idols, ringing bells, organs, piping, indulgences, travelling to churches, brotherhoods, sacrifices, singing, and what he termed the 'mummlen und brummlen' of the old mass. He had been misled, he said, by 'the red whore of Babylon', by which he meant the papacy. At Waldshut that Easter, Hubmaier used normal household leavened bread for communion in place of blessed hosts (wafers). He rejected the doctrine of the real presence because, as he memorably put it in July, just as the pub sign that advertises the new wine is not the actual wine, so also the wine of communion is not Christ's blood.[13]

Even more shocking, he followed through on the implications of his own questioning of infant baptism and baptised seventy or eighty adult citizens, men and women, including many members of the town council. He used ordinary water from a local fountain, not blessed water, and carried it in a milk churn to the font. This was getting rid of the 'useless rubbish' of Catholic tradition, but there was more to it too. Instead of baptism being a sacrament through which everyone joined the church so that the political and religious communities were the same, believer's baptism meant that joining the church was a matter of choice. The Christian had to make a covenant with God and undergo the sacrament; he or she had to decide to be on Christ's side. Those who did not would be excluded from communion. Hubmaier used the ban as a way of creating bonds and discipline; those who joined had to accept that if they committed a serious sin they would be admonished and could be put under the ban, excluded from interaction with any other members of the community. This was a formidable way of creating an ideal community of the elect.[14]

Thomas Müntzer was doing something similar as he created leagues and established a brotherhood of sworn believers who would support and defend one another. At Allstedt, those who wished to follow Müntzer had to raise their hand, swear the oath in front of everyone else, and have their names written down in a book, and he seems to have later tried to form such a league in Mühlhausen too. Yet undergoing believer's baptism at Waldshut may have been an even more life-altering experience, because it meant breaking with the church of one's youth and treating one's original baptism as invalid.

At the same time, Waldshut renewed its alliance with the peasants with Hubmaier's support, 'so that one might come to peace, quiet and a Christian way of being'. How far his theology merged with peasant concerns is less clear. In 1526 Hubmaier insisted that he had always taught obedience to the authorities—which was true, but only in the sense that he supported the authority of the Waldshut town council, which was not obeying its overlord, Austria. He also claimed that he had not rejected the tithe, but then neither had he taught that it was fitting for authorities, bishops, abbots, monks, nuns, and priests to overburden their 'poor people with unheard of, unchristian dues and rip them from the word of God by force'. It is, as we saw, hard to know what Hubmaier actually preached; his enemies, including Fabri, said he developed a theology according to which the fruits of the air, earth, and water should be free for all. The brief printed pamphlets we have of his from the time are accessible, pithy, and clear, and they demonstrate his formidable abilities as a preacher, but they are mainly preoccupied with practical ecclesiastical reform—with abolishing the mass, advocating believer's baptism, and discussing the nature of the church—not freedom or the tithe, which is why it has been suggested that his influence must have been minimal. But his preaching did provide a theological underpinning for establishing a civic community in Waldshut bound together by oaths, the ban, and believer's baptism; it encompassed most of the Waldshuters in opposition to the Austrian Habsburgs. His preaching also furnished a justification for getting rid of the 'useless rubbish'—and so, for plundering churches. And the religious excitement his preaching fostered helped others apply these ideas to their own circumstances.[15]

In addition, Hubmaier clearly influenced the peasant army and its leaders, who had earlier visited Waldshut. By early May, Hans Müller had composed the Sixteen Articles of the Black Forest peasants, which took a leaf out of Hubmaier's book and deployed the ban as a way of punishing those who would not join. Müller now used the language of religious brotherhood as well, writing to the town of Villingen and calling on them to 'help [erect] godly law/rights and the holy gospel of our lord Jesus Christ', and asking them to 'join fraternally in the Christian brotherhood so that the Christian good and brotherly love can be instituted again, established and increased'. Whatever Hubmaier's own views on and interest in peasant issues, evangelicalism like his clearly inspired peasant radicals, who took it in new directions.[16]

Meanwhile, in the nearby Black Forest and in the Hegau, the lords were fighting back. Georg Truchsess of Waldburg, the military leader of the Swabian League, was raising troops; by early March, his forces had slain two hundred peasants near Ebingen, not far from Balingen, in the Swabian Jura in Württemberg. Financiers, including Jacob Fugger, lent money to the Austrians and the league, with Fugger alone providing 10,000 Gulden in March, so that the authorities were soon in a financial position to attack the peasants. But Truchsess Georg's campaign against the peasants, including those on his own lands, was suddenly interrupted when Duke Ulrich of Württemberg, who had been expelled by the Austrians, took advantage of the situation to try to get his duchy back. This effort was initially successful, as his mercenary troops joined with local peasant and townspeople discontented with Austrian rule. The situation grew confused, because though he claimed to support peasants, Ulrich did not support freedom for serfs and had little interest in the gospel of brotherly love. But he did inspire a large popular movement, which continued despite the duke's positions and had some early success. Fears about Ulrich prompted the league to finally mobilise on 7 March. Ulrich managed to take Herrenberg, and having won other towns too, tried to take Stuttgart. In late February the imperial forces had won the battle of Pavia in Italy, and over the following weeks Truchsess Georg, the Austrians' key commander, was able to recruit mercenaries of better quality and lead the forces of the Swabian League against Ulrich in support of the Austrians, while Ludwig von Helfenstein managed to hold Stuttgart. After this ignominious defeat, Ulrich's hired mercenaries soon melted away because he had not paid them, and the attempt to regain his lands fizzled out for the moment, freeing the truchsess to focus on the peasants.[17]

Truchsess Georg was not to have it all his own way, however. For starters, it was still difficult to raise mercenary troops because the mercenaries (Landsknechte) were not willing to fight people who were often their relatives. And even for good pay, locals were not willing to join armies to put down the peasant bands, some of whom also had money to employ mercenaries. As Georg's own herald put it, nobody wanted to take on the peasants.[18] When the truchsess made a speech to his men enjoining them to begin the campaign against the peasants, it fell flat. Not for the last time, at Dagersheim perhaps half the army mutinied after their representatives gathered in the 'ring', and the contingents of Memmingen, Constance, and the Black Forest, strongholds of the Christian Union, simply left. In order therefore to secure his forces for the campaign against the peasants, Truchsess Georg devised a system of threatening the villages they defeated with burning unless they paid a tax, two-thirds of which would go to the league while the rest would go to the soldiers, a strategy that alienated local populations. Technically negotiations with the peasantry were still in progress, but when the Baltringen band attacked the castles of Laupheim and Schemmerberg on 27 March after one of their representatives in the Christian Union was assassinated, hostilities began.

The sheer scope of the peasants' revolt meant that the truchsess could not deal with all places at once; he constantly had to change direction. As a result, some areas around the Black Forest and near Freiburg and Villingen had to wait so long for the promised help to arrive that they had little choice but to capitulate. A cunning strategist, Truchsess Georg could not waste a man, and so he was unwilling to risk further battle until he was sure of victory. But hard-liners in the Swabian League grew doubtful of his strategy as he struggled to capture Duke Ulrich. Tired of waiting, the league ordered him to turn to Leipheim and Günzburg, to the east of Ulm, where a peasant army was massing. The Swabian League under the truchsess would become the major antagonist of the peasants in the southwest, but putting down such a far-reaching, unpredictable, and widely scattered revolt would not prove easy.[19]

The peasants must have felt as if nothing could stop their triumphal advance. We can glimpse something of their excitement that spring through the career of Jakob Wehe, the preacher of Leipheim, who also happened to be the cousin of one of the most successful of the early Reformation pamphleteers, Eberlin von Günzburg. Wehe must have been a riveting preacher, because in a private admonition to him (promptly printed for the benefit of the public), Eberlin specifically warned against the intoxicating sense of power that preaching in a pulpit can confer. But whereas Eberlin had headed for Wittenberg to sit at Luther's feet, and soon retreated from his early radical demands, Wehe remained inspired by dreams of a new world.[20]

In Ulm, the headquarters of the Swabian League, there were fears that the townsfolk might join with the peasants and that Ulm itself might fall. Not far off, the situation in the town of Leipheim was also febrile, for the bishop of Augsburg had placed it under the ban and had forced Wehe's dismissal, which Leipheim had ignored. The imposition of the ban meant there was no prospect of a Catholic Easter mass and confession, and no church burial or other sacraments, and the town was practically forced to adopt the Reformation to celebrate Easter. The church's clumsy attempts to crack down on evangelicals were proving self-defeating, serving only to make people more radical. By March, Leipheim and nearby Günzburg had become the centres of a well-armed peasant army about four thousand strong, and Wehe threw in his lot with them, taking a leading role as they set off on their march. Before battle he is said to have preached that 'they should be brave, the League's cannon would turn around by a special providence of God and shoot their own men, and the same with the lances'.[21]

But on 4 April, the peasant bands met the cavalry of the Swabian League, which by then controlled the corridor between Leipheim and Ulm. The peasants scattered in panic. Trapped in the swampy ground between the knights, the Biber stream, and the Danube River, many rebels who were not cut down drowned 'like pigs'. The town of Leipheim opened its gates for those who survived.[22]

Just over four thousand people are known to have participated in the battle, and we are able to identify which villages they were from. Though some came from long distances away, the geographical concentration in the area is striking, suggesting that pretty much the whole locality sent men to fight, with 250 from Leipheim, 90 from Eberlin's hometown of Günzburg, and far greater numbers from the surrounding villages. Many died in the battle, and another 700 were imprisoned in the Leipheim church.

After their defeat, realising that he faced death, Wehe jumped off the steep wall of the town of Leipheim but was captured by a soldier.

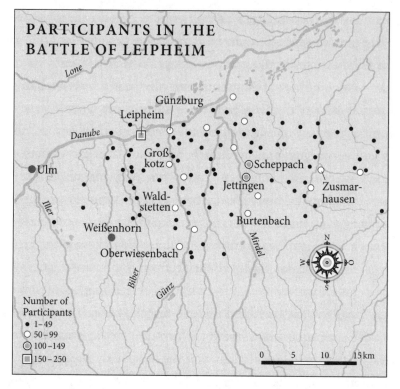

PARTICIPANTS IN THE BATTLE OF LEIPHEIM

Number of Participants
- 1–49
- 50–99
- 100–149
- 150–250

Nearly all the participants came from the same side of the Danube River, which functioned as a natural barrier. Source: Baumann, *Akten*, 181–183. My thanks to Aaron Larsen who compiled the map; and to Susanne Anwander of the Bauernkriegs- und Heimatmuseum Leipheim. Map drawn by Peter Palm.

He would be the last of the leaders to be executed the next day, forced to watch the others die, but he continued encouraging and exhorting them to the end, insisting publicly that he had never preached rebellion. Refusing to 'confess' to a priest, Wehe said, 'I have already confessed to God, my heavenly father, who knows my heart better than any other'. Brought into the ring, he prayed his own heartfelt version of Christ's words: 'Father forgive them, for they know not what they do, not because I think I'm so good, but for the sake of their ignorance'.[23]

Though the villages who had sent men were fined, it was the town that bore the brunt of the punishment, for it had let the surviving rebels in. Leipheim had been bought by Ulm from the Württemberg

government in the mid-fifteenth century and granted a degree of independence, only for its citizens to opt for the Reformation and their
pastor Wehe to join the peasants. The town's penalty was to be opened
to the troops of the league for plunder. 'Who would have thought that
I would become a preacher at Leipheim?' joked the commander of
the Swabian League, Truchsess Georg, as he punished the Lutherans,
compelling them to return to Catholicism. Leipheim's citizens were
punished by hefty fines, and its women, who, one chronicler alleged,
had supported the Reformation enthusiastically, were forced to wear
the town emblem of Ulm on their clothes as if they were prostitutes.[24]

There was worse to follow. On 14 April, Good Friday, under the
leadership of local pastor Florian Greisel, who had been appointed by
the truchsess himself, the peasants from around Wurzach were defeated at a battle just outside the town. The peasants had failed to secure an alliance with Wurzach, and they paid for it dearly when the
town refused to open its gates to them. Many rebels tried to escape by
climbing up trees; others were killed while fleeing towards the town.
The league put several rebellious villages to the torch as punishment.
The Upper German cities meeting at Memmingen drafted a letter begging the league to make peace and negotiate at least a truce with the
Lake Constance and Allgäu peasants; because of the fighting, peasants
were not coming to the weekly markets in towns, and so townsfolk
could not get food. All authorities in the area, prelates, townsfolk, and
nobles, found it unendurable, they said.[25]

As Easter neared, the peasants in the region had suffered reverses,
but they were far from spent: new areas were still joining the revolt.
In Hüfingen in the Black Forest, all it took was fifteen peasants to
appear and demand that the town be given over to them. When the
town complied, it was occupied by two hundred peasants, while three
of the Hüfingers were compelled to march with the peasants so that
the townsmen would share the peasant army's fate, a tactic that other
peasant armies would later use to great effect. Villingen, a much larger

town near Hüfingen, was horrified by the peasants' actions: they were massing 'from the whole Black Forest', and now Villingen feared for its own situation. Zell and Stockach also wrote to the Swabian League asking for help, and Engen, Bräunlingen, and all the Fürstenbergs' castles and towns had defected to the peasants.[26]

Meanwhile at Weingarten, the monastery was forced to feed the peasant armies from its supplies. Only the 'Holy Blood' relic had miraculously saved its buildings from being destroyed, wrote the steward. When Truchsess Georg arrived near the town of Weingarten, where the peasants were encamped, on 15 April, the peasant forces were so large that he was compelled to negotiate, especially since reinforcements from the Hegau and Black Forest bands were about to arrive. His own troops were not reliable and had refused to move when the four Gulden promised to each of them for victory at Leipheim had not been forthcoming. After days of negotiation, Truchsess Georg orally agreed to the truce of Weingarten with the Lake Constance and Allgäu bands on 17 April, allowing them to keep their weapons and letting their leaders go free. But he insisted that the Baltringen band, which he had defeated at Leipheim, surrender without terms. The Christian Union of the Swabian peasants was to be dissolved. The truce effectively ended the war in Upper Swabia for the time being.[27]

Up to this point, the Allgäu and Lake Constance bands had been largely nonviolent, though armed, and they had tried to pursue their aims through uniting with others and getting towns to join the brotherhood. Indeed, though monasteries had been plundered, most had not yet been torched, and violence was more a matter of threats. Not until 26 March was a castle set alight by the Baltringen band, and it belonged to a monastery.[28] A period of optimism had prevailed, with all agreeing to the Twelve Articles and the creation of a new imperial ordinance, and it seemed the world really could be made anew. Like so many leaders of the Poor Conrad and Bundschuh revolts before them, Lotzer, Schappeler, and Ulrich Schmid all escaped to Switzerland, from where perhaps they hoped later to return. Many monasteries had been plundered, and their food and supplies used up, but apart from some isolated incidents, it could have seemed as if the peasants were attacking monasteries alone—this was what many lords assumed, later realising their mistake. Even so, it could have seemed as if, after the truce of Weingarten, negotiations might be concluded successfully with the truchsess and the Swabian League and peace restored, with 'brotherhood', if not victorious, at least gaining some concessions. A different Reformation from Luther's or Zwingli's might have implanted itself in the towns and villages of the southwest. But Leipheim signaled what would happen if the peasants lost.[29]

In the region of Franconia, the war took a markedly different course from the events in Upper Swabia. This was an area of highly complicated rule: there were three major prince bishoprics of Würzburg, Bamberg, and Eichsstätt, alongside the margraves of Ansbach and Kulmbach-Bayreuth, and five imperial cities, Nuremberg, Rothenburg, Schweinfurt, Windsheim, and Weißenburg, with their own territories, along with a host of minor counts. A patchwork of jurisdictions and overlapping rights meant that political and religious questions were difficult to tease apart. Many more knights and nobles were involved as leaders of the peasants, and they had strong links to local notables; many clergy worked as preachers and scribes. This also meant that they could form alliances with townsfolk where there seems to have been considerable support for the 'godly' cause.

As a result, the revolt had less of an antifeudal character, and fewer grievances were formulated. Personal serfdom was rare, and peasants' property rights were comparatively secure. Resentments instead centred on the dues demanded by landlords, as well as on the tithes and the rest of the various imposts, which could demand over half the income of a farm.[30]

Here the Twelve Articles functioned as a default programme, and the revolt reflected a split within the ruling class, though after the war many covered their tracks. Men such as the would-be noble and former bureaucrat Wendel Hipler, and the knights Götz von Berlichingen, Stefan von Mentzingen, and Florian Geyer, were not just dragooned into leading armies or working as secretaries, but willingly chose to fight with the rebels, and individuals like Hans Berlin of Heilbronn, town councillor and rebel leader, managed to straddle both sides. Their success was astonishing, and they even began the process of imagining a world after the war, summoning a peasant parliament and devising a plan for a new order. Any geographical division, though, also fails to do justice to how the armies moved and how events in one region affected another. The defeat of the Upper Swabians at Leipheim had massive consequences for the armies around Heilbronn on the edge of Franconia, while conversely, events in the region around Weinsberg north of Stuttgart and near Heilbronn affected the course of the entire war. This was a region of vineyards and sunshine, and of substantial wealth, where peasants were not producing for subsistence but were deeply engaged in markets, often across long distances.

The uprising around the imperial town of Rothenburg began on 26 March when Georg Metzler, a local innkeeper, formed an armed band. The group quickly attracted people from a wide area, including subjects of the Palatinate, Mainz, and Würzburg, as well as subjects of the Teutonic Knights, whose order was by then weakened by Albrecht of Prussia's defection. They attacked the Cistercian monastery and castle of Schöntal and spent two days and nights drinking out its cellars. They said they wanted to take the dues book (*Zinsbuch*) to strike out everything they thought unfair. Next they moved to Mergentheim, another seat of the Teutonic Knights, where they seized and plundered the castle known as the 'Newhaus', then burnt it down.[31]

The situation in Rothenburg itself was complex. The evangelical movement there had politically influential supporters and included men like Johann Teuschlin, who had preached antisemitism. Jews had consequently been expelled and their debtors allowed to reduce the capital they owed by the interest they had paid. Teuschlin, too, had earlier supported the wonder-working statue of Mary in Regensburg that Hubmaier had vaunted, and had even tried to work miracles by attempting to bring a dead child back to life. But now he had joined the evangelicals and had become something of a hero when he had refused to submit to the bishop's orders to cease Lutheran preaching and had held the mass in German in defiance. A 'blind monk' of the Franciscans also began to agitate for the Reformation, while a member of the Teutonic Knights married the blind monk's sister, publicly breaching his vows. In late 1524, none other than Diepold Peringer, the so-called miraculous preaching Peasant of Wöhrd, appeared in town and with Teuschlin's support began to preach outdoors, while for good measure the pro-Reformation humanist and schoolmaster Valentin Ickelsamer was preaching in town as well.[32]

Into this fevered environment that winter stepped Karlstadt. The renegade noble Stefan von Menzingen and the mayor Ernfried Kumpf began to form a religious faction around him and Teuschlin. Banished from the town in January 1525, Karlstadt continued to live in Rothenburg illegally. His group tried to make common cause with the peasants, but they did not control the council. Meanwhile Teuschlin himself, though critical of the council's failure to support the Word of God, was careful not to preach against lordship. But following in the example of Jakob Strauss, Hubmaier, and Luther himself, he preached against usury. While this fell within the broad sweep of 'Lutheranism', it could also be viewed as incendiary—Jakob Strauss in Eisenach, for instance, had run into trouble for his rousing attacks on usury. Though Luther had distanced himself from antisemitism, publishing his most important philosemitic tract in 1523, it continued to be an occasional strand of evangelical radicalism during the uprising.[33]

Revolt was now spreading ever wider. The peasants' next target was the Counts of Hohenlohe, important rulers and landholders in the region. They attacked the Öhringen castle on 3 April. The chronicler Peter Harer claimed that the count's wife fell at the commander's feet but got no 'pity'. Instead, the peasants took all the arms in the castle and amused themselves by shooting the ornamental drainpipes off the structure's roof. Still, they stopped short of burning the castle to the ground. Meanwhile another group formed at Flein, recruiting men between Heilbronn and Sontheim and across the Neckar, many of whom were also subjects of the Teutonic Knights. They must have known that in February, the grand master of the order, Albrecht of Prussia, had become a supporter of Luther and had secularised his territories, weakening what was left of the knights' power and virtually inviting attack on the order's castles and property in the rest of Germany. The peasants flocked to Grossgartach and drank the cellar of wine that belonged to the noble foundation of Bruchsal there. Meeting no resistance but also few supporters, they moved on to Beilstein and Bottwar before turning back to Sontheim and then to Öhringen. The two bands, only about forty or fifty kilometres from each other, proceeded to join forces at Neckarsulm above Heilbronn, another town with a Teutonic Knights' foundation.[34]

They became known as the 'bright band', the 'Helle Haufen', a term breathing optimism.[35] Linked by hostility to the Teutonic Knights, these groups drew in rebels from a range of different overlords, many of whom—apart from the Counts of Hohenlohe—were religious institutions. It must have seemed as if the whole landscape around the Neckar River would fall to the peasants as they engaged in a three-week-long carnival of drinking out the cellars of the lords and monasteries. 'We found even more wine and household goods than in Schöntal', wrote one exultant peasant leader about a recently plundered monastery.[36]

It all seemed good-humoured as the weather warmed. A group of peasants came upon the local noble Götz von Berlichingen as he was sitting outside a tavern. He would have been unmistakable: he sported a prosthetic iron fist, the legacy of a battle injury. As Götz told the story later, Marx Stumpf accosted him: 'Götz is it you?' He replied, 'What's up?', and was told the peasants had just elected him as their commander. Götz tried to explain that he was a noble and so was on the other side, but they would have none of it. They took him to the army, where his appointment was acclaimed—though Götz later argued that he had signed under duress and for a limited period only, like a salaried condottiere. His appointment seems irrational, a failure by the peasants to recognise that brotherhood had limits. But the locals would not have forgotten Götz's high-profile support for the gospel when he had tried to stage a Reformation disputation to trounce an anti-Lutheran Carmelite monk, nor would the placards he had placed advertising the event have gone unnoticed. Like the famed humanist and supporter of Luther at Worms, the knight Ulrich von Hutten, Götz had made himself a knightly Reformation champion. Now the bemused Götz set to work forming a band of diverse countryfolk into a fighting force.[37]

But this good humour did not last. Not far away, in the hills, lay the town of Weinsberg. From the castle above the town, Count Ludwig von Helfenstein and his men were shooting at peasants and killing passersby. The peasants in Neckarsulm determined that they must capture the castle and stop him. A passing salt-seller alerted the peasant army that the castle was deserted, and so on Easter Sunday, 16 April, a wing of the army easily stormed it, taking the countess and her children hostage; in an hour, the castle was theirs. The sixty horsemen who should have been defending it were down in town, but the town was utterly 'pro-peasant' and let the peasant army in through the gates. They captured the count and many of the soldiers, taking only 'two hours' to secure the town, one peasant commander noted.[38]

Dietrich von Weiler, 'an upright manly person of body', fled up into a church tower, where he was shot and his body thrown down to the churchyard below 'as a spectacle'. Another young noble gave a

Running the gauntlet: *Ein durch die Spieß jagen*, woodcut by Jost Amman, 1573, which has an accompanying verse explaining the procedure: a Landsknecht would be killed by his comrades with their tools of trade. Leonhard Fronsperger, *Kriegsbuch dritter Teil*, fo. 86 r. Bayerische Staatsbibliothek Munich.

peasant eight Gulden to spare his life and kissed him, but when the peasant's companion shouted, 'Stab them all, stab them', he hit the young man in the neck, felling him to the ground, where the other peasants finished him off. The rebels then rounded up twenty-four knights and forced them and two young pages to 'run the gauntlet' on the meadow outside town, a military punishment that strips men utterly of their physical prowess because the victim is made to run towards the flag through two lines of soldiers with lances, so he dies before getting there. The count's own piper, who 'had shared dinner with him', plucked the count's hat from his corpse and put it on his head,

This illustration of the setting of the Weinsberg atrocity from a 1578 chronicle shows no human figures but clearly indicates the castle on its steep slope. The tower from which Weiler's body fell is giant-sized. It is recognizably the view that can still be seen today from the train. State Archives, Stuttgart.

declaring he wished to be a noble, and allegedly smeared his spear in the count's fat. Then they performed 'many unchristian wanton acts' with the ladies of the count's wife (who was of very high social status, an illegitimate daughter of the Emperor Maximilian). Stabbing her young son in the arm—presumably to render him incapable of ever bearing knightly weapons—they 'took all they had and led them on a manure cart to Heilbronn'. They burnt the castle to the ground.[39]

This series of atrocities, the worst committed by the peasant armies, changed the course of the war, it was widely reported and condemned. Leading the violence was Jäcklein Rohrbach, a tough rebel commander with a violent history who was disowned by other peasant bands and expelled from their army. A former soldier who had fought with the Swabian League during the first war against Duke Ulrich, he owned a tavern, a farm with fields, several vineyards, a vegetable garden, three horses, one cow, sheep, and pigs. A man who did not like him described him as looking 'half like a cavalryman, half like a peasant'.[40]

Rohrbach, whose surviving letters indicate that he was highly literate, apparently kept a copy of the Twelve Articles in his bosom and had written to friends in Heilbronn early in March, calling on them to lead their people into the Promised Land. He was late with his payments to the pastor, had not paid the two geese and one hen either, and along with his brother-in-law and a woman known as the 'Schwarze Hofmännin', he had also refused to pay some taxes to the local ruler. When the pastor took him to court, Rohrbach assembled a large group of supporters. The unfortunate pastor, who had stopped at the nearby inn and asked what the crowd was, soon decided discretion was the better part of valour and returned home. From this little victory, Rohrbach may have learned that strength in numbers could overwhelm and unsettle church power.[41]

In early April, Rohrbach began forming his army in earnest. They met at Flein, a village near Heilbronn, and peasants subject to Heilbronn and other villages of the Teutonic Knights, together with citizens of Heilbronn, joined. The council forbade anyone to give them hospitality, but the band simply commandeered wine, drank together, and formed a ring in front of the village, where they swore to the Twelve Articles and chose Rohrbach as their captain. A hostile observer wrote that they all took off their hats and bowed to him as if he were a lord. From there they marched to Sontheim, forcing the villagers to join the group, and on 3 April they crossed the Neckar to Rohrbach's home village of Böckingen. In less than a week they had travelled a little over twenty kilometres in a circle, drained the cellars of the Teutonic Knights at Sontheim, and threatened nearby villages. They had also successfully thumbed their nose at the Heilbronn council's attempts to prevent them forming a band or recruiting its citizens as members. They now joined the much larger Odenwald band, of which Rohrbach was just one amongst many leaders, and the army proceeded to commit the Weinsberg atrocity on Easter Sunday. Though the atrocity became a byword for peasant brutality, it was also a reprisal for the count's killing of a group of peasants shortly before. It was retaliation, too, for the defeat the Swabian League had just inflicted on the peasants at Wurzach.[42]

The following day, Rohrbach and his companion Enderlin von Dürrenzimmer went to Heilbronn, apparently on their own, dressed in the murdered Helfenstein's hat and cloak, and were hosted by the town council. The day after, four representatives of the larger peasant army entered the town, and the council swore to join the peasant league and to levy a fine on the Teutonic Knights. Rohrbach leveraged every ounce of power he could from the atrocity to improve the peasants' military position—and intimidation worked, at least for the moment.

Rohrbach was doubtless a violent and angry man, and he evidently enjoyed exercising power. But this does not mean that his Christian beliefs were insincere: the idea of going to the Promised Land resonated with him, and he probably imagined a land where clerics would not filch the produce of hardworking farmers, and where he, a serf through his mother, would be treated with respect. It was said he liked to call himself Jacob von Böckingen, as if he were a noble. This may not have been audacity but irony. When the Heilbronn council ordered him not to bully its subjects into joining his band, he replied that no one was forced to join, for they accepted only those 'who join of their own power and free will'. Therefore, the council should not 'jump at every bit of gossip and flying rumour'.[43]

He evidently had the measure of the vacillating council, given that the Weinsberg atrocity succeeded in forcing Heilbronn to throw in its lot with the rebels, a major coup that secured the region. Those who had forced the knights to run the gauntlet were now bound together in blood. But to those outside the band, the brutality committed on Easter Sunday did not seem like the work of Christian brothers. Its notorious story lodged in popular memory. Chroniclers often took pains to list by name the twenty-four knights who were killed by running the gauntlet.

Militarily, Weinsberg made it clear that the peasant bands were not aimless revellers offering brotherhood to all, but men capable of killing high-ranking nobles in cold blood and possibly raping their womenfolk. 'Weinbergisch' became a term of infamy, and the bands' opponents soon called the Helle Haufen 'the Weinsbergers'. Their threat—'if you won't come to us, then we will come to you'—had to be taken seriously, and many towns fell to the peasants.

The peasants moved on, plundering the nearby convent of Lichtenstern near Löwenstein and taking the castle of Scheuerberg above it, along with its stores of gunpowder. Rohrbach's band took the Carmelite monastery just outside Heilbronn. It was an important Marian pilgrimage site to 'Maria im Nesselbusch', a miraculous image that had been found in a bush on the Weinsberg road. The pilgrimage and monastery dated to the mid-fifteenth century, but in 1524, after its prior Hans Seitzenweiler had scandalously seduced the mayor's daughter, local preachers had called for the miraculous statue to be burnt. For the Heilbronners it represented the worst of the old corrupt church, and since Rohrbach had connections with the Heilbronn citizens, he would have known that taking the monastery would strengthen the evangelical enthusiasm in the town. Götz von Berlichingen, commander of the bright band, had his own reasons for wanting to get even with Heilbronn: he had been imprisoned in the town for three years from 1519. Heilbronn itself became the next target.[44]

Heilbronn's experience of the war is typical of what happened in many towns, as local political struggles joined with evangelical movements inside town and became galvanised by the presence of peasant armies outside, just as they had in Rothenburg. In Heilbronn, Reformation preaching had been going on for some time, and there was considerable hostility to the oligarchic town council, which did not even have guild representation. When the vine-dressers gathered on the town square in a ring demanding concessions, other craft associations joined, and on 4 April, eight articles were presented to the council. Peasants—who normally had only restricted access into town—were being let in and out of town 'through a small gate'. For the next two weeks leading up to Easter, the situation was very confused; looting apparently occurred, and the Teutonic Order's property was forcibly sold to members of the council. The prior of the order tried to curry favour with the peasants by offering them wine on Easter Sunday—unwisely drawing attention to the old church's refusal to accord layfolk the wine of the sacrament.[45]

After the victory at Weinsberg, the wavering council realised the seriousness of the threat it faced. The council quickly discovered that the peasants knew the extent of internal discontent in town—the peasants had nurtured contacts with townsfolk over the previous months because they had been able to enter and leave freely. Many in the town supported the peasants and considered their demands to be Christian. The women, too, were demanding that the town come to terms. Comprehending that its control was slipping, the council summoned all the citizenry to the market square and tried to get them to renew their oaths of loyalty, the same risky strategy used at Würzburg and at Mühlhausen. It misfired, revealing the scale of anger in public. 'No way will we swear', 'we know how things stand', 'we want the peasant army and not the town', 'we're not going to risk all this danger on the clergy's account', shouted the Heilbronners. Some said that if the council wouldn't let the peasants in, 'they would throw out the "big heads" over the wall'.[46]

The council gave way and agreed that the peasants could 'fine' the town's monastic institutions. The peasants found nine sacks of gold as they looted the Teutonic Order's bell tower. The rebels joked that they were the order's heirs since they had taken the property in there in the first place, and now they wanted it back. Women and poor people carried jugs, bottles, and whatever containers they could find, and filled them with wine from the order's house—all with council permission. In a 'summer house' that formed part of the knights' headquarters, the peasants spread out the fabulous booty on a table—silver, jewels, gold coin. The council and the 'commons' held a joint meeting with the peasant leaders and apparently swore brotherhood with the peasants, although they later denied doing so. The peasants received their own room in the town hall and were permitted to 'fine' the ecclesiastical institutions in the town. Alongside the substantial resources netted by this privilege, they eventually destroyed parts of the hated Carmelite monastery just outside the walls and sold off the stones with which it had been built.[47]

To all intents and purposes, Heilbronn became the local centre of the peasant bands, and it was to Heilbronn that the peasants planned to summon a parliament. Links had been cultivated between the peasant leaders and high-ranking citizens. Hans Müller (alias Flux), a councillor with considerable wealth, was the brother-in-law of the peasant leader Hans Reuter of Bieringen. Somehow the peasants gained supplies of gunpowder, including 'one ton' from the council. We will never know the full extent of the Heilbronners' entanglement with the peasants because the surviving source material was carefully curated to support the council's argument that it was innocent (as is also the case in towns like Mühlhausen). The council even attempted to argue that it never broke its oath of obedience, and if it let the peasants 'punish' the ecclesiastical institutions, that was because the clergy were not citizens.[48]

Towns everywhere faced peasant armies that demanded they introduce the Reformation and punish the hated clergy. At Rothenburg, as peasant bands massed outside the town, a group forced the council to let a 'committee' of rebels work alongside it. At first it looked as if the town would swear brotherhood with the Helle Haufen, but the town delayed sending them the two hundred men and arms they demanded and then insisted it had not formally sworn after all. On 15 May, however, the noble commander of the peasants, Florian Geyer, appeared personally in Rothenburg to ensure that the council swear an oath of loyalty to a 'league' and brotherhood that would last 101 years.[49] The rebels were envisaging a new and permanent world order.

In Würzburg, strong support for the peasants turned it into a citadel for their forces. They massed on the town square with the citizens, intimidating the oligarchic town council, which then had to take account of popular views. The town made links with nearby Kitzingen, which was also letting peasants enter town. In Bamberg the geography tells the story. Built on seven hills, the town was conceived as a second Rome, with a church atop every hill and the town laid out in the form of a cross. The clergy and their personnel, who made up perhaps half the total population of the town, were exempt from tax and from secular courts and mostly resided on the hills, while the townsfolk huddled below. The exclusive cathedral chapter consisted of local noble family members, their shields displayed on their luxurious houses that clustered behind the cathedral and the chapter court; they elected their own members, had aggregated most of the administrative authority, and even chose the bishop, so that the hills were a mirror image of local noble power. Small wonder that they were hated, and that one of the rebels' key demands was that they should be shut out of power altogether. When the peasants formed an encampment at Hallstadt, easy walking distance along the flat land from Bamberg, many from the town joined, uniting against the local ecclesiastical nobility that represented their common enemy.[50]

Towns like Heilbronn, Rothenburg, Bamberg, and Würzburg became regional centres that cemented the peasants' power. They provided a place to store plunder and supplies, and a base for their chancellery. The peasants camped outside, just as the monasteries had been repurposed as army camps. The same thing had happened in Upper Swabia, where Memmingen had functioned as a peasant headquarters, as well as in a host of smaller towns that swore brotherhood. The peasants seized the fabulous wealth of the town monasteries just as they had taken that of the rural foundations, sometimes dividing it up as booty. This was essential not only to ensure that the soldiers stuck with the army but also to pay for supplies and arms and to build a war chest. By creating an infrastructure and working with local citizens, the peasants may have hoped to create an enduring base, loyal territory they could keep even when the army was not there to ensure compliance. Some peasant leaders started issuing passports that guaranteed safe conduct and protection, probably against payment, rather like local warlords. Others used the confusion to feather their nests; Melchior Engelman purchased what was left of the very substantial house of the Heilbronn Carmelite prior, including its wood panelling, from the 'Captain of the Weinsberg Valley', acknowledging him as his liege.[51]

In all these towns, the arrival of the peasants meant that the Reformation proceeded apace, with monks and nuns ordered to don secular clothes for their own safety and monasteries closed or intimidated. The creation of a kind of headquarters in a town or monastery, however, also gave the peasants breathing space to devise an overarching strategy and work towards a settlement, allowing men like the peasant chancellor Wendel Hipler, who had worked for the Counts of Hohenlohe and was highly experienced, to strategise and consider how to unite the Swabian, Alsatian, and other armies. The representatives met in the monastery of Schöntal, which had been looted by the peasants and was now a peasant base. It seemed that a new order could be devised for the peace to come. The fundamental problem for the peasant armies, however, remained: territory could be taken, monastic institutions could be plundered, and so the army could be provisioned and keep moving. But as soon as it left an area—and it had to keep moving to supply itself—it could not be certain of keeping its gains.

From Neckarsulm, peasants marched to take Gundelsheim and its castle Horneck, the seat of the master of the Teutonic Knights that also housed its archives. They liberated substantial supplies from the deserted castle after the master fled to Heidelberg. They moved on through the Schefflenz Valley to the monastery of Amorbach, which they plundered and turned into a base. On 4 May, they formulated the Amorbach Articles, a more moderate document that represented an attempt to adapt the Twelve Articles for conditions outside Upper Swabia. By this point, nine cities in the area had joined with them. It seemed that, as in Heilbronn, a real union could be formed between peasants and townsfolk, united in their hatred of the rich religious institutions and using monasteries to provide supplies for the thousands of armed men who needed to be provisioned. Towns would provide support once supplies from the monasteries ran out; they could not afford to alienate their potential supporters by stealing from peasant farms. They destroyed the castles of Wildenburg and Limbach and forced Count Georg of Wertheim not only to join them but to lend them cannon. Next they headed towards Würzburg, which was already effectively in the hands of another group of peasants.[52]

The rebels now controlled a vast territory, stretching from Rothenburg ob der Tauber, through the Heilbronn region, and right up to Würzburg. On 7 May, Wilhelm of Honstein, bishop of Strasbourg and regent of the archbishop of Mainz, Cardinal Albrecht, capitulated to the peasants and accepted the Twelve Articles at Miltenberg—that huge archbishopric had fallen to the peasants. On 10 May, the peasants of the bishop of Ellwangen rose up, taking the town and two castles. Alongside Götz von Berlichingen, who led one band, the Franconians had the nobleman Florian Geyer leading another contingent, and he had cavalry. In a sign of just how far power had shifted, the marshal of Albrecht of Prussia (who was grand master of the Teutonic Knights, and since February had been a Lutheran and a secular ruler) drafted a letter to Geyer asking him to secure Albrecht's election as master at Horneck as well. After all, both men, Geyer and the marshal, were now on the gospel side, and they were related through marriage too.[53]

About two hundred castles had been destroyed, and monastic foundations plundered and burnt, permanently reshaping the landscape.

Everywhere people were dreaming about how the secular order could be reshaped in ways that could not have been conceived before: a land without monastic rulers, without prince bishops. It seemed that nothing could stop the rebels as they entered what Rohrbach had called the Promised Land.

Meanwhile, on the same day as the Weinsberg massacre, and in response to the rebels' call to join them, the peasants in the region of Bottwar in Württemberg marched to the Wunnenstein, a hill that rises out of the plain to nearly four hundred metres, to symbolically take charge of their landscape. There they elected Matern Feuerbacher, an innkeeper of Bottwar, and they would not be fobbed off with promises that the territory's Landschaft or parliament would meet and discuss their issues. The officials could come at once to them on the hill if they liked, the rebels said. Between 20 and 30 April, the rebels marched through the region, winning over most of it in ten days, sweeping up groups under the leadership of Hans Wunderer and of Jäcklein Rohrbach, who had taken the monastery of Maulbronn. Taking Herrenberg, they marched on Stuttgart, the local capital, on 25 April, and seemed poised to take much of the region. They created a system of government for the Landschaft, with Feuerbacher acting as if he were a territorial ruler, and they even organised a chancellery that employed many notaries and had its own seal. Their success was astonishing, and it was rumoured that the Allgäu peasants, including those who had made peace with Truchsess Georg at Weingarten, were rising again too.[54] Perhaps the flames of revolt might circle back south, reigniting where the Swabian League had seemed to put them out. For a period of over three weeks, the Württemberg rebels ran their own 'state within a state', as the historian Claudia Ulbrich describes it. They had become lords themselves.

CHAPTER 8

MOVEMENT

It is hard to imagine what the remarkable peasant victories felt like to those who experienced them, but it must surely have been exhilarating to be part of a band and to capture so much territory in such a short space of time. The thrill of it must itself have helped drive them on. Peasants who joined a small band or a larger Haufen, a 'heap' or band of peasants, did things they had never done before, met people and saw places they would not otherwise have encountered, and underwent life-changing experiences. They felt what it was to be 'free'. Above all, they went marching, often hundreds of kilometres. Living the dream of brotherhood meant moving.

Peasants did not themselves write about what happened that spring. Even if they could write, they would scarcely have had the time. But this does not mean their experience of revolt is inaccessible to us. We can reconstruct what they did, where they went, and how they spent their days; we have business letters some bands wrote to each other, and we can guess at what they believed from their actions. Indeed, to do so is crucial because revolts are dynamic. Beliefs shift with events and are changed by deeds; those who committed the Weinsberg atrocity, for instance, were hardened by it. Beliefs are formed by what people hear as much as by what they read, especially in an era when print was beginning and when not all were literate. Under the impact of an event so overwhelming, beliefs developed at speed. Key to this process, and to how peasants experienced the revolt itself, was marching together.

When Hans Müller of Bulgenbach led the peasants of the Black Forest in late 1524, he began by marching a troop of men through the region. A herald walked in front and read aloud the printed 'Letter of Articles' of the Christian Union. Müller followed, dressed in a red coat with a matching red hat, and a decorated carriage rolled behind him. Like the itinerant preachers who sold printed indulgences and proclaimed how many years' remission from Purgatory could be gained from a purchase, they passed from village to village. Red—a colour worn by cardinals—would have stood out in a society where most peasants wore grey, but Müller was offering freedom from lordship, a new kind of salvation. And the marches worked: though his December march eventually petered out in the cold, by traversing the villages of the Black Forest, Müller built a band of several thousand men.[1]

Marching was, in a sense, the war. Peasants recruited by marching, adding new members like a rolling snowball as they went from place to place, for only by constant movement could they continue to supply their armies from castles and monasteries that had not yet been looted. If they stayed put, they risked running out of food, having to pay for provisions from cities, or having to steal or loot from local populations, as the lords' armies did. They did not want to alienate the people whose support they needed, and theft was contrary to the ethic of brother-hood. Monastic and church property, by contrast, had been bought with the proceeds of the peasants' tithes, and castles had been built with their and their ancestors' labour.

For the lords and those hostile to the peasants, all this movement was deeply worrying. Everyone, peasant and lord, referred to the revolt with the word 'Aufruhr', 'stirring up' or 'turbulence'. To onlookers, everything seemed to be 'stirred up'—in a terrifying circular movement, not a purposive linear one—as what had been hidden in the depths came to the surface.

It all began with talking, in secret and in public places such as taverns, bathhouses, or at the village oven, as peasants would decide to form a Haufen. In Rappertsweiler the rebels met on a hill that was a recognizable landmark. As the bands became bigger, the scribe would write to the Gemeinde of the next village or town, asking it to 'join' them as brothers. But if they would not come to the peasants, then 'we will come to you'—and 'if however you do not want to join this brotherhood, he [whoever does not join] is against us and [is] our enemy'. The letter would demand an immediate response, or sometimes the recipients might be given a day's grace. In the interval, panicked town councils or Gemeinde groups might write to neighbouring towns and villages, asking for advice on what to answer. Swearing brotherhood meant breaking their oaths to their rulers, but refusing to do so meant they would not be in fellowship with their neighbours and might well be attacked.[2]

Once the new recruits 'came' to the Haufen, they would be asked to swear brotherhood and to accept the Twelve Articles. Generally, as the war gathered speed, the whole Gemeinde would collectively decide whether to join, though there are examples of villages where not everyone joined (or was willing to admit later to having done so). For the most part, the Gemeinde held up as a decision-making body despite the pressure put on it. The numbers involved could themselves intimidate a small community: at Bermatingen near Lake Constance, perhaps ten thousand peasant soldiers gathered, twice the number of the inhabitants of the region, a larger crowd than locals had probably ever seen.[3]

This process blended cooperation and coercion. Sometimes the peasants would require the village to contribute a number of men to the band. Those who left with the peasants would then share responsibility for the band's deeds, and they guaranteed the ongoing loyalty of those at home. Those who did not join were shamed. In some areas, the peasants stuck posts outside their houses so everyone knew who they were. This had a powerful symbolic meaning because doors and thresholds represented the integrity of the house. Anyone who crossed the threshold uninvited attacked the honour of the man of the house; furthermore, protective amulets might be buried under thresholds, which were areas of magical power. Coercion, however, could also be carefully stage-managed. In the village of Alleshausen, the peasants mobbed the house of the local official and forced him to go with them to the Baltringen army. Under pressure, he contacted his lord, the abbot of Marchtal, for permission to go—which, astonishingly, was granted! This ensured, of course, that he could not be punished later, and it also meant that the abbot did not have to dispense with his services.[4]

The same patterns were followed in larger villages or towns. At Tennstedt, the Gemeinde first received a written letter from the peasants, probably delivered by a member of the band. The Gemeinde dithered and appealed frantically to neighbouring towns and officials for advice. Towards evening next day, the whole peasant band arrived outside the town walls, asking to be admitted: 'As the Holy Gospel and Word of God has now come again to the daylight, praise God, we want to know from you, what you are inclined to do for the Word of God for your part'. It was growing late, and the men were tired, so the army tried to make short work of it, explaining, 'Yes, and we also have Twelve Articles, which you have to accept'. The army then asked the citizens to swear to the articles—but without reading them out loud in full, to save time. When the men entered the town, they went to the town square and there insisted on a formal swearing in the ring. The peasant army almost certainly outnumbered the Tennstedters. At

Erfurt, which admitted the peasants on 28 April, eleven thousand entered a town of barely sixteen thousand inhabitants for ten days, creating massive problems of food supply; in Würzburg, a population of a little over four thousand had a peasant contingent in town for weeks, and was then surrounded by armies besieging the bishop's castle.[5]

The authorities found the mobilisation terrifying. The abbot of Weissenau recalled how the peasants always came at night, waking him from sleep, which meant he could not guess how many they were or recognise their faces. Darkness allowed the peasants to assemble without being observed, and they knew their areas well enough not to need light to travel. The pace at which bands formed also frightened the authorities. As Hug, the author of the Villingen chronicle put it, they 'run together like sows'. One army might be defeated, but another soon sprang up in its place. In Swabia, one chronicler listed no fewer than fifteen locations (including all of Württemberg) in which bands had been formed over the space of a month and where, as the usual expression put it, the peasants were 'up'. Bands might be in one place overnight, and the next day somewhere else altogether. Many lords tried desperately to work out where the peasants were, riding around to spy on them and reporting back across their networks of officials. But they could also be caught unawares, like the guards at the castle of Weinsberg, foolishly down in town when the peasants struck.[6]

The list of the leaders who signed the Christian Union in the early weeks of March gives us a glimpse of just how widespread their support was. There were nearly thirty groups, and they came from all over southwestern Germany but did not cluster in any particular part. And yet, composed of three main armies, the Baltringen, Allgäu, and Lake Constance bands, the union probably appeared more coherent on paper than it really was as groups left and joined other bands. The same was true of the Helle Haufen, the 'Schwarze Haufen', the Tauber Valley bands, and the Werra bands, who sometimes intersected. The names the bands gave themselves often referred to where they happened to be, and they reveal how local many were, splinter groups from main armies. At the castle of Schillingsfürst, for example, the bands who gathered at the village below included a mix of soldiers from at least three different groups.[7]

For the peasants themselves, however, the mobilisation could be liberating. It meant leaving homes and farms, families and households, and travelling farther than many of them had ever been. How far they ended up going might vary, even for people from the very same village. Many travelled little more than about twenty to thirty kilometres, an easy day's walk and about the distance between two towns. Seen through their itineraries, life in the bands seems much more chaotic. Andres Tauber and two others, for example, went from the village at Braunshain to Kayna, where a fellow rebel told them to sample the pastor's beer, which they did. Next they went to Hohenkirchen, where they drank two barrels of that pastor's beer, and on to Lunzig, where they took a calf and a sheep from another pastor, which they ate back in Hohenkirchen before returning home. The entire round trip was less than thirty kilometres.[8]

Peasants sometimes travelled as far as the rumours and gossip that summoned them, and apparently spontaneously, off they set. In Mühlberg, not far from Erfurt, some villagers were meeting in the pub to decide what to do and were joined by people from Kirchheim and Rettbach who had heard rumours. The local official had permitted a 'hare hunt' on land that had previously been the lord's preserve, and so the locals concluded this was the first step in freeing all land for hunting. The gossip that freedom was on the way spread within an area of about twenty kilometres. Near the Kyffhäuser Mountains, it was rumoured that the Count of Heldrungen was about to steal the peasants' animals—so they rang the bells to summon neighbouring villages to help, while one Andris Schorlitz rode to Frankenhausen to ask for the town's aid. He was told the town would only help if the peasants joined the 'brotherhood'. From there, Schorlitz rode with the message to

Kannawurf, where he stopped to drink a good Einbeck beer, riding on to Bilzinsleben and finally Oldisleben. As witnesses reported, Schorlitz was wearing only jerkin and hose, without a peasant smock; he probably looked more like a fighter than a peasant. The route he followed was a rough circle barely twenty kilometres long.[9]

Other bands, however, such as what became the Neckartal band under Jäcklein Rohrbach, went long distances. On 2 April peasants from Mergentheim, who were ruled by the Teutonic Order, and those from farther afield met at the village of Flein near Heilbronn. From there, Rohrbach's group planned to attack the Chorherrenstift at Wimpfen but were stopped at Grossgartach by hostile peasants. So they wheeled back in the opposite direction towards Öhringen, going on to commit the Weinsberg massacre. Once they made an accommodation with Heilbronn, they were able to return and pressure Wimpfen to become part of their wider territory. Like Heilbronn, Wimpfen had to permit its citizens to join the peasants if they wished, and many did. The band then moved to Amorbach, where it issued articles on 4 May and finally joined with the Odenwald band, after which it would eventually be defeated. In this case, the band apparently followed a jerkily circular movement in its early days of formation, avoiding the towns and relying on villages. The big tactical problem they faced—how to bring peasants and disaffected townsfolk together—was solved in both Wimpfen and Heilbronn by establishing unions with the towns. Marching together also served to form these disparate groups of townsfolk and peasants, free men and serfs, into a more united fighting force.[10]

In early May 1525, Hans Müller of Bulgenbach led his men of the Black Forest on another march that eventually covered nearly two hundred kilometres, though the geographical distance from starting to end point was only around sixty kilometres. We know about it because the town chronicler of Villingen noted it, as the band came ever nearer his town before moving away, to his great relief. They destroyed several monasteries and many castles while gaining support in the villages and small towns on the route before finally massing with other armies outside Freiburg. The march lasted a little over two weeks, and towards the end the band seems to have moved in a series of circles. By 16 May they had managed to get the peasants of the entire area to rise, and the despairing chronicler noted that 'the whole of the Breisgau everywhere, all villages, small towns, hamlets large and small,...all were on the peasants' side, except for [the towns of] Breisach, Freiburg and Waldkirch, and the peasants all went towards Freiburg to take it by force'. Remarkably, Müller, who used small detachments from the main army to take castles and monasteries and seize supplies, had succeeded in getting the whole region not only to support the army while it marched through but to maintain its support once they had left; indeed, sometimes it seemed as if the abbots were falling over themselves to provide the army with animals to roast and wine to drink—as if they were honouring noble guests.[11]

Marching was itself a rebellious act because many feudal contracts stated that peasants could not move without permission. Peasant livelihoods depended on moving, travelling to the nearest town and its market, but remaining absent for long periods or simply failing to perform labour dues, as for instance the peasants in the Black Forest did over many months, struck at the heart of feudalism, which aimed to tie the workforce to the land. Peasants were not permitted to become town dwellers, so taking over premises in towns to hold meetings and take counsel was also revolutionary. Even though they were free peasants, the Alleshausen peasants were expressly forbidden to leave their villages overnight. They broke this rule by joining an army or even soliciting peasants in other villages at night. Together, the peasant fighters slept out of doors under the open sky; in Alsace, they slept in the vineyards.[12]

Walking was a great equaliser. The troops had horses that pulled their waggons, and some of their number must have had horses that enabled them to leave the main party and spy out monasteries and castles on the route, but for the most part they went on foot, while the laden waggons, probably pulled by draught animals, would have had to go slowly since food supplies had to keep pace with the men. 'Get off your horse' was the first command to nobles who joined the brethren, their surrender accompanied by the final indignity of having to walk at the same slow pace as peasants. Some simply could not manage. Philip von Stein, who had promised to ride with the peasants of Rottershausen to Münnerstadt, begged to be allowed to ride home 'as an old man'.[13]

Horses made nobles imposing because they seemed higher, taller, and more distant. Getting off their horses reduced nobles to peasants, literally putting them on the same footing. Down on the ground, their jangling spurs useless, they had to look their fellows in the eye. Müntzer was infamous amongst nobles for his demand that a prince should have no more than eight horses, and a count, four. He knew that their power depended on their retinues of armed horsemen. Horses also gave lords a different sense of space and of domination because of their ability to easily travel farther. Marching with the brothers meant moving through the landscape at an unaccustomed pace. Jos Wilpurger, a priest from Bregenz who supported the peasants, went so far as to march out in front holding a musket while pipers and drummers followed behind. He had an impish sense of humour, and instead of referring to his ruler as 'your princely illustriousness', he called him 'your princely leichtigkeit', 'your lightness'—that is, 'your nothingness'.[14]

They were leaving their fields in spring and early summer, a busy time in the agricultural year, and setting out into a landscape much of which was not farmed. The peasants therefore worked out a system of rotation, by which a village was required to supply a certain number of men to travel with the peasants to the next village, where they would be replaced. The Tennstedters, who had been so reluctant to swear, had to supply every third man to the army, a total of a hundred over the war. In the village of Alleshausen, a system of lots meant that some men went all the way with the peasants, right down to Lake Constance, over sixty kilometres away; in Alsace, where Erasmus Gerber managed to unite all the peasant armies, a rotation of groups of eight was instituted. Indeed, the composition of the armies was constantly changing as groups of peasants came and went, so that many more individuals were involved than even the estimates we have for the size of armies might suggest.[15]

Marching was like pilgrimage, and in some cases—the monasteries and abbeys of Vessra, Bildhausen, Amorbach—the destination was itself a monastery or even a shrine. The monastery at Bildhausen, after which the Bildhausen band was named, was dedicated to Mary, but the peasants turned it into a temporary headquarters and 'purified' the monastery buildings of Mary and the saints. The official Tham von Herda complained that the peasants wouldn't listen. 'It's just like in the past when they ran to pilgrimages', he wrote, and even when their wives and kin begged them to stay home, nothing helped, and they said 'it must be, it concerns them; and they ran there like crazy folk'. Perhaps he was remembering the pilgrimage mania to nearby Grimmenthal, supported by Tham's own ruler, the Count of Henneberg. Founded little over twenty years before, the pilgrimage was notorious; as Luther put it, people were blinded by the devil, and 'manservants, maids, shepherds, women all left their jobs and ran there as if they were crazy'. And perhaps Tham also recalled hearing about what had happened fifty years before, when peasants joined the Drummer of Niklashausen on his march to Würzburg. For Tham, the peasants were in a state of mass delusion that led them to break their oaths and remain deaf to all appeals, especially his own. Now the peasants were incensed as they attacked pilgrimage centres to which they had once flocked. Soon they were encamped at Grimmenthal itself.[16]

We do not know exactly what routes they took, but it is reasonable to suppose that they largely took back routes, where they would be less easy targets for mounted soldiers. Many were absent from their farms for only three or four days, long enough for a decisive experience but not so long as to sever ties with their local communities. Others, however, could be gone for weeks. The redoubtable Jäcklein Rohrbach left not only his innkeeping business but a farm and vineyard as well; by the time he was executed on 12 May he had been on the march for about six weeks. Normal time evaporated in the band, which may have encouraged listeners to take to heart Thomas Müntzer's appeals that the Last Days were at hand.[17]

Forces of thousands of men were powerfully destructive. If they chose, they could easily destroy monasteries and castles, reshaping the landscape and flattening everything in their path. In the area around Würzburg and Bamberg alone, 292 castles and 52 monasteries were obliterated, a massive total. In the area where the Allgäu army was active, a broadsheet listed 23 monasteries and more castles that had been destroyed. Taking a monastery was comparatively easy, for monasteries outside towns were usually on low ground, unfortified, and lacked soldiers or much in the way of weapons to protect them. Those inside towns were often surrounded by a hostile population. The arrival of a sizeable army in the area was usually enough to cause the monks or nuns to stand aside and allow the peasant soldiers to enter. The peasants did not need force of arms because, aside from the military orders, clergy were not supposed to be armed, and so sheer numbers did the trick.[18]

It must have been sensational to enter these enclosed communities, to find their warm heating ovens, feather beds, down pillows, libraries, jewelled chalices, and massive stores of food, and to see and touch them for the first time. Some monasteries and convents hastily tried to put themselves under the protection of a town or of a nearby knight, but this brought its own dangers. Any monastery that succeeded in gaining citizenship in a town risked losing its tax exemptions and having its goods inventoried and even confiscated. It was a price that might have seemed worth paying. Otherwise they might be occupied, as were the monasteries of Maulbronn, Amorbach, Salem, Schöntal, and many

Portrayal of the destruction of a castle by the Swabian League in 1523, before the Peasants' War. Postcard from author's collection, Bamberger Burgenbuch, Bamberg Staatsbibliothek.

others, which made excellent headquarters for the army and allowed the peasants to regroup, strategise, and rest. At Heilbronn the desperate Carmelite monastery of Mary in the Nettlebush even put itself under the protection of the peasant army, but it was destroyed anyway.[19]

Castles, on the other hand, were usually situated high up on hills or mountains, where they dominated the territory and enemies could be seen from miles away. It was not easy for a peasant force to attack and take a castle, though not all were well defended, and some were poorly maintained. Their capture, though not a serious reversal for the lords, was always a great boost to the peasants' morale. At Schillingsfürst, the castle of the counts of Hohenlohe, some locals from the village below had helped guard the castle, but after the Hohenlohe counts Albrecht and Georg had sworn brotherhood with the peasants, they ceased paying the guards, and left only the gatekeeper, the turner, and two servants up there. That May, two peasant soldiers drinking in the village tavern saw their chance. They said they had letters to deliver to the castle and sent word to its defenders, who sent a boy down to guide them up. But when the gatekeeper opened the castle gate, one soldier stuck his spear forward so the gatekeeper could not shut it, and the two soldiers rushed in. Back in town, the pair were soon boasting that they had seized the castle, and before long, crowds of peasants had arrived to plunder it. Only Hohenlohe peasants were allowed entry. The Rothenburgers, those from the Palatinate, and all peasants from outside the region were not permitted; this was for locals only. Inside, they held a fair that was a cross between a church ale and a market. The peasants ate and drank their lords' supplies and sold the grain, some saying the proceeds were for the army, others that they were for 'the young lord'. On 21 May, when they had cleaned the castle out completely, they set fire to it and burnt it to the ground. The seizure, plundering, and arson were all apparently orchestrated from the pub down in the village of Frankenhain, where many peasants from the region were massed.[20]

In some instances, as in the bishopric of Bamberg, the knights simply gave up and did not even defend their castles.[21] Most castles had high dwellings above the walls built of wattle and daub, which could be set alight, and along with gunpowder, combustible materials were thrown or shot into the castle. Later one rebel confessed how he had ignited a castle by simply taking fire from the kitchen, but usually it was a more organised affair. The fact that the Swabian League had used these techniques so recently during the Knights' War and in its campaign against Thomas von Absberg meant that peasants who had served as mercenaries knew how to do it. The heat generated was so great that even stone was damaged; indeed, the burn marks on the stones of the ruined castle of Ebeleben are still visible today, centuries after the peasants torched it.

Movement, however, was also the peasants' Achilles heel, particularly when they succeeded in creating a super-sized Haufen. The Bildhausen band wrote to the Breitungen band that a huge assembly of the 'Rotembergischen' peasants had assembled at Gerolzhofen, 'and we and all the encampments that belong to us will join together to complete our godly undertaking'. At Würzburg, the men of the Odenwald army of Höchberg joined with the army of the Tauber Valley and the Heidenfeld contingent of the Bildhausen band to form a huge army, somewhere between fifteen thousand and thirty-eight thousand strong. It was, however, very difficult to provision such large numbers. When there were no longer enough monasteries and castles left to loot, they had few options, not wanting to despoil villages. The collective decision-making structures of face-to-face brotherhood were strained, too, because the crowd could often not hear commanders once it grew much beyond five thousand. Armies of this size were visible and less mobile, and hence they lacked the element of surprise. It was hard also to maintain discipline.[22]

Even so, peasants could rise, or be 'up' as the expression had it, in no time, and they were able to raise armies repeatedly. In the Black Forest, Hans Müller was able to gather a force of forty-five hundred men in October 1524, and when they dispersed after being promised that their grievances would be investigated, he was still able to organise another march in November. In May he put together an army of six thousand. In Franconia, after the debacle outside Würzburg, as the besieging armies melted away, a new army of five thousand formed near Königshofen and joined the Odenwälders; even after they were defeated, another army five thousand strong fought the lords' men near the villages of Ingolstadt and Giebelstadt. Such examples suggest that the armies had a reservoir of support to draw on, so that the villagers who had not joined the army the first time were prepared to do so later. The commitments were long-lasting. The men of Allstedt, where Müntzer had been preacher before he went to Mühlhausen, came for the battle of Frankenhausen, their loyalty to the league they had sworn undimmed. Hans Zeiß, the Allstedt official, was left alone to muse on the fact that 'just about everyone' had left and 'only the oldest ones stayed at home', while in Amt Geusa, around Merseburg, not more than thirty men were left in the three villages, 'which should have four hundred'. Fifteen hundred men in the area of Sangerhausen rose up and marched the thirty kilometres or so to Frankenhausen.[23]

Once their bloated size made them more static, the inability to supply or keep armies in the field indefinitely forced them to act. Yet though the armies of Lake Constance and Allgäu proved large enough to make the truchsess negotiate, and though Casimir of Brandenburg-Ansbach had little success against his rebels, peasant armies were generally not a match for the forces of the lords when they met them in the field, even though their knowledge of their own terrain meant that they usually picked their battle sites well. Their hatred of military horses and their lack of mounted soldiers (aside from the cavalry of Florian Geyer's group in Franconia) meant they found it impossible to cope with attacks from the lords' cavalry. Sometimes the peasant armies simply melted away, to the frustration of their opponents like Truchsess Georg, who was then forced to search out where they had gone and pursue them. But if they remained encamped in large numbers, the lords' spies soon realised where they were, and they became sitting targets.

Men anticipating battle to commence could not be kept at fever pitch for long, though the strength of religious passion must have been exhilarating to witness. Charismatic, skilled preachers moved through the crowd, or were raised aloft, expounding the Word at length, vivid mass-audience preaching that many had probably not experienced in their villages. Sometimes this could lead to differences of opinion: in the Bildhausen army a furrier who was a supporter of Müntzer appeared and started preaching that 'one should obliterate the authorities with the sword and shed their blood', but the army's own preacher did not agree with this bloodthirsty line. Soon each side had its supporters, and the army had to ask a nearby town to send two preachers to adjudicate. It was hard to maintain unity and an elevated mood of battle readiness in an army encompassing so many different groups of people, and such spats grew more likely the longer fighting was delayed. As battle neared, preachers tried to raise spirits by reminding men what 'brotherhood' meant and what sacrifice it might entail. And probably, too, the men sang, their voices joining in massed male choirs.[24]

What did it sound like to be part of a peasant army on the march? Military instruments—pipes and drums—went together, and many of the Landsknechte who joined the peasant armies would have been familiar with the sound because the instruments could be played while marching. Originally one person would play the pipe with their free hand while drumming with a single stick, but by the sixteenth century, the drummer used two sticks, allowing rhythms to become more complex and compelling. Ominously, the drum was beaten at Weinsberg when the nobles and their pages were forced to run the gauntlet.

The rebels probably used drums with a wooden body and two animal-hide heads, held in tension with a hoop and a system of ropes that could be tightened by pulling leather tags. Worn in a sling over the shoulder, the drum could be quite large, giving out a loud, low-pitched sound.[25]

Trouble often started with drumming. The steward (*Kellner*) of the bishop of Würzburg wrote in early April to the bishop that the peasants were wandering about with drums all night, going from village to village and waking people. They 'all wanted to be black peasants'; that is, they all wanted to join the 'black peasant band'. They were off to Bildhausen, the monastery where the rebels were assembling, 'and the lowest should become the highest'. At Mellrichstadt, a group went out of town to a tavern and somehow ended up with a drummer; they called 'that they are coming, we want to be up'. The threatening words combined with the drums was enough to rattle the local official, who refused to enter town unless the men were punished. A few days later a group of 'wanton rascals' appeared in the monastery of Vessra with

Albrecht Dürer, *Piper and Drummer* (detail), 1503–1504. This intriguing image is from a triptych depicting the sufferings of Job. The elegant drummer, playing a tiny drum, is clad in a fine pink cloak and sports a fashionable hat of costly black. The roughly dressed piper has his back to us, but the drummer turns to the viewer, his luxuriant, long, curly hair and beard suggestive of Dürer's own. It seems that the musicians are trying to lift Job's spirits, and Dürer, who loved to speculate on the role of the artist, may be suggesting that art's task is to drive melancholy away. Richard Wallraz Museum. Peter Horree/Alamy Stock Photo.

a drum, insulting the priests and demanding food. Another hundred men attacked a different monastery to the sound of a drumbeat, stealing a calf, smashing some windows, and taking wine.[26]

Everyone knew the drum heralded danger. Pastor Johannes Lachmann blamed the master of the local Teutonic Knights for the plunder of his own monastery because he had failed to stop his peasants summoning one another with drums. The hapless gatekeeper of the town of Vacha in Hesse had not been on the job long when he heard a drum in the nearby suburb and shut the gate. The locals persuaded him to let some people in, others rushed through, and then it was too late—he had to explain his failure to the furious Philip of Hesse, who was outraged that his subjects had joined the rebels. Unlike the town's official storm bell, which was rung to call citizens together and was controlled by the authorities, drumming enabled peasants to summon recruits themselves.[27]

Hans Welner of Neckargartach was asked to beat his drum by strangers who promised to pay him and to take responsibility for whatever happened. At first he was reluctant, but then, under pressure from the crowd on the square, he agreed, calling on everyone in town to join them. As he explained, he was paid to beat his drum 'not to sound the alarm, call to robbery, or to take people's goods away, but so that I should help support righteousness'. Welner took responsibility for his actions and did not try to blame those who paid him, but he denied that he had been the one to beat the drum at Weinsberg while the nobles were made to run the gauntlet. It was just as well he convinced the authorities of his innocence, for his was the town where Rohrbach was roasted to death, and where the piper who took the count's hat met the same fate.[28]

Marching was punctuated by eating and drinking. Instead of eating gruel and drinking watery wine or weak beer, the rebels plundered monasteries, dined on stolen fish and livestock, and emptied the monks' fine cellars. And instead of conserving food, saving seed, and husbanding resources for the next year, the rebels threw caution to the winds and feasted like lords. Shocked commentators noted that the peasants killed and roasted sheep 'with wool', without even shearing them. They slaughtered oxen, cows, and even calves, when normally animals would only be slaughtered just before winter, when they would cost money to feed. They took the lords' expensive cattle, cows that had likely just calved or were still pregnant, not so often pigs or poultry, the livestock of the small-scale farmer that could be fed on domestic scraps.[29]

Lent was banished as the cellars of the monasteries and convents were drunk dry. The peasants simply guzzled the fine wine, letting it spill onto the ground, to the stupefaction of the lords and monks. When the peasants from the Hegau were about to arrive at Brettheim, one Michel Hofman of Leutzendorf went through the village telling the innkeeper to prepare, the baker to bake bread, and the butcher to slaughter the calves. They should call the whole community together because 'they wanted to meet and have a good time at Brother Hartman's'. He meant the nearby Premonstratensian convent Bruderhartmann, whose name sounded like a pub sign. Founded by a thirteenth-century nobleman, Hartman von Lobdeburg, it was closely linked to the bishop of Würzburg and housed patrician women from the nearby towns of Schwäbsich Hall, Rothenburg, and Dinkelsbühl, along with women from the lower Franconian nobility. There was apparently little love lost between the nuns and the peasants they ruled, for they had disputed rights over forests, meadow grazing, and dues. The bells were rung, and the Gemeinde assembled and entered the monastery to have 'a good social' with the Hegau band. The political decision to join the peasants was effectively an invitation to a party. It was not such a joyful occasion for the nuns, however, who fled to nearby Rothenburg. For them, it was the beginning of the end: when the last nun died in 1539, the convent was secularised by the town.[30]

Cooking for such large numbers of men was a challenge. The animals had to be butchered and roasted in the open, whereas normally they would have been slaughtered by a butcher. The quantities were vast. Hans Müller's men bullied local abbots and officials into giving them cows and oxen to consume, and the abbot of St Georg gave them a whole waggonload of wine and access to a pond from which they ate three hundred carp; meanwhile, they drove another eight of his oxen with them as they marched to the next town. The man who acted as butcher for one expedition in Thuringia uttered the words 'Das walt gott und kein heilige' over his work: 'in God's name, and not that of any saint'. Preparing and cooking the meat for thousands of hungry men who had walked many miles was a major, time-consuming task, essential to maintaining morale. The animals had to be spit-roasted, or else stewed in giant vats; the Eichsfelders improvised with beer vats to cook the fish. In the Saxon mining mountains (Erzgebirge), the captain of one castle simply fled into town while the townsfolk took it over, 'drinking and shouting...striking down oxen, boiling and roasting them'.[31]

To cook, they needed fuel, and after stealing the abbot of Neuenburg's animals, the peasants near Dorlisheim in Alsace resorted to demolishing stables and dovecotes for the wood. Getting carbohydrates was difficult. Gruel, the standard peasant fare, required big containers and was not easily portable. In Würzburg, they paid the city bakers to produce huge numbers of loaves of bread, which they could carry. These vast communal meals out of doors, when one could eat one's fill, must also have added to what it meant to be a brother, eating what had been captured and cooked by the whole band.[32]

Here, too, the problems started when marching stopped. Food provision was trickier because the peasants lacked supply systems. If the army was encamped outside a town, it was possible to pay for provisions or get them to be given by the town as part of 'brotherhood'. But in towns like Heilbronn, attitudes towards the peasants remained ambiguous, and the army risked being shot at from the city walls as they marched past. Like many other towns, Heilbronn and Rothenburg refused to let the army in, allowing only a small number to enter while the rest camped just outside. Würzburg, in contrast, admitted the peasants, where according to unsympathetic chroniclers like

Martin Cronthal, they sat around all day and got drunk. Some tried to buy them off with food and drink: the *Markgraf* (margrave) of Baden supplied eight *Fuder* of wine and one hundred *Viertel* of corn to the Schwarzach band to prevent them entering his territory.[33]

Taking over a town was a far cry from capturing a castle or monastery, but it also developed its own routines. At Würzburg the peasants massed outside the council chambers, the 'green tree', so called because the tree that grew there symbolized community decision-making, as opposed to rule by the bishop. This was also the place where the peasants could put the most pressure on the council. They sent a series of delegations to negotiate with the councillors, who each time returned to the rebels camped on the square to report on progress. This maximised pressure on the councillors, who were effectively imprisoned inside the town hall, and it also allowed the rebels to present the negotiations to those outside in their terms. At Rothenburg on 24 March the council miscalculated, summoning all the 'watches' of the town to the hall because the peasant armies were outside town and a delegation from the council had been sent to meet with them. This allowed the local noble Stefan von Menzingen to seize his chance. He took command of the watchmen massing outside the council chamber and shouted to the councillors to get out. His supporters then gathered 'in a ring' in the town hall to take counsel, the time-honoured way of representing the Gemeinde. As the watches of the other quarters arrived outside, they were persuaded to join their fellows in the town hall until their sheer numbers made it plain that the council had lost legitimacy. A crowd of men in arms kept matters at fever pitch; they stood on the square or in the town hall to represent the voice of the 'community'.[34]

In this way the peasant armies could precipitate a town revolt, persuading the residents to swear brotherhood with them. Often the councils were not fully democratic, and if there was no guild representation, their lack of legitimacy was vividly exposed. Consequently, the peasant bands created parallel decision-making structures, a Gemeinde that oversaw what the council was doing and negotiated with the peasants, sometimes even meeting in council premises or right next door. These new structures literally circumscribed the actions of the elites and patrician oligarchies that had previously had their own way. And when peasant leaders met in the elegant council rooms decorated with images of justice and shields of the guilds and patrician families, or deliberated in guild parlours or in monastic halls, their surroundings must have conferred a sense of importance. They were men with serious matters to decide.

Yet there were limits to a peasant-town partnership. Even if many townsfolk sympathised with the peasants, for others the rebels' presence was profoundly disconcerting. When large numbers of politically active immigrant peasants suddenly arrived in a town, they rebalanced the Gemeinde, outnumbering the townsfolk. In Würzburg, Martin Cronthal certainly felt threatened by them. Small wonder most towns tried to keep them out. And there were underlying structural tensions between townsfolk and countryfolk. Townspeople's interests lay in low food prices, and they did not want competition from rural crafts; they policed entry to towns, gatekeepers only admitting those with a right to be there. Towns often ruled extensive rural territories, and towns as well as individual citizens were often themselves landlords who owned peasants.

Citizens and peasants were therefore not natural allies. Even though there was sympathy in Rothenburg for the peasant cause, on 11 May a faction of about two hundred peasants from the Helle Haufen tried to attack the town. They demanded corn and only departed when the commander of the whole army, Hans Metzler of Brethain, climbed up onto the town wall and called them off. In Würzburg the peasant army had promised to pay for what they ate, but once they had consumed all the supplies of the town's monasteries and convents, they seized the contents of the civic granaries by force, 'all against the promise and undertaking they had made'. Peasants could also evince a deep-seated hostility to towns. Margareta Renner (the 'Black Hofmännin') said she wanted the walls of Heilbronn to be pulled down so that it would no longer be a town: 'No stone must remain on another here at Heilbronn, it must become a village like Böckingen'. Such comments, later echoed by Michael Gaismair and the Austrian rebels, suggest how profoundly peasants envied richer towns.[35]

The great difference between the German Peasants' War and other peasant revolts before and after was the peasants' ability in this case to get their hands on serious financial resources. Looting monasteries gave them economic muscle. In this respect religion was crucial, because it was only once the Reformation had weakened the institutions' prestige and undermined their point that it was possible to contemplate invading them and treating their holy monstrances, chalices, and plate as so much metal to be melted down for their value. Many monks and nuns had simply left monasteries, especially the male institutions, because they no longer believed in a life of prayer and chastity following a monastic rule, and Luther's teachings had encouraged many layfolk to vent contempt for monks and nuns. Nobles were not always inclined to protect monasteries and convents, even when their own relatives were amongst the members, but rather hoped to profit from their secularisation—and even if the nobles had wanted to, they could scarcely raise troops to defend themselves.

The plunder the peasants secured from the monasteries was legendary. Even so, peasant armies, like the mercenary armies, had to keep their soldiers' greed in check to finance the war. They soon worked out a system of inventorying property, promising their men that they would divide the spoils while ensuring that most of the money was kept for the war effort. Wealth on this scale could be used to buy arms, to pay for provisions like baked bread, and to underwrite the system of messengers. It made peasant leaders powers in the land. Ironically, it was monastic wealth that in large part made the Peasants' War possible, because it at last gave the rebels resources that rivalled those of the lords.

By living off monasteries and paying for food from towns, the peasant armies were able to avoid exploiting the local population. In contrast, the forces of the lords lived off the local peasantry, stole their animals, and alienated them, as when Truchsess Georg forced communities that sympathised with peasants to pay large fines to stop the troops burning their villages. Lack of ready monasteries was partly what drove the peasants to attack lords' castles. There they found beds, pillows, and cloth to be taken, ovens to be smashed, and crockery to be plundered—as well as arms. However, the poorly fortified castles that were easily taken and militarily insignificant were mostly not especially rich. They had supplies that could be used and animals that could be seized, but they lacked the kind of wealth that monasteries possessed as centres of culture, valuable goods, and the arts.[36]

After the war was over, some of the religious houses tried to recuperate their chalices, stolen objects, and animals, mounting legal cases to do so, but they could not recoup much of what was gone, nor did they always discover who had taken it. The looting destroyed many monasteries' and convents' viability, for it removed their 'buffer' for hard times, and they faced exceptionally difficult circumstances after the war, when the climate remained hostile to monasticism. So badly damaged by the war was the monastery of Maulbronn, for example, that it secured permission for its own members to act as priests in all eleven parishes where they had rights of patronage, allowing the monastery to at least claim all the benefice revenues for itself without employing any priests.[37]

In this way the Peasants' War changed the landscape forever. Over its course, more than 500 monasteries and convents were attacked and shrines desecrated, and likely many more suffered minor damage or were compelled to hand over supplies of some kind. When monastic institutions appealed for help to towns or secular rulers, the authorities began by listing their possessions in order to ensure their safe return, but this also meant that the towns and rulers now knew the scale and whereabouts of monastic wealth. Some towns, like Heilbronn, location of the Carmelites, and Zurich, home of the abbot of St Blasius, offered these clerics and their institutions citizenship, but in exchange for this protection they had to pay taxes like other citizens. In the areas that later officially introduced the Reformation, the first step had therefore already been taken during the war, when monastic property was inventoried and taken into 'safekeeping'. And for those who only toyed with the idea of secularising these institutions, the Peasants' War showed just what could be gained for state coffers by seizing their riches. Monasteries, convents, and abbeys—even parish clergy houses, farms, and churches—became objects of attack because they were sites of visible wealth, and communities felt they had a right to them. Better to plunder 'our' church and vicarage, because if we don't, the outsiders will take our goods, some argued. At the village of Weterungen, the locals, returning from Bildhausen, invaded the parsonage and started eating and drinking what they found there—and then, to be on the safe side, they wrote to the bishop to ask him what they should do with the large amounts of wine and corn that remained, since the pastor had run away and the men had already started drinking the wine.[38]

After the war, the Reformation and the resultant secularisation, dissolution, and simple closure of so many monasteries and convents accomplished one of the greatest transfers of land and property ever seen in the German region. This process started in the Peasants' War. But whereas in Protestant England, much of the monastic wealth ended up in the pockets of the gentry and nobility, creating a social group with a vested interest in the success of the Reformation, in German states it mostly passed to secular rulers. There it increased the power of the state and its bureaucracy, contributed to founding schools, universities, and charitable institutions, and in some cases, played its part in financing the military power of princes that enabled them to pursue independent religious policies, a development that would make the Thirty Years' War possible. The peasants began the process of seizing the monasteries' wealth, which financed their armies, but the princes were the ultimate winners of the Peasants' War. Far from supporting the gentry, as monastic wealth did in England, the Peasants' War marked the nadir of the knights, as their castles were smashed and their military prowess was revealed as a sham when many were made to march ignominiously with the peasants.

When the Stühlingen, Fürstenberger, Schellenberger, and Reckenbacher peasants who had sworn together submitted their joint complaints for their legal case to the *Kammergericht* in early April, they were told that a collective complaint was inadmissible. Complaints could only be made against individual lords. So they physically cut the document into pieces.[39]

The events of 1524 and 1525 had transformed the peasants' sense of identity and of place. Back in autumn, they had indeed addressed their complaints to their individual lords, but the marches of the autumn and early spring gave them a new sense of belonging and a wider conception of the region of which they were part. The complaints in the joint document were full and detailed, all in the same hand, many in the same words, and they broadly raised the same issues as the Twelve Articles and referred indirectly to them. The rebels were taking on the lords in a concerted effort, as a group that had sworn together, recognising that they belonged to the same region and that the struggle concerned lordship, not individual lords. The lords naturally wished to prevent this at all costs, because as soon as a united peasantry faced the lords, individual agreements and negotiations would be vitiated. They knew that their position would be profoundly weakened when they could no longer show 'grace' and pick off one group against another.

The peasants might have had to cut their document into pieces for the sake of the legal niceties, but they did not unlearn what their campaign had taught them. Just a few weeks later they submitted another legal document in which they explained why they had joined the peasant armies. They came out with the usual excuses that they had been overpowered, but they also said that they believed they were bound to the wider group by oath and that they were defending the gospel. They were no longer just serfs of a particular lord. Their experience in the 'band' led them to acquire a different sense of space. As peasants walked from place to place, they met with people from farther afield and gained a wider perspective. They saw their own farms within a wider area, a territory, or a Haufen and beyond.[40]

Many areas drew on the idea of the Landschaft, a word that meant landscape but also region. This was the word the peasants of the Christian Union used; they described themselves as an 'honourable region', 'ersamen Lantschaft', which would support the common 'Lantfrid' or land peace. In so doing they deliberately distinguished themselves from the land ruled by a particular spiritual or secular authority, 'geistlicher oder weltlicher Oberkeit', which had different boundaries. It was the Landschaft to which they owed loyalty, and so, they decreed, when anyone left the Landschaft they had to swear not to fight against it and to return to defend it. When Erasmus Gerber in Alsace used the term, it seems to have included the whole of Alsace, while in the Black Forest, Hans Müller of Bulgenbach's men described themselves as 'the band up on the Black Forest', an area that referred to its distinctive landscape. Not surprisingly the lords refused to deal with the Landschaft, insisting that each authority should negotiate with their own peasants separately.[41]

When the peasant leader Florian Greisel tried to get troops at Grönenbach to join him in nearby Wurzach, he had to plead with them to regard his battle as theirs. He reminded them, 'It would be better if we sought the enemy in another land, rather than in our own'. He meant that they should join together against the outsider instead of fighting one another. Indeed, in Württemberg, Matern Feuerbacher supported the Austrians, while Hans Wunderer supported Duke Ulrich, who wanted his dukedom back from the Habsburgs. They did not trust one another and pursued different strategies. But Greisel was also appealing to the Grönenbachers' sense of being part of the same 'land' as him. He did not say, however, what land this might be, or how it could be defined.[42]

During the course of the war, when peasants from different areas made common cause, the boundaries of the 'place' they saw themselves as inhabiting expanded hugely. High up on the Federsee Lake, the peasants of the village of Alleshausen joined with the Lake Constance band, nearly eighty kilometres away and in a very different terrain. Meanwhile, the armies of the entire Alsatian region managed to cohere, despite its patchwork of different lordships and independent towns. In the dying days of the revolt in Alsace, as the peasants tried to persuade Strasbourg and other towns to intervene on their behalf, the leaders of the various Alsatian armies urged them to join together for the sake of 'the common land' against the troops of Duke Anthony of Lorraine, the 'foreign people' invading the 'vaterland'. The 'land' seems to have included all of Alsace or even 'the whole Rhine flow', which one army thought to be at risk. Rumours circulated that Anthony of Lorraine was planning to involve the emperor as well as the king of England, attack Strasbourg, and seize all of Alsace for himself. 'Alsace', even the Rhine itself, was becoming the 'land' to which peasants owed allegiance, and they knew what that 'land' was because they had marched through so much of it.[43]

Marching made peasant theology real. Despite the very wide range of places in which the peasants rose up—from Switzerland through the Black Forest and Alsace, through Swabia, Franconia, and

Thuringia—the central message was consistent. It overrode even differences in theological allegiance such as those between the bloodthirsty passion of Thomas Müntzer and the milder tones of Christoph Schappeler. Everyone insisted on the power of Christian brotherhood, which had become an ideal backed by real experience as the 'brothers' learnt how to trust one another and march together. Everyone insisted, too, on the universal invitation, 'We have formed a Christian union, and we ask you to come to us', as well as on its accompanying threat: 'or else we will come to you'.

Movement—coming to you—was thus at the core of the revolt. 'We are on Christ's side' was the universal cry, and peasant theology was closely related to marching because it divided the world into those who were and those who were not on Christ's side, those who marched and those who did not. Being on Christ's side meant being on the side of the one who had bought our freedom with his blood, and so it expressed a profound critique of lordship and feudalism in practical terms. Being subject to the lords was about staying put, being tied to the land and the lord. Movement meant freedom.

Mary and the saints were excluded. No band invoked the Virgin, put her alone on their banner, or referenced the saints—and this broke with centuries of tradition. It was, after all, the Virgin on whom the pilgrims of Niklashausen had called when they marched to Würzburg. The Peasants' War was a kind of vast antipilgrimage, opposed to shrines, relics, monasteries, and saints, and movement shaped its theology as it reshaped and desacralised the landscape. It smashed monasticism and its outposts. Marching with their brothers, the peasants were free at last as they roamed across the landscape, beyond the narrow confines of lordship.[44]

CHAPTER 9

HIGH SPRING

By late spring, the character of the revolt began to change. The season had begun with the peasants gathering in ever bigger bands. They had swept all before them, plundering monasteries and castles. Then in early April the battles at Leipheim and Wurzach had shown what defeat could mean as hundreds of fleeing peasants drowned in the waters of the Danube and others were slaughtered; in Württemberg a tense peace had been agreed at Weingarten. Yet this had not dampened the fires of revolt—far from it. The revolt was now spreading as peasants were on the move in Alsace, Franconia, Thuringia, and Saxony and joining with supporters in towns. It had all been largely good-humoured, even carnivalesque, as peasants picnicked in monasteries and addressed the lords as brothers. But after the Weinsberg massacre, the mood had darkened. The lords had absorbed the full significance of the taboo the peasants had broken by committing violence against their social superiors.

Positions hardened on both sides. Those who advocated negotiating began to lose the argument, while Truchsess Georg, commander of the Swabian League, carried out reprisals in the areas retaken by his troops, torching rebel villages and looting farms as a way of forcing peasants to pay for what the league's soldiers consumed. Philip of Hesse was putting together a coalition of lords to defeat the peasants, and gradually the lords were beginning to fight back. Peasants also widened the scope of their revolt and began to attack not just the injustices of the rural economy but the structures of class and lordship. 'Free us from the powerful folk of the nobility', one village begged another. Their targets now included the lords as well as the clergy, the rich and the 'grosse Hansen', the 'fat cats'.[1]

The scale of revolt was unprecedented; no one had encountered anything like it. It was chaotic, both for the lords, who had no idea where revolt would break out next and who suddenly had to march in different directions as the enemy moved, and for the peasants, often in the catchment area of more than one army. Its scale was bewildering, now erupting in Franconia, central Germany, the Palatinate, Alsace, Thuringia, and Saxony, and its course was as hard for contemporaries to grasp as it is for the historian to recount. Peasant armies, each with different histories and programmes, were growing larger and had to coordinate; and they moved according to the geography of the valleys and rivers, not political divisions. Many of the lords were humiliatingly forced to join the peasants or found out what it meant to be a lord on sufferance, in hock to the peasants. As the days lengthened and the vivid green of new leaf on the trees faded, the peasants realised that this was a fight to the death, and that the lords were not going to indemnify them for revolt. They had to win.

In middle Germany and Hesse, revolt came slightly later than in the south. Property rights here were more entrenched, serfdom was largely abolished, and services and dues more bearable. Some areas grew less wine and brewed more beer, while Thuringia had a woad-growing industry. Still, as in the south, there was anger about sheep farming and about the lack of access to resources like forests and water. Patterns of rulership were different too. Hesse and the two Saxonies nearby were governed by powerful princes, while areas near Hesse and into Thuringia fell under the control of families of important counts, like those of Schwarzburg, Henneberg, and Mansfeld, as well as lesser counts and individual knights with their own castles. In these territories, administration was comparatively well developed, and bureaucrats were important local figures.[2]

Sandwiched between the apocalyptic drama surrounding Müntzer's Mühlhausen and the radical, articulate peasantry of the south, this region in the middle of Germany has often been treated as incidental, an area without genuine commitment to the war, where developments elsewhere were simply copied and even class conflict failed to get off the ground properly. Many of the lower nobility joined the peasant bands, perhaps as many as twenty-four nobles in the area of Henneberg alone. There are few lists of peasant grievances from here, and those that exist were produced during the course of the war, almost as an afterthought. The Twelve Articles functioned as an off-the-peg set of demands, an import from Memmingen in the south that few apparently even read. The towns do not seem to have allied properly with the peasants but used peasant armies to support their own struggles, turning against the peasants as soon as they could. And even the two dominant armies in the region, the Bildhausen and the Werra bands, failed to unite, fatally weakening their position.[3]

The differences reflected the distinctive social and political economy. Negotiation over lordship does not seem to have been handled through orderly complaint and grievance resolution, and so we lack the kind of evidence we have for the south. Instead of arguing over serfdom, dues, infringements, and encroachments, the revolt addressed the issue of lordship directly. Consequently, when the revolt combusted, it spread rapidly, involved very large numbers, and led to systematic destruction of monastic buildings, followed by attacks on castles. The peasant armies dominated the region, and along with some knights, many rich, politically influential town citizens were 'powerful in the peasant army', as one observer put it. At times it seemed that the whole hierarchy of the region had gone over to the peasants. For nearly two months there was uproar, with some of the most intense fighting of the war. Lordship crumbled, and the war shattered an entire region, strengthening the long-term power of the major princes as a result. Just how this could happen is evident in places like Henneberg and Fulda.[4]

Two days after the Weinsberg massacre, revolt broke out in the town of Fulda, which was ruled by an abbot who was secular authority and religious figure rolled into one. Printed copies of the Twelve Articles from Frankfurt arrived just as Easter approached.[5] Lenten preaching reminded the faithful of Christ's passion, and as the annual Easter communion neared, the issue of how communion was received became unavoidable: Should layfolk receive the wine? Powerful abbeys like Fulda and Hersfeld and ecclesiastical rulers like the bishop of Würzburg dotted the region, so the question of whether churchmen were legitimate secular rulers was an urgent issue. It united the peasants, often exploited by their church overlords, with the townsfolk, for many towns were ruled by bishops or abbots. All this came to a head once the news of the Weinsberg atrocity reached the area.[6]

The coadjutor or assistant abbot, who was the effective ruler of Fulda, was forced to accept the articles of the peasants and the town, including the Twelve Articles. Three days later the peasants captured Hersfeld and the local abbot fled, while the peasant armies of the Werra Valley and Bildhausen built links with towns, just as the bands in the south had done. All this happened against a wider background of revolt; farther away, in Mainz, also ruled by a bishop, the citizens rose on 25 April, and the nearby villages of vintners formulated articles.

By early May the peasants were meeting on Wacholder Heath in front of the abbey of Eberbach, where they reputedly drank two-thirds of its hundred-thousand-litre barrel of wine. As more areas formed their own armed bands, the rebels attacked and plundered monasteries and convents. So far, it all seemed to be about bishops and abbots and abbesses. But that was about to change.[7]

Count Wilhelm von Henneberg was desperate for a horse. Constantly called upon to 'ride out' to confront the peasants, he needed a suitable mount, but his horses had been requisitioned in the feudal levy, and his tackle was rusting to pieces. Wilhelm was a second-rank nobleman, a scion of a well-related, aristocratic family but not a duke or prince. So he turned to Duke Johann of Saxony to lend him a warhorse, repeating an earlier request for a gunsmith, two trumpeters— and the horse. As days went by without reply, Wilhelm's pleas grew more frantic. Finally Duke Johann replied in his own hand, offering a horse that was obedient, steady, and 'carried the wine very gently', but it could also go at a decent trot when needed. Wilhelm promised to send it back as soon as he could.[8]

Wilhelm's peasants were becoming restive. By April 1526, evangelical fervour was high, and a group of six hundred citizens went to Dipperz, a village just twelve kilometres away from Fulda, to hear the evangelical preacher. As Easter neared, matters in Fulda reached a crisis, and Wilhelm could not be indifferent because the coadjutor abbot of Fulda was his son, Johann. Soon the abbot was negotiating with the peasants, while the mayor of Hersfeld himself, Johann Ottensass, took a leading role in the peasant bands and brokered an alliance with Fulda. Wilhelm watched all this from his castle in Schleusingen as his officials wrote him increasingly anxious reports.

Wilhelm was not at first seriously alarmed. Perhaps he saw the chance to finally curb the influence of the bishop of Würzburg, his rival as a major power in the region. In 1516 Wilhelm had managed to get his then twelve-year-old son nominated as coadjutor of the rich abbey of Fulda, which held substantial lands, and he may have dreamed of secularising his young son's abbacy-to-be. He was not particularly helpful to the bishop of Würzburg, Fulda's overlord, whom Johann and his father were obliged to aid, but instead stood back waiting to see how matters might develop to his advantage. He believed the peasants only wanted to attack monks and nuns. But he quickly learnt that he had miscalculated, not for the last time.[9]

On 18 April, as the evangelicals seemed to be taking over in Fulda, Coadjutor Johann fled to Castle Bieberstein, while the town joined in coalition with Hersfeld against him. Johann was reduced to begging his father for help, which Wilhelm could not provide. Johann and the abbot of Hersfeld watched impotently as the towns they had ruled simply disregarded them. In a formal document sealed with the abbatial seal, the abbot of Hersfeld joined the peasants as a brother and swore to follow the Christian principles enshrined in the Twelve Articles and any others that would subsequently be included if they were in line with the gospel. However, the abbot's negotiators somehow managed to insert the cunning proviso that if Landgrave Philip of Hesse, now on the march to put down the revolt, turned out to be even more Christian than the Christian brothers, then the abbot would follow him instead. Not only did Coadjutor Johann himself join the peasant alliance, to his father's disgust, but he made his own officials do likewise, greatly strengthening the peasants. From Johann's point of view, the treaty at least allowed him back into town and his residence and confirmed his rule. His optimism proved naïve when the rebels did not disband their army as promised but blocked his exit out of town. Still, he did manage to get the peasants to recognise him as 'prince in Buchonia' (Buchen), and they dropped his somewhat demeaning religious title of 'coadjutor', bolstering his personal power.[10]

With Hersfeld and Fulda having fallen, and with armies of peasants rising day by day and coming ever closer, Wilhelm knew that it was only a matter of time before the peasants reached him in his castle at Schleusingen. And he knew he did not have the men to defend it.[11]

In Kaltennordheim, Tham von Herda, Wilhelm's loyal local official, began to worry. On 19 April, the day Fulda fell, he wrote philosoph-ically, 'What you can't quieten with force, you have to quieten with kindness'. He hoped for a nonviolent solution. But as Hersfeld fell to the rebels too, the clock was ticking. By 23 April, Tham von Herda was finding it hard to hold the line. He wrote to his brother-in-law Heintz von Wanbach that he needed arms and had very few of them. He had no shot nor any equipment to make it, 'and if I shoot all I have, where will I get more?'[12]

By 24 April the peasants had taken nearby Salzungen and Kray-enburg, and Tham knew that he would soon be surrounded. They had been about to lay siege to his castle, and at the last moment they had mercifully turned away, but who knew when they might wheel back? He tried to curry favour with them, writing to the local villagers that he was happy to be instructed on godly truth in 'brotherly fashion'. The peasants told him roundly that he 'could not resist them: it was not possible'.[13]

In Tham's close-knit world of brothers and brothers-in-law who were all officials of Philip of Hesse or of Wilhelm of Henneberg, the peasants had become ungovernable. The next day, another official had to deal with peasants who had overrun the nearby monasteries of Her-renbreitungen and Frauenbreitungen, and he begged them to remain true to their oath and duty, and to be 'pious subjects', as they had prom-ised just days before. But they were not to be budged. They agreed that they had promised loyalty, but 'we can't resist the force [gewalt], we are unable'. In any case, the rebels had got so drunk on the wine in the cellars that, the official noted, 'I could get nowhere with them'. As if buttonholing his lord, the official addressed him directly: 'Gracious lord, you must not trust citizens or those who are in office; they won't hold firm'; 'I have only two or three men, that's the army I have'. But while the hapless official himself was away checking on the monasteries, his own men had pulled up the castle bridge against him.[14]

Tham, too, ceased to trust those around him. Now he wrote in desperation that he could rely on only seven of his men, not enough to defend the castle—the others were melting away. The local nobles and even Wilhelm's officials had joined the peasantry, becoming 'powerful'—*gewaldig*—in the peasant army, and his own brother and brother-in-law had joined the other side. His lord, Wilhelm von Henneberg, did not seem to realise how serious matters had become but wrote suggesting a clever ruse: he would split the peasant band by priming one group to seize a banner and cause a mutiny by shouting, 'Hennebergers, come over here!' Tham's lord had still failed to grasp that the old days of loyalty to the Hennebergs were finished. Unbeknown to Wilhelm, the rebels were shouting the opposite: 'Today Hennebergisch and for eternity, never again'.[15]

Tham's whole world was falling apart. Every time someone left his castle, he knew they were probably joining the peasants, never to return. On 7 May, he went to survey the peasant army, now close by. 'I was never in more danger of my life than yesterday, one side was screaming: I should be made to run the gauntlet'. After the atrocity of Weinsberg, he knew what this meant. Days later, Tham fled the castle.[16]

In late April, Philip of Hesse's patience snapped when the town of Vacha in his own territory revolted, and he became the first lord in the region to confront the peasants. Outraged by the rebels' impudence, he determined to attack them in the area around Fulda and Hersfeld once he had put down Vacha's revolt. He refused to negotiate, and though an evangelical, he condemned the peasants for 'wanting to do nothing for any authority or be subject to any authority'. He called on Duke Erich of Braunschweig and others to join him.[17]

Philip was staking his claim to authority on the stage of the empire. Barely twenty years of age, he had ruled Hesse in name since 1519, when his mother's regency had ended. In 1523 he had married Christina of Saxony, daughter of Duke Georg of Saxony, a union that strengthened the bonds between Hesse and Ducal Saxony and secured his position in the region. The marriage also underwrote the alliance he would soon make with Georg to defeat the peasants, though it was the younger man who made most of the running. Clever, bold, and independent, Philip would become the most talented statesmen amongst the pro-Reformation German princes—but he had a tragic flaw. His marriage to Christina turned out unhappily, and Philip's constitution, so he argued, required sexual release. As early as 1526 he importuned Luther about what a man in such a situation could do: Might he follow the example of the Old Testament patriarchs and take a second wife? When Luther did not take the bait, Philip let the matter drop, but in 1539 he returned to it, and in 1541, with the tacit knowledge of Luther, Melanchthon, Martin Bucer, and other leading reformers, Philip publicly wed his mistress while remaining married to Christina. The resulting scandal damaged the Lutheran cause and embarrassed Luther, who airily insisted that he would just deny that he had advised bigamy. Philip, however, toughed it out, seeming to regard bigamy as a fully legitimate solution, a stance his own preachers defended. Meanwhile, he continued to father children with both women.[18]

At first Duke Georg seemed reluctant to ally with his son-in-law against the rebelling peasants. Though Georg dealt with most other correspondence the day it arrived, in this instance he made Philip wait eleven full days for a reply.[19] The letter Georg finally sent was largely in his own hand, tidied up by the scribe. He explained that he had worried that Philip, as a supporter of Luther, would not wish to ally with a Catholic. But now he thought that Philip agreed with him that the commands of the authorities should, 'in my opinion', be kept so long as they were not counter to—and here he may well have meant to say 'counter to the word of God'. The scribe deleted the text, so the letter read that Georg did not like to see that 'what men vow and swear, is not kept, whether instituted by God or man', a wider formulation that also removed any echo of peasant rhetoric.[20]

Georg's careful words to Philip suggest that religious differences really had undermined the cohesion of the authorities, and that Friedrich the Wise of Electoral Saxony's cautious policy of negotiation had prevented revolt in his lands, though he may also have experienced difficulty recruiting troops. Indeed, until that point, the trouble had been concentrated in Georg's half, Ducal Saxony. As Georg saw it, religion certainly did play a role: one reason the peasants were attacking him was because he opposed Lutheranism, and he weighed his words so as not to alienate his son-in-law.[21]

Philip turned his attention to Hersfeld, where the abbot had sworn brotherhood with the peasants. Those on the border to Hesse were now caught between the wrath of the landgrave, who was about to march on Hersfeld, and the might of the peasants. Stuck in the town of Vacha, a panicked Rudolf von Waiblingen, a Fulda official, wrote to Coadjutor Johann, explaining that the peasants 'won't let me out of here'.[22] Coadjutor Johann had ordered Rudolf to ally with the peasants, but now he feared 'danger and mischance' (*ebentuer*) from a vengeful Philip. The army of peasants that surrounded him in Vacha had taken the monasteries of Herren- and Frauenbreitingen, parallel male and female monasteries, and they were rumoured to be marching to the town of Schmalkalden. On 29 April, Philip took Hersfeld, sacked the city council, replaced it with his own *Schultheis* or mayor, seized all the valuable goods and silver of the town magistrates, and confiscated their weapons. Philip rounded up the ringleaders and had them interrogated—they were united in blaming Johann Ottensass, the mayor of Hersfeld, who was duly exiled. It was the end of the abbot's rule.[23]

Next it was Fulda's turn. Philip's army of 350 mounted men and 1,400 foot soldiers was only half the size of the peasant force at Fulda. But on 3 May he attacked, and the peasant army dissolved. Fifteen hundred peasants were captured and driven into the castle ditch, where many perished. Only the 'chiefs' were allowed out—to be executed. On Philip's side, just a single soldier and two horses were killed. As in Hersfeld, those interrogated at Fulda were keen to minimise their and the council's role; they had all been 'seduced' by the 'watchmaker' Hans Dahlhopf, who had told them that the gospel meant freedom. Only one of those accused admitted that it was in fact the whole council who had agreed about everything; 'Everyone in the town, poor and rich, were of one voice'. Tham von Herda allowed himself a wry smile at the news of Fulda's defeat: 'If I hadn't become an enthusiastic new Christian and new gospeller, I'd have loved to hear this news, but as it is, I'm not allowed'.[24]

This was not good news, however, for Coadjutor Johann, Wilhelm of Henneberg's son. He had failed to give Philip support, explaining that he could not join Philip's army without breaking his treaty with the peasants, and if he were to do so, the citizens would be unsafe and his subjects would be driven from their houses, their goods plundered, while the town would surely join the Franconian peasants, who now surrounded the city on three sides. But not only had the churchman failed to quell the rebels; he had committed perjury by allying with them and had undermined his position amongst his peers in the empire by trying to turn the abbacy into a secular territory. Still trying to steer a path between Philip and the peasant armies, Johann left Fulda to negotiate but ended up outside the town with the landgrave, unable to do more than warn the town that Philip was coming. He also failed to join with Philip's forces against the rebels, thus destroying his standing with both sides. Philip had the rebel leaders executed, levied a hefty fine on the town for its disobedience, and left Johann utterly humiliated. It was clear that his power now rested on Philip's, and not on Wilhelm's or the Henneberg family's. Next, Philip turned towards Mühlhausen, constructing a grand coalition that would converge on the peasants' forces. With the abbots of Hersfeld and Fulda revealed as incompetent and the local nobles impotent, Philip had become a leading figure in the region.[25]

Philip's victory came too late for Count Wilhelm of Henneberg. On 3 May, the very same day that Philip triumphed over Fulda, Wilhelm had to 'become a peasant', as he noted sarcastically, and swear to the Twelve Articles. He even had to request his own subjects to send in their complaints—and they did. Having begged to become a brother, Wilhelm tried to foment disunity amongst the peasants by seeking to gain protection from other peasant bands. But they saw through this scheme, forcing Wilhelm to explain himself. He had to beg the local band to accept him and to aver that he had always been honest in his dealings. Behind their backs he was of course still negotiating frantically with the landgrave and every other ruler he could. When the peasants had finally hunted him out of Castle Massfeld, they undressed his pregnant wife, leaving her naked in front of everyone before finally throwing her a peasant-woman's shirt—and humiliating both her and her husband. Margrave Joachim of Brandenburg, who told the story to Duke Albrecht of Prussia, doubtless relished the gossip.[26]

Wilhelm's grand strategy had imploded. Instead of his son becoming a secular prince and securing Fulda as a permanent gain for the Henneberg dynasty, the twenty-two-year-old had been ignominiously restored by Philip of Hesse, who now claimed sole sovereignty over the whole town, having previously shared it with the abbot. He punished Fulda with a fine of 36,000 Gulden plus seizure of all the town's provisions, severely damaging its economy. Philip was proving a cunning politician; 'The man is greedy and cruel like a wild boar', wrote

Tham von Herda. Seeing the danger for Wilhelm, he continued, 'You shouldn't rejoice, when the Landgrave comes; whoever doesn't need him should let him stay at home'.[27]

But Wilhelm was still plotting, hoping to salvage something. Next he wrote to Casimir of Brandenburg, suggesting that since the bishop of Würzburg had run away, leaving Casimir's brother, the provost, in charge, perhaps they should try together to install the provost as secular ruler of the region. After all, this would suit the peasants, who wanted to get rid of clergy rulers. Wilhelm had still not grasped how far he had alienated the princes, who viewed him and Johann as traitorous turncoats, meekly doing the peasants' bidding.[28]

At last the money Wilhelm had been waiting for appeared, carefully spirited through peasant-held lands along with his contingent of horsemen, and he joined the landgrave for the attack on the peasant army at Frankenhausen. But once again, Count Wilhelm got his timing wrong. He arrived at the staging point in Salza, only to find that he was too late and the other troops had already left to confront the peasants. An irrelevance, he was stuck in Salza with his armed retinue until the armies returned; he even had to get the landgrave's permission before punishing his own subjects. Wilhelm finally grasped that his subjects hated him. They had fished out all his ponds, he noted indignantly, and 'our whole lordship has been completely overturned'. He wrote to Philip in disgust that Philip's peasants (who had renewed their oaths of loyalty) were better than Wilhelm's, because 'ours... let it be heard that they want neither us nor any other lord at all, but God is their lord'. He was unable to distinguish between peasants not wanting rule by men like him and not wanting rulership at all.[29]

It would be easy to cast this as a contrast of masculine styles, and to see old Wilhelm as too clever by half, so eager to use the war to his advantage that he failed to resist, while the youthful Philip seized the initiative when others temporised. But Philip had a nascent territorial state, troops he could rely on, and status he could use to play a political role in the empire. At a lower level in the political structure, Wilhelm was dependent on more powerful lords and lacked armed forces of his own because he had supplied them for the feudal levy. The Peasants' War exposed the fragility of his lordship, and he proved no match for the peasants. Despite all Wilhelm's scheming, the Hennebergs died out in 1583, and their territories fell to Saxony. Wilhelm's is the story, repeated in many places, of the decline of middle-ranking counts and lesser knights who would find it ever harder to resist the larger states and princes.

Above the town of Würzburg on the opposite bank of the Main River looms the Marienberg Castle. St Mary's church stands in the centre of the fortified area, built on foundations that go back to the eighth century; the original chapel it displaced was probably built over a temple to a heathen goddess. For the peasants, nothing better represented the massive might of the prince bishops than the Marienberg, visible for miles around. When, back in 1476, Hans Behem, the so-called Drummer of Niklashausen, had burnt his drum and called for a pilgrimage of the Tauber Valley to the shrine of Our Lady in Niklashausen, the processions he unleashed had galvanised anticlerical feeling in the whole region. Captured by the bishop's men and taken to the Marienberg, he was burnt at the stake, and his ashes were thrown into the Main. Many of his supporters who had gathered outside the castle were slaughtered as the bishops' men used shot against the rebels' catapults.

Forty-nine years later, on 1 April 1525, the bishop's subjects below the castle rose against him once more and soon assembled a powerful faction within the town as well. Down on the flat square of the town, angry locals who had massed outside the council chamber, the 'green tree', had forced the terrified councillors to agree to let the peasants into town. A regional centre and trading hub situated on the Main, Würzburg stood at a crossroads to wider trade and was at the heart of the prince bishop's expansive territory. But whereas he was safely insulated and protected high up on his hill, the town, safeguarded only by its walls, was unable to defend itself. The peasants threatened to burn the vineyards, a credible warning that would have destroyed the town's wine industry for years to come.

By early May, peasants were massing at Frankenhausen in Thuringia. The Bildhausen and Werra Valley bands had just seen their allies at Fulda, Hersfeld, and the Henneberg lands defeated by Philip of Hesse. Most of the Werra band had melted away. The Württembergers under Matern Feuerbacher had encountered the troops of the Swabian League. Feuerbacher, who proposed peace, was deposed, but the peasants became bogged down in discussion and debate about what to do, giving the truchsess and his troops valuable time, and on 12 May at Böblingen they were bloodily defeated.[30] The town of Eisenach in Saxony had admitted the peasant leaders, but this was a ruse. As soon as the peasants came in, their safe conduct was violated and they were clapped into jail.

Incited by these setbacks and defeats, the peasants wanted revenge. They needed a victory. Würzburg was the citadel they had to take to cement their gains in the south; by this time they had destroyed over sixty castles in the Würzburg bishopric alone.[31] They called on armies all over the region to join them. On 6 and 7 May, two major peasant armies set out for Würzburg, joined by remnants of the bands from Bildhausen. The Heilbronners and the men of the south joined with what was left of the Werra and Odenwald bands under Florian Geyer and the group that had been led by Götz von Berlichingen. For a final moment in mid-May, Würzburg became the beacon for south and central Germany, the fortress against which not only the Würzburgers but all the rebels set their sights, overcoming differences of lordship, belonging, dialect, and belief. Fifteen thousand peasants now surrounded the castle.

The town's garrison had retreated into the castle and the bishop had fled, so it seemed the rebels could take the prize. But how? First they tried negotiations. Down below, the Tauber army called on the bishop, now safely in Heidelberg, to accept the Twelve Articles, pay damages of 100,000 Gulden and hand over the castle, leaving it to the future regional assembly to decide whether to destroy it once and for all. He rejected the terms. Next they attempted an all-out assault on the castle, which lasted for eight days. They came close to victory but failed. The castle was so high that firing at it was difficult, and unlike the castles the peasant bands had destroyed with ease, it was a working castle. The peasants could not ascend without encountering stiff resistance from a small fighting force that knew how to overcome its disadvantage in numbers by defending the narrow entrances and using the castle's advantage of height. The rebels determined therefore to besiege the castle and wait. They had two charismatic leaders, Florian Geyer, a noble, and Götz von Berlichingen, the knight with the iron fist, who later claimed to have been forced to become commander of the army.[32]

But the castle was well supplied, and as a fortnight passed without any development, the bands became impatient with nothing to do. The chronicler and civic secretary Martin Cronthal described with annoyance how the peasants spent their days in the town's taverns. Finally some of the bands encamped on the castle side of the Main River had an idea: there were rumoured to be tunnels under the castle. They planned to dig into the castle from below and destroy it. A later song supposedly written by the castle's defenders mocked the 'drunken miners' amongst the peasants. Digging began and continued for some time. But there was no progress, and time dragged on.[33]

In the region of Baden and the Palatinate, Georg, bishop of Speyer and brother of the Palatine elector, was also finding it impossible to keep his peasants obedient. The peasants of the Bruhrain had summoned him to a meeting, but when he turned up 'in the field' only one peasant met him, saying they would write to him later. During Easter week, a group of peasants at Malsch began encouraging other villages to join them 'to support godly Justice'. Soon they gathered a large group along the Rhine, throughout the Bruhrain, from Wiesloch to Bruchsal. Joining with the town of Durlach, they plundered the monasteries of Herren- and Frauenbreitungen in the Black Forest, moving up the Rhine to threaten Speyer directly. Here they made terms, forcing the clergy in Speyer to provide the army with bread, wine, and meat; and then they dissolved on 8 May, with only those at Bruchsal remaining ready for muster.[34]

Meanwhile, disturbances were continuing in the area around Worms, and clergy were coming under attack. The provost of the St Georgenberg monastery in nearby Pfeddersheim simply gave up, transferring the whole institution to the Palatine elector, 'in consideration of the worrying letters [the Twelve Articles] and times which are now moving the common man to resentfulness particularly against the spiritual estate'. On 10 May, Elector Ludwig of the Palatinate had to make terms with a much more radical group determined to 'root out' the clergy and the nobility. He met the leaders of two armies in person in the forest near his residence of Neustadt, promising to summon a diet and consider their complaints and advising them to disperse in the meantime. The peasants seemed to be finding a hearing. Other peasant groups even suggested that the elector's brother, the bishop of Speyer, should secularise his territory, marry, and become a Palatinate count.[35]

As he promised, Elector Ludwig commissioned reports on the Twelve Articles, which the peasants he was negotiating with had adopted as their programme. Ludwig turned to Philipp Melanchthon, Luther's coworker at Wittenberg, and Johannes Brenz of Schwäbisch Hall, both Lutherans, though tellingly not to Luther himself. Melanchthon thought the princes had responsibility for ensuring 'peace and tranquility', but this meant maintaining a functioning court system, establishing schools, and instituting evangelical preaching—not looking into peasant complaints. In his pamphlet against the peasant articles, Ludwig blamed the peasants themselves, whom he claimed were possessed by the devil, while Brenz continued to advocate a moderate course. But when it came to it, Ludwig did not summon the promised diet, and on 23 May, he seized the chance to force the peasants to disperse.[36]

Mass risings in Alsace also reached a pitch at Easter. In Strasbourg the Reformation was becoming well established, and preaching was extending to the villages, where Clemens Ziegler, a mystic and radical preacher from the gardeners' guild in Strasbourg, was arrested by the lord of Barr. When he was locked out of the church, he had preached the gospel in the churchyard in the village of Heiligenstein. This cause célèbre prompted armed peasants to gather and call for his release. Religious fervour was important elsewhere in Alsace too, and after a local revolt in Saverne, a group formed at Dorlisheim in mid-April that included many pastors. They held a religious disputation to demonstrate the truth of the evangelical faith.[37]

Many of the Alsatian groups used elaborate religious argument in their correspondence. Ludwig Ziegler, leader of the 'Christian brothers assembled at Truttenhausen', wrote a lengthy preamble in a letter to the town council of Obernai describing how the light of God was now emerging but was being darkened by those who had hidden the truth. The monasteries had 'amassed alms through their false appearances, so that they no longer wanted to be called servants but Lords', but the true poor 'who want to fight with the Sword of Faith for his name's sake' were the ones who actually deserved alms. Mixing threats with religious sentiments, the letter concluded that the council should therefore hand over to them any 'wine, grain or other valuables' belonging to all convents or monasteries.[38]

The leader of all the lower Alsatian bands was Erasmus Gerber, an illiterate craftsman from Molsheim, a village subject to the bishop of Strasbourg. On 29 April he proclaimed that they had assembled to confirm the Word of God the Lord, and to comfort and help 'the poor and common man', who had been hitherto exploited by the priesthood. A talented commander, he established a rotational system of military service whereby one man in four from every village should serve in the army for eight days and then return home to wife and family. On 16 May, meeting at Molsheim, the Stechsfeld group sent the Strasbourg council a list of articles which towns and villages should swear when they joined. As with other sets of articles, it gives a flavour of the group's values. It began with the promise 'to actively assist and support the godly word and holy gospel and justice'. No one who was opposed to the gospel should be permitted, everyone was to obey the army authorities and be obedient to all ruling authorities 'which subject themselves to the evangelical view', and all groups should provide military support for each another when needed. Plunder should be handed over to the common fund, and women, children, and maids should not be treated badly in either word or deed.[39]

From Easter until June, Gerber managed to lead the vast forces of the various Alsatian armies in spite of having no political or military experience so far as we know. The excitement of those months enabled his gifts to flower as he and his brothers fought for freedom, and for, as they put it, the free use of the wood in the forest, 'the animals of the earth, the birds of the air, the fish of the sea and all flowing waters'— and as they sought at the end to preserve their Landschaft.[40]

He also tried to gain the cooperation of Strasbourg. On Easter Monday, Gerber wrote to the Strasbourg council and to the preachers 'in christian duty and brotherly love', exhorting them 'to fight for the Word of God against the quivering wolves who are tearing it down', 'zu verfechten das wort Gots vor den inreissenden zuckenden wolfen', using the same imagery as the author of the *An die Versammlung*. He asked the preachers to come in person to the peasants camped at Altdorf 'at 8 o'clock'. Few nonrebel clergy were willing to go to the peasants' camp in person; doing so took considerable courage after the Weinsberg massacre. Johannes Lachmann in Heilbronn had sent an emissary, and Karlstadt would later write about his terror when confronted with a peasant army that he thought threatened him, his wife, and child. But Wolfgang Capito, Martin Bucer, and Matthäus Zell, the Strasbourg preachers, asked the council for permission to go, assuring the councillors that they would exhort the peasants to return home. They entered the peasant ring and made their case.[41]

On the way home, they wrote to Gerber and the other 'regents', 'regenten', of the 'assembly', 'versamlung'—they had not quite absorbed its egalitarian values—making twelve points. They reassured Gerber that the Strasbourgers would act swiftly. Gerber must rightly have worried that he was being strung along while the enemy gathered its forces. They advised the peasants to dissolve their camp, because the longer they stayed together the harder it would be to provision the armies. The peasant leaders should trust them, for not doing so was unchristian, and those who sought their own advantage under cover of the gospel would be punished by God. These were not the kind of arguments Luther was making, and the Strasbourgers did not say that rebellion of any kind was always wrong; rather, starting from the peasants' own values of brotherhood, they sought to demonstrate that the peasants were in reality pursuing their own selfish interests rather than seeking salvation as they claimed. But they forbore from suggesting that the peasants' actions were inspired by the devil, and they addressed them as 'brothers'.

Even more remarkably, the Christian preachers were not the only ones to visit Gerber's army: the leader of Alsatian Jewry, Josel of Rosheim, went as well. He had secured protection for the Jewish communities in Strasbourg and, drawing on the Old Testament, seems to have pleaded likewise with Gerber's army not to rebel, possibly also with the Strasbourg council's support.[42] On Easter Tuesday, even after the Weinsberg massacre had happened, it was still possible for the Strasbourg preachers and the army to talk and for the Bible and Christian brotherhood to mean something to both sides. Throughout the region, just as in Franconia and the southwest, evangelical groups within towns tried to introduce the Reformation in the lead-up to Easter, inspired by the peasants. All the same, few towns in the region made formal partnerships with the peasant armies: Ensisheim, Mulhouse, Schlettstadt, Colmar, Hagenau, Strasbourg, and Weissenau all stood aside; Keysersberg did so under duress and had to hand over its supplies of gunpowder.[43]

The peasant numbers increased rapidly to twenty thousand and beyond as they plundered monasteries and convents to support themselves, and they formed a large army that surrounded Saverne, the residence of the bishop of Strasbourg. Another army, eight thousand strong, formed at Herbitzheim in the territory of the cardinal of Metz, and Strasbourg reported that three thousand of them had handguns. Yet another group formed at Weissenbourg and won the town's support. They stormed the provost's castle at the start of May, attacked Castle Rödern in the Palatinate, and joined with a band known as the Kolbenhaufen. Peasants from Alsace and the Palatinate were now coming together, and it seemed as if the whole region was in revolt. By mid-May they managed to unite all thirteen armies of the Alsace-Palatinate at Molsheim under the 'holy Gospel', a remarkable achievement of coordination.[44]

The spreading revolt put the Habsburgs under pressure. In the Alps in Tyrol, an uprising against the bishop of Brixen began on 9 May when a man named Peter Paßler, who was about to be executed for fish poaching, was freed by onlookers. The next day, the crowd attacked and plundered the houses of nobles and clergy, and on 14 May they looted the house of the Fuggers in Hall. The bishops of Brixen and Trent were forced to flee. Jakob Strauss, a radical Lutheran who preached against usury, had once been preacher at the mining town of Schwaz and had also held a preaching post at Hall (whose salt mines and mint made it one of the most important towns of the empire). His successor had been the now loyal Lutheran Urbanus Rhegius, whom we encountered earlier writing a pamphlet more sympathetic than Luther to the ills of serfdom. Hall thus had a tradition of socially radical and possibly antisemitic evangelical preaching. Salamanca, the Habsburgs' hated representative, who was believed to be Jewish, was forced to flee, and Jews in Brixen were targeted too. Monasteries, especially those of the despised Teutonic Knights, were attacked, and revolt under the leadership of Michael Gaismair soon spread towards the Allgäu.

Although a revolt of the miners at Schwaz in February was quickly averted, the authorities had to tread carefully. On 8 May in Salzburg, a 'heretic' who had been condemned to death was freed by the crowd, and on 25 May miners and peasants in the Gastein Valley rose up and marched to Salzburg, where they plundered the archbishop's residence and forced him to retreat to his castle, Hohensalzburg. The rebels formulated the Merano articles, an ambitious programme designed to deal with long-standing grievances in the region. Ferdinand of Austria was compelled to discuss the articles at a *Landtag* that June, obliged to listen as all ninety-seven were read out in the presence of his wife and foreign dignitaries. Tyrol, Graubünden, and Salzburg—indeed all of Upper Austria, it seemed—were in revolt.[45]

The hilly and mountainous area of Saxony and Thuringia was dominated by the powerful rulers of Saxony, different branches of the Wettin family that took opposite views on the Reformation. Elector Friedrich the Wise supported 'his' professor, Luther, while Duke Georg remained militantly Catholic. This was the region that had formed both Luther and Müntzer. Its wealth was rooted in the profits of the mining industry, then at its height, which had made Georg and Friedrich key players in imperial politics.

The landscape of the 'ore mountains' and the heights of the Harz, where little could grow, spread out towards Bohemia, with copper and silver produced in the county of Mansfeld, while the silver towns of

Schneeberg, Annaberg, and Buchholz lay in Saxony. Miners were set apart from the countryside on which they depended, for the sheer number of shafts and slag heaps the mines required left large areas that could not be farmed. Miners relied on food imports, often from far afield. In the mid-sixteenth century a hundred waggons laden with produce went to the Hettstedt market each Saturday, while dried fish, pickled fish, crabs, and herring made their way from Hamburg. In the county of Mansfeld, locals were being forced out by the influx of mine workers, and this was likely the case in the Erzgebirge and the Tyrol too. In Joachimstal, which had seen little more than a decade of intensive mining, the rapid increase in population meant that although some peasants were employed in the mines, others were pushed out.[46]

Mining brought with it a cadre of officials who ran the mines, educated men who intermarried with local town elites and leading mine-owning families, alongside the officials who ran the highly developed bureaucracies of the two Saxonies and the county of Mansfeld. Increasingly, though, it was the long-distance capitalists of the south, in Nuremberg, Augsburg, and to an extent Leipzig, who profited from the mines. The towns of the region were largely middle-sized and not especially rich; even in Erfurt, three-quarters of the population was only modestly well-off. There was no personal serfdom, and peasants had relatively secure rights to the land, but there had been poor harvests in 1523 and 1524. As in the south, a group of rich peasants with substantial wealth was beginning to crystalise as wealth divisions grew. There were powerful monasteries, too, with large landholdings, like that of Grünhain near Zwickau, but there was also a vein of aggressive hostility towards local priests.[47]

Unrest now exploded in the region, moving outwards from Fulda. In Altenburg and around Allstedt, there was disorder, and the once powerful abbot of Grünhain was hunted out of his abbey by his own peasants on 8 May. One incident reveals how far power had shifted. When the nuns of Kelbra's own provost claimed he had bought their house and now owned 'our monastery's horses, crockery and waggon', he reduced the nuns to begging none other than the peasant army at Frankenhausen for help, for the sake of 'Christian, brotherly love'. The prioress simply had nowhere else to turn. In the Harz towns of Goslar, Halberstadt, and Quedlinburg, the trouble was spreading, and by 8 May, Duke Georg was warning those towns against rebellion. At Aschersleben, one Hans Kupferschmid called for the town bells to be rung and the citizenry to be summoned. He claimed he had orders from the emperor and princes to plunder and destroy all the monasteries, and any towns who refused would themselves be plundered. Not impressed, the city council demanded written proof, which he failed to provide. But though the council managed to see off this threat, Kupferschmid had support amongst the citizenry and had been able to lock the town gates so that fleeing nuns could not enter the town. Even more ominously, Kupferschmid tried to foment revolt by persuading the Hettstedters to plunder monasteries in the hope of booty. Hettstedt, just fifteen kilometres away in the county of Mansfeld, was a major mining town.[48]

As in the Tyrol, the authorities dreaded a miners' revolt, which would have jeopardised not only the wealth of the rich merchants of the south but also that of the rulers of Saxony and the counts of Mansfeld. In the copper mines of Mansfeld, just such a situation seemed to be developing. Three thousand miners were employed in the sixty-six shafts around Mansfeld and Eisleben, while ninety smelters operated in Mansfeld alone. The mining towns were known for rough behaviour and lawlessness but also for their remarkable craft knowledge. Skilled workers with a powerful sense of group identity, they might have seemed just the kind of group to support the peasantry and the Reformation. They had also developed religious brotherhoods to pray for collective salvation and had been eager purchasers of indulgences. Luther's attack on all these Catholic practices as worthless fostered their feeling that the priests had duped them. There were economic tensions too, for the elite of the smelters (who owned the mines) were becoming increasingly indebted to the big refining companies (*Saigergesellschaften*) in Nuremberg, Leipzig, and Augsburg, while many of the smaller mine operators were going to the wall. This was the same development that had led to unrest amongst miners in Schwaz in Austria—and some of the same big merchant firms were involved too.[49] All this made Müntzer's theology—with its attacks on the rich and powerful, the big merchants and capitalists—attractive, and many miners had joined Müntzer's leagues when he was in Allstedt.

In the Saxon mining towns of St Annaberg, Marienberg, Schneeberg, Geyer, and Buchholz—located in the Erzgebirge 'ore mountains'—unrest seemed likely as well. At St Annaberg the local official advised removing the silver reliquaries in the church for safety. The silver came from the miners' own labour, and he worried that they might loot the church while the storm—*ungewitter*—of unrest raged (the miners themselves had paid for a magnificent altar in 1515, still in the church today, which features miners' work). The town council at Annaberg tried to recruit locals as mercenaries to fight on the lords' side—perhaps the councillors thought that miners might be willing to put down peasants—but though fifty had shown interest, none signed up. By 18 May the town was finding it hard to keep its own citizens quiet. In the town of Marienberg, groups of miners were attacking villages and plundering the churches.[50]

Just what might have been afoot is apparent from the town of Schneeberg. Between spring 1524 and August 1525, Georg Amandus was preaching, and he had such support from the miners that the authorities dared not risk trying to expel him. Schneeberg was governed by a collective of rulers—Duke Georg of Saxony, Elector Friedrich, and his brother Duke Johann—who each took a different line on the Reformation: Georg was a fervent Catholic believer, while Friedrich protected Luther. Though Amandus was accused of being a follower of Karlstadt, it is not clear that this was true in any straightforward sense.

He was opposed to images and defended the destruction of two cruci-fixes, and he allegedly had said that the Gemeinde was not ruled by the council but that the council governed for the Gemeinde, views that put him close to the political views of the south and central German peas-antry. We can get some sense of his theology from the sole pamphlet of his that has survived, *How a Spiritual Christian Knight and Hero of God Should Fight in This World* (1524), which contains an obvious appeal to miners, whose patron saint was St George.[51]

With its sharp distinction between the world of the 'creaturely' and that of the spirit, this work owes a great deal to the German mysti-cism that also influenced Karlstadt and Müntzer. But the pamphlet's masculine appeal has a darker side. It concludes by welcoming death, 'a door and entrance...to eternal life' that brings no 'bitterness but a sweet sweetness' to those who have been 'made divine' and have given up all creaturely desires. All has been overcome as 'the red of morning appears' and the 'bridegroom rejoices with the bride...and makes her pregnant with all heavenly joy'. This blissful contemplation of death was unusual, and though Karlstadt praised suffering, neither he nor Müntzer ever eroticised death in this manner. Though there are echoes of Karlstadt in Amandus's emphasis on Gelassenheit—like Müntzer and Karlstadt he mocks the book learning of those trained at the university—his embrace of knightly struggle and death strikes a dif-ferent note.[52]

It was not only the theology of Müntzer's that could radicalise the miners; preachers like Amandus were developing equally powerful the-ologies linked to their own circumstances, and at Schneeberg, where the energetic Catholic Duke Georg was threatening to execute evan-gelicals while the ever-cautious Elector Friedrich counselled hearing them out, martyrdom was in the air. After their terrible defeat at Fulda, where perhaps fifteen hundred peasants were driven into the castle ditch, the appalled remnants of the rebel army wrote to the Bildhau-sen army that the 'tyrant' Philip's men had thrown bread to the rebels in the ditch 'as if they were unreasoning animals'. They had mocked the rebels, saying, 'Where is your black peasant and evangelical God now, that he should come to help and support you?' This is one of the few letters we have from the peasants' side reacting to defeat, and it was probably written by an educated scribe. The language deliberately evoked the mocking of Jesus at the crucifixion, as if the tragedy could only be comprehended by casting it as martyrdom in imitation of Christ's. By 'black peasant' they meant the Odenwald band, those who had not come to the rebels' aid.[53]

The authorities were most worried about Joachimstal in Bohemia, in the territory of the noble Count Stefan Schlick and not far from the Saxon towns of the Erzgebirge. Reformed preachers made headway there as well, and Andreas Karlstadt visited the town in 1520, dedicating at least nine tracts to Joachimstalers between 1520 and 1524. He grasped the burgeoning town's importance and realised that the Reformation would find support amongst miners. If nearby Joachimstal were to revolt, solidarity amongst miners might lead the Saxons to revolt too, causing the Saxon rulers serious difficulties, for a fifth of the production of the Saxon mines went to the rulers.[54]

The mining region around Mansfeld was where, at the behest of the counts of Mansfeld, Luther had undertaken a preaching tour to help calm the situation. Luther had spent his childhood there, but this time his campaign was not a success. He was mocked and treated with sarcasm, and once he had returned home he was not even sure he could rely on the counts to resist the peasants. Don't let those counts get 'soft', he exhorted their official, Johann Rühel.[55] Becoming more hard-line, Luther tried to push his ruler, Friedrich the Wise, into action against the peasants. In early May he wrote the infamous *Against the Robbing, Murdering Hordes of Peasants*, a much shorter piece that was originally printed alongside the earlier, more measured *Admonition* (*Ermahnung*) from April, and it probably appeared in the second week of May. With its forceful verbs, Luther's prose mimicked Müntzer's own rhetorical style. He condemned the peasants as 'turbulent'—or as we might say 'rebellious' (*aufrührerisch*)—no fewer than six times in the very paragraph that called on the reader to 'smite, slay and stab' the rebels as if they were mad dogs. He even went so far as to proclaim that killing peasants was a godly work. He did not discuss the peasant complaints or admit they had any justice. On 14 and 15 May, shortly after the pamphlet was in print, thousands of peasants would be slain at the battle of Frankenhausen, while the Duke of Lorraine wreaked bloody vengeance on the peasants of Alsace at Saverne. Luther of course could not know what would happen when he wrote the tract, and Lutheran historiography has sought to excuse his excessive language for that reason. But even so, Luther should have realised that the outcome of the war would be mass slaughter of peasants. He had already said in print that every peasant who was found to revolt must be 'slain' (*erwurget*), and where their souls will go 'even a child can tell you', 'wo der hyn faren wird, das mugen euch auch die kinder wol sagen'. He meant they were bound for Hell.[56]

This was not naivety on Luther's part, but a deliberate policy that contradicted his own ruler's stance. Elector Friedrich the Wise was still advocating negotiation with the peasants, not slaughter. He wrote to Duke Johann on 28 April, 'It would be no bad idea to send to [the peasants] and hear from them what they plan and why they have complaints against your grace and us, whether one could perhaps find ways and means to quieten the rebellion thereby'. He advised praying to God, the 'true house father', to avoid bloodshed. But the days of such pious patriarchalism were numbered.[57]

As late as 3 May, Luther visited Weimar and was asked for his view of the situation by Duke Johann, the elector's brother. Luther had insisted that the peasants be put down and had ruled out negotiation or acceptance of the Twelve Articles. It is unclear whether Johann was seriously asking for advice, or whether he just wanted Luther to confirm the action he planned to take against the peasants despite Friedrich's opposition. But while the elector's illness became ever more serious, his brother took the field alongside Philip of Hesse and other princes of the Swabian League, though not in time for the battle of Frankenhausen. Until quite late, the representatives of the leading imperial towns Strasbourg and Nuremberg, Clemens Volckamer and Jakob Sturm, had been negotiating with the Swabian League and the peasants. With his tract, Luther was therefore attempting to mobilise rulers he felt were not taking a sufficiently firm line, and trying to carve out a political role for himself.[58]

When Luther's friends wrote to him after the massacres became public, asking him to apologise for his intemperate language, Luther began his *An Open Letter on the Harsh Book Against the Peasants* contritely, only to become even more extreme.[59] The Lutheran Johannes Brenz attempted to excuse him by suggesting that if the peasants 'had still had the sword in their hands', the pamphlet would have been justified. But even he admitted that they no longer did, and so Christians now ought to show mercy. For many at the time, Luther's tract was an embarrassment—'rash', as Luther's supporter the mayor of Zwickau, Hermann Mühlpfort, described it. Ironically, it had been to Mühlpfort that Luther had dedicated *The Freedom of a Christian* back in 1520—a tract whose very title now seemed remote from those optimistic days of the early Reformation. Two clear fronts were forming as the authorities went on the attack, with Luther urging the rulers and their God-fearing subjects to take up arms against the rebels.[60]

Meanwhile, matters were also moving to a crescendo in Mühlhausen. Back in March, just over a week after Müntzer had been installed at St Mary's and had moved into the substantial former headquarters of the Teutonic Knights in the centre of town, a military muster was held. Müntzer rode about on a horse, preaching to the two thousand or so citizens who had gathered and calling upon them to swear an oath to join God's side, just as he had done at Allstedt. But this time the military captain was having none of it; such an oath was simply not needed, he said. 'If you haven't sworn enough oaths already then swear another basket full and hang it around your necks'. Besides, 'it is fitting to preach in churches, not in the field'. It is difficult to know to what degree Müntzer was still able to influence events. But it was clear that the situation would now build to a conflict.[61]

On 16 March, Müntzer backed another call for the election of an eternal council. The venue was his church, the Marienkirche opposite his house, not the town hall. Placing their rainbow flag by the pulpit, Pfeiffer and Müntzer called for a vote. Over two hundred voted in favour, but a sizeable minority voted against, their names also carefully recorded. Despite the involvement of women in so many of the 'actions' of the revolt in Mühlhausen—including one who apparently even conducted mass, 'which is not appropriate for her to do', as the council later put it—women's views were not apparently asked, nor is it clear whether they were even in the church, though the civic secretary reputedly recorded his sister-in-law's vote, so one woman at least may have been there. The voting tallies—Pfeiffer acted as a scribe as well—show that even at that stage, when many of the opponents of the 'godly' had left town, the citizenry was not united. Nor was Müntzer's theological domination unchallenged: in late April, a 'peasant' from Wittenberg appeared, demanding a disputation with Müntzer, so that he could 'overcome him with the Bible'; if he lost, he was happy to be executed with the sword. Some warned that this might be a Lutheran plot, but the disputation was apparently staged in Müntzer's own church, St Mary's. Whoever the Wittenberger really was, the evangelical peasant was still a figure who could insist on a hearing.[62]

Müntzer knew that they would need support outside the town, and he was careful not only to keep in touch with his old comrades the Allstedters but to reach out to the miners as well. On 26 April, ten days after Easter, he wrote to the Allstedters, 'The whole of Germany, France, Italy is awake; the master wants to set the game in motion, the evil-doers are for it', his excitement palpable. In Fulda four collegiate churches (*Stiftskirchen*) had been destroyed at Easter, and the peasants in the Klettgau, Hegau, and Black Forest had 'risen' in revolt. 'We cannot slumber any longer', he wrote. He was envisaging the conflict in which the godless would be plunged into misery, begging for mercy 'like children', and he exhorted them to recruit in villages and towns, 'and especially the mine-workers and other good fellows who will be of use'. 'Let this letter go to the miners', he ordered. 'Go to it, go to it, while the fire is hot! Don't let your sword grow cold, don't let it hang down limply! Hammer away ding-dong on the anvils of Nimrod', metaphors drawn from the blacksmith's work that will also have resonated with miners. The miners of Mansfeld were little more than twenty-five kilometres away from Allstedt, and many had joined the Eternal League when Müntzer had been preacher there.[63]

Mühlhausen's large territory now began to play an important part. Pfeiffer had worked hard with local villages and peasant bands, building their trust and calling for their dues to convents and monasteries to be abolished, their main grievance since serfdom had been eliminated in the region. Meanwhile the Peasants' War was continuing to unfold outside Mühlhausen's gates. At Salza (now Langensalza) on 26 April, evangelical preaching had caused serious unrest; citizens from there were asking Mühlhausen for help against the hated Sittich von Berlepsch, the official of Catholic Duke Georg, who was threatening to imprison evangelicals. About four hundred Mühlhauseners set off for Langensalza, picking up additional peasants on the way, and they assembled outside the town. But by this time the revolt had fizzled out, and perhaps because the citizens of Langensalza did not trust the Mühlhauseners, they sent them politely home, buying them off with two barrels of beer.[64]

Shortly afterwards, however, a group of Mühlhauseners set off on another march, in which they plundered a convent and a castle in Schlotheim, joined by locals. On 29 April the main group decided to set off from Görmar near Mühlhausen for Ebeleben, where they took arms, grain, valuables, 482 sheep, 66 head of cattle, 72 pigs, 120 geese, and about 300 hens, along with down pillows from the counts of Ebeleben. They also plundered all the fortified houses, castles, and priests' houses they could. After camping in Ebeleben for three days, they headed north. They had apparently planned to march to Nordhausen and to Heldrungen, where Müntzer's great enemy, Count Ernst, was ensconced; but when the villagers of the Eichsfeld joined the band and begged for help, they turned towards the village of Niederorschel instead, where they were promised stewed fish stolen from the noble von Bültzingsleben and cooked especially for them. 'Rejoice!', Heinrich Gera twenty years later remembered the villagers saying, 'we have spoken to the army at Ebeleben. They will come and make us all free'.[65]

As they traveled, everything seemed to fall to them, repeating the heady triumph that the rebels of the Black Forest, Swabia, Alsace, Thuringia, and Franconia had enjoyed. The monasteries of Reifenstein and Beuren and the convents of Teistungenburg and Worbis went up in flames; the castles Scharfenstein, Burg Stein, and the Harburg were set on fire. Windows and heating ovens were smashed, featherbeds looted, cellars drunk dry. The local nobility largely conceded defeat and swore brotherhood with Müntzer, first Ernst V von Hohnstein and Günther XL von Schwarzburg, whose father, Heinrich, had fled to the town of Nordhausen, and later Count Bodo of Stolberg with his son Wolfgang and the three counts of Gleichen. They would later have to explain their disloyalty to Duke Georg. Müntzer addressed them as equals, and the band deliberated on whether to accept them as brothers. Once again, it seemed, Müntzer had created a movement that overcame distinctions of class and status. They reached Heiligenstadt, where Müntzer insisted on preaching. The town invited him in—though not the army—and he preached in the city's main church. It seemed the entire region would be theirs.[66]

Finally it was revealed to Müntzer in a dream that they should march after sunrise, so he called the army together, saying that those who did not want to march farther should go home. Those who wished to continue marched back to Mühlhausen, rested for four days, and set off on the fateful journey to join what was now a large army outside Frankenhausen. It was a long trek along the river valley and then a steep climb up from town to where the battle would eventually be fought. The mood must have been electrifying as peasants from all over the region converged on Frankenhausen.[67]

The Allstedters had already heeded Müntzer's summons to join the men at Frankenhausen—Hans Zeiß, the Saxon official, claimed that just about all of them went, and he was left pretty much alone in Allstedt. In Frankenhausen itself, a salt-making town, a revolt had succeeded, and the evangelicals were in power, supporting the peasants. By 7 May, about six thousand men had gathered outside Frankenhausen; many had been there since 4 May and some since late April. Müntzer wrote frenzied letters to the communities at Walkenried, Sondershausen, and Großenehrich, and to the Werra band encamped at Eisenach, the Eisenachers themselves, and the Erfurters, calling on them for support.[68]

Müntzer himself and about three hundred men from Mühlhausen arrived at the town of Frankenhausen around 12 May. That day he poured out a torrent of brilliant abuse in letters to Count Ernst of Mansfeld and to Count Albrecht of Mansfeld, the Lutheran count who had tried to avoid taking sides against the peasants. Albrecht had recently attacked a band of miners and peasants on the way to Frankenhausen, massacring at least twenty of them at Osterhausen. Müntzer summoned the Lutheran Albrecht to appear before the whole camp and give account of his faith, castigating him for being so steeped in his 'Wittenberg soup' and 'Martinian peasant filth' that he could not see Ezekiel's prophecy that God would call on the birds of the heavens to 'consume the flesh of the princes'.[69] To Count Ernst he wrote, 'Just tell us, you miserable, wretched sack of worms, who made you a prince over the people whom God redeemed with his dear blood?' He commanded him to appear in the ring to apologise for his tyrannical behaviour and prove he was a Christian; he must answer this very day or else be attacked by the army (Haufen). The living God had commanded that Ernst should be 'overturned from your seat by force' and had given the army the power to do this, 'for you are no use to the Christian people; you are nothing but a scourge'—a worn-out old dust broom—'which chastens the friends of God'. He signed both letters as 'Thomas Müntzer with the Sword of Gideon', referring to Gideon of the Old Testament, whose small band slew the mighty forces of the Midianites. These shrill letters using the informal 'you' were highly insulting; drenched in apocalyptic expectation, they insisted that the time for battle was now. 'I'm on my way', he concluded his letter to his old enemy Ernst.[70]

Many of the men had been camping in the field for ten days or more, perhaps engaged in digging defensive ditches and building barriers, while others formulated the Frankenhausen articles based on the original Twelve Articles of Memmingen. Wolfgang, Count Bodo von Stolberg's son, who had joined the peasants, arrived in the camp, but the peasants did not trust him and took him and his followers hostage. The enemy was now the 'lords'—not the landlords or even the monks, nuns, and bishops, but those who held the sword, the rulers, the 'tyrants', and their supporters. Müntzer preached daily to the soldiers, proclaiming on the eve of battle, Sunday 14 May, that 'God the Almighty wanted now to purify the world, and had taken power away from the authorities and had given it to the ruled'. God was with them.[71]

Meanwhile the army had to decide what to do with the Mansfeld counts' scouts, Martin von Gehofen, his servant Georg Buchener, the priest Stephan Hartenstein, and two other soldiers, whom they had captured. On 13 May, their passions probably inflamed by Ernst's brother Albrecht's slaughter of men on their way to join the army, they deliberated 'in a ring' and decided to execute the three—von Gehofen, Buchener, and Hartenstein—beheading them on the spot, a decision that Müntzer later argued was 'godly justice'. A line had been crossed.[72]

The hill on which the battle was fought is high, and one can see from it for miles around. For three days before battle, a rainbow or sun halo appeared, as if the banners under which the Mühlhauseners had fought had suddenly sprung to life. The rainbow was traditionally a sign of war, but God had turned it into a covenant at the time of Noah's flood. Now it represented battle, and God's pledge that he was on their side. The insignia 'VDMIA' ('the word of God endures forever') was sewn on the flag. By a strange twist of fate, this slogan would later be taken over by the soldiers of Philip of Hesse, eventually becoming the evangelical logo.[73]

On the evening of 14 May, the peasants built a 'Wagenburg', a castle of waggons, on the steep hill above Frankenhausen, arranging all their carts in a defensible circle. Seemingly in a strong position, they had escape routes into the forest and back into town and views on all three sides. Earlier that day they had succeeded in fighting off an advance party, further raising their spirits. The delay before fighting commenced, however, had allowed Duke Georg's troops to arrive with Ernst of Mansfeld's men and had permitted the Braunschweig troops to recover. These troops moved into the forest, causing the peasants to be surrounded on all sides. Perhaps eight thousand peasants now faced an army led by Georg of Saxony, Philip of Hesse, and Erich and Heinrich of Braunschweig, comprising fifty-five hundred infantry and twenty-five hundred to three thousand mounted men.[74]

The rebel army sang Müntzer's Pentecostal hymn to the Holy Spirit, 'Nun bitten wir den Heiligen Geist', based on the old Latin hymn 'Veni creator spiritus':

> *Come to us, creator, holy ghost*
> *And illuminate your poor Christian folk*
> *Fill our hearts, which sigh to you*
> *In agony and inner turmoil.*
> Kumm zu uns schöpfer, heylger geyst,
> Erleucht deyn arme christenheyt,
> Erfull unser hertz, das zu dir seufftzet,
> Mit innerlichem schmertz.[75]

The mystical elevation of suffering had reached its apotheosis and would be sealed in blood.

CHAPTER 10

BROTHERS

The men who sang together on the Frankenhausen plateau before battle were bound by bonds of brotherhood, a deep commitment to their fellows in battle and in faith. Fraternity had created a collective loyalty between men, and the exclusion of women was part of its cement. For better and for worse, this was a movement that exalted manliness and had little to say about women. Even the Madonna had no place in it, unusual for a peasant revolt. At this moment of greatest spiritual intensity, the Frankenhausen fighters instead invoked the Holy Spirit. Drenched in the new theology of evangelicalism, everywhere the movement focused solely on God, the gospel, and Christ.

Indeed, women are almost completely absent from contemporary images of the war. The new print medium had been producing positive images of peasants, remarkable in a moment when they were otherwise depicted as animalistic, threatening, or crude. The title pages of pamphlets by the so-called Peasant of Wöhrd, Diepold Peringer, who was preaching just two years after Luther had defied the emperor at the

Diet of Worms, featured an upright, gesturing, male peasant hero, and even after Peringer had been unmasked as a fraud, his sermons continued to be printed. Over thirty editions of Peringer's pamphlets were issued between 1522 and 1525, most depicting an image of a peasant on the cover. At least fifty representations of the evangelical peasant appeared on other pamphlets and broadsheets, showing him pointing to the gospel as he importuned cardinals and bishops or argued with monks. These numbers put the evangelical peasant in the same league as Luther himself, whose face became famous because he featured on the cover of many of his writings. The image of the evangelical peasant received a back-handed compliment in 1524, when Johann Rott published a tract whose cover shows the same peasant as the Peringer pamphlets, but holding his rosary in one hand and in the other a banner depicting a fox tail, which stood for flattery, insinuating that the evangelical peasant was a fraudulent flatterer. Everyone would have recognised the Christian peasant immediately.[1]

It was his clothing that made him familiar. He sports a fine pair of boots, a short smock, and a dagger at his side. His legs are visible and his stance confident as he addresses the reader as if to instruct. His felt hat is distinctive peasant attire. When Andreas Karlstadt, Luther's former ally and later bête noir, traveled to Jena to hear Luther preach, he wore this style of felt hat, and Luther did not recognise him. In the highly hierarchical society of sixteenth-century Germany, lifting one's hat in the air denoted surrender. When the flames set by their pursuers in the village of Lupstein reached the church where peasant soldiers had locked themselves in, the men raised their hats up against the windows, but it was too late. In short, although this image of the peasant individualises him and makes him human, every marker of his appearance is male—boots, dagger, jerkin, and hat—all items that women could not wear.[2] Indeed, when the Catholic priest Nikolas Schweygker wanted to disguise himself as a peasant sympathiser to preach against revolt in a tavern, he donned a peasant jerkin, 'peasant shoes', a striped peasant hood, a peasant hat with a sprig of pine, hung a peasant waggon knife by his side, and tucked a peasant sack under his arm, as if he had stepped straight off the cover of one of the pamphlets. When the Twelve Articles of the Swabian peasants and the ordinance were printed, sometimes there was no cover illustration. But some versions repurposed the illustration of the peasant from Peringer's pamphlets, while one remarkably positive image from Zwickau showed a group of peasants deliberating together. These men wear longer jackets, placing them closer to the kind of clothes elite men might have worn. Once again, the gathering is men only.[3]

Just how closely the image Peringer made famous was linked to the peasant cause is suggested by its use after the peasants' defeat. A single-leaf woodcut that lists the castles destroyed by the peasants in 1525 shows the Christian peasant in the centre, indicating that he is to blame for the destruction. Johannes Fundling, another Catholic antagonist, published a tract in 1526 arguing that the war had been Luther's fault. The cover shows Luther the 'double-tongued' in a black cassock debating with a peasant dressed to look like the Christian peasant, but now his dagger has become a long sword and he wears a feather in his hat like a mercenary soldier. Forty years later, the image had not lost its point: a Counter-Reformation pamphlet used it to condemn Luther as a supporter of revolt.[4]

The Christian peasant's pose is as important as his attire. He gestures expansively with his arms, while his legs are apart in the 'power stance' that embodies confidence, feet firmly planted on the ground. He cannot be knocked over and looks ready to move forward. This is not the stance of the refined, horse-riding nobleman whose close-fitting boots reached up over his knee and helped him stand erect, but that of the man who earns his living through physical labour. We see his limbs in outline, not concealed by the loose-fitting gowns that town councillors or academics favoured. Legs hidden by their skirts, women could not visibly adopt the triangular power stance, let alone preach.

Standing up for things was not just a visual trope, for peasants frequently insisted that they wanted to 'stand' by the gospel. Bartel Forster, imprisoned on suspicion of involvement in the Peasants' War, wrote to the Zwickau council on 17 May, reaffirming his commitment to the ideals of the Christian man, to his Christian neighbours and brothers, and to the Twelve Articles 'which have been printed'. God's holy word and the gospel say that 'the powerful will always attack them' (i.e., the word and the gospel), while 'the poor small group'—and here he uses the same word as for the peasant armed bands—'will always remain standing by the truth'. He concluded, 'I will still stand by the holy godly word and what is according to the holy gospel even if it harms me in body or property'.[5]

Bartel Forster expected his brothers to support him and said so, even when he was interrogated with the implicit threat of torture, the language of brotherhood having become dangerous. A highly emotional term, 'brotherhood' evoked sharing, affection, and community. From the outset, peasants called each other 'brother' and addressed the members of other peasant bands as 'brothers' in fraternal rhetoric that was occasionally overwhelming. The Christian army of Stocksberg wrote to 'our Christian, dear brothers', addressing them as 'you elect, beloved, dear brothers' and referring to their 'Christian and brotherly request', which the Stocksbergers had 'received in a brotherly spirit', seeing that the other band wished to deal with them in a 'brotherly and Christian' manner. Writing to the lords, the peasants were at first conspicuously polite. They exhorted them to join the peasants as 'brothers' and were willing to accept them into their band. As the Allgäu articles put it, 'First we will stand by one another and by the Holy Gospel…and lay down life and limb for one another, for we are brothers in Christ Jesus our Saviour. And whoever presents himself to swear an oath as a brother will be accepted, so that everyone may gain justice'. So sacred was this bond that the peasants of the Odenwald band wrote to the peasants of another nearby band warning them not to attack a certain castle because they had made a bond of brotherhood with its owner. If the other band attacked their 'brother', the Odenwald band would be obliged to attack fellow peasants.[6]

And because brotherhood offered amity, it wrong-footed opponents. Even the commander of the Swabian League, Truchsess Georg, borrowed the rhetoric of Christian brotherhood to encourage his troops when they did not want to fight against the peasants, admitting that the peasants 'desire to harm no-one, except that to which they have a right, and they want to erect and institute the word of God'. He went straight on to insist, 'That's what we want too'. The chronicler Heinrich Ryhiner of Basel explained that although 'no-one could deny' that the peasants had seemed only to be asking for an investigation into their complaints on the grounds of 'brotherly love and fairness', it was still not right for them to 'throw off' their burdens themselves.[7]

A series of rituals welded manhood to political capacity. It began with the oath the brothers swore, which destroyed the feudal bond of obedience, replacing loyalty to a lord with loyalty to one's brothers. Swearing the fraternal vow was a risky act, for breaking it was punishable by chopping off the fingers with which the oath had been sworn, a mutilation that prevented the individual from working. The chronicler Peter Harer described how some loyal peasants tried to dissuade those who had formed an army and sworn an oath; they warned them, he says, in a 'manful' (*manlich*) way, because they intended 'as pious, honour-loving people to keep their duty and oath'. For Harer, an opponent of the peasants, piety, honour, and duty went together and were tightly linked to manhood. Some tried to have it both ways, swearing the fraternal oath while claiming they had not broken their oath to their ruler. When the men of Langensalza bullied the men of Tennstedt into swearing brotherhood and admitting them into town, the desperate civic worthies tried to add a proviso to the oath 'insofar as it is not in conflict with our oath to Duke Georg'—or so they later claimed, presenting themselves as victims.[8]

But for those who freely joined the rebels, brotherhood meant taking counsel democratically in a circle ('ring') out of doors, where everyone could voice their view and where all stood on the same level, a model of decision-making that went back to very old customs and ideals of a peasant past. It was also how mercenaries made decisions. It contrasted not only with the decision-making of lords and courtiers, who deliberated indoors while sitting down, but also with the proud civic town halls, which, as rebels saw it, had become the domains of the 'fat cats' and their supporters, who decided matters in secret. True democracy happened out of doors, under the village tree or on the market square outside the town hall, where groups of men could gather together and put pressure on the town council.[9]

Deciding in the ring was not just an empty ritual; decisions could and sometimes did go in ways leaders did not wish. Thomas Müntzer lost the vote to march to Heldrungen when the villagers of Niederorschel called on the army to go to the Eichsfeld first. Deliberating together meant listening to the opinions of both sides and reaching a view—though admittedly when the 'group' consisted of thousands of men, the speeches may have been inaudible to most. In Alsace, the peasants emerged from the monastery at Neuenburg, where they were camped, and formed a ring two thousand strong, and the representatives of the town of Strasbourg had to ride into it to put their case (the Strasbourgers were on horseback, which may have made them easier to hear). They were greeted formally but had to leave and wait while the men deliberated, and were then invited back to learn the decision, a procedure that underlined their supplicant status. At Rappoltstein the townsfolk gathered on the marketplace to decide whether to let the peasants in, and they had the Twelve Articles read aloud to them, but they would not allow the 'grey-headed' schoolmaster to do it, presumably because he was unsympathetic. They let their local official plead his case, but he also had to leave while they decided. Men like the schoolmaster and the local official may have needed strong nerves to appear in the assembly. On a previous occasion, when Strasbourg's representatives were invited to come to the ring at Dorlisheim and put their case, they had demurred. After all, the ring could be dangerous. It was the ring that decided to execute the servants of Count Ernst of Mansfeld. It was the ring that carried out the punishment of running the gauntlet, which meant being killed by the blows of the entire armed group, the penalty meted out to Ludwig of Helfenstein and his men at Weinsberg, and by Hans Müller's band at Vöhrenbach against the former vogt of the area.[10]

Indeed, brotherhood had moral force, and it could be invoked to police a group's own members. A field ordinance from early April established what living in a 'brotherly manner' meant for one peasant army: it banned blasphemy, drunkenness, overeating, swearing, and gaming, and declared that disorderly women were not to be tolerated in the camp. The flags, carried by the bannerman, represented the identity of the band and had to be defended. They were designed with care. Thomas Müntzer's banner, a rainbow, depicted a crucifix as well as a fish, bird, and woodland, because 'all these things will be free'. The bands' strong egalitarian ethos did not preclude their having a structure, with band leaders and officers. The provisioner or cook was one of the most important, because he ensured that the men were fed. The 'war ordinance' of the Rhine peasants reveals an organisation in which two 'Fenlein' of men went first, along with two individuals chosen from every 'Rott'. The 'gewaltig Hauf' of the main army followed. Each 'Fenlein' had its own 'Proviantmeister'. Two preachers preached daily, and four 'Postboten' took messages. 'Courts' punished those who misbehaved, firm rules dictated that all plunder was to be handed over for division, and in theory behaviour was strictly policed, especially in relation to women.[11]

Not all brothers were equal, however. In the village, richer peasants had more animals and so made more use of common pasture; they also had a larger share where the commons were divided. They needed wood and water, and they chafed as much as poorer peasants under the endless dues and impositions, but they had increasingly monopolised the important offices of the Gemeinde. One village with the same landlord might pay more in dues than another, and neighbouring villages under different landlords might have very different obligations. And yet to a considerable extent, brotherhood could override differences of wealth, status, or type of tenure within the peasantry.

In the case of the Weinsberg area, we know something about the comparative wealth and standing of seventy-one of the rebels. They came from fourteen different places in an area of about twenty kilometres at its widest. Only twelve were from the town of Weinsberg itself, including two married women whose husbands were described as 'obedient and honourable', so these women had evidently acted without their approval and had done something significant enough to be included on a comparatively short list; their story would be worth knowing. Eighteen were assessed as owning 'nothing', which meant nothing of value—a tax assessment term, it did not mean they were destitute. But a surprising number, seventeen, had substantial possessions, while several had been *Schultheißen* (mayors) and owned substantial property. One owned a house and barn, meadows, an orchard, parts of two woods, fields for grazing and for crops, and several vineyards valued at 570 fl. Another owned a house, barn, and farm by the brook, a second farm that was his wife's dowry, and extensive fields and vineyards valued at 860 Gulden. These men of substance were local community leaders whose participation suggests that the cause was backed by local elites.[12]

By contrast, Hans Schierkner's property was valued at only 40 fl. Even though his property was 'worth' far less, by his measure he had a lot to lose. As did German von Rapach, who owned possessions valued at 'absolutely nothing' except a 'rotten' little house, a little garden beside it, and some fields and vineyards, all of which would have taken time to build up. Thirty-six of the group had possessions of this order, worth under 100 fl. All were integrated into a complex local economy of interlocking debts, inheritance claims, and dues. The tenant farmers, cottagers, and day labourers depended on each other, the richer peasants employing the cottagers and day labourers at busy times, the poorer needing the oxen and horses of the richer to plough their fields, which together formed a scattered patchwork abutting those of their neighbours. Eight peasants paid the ultimate price for their participation in the revolt and were executed, two of them by the unusual punishment of poison. In the regions where we can work out the wealth of the rebels it is clear that both tenant farmers and day labourers, rich and poor, joined forces, and all could subscribe to the articles because all had a stake in farming—even the poorest day labourer with a garden understood himself as a peasant.

This is not to deny that there were divisions of wealth and power. At the abbey of Ottobeuren, it seems that it was the richer peasants who led the earlier phase of revolt, when negotiations with the lords dominated; when the revolt became more radical, it was the poorer who acted. A week after the revolt had begun, negotiations with the abbot resumed, but the sack of the monastery was led by a poor day labourer and former mercenary. Nearly 80 per cent of those who 'instigated and led' the revolt were tenant farmers, whereas two-thirds of those we can identify as 'radicals' were craftsmen and day labourers. But to conclude that this count defines clear parties of radicals and traditionalists that corresponded to divisions of wealth may push the evidence too far. There was no clear distinction between earlier and 'radical' phases of the revolt, and we do not know exactly who took part in which actions or whether the wealthier peasants also supported (or did not support) storming the monasteries; it would, after all, have made sense for a mercenary with military experience who knew how to storm a monastery to take the lead. The number of town craftsmen amongst those who can be identified as 'radical' also muddies any class reading. Despite differences of wealth and tenure type, in 1525 peasants seem not to have articulated these factors in their demands or their theology. Instead they stressed what joined them together in brotherhood.[13]

Brotherhood could have its darker side. One commander wrote to the community of Bietigheim, 'We want you to come and give us brotherly troth'. But if you won't, he went on, 'we will come to you,…and you won't be laughing'. Near Heidelberg, peasants assembled at church ales (one of the few occasions when, significantly, peasants could bear arms), and they met at night too, waking others from their beds (so this hostile observer wrote) and compelling them to join with them in brotherhood. Many peasant communities said they were 'forced' to join the brothers, though it was politic to say so after the peasants' defeat.[14]

At first, brotherhood was a highly inclusive idea: any man, it seemed, could become a brother. But what did peasants mean by it? And how did it function politically? Offering brotherhood to the lords was a claim to social equality, akin to the demand that lords dismount from their horses to speak with peasants on their level. It was also an emotional appeal, an attempt to lance the potential aggression by offering kinship and love. Brotherly love was about creating a Christian world where there would be no division, class, or enmity, and where injustice would be overturned by the affective bond of fraternity. Many of the Thuringian nobility eventually agreed to swear brotherhood with the peasants, and the peasants compelled them to do so because they believed the oaths would neutralise the nobles' opposition. This was how the noble Florian Geyer could become a leader of the Taubertal peasants, or how peasants could appoint the knight Götz von Berlichingen as their commander; he claimed to have been surprised into it when he was drinking outside a pub. Genuine ties of affection overrode identifying him as an enemy—at least, as he remembered it when writing his memoirs in old age. He was not unique: Hans Hake of Hackpfüffel, a noble, was forced to become a peasant commander 'not out of joy of pleasure' but because of 'fear and compulsion', as he later excused his behaviour to Duke Georg of Saxony. In the Samland, one local notable was forced to interrupt his breakfast, swear brotherhood, and join in the peasants' march after drinking a brandy with their commander, a miller. Towns might be willing to espouse brotherhood with the peasant armies encamped outside them, and many of the townsfolk saw the peasant cause as their own. Brotherhood created bonds of kinship, inviting groups of people together in an open, inclusive manner and calling on them to fight for the gospel. Against whom they were fighting could remain at this point unclear, a naivety that led Engels to conclude loftily that amongst the 'plebeians and peasants', only the 'most advanced section' under Thomas Müntzer was truly revolutionary, 'a small minority of the insurgent masses'.[15]

Once sworn, that bond of fraternity was lived out above all in drinking, eating, sleeping, and marching together. The rights for which the brothers fought were also male: the right of the Gemeinde to appoint the preacher, the right to hunt, the right to be 'free'. Jacob Murer's pictorial chronicle of the war shows the peasants with their swords, hats, and boots refusing the offer of 'frid' (peace) and fighting on. Men for the most part are the ones described as fishing out the monastic ponds and mocking the monks, who, unlike the peasants, did not know how to fish with their hands; the right to hunt stags with their majestic antlers clearly staked a claim to manhood; and though the Twelve Articles does not spell it out, the freedom that Christ bought for us all was not a freedom that compelled men to share property or political rights with women.

There was also respect for age. A certain Lienhart, whose surname we do not know, found himself made a captain 'so that the young ones might be more likely to follow him'. He later claimed that the rebels had threatened to smash his grey head and destroy all his household goods if he refused, but their assumption that his age would mean the younger peasants would obey him is revealing. At meetings of the Gemeinde in the ring at Salem, we know that men spoke in order of age, the eldest first, so their view on whether to join the peasants would shape the discussion.[16]

Joining the rebels gave men agency, allowing them to fight back instead of passively enduring worsening conditions, humiliating treatment, and lack of status. Men who were prospering, growing new crops, and engaging in the market may have felt infantilised by having to obtain permission from the lords to get married or even to leave their village overnight. Their increasing confidence may have led them to feel anger at having to have collective decisions approved by lords, their agency hemmed in at every turn, and it is notable that many village officeholders and richer peasants joined the armies when they might have been expected to support the status quo.

Inside the peasant armies men counted for something. Though peasant leaders might have dominated the assemblies when it was time to make a decision, they could not take their outcome for granted. Mostly their commanders and officials were experienced folk who were used to giving orders, but this was not true of everyone. Hans Müller of Bulgenbach, for instance, was a tavern keeper, Erasmus Gerber a minor craftsman, possibly a leatherworker. The local armed band counted for something too. When a band sent fateful letters to the next village offering it brotherhood but threatening to 'come to you' if it refused to join, there may have been some pleasure gained from bullying a neighbouring, possibly rival, village. Together in the large group, the peasants' sheer numbers made them strong.

Ultimately, brotherhood meant being willing to risk one's life to defend a brother. As the author of the pamphlet *An die Versammlung* put it in an admonition that mixed sacramental theology, militarism, and manly metaphor, 'Remain firmly together in all godly fear, brotherly faithfulness and love, so that you all become one body under the head Jesus Christ. Thus Christ and true God will certainly become your army leader. Therefore be manly, courageous and unshocked, no matter how big and strong the godless army that rushes against you. Your own conscience will beat them and drive them to flight as Solomon said, Proverbs 28'. As the rebels made decisions together, lived in bands far away from their womenfolk, and felt their power in the group, they learnt to trust each other and prepared for what the months of massing together were designed to do: take on the lords by strength of arms and numbers, with whatever weapons they had. They believed they would win because God was on their side.[17]

Monasteries and convents, the institutions of religious brotherhood, were the war's major targets. In the region of the war itself, nearly 45 per cent of all monastic institutions were physically attacked, an astounding figure. Monks and nuns from rich orders were particularly exposed. Premonstratensians, Cistercians, Benedictines—all orders that emphasised prayer and study, and many of whose foundations were wealthy—had nearly two-thirds of their monasteries and convents attacked. Franciscans, Augustinians, and Dominicans, orders vowed to poverty, seem to have fared better. Just over a quarter of the Augustinian houses were attacked, just under one-fifth of the Franciscans. Female monastic institutions do not appear to have been attacked more often than male ones, though there may have been assaults on convents that were not recorded. Nuns of the rich orders seem to have been particularly vulnerable, and half of Dominican nunneries suffered attack compared to only one-third of their male counterparts. By contrast, whereas nearly three-quarters of male Cistercian monasteries were hit, the figure for female Cistercian convents was two-thirds. In total, over 530 institutions at least were attacked, many severely damaged. These were often rich, extensive institutions with large sets of imposing, sometimes heated buildings that were stocked with elaborate furniture, paintings, costly plate, fabric, books, and written records.

By any measure, this was an extraordinary level of destruction, an assault on what had been major cultural and religious centres. In some areas, such as Thuringia and parts of Saxony, the damage was even more extreme there; 70 per cent of the monasteries and convents were attacked. Its extent demonstrates how bitter and how widespread hatred of monasteries and convents had become. For those targeted by the destruction, it was traumatic; for those on the other side, it was liberating. It was about getting rid of the convents and monasteries that had exploited them for so long, the false brothers whose actions were the antithesis of the ethos of brotherhood. It was also an impassioned assault on monastic manhood.

The figures give little sense of the personal indignities the attacks could involve. At Weissenau, Abbot Murer suffered disgrace when a peasant became abbot in his place while he himself scurried to Ravensburg, taking the monastery's silver and valuables with him. The illustrated chronicle he later commissioned shows the peasants driving the monks out of their own refectory but does not give the peasant-abbot's name, perhaps a form of revenge that denied the peasant a place in the monastery's history. Even after the rebels' defeat and Murer's return to the monastery, the peasants would not swear their oath of loyalty to Murer. They all stood before him on the square in front of the tavern, each with weapon in hand, and 'looked at me in rage', Murer wrote, saying they wanted nothing but godly and imperial 'justice'. His abbatial authority lost, Murer then had no choice but to summon troops from the league to compel 'his' peasants to swear. The final image of the chronicle shows the world right way up at last, as the peasants swear allegiance under duress.[18]

The fury and sheer scale of such attacks can scarcely be imagined. After the evangelical Gabriel Didymus had preached in Torgau, the town's Franciscan monastery church was comprehensively destroyed on Ash Wednesday 1525. The votive lamps in front of the sacrament were smashed, an altar recently commissioned from the leading artist Lukas Cranach for the sum of fifty Gulden was destroyed, the ornamented choir stalls were demolished, the curtain in front of the choir

Table 10.1: ATTACKS ON MONASTIC INSTITUTIONS DURING THE PEASANTS' WAR

	ALL INSTITUTIONS	ATTACKED	MALE	ATTACKED	FEMALE	ATTACKED
TOTAL	1,218	534 (44%)	788	342 (43%)	431	193 (45%)
MAJOR ORDERS						
CISTERCIANS	172	113 (66%)	46	34 (74%)	126	79 (63%)
BENEDICTINES	213	138 (65%)	152	98 (64%)	62	40 (65%)
PREMONSTRATENSIANS	49	32 (65%)	34	21 (62%)	15	11 (73%)
CARTHUSIANS	17	10 (59%)				
DOMINICANS	78	33 (42%)	33	11 (33%)	44	22 (50%)
TEUTONIC KNIGHTS	57	23 (40%)			44	
WILLIAMITES	16	6 (38%)				
AUGUSTINIANS	241	91 (38%)	188	74 (39%)	53	17 (32%)
CARMELITES	32	9 (28%)				
HOSPITALERS	58	11 (19%)				
FRANCISCANS	206	39 (19%)	115	31 (27%)	91	8 (9%)
ANTONITES	22	3 (14%)				
SMALLER ORDERS (under 10 houses)						
PAULINES	6	5 (83%)				
SERVITES	9	5 (56%)				
MISCELLANEOUS	42	16 (38%)	2	0	40	16 (40%)

Note: The table is based on the results of the project known as Destruction of Monasteries and Convents During the German Peasants' War 1524–6, funded by John Fell and the British Academy. I am grateful to Louisa Bergold, who compiled the figures (which are based on Jürgensmeier and Schwerdtfeger, *Orden und Klöster*; the database Germania Sacra; all available online sources; and all major printed primary sources from the Peasants' War). She did this by first identifying all the monastic institutions in the region of the Peasants' War, and then establishing those attacked. I also thank my coinvestigator Edmund Wareham Wanitzek. We are preparing an online digital map with the help of Charlotte Gauthier.

was ripped, and the huge breviary from which the monks read mass was slashed through with a sword. The attackers rammed the monastery gate with a big tree, and the crowd then headed for the monks' dormitory, where they smashed all the doors and windows. They tore the hood of the monastery's guardian and almost killed him. They forced another monk to jump out a window and hunted him through a fire, while yet another leapt over a wall, falling and injuring himself. Their targeting of the dormitory, the area where the monks slept, probably reflected popular rumour about what lascivious activities the monks got up to. Shortly after, the monastery was dissolved for good.[19]

Near Altenburg, the Catholic preacher armed himself to give a sermon. For good reason: passing a monastery on his return home, he was shot at by an evangelical and his 'mob' ('lose rotte'). They were tormenting the monks, screaming 'a monk, a wolf, a rascal, a knave, a thief', and trying to throw the monks in the pond. Such terrifying assaults could bring monasteries to collapse. At Coburg, the Franciscan monastery dissolved itself on 4 May, and the fifteen brothers who lived there (plus two who were absent) gave all its property and its building to the town council, explaining that they had entered the monastery out of misunderstanding and ignorance.[20]

Nuns were attacked too. Sophia von Schafstädt was abbess of the convent of Naundorf whose Marian chapel at Mallerbach had already been burnt down by Müntzer's followers in Allstedt a year before. Now that her convent, too, was in danger, she left for Halle and asked Hans Zeiß, the official at Allstedt, and Georg Spalatin, Luther's close friend at the court, for help. All Zeiß could suggest was that she flee because, he warned her, Müntzer was on his way. She returned to find the whole district occupying her convent, but Müntzer was nowhere to be seen. She clearly thought Zeiß was playing a double game, frightening her into leaving the convent and then informing the locals she had gone. The crowd had already helped itself to two barrels of convent beer and a ton of cheese together with other food. They had let out all the animals, the geese, the hens, and even the doves, and had opened the doors of the convent about ten times, insulting the nuns. Schafstädt tried to get the nuns and the children they cared for to safety in the castle at Allstedt, but Zeiß refused even to let them stay overnight in its stables for fear the enraged populace might attack the castle. Zeiß, who had most likely supported Müntzer at first while keeping his employer the elector on side, was a wily character, but respect for convents had gone, and there was probably little he could do. In monastery after monastery, abbots were unable to protect their monks, even by using their knightly connections, and because monks and other clergy were usually unarmed, they were easy prey for peasant bands. When the peasants got in, they destroyed the libraries and archives, especially the documents relating to lordship.[21]

But not all monasteries were destroyed. At Maulbronn, Jäcklein Rohrbach himself ensured that the buildings were spared because, as he explained, they were beautiful. Sometimes monasteries located close to one another met strikingly different fates. In the hills of Alsace, the convent buildings of St Odile (Hohenburg) were left intact, and the peasants even promised to return goods of the abbess that they had in 'safe-keeping' (though the abbess does not seem to have been entirely reassured). Yet at Niedermünster, lower down the same hill, the convent was burnt to the ground. The abbess had tried to protect her convent by becoming a citizen of Strasbourg and invoking its protection, but the peasants regarded her action as a hostile stratagem.[22]

Having kicked out the monks, the peasants sometimes moved in— the buildings were after all ideally suited to housing a different kind of brotherhood. Some abbots cravenly ran away, leaving the brothers to fend for themselves. Especially where the abbot was a local ruler from a noble family with his own castle, he might not even be present in the monastery. The prior at Ochsenhausen pleaded with their abbot to 'take their anxiety to heart as a faithful and either return in person to deal with the peasants or else let them swear brotherhood with them'.

Elsewhere those who could did their best to profit from the situation. In Thuringia the local official placed valuables from the monasteries of Roda and Rohrbach in his own office for 'safe-keeping', but when he tried to do the same at another monastery, its own provost stole two waggons full of valuables and made off in the night over the border. Which of the two was really despoiling the monasteries, official or provost, we do not know.[23]

Brotherhood was not generally open to monks and priests, nor was it offered to Jews and other non-Christians. Balthasar Hubmaier's attraction to the ideal of a pure Christian community bound together by baptism and disciplined by the ban may have been related to his earlier militant antisemitism, when his preaching had incited the expulsion of the Jews from Regensburg and supported the pilgrimage to the 'beautiful Maria' of the chapel built on the site of the former synagogue. In 1520, Johann Teuschlin, another passionate devotee of Mary who later became a Reformation leader in Rothenburg ob der Tauber, wrote a particularly nasty antisemitic pamphlet on usury comparing the Jews to pigeon manure that makes the fields on which it is spread unfertile. If secular judges would not act against usury, religious authorities should use the ban as a weapon against the Jews, he argued, and all contact between Christians and Jews who charged usurious interest should be stopped until the interest was repaid. It is hard to know how much of his earlier antisemitism coloured his preaching during the war. In the Rheingau, the articles of the peasants demanded that 'no Jew should have his dwelling or housing in the territory because of the great harmful damage which they cause the common man', nor should judges uphold Jews' claims for interest payments.[24]

In one of the worst outbreaks of antisemitic violence, a crowd of five thousand in Bergheim in Alsace smashed the tablets of the law and ripped up Jewish books; the Jews were forced into a single building and their pawned goods offered back to their debtors. The articles of the

Sundgau and upper Alsace called for the expulsion of the Jews, as did those of Kastel. The town of Mainz wanted Jews banned from selling clothes, and Frankfurt demanded they be banned from charging usurious interest; pawned items should be returned for free.[25] These same articles also expatiated on the values of Christian brotherhood. Other articles, though, such as those of the Bildhausen band, did allow that Jews might even be permitted to join the armed bands, provided they did not engage in usury, and there is some evidence that the Strasbourg authorities may even have cooperated with Josel of Rosheim when he tried to protect Jewish communities. Overall, though the strong Christian communalism of the Peasants' War and its hostility to monasteries and usury might easily have descended into violent populist antisemitism, it does not appear to have done so. For the most part, antisemitism centred on usury and property and did not turn into violence against people.[26]

Not so for monks. The rebels' position was that no one should be allowed thenceforth to become a monk. Those who wished to could leave, and those who were there 'should die out', while mendicants were forbidden. Or as the Frankfurt articles had it, the monks 'who begged money off the citizens with false spirituality' should no longer be permitted to beg, preach, or hear confession, and should be forbidden to take on novices. The Catholic monks and friars, whose brotherhood the peasants displaced, were taunted for their lack of masculinity because they did not carry arms, were not citizens, were clean-shaven, concealed their bodies under loose-fitting, belted cassocks, and were meant to be celibate. It was the Catholic rural parish clergy whose beer the marauding peasants downed and whose animals and manure they stole; it was the hated monks whom they terrorised. Peasant fraternity was also about despising those who did not conform to the rebels' vision of manhood.[27] In Fulda, where the peasants stormed the monks' property, 'there is no monk left either in the Stift or on the hills'—they had all fled to safety. In Saxony, anticlericalism went further, with peasants reportedly torturing priests with the 'gentleman's rope' ('heren strick'), pulling a rope back and forth through the crotch area, until the priests gave them everything they had. Such sexual humiliation was designed to destroy their authority for good.[28]

For those former priests and monks who became preachers and leaders in peasant armies, the Reformation had upended what it meant to be a man. For some, it meant a discovery of Christ's manhood as well as their own. 'Within two years Christ began to blossom in my heart. I have never been able to preach him so manfully as now, by the Grace of God', wrote Hubmaier, proudly refusing a position as a Catholic priest in Regensburg in 1524. Once tonsured celibates, many of them had by then married, had children, or had grown their hair and wore beards, mostly adopting lay clothing.[29]

These steps were a huge shock for men who had never had to worry about domestic duties and who had been immediately recognised as belonging to particular orders by their clothing. All this was very new during this era of the Peasants' War, for the earliest evangelical clergy had only married within the preceding five years. Some pastors even dressed as soldiers, breaking the taboo against clergy carrying weapons. Luther's adaptation of the scholarly *talar* as the pastor's uniform lay in the future. Perhaps the fact that one route to a paid position was through becoming known as an inspiring preacher—which was how Müntzer and Wehe made their careers—encouraged them to be more radical and win an audience. Preaching outdoors in the field on horseback or held aloft by the peasants was a far cry from preaching in a pulpit, and it required the ability to hold a crowd. Instead of deciding to become a monk in an institution with its own hierarchy, or cultivating a patron to gain a coveted benefice, the evangelical preacher was appointed by the Gemeinde, the community, the group that met in a ring. In a time of revolt, his employer was effectively the military band, his new brothers.

* * *

Brotherhood was not apparently open to women either. Its rituals were male: women could not swear oaths, bear arms, take counsel in the circle with their menfolk, wear the peasant boots and hat, or become part of the peasant military. The common man might be the hero of the Reformation, but in sixteenth-century parlance, the 'common woman' was a prostitute, one of the targets of evangelical moralism.[30]

This did not mean, however, that women did not play an active part in the war, or that the idea of brotherhood did not attract them. The Catholic conservative and anti-Lutheran Johannes Cochlaeus was specifically appalled by the women who joined the movement, whom he regarded as culpable. He believed they followed the preachers more audaciously, and so the 'wives' of the Leipheimers had been rightly punished by being forced to wear the town symbol of Ulm on their clothes for the next thirty years, because they 'were so completely Lutheran that they forced and incited their menfolk to revolt'. Wearing the badge of Ulm made them look like prostitutes since in many towns those who worked in the brothel wore distinctive badges on their clothes. In Allstedt, the electoral official noted after the war that the spirit of Müntzer had so taken root amongst women that it was harder to 'eradicate' it from them than from men. In Rothenburg ob der Tauber, four women staged a riot outside the house of Conrad Volkmaner, priest at Our Lady's chapel. Like French Revolutionary women over two centuries later, they attacked a cart full of grain that was standing outside his house and then broke in and plundered it, crimes that went unpunished. At Rappoltstein, the women went out with their menfolk to the beat of drums to cut large stakes from the trees, as the worried noble official noted, and they marched around the small town with a ragged flag, demanding wine.[31]

In Waldshut, the women joined the men at Pfingsten in 1524 to protect their preacher Balthasar Hubmaier. Müntzer was also known for the enthusiasm of his female followers, but women in Mühlhausen had long broken barriers. One woman said she had held mass herself with the support of the 'preacher', Heinrich Pfeiffer, Müntzer's later ally. If true this would be a remarkable instance of a woman taking on the role of a priest. Contrary to 'female modesty' and what was 'fitting', as alleged in a complaint against her after the war was over, a sister-in-law of the local government official took a prominent role in events, even voting at the key meeting where Müntzer's followers instituted an Eternal Revolutionary Council. At Allstedt, it was reported that back in July 1524, when pressure was growing on Müntzer in the lead-up to his interrogation at Weimar, the women had joined together 'with their weapons' after the early morning sermon and had formed their own band; 'they wanted to ring the storm bell, which was forbidden them'. And after the war was over, there were reports that the Allstedt women continued to support their former preacher. In Windsheim, sixty women planned to attack the Augustinian monastery and met at midnight armed with axes and hacksaws. These were all townswomen, who may have found it easier to act because they could do so locally and without marching long distances. They were certainly not contenting themselves with 'fitting' or 'modest' behaviour. Women were amongst those named as rebels in the area around Freiburg.[32] In January 1525, Müntzer's wife, Ottilie von Gersen, led a group of women in a riot at the village of Mülverstedt, where they interrupted the sung vesper service of the prior of the Wilhelmite monastery, another of the few cases where women are known to have acted as a group, 'completely contrary to Christian order', as the local official put it. After the peasants' defeat, 'all' the women of Dettwang were imprisoned for having mowed the meadow of the commander of the Teutonic Knights and taken his hay, a fragment that suggests women's resistance was ongoing. It is difficult to know how far peasant women were simply subsumed under their menfolk, how often they joined in the marching as part of a baggage train, or how much they supported the cause by assuming the agricultural labour or the mining work the men left behind.[33]

Margareta Renner was notorious. She was known as the Black Hofmännin because she was the widow of the farmer ('Hofmann') of the Teutonic Knights. As a close associate of Jäcklein Rohrbach, the ruthless leader from Böckingen near Heilbronn who led the Weinsberg massacre, she marched with the army from Sontheim to Erlenbach and Binswangen up to Öhringen, and then in the direction of Schöntal before turning back to Lichtenstern, a distance of probably over a hundred kilometres. A Joan of Arc figure, she not only admonished the troops to be brave, 'keck', but also blessed them, so that 'neither lance nor halberd or musket should harm them'. She claimed to have often been Rohrbach's 'advisor', 'ratgebin', an interesting female form of the word. She had been at Weinsberg, she claimed, and she had nothing but contempt for the Heilbronners, who were 'rascals'. 'No stone must remain on top of another; [Heilbronn] must be turned into a village like Böckingen', she proclaimed. She probably meant that its walls must be destroyed. The Heilbronners had tried to keep the peasant army outside town and had even shot at them as they passed by. While the two factions in Heilbronn wrestled for control of the walls and gates, those supporting the council were getting women to bring earth and stones to block the entrances, while the women supporting the peasants tried to keep the gates open and shouted at the others.[34]

Renner boasted that she had stuck her knife into the Count of Helfenstein at Weinsberg and had wiped the grease from his body onto her shoes. She said they should 'cut off the clothes of the stinking gracious ladies in front of their arses, so that they should go about like plucked geese'. When the moderate rebel leader Hans Berlin had explained the peasants' demands in public at Heilbronn and had also insisted that property rights should not be harmed, and tithes, interest, and so forth should be paid as before, she had retorted that, by Christ's sufferings, Berlin was cheating them, and she would be the first to stick a knife in him. It is hard to know what to make of her bloodthirsty Rabelaisian humour. The image of the bare-bottomed noble ladies is unforgettable, as is her fondness for the knife, the only weapon women could use. But when the war was over, her relatives insisted that she had only been imprisoned in Heilbronn because of her 'unguarded mouth', and her lord interceded for her. He added, 'The female sex does not carry out its threats except with their mouths, and they have no effect with deeds'. Perhaps misogynist tropes worked in her favour. Her boldness and lack of reticence under interrogation are remarkable. Or perhaps she was indeed more of a big mouth than a murderess, and though she was imprisoned she escaped Rohrbach's terrible fate.[35]

But so far as we know, she was an exception. Women are not pictured in Jacob Murer's contemporary visual chronicle of the Peasants' War, and men alone are shown storming the convent of Weissenau and massing in peasant bands, though we know that women did take part in plundering the convent there. When the authorities forced rebels to name their coconspirators, they listed men. Everywhere the language of the peasants celebrated maleness, even while some women were defying social expectations of womanhood. The author of the tract *An die Versammlung gemeiner Bauernschaft*, which praised brotherhood so fulsomely, also admonished the peasants to fight for 'your houses, and your wives and children too', a classic statement of patriarchal values.[36]

There may have been more than a streak of misogyny in the rebels' attitude towards nuns, especially those who were allowed by the rules of their order to own property and whose foundations were rich. Such convents were frequently attacked by the peasants. Often situated outside towns and housing noblewomen, they were obvious targets. Women could share this envious antagonism; one group of peasant women threatened the nuns of the convent of Heggbach that if the soldiers killed their husbands, 'they would come into the convent and scratch their eyes out'. The nuns would have to milk the cows and wear poor clothes while the peasant women wore clean ones, and they would be forced to become army camp followers and have 'a taste of the pains of childbirth'.[37]

Soon threats turned into action. Rebel soldiers entered the convent and were only prevented from driving the nuns out and setting the convent on fire when the faithful convent steward pleaded with them not to do so, showing considerable courage. In Schlotheim, the mob stole the convent women's feather pillows along with other valuables; this convent was full of noblewomen whose comforts the peasants envied. Furious abbesses complained that the officials who should have protected them tricked them instead; others used what connections they could to move their valuables and get their nuns to safety. Perhaps these highly articulate, competent, elite nuns were attacked because they were powerful women whose lordship over their peasants may have been especially resented because of their sex. As a group, nuns were hated for their wealth and apparent idleness, and their learning and spiritual accomplishments that had been built up over centuries were trashed. Many nuns certainly feared sexual violence from the bands of armed men, and felt they had no option but to flee to the towns. Some even joined with convents of different orders for protection, which entailed losing their distinct identities and histories. Whereas monks could take up a trade or become preachers, this was not an option for women, who had few choices apart from marriage if they left the convent (Ottilie von Gersen, who married Müntzer, and Katharina von Bora, who married Luther, were both former nuns). Whether or not their fears were justified, there does seem to have been a current of misogyny that helped to hold brotherhood together.[38]

At Frankenhausen, so commentators noted, all the 'burger', the male citizens, were slain—and while we do not know for sure that the word 'burger' excluded women, they are not mentioned in accounts of the bloodbath. By contrast, women do appear in accounts of rituals of surrender. In Mühlhausen the women had to go to the camp to sue for terms. Twelve hundred women and five hundred maidens pleaded with the victors, the women dressed in humble clothes and the maidens decked with wormwood garlands. In Leipheim they did the same, as if wiping out the actions of their menfolk. The Frankenhausen women were forced to punish one priest who had supposedly led them on. He was beaten in the marketplace with such vehemence that the blows continued for half an hour after he was dead, according to a shocked letter writer. Writing to Cardinal Albrecht of Mainz, one clerical dignitary remarked, 'I can tell your grace in truth, that few women cry especially or mourn their men, which amazes everyone a great deal'.Perhaps he mistook indifference for a proud unwillingness to reveal to a member of the hated clergy what defeat meant.[39]

As the authorities in the wider region tried to round up the ringleaders after the war, they turned to the rebels' wives, threatening that they and their children would be turned off their land and their houses burnt to the ground if they did not surrender their menfolk within four days—suggesting that the authorities, at least, regarded the men as guilty and the women as their accessories. Even so, in Mühlhausen the sick, elderly wife of Claus Kreutter, who refused to betray her husband, was locked out of her house; her money was taken and she was left on the street. The keys to her house were seized by the council, and she was humiliated by being carried to prison in Mühlhausen in a baking trough. She was whipped through town, branded on both cheeks, and exiled—this was the woman who had earlier conducted mass herself. More commonly it was the men who had broken their oaths to the authorities, sworn brotherhood with their fellows, and massed in the peasant 'armies', who were punished.[40]

One group amongst the rebels may have played a special role in radicalising the ethos of manhood that brought them to the brink of massing against the lords and implicitly declaring war: the mercenaries, or

Landsknechte. The victory at Pavia in February had allowed Truchsess Georg to recruit the returning mercenary troops for use on German soil. At first he used them to put down the peasant rebels, and then he had to deploy them to defeat Duke Ulrich before resuming his campaign to repress the peasants. But though we cannot know exactly what happened, it seems that many mercenaries were unwilling to join the lords, lending their skill in fighting and their weapons to the peasant army instead, sometimes for pay. They had their own culture, too, one that celebrated manhood just as vigorously.

Mercenaries were generally recruited from the ranks of poor peasants and townsfolk, and military service offered these men social mobility. If a town was sacked, a mercenary could hope to win rich booty, valuable plate, cloth, or even jewels, acceptable spoils of war because pay was often slow in coming or might never appear. All these items then had to be transported, and so an army usually had waggons of plunder in its rear, a practice that the peasants followed too. Reliant on their skill in wielding the pike or lance, mercenaries were proud of their physical strength. They were famed for spending money on fabulous clothes, slashed doublets that allowed the silk lining underneath to show, gorgeous trousers that reached only below the knee to reveal their impressive leg muscles, and hats with extravagant feathers. Uniforms did not exist, and their garments must have created a riot of colour, very different from the monochrome peasant attire. Their clothes became a byword for luxury, the frilly finery creating a kind of hyperbolic manhood that was tempting to mock. Of course, few could have afforded such magnificent clothes, and war would have left them ragged and dirty.

They, too, celebrated brotherhood. They were trained to rely on each other and stand firm in the face of terrifying assaults from men on horseback. Military tactics depended on keeping formation, and foot soldiers were only safe in the group; if some fled, all were at risk. Soldiers were used to eating and sleeping out of doors and knew how to make encampments. They knew how to walk long distances in rough weather and how to live off the land if needed. Brotherhood as a religious value could resonate with them, and the preaching of the clergy who fought with the peasants may have inspired them as well.

Peasants knew their terrain, and they were often surprisingly skilled in choosing the best sites from which to meet their enemies. Indeed, for many the life of a mercenary was a temporary expedient, not a permanent choice. Jäcklein Rohrbach, for example, had fought in the army of the Swabian League in 1519 before returning to his farm in Böckingen. The redoubtable Hans Müller of Bulgenbach, who led the peasants of the Breisgau, had been a mercenary in France. Many had had similar careers, a fact that may help explain why the peasants were able to organise their armies so speedily. They made brotherhood work. Quickly they constructed a system of captains, bands, and larger bands, and a set of officials such as provosts and captains, all of which mimicked the structures of the armies they knew. The rebels realised very early that they needed field ordinances and systems of discipline and justice that would ensure that the large groups of men who were not used to living in such crowds, let alone fighting together, would obey. Some armies even set up prominent gallows in towns to frighten any villains in their own ranks into behaving properly.[41]

Fighting required weapons. Many of the peasant fighters had only easy-to-make short lances (*Sauspiesse*) with crude pointed metal ends, not the long lances that could be used to deadly effect in massed blocs against cavalry. Some had little more than agricultural tools: pitchforks, scythes mounted on long poles, flails studded with nails. But some were quite well armed, with muskets, cannon, and gunpowder, perhaps captured or seized from well-stocked town arsenals and castles. They were also able to purchase arms with plunder. The feudal levy meant that some lords had armed their peasants, to their later regret. Lorenz Fries commented wryly that the peasants apparently obeyed all the lords' orders willingly, checked their weapons, readied their waggons, and remained at home awaiting the bishop's summons; 'and they came without even being asked—only [it was] not to support their lords, but against them, and to their harm'. As the East German historian Siegfried Hoyer has pointed out, the peasant bands were most effective in small, mobile attacking groups, from which they could inflict heavy losses on the enemy. In massed, pitched battle their lack of training showed, and they could not withstand the onslaught of cavalry. Though they often chose good strategic positions, they tended to form a Wagenburg, a circle of waggons, and defend it, losing the advantages of surprise and attack. Theirs was an ethos of defence based on securing the land and its fruits, and protecting their wives and children.[42]

Plunder posed a major challenge to the ethos of brotherhood. Mercenaries and many peasants expected to win booty, and for some at least this was a key reason for joining. After all, the revolt had begun in the early days of spring with people feasting in monasteries, drinking the priests' beer, or simply picnicking outside as if they were celebrating a church ale. It was not much of a step to stealing the priests' vegetables or animals or taking the odd valuable—and many explained that if they had not plundered 'their' priest's house or monastery, outsiders would have stripped it. When these bands coalesced into armies, they had to establish finances to purchase food and weapons on a more permanent basis and could not afford to allow all the capital they took from the monasteries to be divided amongst the fighters. All the ordinances insisted that booty must be noted down and deposited with the central chancellery of the army; no one was to enrich himself, and only limited distributions were permitted.

The possibilities for corruption were huge, but mostly people seem to have respected the rules. Surprisingly few were later accused of having purloined goods or money, even though this was an obvious accusation to make. Though church officials and nobles produced long lists of the goods they had lost, and sought to recover items like stolen chalices, they mostly accepted monetary compensation instead. The few accusations of theft largely concerned objects so trifling that it seems the principles really were honoured. So where was it all? What happened to the fabulous treasure that had been taken from the house of the Teutonic Knights in Heilbronn, or the abbot of Kempten's castle in Liebenthann? It had probably been absorbed by the treasuries of the army and used to finance the war, for the repeated mobilisations of armed men would only have been possible with money. Ironically, the capital of the monks helped pay for the armies of the peasants, one form of brotherhood unwittingly financing another.

As the lords' situation became more desperate, they made ever greater attempts to recruit mercenaries, offering them large sums to join the nobles' forces. It was hopeless, at least at first. In Alsace, they relied on troops who were not local and did not even speak German. We have the bemused account of the French Catholic loyalist Nicolas Vollcyr, who fought against the 'Lutheran' peasantry and could not understand a word they said. The troops of the Swabian League mutinied at Dagersheim and after the battle of Leipheim; they were loyal to one another more than to their commander Truchsess Georg. But the truchsess did eventually recruit the men he needed, and he gradually sent troops to others who needed them, while Philip of Hesse and Georg of Saxony were apparently able to count on their own loyal troops. When the lords' troops camped outside Würzburg, the civic secretary Martin Cronthal observed men who had no compunction about commandeering the waggons of the peasants, plundering and piling them high with their own booty. They threatened him physically even though he had a safe-conduct pass, and they terrorised the citizens, parading their weapons. The peasant soldiers he had witnessed in Würzburg may have been boorish rascals, strutting about or drinking their days away in the town's pubs, but these men were truly terrifying. As victors they felt they had the right to plunder and that it was their job to punish the rebellious population by forcing them to feed and supply the troops. Unlike the peasants, these men had no bonds of loyalty, and townsfolk had not sworn brotherhood with them. Their brotherhood was with each other, a closed group.[43]

It is unclear how many former mercenaries may have slipped into the peasant armies on returning from Italy, or how many peasant leaders had been mercenaries before. But their involvement may have injected a more ruthless element into the bands, a tougher form of brotherhood. The mercenaries hired by the lords followed a code of manhood that was far more brutal and bloodthirsty, as their actions that summer would show.

For the lords, the Peasants' War was an assault on their manhood, and the stories they told afterwards frequently suggested that the peasants were potential rapists who had threatened their women. Trying to raise contributions from the nobility after the war, Landgrave Philip of Hesse wrote that the peasants had not only attacked nobles and burnt buildings but had 'blasphemed [against] the sacrament' and 'undressed honourable women and insulted [raped?] them'. The peasant leader Erasmus Gerber in Alsace was compelled to confess that the peasants planned to kill all the nobles and rape their wives in front of them. Since he was tortured it is hard to know what weight to place on this admission, especially given the widespread credible accusations of rape against his opponents, the soldiers of the Duke of Lorraine in Alsace, but it does reveal the lords' anxieties. Georg von Werdenstein reminisced that the peasants arrived in his castle shouting, 'Come down you old dog, we want to pull out your beard'. Beards were a new luxury fashion item requiring expensive equipment to maintain; the evangelical peasants depicted in sixteenth-century images mostly do not sport facial hair. The peasants supposedly called to Werdenstein's daughters, 'You young whores, we want to screw you, and then we'll rape the old ladies'. The attacks on his beard and his womenfolk went together, separated only by a few sentences.[44]

There is evidence of the peasants sexually humiliating noblewomen, though there is also ambiguity about the extent of their actions. The Count of Helfenstein's widow was reputedly sent off in a cart to Heilbronn after the Weinsberg massacre and her clothes were taken. Nobles were outraged that the rebels took beds and necklaces from Rudolf von Hopfgarten and even stole the rings off the fingers of his wife while she still lay in childbed. There are no direct accounts of rape, though it is possible that these are circumlocutions. Rumours circulated that the peasants planned to rape nuns, but there is no evidence that they in fact did so. The peasants besieging Kitzingen had joked about 'who would be the first to sleep with the Margravess' when they won the town, and they repeatedly imagined how each should have his pick of the virgins 'until they could all have their pleasure'. Yet it was their words, not their deeds, that led Margrave Casimir to have sixty of the Kitzingers blinded.[45]

Despite the importance of male bonding to their cohesion, the peasant armies do not appear to have used rape as a tool of domination, as so often happens in wars of religious and ethnic hatred. By contrast, at Saverne, where the mercenaries were sent to put down the peasants, there are numerous reports that many 'virgins and women were raped'. The apparent absence of rape by peasant soldiers may have been because the ideal of brotherhood created potential kinship even with the lords, constraining the wish to make the enemy's women bear one's children; the Peasants' War was not an ethnic conflict of this kind. The lords nevertheless remained convinced that their women would be dishonoured, and they believed their fears of sexual humiliation entitled them to carry out brutal punishments on the vanquished.[46]

They did not forget that they were dealing with their underlings. Count Wilhelm von Henneberg recalled how the peasants commanded him to go to Meiningen to negotiate. He had no mounted men for they were all with Casimir of Brandenburg, and when he arrived he was surrounded by the peasants. In public, therefore, and not in private, he had to endure the boast of Steffan Mann from the town of Schmalkalden, who said that a rope had been bound in Rome to reach to St Jacob, and no one could cut it in two or break it. He meant the revolt was so big that it encompassed more than Henneberg's lands, and no emperor, king, or prince could resist it. Later, when Mann was captured, Henneberg remembered those words and was not inclined to be merciful.[47]

Joining the peasants, as many lords were constrained to do, meant 'swearing brotherhood' with them, another demeaning experience. Georg von Werdenstein recalled how he was ordered to ride alone into the 'ring' of the peasants, who parted their lances to allow him to enter. He was permitted to speak but had to leave while they discussed the matter, and, returning at their command, he was asked to join the brothers. When he refused, explaining that he was bound by oath to the princes of Austria, 'so that it will not be appropriate for the sake of my honour to join in a league behind his back', one of the peasants addressed him without title, with the informal 'you', and with a curse: 'May God's martyr shame you, you have always tormented us, I would like to stick my lance through you'. Von Werdenstein lived to tell the tale because he had a safe conduct which the peasants honoured, but the sting of the insult is palpable in his account. Duke Georg of Saxony had only contempt for his vassals, who had sworn to Müntzer under duress. For a lord, breaking the oath to your liege was perjury, and it meant you were no longer a proper man. The noble Götz von Berlichingen, with the iron fist, recounted a swashbuckling story of sitting peaceably at a tavern, and being clapped on the back and told he was now a peasant leader and a brother. But most found taking the oath degrading. When they swore allegiance to Thomas Müntzer, they were addressed in the informal 'you', and they had to limit the number of horses they owned and resign their titles, all things that made them lords and men. The Bavarian chancellor Leonhard von Eck was scathing about such turncoats: it was the 'unheard of timidity of all authorities' that was to blame. 'In this matter the greatest war is to bring the authorities to a more manly frame of mind—only then will it be over for the peasants'.[48]

Even for those who did not switch sides, the battles may have been profoundly unnerving. Often, though not always, the peasants were easily defeated, and thousands were bloodily slain. Unused to battle, they tended to scatter when the cannons were fired at them, and then nobles on horseback could simply chase them, slashing them to death as they tried to flee into the woods or towns. But the nobles sometimes admitted that they had been impressed by peasant courage. Many of the chroniclers accepted that the peasants had fought 'manfully'. One Basel chronicler reported on the battles in Alsace, where, even after defeat, the peasants had massed 'so manfully'. Their insistence on the 'manfulness' of the peasants may have been in part because the peasants often ran away. Mostly the rebels were not equal opponents, and defeating them could not bolster a sense of knightly virtue. Slaughtering such numbers of men was hard as well as gory work, and some seem to have felt a sense of guilt. Aschwin von Cramm led the cavalry of Braunschweig at Frankenhausen and later seems to have turned to Luther for help with his conscience.[49] At a time when the status of being an independent 'knight' was in terminal decline, the peasants' assault on masculine authority may have reinforced a sense of diminishment amongst the knights themselves.

Nearly twenty years after the war, the Nuremberg artist Hans Sebald Beham, who had lived through it and had himself been suspected of unorthodox belief, produced this fine copperplate engraving of 'Field Conrad' and 'Klos Wuczer', the soldier (Landsknecht). The bandy-legged 'Conz', whose name evokes the 'Poor Conrad' revolts of the early

Hans Sebald Beham, *Acker Conz und Klos Wuczer*, 1544,
copper engraving, 7 x 4.8 cm. Metropolitan Museum of Art,
New York, gift of Felix M. Warburg and his family, 1941.

sixteenth century, beats the drum and seems to be obeying 'Klos', who
holds the standard and whose fine hat, breastplate, and sword mark
him out as a *Fähnrich* or bannerman. The Peasants' War, this engraving seems to suggest, was an alliance of the peasant and the Landsknecht (whose names echo each other) in which the peasant was misled.
Conz is no longer the upright evangelical peasant of the woodcuts of
1525, but a simple soul led astray; and Klos Wuczer, whose military
stance and attire suggests he may be a poor knight, is the leader. Their
manly partnership defined the moment.[50]

Both sides were obsessed with manliness—the authorities, knights,
and monks who felt their manhood had been impugned, and the
peasants who believed they were fighting for brotherhood. When the

peasants were defeated, their surrender was carefully choreographed by gender, and in some towns women sued for peace, acting as collectives of married women and virgins, not as individuals. Their embodiment of 'the' community indicted their menfolk's failure to be a proper civil body within the existing political structures, the final unmanning of the side that had lost.

Brotherhood was a radically egalitarian ideal binding people together. Interrogated afterwards about their union, Claus Rautenzweig said that he understood nothing but that 'they should be brothers and love one another like the brothers'. It was an idea so powerful that it could overcome the social, wealth, and geographical differences amongst the rebels, one of the greatest challenges they faced. It could facilitate alliance with mercenaries and miners, and between townsfolk and peasants. It was even broad enough to include lords and knights when they, too, were offered brotherhood. Brotherhood provided a symbolic arsenal that everyone understood and a theology that inspired, but it could also be aggressive and exclusionary. The opposite of the 'common man' was not the lord but the 'common woman', the disorderly, sexually available woman whose body was a collective possession of the male members of the commune. And what were the hated clergy but 'courtesans' of the pope who were not real men? When the peasants lined up with their backs against the waggon circle that held all their plunder and supplies—the formation in which they so often chose to fight—they were defending their manhood and standing four-square against the lords. Perhaps the intoxicating experience of being brothers together, massing in their thousands and escaping time and lordship, had also led them to think they were invincible, with God on their side. The trauma of their defeat reshaped the Reformation and ended its dream of a fraternal future.[51]

But before we dismiss brotherhood as a naïve, masculinist ideal that was destined to fail, we need to recognise that in its time, it had transformative power. Brotherhood enabled people to articulate what was wrong with economic relationships that were fundamentally exploitative. In a world where only profit mattered—forcing yet another due out of a new crop, adding an impost here, a tax there, turning yet another old customary act of assistance into a new labour due—brotherhood offered a different way of conceiving relations between people and the environment. If we are all kin, and if we all share in the one body and blood of Christ, then we have obligations to each other that override class and status. We must treat each other fairly, or in what they described as 'a brotherly fashion', allowing for give-and-take, for peasants to perform labour dues for lords willingly but to be treated with respect in return, and not to be compelled. We need, they argued, to share the gifts of the creation that God made for all to use. Brotherhood in this sense reached back to the earliest ideals of Christianity, and yet it was profoundly revolutionary because it proposed a new model of human relationships and so of the economy. As the summer arrived, that brotherhood faced its greatest test.

PART FOUR

SUMMER

Hans Wertinger, *June* (Landshut, 1525–1526). Germanisches Nationalmuseum Nuremberg.

CHAPTER 11

SUMMER

As the weather warmed, the peasants faced battle with the lords on many fronts, in Alsace, in the region around Würzburg, and in the southwest. In Thuringia, the peasant army, which encompassed the Mühlhauseners, the men of Frankenhausen, the Allstedters, what remained of Hans Sippel's peasant army (the Werrahaufen), recently defeated at Eisenach, and others had assembled above Frankenhausen. Up on the hill they could see for miles, over the land for which they fought. The armies of the princes gathered. The peasants wrote to them on 15 May: 'We proclaim Jesus Christ. We are not here to harm anyone (John 2) but to maintain godly justice. We are also not here to shed blood. If you will do the same, we will do nothing to you'. The princes wrote back offering them merciful terms if they would hand 'the false prophet', Thomas Müntzer, and his associates over to them. When the letter was read out to the army, Müntzer reportedly stepped forward, asking them what they should do. 'No, no', they all shouted, in a final affirmation of brotherhood, 'we want to remain together alive or dead'. God was with them.[1]

But victory was not to be theirs. Battle commenced that day under the personal leadership of the princes, with a round of cannon fire and an attack from the mounted soldiers. The waggon fort offered no protection and could not be defended against the artillery. Trained soldiers mowed the peasant soldiers down as they fled downhill towards Frankenhausen, cavalry slashing them to pieces. The blood ran in a gully in the landscape on one escape route to the town below—it is still known as the *Blutrinne*.[2]

Having reached the town, some of the peasants hid in the sewers and in the salt-panning huts, where they were chased by the soldiers, who then plundered the town. Perhaps seven thousand peasants were slaughtered that day; three hundred more were executed in the town the day after. It was claimed that only six soldiers on the princes' side were killed. 'Send me the ear of a peasant', Margrave Joachim of Brandenburg had demanded. 'We can send you over a hundred or more', his commanders joked, 'but it's not a good ware to be sending overland at the moment'.[3] They knew that the peasants were not yet defeated.

After the battle, Müntzer was discovered in town hiding in a bed, pretending to be 'an old sick man'. A Hessian soldier seized him and brought him to the commanders. The letters he still carried, and which he had not destroyed, were his undoing. He was taken to the princes' camp, where he encountered his enemies Duke Georg, Landgrave Philip of Hesse, and Duke Heinrich of Braunschweig. According to Johannes Rühel, who wrote to Luther describing the scene, Duke Georg demanded to know why Müntzer had executed Count Ernst's men, whom they had taken captive, in breach of the rules of war. Müntzer replied that not he, but divine justice, 'das Göttliche recht', had done this. Then in an extraordinary moment, these bitter opponents— the evangelical landgrave and Müntzer—reportedly traded biblical quotations as if they were equals, Müntzer citing the prophets, Philip of Hesse adducing gospel passages to prove rebellion was always wrong.[4]

Next Müntzer was handed over to his archenemy, the Catholic count Ernst of Mansfeld who took him to his castle at Heldrungen, where he was interrogated and tortured. This was the castle Ernst had refortified and turned into a modern redoubt, the very one the peasants had planned to besiege. Now Ernst had Müntzer completely in his power. By 23 May, however, Duke Georg peremptorily ordered Ernst to surrender his prisoner, and Müntzer was transferred to the princes' camp at Schlotheim, about fifteen kilometres from Mühlhausen. There the castle itself was in ruins, having been burnt to the ground by the rebels just a few weeks before.[5]

But the victors were far from united. Shortly after, the Catholic Duke Georg wrote to his son-in-law, Philip of Hesse, upbraiding him for adhering to the 'sect'—by which he meant the Lutherans—and blaming Luther for having caused the uprising. Heresy, in Georg's view, led inevitably to rebellion. The Catholics consistently maintained this analysis despite Lutheran rebuttals. The Lutherans feared that Georg would use victory to impose Catholicism throughout the region. Elector (formerly Duke) Johann of Saxony finally joined the army of the princes but only after the battle, while Wilhelm of Henneberg escaped from his brotherhood with the peasants and, very late, joined the princes.[6]

In Mansfeld, Johann Rühel worried that Müntzer had not really recanted, and indeed was if anything worse than ever, blaming the peasants' self-interestedness for the disaster. He is truly a 'desperat' human being, Rühel wrote, meaning that he was beyond hope: 'Ich besorge, man sage, was man wolle, es sey ein desperat mensch'. Indeed Müntzer's 'confession' was ambiguous, for he did not actually deny his creed, and in a final letter to his followers in Mühlhausen, he interpreted their defeat as the result of their 'eygennutz'—their 'self interest'—'for everyone was more concerned with his own self-interest than in bringing justice to the Christian people'. Luther was incandescent: the wrong questions had been put to Müntzer. 'I would have had him questioned very differently', he wrote to Rühel. 'He did not admit to having done anything wrong'. He continued, 'I did not think it possible that a human heart could be so deeply blocked' ('verstockt'), or as we might say, hardened, a description that drew on the idea of the humours flowing through the body and implied that the natural flows in Müntzer had been obstructed. Johannes Agricola, one of Luther's most loyal lieutenants, took this further, publishing a mock commentary on Müntzer's interpretation of the psalm 'in new prophetical', suggesting that Müntzer was possessed by the devil. He also wrote an anonymous dialogue between a peasant and a follower of Müntzer. The Lutherans wanted to present Müntzer as the sole author of the war. By the time Cyriakus Spangenberg wrote his version of events a generation later, Lutheran 'memory' was callous. Spangenberg described how Müntzer had caved in at the first application of the thumbscrews. He had reneged on his faith, accepting communion in one kind. He had not even been able to recite the creed and had to be prompted by the Duke of Braunschweig.[7]

Yet at the time, a very different story circulated. The Strasbourg theologian Caspar Hedio, one of the adherents of a position closer to that of the Sacramentarians, reported that Philip of Hesse had spoken admiringly of Müntzer's death, saying that he wished he might have such an end, for he had sighed over all his sins from his heart to God. The landgrave had also cited the testimony of the Duke of Braunschweig that Müntzer had not actually recanted but had admitted errors and asked for God's mercy. In death, it seemed, Müntzer might become a hero.[8]

Müntzer's ally Heinrich Pfeiffer, meanwhile, had fled Mühlhausen with about six hundred others. The gates had been shut, but they had been allowed to flee through the town gate leading towards Franconia, almost certainly with the connivance of authorities in Mühlhausen—who promptly told the princes' party in which direction they had gone. Whether intentional or not, this avoided further bloodshed in the town and enabled the authorities to distance themselves from what had taken place. Pfeiffer was caught, and he and Müntzer were executed together, along with another twenty-four rebels, on 27 May in the princes' camp. Their bodies were left unburied, their heads exhibited on spikes outside Mühlhausen—Müntzer's on a hill, Pfeiffer's at a crossroads towards the village of Bollstedt.[9] But they were not forgotten. Around Allstedt, radical preaching continued, and in March of 1526 there were rumours that Mühlhausen would rise again. In 1531 Luther mentioned reports that a path to the site of Müntzer's execution had been worn deep by visitors, and if action were not taken, Luther feared, the man would become honoured as a saint.[10]

It is hard to assess whether Müntzer's was just a local story, or to what extent his influence drove the whole war, an issue that Lutheran mythmaking distorted early on. When asked by his interrogators at the end how far Müntzer intended his kingdom to extend, he answered 'nine miles'—he meant German miles, a distance of about seventy kilometres, which would not have even included Wittenberg. Allstedt, Zwickau, and Mühlhausen, the places where Müntzer worked, seem to have been universes in themselves, and Müntzer's apocalyptic scenarios appear to have been imagined within their confines. Yet the Allstedters remained faithful, converging to a man on Frankenhausen in his support. Furthermore, Müntzer had earlier travelled to Prague, home to the Hussites, and we know that in the fateful final six months, when he was expelled from Mühlhausen, he visited the Black Forest, Nuremberg, Fulda, and Schweinfurt, all in regions that became centres of the peasants' revolt, and where he had contacts with local preachers. The preacher of Dipperz, who inspired the Fuldaers as they rose in revolt, may have known Müntzer; preachers around Schweinfurt may have heard him; Hans Hergot of Nuremberg likely was acquainted with Müntzer too. Hans Hut, the later Anabaptist, was at Frankenhausen as well and took part in the battle.[11]

But was it Müntzer's ideas that inspired those who encountered him? Müntzer had visited Fulda and had even been imprisoned there, yet although the mysterious watchmaker who inspired the Fulda revolt had mocked the lords, joking, 'I'm a lord and you have to do what I want; here I sit on the bench and win castles and towns', this does not sound like Müntzer's bloodcurdling rhetoric against the lords. Preachers like Jakob Strauss, Adam Crafft, Georg Witzel, and others who had been evangelical firebrands soon modified their stance and distanced themselves from Müntzer. They did not see him as an ally. Even Andreas Karlstadt broke with him and took care to distinguish his views from those embraced by the radical as early as 1524. The Zurichers and Swiss who had once corresponded with Müntzer stopped disputing with him because they no longer shared common ground.[12]

So while it suited many to blame Müntzer and to see his influence at work everywhere, it is difficult to grasp the extent to which the rebels could have known of his ideas. After all, most of his few published works did not appear until 1524, and it was the banishment from Mühlhausen that first brought him to the major town of Nuremberg, where his works could be printed on its presses. Ironically, Luther himself made Müntzer famous by denouncing him in print and made his final letter to the Allstedters known by publishing it after his death. As Thomas Müller has shown, even Heinrich Pfeiffer had his own distinctive theological and tactical position, and he, Rothemeler, Hisoldus, and a group of other preachers had got the Reformation underway in Mühlhausen without Müntzer's help; their success was what enabled them to invite Müntzer after his departure from Allstedt. Müntzer had his work printed, but many other influential preachers did not, including Pfeiffer himself, the nameless pastor of Dipperz, Jakob Wehe of Leipheim, and many more who joined with the peasants and who played key roles, preaching and encouraging the peasant bands, reading and writing letters, and formulating the peasants' demands. We cannot assume that even those who met Müntzer shared his eschatological vision, nor conclude that his theology was theirs. Even in Frankenhausen there were powerful radical preachers whose views may not have coincided with those of 'the Allstedter', as he was known, and the Frankenhauseners had their own reasons for forming the peasant army, which the Mühlhauseners joined only after it had been formed.[13]

And though Müntzer apparently tried to recruit the miners to his cause, the mining towns of the Erzgebirge did not rise in sustained revolt. At Schneeberg, Georg Amandus's preaching had been radical, but when he was interrogated by the council, Amandus claimed his views had been taken out of context. He avoided becoming a martyr. Annaberg stayed loyal to its Saxon rulers though some of its citizens attacked local priests and engaged in acts of iconoclasm. At Joachimstal in Bohemia, the revolt the authorities had feared for so long finally broke out—but only after the peasants had been defeated at Frankenhausen. Count Schlick's new castle, the mint, and the town hall were damaged, but though they sought support from other mining areas it was too late, and they came to terms on 29 May, resuming work on 11 June. Some peasants and miners tried to go from Eisleben to Frankenhausen to join the army, and we know of their journey because they were stopped by Count Albrecht of Mansfeld. Sympathetic as many may have been to radical theology, and though some of them may have fought at Frankenhausen, the miners as a group did not harness their concerns—which soon centred on issues to do with mining—to those of Müntzer.[14]

Müntzer's story does not stand in for that of the Peasants' War as a whole, and we must reconstruct peasant theology piecemeal from the fragments of their writings and their actions, not through the fevered speculations of Müntzer. In the end, Müntzer was a townsman who appealed not only to the dispossessed, but, strange as it may seem, to the urban upper-middle class—to the mine owner Christoph Meinhard of Eisleben, the mining entrepreneur Christoph Fürer of Nuremberg, the merchant Hans Pelt of Braunschweig, the bureaucrat Hans Zeiß, the bookseller Wolfgang Juche, the watchmaker of Fulda—and the miners of Stolberg. Müntzer was at home in the busy streets of the middling towns where his dramas played out; he did not, at a deep level, understand the peasant cause but rewrote it into his own apocalyptic drama. The same might be said of Luther.[15]

But Müntzer remains the theologian who articulated social justice like no other. A major thinker, he was Luther's intellectual peer, and his observations on 'Pope' Luther's authoritarianism, as he dubbed him, hit home. His poetic language expressed the anger against the 'fat cats' ('grosse Hansen') and their unjust rule that so many felt. And for all his towering megalomania, he remains the only theologian who articulated the plight of the dispossessed from their point of view. He is the theologian of anger, a prophet giving voice to the righteous rage of the downtrodden, who saw that it was not just tinkering with feudalism or concessions from the rich that were needed. The entire system of earthly lordship and hypocritical deference needed to be swept away. His rhetoric was a flood of bloodthirsty, violent language with barely a pause for breath, and for his opponents he was a demagogue who led thousands to their deaths. And yet he was also a mystic for whom music was centrally important and who spent much of his time designing a new liturgy; a gifted political organiser who knew how to find the lieutenants to help him form the leagues that provided the bedrock of his support; and a compelling preacher who could at first attract the likes of even Hans Zeiß, the Saxon official. He was also a remarkably empathetic pastor who knew how to mobilise the power of dreams, and to whom his followers remained loyal to the end.[16]

In May the tide began to turn in Alsace, just as it had in Franconia and Swabia. Here as in so many places the slaughter was massive, because although the peasants had cannons, muskets, and pikes, they lacked cavalry, and so the forces of the nobles were able to scatter their ranks by charging them. Much of the fighting involved slashing with pikes and swords by men on horseback; guns and cannon were aimed at destroying buildings as much as killing men.

The forces of Anton of Lorraine pressed the peasants into the village of Lupstein, where the houses were soon packed with fleeing peasants carrying the goods they had plundered from nobles and clergy. Many fled to the main church, which is on raised ground, and barricaded themselves in. The troops could not gain access, so on 16 May they set the village on fire 'at all four corners'. Three thousand peasants, perhaps more, perished in the blaze. As the French Catholic chronicler quipped, the Lutherans had finally sought salvation in the church, but too late to save themselves. At four in the afternoon, one official saw the whole of Lupstein standing in flames—he had taken other villagers into his castle for safety after the soldiers had plundered churches and 'run after the women'. Rumours soon spread of how Lupstein had been razed and 'virgins dragged off into the corn and shamed' (raped?). 'They did things to the women, so that the poor women didn't know what to do'. At Kleeburg, the peasant army petitioned the council for help against the 'tyrant'; evoking biblical images, they wrote that the soldiers 'chopped off the heads of women lying in childbed, and they stab small children and hang them on their swords, and display them like King Herod'.[17]

In the town of Saverne, held by the peasants, their leader Erasmus Gerber wrote to the Strasbourg council in desperation on 15 May, begging them to act as 'Christian lords and rulers'. 'Come to our help, gracious lords. ... Do it for God's sake, come to our aid, don't leave us', he wrote at three in the morning as disaster was about to descend. Writing again three hours later, he pleaded, 'If we are unable to resist the enemy, we and all the Lantschaft will be ruined', dating the letter 'in a hurry and in anxiety'. He still believed in an evangelical fraternity and hoped that the peasants and the evangelical city of Strasbourg were on the same side, for the struggle concerned not only the Strasbourgers and their subjects but also the land itself, and its fruits. It was for that fertile earth, God's creation, and for its people, that he was fighting.[18]

Saverne surrendered, but to no avail. Fleeing peasants rushed into the town, and the troops came after them, bent on massacres and plunder. A French chronicler recalled that the atrocity had been sparked by banter between a peasant and a soldier, and then a voice called from heaven in German, 'Strike, we are allowed to'. This was a grisly echo of the peasants' plunder of convents, monasteries, and castles that had evoked Schlaraffenland, a time of plenty when pigs come with knives already stuck in and capons are dressed to be devoured—a time of pure licence, when everything is permitted. The 'Lutherans' were shown no mercy. On 17 May, those who had fought on the Martelberg above the town were routed, the survivors captured. In Saverne, Italian, Dutch, and Lorrainese mercenary troops, with no shared language and no sympathy for the civilians, were let loose on them. 'They took pretty women, daughters and women in childbed with them, and had their way with them. . . . They made their men watch and then slew them'. One local official took in women and children and housed them overnight in barns and outhouses—he estimated there were thirty waggons, 150 children. When the Strasbourg representatives rode to Saverne, they found dead peasants and citizens everywhere, on the streets and in the houses. There were so many dead at the gates that they could barely get the horses to ride over the corpses. They saw the bodies of the Alsatian peasant leaders Erasmus Gerber and Peter Hall hanging on a tree, not far from the ground, men with whom they had been negotiating not long before.[19]

Duke Anton was less fortunate when he turned to Scherwiller, where he encountered eight thousand peasants intent on revenge for the atrocities of Saverne and Lupstein. Five hundred of his Dutch infantry troops were killed, leading the duke to decide against attacking another peasant army. Looking back, Georg Gügi described his life as a pastor in a village outside Strasbourg in those grim days; in the end, he went home to Switzerland because staying was too dangerous. Peasants did not dare return to their farms, and children were hiding in the bushes and stealing food. The worst, he said, were the bishops' cathedral chapter and priests, who lord it over 'the peasants' sweat and blood. Lord God, you alone see the pains of the poor; let their suffering go to your heart!'[20]

At Böblingen in Württemberg, Truchsess Georg's army defeated the rebels on 12 May, killing perhaps four thousand peasants and hunting those who fled as far as Stuttgart; those they took prisoner, they slew. In their panic, everyone fled; 'one had no shoes, the other no hat, the third no knife, dagger, spear or halberd'. The revolt petered out in panic and confusion.[21]

Yet amidst the mass slaughter, there were some successes. Six peasant armies gathered around Freiburg. On 23 May, Hans Müller of Bülgenbach and his men managed to take the town; they had needed little more than ten days. Though he could draw on the armies that had massed near the town, his own group had few weapons, so this victory was an extraordinary achievement. In a daring raid his forces secured control of the *Schlossberg* above the town, which was full of gunpowder and munitions; from this commanding position, as can still be seen today, they could target and destroy any house in the city. The Freiburg humanist Ulrich Zasius had previously been a supporter of Luther, but his growing hostility to the new religion was confirmed when his house and library were hit. Freiburg capitulated, joining the brotherhood and allowing the peasants in, which gave them access to the wealth of the monasteries.[22]

For the Catholic chronicler Heinrich Hug, this victory was the product of the town's shameful cowardice, vanity, and disunity. He expostulated that if the Freiburgers had been attacked by a prince with a full army, they would have defended themselves 'as honourable people'—yet Müller had outmanoeuvred them with nothing but a culverin and two falconets. They had surrendered their town 'shamefully and blasphemously' and joined the 'brotherhood of rascals'. The Catholic chronicler Andreas Lettsch was equally scathing: the peasant fighters wanted to 'get rich with the gospel' and get money for the silver chalices, and the town shamefully paid them off with 3,000 Gulden, money it had extorted from the abbots and clerics who had fled there.[23]

But as in Heilbronn, the rebels' problem was keeping territory they had won; the armies rapidly dissolved, allowing the peasants to return to their fields while remaining on call. To prevent losing their gains, the army forced Freiburg to promise to supply the army with three hundred of its citizens and all their weapons. In mid-June Müller tried to repeat his success by marching the Black Forest troops to Zell, where the Hegau peasants had become bogged down in an unsuccessful siege. But his sense of strategy was no match for the large army composed of Swabian League and Austrian troops, and they were defeated on 1 and 2 July, while Freiburg deserted the peasant cause as soon as it could. The Hegau revolt, which had been one of the very first of the war, collapsed, followed on 12 July by the Stühlingen revolt.

Müller himself fled to the Hohentwiel fortress, a mighty castle in the Hegau built on top of an extinct volcano that towers above the town of Singen. He was briefly captured at Schaffhausen but then freed—a remarkable turn of events at a time when the defeated peasants were on the run; it may suggest that the town, involved earlier as an intermediary in the disputes of the region's peasants, may have known and protected him. But he did not manage to escape for long: the Austrians caught him. This time he was kept and tortured for forty days before being executed at Laufenburg. Execution, unlike hanging, was an honourable punishment, and it hints that even the Austrians—known for brutal punishments of rebels—may have had some respect for him.[24]

Müller emerges not only as a talented strategist but as a speaker who elicited strong loyalty from those under his command. Even the hostile commentators mention his ability to 'schwetzen', his gift of oratory so important in inspiring, enthralling, and uniting an audience. (He was not the only charismatic speaker: Ulrich Schmid, the peasant leader from Sulmingen, was lifted up on poles so he could be heard 'as if the Holy Spirit apparently spoke out of him', an adversary noted.) Like the preachers who played such a powerful role in the leadership of the movement, and who knew how to project the voice in order to be heard by large crowds, Müller had an ability to rouse an audience, one of his chief talents.[25]

He also knew his patch inside out. He roamed between Stühlingen, Waldshut, Hüfingen, Zell, the Hegau, Freiburg, Villingen, and the Black Forest, taking care to persuade tiny village after village to swear brotherhood. This was his domain, and it was a region, not an area ruled by a single lord. It is no accident that his band was named the 'Black Foresters', for the area was hilly and wooded, ideal terrain for peasant fighters who could survive through the network of sworn villages he had nurtured. His ability to move quickly through this landscape explains how he and his followers widened the scope of the revolt in autumn 1524 and maintained its impetus through the winter, keeping it alive through the terrible summer after other regions had been defeated. And he seems to have grasped that the struggle needed part-time soldiers who could come when needed and could farm meanwhile, melting into and out of the forest.

Müller seems to have believed in an exclusivist form of brotherhood, bound by trust and by discipline, values that were probably forged during his time as a mercenary in France. He developed Hubmaier's theology of the ban into a way of defining brothers and enemies, insisting that there must be no fellowship with those who were 'banned' and thus excluded from the religious, political, and economic community. He knew, too, that the struggle had to be won if his and subsequent generations were not to be forced into poverty. This exclusivist, separatist form of brotherhood was stricter than the earlier, more open version of fraternity espoused by those in central Germany. And he realised early on that nobles were not to be trusted. Only if they gave up the trappings of nobility, in particular their houses, could they become 'brothers', he insisted, but then they could keep the rest of their property. Bonds between men were essential in this challenging context, and spies had to be dealt with ruthlessly. Fraternity also required structure and moral discipline, for one of the greatest challenges the rebels faced was how to turn a crowd of amateur soldiers into a fighting force led not by the values of deference but by the power of brotherhood.

As the Austrians and the Swabian League began to tackle the peasants in the central and southern areas of Germany, leaving the Black Forest until last, Müller and his men took the offensive, burning castles at Zindelstein, Triberg, and Neu Fürstenberg, minor outposts of lordship high on the crags. He was not defeated until 19 June at Zell, a fortnight after the peasants were massacred near Würzburg. By then it must have been clear that the situation was becoming desperate, but rather than flee to Switzerland, as he could easily have done, he chose to rally the troops to try to turn the tide by taking Zell.[26]

His vision of brotherhood lived on beyond his death: in autumn 1525 it was the Stühlingen, Klettgau, Hegau, and Black Forest peasants who continued to bring court cases and revolt until the forces of the Swabian League rounded them up after a battle and butchered them 'on a churchyard', 'auf ainen kürchhof', as the notary of the Truchsess Georg noted.[27]

Above all else, Truchsess Georg was determined to avenge the Weinsberg atrocity, and on 21 May he had the town burnt to the ground. As part of its by now familiar tactics, the league also set ten villages belonging to Weinsberg on fire, because they housed people who had supported the rebel armies. Burning villages destroyed the peasants' possessions and culture, but it did not harm the lords' property, including their labour force, the peasants. Those who had taken part in the Weinsberg atrocity were singled out for brutal punishment: Jäcklein Rohrbach, the piper who took Helfenstein's hat and placed it on his own head, was chained to an apple tree with two iron chains and roasted to death while the lords personally placed logs on the fire.[28]

With three peasant armies surrounding or near Würzburg at Heidingsfeld, it seemed the citadel might yet fall, but soon news came that the army of the Swabian League was on its way with the bishop of Würzburg riding with them. The Odenwald band under Hipler gave up the siege on 23 May, and soon afterwards, Götz, who had earlier gathered his men outside Weinsberg, deserted the band, claiming his military contract had expired. Many of the rest of the Odenwald army simply disappeared, but even so, an army of an additional five thousand was raised to fight at Königshofen, not far from Würzburg. On 2 June they tried to prevent the troops of the Swabian League from crossing the river to Würzburg. They gave up, retreating to the heights above. The horsemen mounted the slope, and some of the peasants panicked, untying the horses from the waggons. As the peasant army fled, many were slain, and a group who tried to hide in the woods were surrounded and butchered. Perhaps seven thousand were killed in total, and only fifteen of the three hundred citizens of Königshofen allegedly survived.[29]

On Whitsunday, 4 June, the final battle took place on the plateau between Würzburg and Ochsenfurt. An army of about five thousand faced the Swabian League, which had not been expecting resistance after Königshofen. But between Ingolstadt and Giebelstadt, the league attacked with cavalry, and the peasant army scattered, with only a remnant retreating into a castle. As it happened, the castle belonged to Florian Geyer, the leader of one of the armies, who was in Rothenburg negotiating. The army's remnants mounted a stiff resistance, but it was not enough to save them. Geyer, meanwhile, was expelled from Rothenburg and was assassinated on 9 June by a servant of his brother-in-law Wilhelm von Grumbach, who had tricked him by pretending to suggest a plot to reignite the struggle.

After the battles were over, the atrocities soon began. At Bruchsal so many were captured and put in a tower that they could not move. It was hot, and their 'shock, worry and fear' made them even hotter. The next day they were made to kneel on the square, where five of them were executed before the Pfalzgraf called a halt to it. Mercenaries at Königshofen had captured sixty peasants and slaughtered them in cold blood, because, it was said, the peasants had earlier threatened to kill them. Peasant fighters fled into the village of Ingolstadt to seek sanctuary in the churches. In desperation and lacking arms of any kind, they were reduced to breaking the tiles off the roofs to throw at the enemy. They were all slain. The villages of Buthert, Sultzdorf, and Giebelstadt were torched. In Giebelstadt, where the peasants had barricaded themselves into what was left of the castle, the men hung their hats in the air as a sign of surrender, as the peasants at Lupstein had done, and screamed for mercy. Some fled down to the cellars; the soldiers stuffed straw and gunpowder into the basement and set it alight. Only three escaped. The horror was so great that chroniclers struggled to convey it. Lorenz Fries went through the castle the next day and counted the bodies: he found 206. Trying to escape the cavalry, some peasants fled to the moat ditch in the bushes, where the horses could not follow; mounted men on the lords' side called out that anyone who slew one of his companions would be saved. Hearing this, one peasant killed five of his 'brothers', but when the sixth resisted, they struggled, and both fell into the moat and drowned. The chronicler Hans Fridell described this unforgettable vignette as if it were a 'screen memory' masking yet worse horrors. It vividly conveyed the end of brotherhood, the ideal for which the peasants had fought so bravely.[30]

As if this brutality were not enough, the summer brought retaliation and punishment as the forces of the league and of local rulers wreaked their revenge. In Würzburg, it was marked by carefully choreographed rituals of humiliation, and we know about them because the civic notary Martin Cronthal, who experienced them, wrote about the events. First, the civic representatives had to cross the River Main bridge to the Marienberg fortress side and sue for peace at the military camp, accompanied by the league's trumpeter, who sounded trumpet calls in the middle of the bridge, at the other side, and at St Burkhard's church. As they passed through the Holzgarten to Heidingfelt, they met with shouts of 'Here come the faithless rogues, stab them dead'. Arriving at the tent, they were given soup and something to drink, and were ushered through to the commander. Cronthal himself was ordered to provide a 'narration, of how they came to do it'. But while he was telling the story, they heard that the league soldiers and those in the Marienberg fortress were attacking and plundering the suburb below, on the opposite side of the river, and the rebels were powerless to protect their fellow citizens. When Cronthal and his fellows remonstrated with the soldiers, reminding them they had been given safe conduct, they were told in short order that this applied only to them personally; there was no armistice. If they did not accept the league's conditions, the league's forces would root up all their vineyards, eat all the fruit, and leave no one over age twelve alive in the city. On their way back from the camp towards the bridge, they met the league soldiers as they passed from the suburb, carrying the looted animals, household goods, and bedclothes. Only the authority of the league's trumpeter kept them safe; otherwise they would surely all have been killed.

Cronthal and the councillors had to accept the conditions of surrender, which included a ten-Gulden fine for every house, surrender of all their weapons, an oath of allegiance to the bishop, and punishment of those who had caused Aufruhr. On 8 June, the citizens were summoned for 7:00 a.m. to the market square. 'Foreigners' from other towns were ordered to the Jews' square (*Judenplatz*) in front of Our Lady's Chapel, and those from the villages were sent to the *Rennweg*, the street in the higher part of the town near the bishop's quarter. Ironically these were some of the sites where the peasants had erected gallows when they were in power. The citizens on the square were encircled by soldiers with pikes, and the exits were blocked. Three executioners, 'like ravening wolves', were called forward and set about their work. On the *Judenplatz*, twenty-four were executed, at the *Rennweg* another thirty-six. When the first executions were over, the council representatives were made to walk to the town hall, the 'green tree', where so many events of the revolt had taken place. They had to pass through two lines of soldiers, and on the way, many had their purse belts cut off and stolen; the mayor himself was robbed of the town seal (*Secret*) and all his money. The townspeople no longer had control of their streets. The beheadings went on for days. Cronthal wrote that people 'were valued like chickens'.[31]

Throughout the month of June into early July, during the long summer days, the grim progress through Franconia continued as the commanders went from one village and town to the next in an arc of destruction. In towns, the gates were opened, the night-curfew chains across the streets taken off, the towers destroyed, the walls taken down so the town could no longer control who came in or out. War damages were set. In villages, the lords' representatives arrived to mete out justice and make the peasants swear oaths of obedience anew. And then the beheadings began.[32]

This pattern was followed everywhere, sometimes in even more grisly form. As soon as Casimir von Brandenburg—conspicuous by his lack of success against the peasants up to this point—heard the news of the peasants' defeat at Königshofen, he set forth to punish his own peasants, who had been fighting at Ingolstadt and Gibelstadt. At Leutershausen he destroyed the city gate and the tower and executed six peasants, one priest, and one soldier; he had the fingers of some cut off, and gave the town over to be plundered. He processed from there to Uffenheim, treating the 'guilty' in the same way, and then on to the town of Kitzingen. On 8 June, the citizenry and council were called to the town hall, and those to be punished were made to assemble in a separate place; sixty-two were taken to a cellar, where they had their eyes put out. Casimir said that 'these rebellious citizens had let it be known that they would not see his princely grace or have him as their lord, therefore they should see him no more'. Twelve did not survive; their bodies were left on the public streets. Those who survived were banished with wife and family. They would have been rendered completely dependent, a burden on their households, and a hideous reminder to all.[33]

At Bamberg, the citizens were summoned to the Bishop's square, as was by then customary, and eight were executed while they stood in a ring, free and unbound. One lucky Bamberger, realising he was next in line, quipped, 'I've seen enough of this, I'm off home', and escaped into the crowd. The town was plundered. Next the lords' forces burnt the peasant camp outside Hallstatt. They moved on to Rothenburg, which had been a peasant citadel for so long. Everyone was summoned to the market square for 7:00 a.m. on 28 June, and the names of eighteen who were to be executed were read out. The bodies were simply left on the square 'for punishment and horror'. The executioner wanted to show off by beheading the blind monk, a famous peasant leader, while the monk stood. But his stroke misfired. After the man sank to the ground and then got up, the executioner had to take a second stroke.[34]

The horrors continued. In Hall, a peasant who had dressed in cope and mass vestments and mocked the Host was run through with a spear by a horseman amongst Casimir's troops. The spear was left in his body until the third day as a public reminder.[35] At Feuchtwangen, the head of an executed priest rolled to the ground, opened its mouth three times, and seemed to say, 'Jesus'.[36]

The victors mostly did not hang the rebels, and they did not use the usual execution sites, located outside town. Instead they chose to behead the leaders, an honourable form of punishment, but also one that stained the towns' cobblestones with blood and polluted the market squares, key sites of commerce where residents of town and country met and peasants sold their wares. They chose a spectacle everyone was forced to witness, ensuring that it would be etched in their memories forever. They made the victims stand in a ring, just as they had stood in a ring to agree to their rebellion. After all, peasants were the lords' labour force and, in areas of serfdom, their property, so it was easier to punish townsfolk, whom no one owned. By limiting their victims to the 'leaders'—pastors and commanders—the lords could intimidate their subjects and limit their loss of assets; many insisted on punishing 'their own' peasants to prevent them being punished by others. Villages were often torched and animals stolen in the final chaotic weeks of the war because those houses and animals were the peasants' property, not the lords'. Little by little, as passions cooled, agreements were reached in the years after it was all over, and even notorious rebel leaders managed to get off with fines. But this could not bring back the thousands killed.[37]

Blood was everywhere in the Peasants' War, or as one chronicler put it, 'There was hardly a town or castle so small that blood was not shed there'. The demand for Christ's blood, for the communion wine and not just the bread, is what powered the early Reformation. It was Christ's blood with which he bought us and made all free, the fundamental theological insight of the evangelical peasants. This was what the priests had been denying them, the very thing that had bought freedom, ended serfdom, and made everyone equal, and the sense of outrage at having been cheated of it lay behind much of the religious passion of the Peasants' War. The peasants swore brotherhood, symbolically insisting that they were of one blood. This was what enabled them to reach out to those beyond their own territory and form Christian Unions.[38]

The form the battles took was particularly bloody, and the numbers of those slain was large, even for the period. One peasant band wrote a long appeal to the Strasbourg council in which they seriously pondered 'that it is not possible for the lords to kill us all and live alone on the earth'—but they seemed to be facing 'annihilation'. Rain and blood ran in brooks down the streets of the village of Lupstein when the peasants were slaughtered there. Chroniclers spoke of seeing butchered ('gezetelt') peasants—peasants chopped into little bits—on all the roads into Würzburg. And still it was not over. At Pfeddersheim, near Worms in the Palatinate, a peasant army joined battle on 23 and 24 June in the high fields above the town against the princes, who were better armed and had cavalry. Perhaps four thousand peasants were slain; the blood from the battle was said to have flowed down the hill into town. A group who had fled into town were locked in the church, and when they tried to escape the next day the troops ran amok, killing perhaps eight hundred peasants. The stench in the hot weather must have been unbearable.[39]

Along with the bloodshed that summer came the ritual humiliations. Everywhere, peasants were forced to swear again to their lords, in ceremonies where they lined up obediently, raising their 'swearing fingers' to the single lord and not to the collective. The Weissenau chronicle pictures the moment in a triumphal final image: abbot and abbey officials stand on their balcony while the peasants gather below to swear fealty. In rebel towns and villages, peasants had to hand over all their weapons and were forbidden to wear swords and daggers, a humiliation of their masculinity. Wilhelm Truchsess thought that arming the peasants had caused all the problems in the first place. Every lord had wanted to increase his military power by having the best armed peasants, but this was foolish. They should 'let the peasants be peasants and till the fields and they should be the powerful lords'. For his part, he would never again offer his peasants weapons or armour.[40]

Cronthal's story explaining how the Würzburg town council had been forced to join the peasants succeeded in saving his own skin and that of his fellow councillors. His entire chronicle is an attempt to re-count the councillors' version of events, to supply all the details and dates that might explain how a town could let the rebellious peasants in and form common cause with them. This was his task as civic secre-tary and as repository of the memory of the town. Michael Gross von Trockau, Marx Halbritter, Martin Cronthal, Thomas Zweifel, Lorenz Fries, Götz von Berlichingen, and all the other chroniclers felt the over-whelming need to tell their stories and to justify what they did. Like no other event, the war drove these men to put quill to paper. Some wrote many years later; some remembered particular incidents that made the vast scale of the horror manageable. The Peasants' War chronicles are different from Reformation chronicles: there are more of them, and more that were written by participants, because they were dealing with an event they could only make intelligible by writing it down. And yet they were mostly not public, but manuscript accounts. After the events, there could be no public commemoration, only a covering over of what had happened.

Wendel Hipler, the chancellor of the peasants who had begun to devise the Reformation that would be the charter of the new order, was captured by the troops of the Elector Palatine and handed over to Würzburg, where he ended up in the Marienberg Castle. He was kept in 'knightly' imprisonment, as if his coat of arms with the two fishes entitled him to this special treatment. But before he could be tried, he died—inside the castle the peasants had tried so hard to take. Their other leader, Götz von Berlichingen, had his noble friends swing into action. They interceded with Truchsess Georg, claiming that Götz's 'honour' had been impugned by the league through the imputation that he had been one of the causes of the Peasants' War. He had not acted out of 'his own advantage or pride' but had genuinely done all he could to avoid harm, so much so 'that I can't at this moment write it all at length for you'. Honour, it seems, did not figure in his decision to quit his troops once he had decided his contract had expired.[41]

Soon afterwards a song was printed, supposedly composed by the Würzburg castle's garrison and sung to the tune of 'First We Must Praise Mary', the song of the 'poor knights'. The words accused the peasants of breaking their oaths, of driving out their 'pious and good rulers', of being drunken, and of misusing the gospel. It celebrated the sound of the drums, the 'singing' of the muskets, and the shots ringing out as the troops of the Swabian League arrived and the peasants were slaughtered. Its cover showed a rich burgher clutching a book and sporting the fashionable net cap worn by princes and the rich, facing a proud peasant with a knapsack on his back and gesturing with his hand as if to expound the gospel. Closely modelled on the positive images of the peasant before 1525, it insinuated that these two were in league against 'manly' knights. Würzburg had been saved by the castle's noble defenders. In its iconography and words, it reversed the pamphlets that had glorified the peasant just a year before, and its tune evoked Mary, protectress of the castle.[42]

To the victors go the spoils. The town of Villingen, loyal to the Habsburgs, had spent the spring and summer anxiously watching the progress of the Black Forest peasant band through the surrounding region and begging the Swabian League to come to its aid—in vain. Now the council decided to do its own butchery. In June the council had five huge oxen slaughtered and gave all those above confirmation age a pound of meat, and every child half a pound. Everyone, rich and poor, noble and commoner, clergy and layfolk, could take some of the twenty-five hundredweight of meat, and 'everyone had their fill'.[43]

The danger was not past in Villingen, however, for the band's redoubtable Hans Müller was still in nearby Hüfingen, but it was clear that victory for the authorities and the Swabian League was now a matter of time. Butchering the animals established the event in the collective memory of Villingen, because children would remember the day when there was more meat than you could eat. A few days later, the town finally turned the tables on the peasants. The Villingers assembled at nine in the morning and set off to the nearby village of Schwenningen on a summer carnival. They plundered the village, stealing the animals and burning all but three houses to the ground. They did the same to several other villages and drove the animals back to Villingen. In the words of the Villingen chronicler Heinrich Hug, 'They brought geese, hens, no-one came back empty-handed'. From then on, the fighting degenerated into over a week of cattle rustling and village burning.[44]

Now it was the peasants' animals who paid the price for the townsfolk's fury. Hug describes the desperate women of Schwenningen who had to identify their animals in Villingen and then buy them back: 'it would have moved a heart of stone'. The animals' fate, the pandemonium, the grief-stricken women—Hug finally allowed himself to express the horror of those terrible months through the story of the beasts. Even though he himself was a Villinger, Hug lost thirty Gulden worth of cows, a bull, and beehives in the indiscriminate plundering— 'that was enough war for me'. Throughout the region of the war, men and women had been slaughtered in vast numbers, villages set alight, farms looted—and then peasant and town leaders had been publicly executed on the market squares. This was the grim harvest of the summer of blood.[45]

CHAPTER 12

AFTERMATH

In the months and years that followed the carnage, life continued, and the threads of the various stories and individual lives we have traced reached their diverse conclusions.

Luther's final tract on the Peasants' War was printed before Müntzer's execution, though after he knew Müntzer's fate. *A Judgement on Thomas Müntzer* published Müntzer's last letters, with Luther's annotations in the margins. Luther argued that the letters were damning because they showed that when Count Albrecht of Mansfeld had been trying to reach an accommodation with the peasants and miners, Müntzer, who had claimed that the Holy Spirit spoke through him, persuaded the peasants not to send a reply. No treaty was agreed, and five thousand peasants were slain. Sarcastic throughout, Luther mocks Müntzer's claims to divine inspiration as having been found 'ym rauchloch', that is, in the smoke hole or anus. And when Müntzer reaches his peroration 'We shall conclude, what God has ordered us to do: do your best, I shall go there', signing off as 'Thomas Müntzer with the Sword of Gideon', Luther parses this as 'I'm flying on a knebel into the tower at Heldrungen and have become a shitty prophet'. Both Müntzer and Luther had grown up in mining areas not far from Held-rungen, the castle of Müntzer's great enemy Count Ernst of Mans-feld, where Müntzer was being held and tortured. Luther seems to be imagining him as a witch, flying into the tower not on a witch's broom but on a *Knebel* (miner's carriage), a man of the devil, and a 'shitty' prophet who gets truth from the 'smoke hole'—an insult he would later use against the Jews. His final verdict on Müntzer was a repetition of the words he had already rehearsed when he wrote to Rühel: 'Whoever saw Müntzer may say, he has seen the very Devil in bodily form in his worst raging. O Lord God, where such a spirit is also in the peasants, how necessary it is that they should be slain like the mad dogs', quoting himself again from *Against the Robbing, Murdering Hordes of Peasants*.[1]

On 13 June, a week after the final defeat of the Peasants' War in central Germany and little more than a fortnight after Müntzer's ex-ecution, Luther got married. He did so, he explained, 'to spite' the Devil. The marriage of a monk and a nun, a double breaking of vows, it was Luther's final rupture with monasticism, and it made good on his promise from 1521–1522, when he published *On Monastic Vows*, dedicated to his father, pledging he would no longer disobey him by spurning marriage and joining the monastery. Except that of course he remained in the monastery where he had once been a monk, gifted to him by the Elector of Saxony. Luther's own internal drama of separa-tion from the papal church and reconciliation with his father reached its climax with the end of the war.

Karlstadt, by contrast, had been exiled, and had ceaselessly wan-dered with wife and child to Strasbourg, Zurich, Basel, and Heidel-berg. In a later self-exculpatory pamphlet, Karlstadt describes how from there he went incognito to Rothenburg—which was about to become a major theatre of the Peasants' War. But his idealisations of peasants were shattered when he went to the peasants' camp at Hei-dingsfeld, some fifty kilometres away, and received a rough reception:

the peasants did not want to hear what he had to say. Temperamentally more suited to town reformations, he spent most of the Peasants' War in Rothenburg, where he became involved with the pro-Reformation clique, preaching with considerable success, but there, too, opposition grew against him, and on 18 May a petition of 150 citizens demanded that he and preachers of his ilk be replaced 'with other genuinely Christian preachers, who will preach and teach us the Holy Gospel and God's Word purely and clearly without any clever glosses or human additions'. They objected specifically to his Sacramentarianism, 'that he wants to base in grammar' which ordinary folk could not understand. Now the boot was on the other foot, for it was Karlstadt who seemed to be introducing complex human doctrine instead of the pure Word of God, and the old believers could turn the slogans of the evangelicals against them. He left town secretly, with the advice and help of 'a good friend, one of the City Council'—who was, however, none other than Stefan von Menzingen, a supporter of the peasants.[2]

When the peasants were defeated at Würzburg and Rothenburg, Karlstadt faced mortal danger because he was widely believed to have supported the peasants. He fled—to Wittenberg. There he was offered shelter and hiding by none other than the man who had sworn enmity against him back in the tavern in Jena. Luther invited him and his wife and family to stay in the monastery where he himself had just embarked on married life with Katharina von Bora. But there was a price. Karlstadt had to publish two humiliating pamphlets with Luther's own printer, Hans Lufft, one a justification of his behaviour in the Peasants' War, the other a partial recantation of his position on the sacrament. Luther wrote prefaces to each.[3]

For Luther, the Peasants' War began in the battle over iconoclasm and had its roots in the events in Wittenberg in 1521–1522, when a popular Reformation was introduced under Karlstadt's leadership. From then on, his bitter enmity with Karlstadt determined his response to the peasants. The rhetorical arsenal Luther would use during the Peasants' War was devised in the long treatise *Against the Heavenly Prophets*, the work in which he finally got to grips with Karlstadt's theology. By then he had read the six works that he had prevented Karlstadt from publishing until the declaration of their feud in the Black Bear Inn in Jena. In this tract, Luther condemned the 'murderous spirits' who would bring about Aufruhr and painted Karlstadt as a false prophet who claimed divine inspiration but was led by the devil. Luther's response to the Peasants' War was therefore shaped by his obsession with fighting iconoclasm and attacking the claims of those who professed to having divine inspiration, mystics who trusted dreams.

Luther liked to remember that he was the grandson of a peasant, and his first writings on the Peasants' War had at least started by taking peasant grievances into account. But he had always been on the side of established authority, so there was never any chance that he might have supported the peasantry. That alliance with worldly authorities had been brokered through his close friendship with Georg Spalatin, court preacher and secretary to Friedrich the Wise. It was Friedrich who had saved Luther's life after Worms, hiding him in the Wartburg, and there, he had disguised himself as Junker Jörg, choosing noble, not peasant, dress. The Peasants' War sealed that partnership with the elite as Luther became an advisor to the counts of Mansfeld and worked on their behalf to quieten the miners and peasants. Later, he praised the Mansfeld count, who was, as he wrote, 'the first to put on armour'. The boy who had started out down in the Mansfeld Valley with the miners became a friend of the counts up on the hill; and these links were lasting, for Luther's children would boast men like the electoral Marshall Hans Löser and the elector's younger brother, Duke Johann Ernst, as godparents. Throughout his life, the theologian remained close to the rulers of Mansfeld, and he even undertook his last journey to help settle a dispute between them, dying in Eisleben, where he had been born.[4]

Many of those on Luther's side, including Spalatin and Hermann Mühlpfort, were deeply shaken by the events and by Luther's tone.

Johann Rühel, another close ally, warned him it was being said publicly at Leipzig that because Luther's protector, the old elector, had died, 'you fear for your skin' and so 'you are flattering Duke Georg that you agree with his actions' against the peasants. Even 'your supporters', Rühel warned, were troubled. What worried them most was that Luther had not only failed to condemn the 'tyrants' pitiless slaughter' but had gone so far as to proclaim that those who died slaying the peasants 'could become martyrs'.[5] In Strasbourg, the preacher Wolfgang Capito wrote to Ammeister Kniebis, warning him not to rejoice at the peasants' defeat. Even the Nuremberg patrician Caspar Nützel described the retaliation of the authorities in many areas as approaching a tyranny, 'einer tiranei', which might bring its own reaction, and insisted that no reasonable person could deny 'how unfittingly, unchristianly, and much too extremely the authorities had acted against the subjects'. The orthodox Lutheran Johannes Brenz advocated Christian mercy in a printed pamphlet; so many had been executed as a terrible 'example' that there was no need for further brutal killings. He admonished his own town council of Schwäbisch Hall that Christian authorities should not behave like ravening wolves either, and that faults lay on both sides.[6]

Brenz's pamphlet had several editions, including two in Augsburg, where it was printed with a stunning cover by none other than the renowned local artist Hans Burgkmair, then at the height of his fame. Its artistic brilliance, utterly out of place on a cheap pamphlet barely nine pages long, rewards a closer look. A blindfolded prelate of the church in a cardinal's hat faces an emperor in regal robes whose hat has slipped down his head so that he cannot see. Below them a burgher and a peasant raise their arms in supplication. Perhaps Burgkmair was suggesting that justice must be blind, or that the authorities of the old church and the state were blind to the sufferings of those who were being unjustly punished. Below them a bearded knight carries a globe like Atlas: Does he bear the weight of the world on his shoulders? The peasant is familiar to us from the old woodcuts illustrating the pamphlets of the

Title page, Johannes Brenz, *Von Milterung der Fürsten*, 1525. Württembergische Landesbibliothek.

Peasant of Wöhrd—he has the same hat and gesturing hand. But the figure who holds the globe displaying the pamphlet's title appears to be a portrait, and his finely patterned, noble attire has even been coloured in by one former pamphlet owner. His expression is sad, his eyes downcast, his posture slightly stooped. Whoever he may be, this remarkable image is in keeping with the message of the pamphlet and is certainly not a celebration of victory. It is a mystery: Who ensured that a pamphlet from Schwäbisch Hall was printed in Augsburg? Why did the artist who produced the fabulous triumphal waggon for Emperor Maximilian stoop to designing the cover of a cheap pamphlet and produce an image of such quality and originality? And who might the mysterious nobleman be? Puzzles like this reveal the hidden divisions in opinion about the war and its traumatic end. Not everyone wanted the world to be turned right way up again.

The Peasants' War fulfilled all the baleful prophecies of Luther's Catholic opponents and proved that questioning authority in one area led to questioning in another. Preaching the pure Word of God only radicalised the 'common man', 'the people without understanding and also the poor folk', as Jacob Fugger, then the richest man in the world, put it. It showed, moreover, what happened when Luther's antimonasticism was given free rein and convent women were raped and monasteries plundered and burnt. As the Catholic Johannes Fabri wrote, the 'poor wretched widows and orphans of which there are many hundred thousand within a small area of the German nation' must blame Luther: 'their husbands were slain on account of Luther's counsel and sermons'.[7]

Yet Luther managed to elude blame. Try as they might, Luther's Catholic opponents did not manage to make the idea that Luther was responsible for the peasant insurrection stick. Instead, Luther managed to present himself as the supporter of the authorities, the prophet who told truth to power and who condemned the peasants. He did not go back on his call to 'stab, smite and slay' the peasants, nor did he tone down his antimonastic rhetoric. Instead, in early 1526, he supplied an introduction and conclusion to a picture book on the diabolic papacy and 'all its limbs', with sixty-five illustrations depicting every male order—and it was not flattering. By October 1525, as he preached on the 'friendly' authority of father and mother, he described the authorities—to whom, as he points out, we are *not* kin (let alone brothers, he seems to be implying)—as 'our Lord God's beadles, judges and hangmen, through whom he punishes the evil rascals'. This was an even more dour view of secular authority than he had expressed before, because hangmen and beadles were dishonourable people whose touch polluted. Yet while Luther belittled secular authorities, thus seeming to adopt a critical stance, he simultaneously insisted that they were a

necessary evil and must be obeyed. The theories about secular authority that Luther had elaborated in print in 1523 had been put into practice in Luther's behaviour during the Peasants' War. Luther's outlook
shaped Lutheran insistence on obedience to secular powers no matter how unjust, a legacy that may have shaped the Lutheran church's
behaviour when it accommodated National Socialism and reached an
accord after the war with the East German regime.[8]

Meanwhile, other powers made use of the peasants' defeat. In the area
surrounding the city of Basel, the town council had been busily exploiting the crisis to create a unified territory, forcing those peasants
who were not its serfs to buy letters of freedom at their own expense
and pushing back against the rival claims of Solothurn, which owned
a large number of serfs in the region. But in 1532, the peasants 'volun-
tarily' handed back their letters of freedom, and serfdom was reintroduced, though peasants were allowed to marry others in the region,
not just peasants of the same lord. Serfs once more, cheated of their
freedom, they had at least obtained an extension of the right to marry.
The complicated patchwork of subjects of different lords residing cheek
by jowl was ironed out, a process that may also have weakened peasant
power because they could no longer play different lords off against one
another.

By early July, the Lake Constance peasants were put down; in
Alsace, even despite the bloody defeats at Saverne, the peasants still
managed to raise another army and were not fully defeated until late
autumn. In the Samland in East Prussia, peasants finally rose up on 2
September, and the revolt ended less than a week later, on 8 September.[9] In the Klettgau a truce was agreed at the end of June, which at
least gave both the Klettgau and nearby Waldshut some respite after
more than a year of struggle. Zurich tried to protect the Waldshuters
from the Austrians with Hubmaier's support, but in the event Zurich

failed to help, and the Klettgauers were defeated at Griessen in early November. Their shot went too high, failing to hit the enemy, and they were chased into the churchyard, where hundreds were killed, with fighting continuing all night. 'Strike them dead', called the mounted soldiers. In the same month, Zwingli published an attack on Hubmaier's view of baptism, causing the rift between the two men to become public. Eighty of Waldshut's citizens left town secretly, most Catholic but some evangelicals too, and in December the town met and decided to surrender. Hubmaier fled, but he could not travel towards Basel or Strasbourg because the Habsburgs controlled those roads, so he was forced, like Karlstadt, to return to his enemy's citadel, Zurich. The Austrians took the town of Waldshut, Catholicism was reintroduced, and Hubmaier's Reformation was over.[10]

Once in Zurich, Hubmaier was imprisoned along with his wife, who had joined him later. The Zurichers, however, refused to hand him over to the Austrians. He was protected, but he was humiliated just as Karlstadt had been by Luther. Zwingli forced him to recant his commitment to believer's baptism from the pulpit of the main church in Zurich. But in that moment, Hubmaier mounted the pulpit, raised his voice, lifted his hands towards heaven, and said, 'I can and may not recant', the very words Luther had used at Worms. The staged recantation ended in pandemonium when Hubmaier proceeded to defend believer's baptism from the pulpit, and Zwingli stood up from the floor and argued with him.[11]

Hubmaier was carted off to prison again, and by April, ill and exhausted, he finally renounced his faith publicly in a written pamphlet. This would not be the end of his commitment, however, and he managed to leave Zurich, finally arriving in Nikolsburg in Moravia, where he founded another local Anabaptist church like the one in Waldshut. It lasted over a year until the Austrians finally captured, tortured, and burnt him as a heretic; his wife was drowned in the Danube. This time neither he nor his wife recanted. A purported confession was printed by his opponents, just as Luther had printed Müntzer's incriminating letters when he died, but Hubmaier and his wife became revered as martyrs.[12]

Anabaptism was thus also in a sense a product of the Peasants' War. The same concerns that led a preacher like Hubmaier to use the ban as a form of church discipline so that only the godly received communion also led him to argue for believer's baptism, where only those who entered the new covenant were members of the church. This vision was also taken up by the peasant leader Hans Müller, who used the ban to create a coherent band of fighting brothers. Once again, social issues were inseparable from theological visions: those amongst Zwingli's circle in Zurich who advocated believer's baptism were also those who argued most strongly that the tithe was not biblical and should not be defended. This was of course a leading peasant demand, and so the Peasants' War accentuated the theological split between Zwingli and the radicals who would later become Anabaptists, that is, those advocating believer's baptism. Like Luther, Zwingli chose the side of the authorities and of property.

The views of Hubmaier himself, however, were not universally accepted amongst Anabaptists because he was not a pacifist. His thinking had been forged in the struggle of Waldshut in alliance with the peasants against the Austrian authorities. Hubmaier's antagonist Johannes Fabri claimed that he had an arquebus (*Hackenbüchsen*) in his house, owned another firearm (*Feuerbüchsen*), kept a battle sword by his door, and that he had advised on building fortifications. True or not, Hubmaier certainly disagreed with Hans Hut at Nikolsburg over the issue of pacifism and thought Christians should take up the sword in some circumstances, and eventually the congregation split. Hubmaier stood for a kind of radical, nonquietist Anabaptism that was congregationally based, meaning members were bound together by oaths and baptism. His was a vision that was able to reach outwards to others, perhaps because Hubmaier himself was a sociable and charismatic character, but also because it inspired people to defend themselves against the lords and the hostile Austrian Catholic authorities.[13]

Meanwhile, Hubmaier's congregation in Waldshut had lost its preachers, and perhaps half of the citizenry had gone, leaving behind most of what they owned to start new lives elsewhere. The Waldshuters paid a heavy price for supporting the peasants. The gory punishments continued. In Griessen, the captain of the peasants who was a local had his eyes taken out and his fingers chopped off; the pastor Johann Rebmann, 'who was also a good Lutheran', was blinded; and several from Waldshut who were at the battle had their fingers chopped off and had to swear that they had committed perjury against the House of Austria. Thirty-six of those who were captured were stripped down to their 'hose and doublets', given a white stick each, and made to swear to return home in 'wet, cold weather'. Overall, one chronicler claimed, two were killed on the lords' side, but over five hundred peasants were slaughtered.[14]

For the most part, the war was over; those who had survived now had to make sense of what had taken place. Little agricultural work had been done: the nuns of Heggbach noted in autumn that the peasants had nothing to eat 'because they had sown nothing during Lent'. Even so, the chronicler Heinrich Hug reported a good harvest with corn, oats, barley, a lot of very good wine, apples, beer, nuts, acorns, and beechnuts (eckrid). 'But the great unpeace ruined all the land, and one cannot write what it was like, for the lords fined the peasants so hard it cannot be believed. How it will end is in God's hands, who governs all things'. At Rothenburg, Johann Teuschlin refused confession, saying he had shriven himself. Raising their hands, he and his fellows prayed, 'O Lord Jesus, let the pouring out of your blood be a washing away of our sins'. Teuschlin insisted that they were dying for the gospel; his opponents said he was dying for 'Aufruhr', not for God's Word. Each side wanted to set out its version of truth, and even more extraordinary, the chronicler recorded both. Residents of Allstedt, including many women, said that those who died at Frankenhausen had died 'for the sake of the Word of God', and those who had been executed had died 'for the sake of the princes and the will of man'. Their deaths were martyrdoms.[15]

There were less brutal reckonings as well. Johannes Zwick, a high-born pastor of the tiny town of Riedlingen in the Allgäu, and one of those whom the peasants named as a potential sympathetic judge back in February, found himself expelled from his benefice. He wrote a farewell pamphlet to his congregation that had it both ways: he had been expelled for not joining the brotherhood and the 'field pastors', but he admitted he had later agreed to swear after all, 'insofar as it is not against God', a rider that he claimed meant he had not actually sworn. Ever the patrician, he told his 'subjects' not to rebel against the unjust authorities and castigated them for their addiction to sins. He shared Johannes Lachmann of Heilbronn's gloomy apoliticism and tendency to blame everything on human faults. It was all a far cry from the peasants' insistence that they, not the pastor, were the authority and could hire and fire him. Johannes Schwanhauser also wrote a sad farewell from exile to his congregation in Bamberg when the chapter and bishop were restored to power: just as the cow could not ask God why he had not been created a human being, so men could not ask God why they had been created sinners. This was a man who had concluded a sermon in 1523 from the town parish church of St Gangolf by pointing out that 'if we were true Christians, rather than let the poor suffer need we would first sell monstrances, chalices, church and mass vestments'. Sebastian Lotzer, the energetic pamphleteer who compiled the Twelve Articles and who had acted as notary for the peasants, had fled to St Gallen in Switzerland. There he reminisced about the events of that spring with Johannes Kessler, whose chronicle, the *Sabbata*, records their conversations. After that, we lose Lotzer's trace in the records, and so far as we know, he never published again.[16]

We do not know how many peasants were slain in battle or died in the course of the conflict. Perhaps eighty thousand, perhaps a hundred thousand, most of whom perished within the space of just a few weeks. One historian has estimated that in the regions where the war was fought, 10 to 15 per cent of men capable of bearing arms were killed, a colossal proportion. At the time, most observers put the total deaths at a hundred thousand, though they differed on which areas they included in that sum. It is true that contemporary estimates of numbers are notoriously unreliable, and we will never know the true figure. But whatever the total, this was slaughter on a vast scale.[17] Many households would have been left without a male head, many farms without a farmer. These were losses that were unnameable; they found no commemoration at the time. They left their mark in stubborn mistrust of the established church. Many of the villages that would become sites of Anabaptism had been actively involved in the Peasants' War and retained an undying hatred of the church of the 'grossen Hansen'. The 'blood gutters', as they are known today—places where the peasants' blood flowed at Frankenhausen, on the road to Mörstadt from Pfeddersheim (the Bluthohl), and in Saverne—have left their mark in the landscape itself and are not forgotten.[18]

After the bloodshed and the lords' tours of terror, it was time to restore order. First, all the feudal oaths were resworn, re-creating the system of mutual obligation and loyalty. Some of those who had been most active in the Peasants' War and who had fled were now sought by the authorities for punishment, especially townsfolk. Elector Johann, Duke Georg, and Philip of Hesse ordered the women of the Mühlhausen villages to summon their men home, present themselves to the victors, and hand over their leaders. If they refused, the women would be driven out with their children, their houses would be burned down, and their goods given to 'obedient' communities. Many were banished, which effectively rendered them destitute because they were now landless. Huge fines were imposed on the communities to pay for the damage that had been caused and to defray the costs of employing the soldiers. Margrave Casimir squeezed 100,000 Gulden in fines out of his lands, 13,000 from the town of Kitzingen alone, and he did not return the money and goods he had 'inventoried' from the monasteries. Elector Johann, Friedrich's successor in Saxony, exacted 100,000 Gulden in fines, more than double his annual income. Mühlhausen alone was ordered to pay the princes 40,000 Gulden in fines.[19]

The lords proceeded with a characteristic mix of eye-watering financial demands and apparent mercy. One register has survived for the town of Bamberg, which faced nearly 9,000 Gulden in fines, a huge amount for a medium-sized town to assemble—but a substantial reduction from the league's original demand of 50,000 Gulden. The amount each household paid was based on its weekly tax rate, and their payments are carefully noted, along with payments still outstanding.[20] Another booklet from Bamberg lists the nonpayers in one parish; they were all summoned and ordered to pay, and if they could not and were 'guilty', they were to be exiled from town and their property forfeited. The clergy, those they employed, and those who could prove their innocence were exempt. Yet though the fines were large, the bishop tempered victory with mercy. In a good number of cases, people were let off—because he had 'four underage children', she had 'a sick husband', or they were just too poor. This was government by a bishop who could afford to be charitable and to exercise lordship by granting his subjects merciful exemptions—but he did not allow them independence. The ninth of the Bambergers' articles had called for justice to be administered 'according to the stated penalty' and not according to 'Gunst', 'favour', but now the bishop's men chose those whom he would exempt, exercising authority in the time-honoured way.[21]

The punishments were also carefully limited. After all, it was not in the interests of the lords to slay their own workforce, and it was the lords' systems of controlling labour and resources that had underlain the discontent that had exploded in the war. For two or three years after it was over, individual leaders were pursued, and authorities corresponded with one another when they found them. Kuntz Jehle, who had led the Hauensteiner peasants, was finally caught by the Austrians in 1526, taken to the monastery of St Blasien, and hanged from an oak tree on the road by the mill above Waldshut; in revenge on 11 April 1526, the peasants burnt the monastery to the ground.[22] But two or three years later, retribution was no longer as bloodthirsty; some even managed to escape with fines. Most remarkably, Matern Feuerbacher, the innkeeper at Bottwar who had been a peasant commander until he was sacked before the battle of Böblingen for advocating a more moderate course, fled to Rottweil, where he was eventually caught and tried in 1527 but found innocent. After a decade in Zurich he returned to become master of the kitchens for none other than Margrave Ernst of Baden. Few peasant leaders, however, were able to return to their farms.[23]

Instead, court cases rumbled on for years, providing some of the surviving source material as individuals were questioned about what had happened and who was responsible. In Marchtal, the peasants of Alleshausen stubbornly refused to pay the cavalry tax (*Raissteuer*) their abbot had imposed, because they were free peasants, not serfs, and had only ever paid half the tax that others paid; moreover, they had been included in the treaty made by Georg Truchsess with the Lake Constance Bodensee peasants and had already been fined. The records of the legal proceedings betray how things were stacked against the peasants: those who testified on the abbot's behalf were all his officials or employees, and only the statements of two nobles on the peasants' behalf revealed that the abbot had not even bothered to consult the text of the treaty of Weingarten. The matter was decided by judges of the Swabian League, whose forces had defeated the peasants. The abbot claimed the peasantry had caused 2,000 Gulden in damage, but even his witnesses were unspecific about what had been destroyed, aside from some heating ovens. Even so, the peasants did not give up and were able to state their case, and their sullen determination undercut the abbot's effusive protestations about his generosity in dealing with his disobedient peasants.[24]

At Innsbruck, the Habsburg government managed to quell the revolt in the Tyrol by offering a new territorial ordinance (*Landesordnung*) in 1526 that dealt with some of the peasants' grievances. The government accorded them some fishing and hunting rights, and it seized the propaganda initiative by having its ordinance printed and distributed. Apparently the authorities had finally bought the rebels off, and in 1532 they were secure enough to revoke some of the concessions they had made. Mühlhausen and Heilbronn became embroiled in court cases that aimed to settle liabilities and damages, and in both cases the documents were carefully curated to remove evidence that might have incriminated Johann von Otthera, the Mühlhausen town syndic, or might have revealed the extent of Heilbronn's collaboration with the peasants. In the town of Kempten, the canny mayor exploited the weakness of an abbot who had fled his castle to seek safety in town; he forced the abbot to sell the town its freedom. The abbot never recovered his rights. But in the territory of Cardinal Albrecht of Mainz, the towns of the League of the Nine Towns lost their independence for good, and the league was effectively dissolved.[25]

And yet all was not over. Later in 1525, in a village near Kempten, residents met a well-spoken stranger, a tall, thin man of about thirty-four or thirty-five years of age, sporting a dark-brown, thin beard, with a handsome, small face, a bald head, and a slight stoop. Adelhaid Gaisser recalled meeting him. She did not know his name, though she had been told he would not harm anyone but just wanted 'to protect the gospel and stand by it', in the old words familiar from the Peasants' War. There were about fifty others in the tavern at Trogen, where she met him, but the stranger's presence was betrayed, and she and her husband had helped him escape. Now people were travelling to Switzerland to join him there. By spring 1526 the pastor at Oberdorf had slipped over the border; he had been present when the peasants of the Allgäu had negotiated with the bishop of Augsburg in spring of the previous year, when he had looked 'his grace' directly in the eye. 'Florion', a former priest at Aichstetten, was gone too, and so was Mang Batzer of Wilboldsried, along with other veterans of the war. Agatha Käßin, wife of the pastor Christian Wanner (the 'supposed wife', noted the Catholic Austrian authorities), whose husband had notarised the goods the peasants found at Castle Liebenthann, had met the stranger also.[26]

The handsome stranger was Michael Gaismair, the Tyrolean rebel, and in spring 1526, revolt broke out again in Salzburg under his leadership. It seemed that the cow bellowing on the Schwanenberg had at last been heard in the mountains, and the lords' 'Geitz' (greed) had driven people to 'turn Swiss', to fight for the ideal of politically independent, godly communities. The prophecies of *An die Versammlung* had come true, but a year late. In the end, Gaismair and some of his fellow rebels would even manage to escape again over the border to Venice. Though it was no longer on the scale of the Peasants' War, the tradition of revolt had not died, and the women who were unlucky enough to be caught near Kempten, such as Adelhaid Gaisser and Agatha Käßin, showed remarkable courage and openness when they were interrogated by the Austrian authorities. They had not given up.[27]

Overnight on 7 June 1525, the artist Albrecht Dürer had a dream or 'gesicht'—a vision, as he called it. So disconcerted was he that he painted it, one of the very rare occasions on which he made a private painting about himself. Employing the medium of watercolour, he

Albrecht Dürer, *Dream*. Kunsthistorisches Museum, Vienna.

depicted a landscape being showered with giant blobs of rain. This was just after the feast of Pentecost, the liturgical commemoration of the descent of the Holy Spirit, but in the dream all that descends is water. In a description written below, he notes the terrible noise, speed, and cruelty of this flood, which was so great that it woke him up before the second lot of rain came. The next deluge poured from such a height that it seemed to fall slowly. Shocked by the vision, Dürer wrote, 'When I awoke my whole body trembled and I could not recover for a long time'.[28]

Dürer must have had recent events on his mind. At Frankenhausen in mid-May, Thomas Müntzer's followers were defeated, and Müntzer himself was beheaded on 27 May. Then three days before Dürer's dream, thousands of peasants were slaughtered near Würzburg. Starting on 3 June, six thousand peasants had been besieged in Meiningen, and on 5 June they surrendered. This news had reached Nuremberg, the centre of the world, as the anti-Lutheran Johannes Cochlaeus saw it, by 7 June. From the outset, Luther's opponents had prophesied that his ideas would cause rebellion, and indeed, the peasants had advocated brotherly love and called for evangelical preaching. Now the peasant armies in all directions from Nuremberg were vanquished.[29]

Dürer recorded his dream in Nuremberg, a city that had formally declared for the Reformation just a few months earlier. The artist never wrote about the Peasants' War as such, but he did design a mock monument for the defeated peasants that shows milk pails, peaceful cows, cheese, eggs, and grain; atop the pillar sits a 'melancholy' peasant who has been stabbed in the back. There can hardly be a more vivid demonstration of the tragic reimposition of order—and the end of the Lutheran movement as a gospel of liberation. The treatise in which the illustration appears has nothing to do with the Peasants' War but is a technical work about measurement. Perhaps Dürer did not intend to convey a sense of irony over the unmeasured response of the lords to the peasant uprising. But this work by the acclaimed 'modern Apelles', which revealed the secrets of his craft at a time when he was barely painting any longer, was highly personal and idiosyncratic. Hidden in the sections on measuring is a tiny figure, like a peasant, who seems to carry a pitchfork, so tiny that the casual viewer would not see him.[30]

Scholars and art historians have puzzled over these images and over what Dürer meant by them. We shall never know for sure, because Dürer carefully said nothing direct. But they seem to represent in some way the unspoken nightmare of the Peasants' War. Thousands of peasants had been defeated in real, not metaphorical, blood. Luther's language of 'freedom' had given way to an insistence on obedience. Brotherhood could no longer unite the Strasbourg preachers and the peasants, Götz von Berlichingen and his neighbours. The roar of the Peasants' War had been extinguished just as it had been in Dürer's dream, and water had washed out the gutters of blood. The 'victory' was hollow—one of Dürer's other mock monuments in the treatise on measurement was to a drunkard—for it had not been difficult to mow down the peasants, whose humdrum, peaceable produce (the cows,

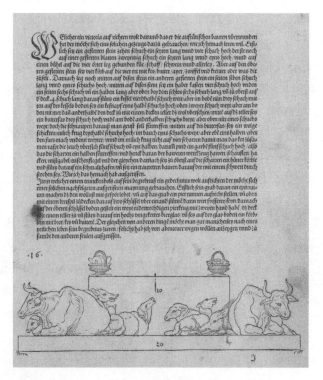

Albrecht Dürer, Peasants' War monument, from *Underweysung der Messung*, 1525. Bayerische Staatsbibliothek, Munich.

sheep, eggs, milk, and grain) form the decorations below the plinth. What noble lord would raise a monument to his slaughter of peasants?[31]

In fact, one did. In 1526, Albrecht of Mainz erected a fountain on the market square at Mainz, a fine piece of red sandstone Renaissance sculpture that celebrated the victory of Charles V at Pavia and the conclusion of the Peasants' War. The monument shows a drunken peasant lying with his legs in the air and his breeches flopping about his ankles; he is pouring copious amounts of wine from a barrel into his open mouth while bottles of wine are spilt on the ground. It mocks the drunken peasants, who tried—and failed—to drink dry the hundred-thousand-litre barrel of wine in the monastery of Eberbach. As legend had it, the devil made the peasants drink the wine and 'blessed' it himself. In one hand the peasant clutches a rooster, a symbol of masculinity but also of the 'red coxcomb', fire, perhaps a reference to the destruction the peasants caused, perhaps a reference to the torching of their own villages in the war. His lost breeches denote his loss of authority and manhood. Above him are the words 'O Bedenck das End'—'O consider the end'—a motto that warns against drunkenness but also refers to the fateful defeat of the peasants. The boorish peasants, the monument insinuates, could not appreciate fine wines, just as they burnt the libraries and melted down the chalices. Opposite the drunken peasant is another column depicting a naked peasant with a loincloth; gold coins tumble out of his sack. He sports the evangelical peasant boots, but he is revealed for what he is: a naked, bestial, wild man and a thief.

The wine the peasants drank may have a deeper resonance, because Albrecht, the cardinal whose sale of indulgences sparked the Reformation, was also a Catholic clergyman who refused to give the laity, the peasants, the wine of communion—the blood with which Christ bought our freedom. Perhaps Albrecht was laughing at Dürer too, for Dürer's mock monument to the drunkard appears in his treatise on measurement just after his design for a monument to the Peasants' War.

These were no heroes, Cardinal Albrecht's monument seems to be saying, but drunken thieving oafs, a powerful message in a town which as a centre of wine-growing valued fine wine. Unlike Dürer's monument, this one's elegant mannerist decorations obscure violence, but it was erected on the marketplace, where the executions of four peasant leaders probably took place, and Mainz itself and the surrounding area of the Rheingau did not surrender until 13 June. And by referring to the legend of Eberbach about the barrel of wine blessed by the devil, which circulated after the Peasants' War, Albrecht's fountain makes the same allegation Luther made: that the war was the work of the devil. Instead of blaming Müntzer or Luther, however, Albrecht blames the peasants.[32]

As Elector Friedrich of Saxony lay on his deathbed early that May in his favourite castle at Lochau, being read to by Georg Spalatin, Luther's great confidante, the castle was nearly empty and a whole world was coming to an end. Friedrich died just ten days before the battle of Frankenhausen, the slaughter he had tried so hard to avert. Zwingli broke with the radicals who had wanted an end to tithes and to infant baptism, and then he broke with Hubmaier altogether, setting the Swiss church on a path of opposition to Anabaptism as he, too, aligned his church with the authorities. In Strasbourg's tolerant milieu, Clemens Ziegler of the gardeners' guild developed his mystical theology and his religious anthropology, complete with diagrams of the human body. Mystical prophets would appear in Strasbourg in the years that followed. But even there, many radical voices were stifled in the reactionary years after the Peasants' War. It is surely no coincidence that Katharina Schütz Zell, wife of the Strasbourg pastor Matthäus Zell, who had visited the Alsatian peasants, stopped writing pamphlets and turned to writing hymns, while the many lay pamphleteers like Sebastian Lotzer and others who had supported the Reformation fell silent. As the Sacramentarians and Lutherans set about establishing churches and structures, evangelical theology ceased being the voice of the dispossessed, losing its radical utopianism and its creative force.[33]

The rebels did not give up entirely. Even after the defeat of the peasants in Switzerland, uprisings continued and peasants went on taking their lords to court and holding them to account. Some settlements did win the peasants a few rights, though they were not always lasting. In 1555, the Legal Ordinance of the Imperial Chamber Court (*Reichskammergerichtsordnung*) accorded peasants, citizens, and everyone else the right to sue their lords. Peasants also resisted by challenging the new forest officials and laws, and by poaching. The theology of brotherhood lived on within Anabaptism, where all addressed each other as 'brother' and 'sister', and where radical utopian ideas, even about sexuality, marriage, and gender, continued to develop. New forms of community, Gemeinde, were tried out in a movement that continued the believer's baptism which underlay Hubmaier's vision of the elective church, and with which Karlstadt had toyed.[34]

But the peasants were unable to defeat feudalism. East of the Elbe, feudalism became reinvigorated as the long-distance trade in grain became lucrative and the lords and upper peasants profited from the labour of serfs, now tied to the land. Perhaps as recent historical writing suggests, this system was not as brutal, not so firmly governed by the whip, as we once thought, and perhaps it allowed many richer peasants to prosper, to marry into the burghers' or even the lords' own class. But for the poor, it spelt a life shorn of possibility. In Upper Swabia, Franconia, and Alsace, feudal dues remained, and while richer peasants may have been able to engage in markets, the hold of the poor on their land was weakened as village elites emerged.[35]

By the eighteenth century, Counter-Reformation clerics were discovering the rural world of the village and recording its dialects and customs; for them, peasants were aliens, their culture an object of curiosity. University-educated Lutheran pastors for the most part had little to say to country peasants who could not read, and theirs became a primarily urban culture. Gone was the vision of the pastor as a man like any other peasant; Lutheran pastors' families typically intermarried, becoming a separate caste.[36] The Peasants' War was perhaps the last moment when the Gemeinde truly outweighed divisions of wealth, where all householders were equal, all brothers fought together, and all brothers decided matters outdoors under the tree. Indeed, later in the century, in the city of Würzburg, the tree outside the council chamber—which had once symbolised the council's power as the voice of the whole community, and where the rebels had gathered to show that they, and not the council, were the people—withered and died. It had to be painted onto the town hall's wall. The fresco of the tree was, of course, a male vision of democracy, yet perhaps with time it would have included women. But then it would have been a different vision.

The peasants must have the last word. 'We're eating goose', they said in late May 1525 as they marched around Alsace. The worried official reported that they were going from village to village, and 'they put their trust in a piece of leather, which I understand to be a shoe'.[37]

'We are up and if you are not coming to us, we are coming to you'.

CONCLUSION

When the Peasants' War was nearly over, Anna Königsfelder, abbess of the St Clare's convent in Bamberg, narrated the story of a mob that gathered in their courtyard demanding entrance to the church so that a mercenary could marry a poor girl 'from the army'. The convent had refused to open its doors. The abbess could see no reason to sully her church for a camp follower who was probably pregnant and a bridal party whom she called 'vermin'. She told the tale about the would-be bride in a letter to a sister nun in Nuremberg, the abbess Charitas Pirckheimer, thinking it would amuse her.[1]

Her contempt speaks volumes about the attitudes of nuns and suggests why monastic institutions were so hated that fully a third of them in the region of the war were attacked, some damaged beyond repair, a figure that rises to more than half the monasteries of rich orders like the Benedictines. Over 100 of the nearly 180 Cistercian monasteries and convents were harmed or damaged, two-thirds of the over 200 Benedictine houses. The sheer scale of the destruction is astonishing, and in the areas of the fiercest fighting in Thuringia, Saxony, Saxon-Anhalt, and Hesse, nearly two thirds of all monastic institutions were attacked.

Clerical personnel, monks, nuns, and priests were threatened and even physically assaulted.

By capturing so many monastic institutions, the peasants fuelled their initial success with secure bases and supplies, while the plunder allowed them to continue the war and buy arms. This helped make the revolt far more effective than previous or future uprisings. It hastened the secularisation of monasteries by revealing how little popular support they had, and it also uncovered exactly what property they owned. When the Württemberg estates met after the war in 1525, the Landschaft demanded that the monks and nuns 'in their splendour and lazy lives' be left to die out; when Duke Ulrich returned to his Württemberg lands in 1534, he secularised them. Elsewhere many convents and monasteries took decades to recover, and some never did. That autumn, the nuns of St Johanniszelle complained that their convent had been plundered by the peasants and they had no dry room in which to sleep; their stores of corn were all wet and ruined, and now the locals were even stealing the convent's 'tiles, wood, bricks [and] doors'. By 1550, the convent was no more. Such stories were repeated in hundreds of convents and monasteries across the empire, creating a situation in which it was easy for Protestant rulers simply to secularise the institutions and seize their wealth. The Peasants' War dealt a huge blow to monasticism, and it would take the Counter-Reformation in the second half of the sixteenth century to begin to reinvigorate the monastic ideal.[2]

The peasants' bloody defeat affected peasant communities for generations and transformed the Reformation from a movement that challenged the social order into one that supported the existing authorities. Luther insisted that revolt could never be justified and that killing rebels was a godly work. The dreams and hopes that inspired scores of thousands of ordinary people to risk all they had were dashed as perhaps as many as a hundred thousand were slaughtered in battle, and hundreds of others were bloodily executed on town squares. With the defeat of the peasants, the vision of a new society was also lost. Theirs had been a theology of creation where the natural world would be used justly, as God intended, where relations between people would be mutually fair and not motivated by 'Geitz'. We have lost sight of this early, socially radical Reformation, and the sheer scale of suffering and loss of life in 1525.

We have also forgotten the excitement. Sebastian Lotzer and Jakob Wehe began as conventional Lutherans, but in barely three months they became impassioned revolutionaries, leaving town to join peasant bands and take leading roles. In Mainz, ordinary craftsmen—including a bath attendant, a metal worker, and a cook's assistant—stayed up all night to write the articles for their revolt. Many, like Georg Vollrath and Mertin Sontag, walked long distances to join peasant armies and were radicalised by their experiences of eating and drinking together and living out of doors. Their 'ideology', as it has been unhelpfully described, developed under the pressure of events as people moved further from the lives they had led, committed to novel ideals, and did new things they would never have dreamed of doing without the inspiration of revolutionary fervour. Revolution transforms people as it alters their emotional and spiritual outlooks.[3]

For three heady months in spring 1525, the peasants were in control of much of what is now Germany, and they began to put plans for a new future into action. They lost because they lacked the military training and cavalry of their opponents, but they were not incompetent. Former mercenaries amongst them knew how to organise, how to destroy castles, and how to seize the best ground for battle. Nor were they without serious weapons. Though peasants sometimes fought with agricultural implements or were reduced to hurling tiles at their enemies, their armies often managed to get hold of well-equipped civic arsenals, found arms in the captured castles, and used plunder to equip themselves better; Florian Geyer even recruited a cavalry unit that fought with the peasants.[4]

Certainly, they were angry at how the lords treated them, but explaining the revolt in economic terms alone is not enough. Many richer peasants and even substantial burghers joined the revolt, as did many poor knights, some under duress, others because they chose to. The relationship between economic conditions and revolt is complex. It does not seem that worsening economic conditions forced the peasants to rebel; indeed, if anything, conditions might have been improving as peasants engaged in markets and as a long period of economic upswing continued after the Black Death. For the twenty years before the revolt, grain prices were stable and harvests broadly good, despite some poorer years and incidents of severe hail damage to crops. Economic circumstances are only part of the explanation. Peasants were angry, but not so much about particular dues, laws, and burdens as by the entire system of lordship itself, which they felt was 'against Christ'.[5]

The Reformation brought a religious transformation that did far more than legitimise or justify previous attacks on the abuses of feudalism; it brought a new vision of creation, of freedom, and of relations between human beings and the environment. Christ had bought us all with his precious blood, and so we should receive the sacrament with both the bread and the wine; we are all 'free' and wish to be free. Or as some put it, all of us, rich and poor alike, are Christ's 'aigen', his 'own', the same word as for serfs. The peasants had not 'misunderstood' Luther and his ideas of freedom. They were using the very paradox that begins Luther's *Freedom of a Christian*—the Christian is lord of all *and* servant of all—to explain why serfdom was wrong. The wild animals and the birds of the forest and the air had been created by God, 'free for' us all; water and woods should be open for all. Labour on God's earth should not be forced—instead we all owed one another brotherly assistance because we are all brothers in Christ. Marching together or taking over monasteries and convents allowed peasants to experience together a life of plenitude, where there was enough meat for all and more wine and beer than you could drink, a life of comradeship and brotherhood, not of dour monastic asceticism. These were the ideals for which people were willing to fight. Despite the differences in lordship, serfdom, and economies, these ideas were broadly the same right across the vast area of the revolt, and even the language in which they were expressed was broadly similar. All could subscribe to the programme of the Twelve Articles, even those who did not know its specific contents.[6]

As the war developed, peasant theology evolved with it, and its attitude towards nobles and the rich hardened. Shortly before the battle, Hans Zeiß, the electoral official at Allstedt, apparently believed that the soldiers at Frankenhausen meant no harm to anyone except those who refused to let themselves be 'reformed'. There should be no more nobles, and all should be equal—'one should be as another'—and their houses, which embodied social inequality, should be levelled. If a noble joined them 'as one of them', then they would gladly have him as a brother. This was a radical, but coercive, vision of social equality that went further than simply forcing nobles to swear brotherhood, and the armed men who gathered at Frankenhausen wanted to make it a reality. After the defeats, some seem to have regarded the deaths as martyrdom for the Word, and near Allstedt, some village preachers were shouting from the pulpit that they should not give up even though the princes were now raging in fury 'in Christian blood', their words recalling Müntzer's own rhetoric. The rebels' hatred of princes and 'top dogs' was now sealed in blood, and gone was any reverence for rulers.[7]

With its rhetoric of brotherhood, its masculine symbols, and its reliance on male fighters, the movement was held together through male bonding as men marched, ate, drank, and lived together in the armies and decided matters democratically 'in the ring'. It is hard to know whether women would have felt included in their men's demands, though the revolt could not have succeeded without women's support in running the farms and gardens their menfolk had left. The intoxicating power that brotherhood conferred may also have led peasant soldiers to overestimate their strength and underestimate their opponents.

At Frankenhausen, Müntzer probably did not assure the troops that he would catch the bullets in his sleeves, as Luther's right-hand man Melanchthon claimed he did, but the apocryphal boast captures the invincibility that soldiers may well have felt as they sang 'Come Holy Spirit' before battle commenced.[8]

So why did the Peasants' War fail? Most strikingly, the miners did not rise in May 1525 despite evangelical fervour and radical preaching, and despite the kinds of splintered rulership that facilitated revolt elsewhere. Nor was it that the worlds of peasants and miners were completely different. Luther's grandfather had been a peasant, and it was his father who ventured into the mines at Mansfeld, while many peasants mined part-time. There were committed revolutionaries amongst the miners, who joined peasant bands and left the mines. But though the miners' articles include demands for Reformation preaching, they concentrated on internal mining matters, while in parts of Mansfeld, the Tyrol, and Saxony, evangelical preaching had already been allowed by the authorities and so was less of an issue. Because they were represented in their own mining organisations with exemptions from some local laws and from tax, the miners' anger was not so readily directed at the authorities.

Because a miner might still hope one day to strike lucky, a theology of the natural world may also have had less appeal. With the ever-rising amounts of charcoal required by smelting, mines were major destroyers of woodlands, for the charcoal was largely imported from areas nearby; and miners used a lot of water to refine and clean ore. It was not very difficult for lords like Ferdinand of Austria, the counts of Mansfeld, or Count Stefan Schlick of Joachimstal to make concessions that would ward off revolt.

Significantly, too, the big towns of Nuremberg, Strasbourg, Augsburg, and Ulm did not join in revolt—even though they had been sites of Reformation agitation and bitter internal civic revolts in the years before 1525. Revolts did occur that year in Frankfurt, Friedberg,

Limburg, Cologne, Münster, Osnabrück, and Minden, but they did not link with the peasants' cause or were outside the region of the peasant revolts. By contrast, Würzburg, Bamberg, Fulda, Hersfeld, Heilbronn, Erfurt, Schmalkalden, Aschaffenburg, Rothenburg, Nördlingen, Memmingen, Schwäbisch Gmünd, Obernai, Mühlhausen, and a host of other towns combusted as internal urban discontent merged with evangelical fervour, especially in the weeks leading up to Easter, when townsfolk could believe that they, like peasants, were fighting for the gospel. After the peasants were defeated, of course, these towns tried to cover their tracks, even removing the traces from the archival record. This makes it easy to overlook just how widespread support for the peasants may have been at the height of the revolt. Afterwards, everyone wanted to forget.[9]

The peasants' failure to bring the large towns into their orbit probably has many reasons. For one thing, cities were simply too populous, rich, powerful, and well armed to be seriously threatened by a peasant army. Yet this is not a complete explanation; just the year before, Augsburg had been forced to employ mercenaries to ensure civic peace, and Erfurt had a decades-long history of bitter internal factionalism. Bamberg, Fulda, Würzburg, Hersfeld, Aschaffenburg, and Mainz were all ruled by ecclesiastical lords, which meant that they found it hard to resist the wave of anticlericalism and antimonasticism. This mood was as powerful in towns as amongst peasants, even in towns that did not ally with the peasants or did so only temporarily. In the end, however, the issues that faced town dwellers and peasants generally diverged, which is why so many towns formulated their own demands and did not adopt the Twelve Articles alone. Although complaints about water, wood, and hunting could resonate with them, in larger towns these grievances were less salient.[10]

Even when town authorities gave the peasants meeting rooms, as they did in Heilbronn and Würzburg, or appointed additional 'monitors' to their councils who represented people who had previously been excluded from power, the peasant systems of government remained separate and autonomous. The townsfolk who supported the pro-peasant, evangelical faction included many middling and elite folk. But it was the coincidence of their revolt with that of the peasants that gave them their chance of success. For the most part, despite large groups in many towns who sympathised with the peasants—especially in the smaller towns that were little more than villages, and in wine-growing areas, where townsfolk often worked in the countryside—the two movements came together only briefly and contingently.

All the same, towns suffered some of the harshest repression and saw some brutal executions. But in 1526, the Diet of Speyer relaxed the provisions of the Diet of Worms, making it possible for authorities to introduce the Reformation in due course, and over the next years many imperial towns did so, including Memmingen, Kempten, Heilbronn, Nördlingen, Windsheim, and later Rothenburg, which had all been involved in the Peasants' War. The events of 1524 and 1525 as well as earlier revolts had shown that civic peace simply could not be maintained without allowing towns to become evangelical, albeit in more moderate form. But though some towns managed in the end to snatch religious change out of the jaws of defeat, the peasantry did not. They had to depend on the religious inclinations of their rulers.[11]

There are many questions this book cannot answer. Why did the revolt fail to spread to the north and west? Why was it apparently so weak in Prussia and in the east, where a German population dominated a local Slavic one? Why was the duchy of Bavaria—admittedly a far smaller and less important area than it is now—able to hold off the rebels? What did Anabaptist thought owe to the Peasants' War, and why did Anabaptist communities later appear in many places that had been involved in it? Thuringia, Hesse, and Alsace became important Anabaptist centres, and the celebration of suffering in Anabaptist theology, the 'baptism of blood' of the true believer, built on ideas developed during the Peasants' War as people came to terms with defeat and persecution.

Why did witch hunts occur fifty years later in many areas that had been caught up in the struggle? Bamberg, Würzburg, Mühlhausen, Gerolzhofen, Mainz, Mergentheim, Eichstätt, Nördlingen, Aschaffenburg, and Alleshausen, amongst others, all saw major witch panics.[12] Perhaps it was mere coincidence. Perhaps tensions between fervent evangelicals and outraged old believers explain both the war and witchcraft. Or maybe the unspoken grief of the Peasants' War—the nameless dead buried unmarked in the fields, the horrific random executions in town centres, the destruction of the landscape, the sheer scale of loss—made people passive and unable to act, and led their descendants to seek a cause for misfortune by blaming it on external forces like witches. They, at least, could be punished and justice meted out.

The Peasants' War failed in its primary goal of shaping society according to the gospel, and the deaths of so many did not succeed in bringing the freedom and brotherhood they sought. In some areas, the lords did make concessions such as reducing death duties, easing marriage regulations, and protecting segments of common land. But serfdom was not abolished, labour dues remained, and tithes continued. Lords continued to exploit the forests and water resources. Over the next generations, the differences between rich and poor peasants became yet more marked when, in many villages, an elite of half a dozen or so families crystallised. They monopolised village offices and dominated the communes, while poorer peasants became more dependent. In eastern Germany, the so-called second serfdom would be introduced and the exploitation of poorer peasants would become more intense. These areas had mostly not been involved in the Peasants' War, but it cannot be said that this was why they underwent the second serfdom, which arose from many long-standing regional differences in economic and political organisation. The war, it seems, did little to stop the erosion of peasant communes' power, and it did not halt the growing differences of wealth and power in rural communities.

After 1525, as Lutheran and Zwinglian preachers set about forming their churches and went out into the countryside, they were shocked by the ignorance and indifference they found amongst rural communities, and they bewailed the Reformation's failure to take root. But peasant alienation was hardly surprising. It sprang neither from peasant irreligiosity nor from lack of interest, for as we have seen, in 1525 peasants rapidly adopted evangelical ideas and made them their own. They used these ideas to formulate a theology of creation that also explained how human beings should treat one another, powerfully condensed in the Twelve Articles. Their alienation may well have been the result of the tragedy of 1525, when their religious hopes had at first been dazzlingly realised and then dashed. The exultation of the marches and the sense of community had been destroyed. They had fought for the right to appoint their own evangelical pastors, and that right had passed to territorial rulers and churches. They had fought for freedom and had lost. What did a 'Reformation' undertaken by the authorities have to offer them?

Despite the disappointments—which were many and enduring—the war did lead to major changes. The peasants flattened the towers of lordship and wiped out the sacred geography of pilgrimage and monasticism. They began the secularisation of the monasteries that Protestant rulers would later complete, and they laid bare the old church's lack of religious engagement with rural communities that the Counter-Reformation would have to address. The war permanently undermined the power of the lesser nobility, continuing the process that was underway in the Knights' War of 1522–1523. Revolts continued, though smaller in scale, and communities went on taking their lords to court.[13]

The Peasants' War cut the tie between the lords' authority and religion by demonstrating that we are all Christ's own and all free, and it showed that feudalism was not divinely sanctioned. Radical religion enabled people to question lordship, to take up the cause of the 'poor', to unite as brothers and experience the power of a crowd of like-minded people, to feel what freedom meant, and even to imagine new political futures. As men like Müntzer, Hubmaier, the author of *An die Versammlung*, and even peasant leaders inveighed in Old Testament language against those they called the 'tyrants', they also evoked the tyrants of Rome and implied that their unjust behaviour must be resisted. And when many who supported the authorities called their repression of the peasants after the war 'tyrannical', they also questioned the rulers' right to behave as brutally as they liked. The concept of tyranny found its way from radical religion and political utopianism into nascent republicanism. It would be developed in centuries to come. In defeat, radical religion sanctified the peasants' suffering, celebrating what Anabaptists would later name a baptism of blood.

The extent of this transformation and the numbers it involved merit the term 'revolution'. Contemporaries nearly universally called it the 'Aufruhr', the turbulence, a word that captures its disruptive motion. It was also a bloody war between two very unequal sides that left traumatic memories. And yet the ideas and dreams that had been formed in the war did not disappear but lived on in Anabaptism and in many varieties of radical thought. The peasants who refused to swear their oaths to their rulers until they were compelled to do so had changed profoundly. They no longer accepted their lord's authority as natural, and they knew they were not alone. The war's legacy of blood desacralised lordship and unmasked it as unchristian and unbrotherly.

The German Peasants' War had legacies greater than its immediate and even longer-term consequences. These are not just historical but intellectual and political, as the event became a primary battleground for arguments between right and left, and a test case for the study of revolution in all periods. Some of the most profound political debates in historical writing of the last two hundred years, and especially over Marxism and its legacies, were fought out on the terrain of the German Peasants' War; indeed, Karl Marx and Friedrich Engels themselves developed their theories of revolution and progress by studying it.

And the story of 1525 is more than just an academic matter; in Germany it is a public issue. After the Second World War and the formation of the two postwar German states, East and West Germany, the Peasants' War became emblematic of their differences. Both sides drew on it to claim national legitimacy. West Germany lauded the Twelve Articles as the first document of human rights, while East Germany made Thomas Müntzer the hero of the early bourgeois revolution, erected statues to him, named streets after him, and even put him on its five-mark banknote. The radically different approaches and the lavish public celebrations that accompanied them encapsulated the distinct, antagonistic identities of the two German states.

By the twenty-first century, the subject had become so weighed down by stale debates and fixed positions, and so tainted by its political appropriations, that there has been no new history of the German Peasants' War for nearly forty years. Small wonder that historians mostly left the subject well alone. But it is vital to return to these old controversies because they reveal what is at stake for us in writing a new history of the war, both for the history of revolutions and for understanding German national identity in the modern era. Reprising them reveals the paths that were not taken, in particular, historians' blindness to the ecological dimensions of the revolt. If we want to understand Germany today, we need to take stock of this freighted history, not forget it. As a historian who has spent my life fascinated by Germany, and who lived through German reunification, I wrote this book for these reasons.

Modern historiography began with Zimmermann's three-volume history of the war, published between 1841 and 1843, a vivid and romantic account that fired the imaginations of many, including Marx's coworker Engels and the artist Käthe Kollwitz. Zimmermann was a

Lutheran theologian, a vegetarian who cared passionately about the natural world and freedom, and soon he put those beliefs into action, becoming a left-wing member of the revolutionary Frankfurt Parliament in 1848. Indeed, Zimmermann's history may well have inspired these later rebels. Another leader of the 1848 revolution, Friedrich 'Carl' Hecker, marched his followers through the Black Forest in a bid to spread the ideas of freedom just as Hans Müller of Bulgenbach had done before him.

Ever since Zimmermann's book, the Peasants' War has occupied a highly contested position in relation to German national identity and to political ideology left and right. Marx's *The Eighteenth Brumaire of Louis Bonaparte* and Engels's *The Peasant War in Germany* were written around the same time and in the wake of the failure of the revolutions of 1848. Both engage with revolution and with peasants, the two works forming two halves of a single intellectual endeavour. Both also reveal the limitations of Marxism in understanding peasants and their communities.[14]

Engels deals with a peasantry that rebelled in a divided, complex Germany, Marx with a French bourgeoisie whose material interests in the end led them to betray the revolution. Both interpret their subjects in the light of the forward march of history. In 1525, the early German bourgeoisie was not strong enough to push through its own interests, while the miners and other proletarians were not yet sufficiently numerous to win; whereas in 1848 in France, the proletariat could not overcome the bourgeoisie but had enough self-consciousness to know that its interests were not theirs. Both authors therefore relegate peasants to the sidelines of history. Engels sees them as part of an old feudal order and hence not truly revolutionary, and he assigns the key historical role to the bourgeoisie even though it was the peasants who acted. But it is impossible to overlook his sympathetic interest in the peasant struggle, and some of his best passages are devoted to the revolts before the war, the meeting places, banners, and even the 'beggar kings', one of whom he cannot resist describing: he had 'spices and wormseeds for sale, and wore a long steel-coloured coat, a red barret with the Baby of Trient attached to it, a sword at his side, and many knives and a dagger in his girdle'. Engels also pays attention to mysticism and religion, arguing that Müntzer 'held the threads of the whole movement' but did not yet have a 'class' that could support him: 'The worst thing that can befall a leader of an extreme party is to be compelled to take over a government at a time when society is not yet ripe for the domination of the class he represents and for the measures which that domination implies'. And so Müntzer is trapped like an impotent time traveller, able to articulate 'the ideas of which he himself had only a faint notion' but incapable of 'transforming society'.[15]

Marx, by contrast, denounces the smallholders, the peasants who won freedom and their own plots of land. They supported Napoleon and they are conservatives, confined because 'their method of production isolates them from one another, instead of drawing them into mutual intercourse'. Infantile creatures, they are incapable of revolution and must be represented by a leader 'who protects them from above, bestows rain and sunshine upon them'. Peasants are all the same, and they make up the vast mass of the French nation, 'much as a bag with potatoes constitutes a potato-bag'; the dismissive metaphor encapsulates his view of them.

An unwillingness to theorise how peasants engaged in revolution was one of Marxism's great failures. Classical Marxism was unable to imagine Maoism and a revolutionary peasantry and had no adequate account of the relationship between human beings and the environment. East German Marxist historiography renamed the German Peasants' War as 'the early bourgeois revolution', obliterating the peasants altogether. Marx and Engels were mesmerised by industrial production, failing to see the environmental harm it caused or why peasants cared so deeply about the land and its resources. And for all Engels's interest in religion, his elevation of Müntzer as the sole true revolutionary leader is just a mirror image of Luther's condemnation of him as the devil in physical form. Both attribute far too much significance to Müntzer, and so they fail to see the number and variety of revolutionary actors, and the wealth of ideas the movement generated.

Marx's attraction to a scientific study of history also led him to reject idealism and, above all, emotion. *The Eighteenth Brumaire* opens with an extraordinary passage where Marx excoriates 'bourgeois revolutions', in which 'men and things seem to be set in flaming brilliants, ecstasy is the prevailing spirit'. By contrast, proletarian revolutions 'criticize themselves constantly;... scorn with cruel thoroughness the half measures, weaknesses and meanesses of their first attempts'. It is hard not to see this contrast between the flighty uprisings of the bourgeoisie and the reason-driven revolutions of the proletariat in gendered terms. Indeed *The Eighteenth Brumaire* is peppered with misogynist metaphor. Marx pronounces that 'a nation, no more than a woman, is excused for the unguarded hour when the first adventurer who comes along can do violence to her'; when Barrot becomes head of Bonaparte's ministry, he 'leads the bride home, but only after she has been prostituted'. Marx's suspicion of emotion also means that he accords little significance to the rebels' dreams and hopes, or to what he termed their 'ecstasy', the experience of revolution which, I have insisted, is so central to the story of the German Peasants' War.[16]

The war did not remain the preserve of the left for long. From the 1930s through the post–World War II era, the Western understanding of the Peasants' War was reshaped by a former member of the SS who may well have worn his uniform when lecturing: Günther Franz, who held the first chair of history at the occupied University of Strasbourg in 1941. In the conclusion to the first edition of his history of the Peasants' War, a popular classic published in 1933, he wrote, 'Everywhere the peasant is on the march and, united, places himself behind the Führer of our people, who has recognised the eternal values of blood and soil and has put them in the service of our "Volk"'. He remained a scholar after the war, albeit banished to the minor university of Stuttgart-Hohenheim, but he continued to reissue his history of the German Peasants' War virtually unaltered, and to coedit collections of source material.[17]

Franz's labours created a vast treasury of published records systematically gleaned and transcribed from the archives—but his selection also shapes how scholars today can perceive the war. Though his National Socialist political views are mostly implicit, he waxes lyrical on the importance of leaders and explains the revolt's lack of success in some areas as due to the absence of charismatic figures. He idealises the Gemeinde, the commune, playing down divisions of wealth and naturalising the feudal order. He assiduously notes the rebels' antisemitism, something that many other historians gloss over. For him, the Peasants' War was an authentic expression of the German people, who formulated grievances against their lords and who wanted Germanic law in place of Roman law. He was scathing about areas that merely adopted the Twelve Articles and failed to produce genuine lists of complaints of their own, or that had poor leaders. For him this included the Ries, the area of the Bildhausen army, and much of middle Germany apart from Thuringia. His idealisation of a German peasant past fitted seamlessly into Nazi culture, and its seeming objectivity enabled it to leach into postwar scholarship.[18]

By the 1960s and 1970s the communist state of East Germany was developing its own Marxist understanding of the war, dominated by historians like Max Steinmetz and Günter Vogler, theologians like Siegfried Bräuer, and a host of others. They developed the class analysis Engels had pioneered, giving it foundations in meticulous social research, but Steinmetz still regarded Müntzer as the key figure. Only when the war moved to 'middle Germany'—the very area Franz thought not properly rebellious—did it become truly revolutionary under Müntzer's leadership, whose influence Steinmetz discerned throughout the region. So important was Müntzer in Steinmetz's view

that he classed everything that occurred after the defeat at Frankenhausen as the 'decline period'.[19]

The East German regime adopted Engels's laudatory assessment of
Müntzer. In 1976, the year after the 450th anniversary of Frankenhausen, the regime commissioned a massive circular monument to the
Peasants' War on the battlefield; it houses a panorama oil painting 14
metres high and 123 metres long by the artist Werner Tübke. Tübke's own attitude to the regime was ambiguous, and his work does not
idealise peasant struggle or subscribe to the onward march of history.
Instead he created a cyclical painting that has no clear end. Crammed
with arresting details lifted from sixteenth-century art, it even employs
that era's rich reds and browns, and like Dürer, who sometimes included himself in his paintings, Tübke depicts himself in it. The work
took him and his assistants twelve years to complete, and it staked
the claim of East Germany to be the true heirs of a populist, cultured
'Germany'.

As the art historian Ulrike Eydinger has shown, Tübke in fact took
nearly all the hundreds of motifs that crowd the work from the *Illustrierte Geschichte der frühbürgerliche Revolution* (Illustrated history of
the early bourgeois revolution), the volume Steinmetz himself edited
to commemorate the 450th anniversary of the war in 1975 and which
made East Germany's interpretation of history available to a mass public. Thus despite Tübke's distance from the regime's orthodoxy, his
work was in a very profound sense an East German artifact. The giant
circular building that houses it still dominates the hill today. And then
in one of history's great ironies, the panorama opened with a fanfare on
14 September 1989 in the presence of the deputy of the leader of the
German Democratic Republic Erich Honecker (Honecker himself was
by then too ill to attend). Just weeks later, the Berlin Wall fell and the
regime came to an end.[20]

In 2017, German celebrations of the 500th anniversary of Luther's posting of the Ninety-Five Theses sought to draw a line under

this division between East and West and bring the country together in commemorating Luther as the hero who was born in and was active on the soil of the former East Germany. As the inventors of the German language, Catholics could celebrate him as well as Lutherans, and the Peasants' War and Müntzer could for the moment be forgotten. In Wittenberg itself, a large circular panorama was constructed that told the story of the dawn of Luther's Reformation, as if deliberately demeaning Tübke's masterpiece.

But not everyone concurred with this adulation of Luther. Alongside the flood of Luther biographies unleashed by the Reformation's quincentenary came a 2016 biography of Thomas Müntzer by Siegfried Bräuer and Günter Vogler. This volume was, in a sense, the swan song of the East German lauding of the heroic Müntzer as well as a counterblast against Lutheran hagiography; it is also a moving monument to the scholarly cooperation of a historian and a theologian critical of the East German regime. More recent work, however, especially by Thomas T. Müller, has demoted Müntzer from his previous centrality, revealing that he was not even the sole theologian of Mühlhausen or Allstedt, still less the inspiration of the entire war. But if we have lost Müntzer as a revolutionary hero, we have gained a far wider sense of the Reformation as a dynamic and variegated movement.[21]

The West German assessment of the Peasants' War was just as ideological. Writing in 1977, Peter Blickle presented the war as the 'revolution of the common man' fired by the ideal of godly law. Equally of its time, his interpretation was infused with the values of postwar social democratic West Germany and, one might say in retrospect, inspired by the revolution of 1968. Blickle's formulation addressed the problem that the revolt had not just involved peasants but townsfolk and miners too, just as 1968 sought to bring workers and students together. He broke with a simple class analysis, arguing that its actors were not a proletariat or an oppressed peasantry but a coalition of those without a stake in power, the 'common man'. He dethroned Müntzer as the revolt's leading ideologue and set the war in the context of the theology of south Germany, which owed little to Luther and was instead influenced by Zwingli and other theologians of the region.[22]

Blickle saw the Gemeinde as providing a lost democratic model for decision-making. Germans, he argued, had not always been Führer-loving conformists. This, too, was one reason why he and many West German historians of those years downplayed Luther's influence, which was associated after the Second World War with Prussian authoritarianism. By recovering the influence of Zwingli in the southwest, they showed that a local non-Lutheran, community-oriented kind of Protestantism had existed and was part of West Germany's historical inheritance. But his idealisation of the Gemeinde rings hollow now. The term 'common man' only worked for men—after all, in sixteenth-century parlance, the 'common woman' was the prostitute, and women were not amongst those who decided matters in the ring. Blickle interrogated neither the masculinism of his own language nor that of the values of the revolt. The rebels themselves used the word 'brother', not 'common man'. His work was based primarily on sources from the southwest, in particular the Black Forest, where the revolt began, because these were the archival materials and landscapes available to him in West Germany. This perspective, however, meant that he assumed that the whole revolt was about 'godly justice' and involved grievances to do with law. And he conceived of the Reformation as the mechanism that legitimated and generalised local demands to address lordship as an institution, not as a wide-ranging, amorphous, religious movement in its own right.[23]

This highly politicised historiography explains why it has been so difficult to approach the subject for the last forty years. Reunification finally offered the chance to bring all regions into our account. It also allows us to move beyond classical Marxism and Western neo-Marxism, and to begin to understand what the Peasants' War has to say to us today.

Neo-Marxists and post-Marxists like E. P. Thompson and Gareth Stedman Jones have argued that economic interest and class alone do not determine how people behave; first, one must recognise oneself as belonging to a class. Thompson brilliantly showed how working people gradually began to see themselves as part of a collective and as proletarians, though he was scathing about Methodism and the false religious vision of collectivity that it offered. Nor did he have much to say about how far women saw themselves as part of a class. We have learned a good deal about the nuances of language, which has led to finer analyses of what the rebels wanted and has opened up the range of voices that our histories now include. But such a focus also has its limits. At its most basic, the language of class only takes us so far with the German Peasants' War because the peasants talked of 'brotherhood', not class.[24]

As we have seen, 'brotherhood' was a capacious term that meant virtually anyone male could be a brother. The language of brotherhood could be used by nobles, peasants, and townsfolk, while symbols like banners or seals were as important as words for creating a group identity that largely excluded women. Much more formative was the experience of brotherhood—the shared experience of finding and then joining the peasant band and marching together as men. But the revolt did not fail because its language was too broad. Indeed, an emphasis on language too easily draws the historian towards the study of print in what was still largely an oral society. If we emphasise the printed word in this manner, we risk amplifying the bias of records, which were dominated by the literate. Most peasants could not read or write, and there are almost no accounts of the war from their perspective. And an emphasis on language and discourse cannot explain how and why people become committed enough to revolution to risk their lives. Hearing a sermon in a large group, perhaps out of doors, or before battle, could itself be a life-changing experience that the printed page does not convey.

The French *Annales* school, and Fernand Braudel in particular, with its concept of *mentalité*, offers a different way of approaching peasant life on its own terms that at first sight might seem to take us further. Works such as Braudel's famous three-volume *Civilization and Capitalism* (1967–1979) sought to examine enduring structures such as climate and landscape and saw events as epiphenomena. *Mentalité* describes a mental disposition mixing emotion, values, and ideas; it is shared by a whole social group, in this case, the peasantry, and linked to the land.

However, though landscape and climate are important, this approach risks presenting peasants as unchanging, closer to natural forces, even less than fully human; indeed, Braudel provides some of his material on the peasantry under the heading of 'Climate'.[25] But peasants are not immutable, and during the Peasants' War many changed their ideas very quickly and reacted to shifting events. The visions they espoused were not all the same, and they disagreed about violence, arguments that the term *mentalité* does not help us to understand. After all, peasants were never romantically aloof from markets; they constantly responded to economic opportunities, growing new crops and selling produce in towns. Nor was the Peasants' War simply a cyclical reprise of earlier European revolts, like the Hussites, the Poor Conrad revolt, or the Bundschuh movements. True, peasants had been involved in revolts before, especially in the southwest, and some of their complaints were similar, but they also learned from their experiences. They learned how to organise; where to meet; how to get flags, fifes, and drums; and how to secure weapons.

My approach has been to try to understand the world the peasants inhabited through uncovering the rich detail of their daily lives, and to reconstruct their beliefs not only from what people said—though I have done that as much as possible, from as many different voices as I can—but through what they did. Instead of deducing an explanation from economic position or social class alone, I have intended to reconstruct what the rebels experienced, felt, and believed. I have argued that the revolt was motivated by religious conviction, a revolutionary religious commitment that our denominational histories have led us to forget, and with it, the social radicalism of the early Reformation. Religion was not a cloak or guise for expressing something else, but a profound worldview that changed lives and aimed to transform society. It included emotions, the 'ecstasy' of revolt that Marx disdained but without which people could not have acted. Indeed, revolutions must be explained in terms of beliefs, experience, and emotions as well as social conditions. Class and injustice are learnt through experience, through daily humiliations and privations, and beliefs are not just rational sets of propositions. The Twelve Articles were important not only because they articulated a theology but because they were a printed object that one could point to, a concrete crystallisation of a set of attitudes and convictions.

The revolt celebrated God and Christ as male figures and dispensed with Mary and the saints. At one convent the rebels even chopped off Mary's head. In this it differed from peasant revolts before it, which so often turned to Mary. The powerful male bonds created a sense of belonging and cohesion that could on occasion even trump class. But this emphasis was also a fatal weakness because it obscured the different interests of the coalitions that 'brotherhood' held together. It also cut the movement off from women and limited its goals. Some of the early demands—such as those connected with marriage and serfdom, with service dues, with the work of preparing and spinning flax, even with the justification for fishing in ponds (pregnant and nursing women needed to eat fish)—were lost as only men formulated the Twelve Articles. Revolutions tend to create male heroes and to celebrate battles, but patriarchal structures were as powerful amongst peasant communities as they were amongst the lords. The intoxication of brotherhood after days of marching may also have led men to exaggerate their own military capabilities and prevented them from realising how little chance they stood against cavalry.[26]

This is not to take away the radical edge of the Peasants' War, or to deny its significance. Indeed, it recognises the sheer breadth of their ideas, which addressed the environment, human agency, animals, and freedom. These were not the issues that interested Marx and Engels, because they did not point the way forward to the industrialisation of the future. But they are the questions that confront us now: Who owns natural resources, timber, rivers, ponds, and common lands? Who controls energy sources? How can we till the land sustainably, in a way that is fair to both small and big producers? How can wealth be shared more equally? These issues also force us to ask what the 'community' consists in, how far it extends, and how to prevent a community becoming exclusive, a problem the peasants were unable to solve. Their anarchic structure of independent yet cooperative bands meant they did not always agree or even show solidarity with one another in times of need. Yet even so, they held fast to the dream of being part of a community, a fellowship of 'brothers' that stretched beyond their village and the structures of lordship.

The war was not the work of any single figure, but of vast numbers of people who joined in bands together, did things they had never imagined doing, and risked their lives for a future they wanted to build. They called for the freedom that Christ had bought with his precious blood, and they wanted creation to be 'free for' all humans to enjoy. They wanted social relations between people to be different too. They wanted to end exploitation and coercion and replace them with mutuality and brotherhood. They did not think in terms of individual rights but of collective obligations, including shared access to the natural resources of the earth, sky, and waters, which God had made. Theirs was a utopian vision; indeed, it could encompass a profound spirituality. And though it was of its time, it has much to say to our time too.

ACKNOWLEDGEMENTS

To understand the Peasants' War, you have to know the landscapes. I began this book by cycling the route taken by Thomas Müntzer and three hundred of his supporters from Mühlhausen to their final battle at Frankenhausen, a journey from which most did not return. I finished the book by cycling six hundred kilometres from Strasbourg to Saverne, along Alsatian vineyards and the regions Erasmus Gerber organised, across the Kaiserstuhl and Colmar to the Upper Rhine, Breisach, and the Black Forest, through which Hans Müller marched his men into Freiburg, and finally down to low-lying Constance on the beautiful lake, where the Seehaufen, the Lake Constance band, formed. The best way to get to know a landscape is to feel it in your legs, and over the nine years it has taken me to write this book, I have walked or cycled most of the places it mentions. I chose to travel at walking or cycling pace because I needed to know the landscape at the speed the peasants moved through it, not with the rapidity the car makes possible, and because I needed to be able to slow down and notice my surroundings. Only then could I fully appreciate the vast scale of the event, and why the peasant armies formed and reformed as they did.

Of course, the landscape we see today is not that of the sixteenth century. Most crassly, the East Germans blew the top off the battle-field at Frankenhausen to build the giant Panorama Museum that commemorates the battle. Roads are routed differently now; modern farming has removed field patterns; woods have vanished. But traces of the old roads remain in the back routes that walkers and cyclists take, while the underlying topography and soils still determine to some extent what can be grown, how hills, mountains, and church towers dominate the landscape, and they shape that intangible, the 'feel' of a place.

I also visited the many battlefields of the war. At Leipheim, the site of the first major peasant defeat, where peasants were cornered on boggy ground between the Danube and the Biber Rivers, the road dips down towards the site, and the area has not been built on, remain-ing one of the few battlefields that still looks pretty much as it did. Königshofen, a hill outside the town, now has wide vistas which would have been wooded then; at Scherwiller, the town is on a wide, flat plain and the hills rise sharply behind. At Freiburg the slopes of the Burghalde hill below the castle are directly opposite the town. When Hans Müller captured it in one of the most stunning peasant victories of the war, he could threaten the Freiburgers into surrender because from the Burghalde you can indeed see and aim at every single build-ing as clearly as if it were a shooting range. I went to as many monaster-ies and convents and their ruins as I could, and saw the sheer size and extent of their buildings that still tower in the landscape today, their gi-ant barns and armouries, and the characteristic defensive quadrangles of the foundations of the Teutonic Knights. No wonder the peasants were angry at where their money was going.

But the most shocking encounter was at Lupstein, the scene of an atrocity where the troops of the Duke of Lorraine set the village on fire from all four corners, incinerating the peasants who had sought sanc-tuary in the church. As you approach the village by the side of a canal, the church stands out; it can be seen from far away because it is on a hill. There is nothing left of the original building, but to the side is an ossuary. Looking in, I encountered the skulls and bones of hundreds of the peasants about whom I had been writing.

My life as a historian and the lives of other historians of my generation have been bookended by the German Peasants' War. As an undergraduate in Australia, I watched the East German celebrations of the Peasants' War in 1975, and its five hundredth anniversary comes as my cohort retires. My generation witnessed the fall of the Berlin Wall and saw social and cultural history displace Marxist materialism. For the last thirty years, historians have in the main been more interested in continuity than in change, in the growth of the state or the crystallisation of Protestantism and Catholicism, and less concerned with moments of rupture when the world turns upside down.

It might seem tempting now to belittle the historians of the previous generation, the postwar 68-ers in East and West who idealised the Peasants' War as the first struggle for democracy, or who named it the early bourgeois revolution, and to claim that the war's importance has been overstated, its revolutionary ideas overhyped, or that it was merely a string of related revolts that lacked an overall coherence. But this would be to duck the methodological challenge its history poses, of how to write the story of a movement that left only limited written sources. And it would be to sidestep the question of how to understand revolution in a post-Marxist era, the foremost intellectual challenge that has confronted my generation. I lived through the period of reunification and spent a year at the Wissenschaftskolleg, the Institute of Advanced Study in Berlin, in 1991–1992, barely two years after the wall came down, and I witnessed that long process and its intellectual ramifications. I am grateful to the WIKO, which made that possible, and to Wolf Lepenies, its then director, who wisely remarked that the point was not to publish a book, but to seize the chance to open oneself up to new experiences. The Humboldt Foundation enabled me first to work in Göttingen for a year and then to spend a year in a very different Berlin in 2006–2007, when writing a biography of Luther meant that I spent time in the former East, getting to know places like Wittenberg, Dresden, Erfurt, Weimar, Halle, Wernigerode, and Mansfeld. The German Peasants' War is the single historical issue that encapsulates the differences between East and West, and that is why it is so urgent to understand it afresh, a full generation after the wall came down.

During my travels I met many people in museums, in archives, and on the road, some of whose names I do not know but all of whom helped me and whom I would like to thank. Amongst them, in Leipheim, Susanne Anwander not only showed me the Bauernkriegsmuseum in the former Blaue Ente Inn but even drove me to the battlefield; in Heilbronn one evening, the museum staff found me maps, recommended books, and answered my endless questions. In Böblingen the staff of the museum were very helpful, as were the staff in Frankenhausen at the Panorama Museum and in the town museum. At the Ashmolean Museum Oxford, An van Camp compiled a huge database of images of peasants and found me a fantastic print by Barthel Beham, while Isabel Holowaty of the Bodleian Library has been unfailingly helpful. In Mühlhausen, Antje Schloms in the archive helped in so many ways. The archivist at Mühlhausen, Helge Wittmann; the director of the Mühlhausen Museums, Susanne Kimmig-Völkner; the archivist of Memmingen, Christoph Engelhard; Anna Aurast at the Stadtarchiv Heilbronn; and Jörg Filthaut, archivist of the Thuringian State archives at Meiningen—all have done much to help the project. The staff at the city archives of Bamberg, Heilbronn, the state archive in Würzburg, and the state archives at Dresden have all been very helpful.

Natascha Mehlers of the University of Tübingen generously discussed her findings about the twenty-four skeletons from the Peasants' War at Leipheim. The Thomas Müntzer Gesellschaft and its *Vorstand* are wonderful friends and colleagues, and I am honoured to be a member. Like all who work on the *Bauernkrieg*, I am profoundly indebted to the army of local historians who care so much about this history and have shared material on the Peasants' War online, collecting forgotten sources and identifying the locations of castles, monasteries, and battles. And last but not least I would like to thank ExperiencePlus! Cycling for accidently compiling exactly the route I needed, and the group of five who cycled it with us.

The award of a two-year Leverhulme Senior Research Fellowship enabled me to write the book. The research was enabled by the award of the Gerda Henkel Prize in 2016, which amongst other things allowed me to purchase the vast library of books needed, to travel, and to write. The Reimar Lüst Prize of the Humboldt Foundation made it possible for me to spend time in Germany, and I am grateful to my host and friend Daniela Hacke of the Freie Universität Berlin. The Faculty of History generously gave me sabbatical leave, without which I could not have written the book. The Oxford-Berlin partnership enabled me to work with Matthias Pohlig and with his and Daniela Hacke's students at the Freie Universität and Humboldt University. Ed Wareham Wanitzek first suggested that I write a history of the Peasants' War, and then co-ran the project Convents and Monasteries During the Peasants' War with me, which was twice funded by the University of Oxford John Fell Fund. It has now become a project to create a map of the destruction the peasants caused, codirected with Beth Plummer and funded by the British Academy. Louisa Bergold, the researcher on the project, has created a superb resource, and all future students of the war will be indebted to her; Charlotte Gauthier is compiling the information in map form for the anniversary year.

Bethan Winter, Michaela Kalcher, Aaron Larsen, and Louisa Bergold all carried out miscellaneous research tasks for me; my warm thanks to them. Ellen Yutzy-Glebe undertook a fact-checking reading, and I am deeply indebted to her eagle eye.

Nina Sillem took the manuscript on trust, and I am grateful for her and Peter Sillem's friendship over many years. At Fischer, Tanja Hommen has been an empathic editor who understood the book at once and provided encouragement at a key point. Holger and Sabine Fock, the German translators, are a joy to work with, and I am fortunate to have them. Clare Alexander, my agent, has been behind me during difficult times, and she and Lisa Baker solved problems that seemed insuperable. At Basic Books, Lara Heimert has been a steadfast and insightful publisher; Brandon Proia is a marvellous line editor with an intuitive sense of what a paragraph needs. Kelley Blewster is a dream copy editor who ironed out countless infelicities. My thanks to Kristen Kim and Melissa Veronesi for keeping the show on the road.

In Oxford, the informal Early Modern Workshop was where the book began, and it owes more than I can say to its members' support and discussion. Many people generously read the manuscript, and all of them helped me immeasurably; the writing was so difficult that I was more than usually reliant on their advice and support. I am more grateful than I can say to Gadi Algazi, Andy Drummond, Daniela Hacke, Joel Harrington, Kat Hill, Beat Kümin, Peter Matheson, Daniel Pick, Mike Roper, Carla Roth, Barbara Savage, Alex Shepard, and Ed Wareham, who each read the entire manuscript and commented on it extensively; they all shaped the book in different ways and are not responsible for its errors. I learnt greatly from conversations with Etienne François, Bruce Gordon, Bridget Heal, Alison Light, Hannah Murphy, Simon Ponsonby, Philipp Rössner, Miri Rubin, Ulinka Rublack, Jenny Spinks, Claudia Ulbrich, Peter Wilson, Karin Woerdemann, Andy Wood, Benjamin Ziemann, Charles Zika, and Oliver Zimmer as well as discussions with Anand Narsey and Sam Stargardt. Gerd

Schwerhoff generously answered questions and shared materials, while Thomas Kaufmann kindly let me read his manuscript on print and the Peasants' War before its publication.

Some truly remarkable people work on the Peasants' War, and this undertaking has brought me many new friends. Amongst them I would like to thank the late Henry Cohn, who first pointed out the economic dimensions of anticlericalism; the late Tom Scott, who generously met and discussed ideas with me until his untimely death; and the late Bob Scribner, my doctoral supervisor who together with Tom created the collection of documents in English that makes it possible to teach the subject, and whose work has inspired so much of this book. Though Bob died in 1999, his scholarship continues to provide the agenda for Reformation studies. Scott and Scribner's overview of the events of the war is still the best short account and the indispensable starting point for German- and English-language scholars alike.

In Mühlhausen, Thomas T. Müller not only shared his research on Thomas Müntzer but took me to Stollberg, Allstedt, Heldrungen, and many other Müntzer sites. I have benefited hugely from his scholarship and inspiration, his hospitality, and his sense of fun; he also read the manuscript and even checked the bibliography. Ulrike Eydinger made me understand Tübke's masterpiece in completely new ways. Doug Miller introduced me to dioramas and showed me how materiality can help you understand military history and the landscape. Andy Miller has been a tower of strength, reading the entire manuscript twice, encouraging me, and brilliantly providing instant online research on the strange monuments to the war I encountered during my travels. Through this research I met Peter Matheson in New Zealand, who read the entire book and urged me on, and whose combination of moral conviction and scholarly rigour remains an inspiration.

But two people in particular have done more to shape this book than anyone else. Ruth Harris read the manuscript innumerable times and developed its argument and style. Years of conversation with her have formed how I think about the role of religion and about how we write history, and I am lucky indeed to have her friendship. My husband, Martin Donnelly, not only read the manuscript many times and tested its arguments but also cycled from Strasbourg to Constance with me. His remarkable eye for detail found me unexpected sources time and again, and his sure sense of what is important in life is an anchor. This book is for him.

ABBREVIATIONS

AGBM	*Akten zur Geschichte des Bauernkriegs in Mitteldeutschland*, ed. Otto Merx, Walter Peter Fuchs, and Günther Franz, 2 vols. in 3 parts. Leipzig, 1923–1942, reprint Aalen, 1964.
HStA	Dresden Hauptstaatsarchiv Dresden
HStAS	Hauptstaatsarchiv Stuttgart
LASA	Landesarchiv Sachsen-Anhalt
LATh Meiningen	Landesarchiv Thüringen (Meiningen)
LW	*Luther's Works*, Fortress Press, Philadelphia, 1957–.
NDB	*Neue Deutsche Biographie*, Berlin: Duncker and Humblot, 1953–.
StA MR	Hessisches Staatsarchiv Marburg
StA Sigmaringen	Staatsarchiv Sigmaringen
StA WÜ	Staatsarchiv Würzburg
StadtA	Bamberg Stadtarchiv Bamberg
StadtA	Mühlhausen Stadtarchiv Mühlhausen
StadtA	Nürnberg Stadtarchiv Nürnberg
StadtAMM	Stadtarchiv Memmingen
TA Zurich	Täuferakten, Zürich
ThMA	Thomas Müntzer Ausgabe, ed. Armin Kohnle et al.
VD 16	Verzeichnis der im deutschen Sprachbereich erschienenen Drucke des 16. Und 17. Jahrhunderts, online resource.
WBr	*D. Martin Luthers Werke*: Kritische Gesamtausgabe, Briefwechsel, 18 vols.

WDB   *D. Martin Luthers Werke*: Kritische Gesamtausgabe, Deutsche Bibel, 15 vols.

WS   *D. Martin Luthers Werke*: Kritische Gesamtausgabe, Schriften, 72 vols., Weimar, 1903.

WT   *D. Martin Luthers Werke*: Kritische Gesamtausgabe, Tischreden, 6 vols.

NOTES

Introduction

1. Contemporaries generally gave a figure of 100,000 dead, though some gave this number for southern Germany alone; Jacob Fugger believed 50,000 had died. Such estimates must of course be treated with caution, and they came from the victors, who also minimised the losses of their own side. Günther Franz, probably the leading modern authority on the war as a whole, accepts a figure of 100,000 for upper and middle Germany alone, *Der deutsche Bauernkrieg*, vol. 1, 299. Peter Blickle estimated a far lower total of 20,700, but his figures included only those killed by the army of the Swabian League (in southwest Germany) and in battles only, *Bauernjörg*, 292–296. Georges Bischoff estimates, for Alsace alone, between 16,000 and 20,000, maybe even 30,000, *La guerre des paysans*, 341, 344. None of these figures include Austria and the Tyrol.

Since most of those killed in the German Peasants' War were men, Franz argues this would be approaching 2 per cent of the whole male population; Franz calculates that 10 to 15 per cent of those men in the regions of the war who were capable of bearing arms died in battle or in the punishments that followed. By comparison, 2 per cent of the British population was killed during World War 1; see Winter, 'Britain's "Lost Generation"', and many current websites. (I am grateful to Michael Roper for this information.) For a recent estimate of population in 1525, see the work of Pfister, 'Urban Population in Germany, 1500–1850', figure 3.1.

We will probably never know the true figure, but it is clear the numbers were very high.

2. *The Freedom of a Christian*, WS 7, 20–38, 49–73 (Latin); LW 31, 333–377.

3. For a superb account of the events of the Diet, see Parker, *Emperor: A New Life of Charles V*, ch. 5.

4. On the Twelve Articles, see Mayenburg, *Gemeiner Mann und Gemeines Recht*; and see also Ruszat-Ewig, *Die 12 Bauernartikel*; *Sebastian Lotzer*.

5. For Götz von Berlichingen's autobiography, see von Berlichingen, *Mein Fehd und Handlungen* (a translation by Joel Harrington is forthcoming, *Götz von Berlichingen: My Feuds and Actions*); on Florian Geyer, see Barge, 'Florian Geyer'; on Truchsess Georg von Waldburg, see Blickle, *Bauernjörg*.

6. Blickle, *Revolution* (Oldenbourg 2004 edition), 323, 'Die zwölf Artikel'; Blickle, *The Revolution of 1525*, 'The Twelve Articles' (appendix), 197 Article 3, trans. Brady and Midelfort (this is the version and translation I shall use throughout).

Chapter 1: Stirrings

1. Arnold, *Niklashausen 1476*, 270 (Trithemius); Wunderli, *Peasant Fires*, 70.

2. Arnold, *Niklashausen 1476*, 271 (Trithemius). On the castle, Helmberger, *Festung Marienberg Würzburg*, 10–16.

3. Wunderli, *Peasant Fires*, and Arnold, *Niklashausen 1476*. The surname 'Behem' or 'Bohemian' led some to suggest that the drummer might have had a link to the Hussites, but this has not been proved and the name is not uncommon in the area, Arnold, *Niklashausen*, 83. The drummer was mentioned in Hartmann Schedel's famous printed *Chronicle*, and songs circulated about it, including one found transcribed in the monastery of Bebenhausen near Tübingen, Maurer, *Bauernkrieg im deutschen Südwesten*, 15.

4. Bischoff, *La guerre des paysans*, 83–97; Virck, *Urkunden und Akten der Stadt Strassburg* (hereafter *Strassburg*), 103; Rosenkranz, *Bundschuh*, vol. 1, 59. See also Rosenkranz, *Bundschuh*, vol. 2 (*Quellen*), 241. In 1514 it was said that they also met on a hill.

5. For examples of peasant shoes, Rückert, *Der 'Arme Konrad' vor Gericht*, 156–159; Bischoff, *La guerre des paysans*, 101–107. On noble boots, Rublack, 'Matter in the Material Renaissance'. On Fritz, Adam, *Joß Fritz*; Scott, *Freiburg and the Breisgau*, 165–189; Klebon, *Im Taumel des Evangeliums*, 34–36. On passwords, Scott, *Freiburg*, 174; Rosenkranz, *Bundschuh*, vol. 1, 137–250, 182–183; and Rosenkranz, *Bundschuh*, vol. 2, 93.

6. For flags, Rosenkranz, *Bundschuh*, vol. 1, 313, and vol. 2, 225, confession of Hans Humel: he saw the flag before it was painted, and he touchingly describes his joy at seeing it. Demands: Rosenkranz, *Bundschuh*, vol. 2, 183. Fate of the revolts: Rosenkranz, *Bundschuh*, vol. 1, 251–394.

7. Miegel, 'Alexander Seitz'. When Seitz was again threatened with banishment in 1516, a petition calling for him to be allowed to remain was presented from 'all schwanger und ander ersam frowen zu Baden', Miegel, 99. In 1525 he was involved in disturbances at Reutlingen. See also Bischoff, *La guerre*, 108–113.

8. Dillinger, 'Freiburgs Bundschuh'; Dillinger, 'Der Bundschuh von 1517'; Rosenkranz, *Bundschuh*, vol. 2, 309. For a different view, Bischoff, *La guerre*, 113–117.

9. See Brant, *Doctor Brants Narrenschiff.* Under the headline 'contempt for Scripture' he cites the 'Sackpfiffers von Nickelshusen', fo. 15 v.

10. WS 1, 233–238, 238 Nr. 17 [*sic*]; LW 31, 33, Thesis 92.

11. *To the Christian Nobility*, WS 6, 404–469; LW 44, 123–219. *On the Babylonian Captivity*, WS 6, 497–573; LW 36, 11–219. Quotation: WS 6, 504:11–18; LW 36, 22.

12. *The Freedom of a Christian*, WS 7, 20–38, 49–73 (Latin); LW 31, 333–377. Luther wrote the German text and dedicated it to Hermann Mühlpfort of Zwickau. Quotations: WS 7, 21:1–4, 22:3–5; LW 31, 345. He put this slightly differently in German than in Latin: 'Hatt die seele keyn ander dinck, widder yn hymel noch auff erden, darynnen sie lebe, frum, frey und Christen sey, den das heylig Evangely, das wort gottis von Christo geprediget', WS 7, 22:3–5, cf. WS 7, 50:33–35. For peasant use of religious rhetoric, Schreiber, *Der deutsche Bauernkrieg*, vol. 2, 104–105 (letters of Black Forest band). This link between Luther's use of the word 'freedom' and peasant unrest was made early on: Luther's opponent Thomas Murner's *Uon dem grossen Lutherischen Narren* included a woodcut of a *Landsknecht* with a banner emblazoned 'Fryheit', fo. P i v.

13. Roper, *Luther*, 191; and see Oberman, 'The Gospel of Social Unrest'.

14. Karlstadt, *Kritische Gesamtausgabe*, vol. 3, 544–545: *Welche Bücher biblisch sind*, 1520. The pamphlet was a German version of a text on 'Which books are biblical', which was designed to help layfolk read the Bible. These words came from a new section he had added, the 'Notabilia', which denounced Pope Leo X as a heretic, and marked his final breach with Rome. The reference to the Councils of the Church is important because conciliarists argued that the councils of the gathered church rather than the pope alone should constitute the church tradition equal in authority to scripture, a reformist position with which Luther broke at Worms in 1521 when he insisted that scripture was the sole authority. Hubmaier, *Schriften*, 74: this was the concluding point of the *Achtzehn Schlußreden*. All 'müssiggenger', regardless of who they might be, were 'verflucht', accursed—this would have included noble rentiers and Catholic clerics. Luther visits Möhra: Roper, *Luther*, 18, 195, 438.

15. There were at least fifty such images that have survived and over thirty editions of his sermons, and they continued to be printed even after he was unmasked. I am grateful to Bethan Winter, who compiled the images from VD 16 and calculated overall numbers. For the Strasbourg Karsthans, Virck, *Strassburg*, 106. There was another 'Karsthans' in Freiburg, Hans Maurer, who had studied at Tübingen and Freiburg, Scott, *Freiburg*, 191. In 1563 a fifty-five-year-old witness remembered hearing a preaching peasant dressed in blue at the marketplace in Heilbronn, who had to come indoors because of the rain, Rauch, *Urkundenbuch der Stadt Heilbronn*, vol. 4 (hereafter *Heilbronn* IV), 7 January 1525. The figure of Karsthans as an evangelical preaching peasant first emerged in 1520, Scribner, 'Images of the Peasant', 30.

16. Wendelstein, *Dorffmayster vnnd Gemaind zu wendelstains fürhalten*; Franz, *Quellen*, 316. The local judge Hans Herbst had taken to writing pro-Reformation pamphlets, criticising his brother-in-law, the pastor Johann Linck, for his lack of

evangelical zeal and advocating that a common chest be established to help the poor (this pamphlet also featured a female textile worker, pictured on the cover): *Eyn gesprech von dem gemaynen Schwabacher Kasten*. Perhaps unsurprisingly, Herbst soon found himself in prison for his pains. Whether or not he wrote the letter of appointment (and its aggressive tone suggests it may even have been a mock piece published by an opponent), its sentiments certainly fitted with the trend of his pamphleteering: he published five such pamphlets in Nuremberg 1524/5. Seewen near Solothurn: Franz, *Der deutsche Bauernkrieg, Aktenband* (hereafter *Akten*), 278.

17. See *Das Bapstum mit seynen glider gemalet und beschriben*, WS 19, 6–43: this illustrated pamphlet appeared the year after the Peasants' War and presents sixty-five different ecclesiastical dignitaries and orders, depicting their habit and providing a mocking verse for each. Luther's return: Roper, *Luther*, 200–204, 475–476 nn. 18–26.

18. Karant-Nunn, *Zwickau in Transition*, 37–39, 187; Rauch, *Heilbronn* IV, 46, 81–83, 899. See Cohn, 'Anticlericalism'.

19. For Grünhain, Karant-Nunn, *Zwickau in Transition*, 37–38, 39, 123–127: in 1522 the monastery had imprisoned a peasant, precipitating a riot, which the council apparently exploited to secularise it—though it failed to gain the abbey's rural jurisdictions. The Cistercians' depot in Zwickau eventually became the new grammar school. AGBM 2, 23–24, complaint of Textor to the Hochmeister of the Deutscher Orden, 5 February 1524; the two institutions belonged to separate Kommenden of the order. See also Müller, *Deutsche Orden und Thüringen*.

20. Seitz, *Ain Warnung des Sündtfluss*, fo. A iii r; a iii v. Seitz was also involved in the Peasants' War and escaped afterwards to Switzerland; he continued publishing and died in 1545. For a slightly different interpretation of his political position, see Barnes, *Astrology*, who argues he was not calling for revolution, 114. For such prognostications, see for example, Hans Virdung, *Practica deutsch*, and warnings earlier, Virdung, *Practica Teütsch*, and on the signs at Vienna, Virdung, *Außlegung vnd Beteütung*; Reynmann, *Practica*; and see on this, Scribner, 'Images', 42. An owner of the copy in the Staatliche Bibliothek Regensburg has coloured the cover image and commented on the predictions, noting that the prognostication for 1524 was wrong but the prediction for 1527 and 1528 that the 'populus communis' would 'vnmüssig vnd starck regiern' (fo. C ii r) had come true in 1525. The owner has also annotated the flag on the cover woodcut, to condemn 'Herr omnes' as 'lotterisch' (Lutheran) and inspired by the devil (*teifel*). Sebastian Brant also wrote a 'Prognosticon' in 1516, predicting flood and various disasters at the conjunction of the planets, and Abbot Murer placed it at the head of his pictorial chronicle of the war, Franz and Fleischhauer, eds., *Jacob Murers Weissenauer Chronik*, 2, 41.

21. Fries, *Geschichte*, vol. 1, 2 f.

22. On labour and tools, Bentzien, 'Arbeit und Arbeitsgerät'. Grain was supplied from late summer through to after Christmas, depending on the type of grain, Weingarten, *Herrschaft und Landnutzung*, 91–92; Robisheaux, 'Peasantries of Western Germany', 114. The size of the rye grain was also smaller, between 4 and 6 mm, whereas today it is 8 mm and longer, Vogt-Lüerssen, *Alltag*, 193.

23. Franz, *Akten*, 100; Anshelm, *Berner-Chronik*, vol. 5, 100: 'muestid schneg-genhusle suchen, garn zewinden'. Anshelm was the civic chronicler of Bern from 1529, and died in 1546/7; he had also lived in Rottweil. A Protestant, he was well placed to know the story. Barack, *Zimmersche Chronik*, vol. 2, 523, supplies a song about their complaints, including collecting snail shells. Martin Gerbert's *Historia Nigrae Silvae*, vol. 2, 317, notes: 'sie solten in der Erndt der Graffin Schneckenheuslin lessen, den sy garn daruff winden khinde'. As Abbot of St Blasien between 1764 and 1793, Gerbert would have had access to local history and sources. Engels also used the story, *Peasant War*, 10. Outbreak, Baumann, *Akten*, 2–3; and see 184–185. The grievances were formulated some time before 4 or 6 April in the course of the case they brought against their lords, Baumann, *Akten*, 188–208.

24. See accounts of Andreas Lettsch (*Chronik*) and Heinrich Hug (*Villinger Chronik*); and Buszello, 'Oberrheinlande'.

25. Hug, *Villinger Chronik*, 99: Sigmund of Lupfen was the overlord of the peasants of Stühlingen; he died that December; Buszello, 'Oberrheinlande'.

26. On Hubmaier at Waldshut, see Scott, 'Hubmaier, Schappeler, and Hergot on Social Revolution'; Scott, 'Reformation and Peasants' War in Waldshut'; Loserth, *Stadt Waldshut*; and Bergsten, *Balthasar Hubmaier*; Kessler, *Sabbata*, 221–222. On the pilgrimage to the 'beautiful Maria', see Creasman, 'The Virgin Mary Against the Jews'.

27. Quotation from Loserth, *Stadt Waldshut*, 20. Hubmaier himself strongly rejected this accusation, but as both Scott and Loserth point out, his hearers may have understood him to be critical of the small tithe and perhaps of the tithe itself. 'Satan's clergy, the soul eaters': Hubmaier, *Schriften*, 16; Kessler, *Sabbata*, 106; Bergsten, *Hubmaier*, 67–87; see also Loserth, *Stadt Waldshut*. Bergsten points out that hostility to the Habsburgs was a leitmotif of his career: his support of the Regensburg pilgrimage and antisemitism had also pitted him against the emperor, 92–93. Hubmaier was at Schaffhausen while negotiations with the Stühlingen peasantry continued, Blickle, *Bauernjörg*, 91. They had resumed negotiations in September while also planning for revolt, perhaps a double policy, perhaps a result of splits over tactics, Scott, 'Reformation and Peasants' War in Waldshut'.

28. Hug, *Villinger Chronik*, 103; he claimed people made them into 'hossben-del', that is, trousers belts; and see also Lettsch, *Chronik*, 46. On Müntzer's sojourn, Bräuer and Vogler, *Müntzer*, 315–319; and see Scott, 'Ein Radikaler auf Reisen'.

29. Women's support for Hubmaier: Küssenberg, *Chronik*; Fabri, *Ursache*, A iii v; Hubmaier, *Schriften*, 94, 108–109, and 111; Roper, 'Luther and Gender', 61.

30. Hug, *Villinger Chronik*, 100; Hecker, Exhibition, *Jetzt machen wir Republik. Die Revolution von 1848–9*, Kulturzentrum am Münster, Konstanz 2023; Clark, *Revolutionary Spring*, 495–496. On Müller: Baumann, *Akten* 27–29; Lettsch, *Chronik*, 46; Schreiber, *Deutsche Bauernkrieg*, vol. 1, 153; Hug, *Villinger Chronik*, 100, 105, who commented, 'dan er kund wol schwetzen'.

31. St Trudpert: Schreiber, *Bauernkrieg*, vol. 1, 172, Urgicht of Peter Ganzenberg from 1526—the authorities tried to paint him as a thug. See Hug, *Villinger*

Chronik, 108; Schreiber, *Bauernkrieg*, vol. 1, 144–146, 155–156, 171–172. Freiburg had to send a hundred soldiers to defend the monastery, Scott, 'Freiburger Talvogtei', 84. Scott points out that appeals to 'godly law' did not dominate at this point, but this is to adopt a narrow definition of 'religion'; smashing sacred objects certainly attests to the influence of Reformation ideas more broadly. For trouser belts, Küssenberg, *Chronik*, 421. This is a standard accusation, made also for Weissenhorn by Nicolaus Thomann, 'Weissenhorner Historie', 81. See also Bergsten, *Hubmaier*, 144–159, who shows that the allegation that Hubmaier was a follower of Müntzer dates back to Bullinger's work on Anabaptism, designed to prove that Anabaptism came out of Müntzer and the Zwickau prophets and not out of the Swiss Reformation. On religion and the revolt, Scott, ed., *Town, Country and Regions*, 3–56; Buszello, 'Oberrheinlande', 70, who argue it was not important. Hug, *Villinger Chronik*, 109–110, reproduces the 'sixteen articles' of the peasants, none of which concern religion, though he also states that they thought they could bring their plots against their lords 'mit dem gottlichen rechten'. Bergsten argues persuasively that religion was important from the outset, *Hubmaier*, 109–110.

32. The Hegau peasants withdrew from the proceedings at Stockach, and discussions in January did not resolve the issue; the Stühlingers withdrew from their case at Esslingen on 20 April 1525, Buszello, 'Oberrheinlande', 68. Scott, Buszello, and others argue that the issues were not religious at this point and concerned only custom and 'das alte Recht'. However, this seems to me to underestimate the gradual way in which exposure to religious radicalism changes minds. Lettsch attributes religious motivations to the peasants at this point, albeit ironically, Lettsch, *Chronik*, 46. He was clear that Hubmaier and his followers had 'ain sondern glouben' because they advocated believer's baptism, though he also terms them Lutheran.

33. Lettsch, *Chronik*, 46. Fabri, *Ursache*, fo. B r. Austrian threats: Loserth, *Stadt Waldshut* (Quellen Beilage), 117; this comes from the Entschuldigung und Klage der gemeinen Stadt Waldshut, possibly from November 1524, though dated 1525; Hubmaier was likely involved in its authorship: Hubmaier, *Schriften*, 58–59.

34. Scott, 'Reformation and Peasants' War in Waldshut'.

35. Schreiber, *Bauernkrieg*, vol. 1, 116, November 1524; Zurich wrote that they knew the peasants' revolt was for the sake of 'God's word and the Gospel' ('Gotzwort und das Evangelium'), so they expected their agreement. By December, the Klettgauers explained their complaints, forty-four in total, including that their Landvogt had threatened them with punishment for swearing to 'protect the gospel and the Word of God', Schreiber, *Bauernkrieg* 1, 184. Potter, *Zwingli*, 198–203; Buszello, 'Oberrheinlande', 67–68.

Chapter 2: Land

1. Cochlaeus, *Kurze Beschreibung Germaniens*, 48. It was published as an appendix to Pomponius Mela's *Cosmographia*, fo. G iv (r) to fo. L ii (v), and it was the first work of German geography of its kind, based in part on Cochlaeus's own journeys.

2. Cochlaeus, *Kurze Beschreibung*, 68, 69, 72; 106–107; 94–98; 82, 88, 89.

3. Metzger, ed., *Dürer*, 118–173; Groschinski, 'Cranach's Animals', 29; Morass and Thalinger, 'Cranach im Fokus der Naturwissenschaft', 163. On the German forest, Schama, *Landscape and Memory*, 75–100. On Dürer, Rublack, *Dürer's Lost Masterpiece*.

4. Zeune, ed., *Fränkische Burgen zur Zeit der Bauernkriege*, for coloured illustrations to the manuscript of the Staatsbibliothek Bamberg depicting the twenty-two castles destroyed. On feuds and knights, Zmora, *State and Nobility*; Algazi, *Herrengewalt und Gewalt der Herren*. On monastic and church property, Ocker, *Church Robbers*, 17–49.

5. See Parker, *Global Crisis*; Mauelshagen, *Klimageschichte der Neuzeit*; Behringer, *A Cultural History of Climate*. On peasant life see, amongst others, Schubert, *Alltag im Mittelalter*; Rösener, *Bauern im Mittelalter*; Vogt-Lüerssen, *Der Alltag im Mittelalter*; Kießling and Troßbach, eds., *Grundzüge der Agrargeschichte*, 1; Wunder, *Die bäuerliche Gemeinde in Deutschland*; Robisheaux, 'Peasantries of Western Europe'; Hagen, 'Village Life'; Rebel, 'Peasantries Under the Austrian Empire'; Rowlands, 'Conditions of Life for the Masses'. On candles, Arnold, *Niklashausen 1476*, 11; Füssel, *Schedel'sche Weltchronik*, includes an account of the Drummer of Niklashausen that shows candles towering above the church; large candles were also used in the Regensburg Marian pilgrimage.

6. For example, see Alter, *Pfeddersheim*, 207–225: in the small wine-growing agricultural town of Pfeddersheim, a group of 10 'big' peasants owned 47.5 to 87 Morgen of land; 23 'middling' peasants owned 20 to 47 Morgen; 20 'small peasants' owned between 10 and 18.5 Morgen; 56 owned between 5 and 9.5 Morgen. Alter reckons this would have sufficed to engage full-time in agriculture. A further 151 people, or 63.4 per cent, owned less than 5.25 Morgen and so would have needed additional occupations. A final 129 had no land, presumably town dwellers only. At Dagersheim, a village of 76 hearths in 1525, a Turk tax list of 1545 shows that 15 individuals owned over 500 Gulden; while 40 owned between 100 and 500 Gulden; 44 between 20 and 100 Gulden; and 53 (about a third of the total) less than 20 Gulden, Lorenz, ed., *Dagersheim*. Sreenivasan, *Peasants of Ottobeuren*, esp. 47–50; Adam, *Joß Fritz*, 28–29; Brun, *Abbot and His Peasants*, 128–129, 145–160; Sabean, *Landbesitz*. Weingarten, *Herrschaft und Landnutzung*: here oats were grown in summer, and probably rye and spelt in winter, 221. Ditches, fences, hedges protected the fields from wild animals. Villages usually had a mayor, court, and treasurer (*Gemeinderechner*). On labour, Bentzien, 'Arbeit und Arbeitsgerät'.

7. Sreenivasan, *Peasants of Ottobeuren*, 7–106. However, his identification of a first less radical and a later more radical stage of revolt led by lower-class peasants cannot necessarily be generalised, and there does not seem to be sufficient evidence to push back the stratification evident in village life after 1560 into this early period. Lorenz et al., eds., *Dagersheim*, 44, argue that *Seldner* as well as day labourers and *Knechte* were not members of the Gemeinde by right and did not automatically have access to the common lands. The 'Allmende' or common lands included pasture,

forest, paths, and the grass areas between fields. Sabean, *Landbesitz*, argues that the upper, richer peasants who dominated the leadership were able to exploit the poorer. However, as Brun points out, if the army's programme had been that of the richer peasants only, 'it could not have won the support of such large numbers of men', Brun, *Abbot and His Peasants*, 119. For a convincing critique of both Sabean and Sreenivasan on common lands, see 145–160. On the social composition of rural rebels in Thuringia, see Rommel, 'Zur sozialen Zusammensetzung der Aufständischen': he does not distinguish different levels of 'Bauern' and treats them together with rural craftsfolk; he finds that 'Lohnarbeiter' did not yet have a separate class consciousness.

8. Sabean, *Landbesitz*, argued that population in Württemberg increased during the period from the late fifteenth century, and that this increased wealth divisions. However, he also states that the only set of articles which expressed interests other than those of the tenant farmers were those of Ochsenhausen, suggesting that the articles were generally broadly agreed. Sabean, 'German Agrarian Institutions', 80. See Brun, *Abbot and His Peasants*, for a critique of Sabean's arguments. Schirmer, 'Ursachen des Bauernkrieges in Thüringen', points out that in areas like the regions around Magdeburg, Querfurt, and Leipzig there were large farms, and in Schweidnitz by 1571 the Gemeinde consisted of five farms. In these areas, which did not engage in revolt, the big division was between rich farmers and those who worked for them.

9. Schirmer, 'Ursachen des Bauernkrieges in Thüringen', 31: Electoral Saxony gained economic control by controlling the parish finances, which it was readily able to do after the first visitation of the new church following the Reformation, 1527. Women: we know that in Salem, only male household heads were members of the Gemeinde, Brun, *Abbot and His Peasants*, 128–129; in Ottobeuren, women could not hold any communal offices (54–55), nor could they be tenants of farms in their own right. Robisheaux, *Rural Society*.

10. Brant, ed., Virgil, *Opera* (Georgica).

11. Müller, 'Albrecht Dürer's Peasant Engravings'. Cranach, *Bauernkopf*, Öffentliche Kunstsammlung Basel. The British Museum has a drawing attributed to Cranach the Younger, SL, 5218.19, which is dated to 1540–1550 and is a well-realised copy of the Cranach watercolour. Its existence suggests that the image was known and valued by the workshop at the time. By contrast, Chrisoph Amberger, Leonhard Beck, and Hans Weiditz, amongst other artists, produced woodcuts of hideous, deformed peasants and lower-class characters.

12. Heinrich Aldegrever, *The Large Wedding Dancers*, 1538.

13. See, for examples of their role in revolt, Hug, *Villinger Chronik*, 98 (Waldshut), 100 (Hiltzingen).

14. Kießling and Troßbach, *Grundzüge*, 46–48; Sabean, *Landbesitz*; Sreenivasan, *Peasants of Ottobeuren*; Robisheaux, *Rural Society*.

15. For authorities' view that burdens on peasants were too harsh, see for example Pfeiffer, *Quellen*, 339; Ludolphy, *Friedrich der Weise*, 483. The Catholic Johannes Salat blamed burdens placed on the peasants by the religious and secular lords (especially those who owned serfs) and said their discontent had been exploited by Luther

and Zwingli, Salat, *Reformationschronik*, 1, 327–328. On the agrarian economy, Schirmer, 'Ursachen'; Joestel, *Geschwinde Zeitläufte*, argues there is evidence for bad harvest and price increases in parts of Saxony in 1523, 315–330.

16. Kießling and Troßbach, *Grundzüge*, 48. On the emptiness of the 'Schutz und Schirm' ideal, see Algazi, *Herrengewalt*, 80–86. Vogt, *Die Correspondenz des schwäbischen Bundeshauptmannes Ulrich Artzt* (hereafter *Artzt*), 555. On labour services (*Frondienste*), Mayenburg, *Gemeiner Mann und Gemeines Recht*, 263–351.

17. Robisheaux, 'Peasantries of Western Germany', 133. Blickle provides an analysis of the subjects dealt with in the fifty-four surviving grievance lists of upper Germany, *Revolution of 1525*, 201–205.

18. See Scott, 'Die Spätmittelalterliche bäuerliche Unfreiheit in Südwestdeutschland', 180–201; as Scott shows, bodily serfdom persisted also in many parts of western Europe. In middle Germany, dues related to the land, not the person, and peasants had more secure tenancies, but they, too, suffered from dues and burdens, Graupner, 'Dorfgemeinden und ihre Artikel'.

19. On testes, see Simons, *Sex of Men in Premodern Europe*; on hens, Ulbrich, *Leibherrschaft*, 123 n. 511; Brun, *Abbot and His Peasants*, 97. See also the articles of the peasants of Obhausen, LASA, A 32a, Nr. 392, fo. 3 r–v (online); AGBM 2, 169 ff, wrongly given as Osterhausen, c. May 1525, where the peasants refused to supply '2 huner, eyn rauchhuen und eyn treydhun', which each household had to pay.

20. Blickle suggests that serfdom emerged only in 1400 on monastic estates, and that peasants had earlier been free to move, to change lords, and to marry as they liked, Blickle, 'Economic, Social and Political Background', 66; Blickle, *Revolution of 1525*. The process was certainly worsening in the fifteenth century as monasteries and convents tried to create unified bodies of subjects who all had the same rights, in place of a myriad of communities each with different rights and traditions; so, for example, Zwiefalten issued an ordinance in 1479 to apply to the whole territory. Quotation: Vogt, *Artzt*, 552. The issue of marriage could also be important in areas without serfdom. In Thambach, peasants demanded that 'no-one be forced against fairness in marriage matters', AGBM 1, 433, while the villages of Geisenheim, Mengersgereuth (now Gerhardsgereuth), Rappelsdorf, and Thambach asked that no one should be forced to give their child in marriage to someone. Here I have learnt from the literature on women, family, and slavery in North America; see for example Stevenson, *Life in Black and White*; Stevenson, *What Sorrows Labour in My Parent's Breast?*; and Knott and Griffin, eds., *Mothering's Many Labours*.

21. See Blickle and Holenstein, *Agrarverfassungsverträge*, 120–167, 122, 122–123. The word Dorn and Necker and the others used was 'gefangen', captured, the same word as for capture of animals. There were three levels of servitude in this region: those who had full freedom; 'zinser', who had to pay small yearly dues in recognition of the abbey's authority and pay the best animal as death duty; and serfs, 'leibeigen'. The monastery was attempting to make all its subjects equal in status, driving them down to serfdom, because this enabled the abbey not only to prevent peasants moving to another lord but also to claim dues in kind, service dues, and up

to half an estate on death. Each entry in the 'Libell' encapsulates a whole life history. See also Haggenmüller, 'Allgäuer Haufen'.

22. Blickle and Holenstein, *Agrarverfassungsverträge*, 125. Nor was it only peasants who were affected by these kinds of practices. Benz Funk, a townsman from a rich Kempten family who owned the castle of Illerberg, got into a dispute with the abbot over a number of issues, including his marriage to a free woman, and rumours, which he denied, that he planned to sell the castle. He was imprisoned in a tower, and 'the old man went into himself and thought should I be punished in my old age for things I'm innocent of?' Funk's castle was occupied by the abbot, his wife was captured, and he was even forced to pay for what the abbot's men had consumed. He became ill and was transferred to a castle chamber on the Eve of Our Lady's Presentation. He prayed to her and tied his bedclothing, rope, and sheets together to climb out of the castle, but the makeshift rope was not long enough, and he fell, dying six months later, 147–148.

23. Franz, *Der deutsche Bauernkrieg, Aktenband* (hereafter *Akten*), 216, 218; the abbess of Buchau, Franz, *Akten*, 150; her reply to other subjects, 161. On Beuggen, Ulbrich, *Leibherrschaft*, 125–128: by 1539 this was extended to include marriages with serfs of the Margrave of Baden, the Komtur of Beuggen, and other lords. At Salem, if a man of the abbey married outside it, the monastery's practice was to penalise him 'as we wish', that is, the penalty was not fixed, Brun, *Abbot and His Peasants*, 97.

24. So, for example, a Katalog of 1520 reveals that 166 peasants from the area of Schmalkalden owed the Stift of Schmalkalden a total of 2,450 Gulden, an average of 14.6 Gulden per debtor, Wölfing, *Bauernkrieg im südthüringisch-hennebergischen*, 12. See also Cohn, 'Anticlericalism', and Blickle, 'Economic, Social and Political Background', 68–69: Weingarten secured about 20 per cent, with some smaller properties paying as much as 40 per cent; Heggbach, 30 per cent. Rents, however, do not seem to have increased.

25. The tithe system could be extremely complex. For example, in the parish of Mainau the tithe revenues were split into sixteen separate shares, and four corporations each had different numbers of those shares. Brun, *Abbot and His Peasants*, 87. Though the legitimacy of the large tithe was generally accepted, it was questioned in the region around Zurich and formed part of the background to the development of Swiss Anabaptism.

26. Quotation: Franz, *Akten*, 182—this is probably a garbled reference to the Exodus story of the parting of the Red Sea for the Israelites as they escaped Egyptian slavery. On increasing dues, Ulbrich, *Leibherrschaft*, 124–125.

27. See Schirmer for the argument on second serfdom, 'Ursachen des Bauernkriegs'. Labour dues: Blickle, *Revolution von 1525*, 325 (German); *Revolution of 1525*, 199 (Article 7).

28. Money as an issue in the Peasants' War: Rössner, *Deflation, Devaluation, Rebellion*, esp. 491–530. Peasant complaints: Vogt, *Artzt*, 319 ff. See also Baumann, *Akten*, 161. Langerringer Articles complained that they and the animals were not given

food and drink when they brought the dues in; subjects of the Teutonic Knights at Ellingen wanted better food and to be paid at the rate they paid their own grain harvesters, Oechsle, *Beiträge zur Geschichte des Bauernkrieges*, 125. In Tübingen, peasants resented having to travel from their distant villages at midnight to perform services and were not given food for themselves or their animals (draft oxen or horses); they had to provide wood for fires more frequently because the duke entertained more there, Maurer, *Der Bauernkrieg im deutschen Südwesten*, 13. It is of course difficult to be certain of the facts because complaints are so often worded in terms of time-honoured custom, and it is hard to know which customs really were old; lords too were coping with changing economic conditions and high expenses. What is clear is the level of resentment. On haulage, see also Bentzien, 'Arbeit und Arbeitsgerät'.

29. Wood: AGBM 1, 279. Nearby Lauenhain complained that the good building wood was being used for charcoal, 282; in the Kraichgau, peasants were forced to buy wood from the lord, Klebon, *Im Taumel des Evangeliums*, 38–42. Baking: LASA, A 32a, Nr. 392, fo. 3r–v, May 1525; concerning Obhausen, also in AGBM 2, Nr. 1270, 169 f. Hay: Vogt, *Artzt*, 561, 560. The peasants of Risstissen complained about 'hay money', and the peasants of Rörwangen begged to be allowed to keep the hay from the tithe for a fair fee. Building wood: AGBM 2, 295. The official of Magdeburg was livid at what the Premonstratension monastery of Berge had done with their woods. They had chopped down too much wood, sold the 'most beautiful' oak tree trunks, and destroyed them. He believed the monks were spending their days drunk and stripping the monastery of its resources because they knew they risked having to hand it over, and they wanted to ensure that they each got 400 or 500 Gulden. Later transactions after the war suggest the kind of sums involved: the Fuggers sold beechwood worth 700 fl (florin or Gulden) to Ulm in 1554, cut from an estate they had recently bought; Gutenzell monastery sold 300 fl worth to Ulm in 1562. Prices for charcoal therefore rose; for instance, the Mansfeld Mining Ordinance of 1521 tried to fix the price of charcoal—as Fessner, 'Steinkohlenbergbau', points out, the real price paid for charcoal was probably much higher. On salt panning, see Miller, *Frankenhausen*, 32–33; in the town museum at Frankenhausen, Doug Miller has created replicas of the saltworks. The smoke caused by burning hay made working conditions impossible for the salt makers, who had to revert to kindling wood.

30. Development of forestry officials: Warde, *Ecology, Economy and State Formation*, and Warde, 'Fear of Wood shortage'. So, for example, Masmünster (Masevaux) complained that the abbess was turning the Waldforster into her 'Amtmann', Franz, *Akten*, 239.

31. Hausen: Baumann, *Akten*, 221, and see 225. Alsace: Virck, *Urkunden und Akten der Stadt Strassburg* (hereafter *Strassburg*), 155–156, no. 275, 12 May 1525. It had previously belonged to the Neuweiler Stift. Alleshausen: StA Sigmaringen, Dep. 30 Marchtal—12 T4_44, p. 25. Bogs in war: Baumann, *Quellen: Chroniken* (Truchsess Schreiber), 550–552, 561–562.

32. Hipler had cut down sections of the local wood; he also alienated a local noble competitor, Taddey, 'Hipler', 71–72. Mining pollution: Schirmer, 'Ursachen

des Bauernkrieges in Thüringen', 29–30. In these areas, the cattle drives were also damaged.

33. Vogt, *Artzt*, 46, Complaints of Busmannshausen, 22 February 1525, no. 12; see also Baumann, *Akten*, 221, peasants of Löffingen complained that they had to cook for the dogs and hunters.

34. AGBM 2, 602, 22 April 1525. On poaching, see the classic by Schindler, *Wilderer*; on hunting, the exhibition in the stables at Jagdschloss Grundewald, which has replicas of the ropes and banners used along with paintings indicating how this was done.

35. Tyrol: Bücking, *Michael Gaismair*, 58–82. It was not a spontaneous reaction, however, but a carefully planned event, and it marked the move of Gaismair, an official, to revolution. Fish was also an important food for pregnant women and the ill. The community of Baustetten did not go so far as to demand free waters, but only the right to fish for a single meal of fish or crab for someone ill or pregnant, Franz, *Akten*, 153. Peasants catching fish with their hands: AGBM 2, 485. Eichstätt: Franz, *Quellen*, 343; see also Eglißau, where on 24 March, the local official at the castle went fishing with his men for 'naßen'. A dozen peasants joined him, and when the official tried to stop them, they reassembled the next day two hundred strong. Stumpf, *Schweizer- und Reformationschronik*, 253. Henneberg: AGBM 1, 593–595. Neustadt: AGBM 2, 658–659; when the Vogt arrived, the witness claimed to have persuaded the peasants to stop fishing since they had caught enough. But he was still persuaded to eat the fish with them afterwards.

36. Lord growing flax: Vogt, *Artzt*, 321. See also Kießling and Troßbach, *Grundzüge*, 47–49. Flax was labour-intensive to grow, too, but this meant that it was economically viable for those who had little land, Weingarten, *Herrschaft und Landnutzung*, 103.

37. It is estimated that for the same area, vines required eight times as much labour as crops. Adam, *Joß Fritz*, 20. On the notable involvement of vintners and wine-growing regions in the revolt, see Robisheaux, *Rural Society*, 56–57, and Scott, *Freiburg*.

38. Endres, 'Franken', 137. See Schirmer, 'Ursachen des Bauernkrieges in Thüringen', 26–29, who shows that sheep farming was a major grievance in Thuringia. Manure: Vogt, *Artzt*, 554. Manure was an important resource, especially for peasants' garden plots.

39. Wilfried Setzler, ' "Sie versammeln sich und beklagen ihre Beschwerden": Die Klöster Bebenhausen und Zwiefalten im Bauernkrieg', lecture, University of Tübingen, 10 May 2023; Weingarten, *Herrschaft und Landnutzung*; Sulger, *Annales Imperialis Monasterii Zwifaltensis*, 120; I am grateful to Setzler for drawing this to my attention.

40. Baumann, *Akten*, 226, 215: 'Deckingen' (Deggingen) claimed not to have been required to give the carnival hen but had given one only, 'von alters her'. But now two were demanded. Not Christian: 'In summa: Es ist nit christlich', as the anonymous author of *An die Versammlung*, put it, 102.

Chapter 3: Freedom

1. See Barge, *Karlstadt*; Krentz, *Ritualwandel*; Müller, *Wittenberger Bewegung*; Joestel, *Geschwinde Zeitläufte*.

2. WS 10, 3, S. 8:5–6; LW 51, 72–73 does not quite capture the sense.

3. WS 15, 339:29, 340:5–6, adding, 'the more boldly you attack me, the dearer you'll be to me', 'ye tafpfferer ir mich angryfft, ye lyber ir mir sein solt'.

4. WS 15, 341–347, for Reinhard's report of the events at Orlamünde; WS 18, 83:33–84:34, for Luther's report of the same events in his *Wider die himmlischen Propheten*; Roper, *Martin Luther: Renegade and Prophet*, 253–254. On Orlamünde's participation in the Peasants' War, see Joestel, 'Karlstadt und der Bauernkrieg'; Joestel, *Geschwinde Zeitläufte*, 315–330.

5. Quotations from: Karlstadt, *Anzeige*, fo. F iv (v), fo. G i (r), fo. A i (v) (VD 16 B6099); *Several Main Points of Christian Doctrine*, in Furcha, ed., *Essential Carlstadt*, 374, 375, and for the list, 341. Here Karlstadt was revisiting the arguments of the Leipzig Disputation, where he had taken a more moderate position on the role of works in salvation than Luther had. From 1522: Karlstadt, *Von Gelübden*, fo. g (i) (r); 'Regarding Vows', in Furcha, *Essential Carlstadt*, 84.

6. Karlstadt, *Entschuldigung*, fo. A iv (v)–A iv (r); I have translated literally. See Furcha, *Esssential Carlstadt*, 381.

7. ThMA 2, 290:2–4. The original letter does not survive.

8. ThMA 2, 285–286; for Karlstadt's Latin letter to Müntzer, 287–292, 292–296. The letter from the congregation of Orlamünde to that of Allstedt of 19 July 1524 rejected physical resistance and brotherhood, and was printed in Wittenberg with Hans Luft to make this absolutely plain. Karlstadt formally resigned his post on 22 July 1524 and was exiled from Saxony in mid-September, after which he actually left in late September, Barge, *Karlstadt*, vol. 2, 140. Volkmar Joestel argues that Karlstadt's published treatise on the Sabbath suggests that his sermons did encourage some resistance to aspects of rule, 'Karlstadt und der Bauernkrieg'. On possible meetings between Karlstadt and Müntzer, Bubenheimer, *Thomas Müntzer und Wittenberg*.

9. Agricola condemned him in 1521 as bent on murder and bloodshed (he put this in large type), ThMA 2, 72–75; an anonymous poem from 1520 'lambasted him as longing to shed blood', ThMA 3, 83, 84, facsimile edition, *Historien Thome Muntzer*. Georg Witzel condemned him as a 'man of blood', ThMA 2, 391–397, though this was a letter supposedly from 1525 which he printed in a pamphlet in 1534, and no original survives. Sectarian: 'factiones excitabat, homo ad schismata et hereses natus', ThMA 3, 98. Reported rude comment to opponent: Interrogation of Hans Moller, 16 December 1525 (this man was clearly trying to distance himself from Müntzer), ThMA 3, 117. But Moller was not the only source for this: see also 1522 Colloquy of Master Wolfgang Stein, Müntzer quoted as saying 'I shit on you', 'ich schiss dir eyn werk'; Spalatin also recorded this discussion, Matheson, *Collected Works of Müntzer*, 455–456; ThMA 3, 114.

10. On Müntzer, see Matheson, 'Language of Thomas Müntzer'; on his mysticism, Goertz, *Nähe Gottes und Veränderung der Welt*; and on his apocalypticism, amongst others, Stayer, 'Prophet'. On his time in Allstedt, Wölbing, *Müntzers langer Schatten*.

11. Bräuer and Vogler, *Müntzer*, ch. 1 and 2; the dating derives from the youngest age he could have matriculated at Leipzig. On Müntzer, there is a vast literature. See in particular Scott, *Thomas Müntzer*; Goertz, *Thomas Müntzer*; the now authoritative Bräuer and Vogler, *Thomas Müntzer*; Müller, *Mörder ohne Opfer*, for the Mühlhausen context; Schloms et al., eds., *Deutscher historischer Städteatlas Mühlhausen*, Tafel 8.2, 8.3, 8.4; and Drummond, *Dreadful History*. On Müntzer's social background and networks, Bubenheimer, *Thomas Müntzer*; and Bubenheimer, *Thomas Müntzer und Wittenberg*.

12. A letter from spring 1521 points to tensions between Müntzer and his father over legacies from his mother that Müntzer believed he was owed; it may suggest that this was in fact his stepfather. ThMA 2, 79–80; Matheson, *Collected Works of Müntzer*, 22. On mining see Agricola, *De re metallica*; its illustrations also show women working.

13. Luther's father was said to have started out as a miner before becoming a smelter and effectively a mine owner, but as Michael Fessner and others have shown, this was almost certainly a myth because he would have needed both capital and connections to become a smeltermaster. Fessner, 'Die Familie Luder'; Vogler, 'Eisleben und Nürnberg, Stahl, Baugeschichtliche Erkenntnisse'.

14. The canny nuns of Quedlinburg managed to resist dissolution when the town became Lutheran in the late 1530s, becoming a remarkable example of a Lutheran convent, an anomaly in a faith dedicated to opposing monasticism; they ruled their territory until 1802 as direct subjects of the emperor, prince vassals in their own right. Bräuer, 'Simon Hoffmann', 305–306; on Lutheran nuns, Plummer, *Stripping the Veil*.

15. No need to swear: ThMA 3, 135, 137. On Quedlinburg, see Wozniak, *Quedlinburg*. Bräuer and Vogler, *Müntzer*, 41, point out that the league was not necessarily directed against Ernst of Magdeburg, and that there is no necessary connection between the confession that he made a league and his opposition to Bishop Ernst.

16. Bräuer and Vogler, *Müntzer*, 54: the Franciscan monk Bernhard Dappen reported he was 'vertrieben' from Braunschweig ('expulsus e civitate Brunsvicksensi', ThMA 3, 44), while Agricola says he 'ran off like an arch rascal', 'wie ein ertzbube entlaufen'; both are hostile to Müntzer. Dappen's report on Müntzer's preaching for the bishop was eventually printed as *Articuli... contra Lutheranos* through Johann Eck; Luther at first defended Müntzer's preaching though without knowing what he had actually preached, Bräuer and Vogler, *Müntzer*, 76–78. Thus ironically the Catholic Johann Eck, Luther's antagonist, was responsible for the first spreading of Müntzer's ideas in print. Johann Dappen, *Articuli... contra Lutheranos*. The humanist Jiri Pisecky thought Müntzer had been forced to leave Prague, but it was likely his own decision to go, Bräuer and Vogler, *Müntzer*, 155.

17. Zwickau sermon: ThMA 3, 82; Bräuer and Vogler, *Müntzer*, 92–124. Attack on Hofer: ThMA 3, 72–74. See also Wappler, *Müntzer in Zwickau*; Bräuer, ed., *Historien von Thomas Müntzer*. It was also reported that 'some priests' in the town believed that when the body dies, the soul dies too, Wappler, *Müntzer in Zwickau*, 50–51. Summoned to bishop: ThMA 3, 77. The council reached an accommodation with the bishop, which suggests they thought Müntzer could not have been entirely to blame; but his rhetoric had serious consequences, and in 1523, after Müntzer had left town, poor Hofer was killed by a supporter of Müntzer's. Letter to Luther: ThMA 2, 48:7–11. Agricola: 'aiebant Te Nihil Spirare nisi Cedes et Sanguinem!', ThMA 2, 72–76; end January/early February 1521, Agricola to Müntzer (the quotation is in large letters in the original and comes from Acts 9:1, describing Saul's hostility to disciples before his conversion). Agricola, not Lang as VD 16 says, wrote the *Dialogus* between a peasant and a Müntzerite fanatic about the defeat of 1525 (see Scott, 'Johannes Agricola's Ein nutzlicher Dialogus', in *The Early Reformation*, 227–246). He also wrote *Auslegung des XIX Psalm: Coeil ernarant*, Wittenberg 1525, VD 16, which is dedicated to Luther's Mansfeld friend Johann Rühel. For Luther's recycling in 1535 of the anecdote about Müntzer's strange attitude to the birth of his son, see WS 44 493:16–26.

18. There are four versions of the Prague Manifesto. One was a longer version in German, one version was in Latin, and a final incomplete version was in Czech. See Scott, *Müntzer*, 32–33; ThMA 1, 411–440 and esp. 413–414, on the dimensions of all four copies. Scott claims the shorter German version was 'over a yard square' (32), but it was in fact 42.5 x 33.5 cm (response of Dresden archive). However, this still makes it unusually large. I am grateful to Andy Drummond and to Ulrike Eydinger for this information. Quotations: ThMA 1, 411–440, 418:2, 418:12, 427:22–23; Matheson, *Collected Works of Müntzer*, 350 ff.; on the Prague Manifesto and translation, 356 ff.

19. After the war was over in Thuringia, the new electoral official for Allstedt described the local churches in shocked terms: 'They have no crucifix or anything in their churches, only an altar in the middle of the church like in a synagogue', 'Haben kein crucifix ader nits in iren kirchen, allein ein altar mitten in der kirchen wi in einer sinagogen', AGBM 2, 478. Words of consecration: ThMA, 1, 192–193, 219–220; Matheson, *Collected Works of Müntzer*, 174–175; the words were sung. In other respects his liturgy was conservative, drawing on medieval traditions: Honemann and Henkel, *Tradition und Erneuerung*. See, on the vast panoply of objects that had developed around the celebration of the mass, Asquez, *Suffering Christ*, 239–392. On Müntzer's liturgy, Schilling, ' "Allen auserwählten Gottesfreunden" '. On the music, I am grateful to Bethan Winter for exploring it musically; see Boyd Brown, *Singing the Gospel*, 37, who maintains that the music was 'wooden', but this may rather have been music based on Gregorian chant and designed to immerse the reader in meditation. Müntzer wrote hymns and wanted Psalms to be sung by the congregation.

20. ThMA 3, 124, Nr. 76, 21 September 1523; Zeiß replied the next day, explaining that he had summoned both preachers in, and they had given written

responses; he refused to arrest them, ThMA 3, 125, Nr. 77. Haferitz's response to the count denied having used these words but insisted that Ernst was a suppresser of the gospel. Ernst then sent copies of these two letters to Friedrich, asking him to arrest Müntzer, ThMA 3, 127, Nr. 79, 24 September 1523. Friedrich, wily and careful as ever, then wrote to Allstedt and Zeiß asking who had employed Müntzer (the authorities should have been informed of such an appointment). In October Friedrich wrote to Ernst assuring him that Zeiß had made Müntzer and Haferitz vow to refrain from unfair attacks in the future—the formulation stopped some way short of an apology or punishment.

21. Four citizens alleged in a letter to Elector Johann that Müntzer had the support of Reichart and Rückert, ThMA 3, 135–136. They had been forced to come to the town hall and told to leave the area if they weren't prepared to join. After the defeat at Frankenhausen, Rückert himself interrogated others about their membership in the league, 136 n. 2, an example of the complex web of guilt and recrimination after the war, as officials still in power tried to clear their names. On Meinhard, see Bräuer, 'Der Hüttenmeister Christoph Meinhard'. Quotation from league member: ThMA 3, 136–138.

22. Storm bell: ThMA 3, 149, 28 July 1524. Mallerbach: Bräuer and Vogler, *Müntzer*, 226; words of Müntzer and Haferitz: ThMA 3, 145:10–11, 146:5–6.

23. Summoning of Müntzer and Haferitz: ThMA 3, 132–133: entries in accounts suggest that there was a meeting with Johannes Lang, two others (probably Aegidius Mechler and Johann Culsamer), Haferitz, Müntzer, and possibly Count Ernst of Mansfeld's men in November 1523 at Allstedt in the castle while the elector was there; and again in early February or March 1524, this time with Justus Jonas as well as Lang. See also Bräuer and Vogler, *Müntzer*, 207. Riot: Wölbing, *Müntzers langer Schatten*, 49–55; Bräuer and Vogler, *Müntzer*, 229–230. Claus Knauth, a council member, however, was arrested and jailed in Allstedt. The following month, when people from Sangerhausen attending sermons in Allstedt were punished, Zeiß argued that he could not advise people to disobey their local lord, in this case von Witzleben. On Müntzer's interrogation at Weimar, Wölbing, *Müntzers langer Schatten*, 61–70. Luther: ThMA 3, 139; WBr 3, no. 753, 305–308, 18 June 1524. Luther went on to mock him: 'he's a bad spirit, let him try travelling elsewhere, as I've done, and take his chances outside this princedom with other princes, and let's see then, where his spirit is', 'ist ein schlechter Geist; er fahr hin einmal, wie ich getan hab und wage es außer diesem Fürstentumb fur andern Fürsten, und laß da sehen, wo sein Geist ist'. WBr 3, 308:79–81. As so often, Luther had recourse to his own life history to justify his position.

24. ThMA 3, 177, 24 August 1524. For more on Hans Zeiß, see ch. 5 below, n. 16. He also tried to refute the allegation that Müntzer had held a mass in which he had sung a passage from the prophets calling for the princes to be slain. Zeiß insisted he had heard no such mass and enclosed a copy of Müntzer's printed mass; but he did admit 'it's public knowledge that he is very turbulent', 'es ist offentlich, das er gantz auffrurisch ist', ThMA 3, 179, 25 August 1524. Zeiß assured the elector that Haferitz

had now seen the error of his ways and had turned against Müntzer. True or not, this enabled Zeiß at least to protect Haferitz.

25. Luther's letter to Mühlhausen: WS 15, 238–240, 21 August 1524.

26. AGBM 2, 13 (no. 1093), point 45: only two of the fifty-four miscellaneous demands concerned religion. See Müller, *Mörder ohne Opfer*, 213–230, for the various versions of the demands, their contents, and the council's response. AGBM 2, 9–10 (no. 1092); 10–15 the Recess (no. 1093); Müller, *Mörder ohne Opfer*, 143–173. Pfeiffer and Hisolidus were banished in August 1523, returning only in December. On Hisolidus and Hildebrandt, Müller, *Mörder ohne Opfer*; Müller, *Frühreformation in Westthüringen*.

27. Jordan, *Chronik der Stadt Mühlhausen*, vol. 1, 179–183 (= Müller, 'Chronicon Mulhusinum', 48–49; this is a more accurate transcription than the Jordan edition of the passages concerning Müntzer, and both references are supplied throughout); Müller, *Mörder ohne Opfer*, 266–268, 317, 322 (wedding); Drummond, *Dreadful History*. Wettich also rode off on an official council horse, AGBM 2, 70. Interestingly a similar conflict arose in nearby Frankenhausen, where, after the war, Peter Wilde was accused of using the town's seal without permission to seal letters from the rebels addressed to princes and nobility, Hahnemann, 'Einwohner', 77. Müntzer and Pfeiffer apparently backed the call of the linen weavers for a new council, drafting a programme of eleven articles, but these were not accepted by a majority of the quarters.

28. Bräuer and Vogler, *Müntzer*, 271–277. Müller, *Mörder ohne Opfer*, supports the view that in the weeks of August and September 1524, Pfeiffer rather than Müntzer may have been the dominant force.

29. Bräuer and Vogler, *Müntzer*, 275, argue that Müntzer actively engaged in secular politics only during the first revolt in Mühlhausen, and that up to that point he had restricted his engagement to the religious realm. It is true that he initially castigated secular powers in the manner of a prophet, just as Luther did. However, it is evident from the correspondence that in Allstedt, Müntzer was closely engaged with the town elite, with whom he met and interacted on a daily basis, especially with Zeiß, so that his engagement with town politics may have been greater than even the written record suggests.

30. Vogler, 'Imperial City', 39–40.

31. Strauß, *Hauptstück und Artickel*, fo. ii r: point 11 explained that usury had arisen because 'sich die Juden vnder den Christen nit meer neren mügen'. In 1524 he published *Das wůcher zů nemen vnd geben, vnserm Christlichem glauben…entgegen ist*. See also Bauer and Haspel, eds., *Jakob Strauß und der reformatorische Wucherstreit*; Dietmann, 'Die Prediger Jakob Strauß und Wolfgang Stein'. He had trained at Wittenberg, and Luther had got him a position with the noble Georg of Wertheim in 1522, who would later become a Peasants' War leader. Luther's admonition: WBr 3, 178–179, Nr. 674, 18 October 1523; 275, Nr. 733, 25 April 1524.

After the war, rumours circulated, falsely, that Strauss had been executed, and Luther repeated the story in a letter to Rühel of 30 May, WBr 3, 877, 515–516. Strauss condemned the rebellion and did not support the peasants, and indeed tried to get the peasant army at nearby Salzungen to disband. After the war, the town council blamed his preaching for Eisenach's brief involvement. In June 1525, Strauss was summoned to Weimar to face interrogation: WBr 3, 877, 516 n. 15. He seems to have been shattered by the experience, and in 1526 he wrote *Aufruhr, Zwietracht und Uneinigkeit* to justify himself. Here he claims to have been maligned and addresses the reports of his execution, fo. A I v–a ii r. He was exculpated by Weimar and returned to Eisenach, where, however, he had lost the support of the council. In 1527 he wrote defending the doctrine of the real presence and condemning the views of Zwingli and Oecolampadius. See also Dietmann, 'Die Prediger Jakob Strauß und Wolfgang Stein'.

32. TA Zurich, 392. For Luther on usury, WS 15, 279–292, 293–322. For full introduction and analysis of the text, see Rössner, ed., *Martin Luther: On Commerce and Usury*.

33. Laube, 'Social Arguments'. Buszello, 'Oberrheinlande', 83–86.

34. Karlstadt, *Von Gelübden Unterrichtung*, fo. 25 r, 'Gott fordert von vns meer freyheit dann dienstbarkeyt... wiewol ein freyher in gott, gottes diener ist, dannoch herschet er allen creature, in lufft, wasser vnd erden'. Karlstadt, 'Regarding Vows' in Furcha, ed., *Essential Carlstadt*, 84–85. Karlstadt, *Anzeyg etlicher Hauptartickeln Christlicher leere*, fos. F iv (v)–G i (r), translated as 'Several Main Points of Christian Teaching' in Furcha, ed., *Essential Carlstadt*, 339–377, 374.

35. Brunfels: Roper, *Martin Luther*, 256. Zwingli: Potter, *Zwingli*, 204–208; Gordon, *Zwingli*, 115–164. Karlstadt, see Karlstadt, *Anzeyg etlicher Hauptartickeln Christlicher leere*, in Furcha, ed., *Essential Carlstadt*. See Burnett, *Karlstadt*; and Zorzin, *Karlstadt*, esp. 35–36, which shows that Karlstadt published little in 1522 and 1523 but a lot between October/November 1524 and May 1525. The split between Luther and Karlstadt was picked up very quickly by Capito, and he published *Was man halten* in October 1524 in Strasbourg, reprinted in Augsburg in 1524 and in Erfurt in 1525 (VD 16 C, 847–849). Karlstadt's eight writings of October/November 1524 had a total of eleven reprints, but the four-page-long *Wider die alte und newue papistische Messe* made up five of these editions. Most of the first printings were in Basel with reprints in Strasbourg; a few were undertaken in Augsburg and Nuremberg-Bamberg. Zorzin calculates that the Strasbourg and Basel printings would all have been done by mid-November, creating a possible eleven thousand to nineteen thousand copies of writings by Karlstadt in circulation—if we assume all were sold. However, these printings are geographically concentrated (Basel, Strasbourg). The first part of Luther's *Against the Heavenly Prophets* did not appear until the last days of December, and Karlstadt only received a copy of the second part on 26 February. However, Karlstadt's explicit replies to Luther in two main pamphlets were printed with the same printer in Augsburg, had no reprints, and in publicistic terms were a failure, Zorzin, *Karlstadt*, 101–103.

36. ThMA 1, *Deutsches Kirchenamt* (1523), 1–188; *Ordnung und Berechnung des Deutschen Amtes zu Allstedt* (1524), 188–198; *Deutsche Evangelische Messe* (1524), 198–266. I am grateful to Bethan Winter and Sam Heywood for advising me on

the difference between Luther's and Müntzer's masses, and to Rose Guok's work on Müntzer, Luther, and music. Müntzer's music remained more chant-like than Luther's settings. See also Honemeyer, *Thomas Müntzer und Martin Luther*, and Leaver, *The Whole Church Sings*.

37. Even as late as the end of 1525, Gerhard Geldenhauer (Noviomagus) could travel between Antwerp and Wittenberg, staying with supporters of both Karlstadt and Luther; while Hans Pelt moved only gradually from supporting Müntzer to Luther, Bubenheimer, *Thomas Müntzer*, 116–144. Numbers of preachers: Justus Maurer identified these for southwest Germany, Allgäu, and Upper Swabia and Franconia, Maurer, *Prediger*; the number would now be far higher because of the possibilities of systematic text searches. Maurer was of course unable to include Saxony and Thuringia.

38. Hubmaier, *Schriften*, 273. Andreas Lettsch, a Catholic monk, also described Hubmaier as a Lutheran, though he was well aware that his views on baptism were far from being Lutheran, Lettsch, *Chronik*, 45–47.

39. Brenz, *Von Gehorsam*, VD B 7932, fo. A ii r. True freedom, he goes on, results in obeying God his 'Lord' ('herren'), and his neighbour, (be they) ruler or subject', 'Christenlich freyheit ain rechte gehorsam in einem Christen, gegen Gott seynem HERREN, und senem nächsten, Oberkait oder vnderthon, würcke'.

40. Baumann, *Akten*, 13 February 1525, Baltringen Haufen.

41. Franz, *Der deutsche Bauernkrieg, Aktenband* (hereafter *Akten*), 190, Alsace before 24 January 1525.

42. Murner, *Uon dem grossen Lutherischen Narren*, fo. s O iii (r) to P I (v). Sold like cows: Vogt, *Die Correspondenz des schwäbischen Bundeshauptmannes Ulrich Artzt* (hereafter *Artzt*), 556. Aepfingen: Franz, *Akten*, 148, 16 February 1525. Their complaints were amongst three hundred submitted to the Swabian League, a tenth of which have survived. See Vogt, *Artzt*, 26–27, 36, 39–49, 50–52, 57–59, 547–577; Franz, *Akten*, 147–166; Baumann, *Akten*, 51–75, 113–117, 133–134; Blickle, *Revolution of 1525*, 201–205. Some were written by the same scribe, some using the same words. The peasants of Mittelbiberach began their complaints by saying, 'Als die götlich geschrift clar anzaigt, das ain cristenmensch kain andern herren hab dan got den almächtigen', Franz, *Akten*, 150. The peasants of the Hospital of Biberach submitted an unusually complex theological elaboration of the importance of the Word in creating brotherhood and salvation, probably written by a highly literate person: 'Item wir mir hie in Christo bruder versamlet send, begeren erstlich yetz und furterhyn fur uns zu nemen das lebedig ewig unvertruckt wort, das hailig evangelium, so doch yetz in diser zeyt unser vatter sich uber uns arm sonder erbormet hat, und uns mit seinem sun Christo Christo Jesu, der dan uns, wie Paulus spricht, worden ist die weyßhait, gerechtigkait und erlösung durch sein unschuldigen todt, den er uns zu guttem ton hat', Franz, *Akten*, 150. But not all used such high-flown language.

43. Attenweiler: Vogt, *Artzt*, 548, and see also the articles of the Alberweilers, which put the point in similar terms: they went straight on to say that they were burdened with carnival hens and with inheritance dues. The link is that the argument

about creation showed that freedom meant 'aigensch', as they termed it, was unscriptural, and so the carnival hens and other dues which followed from it were also not justified. It was all 'aigensch'. Luther's theology of marriage: in 1519, his sermon on marriage argued that marriage was a remedy for sin, WS 2, 166–171; LW 44, 'A Sermon on the Estate of Marriage' ('Ein Sermon von dem ehelichen Stand'). But in 1522 in his sermon on marriage, he developed a theory of marriage that started from the Old Testament and creation. God had created male and female, and 'hence, as it is not within my power not to be a man, so it is not my prerogative to be without a woman', WS 10.II, 276:14–20, 21–26; LW 45, 18, *The Estate of Marriage* (*Vom ehelichen Leben*). It was composed after Luther's return to Wittenberg, probably in September 1522, WS 10.II, 267, introduction.

44. Baltringen: Vogt, *Artzt*, 549. Schmalkalden: AGBM 1, 628.

45. Cronthal, *Stadt Würzburg*, 32.

46. StadtA Bamberg, HV Rep 3 1439, fos. 2–3, Langensendelbach, Neukürch.

47. The Rappertsweiler band did reject feudal labour dues completely, Vogt, *Artzt*, 564–565. Ulrich Schmid: Baumann, *Quellen: Chroniken*, 281; report of his sermon in the Chronicle of the Nuns of Heggbach Article on labour services: Blickle, *Die Revolution*, 325, article 7; Blickle, *The Revolution*, 199, article 7.

48. For a statement of the English neorepublican position, see Skinner, 'Rethinking Political Liberty'. I am grateful to Hannah Dawson for helping me formulate this point.

49. Cornelius, *Studien zur Geschichte des Bauernkrieges*, 32 n. 1, 12 February 1525, Report of Eck. These feudal arrangements were 'not Christian': *An die Versammlung gemeiner Bauernschaft*, 102. In Thuringia a little later, some articles referred to the contents of 'the Word' a little clumsily, though they had clearly heard Luther's ideas and knew Paul was important. So, for example, the articles of Ballenberg and Krautheim wanted to support 'the word of God and the teaching of Paul', 'dem wort gots vnd der leer Pauli', and they called on the community of Buchen to obey 'the Holy Gospel and also the word of Paul', 'dem Heiligen Euangelio auch dem wort Pauli', HStA Dresden, 10024 Geheimer Rat (Geheimes Archiv), loc. 9135/22, fo. 3, 6 April 1525 (contemporary copy).

50. Erolzheim: Franz, *Akten*, 154. On the dualism of Reformation images, see Scribner, *For the Sake of Simple Folk*.

51. On the meaning of 'göttliches Recht', see Hecker, 'Der Bauernkrieg', who points out that the term means not only deriving from God but also 'billig, gerecht, angemessen', so that it does not necessarily propose divine law as superior to human. See also the interesting argument of Schirmer, 'Ursachen des Bauernkrieges in Thüringen', that in middle Germany, conflicts between lords and peasants had been settled through legal means and had not turned into violent conflict because of the power of territorial rule; it will be interesting to see whether this can be generalised for the whole region outside the Saxonies. Schirmer also raises the important question of the significance of the different Saxon and Franconian systems of law. On law and its significance, see Mayenburg, *Gemeiner Mann und Gemeines Recht*.

52. The Rappertsweiler band's articles were especially clear on the importance of the local parish church, Vogt, *Artzt*, 564–565. Luther: *Daß eine christliche Versammlung oder Gemeine Recht und Macht habe, alle Lehre zu urtheilen und Lehrer zu berufen, ein und ab zu setzen, Grund und Ursach aus der Schrift*, 1523, WS 11, 401–416.

Chapter 4: Winter

1. Kessler, *Sabbata*, 173. The revolt seemed good-humoured; as Nicolaus Thomann's 'Weissenhorner Historie' described it, at first fifty, sixty, then a hundred gathered, saying, 'We want to have a party with each other', 'wy wöllen ain gute geselschaft mit ainandren haben', Baumann, *Quellen: Chroniken*, 63. 'Sie woltent ain Danz hon', Baumann, *Quellen: Chroniken*, 279; in 279–295, report of a nun from Kloster Heggbach from 1541. See amongst many other similar examples, the report of the Council of Stadtilm, who say they admonished the rebels not to attack 'such noble, honourable, virtuous and innocent virgins', AGBM 2, 467.

2. *Kirchweih* (church ale): Baumann, *Quellen: Chroniken*, 35. I am grateful to Ed Wareham for pointing this out. See the importance of the *Kirchweih* at Biengen in autumn 1513 for the Bundschuh, Rosenkranz, *Bundschuh*, vol. 1, 320–321. *Kirchweih* and the Peasants' War: in one of the opening acts of the war, peasants from Stühlingen went to Waldshut for its church ale carrying their flag, leading to an alliance between Waldshut and the Stühlingen peasants, Lettsch, *Chronik*, 46; Hug, *Villinger Chronik*, 100, 105. And at Hilzingen in 1524, matters began at a *Kirchweih*: Blickle, *Bauernjörg*, 87, 93–96. In Heilbronn matters began in an assembly in the church, Rauch, *Urkundenbuch der Stadt Heilbronn*, vol. 4 (hereafter *Heilbronn* IV), 238. Steinhaim: Baumann, *Akten*, 35, 36. Volckamer: StadtA Nürnberg, E 29/IV Nr 1575, Helge Weingärtner summary. Wettenhausen: Christoph Franck, *Annales Wettenhusi*, in Baumann, *Quellen: Chroniken*, 243.

3. No lord: Franz, *Der deutsche Bauernkrieg, Aktenband* (hereafter *Akten*), 147 (February); Sabean, *Landbesitz*, 89. Mittelbiberach: Franz, *Akten*, 151 (February). Baltringen: Baumann, *Quellen: Chroniken*, 280.

4. See Baumann, *Akten*; Franz, *Akten*; Vogt, *Die Correspondenz des schwäbischen Bundeshauptmannes Ulrich Artzt* (hereafter *Artzt*), 547–581 (Augsburg Stadtarchiv collection); AGBM 1 and 2; and Fries, *Geschichte des Bauernkriegs*, amongst others, for peasant articles.

5. In 1523 Luther published a letter to all the Teutonic Knights advising them to marry: WS 12, 232–244; and see WBr 3, Nr. 697, December 1523, 207–209, and earlier conversations. In May 1525 he congratulated Albrecht and was suggesting preachers, WBr 3, 876, 26 May 1525, 513–514. Secularisation happened formally on 10 April 1525. On the Teutonic Knights, see Weiß, 'Deutsche Orden'; Christiansen, *Northern Crusades*; Militzer, *Geschichte des Deutschen Ordens*; Sarnowsky, *Deutsche Orden*; Boockmann, *Deutsche Orden*; Schneller, *800 Jahre*. In Thuringia, Müller, ed., *Deutscher Orden und Thüringen*. On Mergentheim and the tomb of Walter von Cronberg, who took over administration of the order in 1527, Arnold and Trentin-Meyer, *Deutscher Orden 1190–2000*.

6. The Bishop of Samland, Georg von Polentz, was also a supporter of Luther; the former Teutonic Knight and chronicler Philip von Creutz accuses him of simply wanting a wife, and he alleges that he broke his costly bishop's seal, turning it into jewellery for her, and took twenty-four golden pieces out of the church to pay for coverings and curtains for his bed. He maintained that he himself was forced to become Albrecht's serf ('aigen man'), and was treated 'alsz wer ich ein Littaw', 'as if I were a Lithuanian'. Hirsch et al., eds., *Scriptores rerum prussicarum*, 5, 378–384.

7. The order's importance is reflected in the space Cochlaeus devoted to it in his brief description of Germany of 1512. He noted that that only 'German[s] and noble[s]' were accepted, that they grew beards, and that few could read and write, Cochlaeus, *Kurze Beschreibung*, 85.

8. Mainau: Schneller, *800 Jahre*, 245–256. Mühlhausen: Sünder, 'Der Deutscher Orden'; Müller, 'Frühreformation'. Beuggen: Franz, *Akten*, 180.

9. Quotation: Hirsch et al., eds., *Scriptores rerum prussicarum*, 5, 359. For the region around Mergentheim, Oettingen, and Ellingen, see, for example, Oechsle, *Beiträge zur Geschichte*, 123–153.

10. Luther and Albrecht of Mainz: WBr 2, 447, Capito to Luther, 20 and 21 December 1521, 416; and Albrecht of Mainz's letter to Luther, WBr 2, 448, 21 December 1521, 420–421; Luther's mistrustful response, WBr 2, 451, 17 January 1522, 428–443. In 1525, rumours about Albrecht's marriage plans even reached Rome. WS18, 408–411, 2 (?) June 1525, for Luther's letter to Albrecht, probably written around 2 June. Rühel suggested he write, WBr 3, 873, 21 May 1525, 503–507, and Luther promised to do so, WBr 3, 877, 30 May 1525, 515–516. It was probably given to Albrecht, perhaps with Rühel as intermediary, shortly before 27 June, when Albrecht showed it to an outraged Duke Georg of Saxony, WS 18, 402–411. However, the first dated printing of the letter is from 1526, so Luther may still have harboured hopes that Albrecht would marry. Albrecht's wedding present of twenty gold Gulden were given to Katharina von Bora through Rühel. Beuggen: Ulbrich, *Leibherrschaft*, 130 n. 558. Beuggen was attacked and plundered and many documents destroyed; Beuggen had pursued a particularly aggressive policy of enserfment in an area surrounded by free peasants.

11. Figures from 1577: Weiß, 'Der Deutsche Orden', KLK, vol. 1. Samland Bishop: Hubatsch, 'Albrecht of Brandenburg-Ansbach', 42. On the Teutonic Knights in the commanderies (*Balleien*) that later became Protestant, including Thuringia, Demel, 'Die Reformation'.

12. Rauch, *Heilbronn* IV, 9–14. Götz passes over this incident in his autobiography.

13. Rauch, *Heilbronn* IV, 16, 14–18, 20–23. It transpired that the woman was the wife of Philipp von Gemmingen, a supporter of the Reformation who appointed a Lutheran preacher to his village of Fürfeld near his castle.

14. Rauch, 'Bauernführer Jäcklein Rohrbach', 25, and *Heilbronn* IV, 287, testimony of Lachmann.

15. Hubmaier was offering to debate the issue of baptism in February 1525, Hubmaier, *Schriften*, 105–107. On Hubmaier's thought, Scott, 'Hubmaier, Schappeler and Hergot'.

16. The Swabian League had been trying to negotiate between Waldshut and the Austrians but was not inclined to intervene in the Habsburgs' support, because although they had taken Ulrich's duchy, they had not paid for it by meeting the costs of the campaign against Duke Ulrich from 1519 as agreed, Horst Carl, 'Der Gegner—Der Schwäbische Bund im Bauernkrieg', Lecture Tübingen, 19 May 2023.

17. For a sense of Hurlewagen's bold, clear written style, see the fragments of his correspondence preserved in the report sent to Archduke Ferdinand by local officials: Franz, *Akten*, 167–172. His seal survives; see the image at the website of Elmar L. Kuhn (accessed April 14, 2024), http://elmarlkuhn.de/aufsaetze-im-volltext/oberschwaben-und-bodenseeraum/bauernkrieg-in-oberschwaben/die-fuehrer/siegel-des-dietrich-hurlewagen-hauptmann-des-rappertsweiler-haufens/index.html. Tyrol: Blickle, 'Alpenländer', 192–193; Ferdinand promised to summon a special *Landtag* for North Tyrol and agreed to administrative changes in the mines. See Laube, 'Der Aufstand der Schwazer Bergarbeiter', 246–255. These were quite extensive, including reinstatement of holidays, reform of payment systems, and investigating complaints about the Fuggers, 236–237; demands that service dues be reduced were not in the end agreed.

18. See Osiander, *Gesamtausgabe*, Bd. 1, 255–266, for a summary of the likely contents of two works Müntzer's coworker Pfeiffer also tried to publish there, now lost.

19. Case of the 'godless painters' of Nuremberg: Bräuer and Vogler, *Müntzer*, 287–293; ThMA 1, 322–375; Pfeiffer, *Quellen*, 25–27, RV (= Ratsverlasse) 189, 190, 192, 196, 198; Kolde, *Hans Denck*. *Von der newen Wandlung* was reprinted in a memorial edition edited by Max Steinmetz to celebrate the 450th anniversary of the Peasants' War. See also Blickle, *The Revolution*, 150–154, and *Die Revolution*, 232–236. Printing of *Hoch verursachte Schutzrede*: Bräuer and Vogler, *Müntzer*, 260, 284–287.

20. Oecolampadius: ThMA 3, 192, Oecolampadius to Willibald Pirckheimer, 21 September 1525; and 194, later account of Oecolampadius from 1526 printed as part of the publication of their debate about the sacrament. Müntzer's travels: Müller, *Thomas Müntzer im Bauernkrieg*, 17–24; Bräuer and Vogler, *Müntzer*, 317–318; according to Heinrich Bullinger he was at Griessen, which is between Schaffhausen and Waldshut, and was subject to the Abbot of St Blasien; and in the Klettgau and Hegau according to his own confession; ThMA 3, 195–196; see also Scott, 'Ein Radikaler auf Reisen'. Case of Ottilie von Gersen: Gess, *Akten und Briefe*, vol. 2, 8; Bräuer and Vogler, *Müntzer*, 321. The outcome is unknown.

21. Zeiß told Spalatin on 22 February that Müntzer had been imprisoned in Fulda without being recognised; AGBM 2, 66, No. 1155, 22 February 1525, Zeiß to Spalatin; Bräuer and Vogler, *Müntzer*, 319. According to Zeiß, now Pfeiffer was trying to get support in the villages around Mühlhausen, saying that he had been

driven out for the sake of truth, 'umb der warheit…willen', the argument made by Karlstadt. As Franz points out, *Der deutsche Bauernkrieg*, 239, the preacher of Dipperz who had many adherents in Fulda was said to be a supporter of Müntzer.

22. Remnants of the well-appointed hearth are still visible in the house, which I was lucky enough to visit; my thanks to Thomas T. Müller.

23. ThMA, 2, 468.

24. Oberndorf: Franz, *Akten*, 163: they did not want to pay the tithe, but they would pay to support their clergy. Kempten: Ulbrich, 'Oberschwaben und Württemberg', 101; Baumann, *Akten*, 348 from the interrogation of Jörg Schmid.

25. Lake Constance band: Baumann, *Akten*, 138, before 6 March. Letter of Baltringen band, Baumann, *Akten*, 131.

26. Baumann, *Akten*, 131: the letter was written to the town of Ehingen, 28 February 1525.

27. Report on Schappeler: Baumann, *Akten*, 1. Schappeler, born in St Gallen, was influenced by Zwingli and presided over the Second Zurich Disputation in 1523, Hätzer et al., *Acta oder geschicht*. His portrait later in life shows a stern, square-bearded man who points an admonishing finger. Trummer, 'Schappeler'. StadtAMM, Schublade 341/5, gives more background on Schappeler.

28. 'Bishop Schappeler': Lotzer, *Ayn außlegung uber das Evangelium*; Lotzer, *Ain vast haylsam*. This text has a long section on confession, discusses the ban, refers to the elements of bread and wine as a 'sign' ('zaychen'), and has many of the characteristics that would be associated with Zwinglian-influenced theology, which he may have picked up from Schappeler, who had spent time in Zurich. But he also has a lot to say about the importance of faith, mentions the 'Babylonian captivity' of the church (E iiii v), insists that Christians must pick up the cross and suffer, and uses the term 'Lutheran' to refer to the true believers. He also takes a Lutheran line on confession. Paul Russell sees his theology as an amalgam of Eberlin von Günzburg, Zwingli, Luther, and mysticism, but more importantly these were ideas 'most of which might have come from any German preacher in the Southwest', Russell, *Lay Theology*, 91. On Lotzer, Russell, 80–111; Ruszat-Ewig, *Sebastian Lotzer*, 7–48. See also Ruszat-Ewig, *Die 12 Bauernartikel*. Concluding paragraph on true Christians: 'Sagt sy seyen Lutherisch/dye seynds von wöllichen Christus sagt', Lotzer, *Ain vast haylsam*, H v (v). There is, however, one significant exception to his avoidance of controversial topics in this pamphlet: he heads his section 27 on secular authority 'The authorities may not command us against God's Word', 'Die obern haben vns nit zu byeten wider Gottes wort'. He gives little commentary aside from insisting that we should be obedient to secular authority in all fitting things concerning body and property, while authorities should not issue orders against God's command. This formulation, though different in emphasis, was hardly very different from Luther's view, and it was not yet a justification for revolt.

29. Lotzer, *Entschuldigung*, fo. A ii (v).

30. Luther, *Passional Christi vnd Antichristi*, originally printed in Wittenberg in 1521, was copied with illustrations by a different artist in a Strasbourg edition (VD

16 L 5583), and pirated in an Erfurt edition (VD 16 L 5581). See also edition and English translation, Wareham et al., eds., *Passional Christi und Antichristi*.

31. 'No lord but God alone': Vogt, *Artzt*, 561, Risstissen. About thirty of these survive and were analysed by Blickle quantitatively to show that they mainly concerned serfdom, especially death duties, restrictions of movement, and marriage; natural resources like hunting, fishing, woods, and common land; and feudal dues and legal rights. He noted that for the most part they did not explicitly legitimate their demands through scripture or law—but this may not be surprising since this was not what they had been asked to do; more striking is their use of religious language at all. See Ulbrich, 'Oberschwaben und Württemberg', 107–109; Blickle, 'Economic, Social and Political Background'; Blickle, *Revolution of 1525*, 25–57; 202–205, for analysis of these and other grievances. Christian Reyter: Vogt, *Artzt*, 573.

32. Carnival hens: Vogt, *Artzt*, 548. For other grievances, Vogt, *Artzt*, 547–578; Baumann, *Akten*, 113–117 (Kisslegg, February); Franz, *Akten*, 143–173. It is notable, too, that as early as mid-February, observers reported that the peasants had joined together 'to help one another introduce the holy gospel and godly justice', Franz, *Akten*, 145, Claus von Villenbach to Archduke Ferdinand; while on 15 February Chancellor Eck wrote to the Duke of Bavaria that the peasants were inspired by the 'Lutheran teachings', because they based their demands on 'The Word of God, gospel and brotherly love', Franz, *Quellen*, 151.

33. Ulbrich, 'Oberwschwaben und Württemberg', 110; Baumann, *Akten*, 119–126; the articles were submitted on 3 March, and the council replied on 15 March. They resemble the Twelve Articles and were probably written by Lotzer too. For the disagreement between the three groups, see Kessler, *Sabbata*, 173–179; they finally resolved matters by handshake after a highly emotional exchange. See also Ulbrich, 'Oberschwaben und Württemberg', 115; Buszello, *Bauernkrieg als politische Bewegung*; Blickle, 'Nochmals zur Entstehung'; Mayenburg, *Gemeiner Mann*. Interestingly the Allgäuers in their instructions for their representatives had insisted strongly on communion in both kinds, Baumann, *Akten*, 138–139. On the three armies, see Haggenmüller, 'Der Allgäuer Haufen'; Diemer, 'Der Baltringer Haufen'; and Kuhn, 'Der Seehaufen'.

34. Cornelius, *Studien zur Geschichte des Bauernkrieges*, 191–196. For a map of the Upper Swabian peasant armies and their shifting boundaries, see Buszello, 'Die Christliche Vereinigung', 156. The three groups do not overlap, and the leaders are not concentrated in any one village or area, suggesting the movement had very broad support. Allgäu Ordinance: Cornelius, *Studien zur Geschichte des Bauernkrieges*, 190.

35. Cornelius, *Studien zur Geschichte des Bauernkrieges*, 186.

36. Blickle, *Revolution of 1525*, 18–22, 195–201. On events in the Kramerzunftstube, see Ruszat-Ewig, *Was geschah . . . ?*

37. Some credit Lotzer alone as the author; some think Schappeler was coauthor. The preacher had certainly influenced Lotzer, but the fact that there are biblical proof texts for the articles does not prove he was involved, because Lotzer had already pioneered this method in earlier writings. He also drew on other documents, including

perhaps an earlier draft of the Memminger Bundesordnung, Ulbrich, 'Oberschwaben und Württemberg', 109–113; see also Marquardt, 'God, Christ and Serfdom'.

38. Blickle, *Revolution von 1525*, 321–322; *Revolution of 1525*, 18–22, 195–196. On events in the Kramerzunftstube, see Ruszat-Ewig, *Was geschah...?*

39. Election of pastor: Wolgast, 'Pfarrerwahl'. Article three: Blickle, *Revolution of 1525*, 196, 197. Article three and blood sacrifice: here the articles drew on a number of New Testament passages about Christ buying our freedom with his blood; these also refer back to Exodus, the blood of Passover, and the deliverance from slavery (which in turn would later inspire Negro spirituals). However, the words themselves that 'Christ redeemed and bought us all with his precious blood, the lowliest shepherd as well as the greatest lord, with no exceptions' are not a direct quotation from the Bible, nor can they be straightforwardly derived from the scriptural 'proof texts' listed in the margin of the text next to article three (these include 1 Cor. 7, 1 Peter 1 and 2, Isaiah 53, Romans 13, and the Book of Wisdom). They do, however, derive from serious engagement with these key biblical texts and with others, and with ideas circulating in the eucharistic theology of the early Luther. I am grateful to Simon Ponsonby for discussion of this issue.

40. It is revealing that only cattle are mentioned, animals often associated with men (death duties, for example, often required the best head of cattle in the case of a man and the best dress in the case of a woman) in relation to the small tithe, and not other animals on which the small tithe was levied, such as pigs and poultry, which were an important issue for women. Offer to rescind any article proved not in accord with Bible, article twelve: Blickle, *Revolution of 1525*, 195–201; Blickle, *Die Revolution*, 319–327.

41. Kessler, *Sabbata*, 176. After the defeat, Lotzer spent some time in St Gallen, where he spoke to Johannes Kessler, author of the Sabbata, so this is as close to Lotzer's voice as it is possible to get.

42. Ulbrich, 'Oberschwaben und Württemberg', 113. On the Twelve Articles, see also Ruszat-Ewig, *Die 12 Bauernartikel*, 1–65; and Hasselhoff and Mayenburg, eds., *Zwölf Artikel*. They and the Bundesordnung are the only printed documents from the peasants' side apart from the pamphlet *An die Versammlung* and the Weingartener Vertrag, which was concluded by the Swabian League and was not exactly a peasant production, Rammstedt, 'Stadtunruhen 1525', 265. On legal dimensions of the articles, see Hecker, 'Der Bauernkrieg'; the National Socialists included the demand for 'German law' as opposed to Roman law in their programme, which they linked to the peasant war demands for 'göttlich recht'. Posting articles: AGBM 2, 538, the local judge at Neustruppen got the articles from his brother Georg, who had brought them from Joachimstal, and on the Friday after Corpus Christi they were read in Kretschmar. They were on a nail in the parlour of Nesel von Stroppen's house, and he had read them out aloud; there were two pages, he recalled. In Heilbronn, the baker Hans Flux was rumoured to carry the Twelve Articles around with him, Rauch, *Heilbronn* IV, 26. On devising 'twelve' articles elsewhere, see, for example, Odenwald-Neckartal Band Articles, in Oechsle, *Beiträge zur Geschichte*, 272–273. See also the

twelve articles of the community of Obhausen, probably drawn up in May, which did not mention freedom as there was no serfdom but refused to give any more money to the chapter (*dompfaffen*) at Merseburg, 'because we don't know why or through what', LASA, Standort Wernigerode, A 32a Grafschaft Mansfeld, Nr. 392, 3r–v.

43. *Handlung, Artickel vnnd Instruktion*. Text also in Cornelius, *Studien zur Geschichte des Bauernkrieges*, 183–186, draft, 186–190; and Franz, *Quellen*, 195–197. See also Seebass, *Artikelbrief*, 55–148, for comparison of all the printed versions. The ordinance compelled tradesfolk who needed to leave the area for work to swear to their parish captain that they would not join an army opposed to the Christian Union, and that they would return to fight if required. The union was a moral union, too, and a final article banned unseemly gambling, blasphemy, and 'Zutrinken', the custom of mutual toasting with excessive alcohol drinking.

44. Baumann, *Akten*, 150–151.

Chapter 5: Lordship

1. So, for example, Hans von Berlepsch, castellan of the Wartburg when Luther was hidden there, bought himself a moated castle at Seebach from Günter von Bünau not far from Mühlhausen. His second wife was Beate von Ebeleben, from a local noble family. On the nature of political authority in the German lands, see Hardy, *Associative Political Culture*.

2. Roper, *Luther*, 397–398; Jankowski, *Mansfeld*; Hahnemann, 'Einwohner', 73 (Schwarzburgs).

3. For example, 'in childly faithful love and good [wishes], Highly born prince, dear beloved lord and father', 'Was ich in kintlichen truen liebs und guts vermag zu-vor. Hochgeborner furst, freuntlicher Lieber herr und vatter', AGBM 1, 133, Johann von Fulda to Count Wilhelm of Henneberg. 'Dear son', 'Lieber son', Hermann von Henneberg to his son Albrecht, referring to 'our cousin', 'unser vetter', Count Wilhelm, AGBM 1, 113–114. 'Dear brother in law and cousin', 'Liber schwager und gefatter', Tham von Herda to Heinz von Wanbach zu Massfeld and to Johann Jeger (von Wanbach was like him an *Amtmann*), AGBM 1, 136. Tham's letters to von Wanbach can be found in the file of Wanbach's letters from the Peasants' War, LATh Meiningen, GHA Sekt II, Nr. 711. On the wealth of the church, Ocker, *Church Robbers*, 17–49.

4. On Albrecht of Mainz's memorials, see Merkel, *Jenseits-sicherung*. The abbot of St Georgen, Stein am Rhein, decorated his monastic apartments with frescoes featuring the fair of his own childhood, and his arms are everywhere; his monastery was soon a target for evangelicals. Becker and Frehner, *St George's Monastery*; Landolt, *Urkunden zur Reformationsgeschichte*, 624–629.

5. Roper, *Luther*, 20; Jankowski, *Mansfeld*.

6. Rathgeber, *Herrschaft Rappoltstein*, 99, 100. Gess, *Akten und Briefe*, vol. 2, and AGBM 2 throughout. Günther Schuhmann, 'Kasimir', in *Neue Deutsche Biographie* 11 (1977), 315–316.

7. AGBM 2, 91. Friedrich finally agreed to arming, 3 May, 158. As late as 28 April, when he was mortally ill, he counselled his brother Johann to pray to God that

'this difficult circumstance can be averted and stilled without bloodshed', and even on 4 May he hoped for a negotiated solution, AGBM 2, 135, 190. Johann of Fulda even suggested that his father thank the council, commune, and captains of Fulda for not rebelling! AGBM 1, 387.

8. Franz, *Der deutsche Bauernkrieg, Aktenband* (hereafter *Akten*), 273–274, 285–286; 70–71, for the original dispute in 1514, though they still had to perform services, give the carnival hen, and pay taxes as before. Solothurn turned its peasants into Ausbürger: peasants with external citizenship who had no political representation or rights, Ulbrich, *Leibherrschaft*, 182–190. Kenzingen: Scott, *Early Reformation*, 122; and Schreiber, *Der deutsche Bauernkrieg. Gleichzeitige Urkunden*, vol. 2, 9, 105, 158–159. Taddey, 'Wendel Hipler', 68–69.

9. Franz, *Akten*, 153; Bumiller, 'Bauernkrieg im Hegau', 314: the monastery of St Georg in Stein am Rhein had the patronage rights over the parish church. Werdenstein: Baumann, *Quellen: Chroniken*, 485–489. Bregenz: Franz, *Akten*, 174. They were not entirely wrong, because the archduke had not agreed to arrest the priest or three other leaders his officials had wanted to proceed against the previous fortnight, instructing them to do 'the best…as before to stilling [i.e., stopping] [matters]', Franz, *Akten*, 173.

10. Werdenstein: Baumann, *Quellen: Chroniken*, 486, 489; Rathgeber, *Herrschaft Rappoltstein*, 78. They tried to get Ulrich to swear to the Twelve Articles too, which he did the next day but with the proviso that he couldn't bind his brother or father. Georg Truchsess: Lutz, *Tagebuch*, 65; Weissenau: Baumann, *Quellen: Chroniken*, 498. Bamberg: Chroust, *Chroniken*, vol. 2, 40–41.

11. Heggbach: Baumann, *Quellen: Chroniken*, 286. Bamberg: Chroust, *Chroniken*, vol. 2, 33: he mentioned Halstatt because that was where they were about to establish their camp.

12. On the feud and on the knights in this period, see Zmora, *State and Nobility*; Algazi, *Herrengewalt und Gewalt der Herren*. Joel Harrington is currently translating Götz's memoirs into English, *Götz von Berlichingen: My Feuds and Action*, forthcoming.

13. See Xenakis, *Gewalt und Gemeinschaft*, 231–264.

14. Franz, *Quellen*, 368; Laube, *Flugschriften*, 109; Baumann, *Quellen zur Geschichte des Bauernkrieges aus Rotenburg an der Tauber.* [sic] *(Chronik Thomas Zweifel)* (hereafter *Rothenburg*), 356: these articles were brought to Rothenburg on 14 May by Florian Geyer. As Marx Halbritter, councillor at Bamberg saw it, they had intended 'to smash all castles and especially the strongest in the land of Franconia', Chroust, *Chroniken*, vol. 2, 25. 'Destruction', however, sometimes meant no more than removing the roof: Endres, 'Franken', 149.

15. Hennebergs: Tham's brother Christoph was in the castle with him, while a brother-in-law, Michel vom Strauch zu Oberkatz, later denied having said, 'We want to root out the nobles just as one roots out the sticks in the field', but he was forced to sell his goods and leave Hohenlohe, AGBM 1, 636. Berlepsches: AGBM 2.

16. Wilhelm von Herda, AGBM 2, 150; AGBM 1, 261, 352. Hans Zeiß: wife attending Müntzer's, Agricola, *Auslegung*, fo. B iii r. It is difficult to reconstruct this tricky character's true views. See such contradictory episodes as AGBM 2, 941; but Luther had warned Zeiß in person against Müntzer on 3 August 1523, WB 3, No. 641, 3 August 1523, 120:27–128. Double-dealing with Sophie von Schaffstedt, abbess of Nauendorf, AGBM 1, 162; AGBM 2, 186–187. On 22 February 1525, Zeiß worried that Mühlhausen would become the centre of an 'emporung' of followers of Karlstadt and Müntzer but did not send this letter until 5 March, AGBM 2, 66–67. And see in particular his seemingly pro-Müntzer letter to Meinhard, AGBM 2, 228. There is good reason to think the letter to Meinhard is genuine even though it is a copy, not in his hand. It is part of a small bundle of contemporary copies of the three letters from Müntzer and one from Salza to Mühlhausen, which are all together (there are further copies of letters from Müntzer in the file). These are annotated on the back by an official, perhaps Spalatin, 'his Grace [gave] me these letters [to read] in the camp at Schlotheim in 1525', 'Disse briff hat mir sein gnadt [zu lesen geben] ym leger Slatheim ym 1525' (my transcription), and formed part of the bundle of material which Elector Johann gave Duke Georg to read, ThMA 2, 446–447. An earlier note just below the annotation describes the contents as 'writings from the Schosser at Allstedt, Müntzer and others, 1525', 'Schrifft von dem Schosser zu Alstedt Muntzer vnd andern etc Anno 1525', so the letter from Zeiß was included amongst the 'letters', 'briff', HStA Dresden, 10024/9351/22 fo. 9 v. Two lines below have been crossed out (they include the words 'Thomas Müntzer'). Therefore the incriminating pro-Müntzer letter from Zeiß to Meinhard (either in copy or original or both) was in the hands of the princes, together with the three letters of Müntzer and the letter from Salza to Mühlhausen, at the time when the princes were still in the camp at Schlotheim, in the second half of May—very bad news indeed for Zeiß.

The letter to Meinhard also contradicts one he wrote just two days later to Spalatin, AGBM 2, 230, 7 May 1525. Zeiß was no longer in post a few months after the war, which suggests he really was playing both sides or was believed to have been doing so. Furthermore, Peter Sauerwein, a known Müntzer supporter, was interrogated after the war in Zeiß's presence and claimed he had attempted to escape from prison because he was 'shocked' when letters had been found 'from him and Zeiß' at the Allstedt Amt, 8 December 1525, AGBM 2, 738; these letters may well have incriminated both men. (Sauerwein had earlier called the elector a 'seller of blood', 'blutvorkeufer', AGBM 2, 408, for which he had been imprisoned by Zeiß in late May 1525, but had managed to escape before Zeiß arrived to question him.) On 30 May, Luther wrote to Rühel that he had heard a rumour that Zeiß had been executed with two others, and he hoped this was not true, WBr 3, no. 877, 516:42–43. While Luther seems to have liked the man, there were clearly rumours he was disloyal. Certainly Zeiß's career came to an abrupt end after the war. See now on Zeiß, Wölbing, *Müntzers langer Schatten*. Zeiß's life merits a novel. Despairing official: AGBM 1, 261.

17. Flux: Rauch, *Urkundenbuch der Stadt Heilbronn*, vol. 4 (hereafter *Heilbronn IV*), 245; Kump: Baumann, *Rothenburg*, 506.

18. Müller, *Mörder ohne Opfer*; Höbelheinrich, *Die neun Städte*; Stievermann, 'Erfurt im Bauernkrieg'; Scribner, 'Civic Unity and the Reformation in Erfurt' in Scribner, *Popular Culture*; Weiß, *Die frommen Bürger von Erfurt*.

19. Wareham, *Spirituality and the Everyday*. Franz, *Der deutsche Bauernkrieg*, vol. 1, 149–152. To add to the complexity, there were also about three hundred 'imperial villages', which, like the imperial towns, were subject directly to the emperor, Kümin, *Imperial Villages*. This did not make them immune from serfdom, however. Interestingly Jörg Weiss of Sennfeld, an imperial village, was a peasant leader, and the villages of Sennfeld and Gochsheim both participated in the Peasants' War, although they were imperial villages.

20. Myconius, *Geschichte*, 11–20; Roper, *Luther*, 17–34.

21. See, for example, Rathgeber, *Herrschaft Rappoltstein*, 101–102. AGBM 1, 337.

22. Baumann, *Akten*, 340; Franz and Fleischhauer, eds., *Jacob Murers Weissenauer Chronik*, image 3.

23. Karlstadt, *Entschuldigung*, fos. B i (v)–B ii (r). Furcha, *Essential Carlstadt*, 382–383; it was printed around July 1525. Cronthal, *Stadt Würzburg*, 26. Müntzer: ThMA 3, 243. Baumann, *Akten*, 235.

24. Franz, 'Aus der Kanzlei'. Fries, *Geschichte*, vol. 1, 19; and there are a number of originals in LATh Meiningen, GHS Sekt. II, some written in well-formed hands, some on tiny pieces of paper. In fact a considerable number of the peasant bands' letters survived because chroniclers included them in their chronicle as original documents, copying them out word for word. Fries was particularly assiduous, so we have many from the Franconian bands, both to towns and lords and between the bands themselves. Remarkably, the second part of his chronicle was dedicated to presenting the story of the war from the point of view of the bands themselves: the Bildhausen, Odenwald, and Neckartal bands as well as other, smaller ones. This part is less extensive as he is unable to identify and follow their trajectories systematically, Fries, *Geschichte*, vol. 1, pp. LIV–LV.

25. AGBM 1, 372, 395; see LATh Meiningen, GHA Sekt. II, Nr. 697, Bl. 3; and Sekt. II, Nr. 626, for the seals. The captain of the 'Christian Assembly' and others before Arnstadt sealed his letter with the seals of the three towns Rudolstadt, Blankenburg, and Königssee, AGBM 2, 188. Reinsdorf: AGBM 2, 233. Chroust, *Chroniken*.

26. AGBM 2, 673: he told the story as part of a petition to Elector Johann and was careful to explain that he had never been involved in the army's military counsels. For the many examples of flags, see Lutz, *Tagebuch*, 72–73, flag with a fish and a plough; AGBM 1, 627–628, flag with a fish, a bird, a tree, and crucifix. Joss Fritz had difficulties in getting a painter to paint his flag: Rosenkranz, *Bundschuh*, vol. 1, 309–315.

27. Schubert, *Alltag*, 166–168. The letter of Georg Metzler of the bright band to Albrecht of Mainz is a wonderful example, full of polite phrases and offering

'brotherly love', 'bruderlich libe zuvor'. It encloses the Twelve Articles and humbly asks him to support 'the godly word, brotherly love and lightening of the unfair burdens on the common man', and to take it to heart with 'the most passionate Christian brotherly consideration'. But despite its emotional, almost religious tone, it is a letter of threat: if Albrecht will not abolish the abuses, then they will be forced to act against him. Kraus, 'Beiträge', 52–53.

28. On Geyer, see Barge, 'Florian Geyer'; on Denner and Hollenpach, Maurer, *Prediger*, 503, 505; Baumann, *Rothenburg*, 164: notwithstanding the treaty, they kept him virtual prisoner in his castle at Mergentheim. Franz, *Akten*, 345, mid-April, undated draft. Simon Haferitz in Allstedt had made the same point, insisting that one should not write to the princes as 'by God's grace duke of Saxony' but 'by God without grace Duke of Saxony and not our lord', ThMA 3, 146. AGBM 1, 260, 268.

29. ThMA 2, 196, 468–469. ThMA 2, 477, 475, Gemeinde of Walkenried to Müntzer. ThMA 2, 432, 460–461. Simon Hoffmann adopted a similar style of address, with a 'peace and grace' at the outset, ThMA 2, 479–480; but his letters follow conventions addressing princes.

30. Trockau, 'Kurtzer Bericht', 75. Franz, *Akten*, 276–277.

31. Blickle, *Die Revolution*, 323; Blickle, *Revolution of 1525*, 197, Article 3.

32. For the version of the oath that insisted on one lord only, Franz, *Quellen*, 197–200, 197 taken from Kraus, 'Beiträge', 110. This version of the oath is, however, appended to a copy of Wendel Hipler's proposals to be considered at Heilbronn, and forms part of a fascicle which Kraus transcribed from the Stadtbibliothek Trier. This was a collection of documents about the war from the circle of the elector of Trier, Kraus, 'Beiträge', 21–23, so it does not come directly from the peasants who planned to meet at Heilbronn; nor is it clear whether this was the complete text of the oath or whether it reflects what the authorities feared about the peasants' intentions. Other versions of the oath are careful not to restrict or deny authority except insofar as it is contrary to the articles, Franz, *Akten*, 166; Franz, *Quellen*, 197–198.

Chapter 6: Dreams

1. For a different approach, see Blickle, *The Revolution*, 125–154, ch. 8; and for a critique of the idea that the war can be understood in terms of its 'goals', Schwerhoff, 'Beyond the Heroic Narrative'.

2. Mötsch, *Wallfahrt zu Grimmenthal*, 46–57, 265–281. The pilgrimage was especially supported by the Hennebergs, and considerable investment had been made in its chalices and furnishings in the period 1500–1520. Its regular income had averaged well over 900 fl per year but collapsed during 1525 because, according to its account book, 'The Lutherans seduced the people with their sermons not to go on pilgrimage in this year', and then the Peasants' War had attacked churches, monasteries, convents, and castles. Normal accounting did not resume for another five years, and the pilgrimage was finally abolished in 1545.

3. Chroust, *Chroniken*, vol. 2, 183–184. The vision came during the monthlong 'truce' between Bamberg and the peasants when their convent had to accept 'guards'.

4. Seitz, *Ein schöner Traktat*, fo. D I r, 'K'. Seitz fell into the hands of the authorities in 1523 but was freed: HStAS, A2 Bü 4a. He appeared in the Peasants' War and escaped later to Switzerland.

5. Luther, *Against the Heavenly Prophets*, WS 18, 62–125; 203:17–21; Part Two, WS 18, 134–214; LW 40, 73–223; translations mine.

6. Karlstadt, *Von Mannigfältigkeit*, fo. H iv (v), G iii (v); Furcha, *Essential Carlstadt*, 218–219, 224.

7. ThMA 3, 82 (Egranus). See also Bräuer, ed., *Historien von Thomas Müntzer* (unpaginated). This was also part of the attack made in Agricola's fictional dialogue between a peasant and a follower of Müntzer, *Ein nützlicher Dialogus oder Gesprächbüchlein*, and it featured as well in Melanchthon's *Histori Thome Muntzers*, fo. Aa iv v, where Melanchthon alleges that he made dreams the basis of everything.

8. ThMA 3, 54–55: according to Ernst Salomon Cyprian, the Lutheran Martin Glaser noted in a now lost edition of Tauler's sermons that Müntzer had understood Tauler's doctrine of the spirit and soul ('Geist und Grunde der Seel'), incorrectly under the influence of Conrad Glitzsch's 'köchin' (euphemism for partner), which they read together. Glaser notes that the woman was famed as 'holy', 'heylig', in Leipzig. See Bubenheimer, *Müntzer*, 182; Bräuer and Vogler, *Müntzer*, 68–69. Glaser, who was an orthodox Lutheran, claimed to have known both Müntzer and Karlstadt well, but made the comment in 1529 after the peasants' defeat, when everyone was distancing themselves from both men.

9. ThMA 1, 312–313; Matheson, *Collected Works of Müntzer*, 240, 242. See also, on Müntzer's dreams, Goertz, *Träume, Offenbarungen und Visionen*; Fauth, 'Träume bei religiösen Dissidenten', 71–106; Baylor, 'Thomas Müntzer's Theory of Dreams'.

10. ThMA, 2, 345–347; ThMA 2, 326–330; Matheson, *Collected Works of Müntzer*, 107–110, for Emmen's transcriptions of the dream. A contemporary commentator on the copy now held in the library at Wolfenbüttel has noted in the margin that he personally saw this too, and that one of them was called 'Herold', ThMA 2, 327 n. 2; Agricola, *Auslegung des XIX Psalm*. The young man was Ambrosius Emmen, Müntzer's *famulus* or secretary, who probably began working for him in 1519, ThMA 2, 40–41 n. 4; Bräuer and Vogler, *Müntzer*, 357. For the dream, ThMA 2, 330; Matheson, *Collected Works of Müntzer*, 110.

11. ThMA 2, 324–326; *Collected Works of Müntzer*, 108.

12. ThMA 3, 149–150. Laube, *Flugschriften*, 535:30–36. See also Melanchthon, *Histori*, in Laube, *Flugschriften*, 531:13–18. Fischer, *Lutherische Pamphlete*. The pamphlet is tendentious but demonstrates that Lutherans were especially concerned about Müntzer's use of dreams and saw it as one of the ways that he got the 'Pöfel' on his side.

13. ThMA 1, 319; Matheson, *Collected Works of Müntzer*, 250; and see, amongst others, Goertz, 'Gegenwart Gottes, Herrschaft und Gewalt' in Goertz, *Nähe Gottes*, 69–92; Wölbing, *Müntzers langer Schatten*. On the location of the sermon, see the exhibition in Schloss Allstedt, viewed in September 2019.

14. Jordan, *Chronik der Stadt Mühlhausen*, 189 (= Müller, 'Chronicon Mulhusinum', 58: 'ime wehre ein traum angezeigt', so it was likely not his own dream); Müller, *Mörder ohne Opfer*, 432–435. Müntzer declared that those who wished to do so could return home, and some of those from Hesse and from elsewhere in the Eichsfeld departed. The *Chronik*, written in hindsight, presents it as a momentous free choice: 'wer nicht gerne will, der mag heim ziehen'.

15. ThMA 2, 130–133. Agricola, *Auslegung*, fo. B iii r. He claims that the wife of the Schösser of Allstedt, that is, of Hans Zeiß, brought the news to Müntzer on Easter Day 1524, but he showed no reaction. When she left, he turned to 'den vnsern', 'our folk', and said, 'Nu sehet yhr furwar, das ich den creaturen gantz entrissen bin'. For Agricola, this was diabolic, because love of your children is natural. In his commentary on Moses of 1535, Luther discusses emotions and how 'the most natural affections remain in parents' and are 'awakened through grace, not removed'. Linking the Peasants' War to 'schismatic spirits trying to introduce apathy of this kind into the church', Luther adduces the story of Müntzer's reaction to the birth of his son: 'He stood before the altar as if he were deaf and dumb [quasi mutus et surdus]. He did not rejoice, give thanks, or make any reply. It was his purpose to show that he was a log and a stock [truncum et stipitem]. Afterwards he had boasted that his nature was completely changed and slain [mutatam et mortificatam]'. Luther here links Müntzer's detachment to 'apathy', a variety of sloth, one of the seven deadly sins. WS 44, 493:16–26; LW 7, 261; ThMA 1, 369:29, 30–31 (Müntzer on Lang).

16. ThMA 2, 491–506, 17 May 1525, from Heldrungen; Matheson, *Collected Works of Müntzer*, 160–161.

17. Franz, *Der deutsche Bauernkrieg, Aktenband* (hereafter *Akten*), 338. The man who boasted had also said outside Wilhelm Flurer's house that he and his associates would be forest officials for a while (in his stead), and if he (Wilhelm) made any further incursions in the woods, he would hang him. Franz, *Akten*, 338. Under severe torture he confessed that they planned to take the town of Rothenburg.

18. AGBM 1, 148–149 (Münnerstadt); Franz, *Quellen*, 457 (Frankfurt); WS 18, 534–540 (Erfurt: Luther printed these in September 1525 with an ironic commentary); AGBM 1, 604–606 (Schleusingen).

19. Laube, *Flugschriften*, 109. Lienhart Denner and Hans Hollenpach, both clerics, were amongst this band's leaders. Denner wrote a 'Complaint', 'Clagschrift', at about the same time as the Twelve Articles which discusses the peasant burdens in detail. Baumann, *Quellen zur Geschichte des Bauernkrieges aus Rotenburg an der Tauber. [sic] (Chronik Thomas Zweifel)* (hereafter *Rothenburg*) (Zweifel), 76–77; and see also Eisenhart in Baumann, *Rothenburg* (Eisenhart), 600 ff., who describes Denner and Hollenpach working together. Baumann, *Rothenburg* (Zweifel), 316–321. Denner later went with Florian Geyer to Rothenburg to take the formal oath of brotherhood there, which suggests his importance: Baumann, *Rothenburg* (Zweifel), 356–357; Maurer, *Prediger*, 502. While the Taubertal band wanted to secularise ecclesiastical land, the Amorbach articles took a more moderate line.

20. Fries, *Geschichte*, vol. 1, 456. Von Bibra: Franz, *Akten*, 346–347. Oechsle, *Beiträge zur Geschichte des Bauernkrieges*, 176. See also Franz, *Akten*, 346–347, 18 April. As Franziska Conrad pointed out, despite its often formulaic nature, the correspondence of the peasant bands is amongst the best sources we have for their views, Conrad, *Reformation in der bäuerlichen Gesellschaft*, 129–134. The chronicler Lorenz Fries includes many of them, thus preserving them for the region around Würzburg.

21. AGBM 1, 179.

22. Laube, *Flugschriften*, 109–111. Taubertal programme: Hug, *Villinger Chronik*, 117–119, Artikelbrief of Black Forest Peasants, which was sent to Villingen and which Hug reproduces. See also Seebass, *Artikelbrief*, 17–47.

23. Aura band: AGBM 1, 192. Salzungen: AGBM 1, 234–235.

24. AGBM 1, 234–235.

25. *An die Versammlung*; Scott, 'Hubmaier, Schappeler, and Hergot', 213–220. Scott argues that the tract is by Schappeler. I incline to the view that Lotzer is a more likely author. The etymological argument about the derivation of 'Hausvater' from 'dominus' comes straight after a passage that cites Paul's letter to the Ephesians, and then 'King David' (Psalm 115, verse 1, uncredited), *An die Versammlung*, 91:37–38, 92:7. Instead of examining the Greek or the Hebrew texts here, as a theologian versed in both languages would have done, he moves straight to his argument about Latin. There are other stylistic similarities: the strong condemnation of 'Geitz' as a sin can be found in Lotzer; there are many variants of the word 'tyrann', another word Lotzer uses; while the long section on Roman kings also suggests a lay author. Our writer has a predilection for bad puns, such as 'beyß-schaff' instead of 'bishop' (100:20). The powerful echoes of the Twelve Articles (now thought to be by Lotzer) extend to the structure of twelve chapters.

26. *An die Versammlung*, 91–95: *Handlohn* and *Hauptrecht* were the very dues one peasant band would later force the commander of the Teutonic Knights to condemn out of his own mouth.

27. ThMA 2, 278–281, 438, 439; Matheson, *Collected Works of Müntzer*, 86, 87, 88, 89; 147, 7 May 1525 (Frankenhausen Haufe); Loserth, *Stadt Waldshut*, Statement of Waldshut Council to Zurich Council, 7 October 1524, 100–102. *An die Versammlung*, 111.

28. The Swiss chronicler Johann Stumpf argued that *Aufruhr* and tyranny went together like the pot and the lid: the punishment of tyranny is revolt (Aufruhr), and tyranny is the punishment of revolt, Stumpf, *Schweizer- und Reformationschronik*, 262.

29. *An die Versammlung*, 113–114.

30. The editors of the 1975 edition of the text interpret this differently, reading it as a general admonition to 'get moving' (160) and to support one another in a brotherly fashion, but this seems to me to miss the reference to the circular movement of the wheel of fortune and the sense of the words here. On the cover image, see Scribner, 'Images', 44.

31. AGBM 1, 609.

32. Fries, *Geschichte*, vol. 1, 443–445; and see also Kraus, 'Beiträge', 109–110. The Trier manuscript chronicle (Kraus) has slight differences from Fries's version of Hipler's text. Fries follows 'hat sein gestalt' with the sentence 'In dem mitel ist man itzund begriffen', as if Hipler were describing the point in the war that had been reached, whereas the Trier manuscript has 'Zu dem mettel iss nu itzo begriffenn', as if he were describing what measures should be taken next, which makes more sense in the context as he moves to propose what the representatives of all the armies should tell each other. The Fries version has a reference to whether the plan of the Odenwald band is to go no farther than Schwäbisch Hall after they have captured Würzburg, whereas the Trier version refers only to whether they plan to go farther after Würzburg, and what the other armies plan. Where Fries talks of the 'milterung' of the Saxon prince towards the 'armen man' (444), Trier has 'vereinigong', that is, the attitude to their union. On Hipler's ideals, see Robisheaux, *Rural Society and the Search for Order*, 63–65, and Blickle, *The Revolution of 1525*, 132–133.

33. This is less clear in the Trier version (Kraus).

34. Fries, *Geschichte*, vol. 1, 441–443, 431–440. The accompanying letter from Weigandt to Hipler also has a tactical dimension, suggesting that all the territories of ecclesiastical princes should be brought into the union on the basis of the Twelve Articles, in line with the example of the Mainz Stift, and it points out the problem the death of Friedrich the Wise has created for the peasant cause. See also Roper, *Martin Luther*, 229–230.

35. Fabri, *Adversvs Doctorem Balthasarvm Pacimontanvm*; and Fabri, *Ursache, warum der Widertäufer Patron*. The Latin text is a vast work of over two hundred pages that purports to give the text of their discussions, proving that Hubmaier was a heretic; the briefer German is a simple propaganda work designed to demonstrate the same thing by including a summary of the papers, an editorial opening, and his confession before execution.

36. Fabri claims that the author's words 'shaming…and tyranny' refer to the Duke of Lorraine's bloody massacre of peasants at Zabern on 16 May 1525, so this is either an interpolation by Fabri or the writing Fabri is summarising dates from after the peasants' defeats at Mühlhausen and Alsace, when Waldshut had not yet surrendered. Tom Scott argued that the original text must actually have been written by Müntzer or at least in part by him, 'Reformation and Peasants' War in Waldshut', 32–33. While Scott argues that the words have the ring of Müntzer and not of Hubmaier, it is difficult to reconcile this with the use of the term 'Landschaft', which Müntzer did not use, and with the reference to the slaughter at Saverne by the Duke of Lorraine, which happened after Müntzer's defeat and capture. Scott used the text in Franz, *Quellen*, but the original pamphlet includes an opening passage that makes further allegations against Hubmaier, as if the views that follow are Hubmaier's, not those of Müntzer. The text has not been included in the editions of Müntzer's works, and it must remain doubtful that it represents Müntzer's views; certainly the importance of the ban and leagues to it, together with the whole system of election of one individual ruler, would seem to place it closer to Hubmaier's ideas. It is also clearly

related to the ideas of the Schwarzwälder Artikelbrief, discussed in ch. 7, see Buszello, 'Oberrheinlande', 317. See also Seebass, *Artikelbrief*, 22–29, 160–172.

37. Fabri, *Ursache*, fo. C ii (r).

38. Blickle, *Die Revolution*, 322; Blickle, *The Revolution*, 196.

39. Franz, *Quellen*, 285–290; see also Stella, *La rivoluzione*, 184–194, with Italian translation; Blickle, 'Alpenländer', 204–209; it built on the 'First' Landesordnung. It also built on an existing tradition of complaints, the Gravamina.

40. Gaismair was particularly opposed to Salamanca, an advisor of Ferdinand's thought to be Jewish.

41. Bücking, *Gaismair*, 139–142, is quite negative about its limitations; Blickle is more positive. There is a whole section on mining, as one might expect given Gaismair's background.

42. Hergot, *Von der newen Wandlung*. Blickle, *Die Revolution*, argues that its first, utopian half may have been written at or in 1525, 150–154, and points out that it does not refer to the second half.

43. Hergot, *Von der newen Wandlung*, fo. A ii r, A ii v. This is environmentalist in the sense that only local products are to be used, including locally produced cloth, and limiting colours to locally grown woad. It would also have abolished much trade and long-distance transport, which some would now see as an environmentalist goal. However, it is not clear that trade and transport at that time had the deleterious effects they have now, and the vision is motivated by hostility to luxury rather than concern for creation.

Chapter 7: Early Spring

1. As Heidenreich, *Ereignis ohne Namen*, demonstrates through linguistic analysis, the members of the bands themselves generally did not use the term 'Aufruhr', 'revolt', to describe their actions, 79–81. For the movement of the bands in the southwest, see Maurer, 'Bauernkrieg als Massenerhebung', and Maurer, 'Beiwort zur Karte 6.11'.

2. Franz, *Der deutsche Bauernkrieg, Aktenband* (hereafter *Akten*), 342.

3. Baumann, *Akten*, 134, 137–138.

4. Kuhn, 'Seehaufen', 119–120. Vogt, *Die Correspondenz des schwäbischen Bundeshauptmannes Ulrich Artzt* (hereafter *Artzt*), 108–109, 113–114. Baumann, *Akten*, 151–156.

5. Baumann, *Akten*, 159–160; Gerwig had, however, earlier gone in person to negotiate with the peasants.

6. Baumann, *Akten*, 358, 266; for chronicle accounts see, for example, Baumann, *Quellen: Chroniken*, 253 (Knebel), 335 (Furter), 384 (Fläschutz), 482–483 (Werdenstein). The abbot's chronicler (Fläschutz) insisted that the castle did not burn; others say it was destroyed. The abbot fled to the town of Kempten, which accepted him against payment of 30,000 Gulden and resignation of his remaining rights over the town, so that through the 'Grosse Kauf' of Kempten on 6 May 1525, the town finally achieved its freedom, Haggenmüller, 'Allgäuer Haufen', 54. The abbot returned to his

position in 1527. Later attempts were made to discover what happened to the booty from Liebenthann. See the interrogation of Georg Mock, Baumann, *Akten*, 342–343; he claimed to have sent what he had collected to Günzburg, but he also knew of a wide range of places to which silver and money had been sent, over 140 parishes. The plunder that was shared out had been carefully noted down by scribes in the presence of named leaders and divided in an organised fashion. Others gave an account that made it sound far less orderly, Baumann, *Quellen: Chroniken*, 358–359. Interestingly, when the abbot listed the damages, he did not specify the lead, 333–334.

7. Franz and Fleischhauer, eds., *Jacob Murers Weissenauer Chronik* (facsimile); the archive at Waldburg-Zeil would not permit me to see the original. See Stumpf, *Schweizer- und Reformationschronik*, 223–225, for a literary equivalent of the picture: Stumpf describes how at the Premonstratensian abbey of Rüti, the abbot was starting to think his time was up, and so he started removing abbey property. When the locals heard this, they summoned a crowd to seize the goods instead. Such a 'thronging, eating, drinking, going wild, raging, screaming, throwing up' took place that whoever had known the people before would have been amazed, Stumpf writes, as wine was even taken away in pig troughs.

8. Weissenau: Bensen, *Geschichte des Bauernkriegs*, 560; the same happened in Ottobeuren. Schussenried: Baumann, *Akten*, 253. Ottobeuren: Baumann, *Akten*, 238. On 2 April, the abbey's own subjects occupied Ottobeuren, causing great damage. Haggenmüller, 'Allgäuer Haufen', 52. Baumann, *Quellen: Chroniken* (Thomann), 81. At Roggenburg, a peasant made himself abbot. Marchtal: Baumann, *Akten*, 248, it seems they later were included in the treaty with the Lake Constance band. In the Baden region, too, it at first seemed that the peasants' targets were ecclesiastical institutions only, Virck, *Urkunden und Akten der Stadt Strassburg* (hereafter *Strassburg*), 196. In the region of the Lake Constance band, monasteries were not targeted so severely—only four later petitioned for damages, and none went up in flames, Kuhn 'Der Seehaufen', 105.

9. Schöntal: Harer, *Berichte*, 27. Anhausen: Baumann, *Quellen: Chroniken*, 256–257; in this case Casimir of Ansbach drove the peasants out, and his soldiers ran a spear through the man who had dressed up as a priest, leaving him to die in agony for three days. In the abbey of Salem the monks decided to swear to the peasants after the nearby towns had fallen without a struggle; the abbey was occupied, and the army took control of their provisions but made sure they did not go short, chronicle of Salem, Mone, ed., *Quellensammlung der Badischen Landesgeschichte*, Band 2, 123. The army also took control of the bells.

10. See Kaufmann, *Der Bauernkrieg: Ein Medienereignis*, ch. 1. I am grateful to Thomas Kaufmann for letting me see his work before publication. On this journey, see Bräuer, 'Luthers Reise in das Bauernkriegsgebiet'. For the text of admonition, WS 18, 280, 291–334; LW 46. We don't, however, know the content of his sermons during this journey, as no notes survive. WS 17, II, xxxii.

11. WS 18, 293:17–294:1; 316:14–18.

12. Rhegius, *Von Leibeigenschaft oder Knechtheit*, fo. A iii v.

13. Hubmaier, *Schriften*, 112–114.

14. Hubmaier, *Schriften*, 27. Küssenberg, *Chronik*, 423. At Togern, Küssenberg reports, the pastor gave the chalice to the sacristan to drink out of it himself. He was not the first evangelical to use the ban; Jakob Strauss the Lutheran preacher had deployed the ban in 1523 against a parishioner who interrupted the service, Müller, 'Frühreformation', 27–28.

15. Hubmaier, *Schriften*, 16. See Scott, 'Reformation and Peasants' War in Waldshut'; Bergsten, *Balthasar Hubmaier*, 109–121; Loserth, *Stadt Waldshut*, 106–121. 'Ein warhafftig enntschuldigung unnd clag gemeiner statt Waldshut', 106-121: because this did not appear under Hubmaier's name, it was not included in Hubmaier, *Schriften*, though Bergsten considered that Hubmaier likely wrote it; see Hubmaier, *Schriften*, 58–59 (Bergsten, 'Bibliographische Bemerkungen'). Quotation: Hubmaier, *Schriften*, 277.

16. The ban had probably been used earlier, see Franz, *Akten*, 172, 174, where in a report of 8 March, repeated on 21 March, the officials in Bregenz describe the peasants as having threatened surrounding villages that if they did not join, 'that they should be excluded and banned and not be counted Christian people'. Those who refused to join had a post placed in front of their houses to prevent them going out of the house; and they were excluded from joint ploughing and fellowship of any kind. See also Buszello, 'Oberrheinlande', 74 n. 21, 74–75. Hug, *Villinger Chronik*, 117. Hug's transcription of the articles is the only record we have of them.

17. Baumann, *Akten*, 137. On the Swabian League and its commander, Blickle, *Bauernjörg*; and Sea, 'The Swabian League and the German Peasants' War', kindly made available by Gerd Schwerhoff. Finance: Baumann, *Akten*, 136, 150; the Welsers also provided funds. For his part, Archduke Ferdinand of Austria warned Fugger when he knew the peasants were likely to attack their castle at Weissenhorn, 172. Fugger was repaid 4,000 fl by the league afterwards, Sea, 'Economic Impact'.

18. Lutz, *Tagebuch*, 618.

19. Lutz, *Tagebuch*; Blickle, *Bauernjörg*; Miller, *Army of the Swabian League*, 52–62.

20. Eberlin von Günzburg, *Wie sich eyn diener*. In his Wolfaria (1521), however, Eberlin had imagined a utopia where property was limited to land, agricultural work was valued, and the tithe abolished.

21. Baumann, *Quellen: Chroniken*, 550 (Truchsess Schreiber). The bishop of Augsburg, Christoph Stadion, had placed Wehe under the ban and had forbidden all other priests in Leipheim to read mass until Wehe had been expelled, Radlkofer, *Eberlin und Wehe*, 218; Baumann, *Quellen: Chroniken*, 552 (Truchsess Schreiber). On Leipheim, see Broy, 'Reformation und Bauernkrieg'.

22. 'wie die schwein', Baumann, *Quellen: Chroniken* (Truchsess Schreiber), 551. The Baltringen and Lake Constance armies did not provide them with assistance, and thus the Christian Union was undermined. There were probably about 5,000 to 6,000 on the peasants' side, and 1,500 knights plus 7,000 to 8,000 soldiers of the

Swabian League, von Trauchburg, 'Gefechte und Schlachten', 185; the battlefield is still visible today, and the road dips as one approaches the low-lying area. The Danube was still untamed and its course fluctuated. There is a list of 4,077 on the peasants' side in the Castle Wolfegg archive; the peasant combatants came from a wide area around Leipheim. For a reconstruction of the battle, Miller, *Army of the Swabian League*, 58–64.

23. 'Das sie keck weren, der puntischen buchsen wurden sich auß sunderer schickung gottes umbkeren und in sie selbs schiessen, deßgleichen die spieß', Baumann, *Quellen: Chroniken* (Truchsess Schreiber), 552; Vogt, *Artzt*, 135 (Nr. 175, 4 April 1525), 140 (Nr. 185, 7 April 1525). At first they intended to hang both the clerics, but then decided to execute Wehe, a more honourable punishment. Baumann, *Quellen: Chroniken*, 553 (Truchsess Schreiber). There is a contrasting unsympathetic account of Wehe in Nicolaus Thomann's 'Weissenhorner Historie', which claims he was not as brave as he had preached, Baumann, *Quellen: Chroniken*, 84; he also supplies an anecdote about an unnamed preacher who nearly escaped by using a small door in the wall to get into town, and who was found to have 800 Gulden, 82–83.

24. Ulbrich, 'Oberschwaben und Württemberg', 120. Baumann, *Akten*, 256; Broy, 'Reformation und Bauernkrieg'. The group included some citizens of Günzburg. Baumann, *Quellen: Chroniken* (Thomann, 'Weissenhorner Historie'), 85; the Leipheimers appealed in 1530, Maurer, 'Verhalten der reformatorisch gesinnten Geistlichen', 116.

25. Amongst them were Truchsess Georg's own peasants of Waldsee, Wolfegg, and Zeil, Blickle, *Bauernjörg*, 167–173. Burning villages was a strategy Truchsess Georg used repeatedly to frighten others into compliance. Clemens Volckamer mentions the killing of 150 peasants at a village near Walse, StadtA Nürnberg, E 29/IV, Nr. 1578, letter of 15 April 1525. By 4 May, the route from Ulm to Constance was apparently safe, StadtA Nürnberg, E 29/IV, Nr. 1580, letter 4 May 1525. Baumann, *Akten*, 240.

26. Baumann, *Akten*, 236, 249; Hug, *Villinger Chronik*, 113.

27. On the manoeuvrings, Hoyer, *Militärwesen*, 153–155. The truce was sealed formally at Ravensburg on 22 April. The treaty was printed in at least six editions, at Leipzig, Nuremberg, Augsburg, and Wittenberg, and the Wittenberg edition had a preface and conclusion condemning the peasants written by Luther. VD 16, S 4575, S 4576, S 4577, S 4578, S 4579, S 4580. It covered only the Bodensee and Allgäu armies. This was why the peasants of Alleshausen and Brasenberg later insisted that they had ended up in the 'Lake Constance Band', not the Baltringen one, and so they were covered by the protection of their treaty, which meant that their overlord, the abbot, could not fine them. The fact that the treaty was printed and so could easily be referred to would have helped the peasants of Alleshausen's cause. See StA Sigmaringen, Dep. 30/12 T 4 (Marchtal: Akten), Nr. 44, Alleshausen: Prozessakten zwischen Marchtal und Alleshausen mit Brasenberg; 1 Band, 1528–1532, certified eighteenth-century copy of the original. The case dragged on for several years. In early May peasants at Kempten decided against accepting the treaty, Ulbrich, 'Oberschwaben und Württemberg', 123. On the treaty, Rudolf, 'Der Weingartner Vertrag'.

28. Castle Schemmerberg, Franz, *Der deutsche Bauernkrieg*, vol. 1, 131; it belonged to the monastery of Salem, and its destruction seems to have unleashed a period of destruction by the Baltringen band, Diemer, 'Der Baltringer Haufen'. Baumann, *Quellen: Chroniken* (Werdensteiner Chronik), 490, mentions the plundering of the castle and stealing of corn and gunpowder but not that it was burnt. By contrast, Truchsess Georg of the Swabian League threatened to set fire to the monastery of Weingarten, to use it as a 'Wachfeuer', as he tried to pressure the peasants to come to terms in mid-April. Later, the monasteries of Ochsenhausen, Schussenried, Zwiefalten, Marchtal, Rot, Robbenburg, Elchingen, Heggbach, Gutenzell, Uttenweiler, and Buchau were all attacked and plundered, Diemer, 'Baltringer Haufen', 84; see the broadsheet *Illustrierte Geschichte*, 236.

29. Schappeler tried to return to his position in Memmingen several times, but the council would not allow it, Trummer, 'Schappeler', 280–283; he preached for some time in St Gallen.

30. Endres, 'Franken', 135: harvests had been bad here between 1517 and 1524, and would be bad again in 1527.

31. Harer, *Berichte*, 20–21.

32. Maurer, *Prediger*, 480–489. The town's population was around 3,150, Pfister, 'Urban Population', 47; Baumann, *Quellen zur Geschichte des Bauernkrieges aus Rotenburg an der Tauber.* [sic] *(Chronik Thomas Zweifel)* (hereafter *Rothenburg*) (Zweifel), 8. Thomas Zweifel, civic notary, wrote an extensive account of the Rothenburg events; Michel Eisenhart wrote a brief one. On Rothenburg, see also Vice, 'Ehrenfried Kumpf', and 'Iconoclasm'.

33. For Luther, see WS 15, 279–292, 293–322; and see Rössner, ed., *Martin Luther: On Commerce and Usury*, which has a very full introduction and analysis. For a wider argument about the role of coinage in the Peasants' War, see Rössner, *Deflation, Devaluation, Rebellion*, 491–530.

34. Harer, *Berichte*, 27–28; they did, however, burn many other castles in the area. Peter Harer, an official who worked for the Palatine counts, wrote a major account of the war. In January of 1525 he had translated Philipp Melanchthon's work on Christian justice (which had been dedicated to Philip of Hesse). In 1530, Harer would marry Melanchthon's sister; so though he would later become a Catholic, he was also part of the inner circle of conservative Lutheranism. On the Peasants' War in Hohenlohe, see Robisheaux, *Rural Society*; and Oechsle, *Beiträge zur Geschichte*.

35. Sometimes the 'hellen liechten haufens', Franz, 'Kanzlei', 87.

36. Rauch, *Urkundenbuch der Stadt Heilbronn*, vol. 4 (hereafter *Heilbronn* IV), 66, letter of Hans Reutter; Harer, *Berichte*, 27–29.

37. Götz, *Mein Fehd*, 123. Götz von Berlichingen, the knight with an iron fist (he had a prosthesis), wrote an account of his life much later, when he was an old man. His rambunctious narrative was the inspiration for Goethe's play, an English version of which was written by Walter Scott. He also explains that he had been unsure which lord to join and thought he should probably join the Palatinate Count; but his mother-in-law hid the letter from Heidelberg that would have summoned him,

so it was therefore her fault that he became mixed up in the Peasants' War—a most unlikely story (122–123). Götz had a history of fighting feuds and had recently commandeered four waggons of goods that were being taken from Nuremberg; he was therefore facing retaliation from the Swabian League as well as hostility from Nuremberg. Klüpfel, *Urkunden zur Geschichte*, 270. He was not alone in arguing that he had been press-ganged into commanding the rebels; Clas Scheffer, innkeeper at Buttlar, claimed he was woken at midnight and told he was a captain (*Hauptmann*), and so had to go with the peasants to the 'Berg', the Gangolfsberg near Fulda, AGBM 1, 610.

38. Chronicle of Michel Leip in Rauch, *Heilbronn* IV, 28–29: he places the Helfenstein attacks before the massacre. The salt-seller Semmelhans had been imprisoned in the castle earlier, so knew its disposition; he warned the Heilbronners after the Leipheim defeat that the peasants were not beaten and more would come, Rauch, *Heilbronn* IV, 78. Account of Hans Reutter, on the peasants' side, 66.

39. Harer, *Berichte*, 30. Peasant killing noble: Rauch, *Heilbronn* IV, 233; he could still describe the youth, who had a small beard. P. 241: other peasant leaders, including Jäcklein Rohrbach, were also said to have greased their *Scheiden* with Dietrich von Weiler's fat; but these are of course the accounts of the peasants' antagonists. Harer, *Berichte,* 31. It is unclear whether Harer means us to think that the countess and her ladies were sexually assaulted or just insulted; but the use of the manure cart suggests that the rebels wanted the countess to smell peasant life up close as they took her like booty to their headquarters in Heilbronn. This detail, not included in all accounts, may be apocryphal, though in a report from 22 April, Jakob Sturm of Strasbourg, who was in Heilbronn, mentions that she was brought to Heilbronn on a waggon, and 'everything she had was taken from her', Rauch, *Heilbronn* IV, 71–72.

40. 'Halb reiterisch, halb bäuerisch gestalt', Rauch, *Heilbronn* IV, 6. On Rohrbach, see Rauch, 'Bauernführer Jäcklein Rohrbach'; on Heilbronn, Sea, 'The Reformation and the Restoration of Civic Authority'. His peasant band grew out of meetings in the baker Wolf Leip's tavern, attended by Rohrbach's wife, Genoveva, whom he had married the previous year; Enderlin von Dürrenzimmer, who probably lived in Heilbronn; Christoph Scherer, a citizen there; and the innkeeper Jörg Martin of Flein.

41. Rauch, *Heilbronn* IV, 374–375: those who had less than others should be helped, monasteries should be closed, the meadows of the Teutonic Knights should be taken and given to the poor, priests should get thirty fl for life; there should be no more foundations for masses for the dead; monks should receive fifty or sixty Gulden. Rauch, *Heilbronn* IV, 212 ff.; and the account of the priest Wolf Ferber, 297.

42. Rauch, *Heilbronn* IV, 299.

43. Rauch, *Heilbronn* IV, 34.

44. The rebels had threatened the monks on their way to Weinsberg, announcing they would 'have an evening meal' with them, Rauch, *Heilbronn* IV, 28. In 1531 the miraculous statue even ended up in the hands of the local Lutheran preacher Lachmann, who was ordered to look after it on the council's behalf.

45. In Rothenburg, the peasant army outside town wanted to plunder the monastic institutions, but the council argued that the townsfolk should rightfully get

their property, especially their grain stores, and asked each craft for its view before it negotiated with the army, Baumann, *Rothenburg* (Zweifel), 338–345. In Dinkelsbühl, the council allowed some of the peasants to occupy the 'dewtsch haws und closter' around 7 May, as it informed Rothenburg, Baumann, *Rothenburg* (Zweifel), 306–307. For the council's later account of the eight articles to the assembly at Ulm, after 9 August 1525, see Rauch, *Heilbronn* IV, 212–217; and to the league at Nördlingen, 221–229. Side gate: 278. The council proposed making clergy become citizens, but this was rejected by the citizens' assembly on 12 April, probably because it would have put ecclesiastical institutions under council protection. Rauch, *Heilbronn* IV, 214. Plundering of Teutonic Knights: Harer, *Berichte*, 32, who states .hey were offered bread and wine; another witness claims the council undertook the distribution in the Teutonic house, Rauch, *Heilbronn* IV, 293.

46. Rauch, *Heilbronn* IV, 212–217, 215. On women and threat to vines, Rauch, *Heilbronn* IV, 71, report of Jakob Sturm. 'Nit ein meit', their angry cry, was not forgotten, and it went into popular song, Steiff and Mehring, *Geschichtliche Lieder und Sprüche*, 235, 281; Rauch, *Heilbronn* IV, 215, 221–229. The council itself claimed it had no choice and had sent a delegation to the peasants; unbeknown to them, three peasant leaders then slipped into town with the delegation the next day. The threat of throwing the councillors over the wall recurs in the testimony of several witnesses—they would throw them on a pitchfork like turning manure, out of the town hall, down the steps, etc. Rauch, *Heilbronn* IV, 209, 289, 293. The council also claimed that after the peasants left town, the army threatened to come back 'and throw them out over the town hall', 217.

47. Rauch, *Heilbronn* IV, 285, 287, 288–289. *Heilbronn* IV, 216: 'Item it is true, that an honourable Council neither vowed to nor swore nor gave help, contributed or advanced their cause nor joined in any of their matters'.

48. On gunpowder, Rauch, *Heilbronn* IV, 214, 243. Though even the council seems to have realised this was stretching credulity too far: a draft letter to Rothenburg ob der Tauber of 8 May deleted this argument, replacing it with the general claim that they were forced to allow it. *Heilbronn* IV, 93. *Heilbronn* IV, 77: a draft letter to Hall of 22 April explains the fines and also states that the commons were incensed, 'erhitzet', against their clergy. But afterwards the council consistently tried to argue that the peasants had carried out the 'fining', not they, and so it was not responsible for repaying the money to the ecclesiastical institutions.

49. Baumann, *Rothenburg* (Eisenhart), 604; (Zweifel), 352–359. Similar events took place in a host of towns. In Nördlingen in early April, the town council was toppled and replaced by a pro-peasant group, and peasants were allowed to enter town, while the main peasant encampment nearby was at Deiningen. Sea, 'Schwäbischer Bund', 146–147.

50. Kitzingen: Böhm, 'Kitzingen und der Bauernkrieg' (Sebald Ranft Chronicle). Bamberg: Chroust, *Chroniken*, vol. 2, 207, articles of the Bambergers, 11 April 1525, article 3; however, they also insisted (article 5) that the Rat and Gemeind

should have the keys to the town gates, not the bishop or chapter. See also Chroust, 211–213, April complaints include objections to the fact that clergy were exempt from tax. See Roß, 'Zur Sozialgeschichte Bambergs', esp. 71–72.

51. When Jäcklein Rohrbach started issuing safe conducts, he was roundly admonished by his former allies, Götz von Berlichingen and Hans Reutter of the Helle Haufen, who had their own system of passports, Rauch, *Heilbronn* IV, 91, 75.

52. Horneck castle was burnt down together with the archives, so it is difficult to reconstruct the order's history. Militzer, *Geschichte des Deutschen Ordens*, 269; Harer, *Berichte*, 33–34.

53. Bishop of Strasbourg: the bishop had been unable to raise troops and had ended up in Aschaffenburg, facing a combination of peasant and urban rebels there, and had been forced to accept their articles, *Chroniken der deutschen Städte*, Mainz 2, 105. There is a memorial to him in the main church of Saverne, which has a three-quarter sculpted likeness of him kneeling below the crucified Christ with Mary and John. He is bareheaded, his mitre and staff on the ground, with the usual adornments of humanist culture, including a mannerist arch. Ellwangen: Baumann, *Quellen: Chroniken*, Cochlaeus, 784. Letter to Geyer, Franz, *Akten*, 361–362: however, the letter probably never reached him. The author, Melchior Rabensteiner, addresses Geyer as 'dear brother-in-law'.

54. Ulbrich, 'Oberschwaben und Württemberg', 127. Worry that peasants would rise again: Clemens Volckamer, 7 May, StadtA Nürnberg, E 29/IV Nr. 1581.

Chapter 8: Movement

1. Seebass, *Artikelbrief*, 23, 28; chronicle of Andreas Lettsch from St Blasius, Lettsch, *Chronik*, 46.

2. Forming a Haufen: for example, a group that met in the bathhouse decided that if the priest used holy water again, they would throw it over him, which they did, Franz, *Der deutsche Bauernkrieg, Aktenband* (hereafter *Akten*), 340–341. Jäcklein Rohrbach was said to have started the uprising in a bathhouse, Rauch, *Urkundenbuch der Stadt Heilbronn*, vol. 4 (hereafter *Heilbronn* IV), 282. On taverns, see Kümin and Tlusty, eds., *World of the Tavern*. Innkeepers were often leaders, for example, Matern Feuerbacher, Georg Metzler, and Clas Scheffer. They knew how to command attention through talk, and they were repositories of news because travellers passed through their taverns, Franz, *Akten*, 166–167. In Prussia in September, the peasants negotiated with the nobles at the Quednau 'mountain' or hill, full of significance as it was named after an Old Prussian god, Richau, 'Historie von dem Aufruhr', 546. Threats to those who would not join, Franz, 'Aus der Kanzlei', 96, to Balingen. At Alleshausen they remembered that someone from Seekirch had threatened them to join, 'oder aber wun vnd waid meiden', StA Sigmaringen, Dep. 30/12 T 4 (Marchtal: Akten) Nr. 44, 85, 33 (part 2); that is, if they did not join they would be excluded from all collective possessions of the village. See also Franz, *Akten*, 346: 'Therefore know, that if you don't come, that we shall come however', Odenwald army to the town of Tauberbischofsheim.

3. Brun, *Abbot and His Peasants*, 87.

4. Baumann, *Quellen: Chroniken*, 305 (Pflummern Chronicle): von Pflummern claims it was a sign that one could 'eat up all his goods or otherwise make him pay the price'. Nicolaus Thomann also mentions stakes and threats of arson, Baumann, *Quellen: Chroniken*, 63; and in Bregenz, officials reported that the peasants put posts in front of those who would not join and put them under the ban, excluding them from churches, mills, smithies, and public taverns, 'and in sum from all fellowship', Franz, *Akten*, 174. Permission to revolt: StA Sigmaringen, Dep. 30 Marchtal—12 T4_44, 33.

5. Tennstedt: AGBM 2, 286–288; the army noted that since the Twelve Articles were printed, probably some of the citizens had them already. Blickle, 'Die Reformation in Erfurt', 253–254; Würzburg: Cronthal, *Stadt Würzburg*.

6. Baumann, *Quellen: Chroniken* (Weissenau), 497; (Cochlaeus), 783–786. Hug, *Villinger Chronik*, 100.

7. For membership of the Christian Union, see Cornelius, *Studien zur Geschichte*, 191–196. For example, the peasants captured by Truchsess Georg after 13 April included peasants from fourteen different places or jurisdictions, including thirteen villages from the truchsess's own lands. Baumann, *Akten*, 234–235. The 'christian army assembled on the Stocksberg' wrote to their brothers assembled 'aus dem Opperthall' (probably Zabertal); the Christian army at 'Nypperg' wrote to the Christian brothers assembled in Zabergau, Franz, 'Aus der Kanzlei', 87, 91. This will also have meant that their names were perforce temporary.

8. AGBM 2, 568.

9. AGBM 2, 602–603, 643–646.

10. See Rauch, *Heilbronn* IV.

11. Hug, *Villinger Chronik*, 115–121.

12. Rathgeber, *Herrschaft Rappoltstein*, 95.

13. AGBM 1, 339; AGBM 2, 216: at Halle, 'his grace' appeared in person and got off his horse, joining the Gemeinde on foot.

14. Müntzer and horses: AGBM 2, 378–379, letter of Johann Rühel to Luther, 26 May 1525. It had also been mentioned earlier in a letter of Hans Zeiß to Christoph Meinhard, 5 May 1525, AGBM 2, 203, so was probably well known; and it was one of the points to which Müntzer later confessed, ThMA 3, 266. Wilpurger: Franz, *Akten*, 183–184.

15. See Franz, *Akten*, 176, for the system developed in upper Germany. Tennstedt: AGBM 2, 288; StA Sigmaringen, Dep. 30 Marchtal—12 T4_44, 319–338; Bischoff, *La guerre*, 319–338 (lots system).

16. AGBM 1, 226. Luther: WT 4, 4779, p. 493 n. 10. Mötsch, *Die Wallfahrt zu Grimmental*, 2: They consumed the shrine's supplies of food but were unable to take any valuables as the counts of Henneberg had hidden them. The pilgrimage ended in 1545.

17. Rauch, *Heilbronn* IV, 147, 148: Rohrbach's goods were all confiscated and sold, but his widow claimed her property, which led to ongoing court cases because she was a 'leibeigen' serf and then remarried a serf of another lord.

18. *Die Summa und Namen der Schloss*; also *Verbrannte vnnd abgebrochene Schlosser vnnd Clöster*. Broadsheet, *Das seind die Clöster...* , 1525, München, Bayerische Staatsbibliothek—Einbl. V,7 d., https://tinyurl.com/c35kafs3. See also, for lists, Bensen, *Geschichte des Bauernkrieges*, 564–566, based on Eisenhart; Baumann, *Quellen: Chroniken* (Eisenhart), 617–620. See Ocker, *Church Robbers*, 50–100.

19. Rauch, *Heilbronn* IV, 46–47, 12 April 1525, and 75. Sea, 'Imperial Cities'; 'Reformation and Restoration... Heilbronn'.

20. This destruction of castles came on top of the damage wrought by the Knights' War (summer 1522–May 1523), while a further twenty-two were destroyed during the Swabian League's campaign against the robber baron Thomas von Absberg (1523 to 1527). While it was thus not unusual for castles to be destroyed, the scale of destruction during the Peasants' War was remarkable. Schillingsfürst: Baumann, *Quellen zur Geschichte des Bauernkrieges aus Rotenburg an der Tauber. [sic] (Chronik Thomas Zweifel)* (hereafter *Rothenburg*) (Zweifel), 381–391. Meanwhile, the 'young lord' and his sister escaped to a house in Rothenburg and stored their valuables with the Franciscan monastery there, another example of the connections between nobles and monastic institutions; by 1541 the monastery had closed.

21. Chroust, *Chroniken*, vol. 2, 41. He does, however, exaggerate.

22. Bildhausen band to Breitungen band: AGBM 1, 413–414.

23. Franz, *Der deutsche Bauernkrieg*, vol. 1, 205–207; Miller and McBride, *Armies of the German Peasants' War*. AGBM 2, 229, report of Hans Zeiß.

24. Radical preacher: Fries, *Geschichte*, vol. 1, 417.

25. See the image in Chapter 10 of Klos Wuczer and Acker Conz. See also Strobach, 'Trommeln und Pfeifen'. On sound in the Peasants' War, see Hacke, 'Hearing Cultures', and Hacke, 'Mit Augen und Ohren'. I am grateful to Gaby Bultmann of the Berlin Instruments Museum for advice and for demonstrating what many sixteenth-century instruments sounded like.

26. AGBM 1, 24–25. AGBM 1, 94–96, 447. The chronicler Sebald Ranft listed the 'drummer' and the piper amongst the 138 citizens who were punished at Kitzingen, Böhm, 'Kitzingen' (Ranft), 96–97.

27. Rauch, *Heilbronn* IV, 275. AGBM 1, 479–480. On bells, see Stockmann, 'Der Kampf um die Glocken'.

28. Rauch, *Heilbronn* IV, 202–203.

29. AGBM 2, 513, 515, 517, 519. One had lost six hundred sheep 'in wool', and would rather have lost 400 Gulden. This remarkable set of claims lists exactly what the peasants were said to have taken and its value. Nicolaus Thomann notes that the peasants ate meat at the convent of Roggenburg. He uses the derogatory word for eating, *fressen*, and he notes it as unusual. Thomann, 'Weissenhorner Historie', 81.

30. Baumann, *Quellen: Chroniken*, 500 (Murer, Weissenau); Cronthal, *Stadt Würzburg*, 66. Attempts were made to buy the peasants off by sending them wine and bread and meat. See Müller, 'Macht Aufruhr durstig?' and Franz, *Akten*, 359. So also in Alsace, it was clear that the rebels planned to 'usessen' the monasteries; when they had 'eaten out' one, they would take the next.

31. Hug, *Villinger Chronik*, 115–121. Müller, *Mörder ohne Opfer*, 387. Interestingly, 'Das walt got' was the final motto on the one surviving pamphlet of Georg Amandus, the radical preacher of Schneeberg, sometimes thought to have been a follower of Karlstadt or possibly of Müntzer, Amandus, *Wie ein geistlicher christlicher Ritter*. AGBM 2, 276.

32. Virck, *Urkunden und Akten der Stadt Strassburg* (hereafter *Strassburg*), 116.

33. Cronthal, *Stadt Würzburg*, 24, 45–46, 68. Virck, *Strassburg*, 204. Supplying an army with bread was a major task: Schweinfurt sent four waggonloads of bread at a cost of 31 fl 3 ort to the Bildhausen army, having been promised supplies of grain from the army to make more; but the grain had not arrived, endangering the town's own citizenry. When collecting material for his history of the war, Fries found many letters from peasant bands concerning supplies, most of which he did not include, Fries, *Geschichte*, vol. 1, 415–416.

34. Würzburg: Fries, *Geschichte*, vol. 1, 172, 203, 205–207; and Cronthal, *Stadt Würzburg*, 28, 47, 49: when the tree sickened and died in the second half of the sixteenth century, a tree was painted on the wall of the council instead, and its successor is still there. Rothenburg: Baumann, *Rothenburg* (Zweifel), 51–53.

35. Baumann, *Rothenburg* (Zweifel), 336–337. Cronthal, *Stadt Würzburg*, 52. Böckingen was her home village, Rauch, *Heilbronn* IV, 198–199.

36. Blickle, *Bauernjörg*, 126, 250.

37. HStAS A 502 U 117, 118, 30 July 1530, 4 August 1530.

38. Fries, *Geschichte*, vol. 2, 272–273.

39. Baumann, *Akten*, 208.

40. Baumann, *Akten*, 251.

41. Hug, *Villinger Chronik*, 117, for the text. Ulbrich, 'Oberschwaben und Württemberg', 119. Later in the conflict some of the groups appeared to have had a narrower understanding of what the Landschaft meant and to have wanted a local solution, 129–130.

42. Baumann, *Akten*, 235.

43. Virck, *Strassburg*, 174: 'The common land', 'powerful foreign folk will invade our *landsart*', Helle Haufen of Upper Elsass. See also the versammlung of Stechsfeld, Virck, *Strassburg*, 161–162, 289, who refer to the 'vaterland' and Duke Anthony as a 'foreign lord', 16 May 1525. Hans Jacob, Freiherr zu Morsperg, also spoke from their opponents' side of the need to defend 'my "vaterland"'. The Kleeburg army, by contrast, called for support against the 'unChristian tyrant', using the religious, nonpatriotic language favoured earlier in the revolt, Virck, *Strassburg*, 174–175, 177.

44. The exception that proves the rule was one banner which, while not Marian, showed Christ crucified with St John and Mary below (it came from early April 1525, near Böblingen), Leah Wegner, 'Böblingen. Die Gemaine Landschaft der württembergischen Aufständischen', Tübingen Bauerkriegsvorträge, 21 June 2023.

Chapter 9: High Spring

1. AGBM 2, 133.

2. Kießling and Wener, eds., *Gründzüge der Agrargeschichte*, 47–49; Schirmer, 'Ursachen des Bauernkrieges in Thüringen'.

3. Mötsch, 'Aufständische Führungselite in Henneberg', and see Franz, *Der deutsche Bauernkrieg*, vol. 1, 238–248, for his assessment of this region.

4. See AGBM 1, 611: Georg Vollrath was 'one of the powerful' in the Bildhausen band, and his companion Heinz Schuster also wanted to be a 'gewaldiger'.

5. In Frankfurt itself, Dr Gerhard Westerburg, a supporter of Karlstadt's, was preaching, and on 13 and 19 April the citizens assembled in arms and submitted articles of complaint. Struck, 'Mittelrhein', 179–180; Struck, *Bauernkrieg*, 16–20.

6. On Fulda, see Struck, *Bauernkrieg*, 20–22.

7. This incident became famous. See, for example, *Chroniken der deutschen Städte*, Mainz 2, 101–118, esp. 105: one manuscript version of this chronicle includes the 'provberb' 'sprichwort' about this incident: 'As I was sitting on the Wacholder heath / we drank out of a big barrel / How did that agree with us? / Like grass agrees with the dog. / The devil blessed it for us'. 'Als ih uff dem Wahholder saß / Da tranken wir auß dem grosen faß: / Wie bekam uns daß? / Als dem hundt daß graß / Der Teutffel gesegnet uns daß!' For the Mainz articles and the cathedral's settlement, see Struck, *Bauernkrieg*, 23–26, 108–123; and Struck, 'Mittelrhein', 183.

8. AGBM 1, 68; see also on Wilhelm, Mandry, 'Reflexionen', 158–160, 166–167; Wölfing, *Bauernkrieg im südthüringischen-hennebergischen Raum*.

9. Leng, 'Bauern vor den Mauern'.

10. AGBM 1, 188, and see Breul-Kunkel, *Herrschaftskrise*, 267, 263–266. For Johann's version of events, Henneberg, *Wahrhafftige vnwidesprechliche vnnd begrundtfeste entschuldigung*. He was confirmed as abbot, not just coadjutor, after the war by Pope Clement, StA MR, Urk. 75, Nr. 1487, 23 August 1532.

11. AGBM 1, 320–321: he asked Casimir of Brandenburg and the bishop of Würzburg to return the knights he had sent them; the counts of Mansfeld were unable to send him knights.

12. AGBM 1, 117, 199–201. He wrote twice on the same day.

13. AGBM 1, 227.

14. AGBM 1, 231.

15. AGBM 1, 351, 352, 324, 606. His own officials warned him that the peasants saw the Hennebergs as their enemy, AGBM 1, 493. Outside Meiningen, a peasant leader insulted the count publicly and personally. 'Herten' Wilhelm's manservant had had his head chopped off and stuck on a pole by the peasant army of Mellrichstadt; the peasants were saying how much he had confessed 'about what your Grace wanted to do against the peasants', AGBM 1, 499.

16. AGBM 1, 449–451; and see for his account to Wilhelm, 451–452, where he does not mention being threatened with the gauntlet.

17. AGBM 1, 236.

18. On the bigamy, see Rockwell, *Doppelehe des Landgrafen Philipp Von Hessen*, and Fichtner, *Protestantism and Primogeniture*.

19. Georg explained that he had only received the letter 'today', 27 April, AGBM 1, 327; but Philip had also sent him urgent requests for help, AGBM 1, 209, on 23 April, and via his officials, on 25 April, AGBM 1, 274.

20. 'Was man globet und sweret, das man dasselbig nicht heldet, es sei von got ader dem menschen gesatzt'. But his original had read, 'Dan al gebot, so der mens thut und di oberkeit, di ist meins gedenkens zu halten, schuldig, wo si nicht gleich wider'. AGBM 1, 30, for letter of Philip, 12 April; AGBM 1, 327, for reply. On 11 March, Philip had written a remarkable long letter to Georg in his own hand, copied out by a secretary to make it easier to read, in which he tried to convert Georg to evangelical belief. His wife, Christina, wrote a much shorter letter to Georg on the same day begging her father to read the Bible, Gess, *Akten und Briefe*, vol. 2, 67–76.

21. On the different attitudes of Philip, Friedrich, Johann, Georg, and Wilhelm, see Mandry, 'Reflexionen'. Wendel Hipler certainly considered Friedrich to be sympathetic towards the poor, or in another version of his plan, to the 'union', Fries, *Geschichte*, vol. 1, 443–445; and see also Kraus, 'Beiträge', 109–110.

22. AGBM 1, 356.

23. Ottensass knew Luther personally and had been trying to introduce the Reformation for two years at least, but Abbot Crato, who ruled Hersfeld, was too timid to act. He had initially permitted evangelical preaching but then expelled some evangelical preachers, replacing them with Adam Crafft, a Lutheran and a gifted reformer, only to banish him in early 1525. Ottensass claimed that they had sworn to the peasants at Fulda but without prejudice to their loyalty to Hesse. When Philip's troops approached, the council decided to negotiate with the landgrave, offering him Hersfeld as a secularised territory in exchange for recognition of 'what the gospel says' and the Twelve Articles. Ottensass was one of the two negotiators, but instead of receiving them, Philip arrested them, while the town decided to surrender to the landgrave despite the armies of peasants camped outside. Ottensass was put in chains and imprisoned in Philip's castle, Spangenberg. Ottensass pleaded to be released, and an intercession from Luther, who had no idea 'how long you were imprisoned, which I didn't know', freed him after eighteen long months. This did not get him back into Hersfeld, though, and he was still petitioning to return in 1539. AGBM 1, 370; Breul-Kunkel, *Herrschaftskrise*, 272–275.

24. 'Jederman in der stat, arm und reich, einen mund gehapt'. AGBM 2, 419–423, 420. AGBM 1, 415.

25. AGBM 1, 356–357. On the complex politics of the Fuldaers, caught between competing pressures, see Breul-Kunkel, *Herrschaftskrise*. On 2 May, the mayor and council of Fulda knew that the coadjutor had set off to see Philip; and indeed that day, Johann asked to see Philip, AGBM 1, 399, 400. For the rival accounts of events by the Hennebergs and Philip, see: Henneberg, *Wahrhafftige vnwidesprechliche vnnd begrundtfeste entschuldigung*, and Hessen, *Zwischen den Durchleuchtigen*. Ironically, Pope Clemens VII wrote, congratulating Philip on having defeated the peasants and admonishing him to continue to fight the heretics, StA MR, Best. 3, Nr. 192, fos. 21r–22v, 23 August 1525.

26. LATh Meiningen, GHA Sekt II Nr. 739, and Sekt II, 626, for original sealed copies of his swearing to the peasants; both copies were carefully slit later with a cross to indicate they are invalid. For the articles of the peasants, LATh Meiningen,

GHA Sekt II, Nr. 552–562; many are suspiciously similar and are written by the same high-quality scribe. Nr. 560 is in the form of a letter to their 'gracious lord', which declined to list any problems and trusted him to fix them—but these peasants were not entirely intimidated, and hoped that 'your princely grace will give us...the freedom which other princes and lords are giving their subjects', 'E f G werde vnns solche zusagung sampt der freyhait so andere fursten vnnd herrn Jren vnderthannen geben', LATh Meiningen, GHA, Sekt II, Nr. 560. AGBM 1, 401, 427; complaints of the peasantry, 427–435. Wilhelm's negotiations: AGBM 1, 459–460, and see Fries, *Geschichte*, vol. 1, 420–421, for allegations that he secretly made an agreement with Hans Schnabel of the Bildhausen band. Story of his wife: AGBM 1, 402.

27. AGBM 1, 439, 451.

28. AGBM 1, 462, 468.

29. AGBM 1, 435.

30. They left one of their mobile chancelleries behind on the battlefield, a rare example of a source from the peasants' own organisation, Franz, 'Kanzlei'.

31. Baumann, *Quellen: Chroniken* (Cochlaeus), 788.

32. The delay also enabled the bishop's side to provision and fortify the castle. For accounts of the attempted siege, see Lorenz Fries, Sebastian von Rotenhan, Peter Harer, and Martin Cronthal. On Rotenhan, see Fuchs, 'Lorenz Fries, Christoph Scheurl und Sebastian von Rotenhan'.

The garrison probably consisted of between 300 and 350 men. On the peasants' side, 100 (or, according to some accounts, 400) fighters were killed and their bodies left in the ditch; the peasants asked for their dead to be properly buried and the captain agreed, but the hangman chopped up the corpses and threw them into a hole, Leng, 'Bauern vor den Mauern'; Cronthal, *Stadt Würzburg*, 65. The peasant army probably had forty wheeled cannon but lacked the kind of big artillery that could damage the huge walls. They had also secured gunpowder from Nuremberg in exchange for stolen wine, and they had weapons that had come from well-stocked civic armouries, including cannon, powder, and heavy weapons from Rothenburg, Wüst, 'Bauernkrieg und fränkische Reichsstädte', 190; Leng, 'Bauern vor den Mauern'.

33. For a description of the siege, see Hoyer, *Militärwesen*, 162–165. Dietrich von Eyb, another eyewitness suspected of disloyalty to the bishop, described the confusion in the town as peasants and soldiers were everywhere, running 'like wild pigs', 'wie die Wildschwein', StA WÜ, Adel, 1333.

34. Adam, 'Zwei Briefe', 699–700. Malsch: Harer, *Berichte*, 37. On the Palatinate, see Harer, *Berichte*; Virck, *Urkunden und Akten der Stadt Strassburg* (hereafter *Strassburg*), 194–250; and Alter, *Aufstand der Bauern und Bürger*.

35. Pfeddersheim: Alter, *Pfeddersheim*, 265. Bossert, 'Zur Geschichte des Bauernkriegs', 250–266, 544–546. Their leader, Anton Eisenhut, was an ex-cleric firmly opposed to the nobility; see Klebon, *Im Taumel des Evangeliums*. The peasants had written to the bishop of Speyer that 'he should become a lord of the peasants and take a wife', Adam, 'Zwei Briefe'. The same thing was happening in Bamberg, where Bishop Weigand von Redwitz was being encouraged to become a duke so that his

lands could be inherited, Franz, *Der deutsche Bauernkrieg*, vol. 1, 209. Even in the third week of May, after the battle of Frankenhausen, Luther's friend Johann Rühel was hoping that Albrecht of Mainz would consider 'changing his estate, you understand what I mean', WBr 3, 873, 21 May 1525, 503–507, 506:45–46.

36. For the letter, HStAS, J 1, Nr. 127, Bd. 4, fo. 180r–v, 18 May 1525: Ludwig claims to want to avoid bloodshed and says he will hold a disputation in the week following Pfingsten to discuss the Twelve Articles. Melanchthon and Brenz had been named by the peasants as potential judges. See Melanchthon, *Eyn schrifft Philippi Melanchthon*, fo. D iii v; in an appendix added after the peasants' defeat, he called for measured punishment. Greschat, *Philipp Melanchthon*, 62–64.

37. Virck, *Strassburg*, 107 ff., and see especially the report of Martin Bescholt, 107–111, which makes it clear that the preacher of Dorlisheim played a powerful role there; people came to hear his Easter sermons from miles around, and a hundred had to stand outside the church, unable to get in. Virck, *Strassburg*, 185; see also Franz, *Der deutsche Bauernkrieg, Aktenband* (hereafter *Akten*), 200–201. On the course of the war in Alsace, see Bischoff, *La guerre des paysans*.

38. Gyss, *Histoire de la ville d'Obernai*, 356.

39. Virck, *Strassburg*, 128, 162–163.

40. Virck, *Strassburg*, 118, as the articles of the peasants had put it on 20 April; 'lantschaft', 161. Afterwards, the Strasbourg council sought to blame Gerber, now safely dead. He was a subject of the bishop's, not one of theirs, and he had compelled ('us zwang') others to join. They insisted that they had constantly told him to leave their property alone, that they had feared assault on the town by his men, and that they had had to fortify their territory. But they also admitted that their villages and property had not been harmed, which must have added to the impression that they had an agreement with him. Strasbourg at this point was desperately trying to distance itself from seeming sympathetic to the peasants amidst rumours that it would be attacked and punished by the princes. On the term 'landschaft' and the idea of region, see Scott, *Raum und Region*, 11–17. On the values of Christian brotherhood as expressed in the correspondence of many of the Alsatian bands, Conrad, *Reformation in der bäuerlichen Gesellschaft*, 125–134; and on anticlericalism in the interrogations of rebels afterwards, 134–139.

41. Gerber to the Strasbourg council: Virck, *Strassburg*, 113, and for Gerber to the preachers, Bucer, *Correspondance*, vol. 2, 16–17; the preachers' report to the council, 17; the letter of the preachers to the peasant band, 17–20. The radical Valentin Ickelsamer of Rothenburg went to the peasant camp as a representative of the town, Baumann, *Quellen zur Geschichte des Bauernkrieges aus Rotenburg an der Tauber. [sic]* *(Chronik Thomas Zweifel)* (hereafter *Rothenburg*), 143. Jakob Strauss also went to the peasant army outside Eisenach, Dietmann, 'Die Prediger Jakob Strauß und Wolfgang Stein'. So too did Eberlin von Günzburg in Erfurt, visiting both the peasants in town and those encamped outside; he went with a group of other preachers and councillors, Eberlin, *Eine getreue Warnung*, 1526, fo. D iii r–D v (v). Eberlin used the technique of getting the peasants to kneel to calm the situation, a posture both devotional and subservient. For the preachers and negotiations with the Strasbourg council, Virck,

Strassburg, 113–116; Bucer, *Correspondance*, vol. 2, 17–20. For Capito's later account of events in a commentary on Habbakuk published in 1526, Virck, *Strassburg*, 203, who points out that it accords with the preachers' account, Wolfgang Capito, *Habacuc*, fo. 20 r. However, Capito's account is also from the preachers' point of view.

42. Gerber may also have warned Rosheim that the army intended to attack them: they locked the gates and repelled the peasants, Kaplan, 'Entangled Negotiations'.

43. Scott, 'South-West German Towns', 151–152. In an interesting postscript, after the war the Strasbourg preachers Matthäus Zell and Wolfgang Capito were accused of having given advice to the rebels at Wickersheim and even of having written a long document of defence for them before the revolt broke out. Capito and Zell demanded more detail of the allegations, rejecting them as slanderous. In the event, none were forthcoming—perhaps they were baseless, perhaps so serious that they were thought too risky to pursue, Virck, *Strassburg*, 188–190.

44. Virck, *Strassburg*, 147, see also Boell, *Der Bauernkrieg um Weissembourg*: the Herbitzheimers had eight flags of white cloth with a red cross. Buszello, 'Oberrheinlande', 81–83, 93; Alter, *Der Aufstand*, 49–51.

45. Schweyger, *Chronik der Stadt Hall*, 83–84. The miners set out to march from Schwaz to Innsbruck and overnighted in Hall, a salt-mining town about twenty kilometres away, where they were met by the archduke, and on 18 February the authorities agreed to most of the miners' demands. There were apparently Lutheran miners in 1523 who were leaving, and some ex-monks working as miners, Laube, 'Der Aufstand', 233. However, though there is some evidence that the miners wanted 'preaching of the gospel according to Luther', this was not included in the settlement or articles. In April, unrest continued to worry the rulers. Individual miners did engage in the Peasants' War, but the miners did not rally as a group; and about two thousand to three thousand miners probably left Schwaz. Blickle, 'Alpenländer', 194: The Paßler family had a history of grievance against the archbishop, Stella, *La rivoluzione*, 45–49. Schwaz produced more silver than Joachimstal or Mansfeld. The miners had a privileged status, including tax exemption, and many were highly skilled. Though many originally came from peasant families, they may have felt superior to peasants. In Tyrol, the peasants had their own political representation in the Landschaft, but the miners did not, Franz, *Der deutsche Bauernkrieg*, vol. 1, 161–162.

46. Hettstedt: Fessner, 'Montanwesen'. Laube estimates between ten thousand and fifteen thousand miners with over twenty different specialisations for Schwaz, Laube, 'Der Aufstand', 228–229.

47. Weiß, *Die frommen Bürger von Erfurt*; Karant-Nunn, *Zwickau*.

48. Abbot of Grünhain, AGBM 2, 256, report of 9 May. On peasant articles in the region, Graupner, 'Dorfgemeinden und ihre Artikel': those of Ichtershausen omitted the demands concerning personal serfdom, which did not exist in Thuringia, but otherwise follow the Twelve Articles closely, while also borrowing from town demands of Stadtilm and Rudolstadt, suggesting less independence. Other villages merely added specific complaints to the articles. Nuns of Kelbra: AGBM 2, 273. Disturbances in the Harz: rioters had mistreated the sacrament, 'throwing [the host]

out of the monstrances and liborien [*sic*, probably *ciborien*] contemptuously on the ground and treading them underfoot', AGBM 2, 237. This spread to Quedlinburg, which was also later fined for its participation in the revolt. The Goslar unrest issued in a series of demands to the council, including for evangelical preaching, AGBM 2, 416–421; and at Halberstadt convents and churches had been attacked, AGBM 2, 646. In Aschersleben the peasants had also been restive, particularly aggrieved about sheep pasturing, and on 8 May it was thought best to make them concessions, AGBM 2, 226. Kupferschmid: AGBM 2, 271.

49. Laube, 'Der Aufstand', 226–227.

50. AGBM 2, 242–245, 245, 326, 328.

51. Amandus was accused of being at one time 'inclined to Doctor Karlstadt', Gess, *Akten und Briefe*, vol. 2, 50, and of arguing that the council should not govern the 'gemeyn' but the 'gemeyn' should govern ('regieren') the council, going one step further later to argue that a prince should not govern a 'land' but a 'land' the prince. He allegedly called the church a 'Devil's house', supported iconoclasm, and condemned Corpus Christi processions. He denied having preached that 'those below should govern those above' (*dye under dye oben sollen regiren*). He did, however, support the miners' demands for holidays, 'considering the danger of their work', Gess, *Akten und Briefe*, vol. 2, 120–128. In late June 1525 he again claimed to be falsely accused of being pro-rebel, but preached against the reintroduction of the Latin mass, Gess, *Akten und Briefe*, vol. 2, 330.

52. Amandus, *Wie ein geistlicher christlicher Ritter*, fo. B iii v. The pamphlet concludes, 'VDMJE', 'Dass waldt Gott', mottos that would be famously used by the peasants. On Amandus, see Neumann, 'Reformation als religiöse Devianz?' He may have written to Müntzer and visited him at Allstedt; it has been suggested that a letter from a certain 'Jeori' that refers to a visit to Allstedt was from him, ThMA 2, 224–234; see Drummond, *Dreadful History*.

53. AGBM 1, 438, 439; Gess, *Akten und Briefe*, vol. 2, 340–341. Letter to Bildhausen band, Fries, *Geschichte*, vol. 1, 372–373.

54. AGBM 2, 267–268, 353, 535 ff., 571; Boyd Brown, *Singing the Gospel*, 26–42; Zorzin, *Karlstadt als Flugschriftenautor*, 141–163.

55. Bräuer, 'Luthers Reise'; WBr 3, Nr. 860, 4 (?5) May 1525, 479–482. On 5 May at Osterhausen, Count Albrecht, with sixty knights, attacked and killed twenty peasants who were going to Frankenhausen, taking some of the rest prisoner and burning the village to the ground. (See also AGBM 2, 230, report of Zeiß; and Bräuer and Vogler, *Müntzer*, 355. The Eisleben Chronicle gives the total of seventy killed, Grössler and Sommer, eds., *Chronikon Islebiense*, 4–5.) Luther's letter may be referring to this incident when he encourages the count to continue as he had started, and admonishes Rühel not to let the count become 'weich', 'soft'. If so, its upbeat tone is particularly unpleasant; it argues that those in revolt are the devil's possessed limbs and concludes by announcing that, to spite the devil, he will 'take my Katie in marriage before I die, when I hear that they have gone'. WBr 3, Nr. 860, 4 (5?) May 1525, 482:1–2. The Osterhausen massacre was probably also the incident that the

Lutherans praised as marking the turning point in the war, the very moment Friedrich the Wise died; see Neudecker and Preller, eds., *Georg Spalatin*, 66–68. In 1526 Luther praised Albrecht as the man who 'was at that time the first to put on armour', 'dazumal der Erste auff war in den Harnisch', WS 19, 279:19. This was not actually true, and Luther's brief history of the war attempted to blame the revolt on the Catholics as coming 'from Franconia over the forest' and from Mühlhausen through a strip of Georg's land. This was part of Luther's attack on the Mainz proposal to abolish Lutheranism because of the war, *Wider den rechten auffrührischen, verrätherischen und mordischen Rathschlag der ganzen Mainzischen Pfafferei Unterricht und Warnung*, WS 19:260–281, a title that turns Luther's rhetoric against the peasants against the Catholics.

56. Luther, *Wider die räuberischen und mörderischen Rotten der Bauern*, WS 18, 357–361; *Against the Robbing, Murdering Hordes of Peasants*, LW 46; Kaufmann, *Bauernkrieg*, ch. 1. See also Bräuer, 'Luthers Reise', which persuasively argues that the tract is not an outbreak of rage on Luther's part but a carefully constructed, long-standing position. For the text of the treaty of Weingarten published by Luther with his own introductory and concluding remarks, *Vertrag zwischen dem löblichen Bund zu Schwaben...* , WS 18, 336–343, which includes the remark 'wo der hyn faren wird' in Luther's conclusion. Luther compares them to Judases as well.

57. AGBM 2, 135, 28 April 1525, Friedrich to 'Herzog' Johann.

58. Nuremberg and Ulm had also been reluctant to contribute to funding the Swabian League and refused at first; Augsburg was a major contributor, Sea, 'Economic Impact'.

59. *Ein Sendbrief von dem harten Büchlein wider die Bauern*, WS 18, 375–401. It probably followed on a sermon he gave at Pentecost: *Verantwortung D. M. Luthers auf das Büchlein wider die räuberischen und mörderischen Bauern*, WS 17, 264–268. Even so, as late as 10 May, as part of their accord with those engaged in revolt in the town, the Erfurt council asked Melanchthon and Luther to come to Erfurt in person as soon as possible to discuss the Erfurt articles, AGBM 2, 261. In 1525 Urbanus Rhegius wrote a postscript to an edition of the tract that reaffirmed the hard line on obedience: your 'Oberherrn' was instituted by divine authority (fo. D ii v) and you could not rebel; even if he was evil this did not diminish his authority. 'Freiheit' was about being a 'knecht Gottes'; it was not a cover for evil (fo. D iv r). Rhegius, *Ain Sendbrieff von dem harte[n] büchlin wider die bauren*.

60. Brenz, *Von Milderung der Fürsten*, fo. B i a–v: there are four surviving editions of the pamphlet, suggesting that it was fairly widely disseminated. Brenz points out that those involved in the Peasants' War had different levels of responsibility; some merely wrote or spoke seditiously, and some were compelled to join the peasants. Now that the authorities had been reinstituted, Brenz believed that they should not start their regime in blood. See also WBr 3, 878, 517, 30 May 1525, Luther to Amsdorf. Here Luther defends himself against the accusation many in Magdeburg made that Luther was a flatterer of the princes, but does so by repeating his arguments yet more firmly. Similar accusations were apparently still being made on 12 June 1525, WBr 3, 888, p. 528, 12 June 1525, Luther to Amsdorf. For Mühlpfort's

long and impassioned letter condemning the lack of care for the poor and the unbridled seeking of revenge by the nobles, AGBM 2, 437–440.

61. ThMA 3, 213–214, according to the hostile report of the official Sittich von Berlepsch to Duke Georg; and see Müller, *Mörder ohne Opfer*, 337.

62. Jordan, *Chronik der Stadt Mühlhausen*, vol. 1, 185–186 (= Müller, 'Chronicon Mulhusinum', 55); ThMA 3, 215–216, report of Sittich von Berlepsch. Report of woman celebrating mass, AGBM 2, 754 n. 1, Katharina Kreutter. She claimed she had done so with the encouragement of Pfeiffer and had also been baptised by him. It is unclear, however, exactly when either event happened, StadtA Mühlhausen, 10 K 3, Nr. 13, fo. 13 (r). 'Wuhr umb sie Messe gehalden das ir doch nicht gebuert'. She tried to ring the storm bell, and she emphatically hated priests. See also Müller, 'Ein ehrbarer Rat, entlaufene Mönche und streitbare Weiber'; and Müller, *Mörder ohne Opfer*, 558. For the woman who voted, AGBM 2, 535, 773, 834: Dorothea Ziegler, see ch. 10, 'Brotherhood'. The allegation was used to argue that Otthera (to whom she was related) was a supporter of Müntzer. On the peasant preacher, AGBM 2, 98, report of Sittich von Berlepsch. Other reports say that the peasant barely escaped with his life.

63. ThMA 2, 26 April 1525, 403–417, esp. 411, 413, 415; Matheson, *Collected Works of Müntzer*, 140–142.

64. See Gess, *Akten und Briefe*, vol. 2, 256–266, for the self-exculpatory account of the events by the Salza council to Duke Georg after the Frankenhausen defeat. For the letter of Salza to the Mühlhauseners, ThMA 2, 403, 26 April 1525. See Bräuer and Vogler, *Müntzer*, 337–338; Müller, *Mörder ohne Opfer*, 345–367. For attacks on monasteries and convents in the whole region in late April through 5 May, see Gess, *Akten und Briefe*, vol. 2, 119–186.

65. Bräuer and Vogler, *Müntzer*, 337–338; ThMA 2, 429–430. Müller, *Mörder ohne Opfer*, 435; see also 393–405. For a brilliant reconstruction of the Eichsfeldzug, Müller, *Mörder ohne Opfer*, 415–447.

66. Whether the Eichsfelders were responsible for burning Harburg is unclear, but it was destroyed, Müller, *Mörder ohne Opfer*, 462–463. Günther von Schwarzburg brought with him his vassals Kurt von Dittichenrode, Heinrich Hacke, Christoph von Altendorf, and Balthasar von Bendeleben, ThMA 2, 430. Von Schwarzburg did not, however, appear at Frankenhausen, pleading that he needed his troops to put down his own peasants, ThMA 2, 460. Duke Georg's report on discussions with Bodo von Stolberg, Heinrich XXX von Schwarzburg-Blankenburg, and Ernst V von Hohnstein, ThMA 2, 428–429, 7 July; Gess *Akten und Briefe*, vol. 2, 334–340 n. 1075.

67. Jordan, *Chronik der Stadt Mühlhausen*, vol. 1, 189 (= Müller, 'Chronicon Mulhusinum', 57–58). Some of those from the Eichsfeld and from Hesse departed at this point, while the rest went back to Mühlhausen. There already was a large army at Frankenhausen, and an urban revolt had involved the salt workers. The castle of the Count of Schwarzburg had been stormed. See also Miller, *Frankenhausen*.

68. Hans Zeiß to the elector, AGBM 2, 228, 7 May. It was not just Allstedt; he claimed that in the whole Amt, only thirty men had remained where there should have been four hundred.

On Frankenhausen, see Hahnemann, 'Die Einwohner von Frankenhausen'. The town was under the overlordship of the von Schwarzburg counts, who were in turn subject to Duke Georg of Saxony. Comparatively rich, it had a population of between seventeen hundred and nineteen hundred, and its revolt and Reformation history were in some respects similar to those of Mühlhausen. The Frankenhausen articles were closely based on the Twelve Articles, with additions concerning the salt industry and limiting the Schwarzburg counts' power. Miller, *Frankenhausen*, 33; Hahnemann, 'Einwohner', 79–80. Müntzer's letters, ThMA 2, 437–490, which carefully reconstitutes the sequence of missing letters; Matheson, *Collected Works of Müntzer*, 150, 8 May 1525 (Sonderhausen); 150, 9 May 1525 (Eisenach); 157, mention of letter to Walkenried; 158, 13 May 1525 (Erfurt).

69. For Osterhausen, AGBM 2, 320; ThMA 2, 456–459, 461–465. Bräuer and Vogler, *Müntzer*, 355, give a higher figure of seventy, which they take from the *Chronicon Islebensi*. This fuller but later account adds that the village was set on fire and that hardly twenty houses remained. Müntzer to Albrecht, ThMA 2, 464; Matheson, *Collected Works of Müntzer*, 157.

70. ThMA 2, 469, 472; Matheson, *Collected Works of Müntzer*, 155, 156: the word is 'staubbesem', the whip used to punish prostitutes, and is more demeaning than 'scourge'.

71. ThMA 3, 240, report of Hans Hut. Brauer and Vogler, *Müntzer*, 365–368. Elector John the Steadfast of Saxony and Wilhelm von Henneberg arrived after the battle.

72. AGBM 2, 278, 13 May: officials of the elector wrote, demanding the two men be set free because they had had nothing to do with Ernst's attacks. Ernst was a subject of Duke Georg, not of the elector. See also ThMA, 234–235: two years later, the town council of Frankenhausen claimed that they had tried to prevent the executions but they had happened too quickly.

73. ThMA 3, 240 n. 17. Centuries later, the top of the hill was destroyed by the East Germans to build the Panorama Museum, so it now appears more plateau-like than it was originally.

74. Estimates of Miller, *Frankenhausen*, 78. Albrecht of Mainz also supplied three hundred horses, and there were further contingents from Heldrungen, along with the counts of Mansfeld and Count Wolf von Schönburg, who led the Mainz troops.

75. Bräuer and Vogler, *Müntzer*, 368 n. 139; ThMA 1, 184–185, Deutsches Kirchenamt of 1523, Das Ampt auff das Pfingst Fest, including music. That September, the Prussian rebels would also sing this hymn as they reached agreement with the nobility at Quednau, Carsten, 'Bauernkrieg in Ostpreussen', 403. Luther also translated it the year after Müntzer, and it is included in Walther, *Gesangbüchlein* (1524) in Walther's four-part setting, fo. A iii v–A iv r.

Chapter 10: Brothers

1. Johann Locher (Rott), *Ein vngewonlicher, vnd der Ander Sendtbrieff*, he published under the name of Locher. On images of Luther and their ubiquity, see Roper,

Living I Was Your Plague. I am grateful to Bethan Winter, who collected images of peasants on pamphlets for me and compiled the figures.

2. StadtAMM, A 342/2, Bayerische Staatsbibliothek Handschriftenateilung Cgm 4968, for the full case; and see Blickle, 'Memmingen', 1. On boots, see Hahn, 'The Emperor's Boot'; Rublack, 'Matter in the Material Renaissance'.

3. *Die gründtlichen und rechten Hauptartikel.* Another edition from Worms shows two peasants squaring up (VD 16 G 3559), an image which may well have been taken from a block illustrating something else—and it had already been used in the same year in Speyer to illustrate two of Peringer's sermons, *Zwo Sermon.*

4. Fundling, *Anzaigung zwayer falschen Zungen des Luthers*, reused in 1562 by Alexander Weissenhorn, one of the most successful anti-Lutheran propagandist presses of the Counter-Reformation, Weissenhorn, *Vrsprung und Anfang... wittenbergischen Euangeliumbs.*

5. AGBM 2, 322. See also, for example, Schreiber, *Der deutsche Bauernkrieg*, 138: Jörg Bechstein confessed that he had said, 'Welche die seien, die auf den Bauren Seiten ston wöllen, sollen zu mir ston'. He was fined 200 fl and banished.

6. Stocksberg: Franz, 'Aus der Kanzlei', 86–87. Allgäu articles: Cornelius, *Studien zur Geschichte*, 199–201, translation Scott and Scribner, *German Peasants' War*. On forms of address and their importance, see Sternberg, 'Epistolary Ceremonial'. Matern Feuerbacher issued letters of protection to nobles, Franz, *Der deutsche Bauernkrieg* (1933), vol. 1, 353.

7. Lutz, *Tagebuch*, 65. The rest of the speech rather undercut this as the truchsess then described how the peasants had attacked his own lands, 'unn habe mir das mein eingenomen, wider got, err un recht'. (Also in Baumann, *Quellen: Chroniken*, 619, slightly different text.) Rhyiner, 'Chronik', 498.

8. Harer, *Berichte*, 56–57. Tennstedt: AGBM 2, 286–288.

9. Xenakis, *Gewalt und Gemeinschaft*, 127–129; Fronsperger, *Kriegsbuch*, Teil 1, fo. 13 r.

10. Virck, *Urkunden und Akten der Stadt Strassburg* (hereafter *Strassburg*), 136; Rathgeber, *Herrschaft Rappoltstein*, 96–98. Virck, *Strassburg*, 111. Hans Müller's use of running the gauntlet, Hug, *Villinger Chronik*, 116.

11. Fries, *Geschichte*, vol. 1, 143–149; and see similar values expressed in the mandate of the Württemberg peasantry, Vogt, *Die Correspondenz des schwäbischen Bundeshauptmannes Ulrich Artzt* (hereafter *Artzt*), Augsburg 1880, 199–201. Banners and flags: in Heilbronn the council insisted that the Heilbronners should not have town insignia on their flag. In Schaffhausen, one of the conditions of truce arranged with the Stühlingers was that they surrender their banners along with apologising; they refused to accept this humiliation, Miller, *German Peasants' War*.

12. Baumann, *Akten*, 361–378. The low number of rebels in the town may be because others had already been punished and their property dealt with; the list was only made in November 1525. Dionysius Schmid, also a mayor, owned a vast inventory of goods valued at 1,400 fl; Kaspar Küwbuch had been mayor for the abbot of Schöntal and had goods worth 500 fl.

13. Sreenivasan, *Peasants of Ottobeuren*, 9–106. Sreenivasan examines the longer-term crystallisation of an elite here around and after 1560, but the future developments would not necessarily have been evident in 1525. It is also difficult to generalise from the 'pattern' of revolt that Sreenivasan identifies for Swabia and the Black Forest, which does not hold in Thuringia or large parts of Franconia.

14. 'Das irs von Buttika [= Bietigheim] nit werden lachen', Franz, 'Aus der Kanzlei', 88. For similar threats, see 89, 92–93, 96: Balingen, for example, was ordered 'zukommen in disse bruderschaft', 'to enter this brotherhood', with threats if they did not. This collection is particularly interesting because it is a rare example of a set of letters from a peasant chancellery that were captured; it contains draft copies of letters sent and others received. After the war, Joerg Schmid or Knopf was made to confess that all the armies had decided they would seize the property of those who would not join their brotherhood and hunt away their wives and children and send them after them, Baumann, *Akten*, 349; but it is difficult to know how far to trust this confession. For further such letters, see Maurer, *Bauernkrieg 1525*, 37–41. Peasants waking people in their beds: 'weckten sie in Betten uff', Harer, *Berichte*, 49.

15. Götz, *Mein Fehd*, 123. Hans Hacke: 'aus keinem frolucken ader wollust', 'aus forchte und bedrangnisse', AGBM 2, 355. He added that he had not sworn an oath to them, and while he himself could not read or write, he was sure that even the notary had not understood what they had signed. The supplements to Lorenz Fries's chronicle repeat the anecdote of Count Georg of Wertheim, who appeared outside the castle at Würzburg on the peasants' behalf to demand its surrender. The incredulous nobles defending it wanted to know how he could be their enemy and, as Count Wolf of Castel put it, 'be married to my sister'. It was inconceivable to them that he could have joined the peasant brothers. For his part, Wertheim even boasted that his was the best-armed company in the army, Fries, *Geschichte*, vol. 2, 400–401. For Samland case, Richau, 'Historie von dem Auffruhr', 328–357. See 531–566 for report of Nikolaus Richau, town councillor of Königsberg, manuscript in library of Camerarius, Wallenrod. In this revolt, the noble was forced to swap clothes with a peasant; he had to wear 'Hosen und wams' and a felt coat (340). The hostile account of what took place describes how the peasants demanded that the noble surrender ('Gib dich gefangen!'). When, as a man of honour, he demanded to know to whom he must give himself captured, they had no answer—an anecdote mocking the rebels' ignorance of the chivalric code. It may also, however, reveal their self-understanding as a group, not as individuals.

Engels, *Der deutsche Bauernkrieg*, 358; *Peasant War*, 62. Engels's analysis is subtle and recognises the importance of mysticism in peasant revolt. See also János Bak and others, '*The Peasant War in Germany* by Friedrich Engels—125 Years After', in Bak, ed., *German Peasant War of 1525*. On brotherhood, see Hill, *Baptism, Brotherhood, and Belief*.

16. Virck, *Strassburg*, 183–184, no. 326, 1 July 1525. Brun, *Abbot and His Peasants*, 124–125.

17. *An die Versammlung*, 117:5–10. Proverbs 28: the wicked flee though no one pursues, but the righteous are as bold as a lion. The sentiment here is reminiscent of

what Melanchthon accused Müntzer of boasting before battle: that he would catch the bullets of the enemy in his sleeve. Jakob Wehe was also accused of saying they would not be harmed. These may not have been irrational boasts but metaphorical expressions of the biblical sense.

18. Franz and Fleischhauer, eds., *Jacob Murers Weissenauer Chronik*, vol. 1, 34–35. On antimonasticism, see Cohn, 'Anticlericalism'; and see Wolgast, 'Pfarrerwahl'.

19. AGBM 2, 74–76, 79. Town councillors were amongst those involved, and though Friedrich demanded the culprits be punished, he died before they could be, and his successor pardoned them.

20. AGBM 2, 134, 198.

21. AGBM 2, 186.

22. Virck, *Strassburg*, 125, 142 (Niedermünster).

23. Vogt, *Artzt*, 108–109, 113–114 (Ochsenhausen). Gess, *Akten und Briefe*, vol. 2, 146–147 (Roda).

24. Just how far Teuschlin had moved is evident in his 'Schlussreden' against Eck of 1524, when he barely mentioned Mary except to imagine her as sitting in humility by the feet of the Lord, Hubmaier, *Schriften*, 92. When the people of Waldshut defended their preacher in 1525, they expressly denied that anyone insulted or allowed anyone to insult 'our dear lady'. They had insisted on Mary's virginity 'before, in and after the birth', and that she had not borne any other children—they had to defend themselves against anti-Marianism. But nor did they describe her as a queen of heaven or praise her as a mediator, Loserth, *Stadt Waldshut* (Quellen Beilage), 113. Teuschlin, *Auflosung ettlicher Fragen...*, fo. B iv r–v. See Maurer, *Prediger*, 480 ff. Rheingau articles: the capital was to be repaid however, Franz, *Quellen*, 450, 10 May 1525. The Pruntrut band called for all the goods of the Jews to be confiscated and given to them, though the emperor should give them 'a land...so that they can support themselves', 'ein land...damit sye sich neren mogen', Franz, *Der deutsche Bauernkrieg, Aktenband* (hereafter *Akten*), 257. There probably was plundering of Jews' houses, about which we sometimes only know indirectly; for instance, the house of a Jew in Sulzfeld near Königshofen was seriously damaged, but we know about it only because the abbess of the local convent complained that her convent was being used to provide building materials to fix it, AGBM 1, 638–639. See also Wolgast, 'Pfarrerwahl', 101–103.

25. Rathgeber, *Herrschaft Rappoltstein*, 94; the rebels had also earlier repeatedly taken wine belonging to the Jews. For other antisemitic provisions, Franz, *Akten*, 215, 381. The Vorderösterreichischen Landschaft (Alsace, Sundgau, Breisgau, and the Black Forest) had demanded the expulsion of the Jews in 1523 'as enemies of the Christian faith' who impoverish many in town and country, Franz, *Akten*, 134. See also Kraus, 'Beiträge', 68 (Rheingau), 66 (Mainz); Franz, *Quellen*, 457, 459 (Frankfurt).

26. Fries, *Geschichte*, vol. 1, 368–369. On Josel, see Kaplan, 'Entangled Negotiations'. For other indications suggesting that some Jews may have fought with the rebels, see Vogt, *Artzt*, 238: Rabbi Jon of Günzburg and his community was admonished by the league on 9 May 1525 to pay 30 Gulden of the 200 Gulden they were

assessed as having to pay, suggesting they had been involved on the side of the peasants along with the town of Günzburg. Heinrich Burkhart, Marshall of Pappenheim, interceded with the truchsess to reduce the fine levied against his doctor, Jacob, a Jew of Würzburg, because he had already had to pay money to the peasants, Baumann, *Akten*, 308.

27. Franz, *Quellen*, 455, 459, Frankfurter Artikel. On the requirement that clergy must not have any physical deformity, see Röder, *Körper des Priesters*. Interestingly, Sebastian Lotzer, the lay pamphleteer who was centrally involved in drafting the Twelve Articles, mentioned back in 1524 that the old priests had insisted the laity could not receive communion in both kinds because some of them had beards and drops of wine might be spilt, *Ain vast haylsam*, fo F i (r). This is the first argument he cites, and it may suggest that an element of issues surrounding masculinity was at work here, for priests were tonsured and clean-shaven, while beards for men were becoming fashionable amongst townsfolk as well as amongst the nobility. Peasants, by contrast, were not for the most part depicted as bearded, but as clean-shaven. He also spoke of 'manly' ('manhaffter') preaching and called on Christians to 'fight in a knightly manner', 'rytterlich streytten', to reach the 'eternal knighthood', 'ewig Rytterschafft', fo. H vi. He could not have known in 1524 when this was printed that it would in fact come to physical fighting for the gospel.

28. Fulda: AGBM 1, 134. Herrenstrick: AGBM 2, 268. See also AGBM 2, 609, where this was threatened against a priest so as to get all his money: 'We want to pull a gentleman's rope through his buttocks, so that we can get the money out of him', 'wollen wir im ein heren strickt durch die arskerbe zihen, domit wir das geld von im brenken' ('Kerbe' means groove, nick, or notch).

29. Hubmaier, *Schriften*, 19.

30. Roper, 'The "Common Man"'; and see Neumann, 'Der selektive Blick'.

31. Women did play an active role in the risings in the years before the Peasants' War. For example, one Anna Kaiser was made to swear an *Uhrfehde* after being imprisoned at Stuttgart in the wake of the Armer Konrad revolt of 1514 because she had composed a poem that insulted the government and other important people, Rückert, ed., *Der 'Arme Konrad' vor Gericht*, 271. On women and the Peasants' War, see Scott, 'The Collective Response of Women'; and Kobelt-Groch, 'So waren sie in meiner Erinnerung'. Cochlaeus wrote of 'their wives, who were so completely Lutheran that they forced and incited their men to rebel', Cochlaeus, *Wider die Reubische[n] und Mordischen rotten*, fo. E iii (v). This pamphlet by the indefatigable Johannes Cochlaeus, Luther's antagonist and earliest antibiographer, first provides a refutation of Luther's theological views, then an imaginary dialogue between himself and Luther, and next a brief panoramic history of the Peasants' War, including even a rebuttal of Luther's refutation of Thomas Müntzer's final letters. Allstedt, Bernhard Walde: AGBM 2, 478, 565. For the riot at Rothenburg, Baumann, *Quellen zur Geschichte des Bauernkrieges aus Rotenburg an der Tauber*. [sic] *(Chronik Thomas Zweifel)* (hereafter *Rothenburg*) (Zweifel), 217, (Eisenhart) 600: it took place on 20 April, at the height of disturbances. After the defeat of the rebels, on 26 July two of

these women were put in the stocks and banished from town, 609. For Rappoltstein, Rathgeber, *Herrschaft Rappoltstein*, 85–86. Peasant women's anger could be directed at townsfolk too. As they pillaged the house of the Teutonic Knights in Heilbronn, women from the surrounding villages belonging to the knights were heard to say that they wanted to spend time in town, and the citizens would have to go to the villages, Rauch, *Urkundenbuch der Stadt Heilbronn*, vol. 4 (hereafter *Heilbronn* IV), 291.

32. Hubmaier: Küssenberg, 'Chronik', 420. Mühlhausen: StadtA Mühlhausen, 10 K 3, Nr. 13, fo. 13 (r), 'Wuhr umb sie Messe gehalden das ir doch nicht gebuert'. See also Müller, 'Ein ehrbarer Rat'; AGBM 2, 535, 773, 834 (Dorothea Ziegler); StadtA Mühlhausen, K 3, Nr. 1 b, fo. 10–32. For Allstedt, see Wölbing, *Müntzers langer Schatten*, 144–149 and esp. 147: it is possible but unlikely that 'predigt frue' might be read as 'sermon wife' and refers to Ottilie von Gersen, Müntzer's wife; report of Hans Zeiß, ThMA 3, 149. For Windsheim, see Engelhard, 'Rechtsrathe zu Windsheim', 27. The women were foiled, however. In Freiburg, Agatha Haimlichin, wife of the guildmaster of the vintners, moved repeatedly between the town and the peasant camp; she believed the peasants would win because they were so well armed, Scott, *Freiburg*, 215. In Kempten in Our Lady's Church, we know that a Catholic priest was hunted into the sacristy by 'the Lutheran women and men', who apparently threw stones at him and broke windows, Litz, *Die reformatorische Bilderfrage*, 211–223. Some women were apparently amongst the twenty names of rebels in the countryside around Freiburg, Scott, *Freiburg*, 211.

33. Gess, *Akten und Briefe*, vol. 2, 8. Sittich von Berlepsch described their actions as 'unpleasant actions, quite opposed to Christian order'—they prevented the prior from continuing. They were imprisoned; the final outcome is unclear. See, on this case, Kobelt-Groch, 'So waren sie in meiner Erinnerung': as Kobelt-Groch points out, Müntzer was in the Hegau at the time, so her role was independent. It was also alleged that her husband had had clothes made for her out of the liturgical vestments captured by the peasants, which would have been particularly sacrilegious. For Dettwang, Baumann, *Rothenburg* (Zweifel), 209. The women of Bütthart were said to have helped the peasant cause, one of them by getting the knights who were billeted with her drunk, offering them fresh sheets, and trying to make them unaware of danger, Fries, *Geschichte*, vol. 1, 115.

34. Rauch, *Heilbronn* IV, 198–200. There was a prehistory with Böckingen: Rohrbach, who was in a legal dispute with a cleric named Ferber, had threatened to appear with three hundred men when the case was heard at Böckingen, some later saying he had bribed them with a promise of a meal of 'duck'. (Here Rohrbach had form: an innkeeper by trade, he also tried to get the Heilbronners to go to the village of Flein just outside town to join with the peasant band in a meal of slaughtered calf, much to the council's alarm.) But the dispute with Böckingen, partly a matter of Rohrbach's own personal stake in two water meadows, may also have been more. Böckingen was subject to Heilbronn, and the cleric's insistence on his rights may have angered the Böckingers, who saw it as part of civic arrogance. And Margareta

was involved in another Bockingen saga too: the village mayor had been allegedly murdered by the Schad brothers on St Nicholas's Eve 1524, and the Heilbronn mayor, Hans Berlin, perhaps related to Bockingen's Vogt Caspar Berlin, apparently became involved in the case. Renner had housed the Schad brothers and protected them from being sent to Heilbronn, and, so said the Heilbronn council, she took 'great pleasure' in their deeds.

35. Rauch, *Heilbronn* IV, 200; this was in August 1525, so she had not been executed in the first wave of reprisals. See also Franz, *Der deutsche Bauernkrieg*, 189–190.

36. Franz and Fleischhauer, eds., *Jacob Murers Weissenauer Chronik*. The one exception is what appears to be a woman near a church, her arms raised in terror, as an armed knight approaches, image 8. See, for example, the testimony of the shepherd Valentin Sachs, who listed forty men, often 'brothers' or 'sons' from the same family, but named no women: LATh Meiningen, GHA Sekt II, Nr. 581. *An die Versammlung*, 115, 117. 'Therefore be manly, courageous and do not be shocked even if the godless army rushes against you no matter how big and strong it may be'; 'Darumb sind manlich, mutsam und unerschrocken, es komme der gotlosisch hauf, wie groß und wie starck er woelle wider euch gerauschet'.

37. Baumann, *Quellen: Chroniken*, 283.

38. AGBM 2, 186; see also AGBM 1, 118, 413, and the Heggbach chronicle.

39. Mühlhausen: Jordan, *Chronik der Stadt Mühlhausen*, vol. 1, 194 (= Müller, 'Chronicon Mulhusinum', 60). Leipheim: Baumann, *Quellen: Chroniken*, 552 (Truchsess Schreiber). A petition from a number of women from Günzburg and surrounding villages has survived, asking for their husbands to be given safe conduct and allowed to return to their families, StadtAMM, A fo. 299a, f. 67 r–v, 19 September 1525; and women interceded with Philip of Hesse, AGBM 1, 339, 459. Frankenhausen: WBr 3, Nr. 873, Johann Rühel to Luther, 21 May 1525, 504–507. Rühel comments, 'Whoever does not pity such an event is truly no human being', 'Welcher sich solches thuns nicht erbarmet, ist warlich kein Mensch', 505:18–19. Letter to Cardinal Albrecht, AGBM 2, 319, 17 May, Wolf von Schönburg.

40. AGBM 2, 347. AGBM 2, 752–754 n. 1.

41. Lettsch, *Chronik*, 46; his band established military offices very fast, as Lettsch notes. Captainships were open to people of all backgrounds and were merit-based, so peasants could gain substantial leadership experience. Xenakis, *Gewalt und Gemeinschaft*, 135–140; and for the peasants' military structures, Miller, *German Peasants' War*.

42. Reconstructions of peasant weapons can be seen in the Böblingen, Frankenhausen, and Leipheim Bauernkriegsmuseums. After the battle of Königshofen, the victors found forty-nine pieces of wheeled artillery, fifty-one 'arquebuses' (Hakebüchsen), and fifteen half-calibre firearms, Miller, *German Peasants' War*; Leng, 'Bauern vor den Mauern'. They could still produce firearms at the subsequent battles of Sulzfeld and Ingolstadt. Fries on the feudal levy, Fries, *Geschichte*, vol. 1, 20. Hoyer, *Militärwesen*, 149; and on the Wagenburg, Fronsperger, *Kriegsbuch*, vol. 2.

43. Volcyr, *L'histoire*, fos. xlvi r–xlviii r. Mutiny at Dagersheim: Blickle, *Bauernjörg*, 100–105; and after Leipheim, Baumann, *Quellen*, 550–554; and see Lutz's version of this, Lutz, *Tagebuch*, 71. Cronthal, *Stadt Würzburg*, 68, 86–87.

44. Philip of Hesse: AGBM 2, 324. Gerber: counsellors of Bishop Wilhelm of Strasbourg wrote to the Strasbourg council that Gerber's trial records, which the council had requested, did not exist, and neither were there any records of others. But 'credible Lothringers' had told them that before Gerber was hanged, he had let it be heard 'that their intention was, when they had defeated castles and towns, that they would confiscate the goods… [of the rich] and rape [*schmehen*] their women in front of their menfolk' and kill the nobles. Virck, *Strassburg*, 182. This is hardly a credible report. Baumann, *Quellen: Chroniken* (Werdensteiner Chronik), 486; and on beards, see Hanß, 'Face-Work', 314–345.

45. Von Hopfgarten: AGBM 2, 151. Rumours of rape: Tham von Herda worried that the peasants planned to take the nuns of Allendorf into their camp, and 'then without doubt they would have had their way with them', 'alsdan an zwiffel irn wilen mit in gehabt'; but his brother had prevented this, and he himself had brought the nuns of Zella to safety, AGBM 1, 351–353. Jörg Haide, a peasant leader in Sundgau, was accused of raping a noble nun, Maurer, *Bauernkrieg 1525*, 109. Ulrich Artzt wrote to the town council at Augsburg that this had been the Kitzingers' plan, Vogt, *Artzt*, 327, letter of 17 June 1525.

46. Ryhiner, 'Chronik', 501—the author was also shocked by the fact that 'many young boys, eight or ten years old', were slain. Virck, *Strassburg*, 164–165 (Alsace), for reports that women were 'geschent'; see also 174, 176. For the lords' fears, see also Richau, 'Historie von dem Auffruhr', 339: this hostile account claims that peasants of the Samland threatened to make their lord swap places with them, so that he would have to perform labour services ('scharwercken'), while the peasants would perform services 'especially to the castle women'. However, this account of Nikolaus Richau is so harsh that it is hard to attach much credence to it; see 328–357, 531–566.

47. AGBM 1, 464, 473, 521, 608–609; and StA MR, Best. 3, Nr. 1928, fo. 183v–r, 6 November 1525. Steffan Mann, a Sichelschmidt, may have had experience as a mercenary. He was considered to be a substantial and honourable man but had acted as bursar in the army; he denied this and denied being a Lutheran. He tried to get Philip of Hesse to intercede for him, but Count Wilhelm remained adamant.

48. Baumann, *Quellen: Chroniken*, 488–489 (Werdenstein). ThMA 3, 224–225: Botho von Stolberg, Heinrich von Schwarzburg XXXI, and Ernst V of Hohnstein. Eck: Franz, *Quellen*, 152.

49. 'Manfully': Ryhiner, 'Chronik', 502. Aschwin von Cramm: Luther dedicated his tract *Ob Kriegsleute auch in seligem Stande sein können*, WS 19, 623–662 (*Whether Soldiers Too Can Be Saved*, LW 46) to him. This tract reflects on the Peasants' War and justifies the role of soldiers in carrying out God's judgement.

50. The *Fähnrich* or bannerman was the key symbolic person in a battalion, and he was usually patrician or noble. Xenakis, *Gewalt und Gemeinschaft*, 60–65.

51. Rautenzweig: AGBM 2, 453.

Chapter 11: Summer

1. ThMA 2, 486–488, 489–490; see *Ein Gloubwirdig vnd warhafftig vnderricht*, fo. A iii v, and *Eyn warhafftig*, 57–94. On the battle, see Melanchthon, *Histori Thome Muntzers*, which is a work of Lutheran propaganda and purports to reproduce the speech Müntzer gave to the troops, Fischer, *Die Lutherische Pamphlete*, 35–36. For accounts of the battle, see AGBM 2, 302 (Herzog Georg to Cardinal Albrecht of Mainz), 302 (Herzog Georg, Herzog Heinrich d J, and Landgraf Philip to Elector Johann of Saxony), 305 (Philip of Hesse to Archbishop of Trier), 308 (Count Philipp von Solms to his son Reinhard), 310 (Herman Gyßen to his father). ThMA 3, 238–340, account of the later Anabaptist Hans Hut. And for detailed reconstruction, Miller, *Frankenhausen*; Hoyer, 'Die "Schlacht" bei Frankenhausen'; Hoyer, *Militär-wesen*, 155–161.

2. Johann Rühel reported the accounts of two miners, eyewitnesses according to whom Müntzer insisted that when they arrived at Heldrungen castle, the very stones would give way before them; and when the first shot of the battle fell short, he had said, 'I prophesied that no shot would harm you'. WBr 3, 875, 26 May 1525, 509–513. The *Histori Thome* claimed that Müntzer said they would catch the bullets in their sleeves. The same allegation is made in the account produced on the press of the Catholic Hieronymus Emser, who reports Müntzer as saying he personally would catch all the arrows and bullets in his sleeves, *Ein gloubwirdig vnd warhafftig vnderricht*, fo. A iii v.

3. The town chronicler Müldener in 1747 estimated 7,323 victims; others reckon about 6,000. Shortly after Müldener wrote, the archives were destroyed by fire. The total of six dead on the princes' side is probably unrealistically low. Hahnemann estimates the number of dead at no more than 7,000 with 600 taken captive, Hahnemann, 'Einwohner', 84–85. For letter to Margrave Joachim, AGBM 2, 293, 15 May. On the battle, see also AGBM 2, 308–309, account of Philip von Solms; AGBM 2, 318, account of Wolf von Schönburg; Gess, *Akten und Briefe*, vol. 2, 233 ff., report of Georg of Saxony and Philip of Hessen to Johann of Saxony. See Hoyer, 'Die "Schlacht" bei Frankenhausen'; Vogler, ed., *Bauernkrieg zwischen Harz und Thüringer Wald*; Miller, *Frankenhausen*, who has also created a series of three-dimensional models of battle scenes, including one of the Blutrinne, at Museum Frankenhausen (Stadt).

4. WBr 3, 875, 26 May 1525, 509–513; it was the letter from Albrecht of Mansfeld that gave him away—since Albrecht was unlike Ernst a Lutheran, this has an especial propagandist point. See also Melanchthon, *Histori*; Laube, *Flugschriften*, 541. The story was later embroidered by Cyriakus Spangenberg in his history, ThMA 3, 243. The house where he was found in Frankenhausen was at the Angertor, through which many of the fleeing peasants entered. It no longer exists, but there is a memorial stone.

5. Luther had little time for Count Ernst either, and gloated that he died with-out the sacrament or confession. He also told a story that when Ernst first heard Luther's hymn 'Ein fester Burg', he had retorted that he would shoot down such a

castle—only to die within three days. WT 2, 2428, 2566. For transfer of Müntzer, AGBM 2, 362, 23 May. The original castle at Schlotheim has been replaced by a charming eighteenth-century villa, oddly situated atop a castle mound and deep moat, now dry. The next day, the army moved to Görmar, the base the Mühlhausen-ers had used for their marches into the Eichsfeld.

6. See also Gess, *Akten und Briefe*, vol. 2, 398–401, 15 September 1525. Elector Johann and Philip of Hesse both wrote to Georg refusing to persecute Lutherans.

7. WBr 3, 875, 26 May 1525, 509–513, 510:12. Rühel also claimed that Müntzer had received the sacrament in one kind only before his execution, and had become 'ganz Papistisch' at the end, WBr 3, 873, 21 May 1525, 505:11. Müntzer's final letter: ThMA 2, 498; Matheson, 161. Luther: WBr 3, 877, 30 May 1525, 515–517; he writes too of 'teufelische, verharte Verstockung in seinem Furnehmen', 515:28, 516:30. By 'rechte interrogatoria', Luther means a systematic set of questions based on the evidence of testimonies and used in criminal interrogations. 'Wohlan, wer den Münzer gesehen hat, der mag sagen, er habe den Teufel leibhaftig gesehen in seinem höchsten Grimm', 516:34–35. 'O Herr Gott, wenn solcher Geist in den Bauern auch ist, wie hoche Zeit ist's, daß sie erwürget werden wie die tollen Hunde'. Agricola, *Auslegung des XIX*, Psalm. He used the manuscript that had been sent to Christoph Meinhard, which addressed Meinhard on the first page as his 'dilecto Cris. Meni', thus making Meinhard's friendship with Müntzer public; the original had been dedicated to an anonymous supporter. For Spangenberg's account, ThMA 3, 241–242.

8. ThMA 3, 254–255.

9. Endres, 'Franken', 175; Bräuer and Vogler, *Müntzer*, 379. The role of the civic secretary of Mühlhausen, Johann von Othera, is particularly interesting—he seems to have advised Pfeiffer which way to leave and then betrayed him. According to the author of *Ein gloubwirdig und warhafftig vnderricht*, the town revealed where Pfeiffer had gone as part of its surrender. Von Othera's involvement in the story of Mühl-hausen deserves investigation in its own right, for he remained in power as secretary, the town's most senior official, after the town surrendered and so was well placed to control the archives, which have been carefully redacted and purged—and can still be seen today in their seventeenth-century cupboards. I am grateful to Thomas T. Müller for discussion of Othera's role.

10. ThMA 3, 259, 263 (TR 1, 99, p. 38), 264: In June Mühlhausen had to pay the executioner to put Müntzer's head back up on display. Spangenberg wasted little ink on Pfeiffer, who did not play a central role in the Lutheran demonology. Dismiss-ing him in a few lines, Spangenberg wrote that he had not recanted and had died with-out receiving communion, like an 'unvernunfftig Bestia', an unreasoning beast. Many women at Allstedt reportedly said that those who died at Frankenhausen died 'for the sake of the Word of God', and that those who were now being executed by the electoral authorities in Saxony died 'for the sake of the princes and men', AGBM 2, 565 (report by Bernhard Walde, the new official at Allstedt who had replaced Hans Zeiß).

11. For example, Melanchthon's *Histori*; Luther, *Ein schrecklich Geschicht*, WS 18, 362–374. Eobanus Hessus also blamed Müntzer in his long Latin poem about the war, 'Bellum servile'; see Hamm, 'Traum und Zeitklage', 340–349. Friedrich Myconius's history of the Reformation blamed Thomas Müntzer, and 'one, named Schappler', Myconius, *Geschichte*, 62. He also blamed the uprising on the devil, who was trying to prevent the progress of the gospel. A Lutheran loyalist, Myconius insisted that Luther's two books against the peasantry 'accomplished more than all the princes' spears and armour'—but he was looking back from 1540; at the time, even Lutheran supporters took more mixed views.

12. AGBM 1, 420.

13. Müntzer may have been named 'the Allstedter' because his dialect sounded like that of Allstedt, which would have been different from that spoken in Mühlhausen and may even have been hard to understand. I am grateful to Thomas T. Müller for this insight. It was also a pointed reminder that Müntzer was not a local.

14. ThMA 2, 324, 413–414. On the miners, AGBM 2, 388, 391; and see Gess, *Akten und Briefe*, vol. 2, 271 (Nr. 1019), for their complaints about religion. In Joachimstal, now in the Czech Republic, and part of the Bohemian side of the Erzgebirge, the miners had formulated articles of grievance, but they concerned mining matters. In particular they were angry that coins were not being minted in Joachimstal as had been promised, but that the ore was being exported, an issue that concerned local, not supraregional, prosperity. The miners of Count Schlick rose up against him, but by 11 June the local official had succeeded in granting enough concessions to the miners that they had started work again—he had also taken care to imprison the leaders. For their *Urgichten*, see HStA Dresden, 10024, 9135/22.

15. Bubenheimer, *Thomas Müntzer: Herkunft und Bildung*, 37–40, and on Müntzer's social origins, 26–40. On Fürer, Meinhard, and others, see Bräuer and Vogler, *Müntzer*, 220–222, 303, and 396. By May 1525 at the latest, however, Meinhard seems to have returned to the Lutheran fold, WB 3, Nr. 874, 23 May 1525, p. 509. Meinhard may have been Zeiß's cousin and perhaps was related to Agricola as well, who apparently converted him back to Lutheranism, though see Bräuer, 'Hüttenmeister Christoph Meinhard', for scepticism about this. There are three surviving letters of Müntzer to Meinhard. See also on Meinhard, Vogler, 'Eisleben und Nürnberg', 57. Bubenheimer, *Müntzer: Herkunft und Bildung*, 37: Luther may well have interceded for Meinhard after the war, because in 1526 Meinhard presented him with a silver cup (*Becher*). On Hans Pelt and Müntzer's kinship with members of the Braunschweig elite, Bubenheimer, *Müntzer: Herkunft und Bildung*, 116–144; Bubenheimer shows that Müntzer was not as hostile to early capitalism as Luther. I am grateful to Andy Drummond for discussion of Meinhard.

16. Müntzer does not seem, however, to have advocated community of goods, an allegation that goes back to Melanchthon, Stengel, 'Omnia sunt communia'. On Zeiß, who knew Luther personally: the reformer had tried to persuade him in a visit in 1523 not to follow Müntzer, WBr 3, Nr. 641, 3 August 1523, 120:27–33. After

Frankenhausen, in May 1525, Luther had heard a rumour that Zeiß had been executed; he wrote to Rühel, hoping it was not true, WBr 3, 877, 30 May 1525, 516:42. Luther apparently wrote to Johann Friedrich, son of the Saxon elector Johann, to intercede for Zeiß on 5 June, WBr 3, Nr. 885, 5 June 1525, 524–525. Zeiß probably played a double game, supporting the electoral administration as a good official while sympathising with Müntzer; see Chapter 5, note 16, of this book.

17. Lupstein: Virck, *Urkunden und Akten der Stadt Strassburg* (hereafter *Strassburg*), 163. The soldiers had dragged women into the cornfields and 'geschent' (raped) them, doing 'dermossen stuck mit Weibern', also 'dasz die armen wiber nit wissen wonus', Virck *Strassburg*, 164–165, 175; Bischoff, *La guerre*, 341–359.

18. Virck, *Strassburg*, 160–161, doc. 285, 286, 287. The army at Stechsfeld also argued that Anton of Lothringen was a foreign power, and they wanted help from Strasbourg to support their 'vaterland', 162.

19. Virck, *Strassburg*, 177, 179, 24 May 1525: those surrendering had processed out of town holding white sticks, as was customary to indicate surrender. The writer thought twenty thousand had been slaughtered. Volcyr thought twenty-two thousand, Volcyr, *L'histoire*, fo. lii (r) (ch. 18). Rathgeber, *Herrschaft Rappoltstein*, 89. On the slaughter: Virck, *Strassburg*, 164–165, 166–167, 172–173, 179, 182–183.

20. Even so, perhaps three thousand or four thousand peasants were slain, Virck, *Strassburg*, 177. They had taken advantageous positions, and the mounted men could not get at them. Estimates of the size of the peasant forces varied between ten thousand and sixteen thousand. Estimates of the total killed vary between seven thousand and thirty-eight thousand; the generally accepted figure is twenty-five thousand. See Bischoff, *La guerre*, 341–358; Miller, *The German Peasants' War*. On 20 May, battle was joined at Scherwiler near Dambach, below the castles of Ramstein and Ortenbourg, where between six thousand and thirteen thousand peasants were slaughtered; here some of the Dambach townsfolk supported the peasants and let them into town, Fischer, 'Documents relatifs à la guerre', 133–150, 144. Thirty-nine were named as supporters of the peasants, thirteen of whom had died in the battle; Bischoff, *La guerre*, 344. Pastor Guggi: Kessler, *Sabbata*, 184. Only the Sundgau army managed to evade destruction, trying eventually under Heinrich Wetzel to join the Swiss, and finally submitting to the lords on 24 September without conditions.

21. Lutz, *Tagebuch*, 81–83.

22. Lettsch, *Chronik*, 49. See, on the siege, Hoyer, *Militärwesen*, 165–168. Müller also diverted the town's river, cutting off its water supply and removing power from its mills, which was needed to grind grain for bread, Scott, *Freiburg*, 208. See also Schreiber, *Der deutsche Bauernkrieg*, vol. 2, January to July 1525, 113, 118, 120: Müller wrote to Freiburg, calling on them to accept 'our brotherhood', 'unser Brüderschaft', and saying that they wanted only what was in 'the word of God and the holy gospel', 'das Gotzwort und das Heilig Evangelium'.

23. Hug, *Villinger Chronik*, 122. Lettsch, *Chronik*, 49.

24. Scott, 'Reformation and Peasants' War in Waldshut and Environs', 46.

25. 'Dass man in uf stangen erhöchte,...und der hl. Geist redte scheinberlich uß im', Heggbach Chronik, Baumann, *Quellen: Chroniken*, 281; see Ulbrich, 'Oberschwaben und Württemberg', 106.

26. He may, however, have left early. Christopf Schultheiss's Constanzer Collectaneen says that his departure precipitated the collapse of the peasants' siege; they were tired after six weeks and needed to return to harvest. Baumann, *Quellen: Chroniken*, 521.

27. Baumann, *Quellen: Chroniken,* 606; and see Scott, 'Freiburger Talvogtei'.

28. Hug, *Villinger Chronik*, 123. The tactic of burning villages was widely used by the lords. Count Ernst of Mansfeld burnt two rebellious villages on 12 May, Gess, *Akten und Briefe*, vol. 2, 225. For Rohrbach: Nicolaus Thomann, 'Weissenhorn Historie', 109; Lutz, *Tagebuch*, 83, 84.

29. Fries, *Geschichte*, vol. 1, 313 ff. (Königshofen), 321–325 (Ingolstadt), 152–156 (report of Hans Fridell, Königshofen). Endres, 'Franken'.

30. Fries, *Geschichte*, vol. 1, 287; the Bruchsal story is also told by Peter Harer. Ingolstadt: Fries, *Geschichte*, vol. 1, 325. Merx, 'Beiträge zur Geschichte' (report of Hans Fridell, Königshofen, 152–156).

31. Cronthal, *Stadt Würzburg*, 84–93. The artist Tilman Riemenschneider was amongst a group who were held in the coal storeroom of the castle. He was so badly tortured that it is said he was unable to work again.

32. On street chains, Garrioch, 'Sounds of the City': the chains could also have prevented unwanted cavalrymen riding through the streets. Between 20 June and mid-August, the bishop of Würzburg and his officials processed around his territory, executing the ringleaders; 186 individuals are listed in the record of the tour of retribution. The chronicler Lorenz Fries, who worked for the bishop, accompanied many of these expeditions. The memory of the daily executions may well have led him to write his three-volume chronicle of the war. See StA WÜ, Standbücher 903, fos. 76 r–91 v. Many were people of consequence in their communities: council members and the like. No women are listed. At Münnerstadt, the bishop had been preceded by Wilhelm of Henneberg, who had executed twenty-two people; the bishop's men decapitated another twelve.

33. Some reports say sixty, some fifty-eight. See Böhm, 'Kitzingen' (Sebald Ranft), 101–102, who lists them all by name, as does Hammer (in Cronthal, *Stadt Würzburg*, 151–152). The drummer and the piper were both punished 'in the face'; that is, their eyes were put out. Michael Gross von Trockau, commander of Casimir's infantry, provides a long description of the campaign of revenge, Gross von Trockau, 'Kurtzer Bericht', 113–116, 137–140.

34. Marx Halbritter describes how the Bamberg councillors made a personal visit to the bishop, weeping and falling on their knees and begging him to remove a passage in the treaty of their surrender that offended their honour, for if it were not expunged they would never be able to employ honourable apprentices, and so on. The bishop listened to their request on his own. This long set-piece passage describes

the event in detail, reproducing what everyone said, describing their kneeling posture and their bitter tears, as if the narrative itself restored their honour, salvaging a victory out of their comprehensive defeat: Chroust, *Chroniken*, vol. 2, 78–92. It did not, of course, remove the fines.

35. Baumann, *Quellen: Chroniken* (Johann Knebel), 257.

36. Report of Michael Gross von Trockau, captain of Markgräfl. Infantry, 'Kurtzer Bericht', NF 3, nos. 4 to 6, no. 6, 139: he describes him as a pious, learned monk.

37. In Thuringia and Saxony, beheadings were typical. At Arnstadt, nine leaders were executed on the marketplace, and in Rudolstadt the same happened, Sladeczek, 'Mächtige Aufrührer', 239. In Mühlhausen, fifty were executed and many fined or exiled, Schloms, 'Nach dem Ende', who establishes who exactly was punished. For the area around Uberlingen, Göpfert, *Bauernkrieg am Bodensee und Oberrhein*, 77–79, from a seventeenth-century chronicle transcribed in the eighteenth century. For Weißenburg, see Alter, *Aufstand*, 104: nine were executed on the marketplace on 8 July, while two had fingers chopped off. The master of the Teutonic Order at Mergentheim employed an executioner for a period of three months, supplying him with a waggonload of wood, a small house, a fee of five Gulden, and an undershirt, as well as the clothes and personal possessions of those he executed, Oechsle, *Beiträge zur Geschichte*, 228. It was said that Wilhelm of Henneberg executed so many of his subjects that in one village, only two brickmakers escaped execution. One of them, who cried on the way to execution, was asked why, and responded that if he died, the brickworks wouldn't work properly, so he was freed. The other, who laughed, said he was laughing because if they cut his head off, he wouldn't know where to put his hat; he was also freed. The anecdote is another example of the kind of grisly humour that circulated about the Peasants' War executions, Güthe, *Chronica Meiningen*.

38. Stumpf, *Schweizer- und Reformationschronik*, 262.

39. Peasants to Strasbourg council: Virck, *Strassburg*, 170, 17 May 1525. For Pfeddersheim, Baumann, *Quellen: Chroniken*, 120–121 (Nicolaus Thomann); Alter, *Pfeddersheim*, 255–263; Harer, *Berichte*. Alter shows that the support for the peasants came from a large area north of Pfeddersheim with known representatives of thirty-two different places.

40. Franz and Fleischhauer, eds., *Jacob Murers Weissenauer Chronik*, vol. 1, image 11. Franz, *Der deutsche Bauernkrieg, Aktenband*, 386; he was writing to Georg of Saxony.

41. Hipler: Rauch, *Urkundenbuch der Stadt Heilbronn*, vol. 4 (hereafter *Heilbronn* IV), 310. Baumann, *Akten*, 298–299. Georg of Wertheim, who interceded for Götz, was Truchsess Georg's 'Schwager' brother-in-law. It is striking that Humpis, Hurlewagen, and Ziegelmüller, all noble or socially upper strata from the Lake Constance band, were not punished, and their careers even advanced after the war. This was partly because they had signed the Weingarten treaty and secured peace, but it also reflected the fact that elite rebels were more likely to escape unpunished, Kuhn, 'Seehaufen', 126.

42. A song from the same printer using the same cover in reverse mocked the peasants as drunkards, while another accused them of having drunk the cellars of Ochsenfurt dry. See VD 16, ZV 11084, ZV 11605, ZV 11616. All three, and another by Fritz Becker in manuscript only (Gropp, *Wirtzburgische Chronick*, 142–168), concern the Würzburg garrison and its survival of the peasant onslaught. The description of their success by Rotenhan, the commander, also helped make the event a heroic episode, so far as the lords were concerned. The songs that survive do not reflect peasant views. Brunner, 'Von uppiglichen dingen'; Strobach, 'Die Bauern sind aufrührig worden'.

43. Hug, *Villinger Chronik*, 129; next day they slaughtered four more.

44. Hug, *Villinger Chronik*, 130–135. Meanwhile, the Black Forest peasants tried to take Zell but were finally defeated on 1 and 2 July at Hiltzingen, ending the Hegau uprising. On 12 July the Stühlinger and Fürstenberger peasants had to accept similar terms to those of the Hegau peasants. Near Mühlhausen at the height of the war, Hans von Berlepsch also became involved in an animal-rustling feud, Müller, *Mörder ohne Opfer*, 407–414. For similar revenge attacks on villages after the Eichsfeldzug, see Müller, *Bauernkrieg nach dem Bauernkrieg*.

45. Hug, *Villinger Chronik*, 130–133.

Chapter 12: Aftermath

1. Müntzer's final letters are signed 'with the sword of Gideon', a reference to the Old Testament. On whether there was an actual sword, and on the sword supposedly used by Müntzer at the battle with runic characters, see Müller, 'Thomas Müntzers Runenschwert'. 'A Judgement': WS 18, 362–374, 368:29, 371:10–15. On the history of the copies of Müntzer's letters which Luther printed, see Vogler, *Thomas Müntzer und die Gesellschaft seiner Zeit*, 141–143, and on the history of the edition of Müntzer's works and on the image of Müntzer, Vogler, *Müntzerbild*. Johannes Agricola, a Lutheran loyalist, rushed out a condemnation of Müntzer through a dialogue between a Müntzerite and an 'evangelical pious peasant', *Ein nützlicher Dialogus*. This work repurposed the evangelical peasant, using him to undermine Müntzer's claims. Tom Scott has argued that the pamphlet nonetheless contains useful biographical information about Müntzer, *The Early Reformation*, 227–245. For Luther's final condemnations of Müntzer, WBr 3, No. 877, 30 May 1525, 516:34–37. And in *Ein Sendbrief*, WS 18, 375–401, ostensibly a clarification and modification of *Against the Robbing, Murdering Hordes*, but even harsher, he called those who wanted the rebels not to be punished 'blood hounds', 'bluthunde', and repeated his words: 'Therefore as I wrote then I still write now: no-one should have pity for the stiff-necked, obstinate, blinded peasants, who would not let themselves be told, but hit, stab, choke and slay them, get in there everyone as if you were dealing with mad dogs, whoever and however you can', WS 18, 392:22–25.

2. Karlstadt's visit to the peasants became public knowledge, see Baumann, *Quellen zur Geschichte des Bauernkrieges aus Rotenburg an der Tauber. [sic] (Chronik Thomas Zweifel)* (hereafter *Rothenburg*), 368. He argued for nonviolence, or so he claimed, a position which isolated him from the peasants and rebels. Joestel, 'Karlstadt und der

Bauernkrieg in Ostthüringen'. Karlstadt's version of what happened, Furcha, *Essential Carlstadt*, 382; Karlstadt, *Entschuldigung*, fo. B (i) (r). The petition against Karlstadt had been started by a group who went from house to house gaining signatories; Stefan von Menzingen then did the same, asking people to support Karlstadt, Baumann, *Rothenburg* (Zweifel), 374; petition 371–374. For Karlstadt's departure, Baumann, *Rothenburg* (Zweifel), 523. Georg Truchsess, for one, was looking for him, asking the authorities in Rothenburg on 23 June to imprison him if they found him. Teuschlin and Herr Hans, 'the blind monk', were executed in Rothenburg on 23 June, but Karlstadt and others escaped, and 'were not to be seen for dust', according to Michael Eisenhart's chronicle, Baumann, *Rothenburg*, 607.

3. He wrote on 12 June asking Luther to intercede with the elector for the sake of his wife and child. Asking for forgiveness, he said he had decided not to preach, write, or teach anything further, WBr 3, 889, pp. 529–530. WS 18, 436–438; 453–454, for the two prefaces by Luther. Karlstadt promised that in the future, only those writings published with the letters *H.G.B.B.M.* ('God help and keep me') on the first page and printed at Wittenberg were genuine. This effectively put him back under Luther's censorship and control. Whether he meant it or not, it looked as if the motto also meant 'this is how I saved my own skin'—certainly, no further pamphlets by Karlstadt were ever printed in Wittenberg, with or without the acronym. See also Nelson Burnett, *Karlstadt and the Origins of the Eucharistic Controversy*.

4. Roper, *Luther*, 517 n.13; earlier he had chosen Johann Rühel, the official of the Mansfeld counts, and Johann Riedesel, a high-ranking Saxon administrator, as friends and confidantes. Praising Albrecht as the first to put on armour probably referred to his brutal massacre of peasants at Osterhausen, for which the army at Frankenhausen wanted revenge, WS 19, 279.

5. WBr 3, Nr. 875, 26 May 1525, 511:64–69. It is interesting that Rühel repeats the allegation that 'you fear for your skin'.

6. Capito's letter to Kniebis, Greschat, *Bucer*, 66–67; Franz, *Der deutsche Bauernkrieg, Aktenband* (hereafter *Akten*), 384, letter of 5 August 1525 to Albrecht von Preussen. See also the pamphlet sermon *Ain demütige, brüderliche, vnnd Christliche Suplication*, by the preacher Arnold Fesser, who called on the princes who had defeated the peasants to show mercy, and reminded them that God could put down the mighty from their seats. He also stressed that many an honest peasant had been 'forced' ('getzwungen') to join the evil peasants ('böse'), VD 16 F 803, fo. A iv v. Brenz, *Von Milderung*; and see Oechsle, *Beiträge zur Geschichte*, Heilbronn 1830, 444–448.

7. For Fugger's view, Franz, *Akten*, 385, 16 October 1525, Jacob Fugger to Jorigen Hegel; and blaming Luther, Fugger to Duke Georg, Gess, *Akten und Briefe*, vol. 2, 333–334. Margrave Casimir of Brandenburg-Ansbach also blamed the preachers, *Anzeigen, wie die gewesen Empörung*, 4. Johannes Fabri's comments were published as a commentary on the letters of Wolfgang Capito to Zwingli, which Fabri had seized and published, Capito, *Correspondence*, vol. 2, 214; Fabri, *Neüwe Zeitung*, fo. B 1 (v). Other Catholic opponents made the same case, one they had been making long

before the war. The Catholic Hieronymus Emser, the 'goat', as Luther dubbed him, issued a long rhyming poem blaming the Lutherans, *Der Bock tritt frei auf diesen Plan*. Another rhyming pamphlet issued some time after 1527 blamed Luther; it was complete with woodcuts showing Luther as the devil tempting a woman and as a fool in the garden of Eden, *Eyn warhafftig erschröcklich Histori*. It is interesting how much antipeasant commentary after the war is in the form of verse or song. Georg von Werdenstein includes this melancholy rhyme in his chronicle: 'Such an end met the Peasants' War in the Summer, / in Allgäu that is true, / they are left with neither skin nor hair, / and it did not go well for them. / They lost their bodies and lives, / this is not false, but true, / in 26 Year' ('Ein sollich end hat genumen / Der pawren krieg in der sumen / Im Allgew, das ist war. / Iren ist weder haut, noch, har, / Und inen ubel gelungen, / Sind von leib und leben kumen, / ist nit erlogen, sunder war, / Im 26 jar'). Baumann, *Quellen: Chroniken*, 490.

8. WS 19, 1–43, *Das Papstthum mit seinen Gliedern*, 1526: the verses may have been written by Hans Sachs, and the woodcuts are possibly from the Cranach workshop; fifty-eight different orders are shown, each with an individual woodcut. Luther's conclusion warns that since the defeat of the peasants, the monks had been trying to regain their position and recover from the 'slap in the face' (*schlappen*) they had been given by the peasants, but if they don't want to truly convert, and realise how their 'diabolic way of life should be praised', we should help them, 'and give the dirt a good stirring, which would love to stink, until they get a mouthful and a noseful of it' ('und den dreck, der so gerne stincken wollt, weydlich ruren, bis sie das maul und nasen vol kriegen'), WS 19, 43:10–15. Here Luther is very aware that the Peasants' War had indeed inflicted a serious blow on monasticism. His resort to irony and excremental rhetoric is typical of his style. Because the monks are 'limbs of the Pope' and thus of the devil, they must be countered with excremental stink. No copy of the 1526 Wittenberg edition survives, but there was a Nuremberg edition of 1526 with pictures by Hans Guldenmund. It was reprinted at Wittenberg in the second half of the sixteenth century with different woodcuts and additional pictures, including one of the 'Indian' order. Luther on authority, October 1525, WS 16, 488: 20–21; see also Zapalac, *'In His Image and Likeness'*, 151–152. On the Lutheran church and resistance: there were many in the church who resisted Nazism, and there was also a strong Lutheran tradition of opposition to the regime in East Germany.

9. See Wunder, 'Der samländische Bauernaufstand von 1525'; Wunder, 'Zur Mentalität aufständischer Bauern'; Carsten, 'Der Bauernkrieg in Ostpreussen', which relies heavily on Nikolaus Richau's chronicle; and Hubatsch, 'Albert of Brandenburg-Ansbach'. This late revolt has many interesting features. Mainly directed against the nobility, it involved ethnic, linguistic, and status differences; there were German and 'Prussian' peasants who had less land and fewer legal rights and who had their own villages and organisations, but these lacked the privileges of the German ones. The German and Prussian populations were not fully Christianised. There seems to have been a group of mercenary soldier leaders who had established themselves, and against whom the revolt may also have been directed. Lutheran preaching in

Königsberg apparently played a part in radicalising the leader, the miller Kaspar von Kaymen; but this only explains the German involvement. We do not know the ethnic composition of the peasant armies, and whether German and Prussian peasants fought alongside each other. It seems the rebels were mostly loyal to Duke Albrecht of Prussia. Günther Franz believed that the revolt had little to do with the Peasants' War. However, it revealed the weakness of the Teutonic Knights, recently secularised, and suggests that their values of military honour and loyalty may have been under stress. In the aftermath of the revolt, conditions for the peasants were worsened; the status of free peasants was undermined and regulations increased.

10. Waldshut sent weapons to support the Griesseners, but the opponents drew up their formation in such a way that the shot went too far and failed to hit. The peasants panicked and fled to the village; five hundred were killed, and the fighting continued into the night. Hug, *Villinger Chronik*, 149. Bergsten, *Balthasar Hubmaier*, 273–297; Hubmaier, *Schriften*, 27–34.

11. Kessler, *Sabbata*, 150–151; TA Zurich, 148–149, for his December recantation, where he insisted that he had not rejected authority or argued that Christians could not serve 'in der obrigkeit'; nor had he argued that all things should be held in common, only that alms should be given to one's neighbour; and he had not been the first to be rebaptised even in Waldshut. See also TA Zurich, 193–197, interrogation of 4 April 1526; undated fragment after 5 January 1525, 390–393, explains that he did not know what made him deviate from his intention of reading out his recantation. See Potter, *Zwingli*, 186.

12. Fabri, *Ursache*. This accuses him primarily of fomenting rebellion. Hubmaier's place within Anabaptism remains contested because he was not a pacifist and did not believe in separation from the world.

13. Fabri, *Ursache*, fo. B I (r–v). Nikolsburg: Bergsten, *Hubmaier*, 370–377. So when Hubmaier wanted to make his new faith public, he dedicated his tract to the residents of Regensburg and Ingolstadt, where he had formerly been an orthodox Catholic preacher, and of Friedberg, the small town near Augsburg where he had been born. He also published his eighteen points in conjunction with Nicolas Prugner at Mulhouse.

14. Hug, *Villinger Chronik*, 149–150.

15. Baumann, *Quellen: Chroniken* (Heggbach), 292. Hug, *Villinger Chronik*, 151. Teuschlin: Gross von Trockau, 'Kurtzer Bericht' (NF 6), 138; Maurer, *Prediger*, 488–489; the bodies remained unburied on the marketplace all day. Baumann, *Rothenburg* (Eisenhart), 609, who says they died without the sacrament and without confessing, and remarks, 'O Deus!' Allstedt: AGBM 2, 565.

16. Zwick, *Geschrifft Doctor Johanns*, fo. B I (r); Zwick was a patrician from Constance who had been given the benefice as a child by his uncle, who had held it; he was converted by Zwingli and married. Johannes Schwanhauser, *Ain Trostbrief*, fo. A iii r. Schwanhauser had not taken the side of the rebels and he admonished his flock to remain true to their faith, and not be distracted by the Catholics with their Maria of Regensburg. For his views in 1523, Johannes Schwanhauser, *Ein Sermon*.

He argued then that the New Testament speaks of living saints, not of dead ones; but that we leave the poor 'without houses, suffering all evils like frost, hunger, thirst and sickness', fo. B iv v. This is, however, the only point where he mentions the poor, so the extent to which he took a social critical line was limited. The pamphlet was published in several editions in Bamberg and Augsburg. Lotzer: Kessler, *Sabbata*, 176.

17. Franz, *Der deutsche Bauernkrieg*, vol. 1, 'wehrfähige Mannschaft' (299–300). Even in his edition of 1969, Franz left unchanged his sentence from the 1933 edition that said, 'Thus the Peasants' War was also a huge loss in biological respects for our entire Volk' ('Der Bauernkrieg bildete daher auch in biologischer Hinsicht einen ungemein schweren Verlust für unser gesamtes Volk').

For other estimates, see Blickle, *Bauernjörg*, 292–296: he estimated a total of 20,700 killed by the army of the Swabian League in battles only, a figure which excludes most of the regions of the war; Georges Bischoff, *La guerre des paysans*, estimates between 16,000 and 20,000, maybe even 30,000, for Alsace alone, 341, 344. For contemporary estimates: Baumann, *Quellen: Chroniken* (Ambrosius Geyer), 747, over 100,000; Baumann, *Quellen: Chroniken* (Johannes Cochlaeus), 795, 100,000 by the soldiers of the Swabian League alone—Cochlaeus attempts to provide systematic figures for all battles; Fabri, *Neüwe Zeitung*, fo. A ii (r), 'ob', 100,000.

18. There may have been other forms of commemoration, and we glimpse one in reports that peasants from Mergentheim and surrounding areas were meeting on the battlefield at Königshofen; the master of the Teutonic Order forbade such assemblies. They had passwords, too, like the participants in the Poor Conrad revolt: on entering a tavern they would say 'Was leit dir an?' to which the answer was 'Das dir anleit, ligt mir auch an'. Oechsle, *Beiträge zur Geschichte*, 243.

19. AGBM 2, 347, issued from the military camp at Schlotheim. Casimir: Endres, 'Franken', 152–153, 175; Sea, 'Economic Impact'; Falk, 'Strafgeldregister', 126–133; Straube, 'Strafgeldregister, Türkensteuerregister und Amtserbbücher', who tries to conclude direct participation in the war from the fines, and for the fines, see 281–284. For fines in the bishoprics of Trier and Mainz and the Palatinate, Kraus, 'Beiträge', 92–96. For fines levied by more than one ruler on Frankenhausen, see Hahnemann, 'Einwohner'. The Swabian League continued armed patrols, Sea, 'Schwäbischer Bund'.

20. At the town of Schweinfurt, every house had to pay a ransom of seven fl; at Hassfurt, Zeil, Hollfeld, and Schesslitz all had to pay damages and swear an oath of loyalty to their ruler. For the executions in the bishopric of Würzburg, StA WÜ Standbücher 903, fo. Lxxvi ff.

21. StadtA Bamberg, D3, 652, 654. See also Hasselbeck, *Folgen des Deutschen Bauernkriegs im Hochstift Bamberg*.

22. On reprisals in southern Germany, see Sea, 'Schwäbischer Bund'; Sea, 'Swabian League and the German Peasants' War', 662–746; Sea, 'Economic Impact'. The Strasbourg officials suggested comparatively mild punishments: Dettweiler, 200 fl for a village of sixty households, excluding those who had been widows before the revolt; Dossenheim, with seventy households, was assessed at the same amount even though

they had mostly not joined. Ittenheim and Handschuhheim, because of their poverty, were assessed at 100 fl even though some had joined out of free will. In Schiltigheim, four had joined of their own free will, of whom two had been killed, so the men were fined at ten fl and their widows at six fl. In another two villages, the guilty had to collectively pay fines of over 6 per cent of their total assessed assets. Virck, *Urkunden und Akten der Stadt Strassburg* (hereafter *Strassburg*), 193. For Thuringia and fines, see Straube, 'Strafgeldregister'. Duke Georg of Saxony even threatened the mayor of Bautzen, whose name was Müntzer, with punishment if the town did not return to the old faith; while he accepted that kinship did not mean guilt, he did think the town had been sympathetic to Müntzer, Gess, *Akten und Briefe*, vol. 2, 395. Kuntz Jehle: Buszello, 'Oberrheinlande'; Lettsch, *Chronik*, 50–52, who says that the monastery had lost all its doors and windows by this time. There was ongoing bitter hostility to the abbey of St Blasius; that April the abbot had attempted to move some relics to get them out of danger, but as he passed Waldshut with them, he was attacked.

23. Matern Feuerbacher, NDB (Günther Franz); Maurer, *Bauernkrieg 1525*, 112. Eitelhanns Ziegelmüller and other leaders of the Lake Constance band who signed the truce of Weingarten were, however, able to resume their former lives, and even prospered; indeed Ziegelmüller ended up working for the truchsess, Brun, *Abbot and His Peasants*, 119–120. In Heilbronn, Hans Müller, known as Flux, argued that he had acted with the support of the whole council. The case rumbled on until 1531, and in the end, the council simply fined him 100 fl. Sea, 'Schwäbischer Bund', 145. In Alsace, Eckart Wigersheim, who had fought with the peasants at the battle of Scherwiller, where thousands were killed, and who wrote a report about it, became vogt of Bergheim, Pfister, *La guerre des paysans*, 27. A 'Blood Book' from Kempten lists 173 peasants who rebelled or led people. Some of them were executed; only 80 of those listed were working on their farms a year later, 'Jorg Schmid', NDB (Nelly Ritter). A document from Königshofen sheds light on what damage the absence of farmers like these left in their communities: their creditors were left unpaid, those who stood bail for them had responsibilities they could not meet, wives were left alone on farms without their menfolk, StA WÜ, Gericht Königshofen, 290.

24. StA Sigmaringen, Dep. 30/12 T 4 (Marchtal: Akten), Nr. 44, Alleshausen: Prozessakten zwischen Marchtal und Alleshausen mit Brasenberg; 1 Band, 1528–1532, certified eighteenth-century copy of the original.

25. Tyrol: Blickle, 'Alpenländer', 211. Many tried to profit by seizing property that had belonged to those accused of involvement in the revolt or inflating the value of what had been destroyed, see Cronthal, *Stadt Würzburg*, 110–115; Ocker, 'After the Peasant's War'. On Otthera, Müller, *Mörder ohne Opfer*, 425–427, 495; Rauch, *Urkundenbuch der Stadt Heilbronn*, vol. 4. So also, Sebald Ranft's chronicle of Kitzingen tries to present the town as a victim and does not include incriminating documents; Ranft was civic secretary.

There is some evidence that the war brought about some easing of the feudal system, but it is hard to be certain how extensive or long-lasting this was. For example, in the village of Rötenbach, villagers succeeded in getting the ban on marriages outside the lordship reduced to a fixed fine of four fl for women and three fl for men (but they did not get rid of the fines); you could buy yourself out of serfdom, whereas before the lord had to agree to allow someone to leave; death duties were reduced. But this was not abolition of serfdom. In Kempten there was also some relaxation but not abolition of serfdom or of marriage restrictions, Rudolf, 'Weingartener Vertrag', 231–232. For Mainz, Höbelheinrich, *Die neun Städte des Mainzer Oberstifts*, 129–138.

26. Baumann, *Akten*, 404–409.

27. Laube, *Flugschriften*, 139–143; Schweyger, *Chronik der Stadt Hall*, 87–88; Stella, *La rivoluzione*, and text of the ordinance, 184–194, with Italian translation. Gaismair would eventually be assassinated in Padua in 1532; the Austrians had put a bounty on his head. On Gaismair, see esp. Bücking, *Michael Gaismair*.

28. Smith, 'Dürer's Losses'. The shape of the water suggests that Dürer must have seen the pamphlet by Leonhard Reynmann, *Practica*, Nuremberg 1523 (image 1.9), which shows the flood predicted for 1524. The woodcut shows a piper and drummer in the background, suggesting conflict. The faces of the individual peasants are individual and well realised. In particular, the shower of rain and the deluged houses are reminiscent of elements of Dürer's dream.

29. On the origins of the argument that evangelical preaching would cause unrest, see Oberman, 'The Gospel of Social Unrest'.

30. Albrecht Dürer, *The Dream*, 1525, Vienna, Kunsthistorisches Museum. I am grateful to Katja Schmitz-von Ledebur of the Kunstkammer, Kunsthistorisches Museum Wien, and Christof Metzger, Albertina, Vienna, for allowing me to view the image, and for discussions of it. I have also learnt a great deal from Jenny Spinks. See also Ashcroft, *Dürer*, vol. 2, 767–768, for an interpretation and an English translation of the German text. For a brilliant interpretation of both the dream and the monument, see Greenblatt, *Learning to Curse*, 99–130. Greenblatt challenges us to see not only the 'ironic dissent'; 'the difficult task is to perceive the celebration of order' (110). However, Greenblatt himself points out the similarities in the pose of the peasant to Christ in distress, and he may underestimate the extent of unease over the defeat and slaughter of the peasants amongst contemporaries. In fact, the monument to the peasants follows a passage in which Dürer describes how to make a monument to a victory over a major foe and how to stack it with weapons and armour; the monument to the peasants is of course not to victory over a powerful foe, and the items in the monument are not weapons but peaceable agricultural produce, Dürer, *Unterweisung der Messung*, fo. H iv–J; fo. J I (r–v) for monument to the peasants. The next monument he proposes (fo. J I r) is to a 'truncken boltz', suggesting that the grave display a beer barrel and a playing board covering it and so on, including an upended beer glass; and see fo. J ii r for the design, also inscribed with the date 1525. This may be a reference to the barrel of Ebersbach, which the peasants could not drink dry. The sequence certainly suggests that the monument to the Peasants' War is ironically intended. On the dream, see also Hamm, 'Traum und Zeitklage', who understands the work as a subjective response to the Peasants' War; and Bredekamp, 'Wasserangst

und Wasserfreude'. There was reputed to be sympathy for the peasants amongst the Nuremberg populace, and 136 people did not appear for the oath-swearing that summer, and so were regarded as potential supporters, though punishments for actual involvement were light. Nuremberg officials had acted as mediators between peasants and rulers in the wider region. Wüst, 'Bauernkrieg', 189–190; and Foister and Brink, *Dürer's Journeys*.

31. Ashcroft, *Dürer*, vol. 2, 774–789. Perhaps another coincidence is that in the section on how to write in larger script on a tower so that the top line can be easily seen from below, Dürer uses 'Das W. Gotes Bleibt Ewiglich Dis Wort ist Cristvs Aller Crist glavbigen heil' as his sample text. Ashcroft argues that this statement of faith aligns him with Philip of Hesse and Elector Johann of Saxony, who wore 'VDMIAE' on their sleeves when they attended the Diet of Speyer, (1526), proclaiming their faith. With this choice, Ashcroft claims, Dürer was therefore distancing himself from the heresies of the Beham brothers and Georg Pencz, who had been tried for their unorthodox beliefs in November 1524 (789). However, this was the motto that the peasants had made famous, and it is more likely that in 1525 this was what Dürer had in mind. Fo. K I (r) for the tower. On images of the war from the sixteenth century and later, see Jürgen von Ahn, 'Schubladendenken'.

32. On its position, see Lühmann-Schmid, 'Der Mainzer Marktbrunnen'. As a result of the citizens' revolt, the authorities had to accept the rebels' thirty-one articles, which they rescinded when the revolt was over, Struck, 'Mittelrhein', 187. There had also been unrest in the town of Mainz itself, directed against the cathedral clergy in particular. By November, the cathedral was trying to reverse these measures. Otthein Rammstedt, 'Stadtunruhen 1525'. I am grateful to Johannes Paulmann for showing me this fountain. It is one of a number of works that deal with the legacy of the Peasants' War. See also Vogler, ed., *Bauernkrieg*, 425–427. I am currently writing a book on cultures of commemoration in the Peasants' War, including hidden contemporary monuments.

33. On Friedrich's death, Ludolphy, *Friedrich der Weise*, 483. On Schütz Zell, see McKee, *Schütz Zell*; on the pamphleteer Argula von Grumbach, see Matheson, *Argula von Grumbach*; and on lay pamphleteers, see Russell, *Lay Theology*.

34. For example, the peasants of Rötteln, Sausenberg, and Badenweiler got the death tax and marriage fines removed, 12 September 1525, Buszello, 'Oberrheinlande', 77, but it is not known for sure that this persisted, and the much more important demands for free movement and abolition of serfdom were rejected. The Renchener treaty of 25 May for the northern Ortenau is cited by Buszello as an example of a treaty that was based on the Twelve Articles, and thus suggests that a negotiated settlement was possible, 78–79. We do not, however, know for certain that it was maintained. For a more positive view of the achievements, see Blickle, *Der Deutsche Bauernkrieg*, 103–126. See Schulze, *Bäuerlicher Widerstand*, and Robisheaux, 'Peasant Revolts', for the view that resistance continued and was expressed after the Peasants' War in legal cases. There are also many examples of what Scott might term resistance, even public stubbornness. For instance, some of Georg Werdensteiner's

peasants simply left, and he found two 'absagbriefe' on his gate ('Tor'), Baumann, *Quellen: Chroniken*, 490. Belouschek, Dick, and Laufs, eds., *Die Reichskammergerichtsordnung von 1555*, 175, 178. Those so entitled in relation to taking back possession of goods include 'his own subjects, living under himself, be they clerical or lay, noble or not', 'seiner eigen underthanen, under ihme selbst gesessen, er were geystlich oder weltlich, vom adel oder nit vom adel' (178), but in general the wording does not specifically refer to peasants. P. 132, s. 15. refers to the power to call together 'ein gemein' in a town or village (1, s. 15) in a case concerning a whole 'gemeyn', and the ordinance does envisage cases involving a *Fürst, oberkeit*, or '*commun*', in town or country. For ongoing resistance and poaching, Schindler, 'Der "Lange Atem" der bäuerlichen Empörung'; Schindler, *Wilderer*. On Anabaptism, Hill, *Baptism, Brotherhood, and Belief.*

35. On Prussia, Hagen, *Ordinary Prussians*. Sabean, *Landbesitz*; Robisheaux, *Rural Society*; Sreenivasan, *Peasants of Ottobeuren*; Brun, *Abbot and His Peasants*; Bumiller, 'Hilzingen'. Robisheaux, *Rural Society*, also points to the importance of age, as older men gained power over younger ones.

36. Roper, 'Witchcraft and Village Drama' (on the Swabian dialect poet Sebastian Sailer). On Lutheran culture, Hill, 'Making Lutherans'; and 'Fun and Loathing'. The exception here is the Pietist tradition in Swabia; see Medick, *Weben und Überleben in Laichingen*.

37. Franz, *Akten*, 372, 1525 after 26 May; the piece of leather was of course a Bundschuh.

Conclusion

1. Chroust, *Chroniken*, vol. 2, 179–180. The apparently well-appointed convent was inside the walls near the river, one of the few ecclesiastical buildings in the lower part of a town that had only two parish churches, while there was a large cathedral and a multitude of rich churches and monasteries on the hills above. Charitas Pirckheimer's chronicle has almost nothing to say about the Peasants' War, mentioning only the temporary flight of the nuns of Pillenreuth and Engeltal to Nuremberg, and concentrating on the attempts of the pro-Lutheran council to close or reform the nuns of her monastery, *Die Denkwürdigkeiten*, 67.

2. Destruction of convents and monasteries: see Table 10.1 for the results of the research project Destruction of Convents and Monasteries during the German Peasants' War, which for the first time has systematically surveyed the figures and charted the extent of the destruction. On the monasteries of Zwiefalten and Bebenhausen, I am indebted to Wilfried Setzler, Ringvorlesung Bauernkrieg, Tübingen, 'Sie versammeln sich und beklagen ihre Beschwerden. Die Klöster Bebenhausen und Zwiefalten im Bauernkrieg' (lecture). An exception, Zwiefalten managed to survive and maintain independence. Johanniszelle: AGBM 1, 638, 9 October 1525, Dorothea Abbess of St Johanniszelle unter Wildberg to Bishop Conrad. The Sulzfelders were using the convent's building materials to rebuild the houses of the 'Jew of Sulzfeld', which they had also plundered and had been ordered to rebuild.

3. AGBM 1, 612–615.

4. On weapons and experience with arms, Hoyer, *Militärwesen*, 35–54; see Miller, *German Peasants War, 1524–6*; and for examples see the Böblingen, Leipheim, and Frankenhausen museums, which have reproductions of weapons they believe were probably used.

5. Kießling and Troßbach, eds., *Grundzüge der Agrargeschichte*, 47–49.

6. As the writer of *An die Versammlung* put it, 'In summa: wir seind alle gottes aygen mit leyb und seel', 92:3–4. Back in February 1525, the Baltringen peasants had said, 'So beger wir, daß wir ken lipheren sol han dan got alen', Franz, *Der deutsche Bauernkrieg, Aktenband* (hereafter *Akten*), 147. In areas where there was no serfdom, the word 'freedom' still had resonance, see for example LATh Meiningen, 4-10-1020 GHA Sekt II, 560, for Schönau, who asked for the 'freyhait' that other communities were getting from their rulers; or the Bildhausen band to the surrounding area, calling on them to join them 'zu erhaltung christlicher freyhait und gerechtickait', Fries, *Geschichte*, vol. 1, 348; while Wilhelm of Henneberg had to swear to uphold the 'twelve articles of Christian freedom', 'Zwelff Artickel von chrystlicher freyheit', LATh Meiningen, GHA Sekt III, Nr. 739.

7. AGBM 2, 202–203, report of Hans Zeiß in a letter to Christoph Meinhart. AGBM 2, 478, report of 14 June from Bernhard Walde, the official who had replaced Zeiß at Allstedt.

8. Melanchthon, *Histori*; Ludwig Fischer, *Die Lutherischen Pamphlete*, 36:26–27, which purports to reproduce the speech Müntzer gave to the troops, 35–36. The *Histori* is a work of Lutheran propaganda.

9. See Otthein Rammstedt, 'Stadtunruhen 1525', 239. Interestingly, although some of these were inspired by the articles of the town of Frankfurt, which were printed in at least three editions, each town compiled its own. Freiburg is an interesting case: Scott argues that sympathy for the peasants amongst the population has been exaggerated, and relies on the description of the events from a rebel who fled to Strasbourg; others argue that there was considerable support. There was a short-lived revolt of the vintners in mid-June after the main danger had passed—including the cry that there should be no lord but God and the emperor, Scott, *Freiburg*, 217. Sea, 'Imperial Cities and the Peasants' War in Germany'.

10. Uwe Schirmer, 'Ursachen des Bauernkrieges', has pointed out that it was in particular the slightly larger villages who seem to have been most involved in the revolt, especially those with amenities like churches, bathhouses, taverns, and places where people could meet; while it was the middling and smaller towns, sometimes little more than large villages, that also appear to have been most active. This may of course be an artefact of our sources, because very small villages were less worth punishing and leave fewer archival traces.

11. See Sea, 'Imperial Cities and the Peasants' War'. Schwäbisch Gmünd, where the council had also been overthrown, is an interesting exception which remained Catholic.

12. Behringer, *Witches and Witch Hunts*, 130, for a table of the areas of greatest persecution.

13. See Schulze, *Bäuerlicher Widerstand*.

14. On the seventeenth-century historiography and on differences in scholarship on the two sides of the Iron Curtain, see Schulze, *Bäuerlicher Widerstand*, 21–48. Marx, *Brumaire*, was published in 1852; Engels's *The Peasant War in Germany* in 1850.

15. Engels, *Peasant War*, 65–74, on earlier revolts; 115, 116.

16. Marx, *Brumaire*, 7, 8, 20. One contemporary chronicler wrote that the subjects of the Mainz region wanted to join the revolt; they felt 'hierzu lustig worden', referring also to the 'lust' that the citizens of Mainz had for revolt. The German conveys the sense of wanting to revolt, almost of enjoyment. *Chroniken der deutschen Städte, Mainz* 2, 101–112, 105.

17. On Franz's career, his networks of influence, his antisemitic propaganda work, and his postwar rehabilitation, see Behringer, 'Bauern-Franz und Rassen-Günther', who points out that many of Franz's key terms—'Volk und Blut', 'Bauer und Rasse', 'Krieg und Reich', and, one might add, 'Führer'—are apparently neutral but are semantically laden, dog-whistle words that 'insiders' would have understood, 131. See also Müller, *Diktatur und Revolution*. For quotations, Franz, *Der deutsche Bauernkrieg*, 1933 ed., vol. 1, 477. The 1939 edition has a final paragraph (307) that later editions omitted. It praised the Nazi regime as a peasant movement and proclaimed that the defeat of 1525, 'through which the life of our Volk was weakened for centuries, is overcome. For the new Germany, according to a saying of the Führer, will be a peasant Reich or it will be nothing' ('Denn das neue Deutschland wird nach einem Worte des Führers ein Bauernreich sein oder es wird nicht sein'). After the war, Franz replaced this with a quotation from Alexander von Humboldt. However, the sentence immediately preceding it, which laments the lost 'biological' potential through the slaughter of so many peasants, remained intact ('durch die das Leben unseres Volkes Jahrhunderte hindurch geschwächt und ärmer gemacht worden ist, ist überwunden').

18. Franz, *Der deutsche Bauernkrieg*, vol. 1, 201–202, 212–213, 245, 263–264. Franz, *Der deutsche Bauernkrieg*, 1969, remains the classic history (the first edition, 1933, was printed in Gothic type). Franz was also instrumental in various roles in collecting and curating many volumes of the war's massive published source materials and hence shaping how the events are understood even today. He was involved in Walther Fuchs's vast collection of 'Middle German' documents of some two thousand pages, which includes the crucial region where Thomas Müntzer was active; he published a collection of *Akten* of the Peasants' War (Franz, *Akten*, Darmstadt 1968, 1972, reprint of first edition of 1935) and many other source collections; he (in collaboration with Werner Fleischhauer) edited the facsimile edition of the *Weissenauer Chronik*; with Paul Kirn he edited Thomas Müntzer's writings and letters (*Schriften und Briefe*—the edition is now superseded by ThMA); and his brief documentary overview of the Peasants' War remains an invaluable starting point (Franz, *Quellen zur Geschichte*, Darmstadt 1963). Fuchs, also a Nazi sympathiser, was a student of Franz's, and Fuchs's most famous doctoral student was Helmut Kohl. See also Müller, *Diktatur und Revolution*.

19. Steinmetz, 'Die dritte Etappe', 80, taken from Deutsche Geschichte, Berlin, 3rd ed., 1974. See Müller, *Diktatur und Revolution*.

20. Eydinger, 'Motive'.

21. Bräuer and Vogler, *Müntzer*. Its accessible writing continues the East German tradition of popularising history and draws on detailed social historical investigation. Müller, *Mörder ohne Opfer*.

22. Blickle, *The Revolution of 1525*. It shared some of the perspectives of Bernd Moeller's *Reichsstadt und Reformation*, 1962 (published in English as *Imperial Cities and Reformation*, trans. H. C. Erik Midelfort and Mark U. Edwards, 1972), the landmark essay which tried to create a Reformation history that was not just the story of Luther and Lutheran theology.

23. Over the course of his scholarly career he provided studies of many other areas and a brilliant biography of Truchsess Georg von Waldburg, *Bauernjörg*. See also his later reflections in *Der Bauernkrieg. Die Revolution des Gemeinen Mannes*, 1998; 2012, 103–126.

24. Thompson, *The Making of the English Working Class*, 26–54. Stedman Jones, *Languages of Class*; 'The Determinist Fix'.

25. Braudel, *The Structures of Everyday Life*, 49.

26. Chopping off Mary's head: Maurer, *Bauernkrieg 1525*, 72. There are some exceptions: Leah Wegner notes a white peasant flag with an image of Christ and, below, of Mary, in early April near Böblingen, Wegner, 'Böblingen. Die Gemaine Landschaft der württembergischen Aufständischen', Tübingen Bauerkriegsvorträge (lectures), 21 June 2023.

BIBLIOGRAPHY

British Academy Small Grants Fund Project: Louisa Bergold, Charlotte Gauthier, Lyndal Roper, and Edmund Wareham Wanitzek, "Visualising the Destruction of Convents and Monasteries During the German Peasants' War" (earlier supported by the John Fell Fund, University of Oxford).

Primary Works

Adam, A., 'Zwei Briefe über den Bauernaufstand im Bistum Speyer 1525'. *Zeitschrift für die Geschichte des Oberrheins* 45 / NF 6 (1891): 699–701.

Agricola, Georg, *De re metallica libri XII*. Basel: Froben, 1556. VD 16 A 933.

Agricola, Johannes, *Auslegung des XIX Psalm. Coeli enarrant.* Wittenberg: Schirlentz, 1525. VD 16 A 946.

Agricola, Johannes, *Ein nützlicher Dialogus oder Gesprächsbüchlein zwischen einem münzerischen Schwärmer und einem evangelischen frommen Bauern*. Wittenberg: Lufft, 1525. VD 16 L 314 and 315.

Amandus, Georg, *Wie ein geistlicher christlicher Ritter und Gottes Held in dieser Welt streiten soll*. Zwickau: Schönsperger, 1524. VD 16 A 2147.

An die Versammlung gemeiner Bauernschaft. Eine revolutionäre Flugschrift aus dem Deutschen Bauernkrieg. Edited by Bernd Rüdiger and Siegfried Hoyer. Gotha: Bibliographisches Institut, 1975.

Anshelm, Valerius, *Die Berner-Chronik des Valerius Anshelm. Fünfter Band*. Bern: K. J. Wyss, 1896.

Arnold, Klaus, ed., *Niklashausen 1476. Quellen und Untersuchungen zur sozialreligiösen Bewegung des Hans Behem und zur Agrarstruktur eines spätmittelalterlichen Dorfes*. Baden-Baden: Valentin Koerner, 1980.

Baumann, Franz Ludwig, *Akten zur Geschichte des deutschen Bauernkrieges aus Oberschwaben*. Freiburg: Herder'sche Verlagshandlung, 1877.

Baumann, Franz Ludwig, *Quellen zur Geschichte des Bauernkrieges aus Rotenburg an der Tauber.[sic] (Chronik Thomas Zweifel)*. Tübingen: Litterarischer Verein, 1878.

Baumann, Franz Ludwig, *Quellen zur Geschichte des Bauernkrieges in Oberschwaben. Chroniken*. Tübingen: Lit. Verein, 1876.

Bensen, Heinrich W., *Geschichte des Bauernkriegs in Ostfranken aus Quellen bearbeitet*. Erlangen: Palm, 1840.

Boell, Balthasar, *Der Bauernkrieg um Weissenburg. Anno 1525*, Hrsg. Ohleyer, Professor, Weissenburg [= Wissembourg], 1873.

Böhm, Ludwig, 'Kitzingen und der Bauernkrieg: Nach den Originalakten' (Sebald Ranft Chronicle). *Archiv des historischen Vereins von Unterfranken und Aschaffenburg* 36 (1893): 1–186.

Brandenburg-Ansbach, Kasimir [Casimir] Markgraf, *Anzeigen, wie die gewesen Empörung vn[d] auffruren nit den wenigsten tayl auß vngeschickten predigen entstanden sindt*. Augsburg: Ramminger, 1525. VD 16 B 6934.

Brant, Sebastian, *Doctor Brants Narrenschiff*. Basel: Nikolaus Lamparter, 1506. VD 16 B 7065.

Brant, Sebastian, ed., Virgil, *Opera* .... Strasbourg: Johann Grüninger, 1502. VD 16 V 1332.

Bräuer, Siegfried, ed., *Historien von Thomas Müntzer: Handschrift von 1520*. Weinheim: VCH, Acta Humaniora, 1989.

Brenz, Johannes, *Vom Gehorsam der Untertan gegen ihrer Oberkeit*. Augsburg: Ulhart, 1525. VD 16 B 7932.

Brenz, Johannes, *Von Milderung der Fürsten gegen den aufrührerischen Bauern*. Augsburg: Ramminger, 1525. VD 16 ZV 8650.

Bucer, Martin, *Correspondance de Martin Bucer*, vol. 2 (1524–1526). Edited by Jean Rott. Leiden: Brill, 1989.

Capito, Wolfgang, *The Correspondence of Wolfgang Capito*, vol. 2 (1524–1531). Edited by Milton Kooistra, translated by Erika Rummel. Toronto: University of Toronto Press, 2010.

Capito, Wolfgang, *Habacuc*. Strasbourg: Köpfel, 1526. VD 16 B 3953.

Capito, Wolfgang, *Was man halten vnnd Antwurten soll, von der Spaltung zwischen Martin Luther and Andreas Carolstadt*. Augsburg: Ulhart, 1524. VD 16 C 847.

Chronicon Islebiense. Eisleber Stadt-Chronik aus den Jahren 1520-1738, Hg. Hermann Grössler und Friedrich Sommer, Eisleben: August Kloeppel, 1882.

Chroniken der deutschen Städte vom 14. Bis ins 16. Jahrhundert: Band 17, 18: Die Chroniken der mittelrheinischen Städte. Mainz. Leipzig: Hirzel, 1968.

Chroust, Anton, ed., *Chroniken der Stadt Bamberg*, 2 vols. Neustadt an der Aisch: PH.C.W. Schmidt, 2005.

Cochlaeus, Johannes, *Kurze Beschreibung Germaniens. Brevis Germanie Descriptio (1512)*. Translated by Karl Langosch, introduction by Volker Reinhardt. Darmstadt: WBG, 2010.

Cochlaeus, Johannes, *Wider die Reubischen und Mordischen rotten*. Cologne: Quentell, 1525.

Cornelius, C. A., *Studien zur Geschichte des Bauernkriegs*. Munich: Verlag der k. Akademie, 1861.

Cronthal, Martin, *Die Stadt Würzburg im Bauernkriege*. Edited by Michael Wieland. Würzburg: Stürtz, 1887.

Dappen, Bernhard, *Articuli... contra Lutheranos*. Ingolstadt: Lutz, 1519. VD 16 D 117.

Die gründtlichen und rechten Hauptartikel aller Bauernschaft. Zwickau: Schönsperger, 1525. VD 16 G 3562.

Die Summa und Namen der Schloss, auch wem ein jedes zugehört ist. Strasbourg: Schürer, 1525. VD 16 S 10194.

Dürer, Albrecht, *Unterweisung der Messung mit dem Zirkel und Richtscheit in Linien, Ebenen und ganzen Körpern*. Nuremberg: Andreae, 1525. VD 16 D 2857.

Eberlin von Günzburg, Johann, *Eine getreue Warnung an die Christen in der Burgauischen Mark, sich auch fürohin zu hüten vor Aufruhr und vor falschen Predigern*. Nuremberg: Andreae, 1526. VD 16 E 126.

Eberlin von Günzburg, Johann, *Wie sich eyn diener Gottes wortts ynn all seynem thun halten soll*. Wittenberg: Rhau-Grunenberg, 1525. VD 16 E 163.

Ein gloubwirdig, vnd warhafftig vnderricht wie die Dhoringischen Pawern vor Franckenhawszen... vnd Molhawsen erobert worden. Dresden: Emserpresse, 1525. VD 16 G 2205.

Ein neues Lied von der [Bauerschaft] im Frankenland. Würzburg: Balthasar Müller, 1525. VD 16 ZV 11605. VD 16 ZV 11616.

Emser, Hieronymus, *Der Bock tritt frei auf diesen Plan, hat wider Ehre nie getan*. Augsburg: Ulhart, 1525. VD 16 E 1100.

Engelhard, Rechtsrathe zu Windsheim, 'Extract aus der Chronik der Stadt Windsheim'. *Jahresbericht des historischen Vereins in Mittelfranken* 12, Beilage 2, (1842): 25–32.

Eyn warhafftig erschröcklich Histori von der Bewrischen uffrur.... Faksimile. Edited by Günter Scholz. Ramseck: Ed. Libri illustri, 1990.

Fabri, Johann, *Adversvs Doctorem Balthasarvm Pacimontanvm*. Leipzig: Melchior Lotter d.Ä., 1528. VD 16 F 190.

Fabri, Johann, *Neüwe Zeitung und heimliche, wunderbarliche Offenbarung etlicher Sachen und Handlungen*. Freiburg i. Breisgau: Johann Wörlin, 1526. VD 16 F 216.

Fabri, Johann, *Ursache, warum der Widertäufer Patron und erster Anfänger, Doktor Balthasar Hubmaier, zu Wien... verbrannt sei*. Landshut: Johann Weißenburger, 1528. VD 16 F 242.

Feßer, Arnolt, *Eine demütige, brüderliche und christliche Supplikation an den römischen Kaiser Karolum den Fünften*. Augsburg: Steiner, 1525. VD 16 F 803.

Fischer, Dagobert, 'Documents relatifs a la guerre des Paysans'. *Curiosités d'Alsace II*. Colmar: Barth, 1863.

Franz, Günther, 'Aus der Kanzlei der württembergischen Bauern im Bauernkrieg'. *Württembergische Vierteljahrshefte für Landesgeschichte* 41 (1935): 83–108, 281–305.

Franz, Günther, *Der deutsche Bauernkrieg, Aktenband.* Munich: R. Oldenburg, 1935.

Franz, Günther, *Quellen zur Geschichte des Bauernkrieges.* Darmstadt: Wissenschaftliche Buchgesellschaft, 1963.

Franz, Günther, and Fleischhauer, Werner, eds., *Jacob Murers Weissenauer Chronik des Bauernkrieges von 1525,* 2 vols. Sigmaringen: Jan Thorbecke, 1977.

Fries, Lorenz, *Die Geschichte des Bauern-Krieges in Ostfranken,* 2 vols. Würzburg: Thein'sche Druckerei Stürtz, 1883.

Fronsperger, Leonhard, *Kriegsbuch anderer Teil.* Frankfurt: Feyerabend, 1573. VD 16 F 3122.

Fronsperger, Leonhard, *Kriegsbuch dritter Teil.* Frankfurt: Feyerabend, 1573. VD 16 F 3123.

Fronsperger, Leonhard, *Kriegsbuch Erster Teil.* Frankfurt: Feyerabend, 1573. VD 16 F 3121.

Fronsperger, Leonhard, *Von kaiserlichen Kriegsrechten.* Frankfurt: Feyerabend, 1596. VD 16 F 3125.

Fundling, Johann, *Anzaigung zweier falscher Zungen des Luthers.* Landshut: Weißenburger, 1526. VD 16 F 1088.

Furcha, Edward J., ed., *The Essential Carlstadt: Fifteen Tracts by Andreas Bodenstein (Carlstadt) from Karlstadt.* Walden, NY: Plough Publishing House, 1995.

Füssel, Stephan, ed., *Schedel'sche Weltchronik—1493. Kolorierte Gesamtausgabe.* Cologne: Taschen, 2013.

Gerbert, Martin, *Historia Nigrae Silvae Ordinis Sancti Benedicti Coloniae. Opera Et Studio Martini Gerberti Monasterii Et Congreg. S. Blasii In Eadem Silva Abbais S. Q. R. I. P. Collecta Et Illustrate: Liber 2.* Sankt Blasien: Monasterium Sankt Blasius, 1783.

Gess, Felician, *Akten und Briefe zur Kirchenpolitik Herzog Georgs von Sachsen.* 2 vols. Cologne: Böhlau Verlag, repr. 1985 (1905–1917).

Götz von Berlichingen, *Mein Fehd und Handlungen.* Edited by Helgard Ulmschneider. Sigmaringen: Jan Thorbecke Verlag, 1981.

Gropp, Ignaz, *Wirtzburgische Chronick.* Würzburg: Marco Antonio Engman, Hoff-Buchdrucker, 1748.

Grössler, Hermann, and Sommer, Friedrich, eds., *Chronikon Islebiense. Eisleben Stadt-Chronik aus den Jahren 1520–1738.* Eisleben: Kloeppel, 1882.

Gross von Trockau, Michael, 'Kurtzer Bericht vom Bauern krieg Anno 1525'. *Anzeiger für Kunde der Deutschen Vorzeit* NF 3, NF, Nr. 4, 5, and 6, 1855, pp. 73–77 (Nr. 4), 113–116 (Nr. 5), 137–140 (Nr. 6).

Güthe, Johann Sebastian, *Chronica Meiningen 1676.* Edited by Eduard Schaubach, *Poligraphia Meiningensis.* Meiningen: Brückner und Renner, 1861.

Hammer, Hieronymus, 'Geschichte des Kitzinger Bauerkrieges'. *Die Stadt Würzburg im Bauernkriege.* Edited by Michael Wieland. Würzburg: H. Stürtz, 1887.

Handlung, Artickel vnnd Instruktion, so fürgenommen worden sein von allen Rotten und Haufen der Bauern. Augsburg: Steiner, 1525. VD 16 H 488, 489, 490, 491, 492, 493, 495, 496, 497, ZV 31952.

Harer, Peter, *Die Berichte von Peter Harer und Johannes Keßler vom Bauernkrieg*. Edited by Willi Alter. Speyer: Verlag der Pfälzischen Gesellschaft zur Förderung der Wissenschaften in Speyer, 1995.

Hätzer, Ludwig, et al., *Acta oder geschicht*. Zurich: Froschauer, 1523. VD 16 H 136.

Henneberg, Johann Graf, *Wahrhafftige vnwidesprechliche vnnd begrundtfeste entschuldigung*. Mainz: Schöffer, 1526. VD 16 F 3340.

Herbst, Hans, *Eyn gesprech von dem gemaynen Schwabacher Kasten, als durch brüder Hainrich, Knecht Ruprecht, Kemerin, Spůler, vnd jrem Maister, des Handtwercks der Wüllen Tůchmacher*. Nuremberg: Hieronymus Höltzel, 1524. VD 16 H 2228.

Hergot, Hans, *Hans Hergot und die Flugschrift 'Von der newen Wandlung eynes christlichen Lebens': Faksimilewiedergabe*. Edited by Max Steinmetz. Leipzig: Fachbuchverlag, 1977.

Hessen, Philipp von, *Zwischen den Durchleuchtigen vnnd Hochgebornen Fürtsten vnd Herren Herrn Philipsen Landtgraffen zu Hessen und… Herren Johansen Graffen… zu Henneberg*. Erfurt: Johann Loersfeld, 1526. VD 16 H 2850.

Hirsch, Theodor, Töppen, Max, and Strehlke, Ernst, eds., *Scriptores Rerum Prussicarum. Die Geschichtsquellen der Preussischen Vorzeit bis zum Untergang der Ordensherrschaft*. Band 5. Leipzig: Hirzel, 1874.

Hoffmann, Simon, 'Ein lybhaber ewangelischer warheytt'. In *Erfurt Geschichte und Gegenwart*, edited by Ulman Weiß. Weimar: Böhlaus Nachfolger, 1995.

Hubmaier, Balthasar, *Schriften*. Edited by Gunnar Westin and Torsten Bergsten. (= *Quellen und Forschungen zur Reformationsgeschichte: Quellen zur Geschichte der Täufer, Band 9): Balthasar Hubmaier. Schriften*. Gütersloh: Gerd Mohn, 1962.

Hug, Heinrich, *Villinger Chronik von 1495 bis 1533*. Edited by Christian Roder. Tübingen: L. F. Fues, 1883.

Johann III, Graf, *Entschuldigung mit warer vermeldung… ergangener Handlung wider des Herrn Philipsen Landtgraffen zu Hessen jüngst offentlich außgangen und angeschlahen außschreiben*. N.p., 1526. VD 16 F3339 H2850 and reply VD 16 F 3340.

Jordan, Reinhard, *Chronik der Stadt Mühlhausen in Thüringen*. Vols. 1 and 2. Bad Langensalza: Rockstuhl, 2001 reprint (1st ed. vol. 1, 1900; vol. 2, 1903).

Karlstadt, Andreas, *Anzeige etlicher Hauptartikel christlicher Lehre*. Augsburg: Ulhart, Philipp d.Ä., 1525. VD 16 B 6099.

Karlstadt, Andreas Bodenstein von, *Auszlegung dieser wort Christi. Das ist mein leyb* …. Basel: Johann Bebel, 1524. VD 16 B 6111.

Karlstadt, Andreas Bodenstein von, *Entschuldigung*. Wittenberg: Johann Rhau-Grunenberg, 1525. VD 16 B 6152.

Karlstadt, Andreas Bodenstein von, *Kritische Gesamtausgabe der Schriften und Briefe Andreas Bodensteins von Karlstadt*. Edited by Thomas Kaufmann et al. Gütersloher Verlagshaus: Gütersloh, 2012–ongoing; now also digital.

Karlstadt, Andreas Bodenstein von, *Von Gelübden Unterrichtung*. Basel: Adam Petri, 1522. VD 16 B 6246.

Karlstadt, Andreas Bodenstein von, *Von Mannigfältigkeit des einfältigen einigen Willen Gottes*. Cologne: Arnd von Aich, 1523. VD 16 B 6251.

Kessler, Johannes, *Johannes Kesslers Sabbata. Mit kleineren Schriften und Briefen.* Edited by Emil Egli and Rudolf Schoch. St Gallen: Fehr'sche Buchhandlung, 1902.

Klüpfel, Karl, *Urkunden zur Geschichte des schwäbischen Bundes: 1488–1533, Teil 2.* Stuttgart: Literarischer Verein, 1853.

Kobuch, Manfred, and Müller, Ernst, *Der deutsche Bauernkrieg in Dokumenten. Aus staatlichen Archiven der Deutschen Demokratischen Republik.* Weimar: Herman Böhlaus Nachfolger, 1977.

Kraus, Franz Xaver, 'Beiträge zur Geschichte des deutschen Bauernkriegs 1525'. *Annalen des Vereins für Nassauische Altertumskunde und Geschichtsforschung*, Band 12 (1873): 21–141.

Küssenberg, Heinrich, 'Heinrich Küssenbergs Chronik der Reformation in der Grafschaft Baden, in Klettgau und auf dem Schwarzwalde'. Edited by Johann Huber. *Archiv für die schweizerische Reformations-Geschichte*, 411–474. Solothurn: B. Schwendimann, 1875.

Landolt, Justus, *Urkunden zur Reformationsgeschichte des Städtchens Stein am Rhein.* Solothurn: B. Schwendimann, 1876.

Laube, Adolf, *Flugschriften der Bauernkriegszeit.* Berlin: Akademie Verlag, 1975.

Lettsch, Andreas, 'Chronik des Andreas Lettsch von 1519 bis 1531'. In Mone, ed., *Quellensammlung der Badischen Landesgeschichte*, Band 2.

Locher, Johann, *Ein vngewonlicher vnd der Ander Sendtbrieff des Bauernfeyndts zu Karsthannsen.* Zwickau: Schönsperger, 1524. VD 16 R 3387.

Lotzer, Sebastian, *Ain vast haylsam trostlich.... Beschurmubechlin.* [Augsburg]: Ramminger, 1524. VD 16 L 2880.

Lotzer, Sebastian, *Ayn außlegung uber das Evangelium ....* Augsburg: Melchior Ramminger, 1524. VD 16 L 2877.

Lotzer, Sebastian, *Entschuldigung einer frummen Christlichen Gemain zu Memmingen ....* [Augsburg]: 1525. VD 16 L 2879.

Luther, Martin, *Ain Sendbrieff von dem harte[n] büchlin wider die bauren.* Augsburg: Ruff, 1525. VD 16 L 5938.

Luther, Martin, *Das Babstum mit seynen gliedern gemalet vnd beschryben gebessert vnd gemehrt.* Nuremberg: Guldenmund, 1526. VD 16 P 353, 354.

Luther, Martin, *Epistel (II.) S. Petri, gepredigt und ausgelegt.* Augsburg: Ruff, 1524. VD 16 L 4579 and 4580.

Luther, Martin, *Passional Christi vnd Antichristi.* Wittenberg: Rhau-Grunenberg, 1521. VD 16 L5584–L5587.

Luther, Martin, *Vertrag zwischen dem löblichen Bund zu Schwaben und den zwei Haufen und Versammlung der Bauern am Bodensee und Allgäu.* Wittenberg: Klug, Josef, 1525. VD 4579.

Luther, Martin, and Melanchthon, Philipp, *Passional Christi und Antichristi.* Edited by Johann Schwertfeger and Volkmar Joestel. Wittenberg: Stiftung Luthergedenkstätten in Sachsen-Anhalt, 1998.

Lutz, Hans, *Das Tagebuch des Herolds Hans Lutz von Augsburg; wieder aufgefundener Text.* Edited by A. Adam. Karlsruhe: Braun, 1893.

Matheson, Peter, ed., *The Collected Works of Thomas Müntzer*. Edinburgh: T&T Clark, 1988.

Maurer, Hans Martin, *Der Bauernkrieg im deutschen Südwesten. Dokumente, Berichte, Flugschriften, Bilder*. 2nd ed. Stuttgart: Hauptstaatsarchiv Stuttgart, 1975.

Mela, Pomponius, *Cosmographia*. Nuremberg: Johann Weißenburger, 1512. VD 16 M 2307.

[Melanchthon, Philipp], *Die Histori Thome Muntzers*. Hagenau: Johann Setzer, 1525. VD 16: M 3431.

[Melanchthon, Philipp], *Eyn schrifft Philippi Melanchthon*. In *Flugschriften vom Bauernkrieg zum Täuferreich (1526–1535)*, edited by Adolf Laube. Berlin: Akademie Verlag, 1992.

Merx, Otto, 'Beiträge zur Geschichte der religiösen und sozialen Bewegung in den Stiftern Mainz, Würzburg und Bamberg (1524–1526)'. *Archiv des historischen Vereins für Unterfranken* 49 (1907): 135–158, 152–156 (= Chronik Hans Fridell).

Moibanus, Ambrosius, *Catechismi capita decem*. Breslau: Winkler d.Ä., 1546. VD 16 ZV 11084.

Mone, F. J., ed., *Quellensammlung der Badischen Landesgeschichte*, Band 2. Karlsruhe: Madlot, 1854.

Müller, Thomas T., 'Neuedition der den Bauernkrieg betereffenden Abschnitte des Chronicon Mulhusinum'. In Müller, *Thomas Müntzer in der Mühlhäuser Chronistik*.

Müntzer, Thomas, *Auszlegung des andern vnterschyds Danielis*. Allstedt: Müntzerpresse, 1524. VD 16 M 6746.

Müntzer, Thomas, *Kritische Gesamtausgabe*. 3 vols. Edited by Armin Kohnle et al. Leipzig: Evangelische Verlagsanstalt, 2004–2017.

Muralt, Leonhard, and Schmid, Walter, eds., *Quellen zur Geschichte der Täufer in der Schweiz. Band 1: Zürich*. Zurich: Theologischer Verlag Zürich, 1974.

Murner, Thomas, *Uon dem grossen Lutherischen Narren wie in doctor Murner beschworen hat*. Strasbourg: Johann Grüninger, 1522. VD 16 M 7088.

Myconius, Friedrich, *Geschichte der Reformation*. Leipzig: R. Voigtländer, 1914.

Neudecker, C. G., and Preller, Ludwig, eds., *Georg Spalatin: Historischer Nachlass und Briefe. Aus den Originalhandschriften*. Jena: Mauke, 1851.

Oechsle, Ferdinand Friedrich, ed., *Beiträge zur Geschichte des Bauernkrieges in den schwäbisch-fränkischen Grenzlanden*. Leipzig: Carl Drechsler Verlag, 1830.

Osiander, Andreas, *Gesamtausgabe. Band 1: Schriften und Briefe 1522 bis März 1525*, edited by Gottfried Seebass and Gerhard Müller. Gütersloh: Gütersloher Verl., 1975.

Peringer, *Zwo Sermon geprediget vom Pawren zů Werdt bey Nürmberg am Sontag vor Faßnacht vonn dem freyen willen des Mennschen*. Speyer: Jakob Schmidt, 1525. VD 16 P 1414.

Pfeiffer, Gerhard, *Quellen zur Nürnberger Reformationsgeschichte; von der Duldung liturgischer Änderungen bis zur Ausübung des Kichenregiments durch den Rat (Juni 1524–Juni 1525)*. Nuremberg: Verein für Bayerische Kirchengeschichte, 1968.

Pirckheimer, Charitas, *Die Denkwürdigkeiten der Äbtissin Caritas Pirckheimer*. St. Ottilien: EOS-Verlag, 1982.

Rathgeber, Julius, *Die Herrschaft Rappoltstein. Beiträge zur Geschichtskunde des Ober-Elsasses, zum Theil aus urkundlichen Quellen*. Strasbourg: Wolff, 1874.

Rauch, Moritz von, *Urkundenbuch der Stadt Heilbronn. Vierter Band: Von 1525 bis zum Nürnberger Religionsfrieden im Jahr 1532*. Stuttgart: W. Kohlhammer, 1922.

Reynmann, Leonhard, *Practica über die großen und mannigfaltigen Koniunktion der Planeten, die im Jahr M.D.XXIV. erscheinen*. Nuremberg: Hieronymus Höltzel, 1523. VD 16 R 1620.

Rhegius, Urbanus, *Von Leibeigenschaft oder Knechtschaft*. Augsburg: Simprecht Ruff, 1525. VD 16 R 2000.

Rhegius, Urbanus, *Wider den newen irrsal Doctor Andres von Carlstadt des Sacraments halb warning*. Augsburg: Simprecht [?]. Ruff, 1524. VD 16 R 2014.

Rhegius, Urbanus, and Luther, Martin, *Ain Sendbrieff von dem harte[n] büchlin wider die bauren (Schlussred)*. [Augsburg]: Simprecht Ruff, 1525. VD 16 L 5938.

Rhyiner, Heinrich, 'Heinrich Rhyiners Chronik des Bauernkrieges 1525'. Edited by August Bernoulli. *Basler Chroniken, Band 6*. Basel: Schwabe, 1902.

Richau, Nikolaus, 'Historie von dem Auffruhr der Samländischen Bauern'. *Erleutertes Preußen 2*. Königsberg: 1725, 328–357, 531–566.

Ruszat-Ewig, Heide, *Die 12 Bauernartikel*. Memmingen: Historischer Verein Memmingen, 2018.

Ruszat-Ewig, Heide, ed., *Sebastian Lotzer: Fünf Flugschriften aus der Reformationszeit*. Memmingen: Historischer Verein Memmingen e.V., 2015.

Salat, Johannes, *Reformationschronik: 1517–1534*. 3 vols. Edited by Ruth Jörg. Basel: Allgemeine Geschichtsforschende Ges. D. Schweiz, 1988.

Schaubach, Eduard, ed., *Poligraphia Meiningensis, das ist, gründliche Beschreibung der uhr-alten Stadt Meiningen*. Meiningen: Reydern, 1676.

Schreiber, Johann Heinrich, ed., *Der deutsche Bauernkrieg. Gleichzeitige Urkunden*. 3 vols. Freiburg im Breisgau: Franz Xaver Wangler, 1866.

Schwanhauser, Johannes, *Ein Sermon geprediget durch Johanem Schwanhausen*. Bamberg: Erlinger, 1523. VD 16 S 4609.

Schwanhauser, Johannes, *Ein Trostbrief an die christliche Gemeine zu Bamberg*. Augsburg: Ulhart, 1525. VD 16 S 4610.

Schweyger, Franz, *Chronik der Stadt Hall, 1303–1572*. Edited by David Schönherr. Innsbruck: Wagner, 1867.

Scott, Tom, and Scribner, Robert W., eds., *The German Peasants' War: A History in Documents*. Amherst, NY: Humanity, 2006.

Seebass, Gottfried, *Artikelbrief, Bundesordnung und Verfassungsentwurf*. Heidelberg: Carl Winter, 1988.

Seitz, Alexander, *Ein schöner Traktat, darinnen begriffen ist die Art und Ursach des Traumes, wann ihm zu glauben sey oder nicht*. Landshut: Johann Weißenburger, 1515. VD 16 S 5359.

Seitz, Alexander, *Ain Warnung des Sündtfluss oder erschrockenlichen wassers des xxxiij jars*.... Augsburg: Erhard Oeglin, 1520. VD 16 S 5396.

Strauß, Jakob, *Aufruhr, Zwietracht und Uneinigkeit zwischen wahren evangelischen Christen fürzukommen, kurz auch unüberwindliche Lehre*. Augsburg: Steiner, 1526. VD 16 S 9474.

Strauß, Jakob, *Hauptstück und Artikel christlicher Lehr über den unchristlichen Wucher*. Augsburg: Steiner, 1523. VD 16 S 9481.

Strauß, Jakob, *Das wůcher zů nemen vnd geben, vnserm Christlichem glauben... entgegen ist, vnüberwintlich leer, vnd geschrifft*. Strasbourg: Schwan, 1524. VD 16 S 9479.

Stumpf, Johann, *Johannes Stumpfs Schweizer- und Reformationschronik*. Edited by Hans Müller and Ernst Gagliardi. Basel: Birkhäuser, 1952.

Sulger, Arsenius, *Annales Imperialis Monasterii Zwifaltensis*. Augsburg: Utz Schneiderin, 1698.

Teuschlin, Johannes, *Auflosung ettlicher Fragen zu lob vnd ere Christi Jesu, auch seiner lieben mutter*. Nuremberg: Friedrich Peypus, 1520. VD 16 T 623.

Thomann, Nicolaus, 'Weissenhorner Historie'. *Quellen zur Geschichte des Bauernkrieges in Oberschwaben*. Edited by Franz Ludwig Baumann. Stuttgart, 1876.

Verbrannte vnnd abgebrochene Schlosser vnnd Closter. Altenburg: Kantz, 1525. VD 16 V 587.

Virck, Hans, ed., *Urkunden und Akten der Stadt Strassburg: 1517–1530*. Berlin: De Gruyter, 1882.

Virdung, Johann, *Außlegůg vnd Beteütung der Wůnderbarlichen zeichen wie die zů viel malen Jn den Lüfften vnd vff dem Ertrich erscheinen vnd gesehen worden*. Oppenheim: Jakob Köbel, 1520. VD 16 V 1256.

Virdung, Johann, *Practica deutsch über die neue erschreckliche vorher nie gesehene Konjunktion...der Planeten im Jahre 1524*. Oppenheim: Jakob Köbel, 1523. VD 16 V 1310.

Virdung, Johann, *PRACTICA || Teütsch. || Uber die newe erscho=||kenliche: vor nye gesehen: Coniunction /|| oder Zůsammen vereynigung der Planeten / imm Jare || M.CCCCC.XXIIII*. Oppenheim: Jakob Köbel, 1522. VD 16 V 1305.

Virdung, Johann, *Pronostication gemacht durch...Johansen Virdung..., auf das xxiiii. Byß in das. lx. Vnnd lxiii jar*.... [Landshut]: 1523. VD 16 V 1308.

Vogt, Wilhelm, ed., *Die Correspondenz des schwäbischen Bundeshauptmannes Ulrich Artzt von Augsburg aus den Jahren 1524–1527: Ein Beitrag zur Geschichte des Bauernkrieges in Schwaben*. Augsburg: Hist. Verein für Schwaben u. Neuburg, 1880.

Volcyr de Sérouville, Nicole, *L'histoire et recueil de la triumphante et glorieuse victoire obtenue contre les seduyctz et abusez Lutheriens mescreans du pays D'Aulsays*.... Paris: Galiot Du Pré, 1527. First published Lyon, 1526.

Walther, Johannes, *Geistliche Gesangbüchlein*. Wittenberg: Josef Klug, 1524. VD 16 L 4776.

Wareham, Edmund Hugh, Bubenheimer, Ulrich, and Lähnemann, Henrike, eds., *Passional Christi und Antichristi: Antithesis figurata vitæ Christi et Antichristi*. Oxford, UK: Taylor Institution Library, 2021.

Wendelstein, Rat, *Dorffmayster vnnd Gemaind zu wendelstains fürhalten den Amptleüten zu Schwabach vnd jrem new angeendem Pfarrherrn gethan.* Nuremberg: Jobst Gutknecht, 1524. VD 16 W 1904.

Zimmern, Froben Christoph von, *Zimmerische Chronik, Chronik der Grafen von Zimmern.* 4 vols. 2nd ed. Edited by Karl August Barack. Tübingen: Mohr, 1881.

Zwick, Johannes, *Geschrifft Doctor Johanns Zwicken an seyne yhm von got bevolhen Vnderthonen zu Rüdlingen.* Augsburg: Ramminger, 1526. VD 16 Z 735.

Secondary Works

Adam, Thomas, *Joß Fritz—das verborgene Feuer der Revolution.* Ubstadt-Wiher: Verlag Regionalkultur, 2013.

Ahn, Jürgen von, 'Schubladendenken in der Kunstgeschichte? Der Bauernkrieg in der zeitgenössischen Kunst'. In Müller, Schirmer, and Greiling, eds., *Reformation und Bauernkrieg.*

Algazi, Gadi, *Herrengewalt und Gewalt der Herren im späten Mittelalter: Herrschaft, Gegenseitigkeit und Sprachgebrauch.* Frankfurt am Main: Campus Verlag, 1996.

Alter, Willi, *Der Aufstand der Bauern und Bürger im Jahre 1525 in der Pfalz.* Speyer: Verlag der Pfälzischen Gesellschaft zur Förderung der Wissenschaften in Speyer, 1998.

Alter, Willi, *Pfeddersheim um 1525: Zugleich ein Beitrag zur Erforschung des Bauernaufstandes in Südwestdeutschland.* Worms: Stadtarchiv, 1990.

Arnold, Klaus, 'Art. Böhm, Hans (auch Behem), der "Pfeifer von Niklashausen" (um 1450–1476)'. In *Lexikon des Mittelalters (Vol. 1–9)*, edited by Gloria Avella-Widhalm, Liselotte Lutz, Roswitha Mattejiet, and Ulrich Mattejiet. Darmstadt: Wissenschaftliche Buchgesellschaft, 2009.

Arnold, Klaus, 'Neues zu Niklashausen 1476'. In *Reformation und Revolution. Beiträge zum politischen Wandel und der sozialen Kräfte am Beginn der Neuzeit. Festschrift für Rainer Wohlfeil zum 60. Geburtstag*, edited by Rainer Postel and Franklin Kopitzsch. Stuttgart: Franz Steiner Verlag, 1989.

Arnold, Klaus, *Niklaushausen 1476. Quellen und Untersuchungen zur sozialreligiösen Bewegung des Hans Behem und zur Agrarstruktur eines spätmittelalterlichen Dorfes.* Baden-Baden: Verlag Valentin Körner, 1980.

Arnold, Klaus, 'Novissima Niclashusiana: Weitere Quellen zur "Niklashäuser Fahrt" 1476'. *Würzburger Diözesangeschichtsblätter* 76 (2013): 247–277.

Arnold, Udo, and Trentin-Meyer, Maike, *Deutscher Orden 1190–2000: Ein Führer durch das Deutschordensmuseum in Bad Margentheim.* Baunach: Spurbuchverlag, 2019.

Ashcroft, Jeffrey, *Albrecht Dürer: Documentary Biography: Dürer's Personal and Aesthetic Writings, Words on Pictures, Family, Legal and Business Documents, the Artist in the Writings of Contemporaries.* New Haven, CT: Yale University Press, 2017.

Asquez, Ryan, 'The Suffering Christ: An International Symbol of Piety and Identity, 1450–1550'. PhD diss., University of Oxford, 2020.

Bak, János M., ed., *The German Peasant War of 1525.* London: F. Cass, 1976.

Barge, Hermann, *Andreas Bodenstein von Karlstadt*, 2 vols. Leipzig: Friedrich Brandstetter, 1905.

Barge, Hermann, 'Florian Geyer: Eine biographische Studie'. *Beiträge zur Kulturgeschichte des Mittelalters und der Renaissance* 26 (1920): 1–39.

Barnes, Robin, *Astrology and Reformation*. Oxford, UK: Oxford University Press, 2016.

Barnes, Robin, *Prophecy and Gnosis: Apocalypticism in the Wake of the Lutheran Reformation*. Stanford, CA: Stanford University Press, 1988.

Bauer, Joachim, and Haspel, Michael, eds., *Jakob Strauß und der reformatorische Wucherstreit: Die soziale Dimension der Reformation und ihre Wirkungen*. Leipzig: Evangelische Verlagsanstalt, 2018.

Baumgarten, Karl, 'Bauer und Bauernhaus im Hochschwarzwald um 1520'. In Strobach, ed., *Der arm Man 1525*.

Baylor, Michael, 'Thomas Müntzer's Theory of Dreams'. In Dammaschke and Müller, eds., *Thomas Müntzer im Blick*.

Becker, Maria, and Frehner, Matthias, *St. George's Monastery at Stein am Rhein*. Bern: Society for the History of Swiss Art, 1999.

Behringer, Wolfgang, 'Bauern-Franz und Rassen-Günther: Die politische Geschichte des Agrarhistorikers Günther Franz (1902–1992)'. In *Deutsche Historiker im Nationalsozialismus*, edited by Winfried Schulze. Frankfurt: Fischer, 2000.

Behringer, Wolfgang, *A Cultural History of Climate*. London: Polity, 2009 (German 2007).

Behringer, Wolfgang, *Witches and Witch Hunts: A Global History*. Cambridge, UK: Polity, 2004.

Belouschek, Christa, Dick, Bettina, and Laufs, Adolf, *Die Reichskammergerichtsordnung von 1555*. Cologne: Böhlau, 1976.

Bentzien, Ulrich, 'Arbeit und Arbeitsgerät der Bauern zur Zeit des deutschen Bauernkriegs'. In Strobach, ed., *Der arm Man 1525*.

Bergsten, Torsten, *Balthasar Hubmaier: Anabaptist Theologian and Martyr*. Valley Forge, PA: Judson Press, 1978.

Bischoff, Georges, *La guerre des paysans*. Strasbourg: La Nuée Bleue, 2010.

Blickle, Peter, 'Alpenländer'. In Buszello, Blickle, and Endres, eds., *Der deutsche Bauernkrieg*.

Blickle, Peter, *Der Bauernjörg: Feldherr im Bauernkrieg: Georg Truchsess von Waldburg, 1488–1531*. Munich: C. H. Beck, 2015.

Blickle, Peter, *Der Bauernkrieg: Die Revolution des Gemeinen Mannes*. Munich: C. H. Beck, Beck'sche Reihe, 1998 (ed. 2012).

Blickle, Peter, *Der Deutsche Bauernkrieg von 1525*. Darmstadt: Wissenschaftliche Buchgesellschaft, 1985.

Blickle, Peter, 'The Economic, Social and Political Background of the Twelve Articles of the Swabian Peasants of 1525'. In Bak, ed., *German Peasant War of 1525*.

Blickle, Peter, 'Memmingen—Ein Zentrum der Reformation'. In *Die Geschichte der Stadt Memmingen, Band 1*, edited by Joachim Jahn, Hans W. Bayer, and Uli Braun. Stuttgart: WBG, Theiss, 1997.

Blickle, Peter, 'Nochmals zur Entstehung der Zwölf Artikel im Bauernkrieg'. In *Bauer, Reich und Reformation: Festschrift für Günther Franz zum 80. Geburtstag am 23. Mai 1982*, edited by Peter Blickle. Stuttgart: Eugen Ulmer, 1982.

Blickle, Peter, 'Die Reformation in Erfurt'. In *Erfurt 742–1992. Stadtgeschichte, Universitätsgeschichte*, edited by Ulman Weiß. Weimar: Hermann Böhlaus Nachf, 1992.

Blickle, Peter, *Die Revolution von 1525*. Munich: Oldenbourg Verlag, 1977 (4th ed., revised and extended, Munich: Oldenbourg Verlag, 2004).

Blickle, Peter, *The Revolution of 1525: The German Peasants' War from a New Perspective*. Translated by Thomas A. Brady and H. C. Erik Midelfort. Baltimore, MD: Johns Hopkins University Press, 1981.

Blickle, Peter, and Holenstein, André, *Agrarverfassungsverträge: Eine Dokumentation zum Wandel in den Beziehungen zwischen Herrschaften und Bauern am Ende des Mittelalters*. Oldenbourg: De Gruyter, 2016.

Boockmann, Hartmut, *Der Deutsche Orden: Zwölf Kapitel aus seiner Geschichte*. Munich: C. H. Beck, 2012.

Bossert, Gustav, 'Zur Geschichte des Bauernkriegs im heutigen Baden', *Zeitschrift für die Geschichte des Oberrheins* 65 / NF 26 (1911): 250–266.

Boyd Brown, Christopher, *Singing the Gospel: Lutheran Hymns and the Success of the Reformation*. Cambridge, MA: Harvard University Press, 2005.

Braudel, Fernand, *The Structures of Everyday Life: Civilization and Capitalism, 15th–18th Century*. New York: Harper and Row, 1979.

Bräuer, Siegfried, 'Der Hüttenmeister Christoph Meinhard in Eisleben und seine Beziehung zu Thomas Müntzer'. In *Europa in der Frühen Neuzeit, Bd. 6, Vormoderne*, edited by Erich Donnert. Berlin: Vandenhoeck & Ruprecht, 1997.

Bräuer, Siegfried, 'Luthers Reise in das Bauernkriegsgebiet'. In Vogler, ed., *Bauernkrieg zwischen Harz und Thüringer Wald*.

Bräuer, Siegfried, 'Simon Hoffman "Ein lybhaber ewangelischer warheytt"'. In *Erfurt Geschichte und Gegenwart*, edited by Ulman Weiß. Weimar: Böhlaus Nachfolger, 1995.

Bräuer, Siegfried, and Vogler, Günter, *Thomas Müntzer: Neue Ordnung machen in der Welt. Eine Biographie*. Gütersloh: Gütersloher Verlagshaus, 2016.

Bredekamp, Horst, 'Wasserangst und Wasserfreude in Renaissance und Manierismus'. In *Kulturgeschichte des Wassers*, edited by Hartmut Böhme. Frankfurt am Main: Suhrkamp, 1988.

Breul-Kunkel, Wolfgang, *Herrschaftskrise und Reformation*. Gütersloh: Gütersloher Verlagshaus, 2000.

Broy, Erich, 'Reformation und Bauernkrieg'. In *Leipheim. Heimatbuch einer schwäbischen Stadt an der Donau*, edited by Erich Broy. Weißenhorn: Anton H. Konrad Verlag, 1991.

Brun, Katherine, *The Abbot and His Peasants: Territorial Formation in Salem from the Later Middle Ages to the Thirty Years War*. Berlin: De Gruyter, 2016.

Brunner, Horst, 'Von uppiglichen dingen / so will ichs heben an von leidigen baurn singen / wie sie es griffen an. Literatur und Öffentlichkeit im Bauernkrieg'. In Fuchs and Wagner, eds., *Bauernkrieg in Franken.*

Bubenheimer, Ulrich, *Thomas Müntzer: Herkunft und Bildung.* Leiden: Brill, 1989.

Bubenheimer, Ulrich, *Thomas Müntzer und Wittenberg.* Mühlhausen: Thomas-Müntzer-Gesellschaft e.V., 2014.

Bubenheimer, Ulrich, *Wittenberg 1517–1522 Diskussions-, Aktionsgemeinschaft und Stadtreformation.* Tübingen: Mohr Siebeck, 2023.

Bücking, Jürgen, *Michael Gaismair, Reformer, Sozialrebell, Revolutionär: Seine Rolle im Tiroler 'Bauernkrieg' (1525/32).* Stuttgart: Klett-Cotta, 1978.

Bumiller, Casimir, 'Der Bauernkrieg im Hegau 1524/5. Rekonstruktion einer revolutionären Bewegung'. In *Hilzingen. Geschichte und Geschichten,* edited by Gemeinde Hilzingen. Konstanz-Hilzingen: Gemeinde Konstanz-Hilzingen: 1998.

Buszello, Horst, 'Die Christliche Vereinigung'. In Kuhn, ed., *Der Bauernkrieg in Oberschwaben.*

Buszello, Horst, *Der deutsche Bauernkrieg von 1525 als politische Bewegung.* Berlin: Technische Universität Berlin, 1969.

Buszello, Horst, 'Oberrheinlande'. In Buszello, Blickle, and Endres, eds., *Der deutsche Bauernkrieg.*

Buszello, Horst, Blickle, Peter, and Endres, Rudolf, eds., *Der deutsche Bauernkrieg.* Paderborn: Ferdinand Schöningh, 1984.

Carsten, F. L., 'Der Bauernkrieg in Ostpreussen 1525'. *International Review of Social History* 3 (1938): 398–410.

Christiansen, Eric, *The Northern Crusades: The Baltic and the Catholic frontier, 1100–1525.* London: Macmillan, 1980.

Clark, Christopher, *Revolutionary Spring: Fighting for a New World 1848–1849.* London: Penguin Books, 2023.

Cohn, Henry J., 'Anticlericalism in the German Peasants' War 1525'. *Past and Present* 83, no. 1 (1979): 3–31.

Conrad, Franziska, *Reformation in der bäuerlichen Gesellschaft. Zur Rezeption reformatorischer Theologie im Elsass.* Stuttgart: Franz Steiner Verlag, 1984.

Creasman, Allyson F., 'The Virgin Mary Against the Jews: Anti-Jewish Polemic in the Pilgrimage to the Schöne Maria of Regensburg, 1519–25'. *Sixteenth Century Journal* 33, no. 4 (2002): 963–980.

Dammaschke, Marion, and Müller, Thomas T., eds., *Thomas Müntzer im Blick. Günter Vogler zum 90. Geburtstag.* Mühlhausen: Schriftenreihe der Thomas Müntzer Gesellschaft, 2023.

Demel, Bernhard, 'Die Reformation in ihrer Auswirkung auf den Deutschen Orden in Thüringen unter Berücksichtigung von Kardinal Christian August von Sachsen-Zeitz'. In Müller, ed., *Der Deutsche Orden und Thüringen.*

Diemer, Kurt, 'Der Baltringer Haufen'. In Kuhn, ed., *Der Bauernkrieg in Oberschwaben.*

Dietmann, Andreas, 'Die Prediger Jakob Strauß und Wolfgang Stein im Bauernkrieg'. In Müller, Schirmer, and Greiling, eds., *Reformation und Bauernkrieg*.

Dillinger, Johannes, 'Der Bundschuh von 1517. Neue Quellen, eine Chronologie und der Versuch einer Revision'. *Zeitschrift für die Geschichte des Oberrheins* 153 (2005): 357–378.

Dillinger, Johannes, 'Freiburgs Bundschuh: Die Konstruktion der Bauernerhebung von 1417'. *Zeitschrift für historische Forschung* 32, no. 3 (2005): 407–435.

Drummond, Andrew, *The Dreadful History and Judgement of God on Thomas Müntzer: The Life and Times of an Early German Revolutionary*. London: Verso Books, 2024.

Endres, Rudolf, 'Franken'. In Buszello, Blickle, and Endres, eds., *Der deutsche Bauernkrieg*.

Engels, Friedrich, *Der deutsche Bauernkrieg*, first published in *Neue Rheinische Zeitung*, 5 and 6, 1850; ed. of 1875 in *Werke, Band 7*, by Karl Marx and Friedrich Engels, 327–413.

Engels, Friedrich, *The Peasant War in Germany*. Edited by Vic Schneierson. Moscow: Progress Publishers, 1956 (2nd ed. 1965; 1977 printing). Orig. pub. 1850.

Eydinger, Ulrike, 'Motive historischer Flugblätter und Druckgraphiken im Bauernkriegspanorama von Werner Tübke. Zur Genese des Kunstwerkes'. In Müller, Schirmer, and Greiling, eds., *Reformation und Bauernkrieg*.

Falk, Gebhard, 'Strafgeldregister, unausgeschöpfte Quellen zur Geschichte des Bauernkrieges 1525 in Thüringen'. In *Die Frühbürgerliche Revolution in Deutschland*, edited by Gerhard Brendler. Berlin: Akademie Verlag, 1961.

Fauth, Dieter, 'Träume bei religiösen Dissidenten in der frühen Reformation'. In *Religiöse Devianz in christlich geprägten Gesellschaften: Vom hohen Mittelalter bis zur Frühaufklärung*. Würzburg: Religion & Kultur Verlag, 1999.

Fessner, Michael, 'Die Familie Luder in Möhra und Mansfeld. Archivalische Überlieferungen zum Elternhaus von Martin Luther'. In *Fundsache Luther: Archäologen auf den Spuren des Reformators*, edited by Harald Meller. Halle an der Saale: WBG, 2008.

Fessner, Michael, 'Die Familie Luder und das Bergwerks- und Hüttenwesen in der Grafschaft Mansfeld und im Herzogtum Braunschweig-Wölfenbüttel'. In Knape, ed., *Martin Luther und Eisleben*.

Fessner, Michael, 'Das Montanwesen in der Grafschaft Mansfeld zu Luthers Zeiten'. *Montanregion als Sozialregion: Zur gesellschaftlichen Dimension von 'Region' in der Montanwirtschaft*. Husum: Matthiesen Verlag, 2012.

Fessner, Michael, 'Der Steinkohlenbergbau in der Grafschaft Mark und seine konjunkturelle Entwicklung im 17. Und 18. Jahrhundert'. In *Konjunkturen im europäischen Bergbau in vorindustrieller Zeit: Festschrift für Ekkehard Westermann zum 60. Geburtstag*, edited by Christoph Bartels and Markus A. Denzel. Stuttgart: Steiner, 2000.

Fichtner, Paula S., *Protestantism and Primogeniture in Early Modern Germany*. New Haven, CT: Yale University Press, 1989.

Fischer, Ludwig, *Die Lutherische Pamphlete gegen Thomas Müntzer*. Berlin: De Gruyter, 1976.

Foister, Susan, and Brink, Peter van den, *Dürer's Journeys: Travels of a Renaissance Artist*. London: National Gallery Company, 2021.

Franz, Günther, *Der deutsche Bauernkrieg*, vol. 1. Darmstadt: Wissenschaftliche Buchgesellschaft, 1969. (Also consulted 1st ed. of 1933; and 1939 edition.)

Franz, Günther, 'Matern Feuerbacher', in NDB.

Fuchs, Franz, 'Lorenz Fries, Christoph Scheurl und Sebastian von Rotenhan. Ein neuer Bericht über die "beurisch auffrur" 1525'. In *Lorenz Fries und sein Werk. Bilanz und Einordnung*, edited by Franz Fuchs, Stefan Petersen, and Ulrich Wagner. Würzburg: Schöningh, 2014.

Fuchs, Franz, and Wagner, Ulrich, eds., *Bauernkrieg in Franken*. Würzburg: Königshausen & Neumann, 2016.

Garrioch, David, 'Sounds of the City: The Soundscapes of Early Modern European Towns'. *Urban History* 30 (2003): 5–25.

Goertz, Hans-Jürgen, *Nähe Gottes und Veränderung der Welt: Aufsätze zu Thomas Müntzer und den Täufern*. Mühlhausen: Thomas-Müntzer-Gesellschaft e.V., 2020.

Goertz, Hans-Jürgen, *Thomas Müntzer. Revolutionär am Ende der Zeiten*, Munich: C. H. Beck, 2015.

Goertz, Hans-Jürgen, *Träume, Offenbarungen und Visionen in der Reformation*. Wiesbaden: Franz Steiner, 1989.

Göpfert, Dieter, *Bauernkrieg am Bodensee und Oberrhein: 1524–1525*. Freiburg: Rombach, 1980.

Gordon, F. Bruce, *Zwingli: God's Armed Prophet*. New Haven, CT: Yale University Press, 2022.

Graupner, Volker, 'Die Dorfgemeinden und ihre Artikel im Bauernkrieg'. In Vogler, ed., *Bauernkrieg zwischen Harz und Thüringer Wald*.

Greenblatt, Stephen, *Learning to Curse: Essays in Early Modern Culture*. New York: Routledge, 1990.

Greschat, Martin, *Martin Bucer: A Reformer and His Times*. Translated by Stephen E. Buckwalter. Louisville, KY: Westminster John Knox Press, 2004.

Greschat, Martin, *Philipp Melanchthon: Theologe, Pädagoge und Humanist*. Gütersloh: Random House GmbH, 2011.

Groebner, Valentin, 'Losing Face, Saving Face: Noses and Honour in the Late Medieval Town'. *History Workshop Journal* 40 (1995): 1–15.

Groschinski, Niklas, 'Cranach's Animals: A Study of Their Form and Function'. MA diss., Warburg Institute, 2022.

Gyss, Joseph Meinrad, *Histoire de la ville d'Obernai et environs immédiats*. Strasbourg: Salomon, 1866.

Hacke, Daniela, 'Hearing Cultures. Plädoyer für eine Klanggeschichte der Bauernkriege'. *Geschichte in Wissenschaft und Unterricht* 66 (2015): 650–662.

Hacke, Daniela, 'Mit Augen und Ohren die Welt betrachten. Sinnesirritationen in englischen Reisenberichten über Nordamerika im 16. Und 17. Jahrhundert'. *L'Homme. Europäische Zeitschrift für Feministische Geschichtswissenschaft* 31 (2020): 27–47.

Hagen, William W., *Ordinary Prussians: Brandenburg Junkers and Villagers, 1500–1840*. Cambridge, UK: Cambridge University Press, 2007.

Hagen, William W., 'Village Life in East-Elbian Germany and Poland, 1400–1800: Subjection, Self-Defense and Survival'. In Scott, ed., *Peasantries of Europe*.

Haggenmüller, Martina, 'Der Allgäuer Haufen'. In Kuhn, ed., *Der Bauernkrieg in Oberschwaben*.

Hahn, Philip, 'The Emperor's Boot, or: Perceiving Public Rituals in the Urban Reformation'. *German History* 35, no. 3 (2017): 362–380.

Hahnemann, Ulrich, 'Die Einwohner von Frankenhausen vor, im und nach dem Bauernkrieg 1525'. In Müller, Schirmer, and Greiling, eds., *Reformation und Bauernkrieg*.

Hamm, Joachim, 'Traum und Zeitklage. Dürers "Traumgesicht", Eobans "Bellum servile Germaniae" und der Bauernkrieg in Franken'. In Fuchs and Wagner, eds., *Bauernkrieg in Franken*.

Hanß, Stefan, 'Face-Work: Making Hair Matter in Sixteenth-Century Central Europe'. *Gender and History* 33, no. 2 (2021): 314–345.

Hardy, Duncan, *Associative Political Culture in the Holy Roman Empire: Upper Germany, 1346–1521*. Oxford, UK: Oxford University Press, 2018.

Hasselbeck, Johannes, *Die Folgen des Deutschen Bauernkriegs im Hochstift Bamberg*. Bamberg: University of Bamberg Press, 2012.

Hasselhoff, Görge, and Mayenburg, David, eds., *Die Zwölf Artikel von 1525 und das 'Göttliche Recht' der Bauern*. Würzburg: Ergon, 2012.

Hecker, Hans-Joachim, 'Der Bauernkrieg'. In Fuchs and Wagner, eds., *Bauernkrieg in Franken*.

Heidenreich, Benjamin, *Ein Ereignis ohne Namen?: Zu den Vorstellungen des 'Bauernkriegs' von 1525 in den Schriften der 'Aufständischen' und in der zeitgenössischen Geschichtsschreibung*. Oldenbourg: De Gruyter, 2019.

Helmberger, Werner, *Festung Marienberg Würzburg mit Fürstenbaumuseum: Amtlicher Führer*. Munich: Bayerische Verw. d. staatl. Schlösser, 2013.

Hill, Kat, *Baptism, Brotherhood, and Belief in Reformation Germany: Anabaptism and Lutheranism, 1525–1585*. Oxford, UK: Oxford University Press, 2015.

Hill, Kat, 'Fun and Loathing in Later Lutheran Culture'. *Past and Present* 234, suppl. (2017): 67–89.

Hill, Kat, 'Making Lutherans'. *Past and Present* 234, suppl. (2017): 9–32.

Höbelheinrich, Norbert, *Die neun Städte des Mainzer Oberstifts: Ihre verfassungsmäßige Entwicklung und ihre Beteiligung am Bauernkrieg, 1346–1527*. Hildesheim: Georg Olms, 1994.

Honemann, Volker, and Henkel, Mathias, *Tradition und Erneuerung: Mittelalterlicher Hintergrund der Gottesdienstreform Thomas Müntzers in Allstedt: Zwei Beiträge*. Mühlhausen: Thomas-Müntzer-Gesellschaft e.V., 2015.

Honemeyer, Karl, *Thomas Müntzer und Martin Luther: Ihr Ringen um die Musik des Gottesdienstes: Untersuchungen zum 'Deutzsch Kirchenampt' 1523*. Berlin: Verlag Merseburger, 1974.

Hoyer, Siegfried, *Das Militärwesen im deutschen Bauernkrieg 1524–1526*. Berlin: Militär Verlag der Deutschen Demokratischen Republik, 1975.

Hoyer, Siegfried, 'Die "Schlacht" bei Frankenhausen'. In Vogler, ed., *Bauernkrieg zwischen Harz und Thüringer Wald*.

Hubatsch, Walther, 'Albert of Brandenburg-Ansbach'. In *Studies in Medieval and Modern German History*. Houndmills: Macmillan, 1985.

Hubatsch, Walther, *Albrecht von Brandenburg-Ansbach Herzog von Preussen. Deutschordens-Hochmeister und Herzog in Preußen, 1490–1568*. Heidelberg: Quelle und Meyer, 1960.

Jankowski, Günter, *Mansfeld: Gebiet—Geschlecht—Geschichte; Zur Familiengeschichte der Grafen Mansfeld*. Trier: Kliomedia, 2005.

Joestel, Volkmar, *Geschwinde Zeitläufte. Wittenberg und die Reformation in Kursachsen 1521–1522*. Leipzig: Evangelische Verlagsanstalt, 2023.

Joestel, Volkmar, 'Karlstadt und der Bauernkrieg in Ostthüringen'. In Müller, Schirmer, and Greiling, eds., *Reformation und Bauernkrieg*.

Joestel, Volkmar, *Ostthüringen und Karlstadt. Soziale Bewegung und Reformation im mittleren Saaletal am Vorabend des Bauernkrieges (1522–1524)*. Berlin: Schelzky and Jeep, 1996.

Jürgensmeier, Friedhelm, and Schwerdtfeger, Regina, eds., *Orden und Klöster im Zeitalter von Reformation und katholischer Reform 1500–1700*. 3 vols. Münster: Aschendorff Verlag, 2005–2007.

Kaplan, Debra, 'Entangled Negotiations: Josel of Rosheim and the Peasants' Rebellion of 1525'. *Association for Jewish Studies* 40, no. 1 (2016): 125–143.

Karant-Nunn, Susan C., *Zwickau in Transition, 1500–1547: The Reformation as an Agent of Change*. Columbus: Ohio State University Press, 1987.

Kaufmann, Thomas, *Der Bauernkrieg—Ein Medienereignis*. Berlin: Herder Verlag, 2024.

Kaufmann, Thomas, *Erlöste und Verdammte: Eine Geschichte der Reformation*. Munich: C. H. Beck, 2017.

Kießling, Rolf, and Troßbach, Wener, eds., *Grundzüge der Agrargeschichte: Band 1: Vom Spätmittelalter bis zum Dreißigjährigen Krieg (1350–1650)*. Cologne: Böhlau, 2016.

Klebon, Michael, *Im Taumel des Evangeliums. Anton Eisenhut und der Kraichgauer Haufen im 'Bauernkrieg'*. Ubstadt-Weiher: verlag regionalkultur, 2020.

Knape, Rosemarie, ed., *Martin Luther und Eisleben*. Leipzig: Evangelische Verlagsanstalt, 2007.

Knott, Sarah, and Griffin, Emma, eds., *Mothering's Many Labours*. Oxford, UK: Oxford University Press, 2021.

Kobelt-Groch, Marion, *Aufsässige Töchter Gottes. Frauen im Bauernkrieg und in der Täuferbewegung*. Frankfurt: Campus Verlag, 1993.

Kobelt-Groch, Marion, 'So waren sie in meiner Erinnerung, die Frauen der Bauern'. In Vogler, ed., *Bauernkrieg zwischen Harz und Thüringer Wald*.

Kolde, Theodor, *Hans Denck und die gottlosen Maler von Nürnberg*. Erlangen: Verlag von Fr. Junge, 1901.

Krentz, Natalie, *Ritualwandel und Deutungshoheit: Die Frühe Reformation in der Residenzstadt Wittenberg (1500–1533)*. Tübingen: Mohr Siebeck, 2014.

Kuhn, Elmar L., 'Der Seehaufen'. In Kuhn, ed., *Der Bauernkrieg in Oberschwaben*.

Kuhn, Elmar L., ed., *Der Bauernkrieg in Oberschwaben*. Tübingen: De Gruyter, 2011.

Kümin, Beat A., *Imperial Villages: Cultures of Political Freedom in the German Lands, c. 1300–1800*. Leiden: Brill, 2019.

Kümin, Beat, and Tlusty, B. Ann, eds., *The World of the Tavern: Public Houses in Early Modern Europe*. London: Routledge, 2002.

Laube, Adolf, 'Der Aufstand der Schwazer Bergarbeiter 1525 und ihre Haltung im Tiroler Bauernkrieg'. *Jahrbuch für Geschichte des Feudalismus* 2 (1978): 225–258.

Laube, Adolf, 'Social Arguments in Early Reformation Pamphlets, and Their Significance for the German Peasants' War'. *Social History* 12 (1978): 361–378.

Laube, Adolf, Steinmetz, Max, and Vogler, Günter, *Illustrierte Geschichte der deutschen frühbürgerlichen Revolution*. Berlin: Dietz, 1974

Leaver, Robin A., *The Whole Church Sings: Congregational Singing in Luther's Wittenberg*. Grand Rapids, MI: Eerdmans, 2017.

Leng, Rainer, 'Bauern vor den Mauern: Technische und taktische Aspekte des Sturms auf die Festung Marienberg in Würzburg'. In Fuchs and Wagner, eds., *Bauernkrieg in Franken*.

Litz, Gudrun, *Die reformatorische Bilderfrage in den schwäbischen Reichsstädten*. Tübingen: Mohr Siebeck, 2007.

Lorenz, Sönke, et al., eds., *Dagersheim vom Frühmittelalter bis zur Gegenwart*. Böblingen: Stadt Böblingen, 1998.

Loserth, Johann, *Die Stadt Waldshut und die vorderösterreichische Regierung in den Jahren 1523–1526*. Vienna: Tempsky, 1891.

Ludolphy, Ingetraut, *Friedrich der Weise: Kurfürst von Sachsen 1463–1525*. Göttingen: Vandenhoeck & Ruprecht, 1984.

Lühmann-Schmid, Irnfriede, 'Der Mainzer Marktbrunnen, seine Denkmals- und Bildideen'. *Mainzer Zeitschrift. Mittelrheinisches Jahrbuch für Archäologie, Kunst und Geschichte* 69 (1974): 180–186.

Mandry, Julia, 'Die Reflexionen der thüringischen, sächsischen und hessischen Fürsten über die Aufständischen im Bauernkrieg'. In Müller, Schirmer, and Greiling, eds., *Reformation und Bauernkrieg*.

Marquardt, Frederick, 'God, Christ and Serfdom. Christian Egalitarianism in the Twelve Articles of the Upper Swabian Peasants (1525)'. *Archiv für Reformationsgeschichte* (2016): 35–60.

Marx, Karl, *The Eighteenth Brumaire of Louis Bonaparte* (1851). In *Karl Marx, Friedrich Engels: Collected Works*, vol. 11. Moscow: Progress Publishers, 1937, 1979.

Matheson, Peter, *Argula von Grumbach: A Woman Before Her Time*. Eugene, OR: Cascade Books, 2013.

Matheson, Peter, *The Imaginative World of the Reformation*. Edinburgh: T&T Clark, 2000.

Matheson, Peter, 'The Language of Thomas Müntzer'. In Dammaschke and Müller, eds., *Thomas Müntzer im Blick*.

Matheson, Peter, *The Rhetoric of the Reformation*. London: T&T International, 2004.

Matheson, Peter, 'Thomas Muntzer's Vindication and Refutation: A Language for the Common People'. *Sixteenth Century Journal* 20, no. 4 (1989): 603–615.

Matthes, Christian, 'Die archäologische Entdeckung des originalen Luther-Geburtshauses'. In Knape, ed., *Martin Luther und Eisleben*.

Mauelshagen, Franz, *Klimageschichte der Neuzeit, 1500–1900*. Darmstadt: Wissenschaftliche Buchgesellschaft, 2009.

Maurer, Hans-Martin, 'Der Bauernkrieg als Massenerhebung. Dynamik einer revolutionären Bewegung'. In *Bausteine zur geschichtlichen Landeskunde von Baden-Württemberg*, edited by Kommission für geschichtliche Landeskunde in Baden-Württemberg. Stuttgart, 1979, 255–295.

Maurer, Hans-Martin, 'Beiwort zur Karte 6.11, Bauernkrieg 1524–5, Heereszüge der Aufständischen und des Schwäbischen Bundes'. *Historischer Atlas von Baden-Württemberg*, ed. Kommission für geschichtliche Landeskunde in Baden-Württemberg. Stuttgart, 1972–1988. Vol. 6, Karte 6.11 (unpaginated).

Maurer, Justus, *Prediger im Bauernkrieg*. Stuttgart: Calwer Verlag, 1979.

Maurer, Justus Hermann, 'Das Verhalten der reformatorisch gesinnten Geistlichen Süddeutschlands im Bauernkrieg 1525'. PhD thesis, University of Tübingen, 1975.

Mayenburg, David von, *Gemeiner Mann und Gemeines Recht: Die Zwölf Artikel und das Recht des ländlichen Raums im Zeitalter des Bauernkriegs*. Frankfurt am Main: Klostermann, 2018.

McKee, Elsie Anne, *Katharina Schütz Zell: The Life and Thought of a Sixteenth-Century Reformer*. Leiden: Brill, 1999.

Medick, Hans, *Weben und Überleben in Laichingen, 1650–1900. Lokalgeschichte als Allgemeine Geschichte*. Göttingen: Vandenhoeck & Ruprecht, 1997.

Merkel, Kerstin, *Jenseits-sicherung. Kardinal Albrecht von Brandenburg und seine Grabdenkmäler*. Regensburg: Schnell und Steiner, 2004.

Metzger, Christof, ed., *Albrecht Dürer*. Vienna: Albertina, 2019.

Miegel, Annekathrin, 'Der Mediziner Alexander Seitz aus Marbach. Ein Freund des "Armen Konrad" und Agitator'. In Rückert, ed., *Der 'Arme Konrad' vor Gericht*.

Militzer, Klaus, *Die Geschichte des Deutschen Ordens*. Stuttgart: Kohlhammer, 2005.

Miller, Douglas, *The Army of the Swabian League 1525*. Warwick: Helion & Company, 2019.

Miller, Douglas, *Frankenhausen 1525*. Seaton Burn: Blagdon, 2017.

Miller, Douglas, *The German Peasants' War 1524–26*. Warwick: Helion & Company, 2023.

Miller, Douglas, and McBride, Angus, *Armies of the German Peasants' War 1524–25*. Oxford, UK: Osprey, 2003.

Morass, Peter, and Thalinger, Michael, 'Cranach im Fokus der Naturwissenschaft'. In *Cranach natürlich, Hieronymus in der Wildnis*, edited by Wolfgang Meighörner. Innsbruck: Haymon, 2018.

Mötsch, Johannes, 'Aufständische Führungselite in Henneberg'. In Müller, Schirmer, and Greiling, eds., *Reformation und Bauernkrieg*.

Mötsch, Johannes, *Die Wallfahrt zu Grimmenthal: Urkunden, Rechnungen, Mirakelbuch*. Cologne: Böhlau, 2004.

Müller, Jürgen, 'Albrecht Dürer's Peasant Engravings: A Different Laocoön, or the Birth of Aesthetic Subversion in the Spirit of the Reformation'. *Journal of Historians of Netherlandish Art* 3, no. 1 (2011).

Müller, Laurenz, *Diktatur und Revolution. Reformation und Bauernkrieg in der Geschichtsschreibung des 'Dritten Reiches' und der DDR*. Berlin: De Gruyter Oldenbourg, 2004.

Müller, Nikolaus, *Die Wittenberger Bewegung: 1521 und 1522: Die Vorgänge in und um Wittenberg während Luthers Wartburgaufenthalt, Briefe, Akten u. dgl. und Personalien*. Leipzig: Verlag von M. Heinsius Nachfolger, 1911.

Müller, Thomas T., *Bauernkrieg nach dem Bauernkrieg*. Duderstadt: Mecke, 2001.

Müller, Thomas T., ed., *Der Deutsche Orden und Thüringen. Aspekte einer 800-jährigen Geschichte*. Petersberg: Michael Imhof Verlag, 2014.

Müller, Thomas T., 'Ein ehrbarer Rat, entlaufene Mönche und streitbare Weiber: Zu den reformatorischen Bestrebungen in der Reichsstadt Mühlhausen in Thüringen bis zum Jahr 1525'. In *Vor- und Frühreformation in thüringischen Städten (1470–1525/30)*, edited by Joachim Emig, Volker Leppin, and Uwe Schirmer. Cologne: Böhlau, 2013.

Müller, Thomas T., 'Frühreformation, Bauernkrieg und Deutscher Orden—das Beispiel Mühlhausen in Thüringen'. In Müller, ed., *Der Deutsche Orden und Thüringen*.

Müller, Thomas T., *Frühreformation in Westthüringen: Jakob Strauß in Eisenach und Matthäus Hisolidus in Creuzberg*. Jena: Vopelius, 2019.

Müller, Thomas T., 'The German Peasants' War (1524–5)'. In *War and Peace in the Religious Conflicts of the Long Sixteenth Century*, edited by Gianmarco Braghi and Davide Dainese. Göttungen: Vandenhoeck & Ruprecht, 2023.

Müller, Thomas T., 'Macht Aufruhr durstig? Zur Rolle des Bieres im Bauernkrieg'. *Mühlhäuser Beiträge* 27 (2004): 82–90.

Müller, Thomas T., *Mörder ohne Opfer. Die Reichsstadt Mühlhausen und der Bauernkrieg in Thüringen*. Petersberg: Michel Imhof Verlag, 2021.

Müller, Thomas T., *Thomas Müntzer im Bauernkrieg: Fakten—Fiktionen—Desiderate*. Mühlhausen: Thomas-Müntzer-Gesellschaft e.V., 2016.

Müller, Thomas T., *Thomas Müntzer in der Mühlhäuser Chronistik. Untersuchung und Neuedition der den Bauernkrieg betreffenden Abschnitte des 'Chronicon Mulhusinum'*. Mühlhausen: Thomas Müntzer Gesellschaft e.V., 2004.

Müller, Thomas T., 'Thomas Müntzers Runenschwert. Einem Mythos auf der Spur'. In Dammaschke and Müller, eds., *Thomas Müntzer im Blick*.

Müller, Thomas T., Schirmer, Uwe, and Greiling, Werner, eds., *Reformation und Bauernkrieg*. Vienna: Böhlau Verlag, 2019.

Nelson Burnett, Amy, *Karlstadt and the Origins of the Eucharist Controversy: A Study in the Circulation of Ideas*. Oxford, UK: Oxford University Press, 2011.

Neumann, Franziska, 'Reformation als religiöse Devianz? Das Schneeberger Kondominat und der Fall Georg Amandus (1524/25)'. In *Göttlicher Zorn und menschli-*

ches Maß. Religiöse Abweichung in frühneuzeitlichen Stadtgemeinschaften, edited by Alexander Kästner and Gerd Schwerhoff. Tübingen: UVK Verlag, 2013.

Neumann, Franziska, 'Der selektive Blick. Frauen im Bauernkrieg zwischen Frauen und Geschlechtergeschichte'. In *Frauen und Reformation. Handlungsfelder, Rollenmuster, Engagement*, edited by Martina Schattkowsky. Leipzig: Leipziger Universitätsverlag, 2016.

Oberman, Heiko A., 'The Gospel of Social Unrest: 450 Years After the So-Called "German Peasant's War" of 1525'. *Harvard Theological Review* 69, no. 1–2 (1976): 103–129.

Ocker, Christopher, 'After the Peasants' War: Barbara (Schweikart) von Fuchstein Fights for Her Property'. *Renaissance and Reformation* 40 (2017): 141–159.

Ocker, Christopher, *Church Robbers and Reformers in Germany, 1525–1547: Confiscation and Religious Purpose in the Holy Roman Empire*. Leiden: Brill, 2006.

Oka, Hiroto, *Der Bauernkrieg in der Landgrafschaft Stühlingen und seine Vorgeschichte seit der Mitte des 15. Jahrhunderts*. Constance: Hartung-Gorre Verlag, 1998.

Parker, Geoffrey, *Emperor: A New Life of Charles V*. New Haven, CT: Yale University Press, 2019.

Parker, Geoffrey, *Global Crisis: War, Climate Change and Catastrophe in the Seventeenth Century*. New Haven, CT: Yale University Press, 2013.

Pfister, Christian, *La guerre des paysans dans les Seigneuries de Riquewihr et de Ribaupierre*. Ribeauville: Rene Brunschwieg, 1924.

Pfister, Ulrich, *Urban Population in Germany, 1500–1850*. Department of Economics, University of Münster, 2020. www.wiwi.uni-muenster.de/cqe/sites/cqe/files/CQE_Paper/cqe_wp_90_2020.pdf.

Plummer, Marjorie Elizabeth, *Stripping the Veil: Convent Reform, Protestant Nuns, and Female Devotional Life in Sixteenth-Century Germany*. Oxford, UK: Oxford University Press, 2022.

Potter, G. R., *Zwingli*. Cambridge, UK: Cambridge University Press, 1976.

Radlkofer, Max, *Johann Eberlin von Günzburg und sein Vetter Hans Jakob Wehe von Leipheim*. Nördlingen: Verlag der C H Beck'schen Buchhandlung, 1887.

Rammstedt, Otthein, 'Stadtunruhen 1525'. In Wehler, ed., *Der Deutsche Bauernkrieg 1524–1526*.

Rauch, Moritz von, 'Der Bauernführer Jäcklein Rohrbach von Böckingen'. *Württembergische Vierteljahreshefte für Landesgeschichte, NF* 32 (1926): 21–35.

Rebel, Hermann, 'Peasantries Under the Austrian Empire'. In Scott, ed., *Peasantries of Europe*.

Robisheaux, Thomas, 'The Peasantries of Western Germany, 1300–1750'. In Scott, ed., *Peasantries of Europe*.

Robisheaux, Thomas, 'Peasants and Pastors: Rural Youth Control and the Reformation in Hohenlohe, 1540–1680'. *Social History* 6, no. 3 (1981): 281–300.

Robisheaux, Thomas, *Rural Society and the Search for Order in Early Modern Germany*. Cambridge, UK: Cambridge University Press, 1989.

Robisheaux, Thomas Barnett-, 'Peasant Revolts in Germany and Central Europe After the Peasants' War: Comments on the Literature'. *Central European History* 17 (1984): 384–403.

Rockwell, William Walker, *Die Doppelehe des Landgrafen Philipp von Hessen*. Marburg: N. G. Elwert, 1904.

Röder, Brendan, *Der Körper des Priesters: Gebrechen im Katholizismus der Frühen Neuzeit*. Frankfurt: Campus Verlag, 2021.

Rommel, Ludwig, 'Zur sozialen Zusammensetzung der aufständischen Landbevölkerung in Thüringen'. In Vogler, ed., *Bauernkrieg zwischen Harz und Thüringer Wald*.

Roper, Lyndal, ' "The Common Man", "The Common Good", "Common Women": Gender and Meaning in the German Reformation Commune'. *Social History* 12, no. 1 (1987): 1–21.

Roper, Lyndal, *Living I Was Your Plague*. Princeton, NJ: Princeton University Press, 2021.

Roper, Lyndal, 'Luther and Gender'. In *Cultural Shifts and Ritual Transformations in Reformation Europe: Essays in Honor of Susan C. Karant-Nunn*, edited by Victoria Christman and Marjorie Elizabeth Plummer. Leiden: Brill, 2020.

Roper, Lyndal, *Martin Luther: Renegade and Prophet*. London: Bodley Head, 2016.

Roper, Lyndal, *The Witch in the Western Imagination*. Charlottesville: University of Virginia Press, 2012.

Roper, Lyndal, 'Witchcraft and Village Drama'. In *The Witch in the Western Imagination*.

Rösener, Werner, *Bauern im Mittelalter*. Munich: C. H. Beck, 1985.

Rosenkranz, Albert, *Der Bundschuh, die Erhebungen des südwestdeutschen Bauernstandes in den Jahren 1493–1517*. 2 vols. Heidelberg: C. Winter, 1927.

Roß, Hartmut, 'Zur Sozialgeschichte Bambergs vor dem Bauernkrieg'. PhD thesis, Humboldt University, 1956.

Rössner, Philipp Robinson, *Deflation, Devaluation, Rebellion: Geld im Zeitalter der Reformation*. Stuttgart: Franz Steiner Verlag, 2012.

Rössner, Philipp, ed., *Martin Luther: On Commerce and Usury (1524)*. Cambridge, UK: Cambridge University Press, 2015.

Rowlands, Alison, 'The Conditions of Life for the Masses'. In *Early Modern Europe: An Oxford History*, edited by Euan Cameron. Oxford, UK: Oxford University Press, 1999.

Rublack, Ulinka, *Dürer's Lost Masterpiece: Art and Society at the Dawn of a Global World*. Oxford, UK: Oxford University Press, 2023.

Rublack, Ulinka, 'Matter in the Material Renaissance'. *Past and Present* 219 (2013): 41–85.

Rückert, Peter, ed., *Der 'Arme Konrad' vor Gericht. Verhöre, Sprüche und Lieder in Württemberg 1514: Begleitbuch und Katalog zur Ausstellung des Landesarchivs*. Stuttgart: W. Kohlhammer GmbH, 2014.

Rudolf, Hans Ulrich, 'Der Weingartener Vertrag von 1525'. In Kuhn, ed., *Der Bauernkrieg in Oberschwaben*.

Russell, Paul A., *Lay Theology in the Reformation: Popular Pamphleteers in Southwest Germany, 1521–1525*. Cambridge, UK: Cambridge University Press, 1986.

Ruszat-Ewig, Heide, *Was geschah im März 1525 in der Kramerzunftstube in Memmingen?* Memmingen: Historischer Verein Memmingen, 2022.

Sabean, David W., 'German Agrarian Institutions at the Beginning of the Sixteenth Century: Upper Swabia as an Example'. In Bak, ed., *German Peasant War of 1525.*

Sabean, David W., *Landbesitz und Gesellschaft am Vorabend des Bauernkriegs: Eine Studie der sozialen Verhältnisse im südlichen Oberschwaben in den Jahren vor 1525.* Oldenbourg: De Gruyter, 2016.

Sarnowsky, Jürgen, *Der Deutsche Orden.* Munich: C. H. Beck, 2022.

Schama, Simon, *Landscape and Memory.* London: Harper Collins, 1995.

Schilling, Johannes, '"Allen auserwählten Gottesfreunden". Thomas Müntzers Erneuerung des Gottesdienstes für den gemeinen Mann'. In Dammaschke and Müller, eds., *Thomas Müntzer im Blick.*

Schindler, Norbert, 'Der "lange Atem" der bäuerlichen Empörung'. *Zeitschrift für historische Forschung* 49, no. 2 (2022): 209–242.

Schindler, Norbert, *Wilderer im Zeitalter der Französischen Revolution: Ein Kapitel alpiner Sozialgeschichte.* Munich: C. H. Beck, 2001.

Schirmer, Uwe, 'Die Ursachen des Bauernkrieges in Thüringen. Eine sozial-, verfassungs- und reformationsgeschichtliche Spurensuche'. In Müller, Schirmer, and Greiling, eds., *Reformation und Bauernkrieg.*

Schloms, Antje, 'Nach dem Ende Thomas Müntzers—Abrechnung (mit) einer Stadt'. In Müller, Schirmer, and Greiling, eds., *Reformation und Bauernkrieg.*

Schloms, Antje, Stracke, Daniel, and Wittmann, Helge, eds., *Deutscher historischer Städteatlas*, Bd. 6, *Mühlhausen/Th.* Münster: Ardey-Verlag, 2020.

Schneller, Pascal Paul, *800 Jahre Deutscher Orden an Ober-, Hochrhein und in der Schweiz.* Freiburg: Selbstverlag der Komturei 'Am Oberrhein' des Deutschen Ordens, 2021.

Schrenk, Christhard, and Weckbach, Hubert, *Der Vergangenheit nachgespürt: Bilder zur Heilbronner Geschichte von 741–1803: Katalog zur Ausstellung des Stadtarchivs Heilbronn im Deutschhof.* Heilbronn: Stadtarchiv Heilbronn, 1993.

Schubert, Ernst, *Alltag im Mittelalter: Natürliches Lebensumfeld und menschliches Miteinander.* Darmstadt: Primus, 2002.

Schulze, Winfried, *Bäuerlicher Widerstand und feudale Herrschaft in der frühen Neuzeit.* Stuttgart: Frommann-Holzboog, 1980.

Schwerhoff, Gerd, 'Beyond the Heroic Narrative: Towards the Quincentenary of the German Peasants' War, 1525'. *German History* 41, no. 1 (2023): 103–126.

Scott, Tom, 'The Collective Response of Women'. In *The Early Reformation in Germany.*

Scott, Tom, *The Early Reformation in Germany: Between Secular Impact and Radical Vision.* Farnham: Ashgate Publishing, 2013.

Scott, Tom, *Freiburg and the Breisgau: Town-Country Relations in the Age of Reformation and Peasants' War.* Oxford: Clarendon Press, 1995.

Scott, Tom, 'Die Freiburger Talvogtei im Bauernkrieg'. In *Schätze der Welt aus landeshistorischer Perspektive: Festschrift zum 65. Geburtstag von Wolfgang Wüst*, edited by Sabine Wüst. St Ottilien: EOS Verlag, 2018.

Scott, Tom, 'Hubmaier, Schappeler, and Hergot on Social Revolution'. In *The Early Reformation in Germany.*

Scott, Tom, ed., *The Peasantries of Europe: From the Fourteenth to the Eighteenth Centuries.* London: Longman, 1998.

Scott, Tom, 'Ein Radikaler auf Reisen. Zum Aufenthalt Thomas Müntzers in Südwestdeutschland'. In Dammaschke and Müller, eds., *Thomas Müntzer im Blick.*

Scott, Tom, *Raum und Region. Studien zum Oberrhein im europäischen Kontext.* Freiburg: Verlag Karl Alber, 2021.

Scott, Tom, 'Reformation and Peasants' War in Waldshut and Environs: A Structural Analysis'. In Scott, ed., *Town, Country, and Regions in Reformation Germany.*

Scott, Tom, 'South-West German Towns in the Peasants' War: Alliances Between Opportunism and Solidarity'. In Scott ed., *Town, Country, and Regions in Reformation Germany.*

Scott, Tom, 'Die Spätmittelalterliche bäuerliche Unfreiheit in Südwestdeutschland'. In Scott, ed., *Town, Country, and Regions in Reformation Germany.*

Scott, Tom, *Thomas Müntzer: Theology and Revolution in the German Reformation.* Basingstoke: Macmillan, 1989.

Scott, Tom, ed., *Town, Country, and Regions in Reformation Germany.* Leiden: Brill, 2005.

Scribner, Robert W., *For the Sake of Simple Folk: Popular Propaganda for the German Reformation.* Oxford, UK: Clarendon Press, 2004.

Scribner, Robert W., 'Images of the Peasant, 1514–1525'. *Journal of Peasant Studies* 3, no. 1 (1975): 29–48.

Scribner, Robert W., *Popular Culture and Popular Movements in Reformation Germany.* London: Hambledon Press, 1987.

Sea, Thomas, 'The Economic Impact of the German Peasants' War: The Question of Reparations'. *Sixteenth Century Journal* 8 (1977): 75–97.

Sea, Thomas F., 'The German Princes' Responses to the Peasants' Revolt of 1525'. *Central European History* 40 (2007): 219–240.

Sea, Thomas F., 'Imperial Cities and the Peasants' War in Germany'. *Central European History* 12, no. 1 (1979): 3–37.

Sea, Thomas F., 'Predatory Protectors? Conflict and Cooperation in the Suppression of the German Peasants' Revolt of 1525'. *Sixteenth Century Journal* 39 (2008): 89–111.

Sea, Thomas F., 'The Reformation and the Restoration of Civic Authority in Heilbronn, 1525–32'. *Central European History* 19, no. 3 (1986): 235–261.

Sea, Thomas S., 'Schwäbischer Bund'. In Wehler, ed., *Der Deutsche Bauernkrieg 1524–1526.*

Sea, Thomas, 'The Swabian League and the German Peasants' War'. PhD diss., University of California, Berkeley, 1974.

Sea, Thomas, 'The Swabian League and Peasant Disobedience Before the German Peasants' War of 1525'. *Sixteenth Century Journal* 30 (1999): 89–111.

Sea, Thomas S., and Meyer, G., 'Schwäbischer Bund und Bauernkrieg: Bestrafung und Pazifikation'. *Geschichte und Gesellschaft,* Sonderheft, no. 1 (1975): 129–167.

Sider, Ronald J., *Andreas Bodenstein von Karlstadt: The Development of His Thought*. Leiden: E. J. Brill, 1974.

Simons, Patricia, *The Sex of Men in Premodern Europe: A Cultural History*. Cambridge, UK: Cambridge University Press, 2011.

Skinner, Quentin, 'Rethinking Political Liberty'. *History Workshop Journal* 61 (2006): 156–170.

Sladeczek, Martin, 'Mächtige Aufrührer—machtloser Graf? Der Bauernkrieg in der schwarzburgischen Oberherrschaft'. In Müller, Schirmer, and Greiling, eds., *Reformation und Bauernkrieg*.

Smith, Jeffrey Chipps, 'Dürer's Losses and the Dilemmas of Being'. In *Enduring Loss in Early Modern Germany*, edited by Lynn Tatlock. Leiden: Brill, 2010.

Sreenivasan, Govind P., *The Peasants of Ottobeuren, 1487–1726: A Rural Society in Early Modern Europe*. Cambridge, UK: Cambridge University Press, 2004.

Sreenivasan, Govind P., 'The Social Origins of the Peasants' War of 1525 in Upper Swabia'. *Past and Present* 171 (2001): 30–65.

Stahl, Andreas, 'Baugeschichtliche Erkenntnisse zu Luthers Elternhaus in Mansfeld'. In Knape, ed., *Martin Luther und Eisleben*.

Stayer, James M., 'Prophet, Apokalyptiker, Mystiker: Thomas Müntzer und die "Kirche" der Patriarchen, Propheten und Apostel'. In *Endzeiterwartung bei Thomas Müntzer und im frühen Luthertum: Zwei Beiträge*, edited by James M. Stayer and Hartmut Kühne. Mühlhausen: Thomas-Müntzer-Gesellschaft e.V., 2011.

Stedman Jones, Gareth, 'The Determinist Fix: Some Obstacles to the Further Development of the Linguistic Approach to History in the 1990s'. *History Workshop Journal* 42 (1996): 19–35.

Stedman Jones, Gareth, *Languages of Class: Studies in English Working Class History 1832–1982*. Cambridge, UK: Cambridge University Press, 1983.

Steiff, Karl, and Mehring, Gebhard, *Geschichtliche Lieder und Sprüche Württembergs*. Stuttgart: Kohlhammer, 1912.

Steinmetz, Max, 'Die dritte Etappe'. In Wohlfeil, ed., *Der Bauernkrieg 1524–26*.

Stella, Aldo, *La rivoluzione Contadina del 1525 e l'utopia di Michael Gaismayr*. Padua: Liviana Editrice, 1975.

Stengel, Friedemann, 'Omnia sunt communia. Gütergemeinschaft bei Thomas Müntzer?' *Archiv für Reformationsgeschichte* 102 (2011): 133–174.

Sternberg, Giora, 'Epistolary Ceremonial: Corresponding Status at the Time of Louis XIV'. *Past and Present* 204, no. 1 (2009): 33–88.

Stevenson, Brenda E., *Life in Black and White: Family and Community in the Slave South*. Oxford, UK: Oxford University Press, 1996.

Stevenson, Brenda E., *What Sorrows Labour in My Parent's Breast?: A History of the Enslaved Black Family*. Lanham, MD: Rowman and Littlefield, 2023.

Stewart, Alison, 'Large Noses and Changing Meanings in Sixteenth-Century German Prints'. *Print Quarterly Publication* 12, no. 4 (1995): 343–360.

Stewart, Alison, 'Paper Festivals and Popular Entertainment in the Kermis Woodcuts of Sebald Beham in Reformation Nuremberg'. *Sixteenth Century Journal* 24, no. 2 (1993): 301–350.

Stewart, Alison, 'Taverns in Nuremberg Prints'. In Kümin and Tlusty, eds., *World of the Tavern.*

Stewart, Alison G., *Before Bruegel: Sebald Beham and the Origins of Peasant Festival Imagery.* Aldershot: Ashgate, 2008.

Stievermann, Dieter, 'Erfurt im Bauernkrieg von 1525'. In Vogler, ed., *Bauernkrieg zwischen Harz und Thüringer Wald.*

Stockmann, Doris, 'Der Kampf um die Glocken im deutschen Bauernkrieg'. In Strobach, ed., *Der arm Man 1525.*

Stockmann, Erich, 'Trommeln und Pfeifen im deutschen Bauernkrieg'. In Strobach, ed., *Der arm Man 1525.*

Straube, Manfred, 'Strafgeldregister, Türkensteuerregister und Amtserbbücher als Quellen über Teilnehmner und Folgen des Bauernkrieges in Thüringen'. *Jahrbuch für Geschichte des Feudalismus* 2 (1978): 279–291.

Strobach, Hermann, ed., *Der arm Man 1525.* Berlin: Akademie Verlag, 1975.

Strobach, Hermann, 'Die Bauern sind aufrührig worden. Lieder aus dem Bauernkrieg'. In Strobach, ed., *Der arm Man 1525.*

Struck, Wolf-Heino, *Der Bauernkrieg am Mittelrhein und in Hessen.* Wiesbaden: Selbstverlag der Historischen Kommission für Nassau, 1975.

Struck, Wolf-Heino, 'Mittelrhein'. In Buszello, Blickle, and Endres, eds., *Der deutsche Bauernkrieg.*

Stupperich, Martin, *Osiander in Preußen: 1549–1552.* Berlin: De Gruyter, 2011.

Sünder, Martin, 'Der Deutsche Orden in der Reichsstaddt Mühlhausen. Ein Überblick'. In Müller, ed., *Der Deutsche Orden und Thüringen.*

Taddey, Gerhard, 'Wendel Hipler: Um 1465–1526'. In *Veröffentlichungen Gesellschaft für Fränkische Geschichte. Reihe 7.A, Fränkische Lebensbilder 22.* Leipzig: Degener, 2009.

Thompson, E. P., *The Making of the English Working Class.* London: Victor Gollancz, 1963.

Trauchburg, Gabriele von, 'Gefechte und Schlachten'. In Kuhn, ed., *Der Bauernkrieg in Oberschwaben.*

Trummer, Natalie, 'Christoph Schappeler: Fragmente seiner Biographie'. In Kuhn, ed., *Der Bauernkrieg in Oberschwaben.*

Ulbrich, Claudia, *Leibherrschaft am Oberrhein im Spätmittelalter.* Göttingen: Vandenhoeck & Ruprecht, 1979.

Ulbrich, Claudia, 'Oberschwaben und Württemberg'. In Buszello, Blickle, and Endres, eds., *Der deutsche Bauernkrieg.*

Vice, Roy L., 'Ehrenfried Kumpf, Karlstadt's Patron and Peasants' War Rebel'. *Archiv für Reformationsgeschichte* 86 (1995): 153–174.

Vice, Roy L., 'Iconoclasm in Rothenburg ob der Tauber in 1525'. *Archiv für Reformationsgeschichte* 89 (1998): 55–78.

Vice, Roy L., 'The Leadership and Structure of the Tauber Band During the Peasants' War in Franconia'. *Central European History* 21 (1988): 175–195.

Vice, Roy L., 'Valentin Ickelsamer's Odyssey from Rebellion to Quietism'. *Mennonite Quarterly Review* 69 (1995): 75–92.

Vice, Roy L., 'The Village Clergy near Rothenburg ob der Tauber and the Peasants' War'. *Archiv für Reformationsgeschichte* 82 (1991): 123–146.

Vice, Roy L., 'Vineyards, Vinedressers, and the Peasants' War in Franconia'. *Archiv für Reformationsgeschichte* 79 (1988): 138–157.

Vogler, Günter, ed., *Bauernkrieg zwischen Harz und Thüringer Wald*. Stuttgart: Franz Steiner, 2008.

Vogler, Günter, 'Bauernkrieg und bäuerlicher Widerstand. Eine persönliche Sicht auf Forschung und Erinnerungskultur' in Müller, Schirmer, and Greiling eds., *Reformation und Bauernkrieg*.

Vogler, Günter, 'Eisleben und Nürnberg'. In Knape, ed., *Martin Luther und Eisleben*.

Vogler, Günter, 'Imperial City Nuremberg, 1524–5: The Reform Movement in Transition'. In *The German People and the Reformation*, edited by Ronnie Po-Chia Hsia. Ithaca, NY: Cornell University Press, 1988.

Vogler, Günter, *Müntzerbild und Müntzerforschung vom 16. Bis zum 21. Jahrhundert. (1519–2017)*. 2 vols. Berlin: Weidler, 2019, 2021.

Vogler, Günter, *Nürnberg 1524/25: Studien zur Geschichte der reformatorischen sozialen Bewegung i. d. Reichsstadt*. Berlin: Deutscher Verlag der Wissenschaften, 1982.

Vogler, Günter, *Thomas Müntzer in einer Bildergeschichte. Eine kulturhistorische Dokumentation* (= *Schriften des Vereins für Reformationsgeschichte*. Bd. 211). Gütersloh: Gütersloher Verlagshaus, 2010.

Vogler, Günter, *Thomas Müntzer und die Gesellschaft seiner Zeit*. Mühlhausen: Thomas-Müntzer-Gesellschaft, 2003.

Vogt-Lüerssen, Maike, *Der Alltag im Mittelalter*. Munich: Probst Ernst Verlag, 2001.

Wappler, Paul, *Thomas Müntzer in Zwickau und die 'Zwickauer Propheten'*. Gütersloh: Mohn, 1966.

Warde, Paul, *Ecology, Economy and State Formation in Early Modern Germany*. Cambridge, UK: Cambridge University Press, 2010.

Warde, Paul, 'Fear of Wood Shortage and the Reality of the Woodland in Europe, c. 1450–1850'. *History Workshop Journal* 62, no. 28 (2006): 28–57.

Wareham, Edmund Hugh, 'Spirituality and the Everyday: A History of the Cistercian Convent of Günterstal in the Fifteenth and Sixteenth Centuries'. DPhil thesis, University of Oxford, 2016.

Wareham Wanitzek, Edmund Hugh, '"More Akin to a Brick-Kiln than a Monastery": The Material and Emotional Effects of the German Peasants' War (1524–6) on Cistercian Nuns and Monks'. *Citeaux: Commentarii cistercienses* (2022): 295–319.

Wehler, Hans-Ulrich, ed., *Der Deutsche Bauernkrieg 1524–1526. Sonderheft 1*. Göttingen: Vandenhoeck & Ruprecht, 1975.

Weingarten, Hendrik, *Herrschaft und Landnutzung: Zur mittelalterlichen Wirtschaftsgeschichte Kloster Zwiefaltens*. Stuttgart: Jan Thorbecke, 2006.

Weiß, Dieter J., 'Der Deutsche Orden'. In Jürgensmeier and Schwerdtfeger, eds., *Orden und Klöster im Zeitalter von Reformation und katholischer Reform, Band 1.*

Weiß, Ulman, *Die frommen Bürger von Erfurt: Die Stadt und ihre Kirche im Spätmittelalter und in der Reformationszeit.* Weimar: Böhlau, 1988.

Winter, J. M., 'Britain's "Lost Generation" of the First World War'. *Population Studies* 31, no. 3 (1977): 449–466.

Wohlfeil, Rainer, ed., *Der Bauernkrieg 1524–26.* Munich: Nymphenburger Verlagshandlung, 1975.

Wölbing, Lucas, *Müntzers langer Schatten. Das Amt Allstedt, der Bauernkrieg und die Nachwirkungen (1523–1533).* Mühlhausen: Thomas-Müntzer Gesellschaft e. V. Mühlhausen, 2024.

Wölfing, Günther, *Der Bauernkrieg im südthüringisch-hennebergischen Raum.* Suhl: Kulturbund der DDR, 1989.

Wolgast, Eike, 'Pfarrerwahl und Klosterexistenz in Bauernkriegsprogrammen 1525'. In Dammaschke and Müller, *Thomas Müntzer im Blick.*

Wozniak, Thomas, *Quedlinburg im 14. und 16. Jahrhundert: ein sozialtopographischer Vergleich.* Berlin: Akademie Verlag, 2013.

Wunder, Heide, *Die bäuerliche Gemeinde in Deutschland.* Göttingen: Vandenhoeck & Ruprecht, 1986.

Wunder, Heide, 'Der samländische Bauernaufstand von 1525'. In Wohlfeil, ed., *Der Bauernkrieg 1524–26.*

Wunder, Heide, 'Zur Mentalität aufständischer Bauern. Möglichkeiten der Zusammenarbeit von Geschichtswissenschaft und Anthropologie, dargestellt am Beispiel des Samländischen Bauernaufstandes von 1525'. *Geschichte und Gesellschaft. Sonderheft* 1 (1975): 9–37.

Wunderli, Richard, *Peasant Fires: The Drummer of Niklashausen.* Bloomington: Indiana University Press, 1992.

Wüst, Wolfgang, 'Bauernkrieg und fränkische Reichsstädte—Krisenmanagement in Nürnberg, Rothenburg ob der Tauber und Schweinfurt'. In Fuchs and Wagner, eds., *Bauernkrieg in Franken.*

Xenakis, Stefan, *Gewalt und Gemeinschaft: Kriegsknechte um 1500.* Paderborn: Ferdinand Schöningh, 2015.

Zapalac, Kristin Eldyss S., *'In His Image and Likeness': Political Iconography and Religious Change in Regensburg, 1500–1600.* Ithaca, NY: Cornell University Press, 1990.

Zeune, Joachim, ed., *Fränkische Burgen zur Zeit der Bauerkriege.* Bamberg: Babenberg Verlag, 2000.

Zmora, Hillay, *State and Nobility in Early Modern Germany: The Knightly Feud in Franconia, 1440–1567.* Cambridge, UK: Cambridge University Press, 1998.

Zorzin, Alejandro, *Karlstadt als Flugschriftenautor.* Göttingen: Vandenhoeck & Ruprecht, 1990.

Zorzin, Alejandro, 'A Portrait of Andreas Bodenstein von Karlstadt by Lucas Cranach the Elder'. *Reformation and Renaissance Review* 22, no. 3 (2020): 238–252.

INDEX

abbeys. *See* monasteries; *specific abbeys*

Absberg, Thomas von, 40, 225

Acker Conz und Klos Wuczer (Beham), 313 (fig.)

Adelphus, Johannes, 15 (fig.)

Admonition to Peace (Luther), 186–188, 269

Against the Heavenly Prophets (Luther), 86, 149, 186, 346

Against the Robbing, Murdering Hordes of Peasants (Luther), 269–270, 344

Agricola, Johannes, 77, 151, 154, 322

agriculture, 40–41, 63–65

Ain Sermon geprediget vom Pawren zu Werdt (Peringer), 20 (fig.)

Albrecht, Cardinal of Mainz, 10, 104–105, 126, 211, 304, 358, 363–364

Albrecht, Count of Mansfeld, 127, 275–276, 325, 343

Albrecht, Duke of Prussia, 102–104, 198, 200, 211, 224, 254

Allegory of the Reformation (Vischer), 22 (fig.)

Alleshausen, 61, 216, 220, 221, 240, 357

Allgäu band, 32, 38, 111, 115, 117, 195, 196, 217, 227, 282

Allgäuer Bundesordnung, 121–122

alliances, 76. *See also* leagues

Allstedt, 78–79, 151–152, 265, 294, 299, 300, 323, 353–354, 371

Allstedt league, 73, 76, 79–81, 189, 226, 267, 272–273

Alps, 37, 38, 263

Alsace, 12, 38, 54, 85, 130, 180, 220, 222, 233, 239–240, 243–244, 260, 263, 270, 274, 284, 297, 308, 312, 319, 326, 365

Altdorf, 182

Altdorpher, Albrecht, 38

Altenburg, 265, 294

Amandus, Georg, 267–268, 325

Amman, Jost, 202 (fig.)

Amorbach, 211, 219, 223

Amt Geusa, 226–227

Anabaptism, 351–352, 355, 364, 374–375, 377

An die Versammlung (*To the Assembly of the Common Peasantry*), 161–165, 164 (fig.), 174, 176, 261, 290–291, 302, 359

Andreas, Abbot of Ochsenhausen, 181

Anfechtungen (temptations/trials), 78

Anhausen, 186

Anna, St, 137

anticlericalism, 12, 16, 29–31, 78, 84–85, 94, 297–298, 373

antimonasticism, 24–25, 84, 94–95, 349, 373

antisemitism, 15, 30, 85, 199, 296–297
Anton, Duke of Lorraine, 240, 270, 309, 327, 328
Äpfingen, 90
apocalypticism, 152–154, 175, 223, 245
apprenticeships, 75
armies
  banners, 15, 141, 241, 277, 285
  drummers, 228–230
  Haufen, 111–112, 114–116, 138–141, 158–159, 200, 206, 209, 213, 215–218, 225–227, 245
  marching, 214, 219–225
  provisions for, 230–233, 262
  raising up of, 217, 226–227
  religious passion within, 227–228
armour, 132
art and artists
  'godless painters' case, 108
  landscape depictions, 38–39
  peasant depictions, 43–48, 279–281, 289, 313 (fig.), 347–348, 363
  revolt depictions, 183 (fig.), 184 (fig.), 185 (fig.)
'Articles of Christian Freedom.' See Twelve Articles
Aschaffenburg, 373
Aschersleben, 266
astrological predictions, 25–27
atrocities, 202–204, 203 (fig.), 205–206, 214, 219, 230, 246, 327–329, 332–336, 353
Aufruhr (turbulence), 1, 169, 215, 270, 335, 346, 353, 377. See also Peasants' War
Augsburg, 37, 38, 40, 63–64, 84, 111, 135, 136, 193, 265, 267, 348, 372
authority
  challenging of, 5, 11–12, 130–131, 349
  collapse of, 123–124, 137, 245–246
  height as a representation of power, 39–40, 221
  as Herren, 124–125
  judicial, 129–130
  peasants' vision of, 143–145
  scattered systems of, 58–59, 124
  secular, 160–162, 349–350
  See also lords and lordship
autumn, season of, 27–28

Baden, 234, 258
Balingen, 190
Baltringen band, 32, 35, 88, 90, 91, 100, 102, 111, 115, 119, 185, 192, 196, 217
Bamberg, 91, 131, 133, 141, 209, 223, 225, 337, 354, 356, 367, 373
bands, 111–112, 114–116, 138–141, 158–159, 213, 217–218, 245. See also armies; Haufen formation
banners, 15, 141, 241, 277, 285
ban theology, 331, 352
baptism, 188–190, 351–352. See also infant baptism
Barchent production, 63–64
Basel, 109, 350
Batzer, Mang, 359
Baumgartner family, 136–137
Bavaria, 374
beards, 309–310
beer, 25, 27, 38, 64, 82, 218, 244, 273
Beham, Barthel, 48–49 (fig.), 108
Beham, Hans Sebald, 47 (fig.), 312–313, 313 (fig.)
beheadings, 13, 109, 336–338
Behem, Hans, 7 (fig.), 10–11, 14, 108, 256
Belstein, 200
Bergheim, 296
Berlepsch, Hans von, 133
Berlepsch, Sittich von, 109, 133, 273
Berlichingen, Götz von, 4, 105–106, 131–132, 197, 200–201, 206, 211, 257–258, 288, 311, 333, 340, 361
Berlin, Hans, 197, 301–302
Bermatingen, 215
Beuggen, 56, 104–105
Beuren, 274
Bible. See scripture
Biblicism, 147, 150
Bibra, Wolfgang von, 158
bigamy, 251
Bildhausen band, 139, 158, 222, 225–226, 228, 245, 246, 257, 268, 297
Binnrot, 94
Binswangen, 301
Black Death, 48, 53

Black Forest
  bands, 38, 157, 191, 195, 239, 274,
    331, 332, 341
  marches through, 32, 34, 214, 219–220
  revolts, 11, 14, 180, 190–192, 273, 323
  Sixteen Articles of, 190
Black Hofmännin. *See* Renner, Margareta
    ('Schwarze/Black Hofmännin')
Blickle, Peter, 384–385
Böblingen, 257, 329, 357
Böckingen, 204, 301
Böckingen, Jacob von. *See* Rohrbach,
    Jäcklein
Bodo, Count of Stolberg, 274, 276
Bohemia, 264, 269, 325
Bollstedt, 323
boots, as symbol of revolts, 12, 15 (fig.)
Bora, Katharina von, 303, 345
Bottwar, 200, 212, 357
Brant, Sebastian, 14, 43
Braudel, Fernand, 386–387
Bräuer, Siegfried, 382, 384
Bräunlingen, 32
Braunschweig, 76–77, 277
Braunshain, 218
Bregenz, 129, 221
Breisgau, 12–13, 38, 220, 306
Breitenstein, Sebastian von, 182
Breitungen, 225
Brenz, Johannes, 88, 259–260, 271,
    347–348, 348 (fig.)
Brief Description of Germany (Cochlaeus), 37
'bright band.' *See* Helle Haufen
    ('bright band')
Brixen, 62–63, 263
Bronnen, 53
brotherhood
  agency via, 290
  Christian, 1, 88, 102, 120, 262,
    283, 315
  in Christian theology, 93
  clergy excluded from, 296
  decision-making ring, 284–285, 371
  'forced,' 288
  inclusivity of, 288–289, 386
  Jews excluded from, 296
  meanings of, 282–283
  mercenary, 305–306, 309
  as a moral value, 96, 228, 285

oath-swearing, 61, 76, 100, 138–139,
    209, 233, 282, 283
  plunder and, 307–309
  religious, 190, 306
  respect for age, 289–290
  as revolutionary, 314–315
  separatist, 331–332
  as a slogan, 89, 158
  social status and, 285–287
  sworn by lords, 288–289, 311–312
  and willingness to risk one's life, 290–291
  women excluded from, 279, 289, 291,
    299, 386
  See also fraternalism
brotherly love, 85, 93, 96, 113, 161, 187,
    283, 288
Bruchsal, 200
Brudehartmann convent, 231
Bruhrain, 258–259
Brunfels, Otto, 86
Bucer, Martin, 251, 262
Buchener, Georg, 277
Buchholz, 265, 267
Bundschuh rebellions, 12, 101, 119, 196
Burgkmair, Hans, 347
Burg Stein castle, 274
Bußmannshausen, 62
Buthert, 334

Calvinism, 72
capitalism, 5, 84
Capito, Wolfgang, 104, 262, 348
Carpathians, 37
Casimir, Margrave of Brandenburg-
    Kulmbach, 127, 142, 143, 227, 255,
    310–311, 336–337, 356
Castle Church, 16
castles, 39–40, 132–133, 171, 200,
    223, 224 (fig.), 224–225,
    256–258, 274, 281
Catholicism, 2, 24–25, 31, 71, 125, 137,
    151, 188, 266, 321, 351. *See also*
    monasteries; priests
chancelleries, 139–140, 212
charcoal, 59, 60, 372
Charles V, 3, 123, 363
Christ, 15, 16, 114, 150, 279, 370, 388
Christian brotherhood, 1, 88, 102, 120,
    262, 283, 315

Christian freedom, 158, 159
Christian Union, 111–112, 114–116, 116
    (fig.), 121, 134, 144, 191–192, 196,
    214, 217, 239
Christina of Saxony, 251
Chronicle of the World (Schedel), 11 (fig.)
church ales, 46, 47–48, 101
Civilization and Capitalism (Braudel),
    386–387
class, 386, 388
clergy
    anticlericalism, 12, 16, 29–31, 78, 84–85,
        297–298, 373
    attacks on, 68, 77, 82, 259
    communion reserved for, 17, 18
    evangelical preachers, 18, 22, 24, 79, 82,
        87, 110, 180, 298
    excluded from brotherhood, 296
    Hubmaier's preaching against Catholic,
        30–31, 34
    laity and, 70–71
    as landowners, 59, 63, 68
    Lutheran, 365–366
    in Luther's theology, 95–96
    Luther's understanding of priesthood,
        20–23
    as members of military orders, 24
    preaching to armies, 227–228
    predictions of impending disaster
        about, 25
    role of, 70–71
    tithes supporting, 27
    Twelve Articles' demands to appoint
        pastors, 118–119, 120, 170
cloth-making industry, 82
Cochlaeus, Johannes, 37–38, 39, 299, 359
code words, 14
Colmar, 263
Cologne, 373
commercialisation of farming, 50, 51, 63–65
communion, 17, 18, 68, 71–72, 77, 78–79,
    86, 100, 180, 182, 188, 246, 322, 363
community, 21–23, 111–112, 187, 189
congregations, 21–23
Constance, Bishop of, 31
consubstantialism, 150–151
convents, 2, 13, 24, 53, 80, 84, 100–101,
    131, 231, 236–237, 274, 291–292,
    294–295

councils, 233–235, 272, 373–374
Counter-Reformation, 281, 365,
    368, 376
courtesy titles, 142–143
Crafft, Adam, 324
craft workshops, 75
Cramm, Aschwin von, 312
Cranach, Lukas, 39, 46, 292
creation theology, 4–5, 90–94, 119, 369
crockery, 59
Cronthal, Martin, 91, 139, 234, 308,
    335–336, 339–340

Dagersheim, 191, 308
Dahlhopf, Hans, 253
Daniel, Book of, 154
Danube river, 37, 38, 193
David of Winkelsheim, 126
death dues, 57, 119
December (Wertinger), 97 (fig.)
*Defense of the Book Against the Robbing and
    Murdering Peasants* (Luther), 271
Denck, Hans, 108
Denner, Lienhart, 142
Des Christlichen Pawern getrewer Rath
    (Peringer), 21 (fig.)
Dettwang, 300
Didymus, Gabriel, 292
Diet of Speyer, 374
Diet of Worms, 18, 279–280, 374
Dinkelsbühl, 231
Dipperz, 247, 323
dogs, 62, 184 (fig.)
Donauwörth, 38
Dorlisheim, 233, 260, 285
Dorn, Hainrich, 54
Dream (Dürer), 360 (fig.)
dreams and visions
    Dürer's, 359–361
    interpreting, 26–27, 148–149
    Karlstadt's approach to, 149–150,
        175–176
    messages in, 148
    Müntzer's approach to, 150–156, 157,
        174–175
    of peasants, 156–157
    of a perfect world, 172–174
    in Reformation theology, 149
    in scripture, 147–148, 150

Drummer of Niklashausen revolt,
10–11, 14, 34, 222
drummers and drumming, 228–230, 229
(fig.), 313 (fig.)
dues, 10, 29, 31, 33, 49, 52, 55, 57, 91,
120, 197, 244
Dürer, Albrecht, 38–39, 44–46, 61, 108,
359–364, 383
Dream, 360 (fig.)
Peasant Couple at Market, The, 45 (fig.)
Piper and Drummer, 229 (fig.)
Three Peasants in Conversation, 44 (fig.)
Underweysung der Messung, 362 (fig.)
Durlach, 259
Dürrenzimmer, Enderlin von, 205

East Germany, 378, 384
Ebeleben, 274
Ebeleben castle, 225
Eberbach, 364
Ebingen, 190
Eck, Johannes, 30, 77
Eck, Leonhard von, 312
ecology, 172. See also natural resource
management
economic conditions, 50, 370
egalitarianism, 156, 158
eggs, symbolism of, 45 (fig.), 53
Egranus, Johannes Sylvius, 150
Eichsfeld, 154, 233, 274
Eichstätt, 10, 63
Eighteenth Brumaire of Louis Bonaparte, The
(Marx), 379, 381
Eilenburg, 78
Ein durch die Spieß jagen (Amman),
202 (fig.)
Eisenach, 257, 275, 319
Eisleben, 74, 266, 325, 347
Elbe river, 37, 49, 61
Elector of Saxony. See Friedrich the Wise,
Elector of Saxony
Ellwangen, 211
Engelman, Melchior, 210
Engels, Friedrich, 4, 289, 378, 379–380,
382–385, 389
English Civil War, 92
Ensisheim, 263
entrance fines, 57, 158
Erfurt, 68, 135, 157, 217, 265, 275, 373

Erich, Duke of Braunschweig, 251, 277
Erlenbach, 301
Ernst, Count of Mansfeld, 40, 79, 110,
126–127, 142, 154, 162, 274,
275–277, 285, 320–321, 344
Ernst, Johann, 347
Ernst, Margrave of Baden, 357
Erolzheim, 94
Erzgebirge, 233, 265, 325
Esenach, 84
Esleben, 60
Eternal League, 83, 273
Eternal Revolutionary Council, 300
Eucharist, 71, 86, 95, 109, 150–151, 176.
See also communion
evangelicalism, 3, 18–20, 22, 24–25, 31, 35,
67, 68, 84, 86, 87–88, 113, 190, 279
executions, 13, 29, 108–109, 172, 194, 223,
253, 256, 277, 285, 287, 323, 330,
336–338, 368
Eydinger, Ulrike, 383

Fabri, Johann, 33–34, 168–170, 188–189,
349, 352
facial hair, 309
Federsee Lake, 240
Felchta gate, 83
Ferdinand, Archduke of Austria, 108, 129,
264, 372
Feuchtwangen, 337
feudalism, 30, 52, 93, 220, 355, 365,
370, 376
feuds, 131–133
Feuerbacher, Matern, 212, 240, 257, 357
Fichtelgebirge, 37
fines, 52, 53–55, 57, 158, 195, 236,
338, 356–357
firearms, 132, 181
fishing, 62–63
flax crops, 63–64
Flein, 200, 204, 219
flesh, vs spirit, 113, 150–151, 155, 162
Foeditzsch, Hans, 141
food and drink provisions, 230–233
Forchheim, 132
forest officials, 60
Forster, Bartel, 282
Franconia, 38, 64, 105, 157, 167, 197–199,
226, 243, 244, 274, 336, 365

Frankenhain, 225
Frankenhausen, 59–60, 154, 218, 226–227,
    257, 266, 270–271, 275–278,
    303–304, 312, 319–320, 323, 325,
    354, 360, 371–372, 383
Frankfurt, 157, 372
Franz, Günther, 381–383
fraternalism, 94–96. *See also* brotherhood
Frauenbreitungen, 249, 252, 259
freedom
    Christian, 158
    civic, 135
    in creation theology, 90–94, 370–371
    'islands of,' 136
    Karlstadt on, 72, 85–86
    in legal context, 89–90
    Luther on, 2, 17–18, 67, 86
    meanings of, 88, 89–90, 93
    missing from Müntzer's theology, 73, 87
    peasants' loss of, 54
    rumours and gossip about, 218–219
    social consequences of, 70–71
    in Twelve Articles, 144, 159
    works and, 85–86
Freedom of a Christian, The (Luther), 2,
    17–18, 89–90, 118, 161, 271, 370
Freiburg, 192, 220, 300, 329–331
Fridell, Hans, 334
Friedberg, 372
Friedrich, Johann, 80
Friedrich I of Brandenburgh-Ansbach, 102
Friedrich the Wise, Elector of Saxony, 40,
    69, 79, 81, 125, 127–128, 252, 264,
    267, 268, 270–271, 347, 364
Fries, Lorenz, 27, 140, 306, 334, 340
Fritz, Joss, 12–14, 141
Fugger, Jacob, 190, 349
Fugger family, 5, 64, 84, 136–137, 263
Fulda, 110, 246–249, 253–255, 265, 273,
    297–298, 323–332, 373
Fundling, Johannes, 281
Fürer, Christoph, 325
Fürstenberger, 238

Gaisbeuren, 61
Gaismair, Michael, 57, 171, 235,
    264, 359
Gaisser, Adelhaid, 358–359
Gastein Valley, 264

Gebelstadt, 226, 333
Gehofen, Martin von, 277
Gels, 263
Gemeinde, 41–43, 51, 60, 93, 96, 121,
    159, 174, 215–216, 233–234, 268,
    365–366, 385
Georg, bishop of Speyer, 258–259
Georg, Count of Wertheim, 211
Georg, Duke of Saxony, 79, 83, 125,
    127, 224, 251–252, 264, 266–268,
    273, 277, 289, 308, 311,
    320–321, 355
George, St, 15
Georgics (Virgil), 43
Georg of Ebeleben, 81
Georg of Werdenstain, 130, 131
Gera, Heinrich, 274
Gerber, Erasmus, 222, 239, 260–262, 290,
    309, 327, 328
Germany
    artistic landscapes, 38–39
    geography of, 37–38
    prosperity in, 50
    social organization, 41–43
    weather and climate, 40
Gerolzhofen, 225
Gersen, Ottilie von, 109, 154, 300, 303
Gerwig, Abbot of Weingarten,
    180–182, 184
Geyer, 267
Geyer, Florian, 4, 132, 142, 197,
    209–210, 211, 227, 257–258, 288,
    333–334, 369
Giebelstadt, 334
godly right, 94
Goethe, Johann Wolfgang von, 22
Görmar, 274
Goslar, 266
gospel. *See* scripture
government, 41–43, 134–135, 245, 374
Graubüunden, 264
Gravamina, 17
Greisel, Florian, 195, 239–240
Griesingen, 51
Griessen, 31, 351, 353
Grimmenthal, 222
Grönenbach, 239–240
Großenehrich, 275
Grossgartach, 200, 219

Index

Grumbach, Argula von, 32
Grünhain abbey, 25, 265
Gügi, Georg, 328–329
guilds, 135, 206, 233–234, 260, 364
Gundelsheim, 105, 210
Günzburg, 192, 193
Günzburg, Eberlin von, 94, 192

Habsburgs, 31, 54, 107, 124–125, 136,
     162, 190, 263–264, 341
Haferitz, Simon, 78–81
Hagenau, 263
Hake, Hans, 288–289
Halberstadt, 266
Halbritter, Marx, 340
Hall, 84, 263–264, 337
Hall, Peter, 328
Halle, 294
Hallstadt, 209
Hallstatt, 337
Hamburg, 265
Hanseatic League, 75–76
'Hans the Hoe,' 20
Harburg castle, 274
Harer, Peter, 200, 283
Hartenstein, Stephan, 277
harvest time, 27–28
Harz Mountains, 60, 264, 266
Hauenstein uprising, 33
Haufen formation, 200, 206, 209, 213,
     215–217, 225–227
Hausen, 60
Hecker, Friedrich 'Carl,' 32, 379
Hedio, Caspar, 322
Hegau, 30, 33, 38, 100, 179–180, 190, 196,
     231, 273, 330, 332
Heggbach, 119, 131, 302, 353
Heidelberg, 210
Heidenfeld, 226
Heidingsfeld, 333, 344–345
Heilbronn, 25, 100, 103, 105–107, 132,
     135, 165, 198, 204–209, 211, 219,
     224, 233, 235, 237, 301–302, 308,
     358, 373, 374
Heiligenstadt, 274–275
Heiligenstein, 260
Heinrich, Duke of Braunschweig, 277, 320
Heldrungen, 274
Heldrungen, Count of, 218

Heldrungen castle, 39–40
Helfenstein, Ludwig von, 201, 205, 285,
     301, 310, 333
Helle Haufen ('bright band'), 200, 206,
     209, 217, 234
Henneberg, 63, 148, 222, 245
Henneberg, Johann von, 247, 252–255
Henneberg, Wilhelm von, 125, 127,
     133, 247–249, 250, 253–256,
     310–311, 321
Herbitzheim, 263
Herda, Tham von, 133–134, 222,
     249–250, 253, 255
Hergot, Hans, 108–109, 172–174, 323
Hermann of Henneberg, 125
Herren, 124–125
Herrenberg, 191, 212
Herrenbreitungen, 249, 252, 259
Hersfeld, 246–248, 252–253, 373
Hesse, 230, 244–245, 367
Hettstedt, 60, 265
Hildebrandt, Simon, 82
Hipler, Wendel, 61, 128, 165–167, 174,
     210, 333, 340
Hisolidus, Matthäus, 82
Höchberg, 226
Hofer, Nikolaus, 77
Hofman, Michael, 231
Hohenburg, 295
Hohenkirchen, 218
Hohenlohe, 42, 165, 186, 199–200,
     224–225
Hohensalzburg, 264
Hohentwiel fortress, 330
Hohenzollerns, 102–103
Hohnstein, Ernst V von, 274
Hollenpach, Hans, 142
Höltzel, Hieronymus, 109
holy blood relics, 182, 196
Holy Roman Empire, 123–124
Honecker, Erich, 383
Hopfgarten, Rudolf von, 310
Horneck castle, 105, 210
horses, as symbols of power, 221,
     227, 247
*How a Spiritual Christian Knight and Hero
     of God Should Fight in This World*
     (Amandus), 268
Hoyer, Siegfried, 307

Hubmaier, Balthasar
  antisemitism of, 85, 296
  ban theology, 331, 352
  death of, 351
  discovery of Christian manhood, 298
  Fabri's claims against, 168–170, 189, 352
  female followers, 299
  imprisonment of, 351
  political reformation ideas, 168–169
  theology of, 88, 188–190, 352
  on usury, 199
  at Waldshut, 19, 30–32, 33–34, 84,
    107–108, 109, 124–125, 169,
    188–190
  Zwingli and, 30, 107, 351, 364
Hüfingen, 195–196
Hug, Heinrich, 86, 125, 217, 329–330,
  342, 353
humiliations, 254, 339–341
hunting, 62, 119, 142, 162, 218
Hurlewagen, Dietrich, 108
Hürnheim, Wolf von, 128
Hussite movement, 77
Hut, Hans, 108, 323, 352
Hutten, Ulrich von, 167, 201

Ickelsamer, Valentin, 199
Imperial Diets, 17
indulgences, 18, 137, 188, 266, 363
infant baptism, 107, 188
Ingolstadt, 226, 333, 336
Ingolstadt University, 32
inheritance practices, 42, 51, 92
Inner Councils, 43
Innsbruck, 358
Isny, 185
Italian Wars, 123

Jacob, Abbot of Weissenau, 180–181, 183
Jagiellonians, 102–103
Jehle, Kuntz, 357
Jena, 69, 345–346
Jewish people
  antisemitism, 15, 30, 85, 199, 296–297
  calls for expulsion of, 12, 171, 199, 296, 297
  excluded from brotherhood, 296
  as moneylenders, 55, 85
  protections sought for, 262
  targeting of, 264

Joachim, Margrave of Brandenburg,
  254, 320
Joachim of Fiore, 153
Joachimstal, 265, 269, 325
Johann, Duke of Saxony, 79, 81, 126,
  128, 152, 154, 247, 267, 270,
  321, 355, 356
John the Baptist, 15
Jonas, Justus, 80
Jones, Gareth Stedman, 386
Josel of Rosheim, 262, 297
Juche, Wolfgang, 326
Judgement on Thomas Müntzer, A
  (Luther), 343–344
judicial authority, 129–130
June (Wertinger), 317
justice, 129–130, 385
Jüterborg, 77

Kahlenberg, 37
Kaltennordheim, 249
Kannawurf, 219
Karlstadt, Andreas
  approach to dreams and visions,
    149–150, 175–176
  on Christian freedom, 72, 85
  on the Eucharist, 86, 109
  exile of, 344–345
  on flesh vs. spirit, 162
  influence on Peasants' War, 67
  at Joachimstal, 269
  literacy, 139
  Luther and, 68–72, 86–87, 107,
    149–150, 280, 345–346
  Müntzer and, 69, 72–73, 74, 324
  as a 'new layperson,' 70–71
  at Orlamünde, 30, 68–72, 73
  on primacy of scripture, 19
  Reformation implementation, 68–69
  in Regensburg, 199
  *Several Main Points of Christian
    Teaching*, 86–87
  terror at peasant army, 262
  theology of, 268
  view of the Eucharist, 71
Karsthans, 20
Käßin, Agatha, 359
Kastel, 297
Kayna, 218

Kelbra, 265
Kempten, 12, 54, 111, 182, 308, 358, 374
Kessler, Johannes, 354
Keysersberg, 263
Kirchheim, 218
Kitzingen, 209, 310, 337, 356
Kleeburg, 327
Klettgau, 30, 35, 273, 332, 350–351
Kniebis, Ammeister, 348
knights, 40, 103, 128–129, 130, 131–133,
    165, 225
Knights' War, 132, 167, 225, 376
Kolbenhaufen, 263
Kollwitz, Käthe, 378
Königsfelder, Anna, 367
Königshofen, 226, 333
Kramerzunft, 117
Krayenburg, 249
Kreutter, Claus, 304
Kumpf, Ernfried, 134, 199
Kupferschmid, Hans, 266
Kyffhäuser Mountains, 218

labour
    in creation theology, 91–92
    services, 41, 48–50, 56–57, 119
    strikes, 11, 51
Lachmann, Johann, 106, 229–230,
    261–262, 354
laity, 70–71
Lake Constance band, 32, 108, 111,
    115, 191, 195, 196, 217, 227,
    240, 350, 357
landowners
    acquisition of land, 58–59
    clergy as, 59, 63, 68
    as Herren, 124–125
    inheritance practices and, 92
    lords, 39–40
    monasteries as, 23–25, 59, 102
    property transfer, 237–238
    relationships with peasants, 50–52
Landschaft (league), 169–171, 212,
    239, 368
Landsknechte. See mercenaries
Lang, Johannes, 80, 155
Langensalza, 83, 273, 283
Large Councils, 43
Larsen, Aaron, 194 (fig.)

Last Days, 78, 110, 147, 153, 223
Laufenburg, 330
Laupheim, 192
League of the Nine Towns, 358
leagues, 76, 169–171, 209
Legal Ordinance of the Imperial
    Chamber Court, 365
legal proceedings, 11, 129–130, 357–358
legal reform, 167–168, 365
Leibeigenschaft system, 52–54, 56
Leipheim, 61, 116, 192–197, 194 (fig.),
    243, 299, 304, 308
Leipzig, 265, 267, 348
Lenten hen, 11, 28, 53, 115
Leonhard, Abbot of Ottobeuren, 185
letters and correspondence, 139–140,
    158, 215–216, 225–226, 249–250,
    268–269
Lettsch, Andreas, 33, 330
Leutershausen, 336
Leutzendorf, 231
liberty, 92–93
Lichtenstern, 206, 301
Liebenthann, 182
Limbach, 211
Limburg, 373
literacy, 139–140, 160, 214, 386
liturgical calendar, 180
livestock, 64–65
Lobdeburg, Hartman von, 231
looting, 207–210, 235–238, 244, 247, 259,
    263, 266, 296, 307–308
lords and lordship
    attacks on, 244
    brotherhood with peasants, 288–289,
        311–312
    collapse of authority, 123–124, 245–246
    collective nature of, 144–145
    formalization of customs in writing, 65
    grievances against, 101–102
    height as a representation of power,
        39–40, 221
    kin relationships among, 125–127
    knights, 131–133
    legal actions against, 11, 129–130, 365
    mercenary recruitment, 308–309
    order restored by, 355–359
    pawning and selling of, 58, 128–130
    peasants as, 212

lords and lordship (*continued*)
  peasants' opposition to, 130–131, 145
  scattered systems of, 129
  servants of, 133–134
  social distinctions, 141–143
  structures of, 56–57
  war financing, 236
Löser, Hans, 347
Lotzer, Sebastian, 3, 113–115,
    117–120, 156, 160, 196, 354,
    364, 369
Löwenstein, 206
Ludwig, Elector of the Palatinate, 259–260
Ludwigstadt, 59
Lufft, Hans, 345
Lupfen, Countess of, 28
Lupstein, 280, 327, 339
Luther, Martin
  Admonition to Peace, 186–188, 269
  On the Babylonian Captivity, 17, 159
  background, 74, 372
  blamed for Peasants' War, 281, 349–350
  To the Christian Nobility, 16–17, 160
  comparisons of to Christ, 18
  condemnation of usury, 85
  death of, 347
  *Defense of the Book Against the Robbing
    and Murdering Peasants*, 271
  Diet of Worms, 18, 279–280
  elites as audience of, 75, 80
  on flesh vs. spirit, 150–151, 162
  on freedom, 2, 17–18, 67, 86
  Freedom of a Christian, The, 2, 17–18,
    89–90, 118, 161, 271, 370
  on Grimmenthal pilgrimage, 222
  Against the Heavenly Prophets, 86, 149,
    186, 346
  in hiding, 68
  influence on Peasants' War, 67
  Judgement on Thomas Müntzer, A,
    343–344
  Karlstadt and, 68–72, 86–87, 107,
    149–150, 280, 345–346
  knowledge of Philip of Hesse's
    bigamy, 251
  at Mansfeld, 269
  marriage and family, 303, 344, 345
  on monasteries, 23–25
  On Monastic Vows, 344

  Müntzer and, 73, 77, 80–88, 108,
    150–151, 155–156, 322, 326,
    343–344
  Ninety-Five Theses, 16, 78, 104
  opposition to peasant revolt, 2, 3,
    269–271, 346–347, 349
  on the priesthood, 20–23
  as Reformation leader, 2–3, 180
  rejection of monasticism, 94
  reversal of reforms, 68–69
  *Against the Robbing, Murdering Hordes of
    Peasants*, 269–270, 344
  On Secular Authority, 160–161
  on serfdom, 187
  theology of, 95–96, 156, 176
  on tithes, 187
  on usury, 199
  views on the Eucharist, 150–151, 176
Lutheranism, 72, 84–85, 112–114, 199,
    364, 365–366, 376

Mainau, 103
Mainz, 38, 135–136, 246, 297, 364,
    369, 373
Mallerbach, 80, 294
Malsch, 259
manhood, 279, 283, 298, 309,
    313–314, 371, 388
Manifest Exposé of False Faith, A
    (Müntzer), 108
Mann, Steffan, 165, 167, 311
Mansfeld, 60, 75, 125, 136–137, 245,
    264–266, 269, 347, 372
March (Wertinger), 177 (fig.)
marching
  as brotherhood, 240–241
  castles as destinations, 224–225
  drumming while, 228–230
  eating and drinking while, 230–233
  monasteries as destinations, 222–224
  as a rebellious act, 220
  as recruitment, 214
  rotation system for, 221–222
  routes, 222–223
  through the Black Forest, 32, 34,
    214, 219–220
  women's participation in, 300–301
Marchtal, 185, 357
Marienberg, 10, 267, 335

Marienberg Castle, 256–258, 340
marriage fines, 52, 53–55
Martelberg, 328
Marx, Karl, 378–381, 389
Marxism, 378, 380
Mary in the Nettlebush monastery, 224
Mathilda, St, 75
Matthew, Gospel of, 16
Maulbronn, 223, 236, 295
Maximilian, Emperor, 203, 348
meadows, 60–61
Meinhard, Christoph, 79, 325
Meiningen, 360
Meissen, 38
Melanchthon, Philipp, 114, 153, 251, 259, 372
Mellrichstadt, 228
Memmingen, 101, 112–115, 160, 171, 191, 195, 209, 245, 276, 373, 374
Memminger Bundesordnung, 121–122
mentalité concept, 386–387
Mentzingen, Stefan von, 197, 199, 233, 345
Merano articles, 264
mercenaries, 40, 191, 304–309, 310, 369
Mergentheim, 105, 198, 219
Merseburg, 226
Metzler, Georg, 198
Metzler, Hans, 234
military monasticism, 103–105
Miltenberg, 211
Minden, 373
miners and mining industry, 74–75, 136–137, 264–270, 273, 276, 325, 344, 372
Mittelbiberach, 101
Mittelgebirge, 37
Molsheim, 260–261, 263
monasteries
    antimonasticism, 24–25, 84, 94–95, 349, 373
    criticism of, 102
    as destination for marches, 222–224
    destruction of, 223, 274, 287, 291–295, 293 (table), 357, 367–368
    height of as representation of power, 39
    Heilbronn Carmelites, 106
    as landowners, 23–25, 58–59, 102
    looting of, 207–210, 235–238, 247, 259, 266, 296
    military monasticism, 103–105
    as moneylenders, 55, 84
    occupation of, 223–224
    revolts against, 171, 180–186, 197, 211–212, 264
    secularization of, 368, 376
    tithes paid to, 53
money, 57
monks, 3, 19–20, 23–25, 29, 53, 63, 79, 84, 95, 103–106, 113, 181, 184 (fig.), 185–186, 199, 210, 223, 230–231, 235, 291–295, 297–298, 303
movable type, 3
Mühlberg, 62, 218
Mühlhausen, 25, 73, 76–77, 81–84, 103–104, 109–110, 135, 153–154, 189, 208, 226, 245, 254, 271–278, 300, 303–304, 322–324, 356, 358, 373
Mühlpfort, Hermann, 271, 347
Mulhouse, 263
Müller, Hans, 29–30, 32, 34, 134, 190, 208, 214, 219–220, 226, 231, 239, 285, 290, 306, 329–332, 341
Müller, Thomas, 324, 384
Mülverstedt, 109, 300
Münnerstadt, 157
Münster, 373
Müntzer, Thomas
    Allstedt league, 73, 76, 79–81, 189, 226, 267, 272–273
    approach to dreams and visions, 150–156, 157, 174–175
    background, 74–76
    banishments and expulsions, 76–77, 83, 108–110, 324
    banner of, 277, 285
    capture and imprisonment, 320–322, 344
    death of, 322, 323
    female followers, 299–300
    on flesh vs. spirit, 150–151, 155, 162
    at Frankenhausen, 275–278, 319–320, 372
    freedom missing from theology of, 73, 87
    as a hero, 378
    imprisonment of, 110
    influence on Peasants' War, 4, 67, 323–326, 379–381, 382–383
    Karlstadt and, 69, 72–73, 74, 324

Müntzer, Thomas (*continued*)
at Klettgau, 31
Last Days messaging, 78, 110, 147,
153, 223
literacy, 139
Luther and, 73, 77, 80–81, 86, 108,
150–151, 155–156, 322, 326,
343–344
Manifest Exposé of False Faith, A, 108
marriage and family, 154, 303
miners as audience of, 75
at Mühlhausen, 82–83, 110, 271–275
'Nun bitten wit den Heiligen Geist,' 278
opposition to Ernst of Mansfield,
126–127, 154, 275–277
political philosophy, 76, 221
Prague Manifesto, 77–78
theology of, 73–74, 78, 87, 150, 267, 268
Vindication and Refutation, 109
vote to march to Heldrungen, 284
Weimar interrogations, 81
withholding of courtesy titles in
correspondence, 142–143
Zeiß and, 134
Müntzmeister, 74
Murer, Abbot, 292
Murer, Jacob, 289, 302
Murner, Thomas, 90
mutinies, 191, 308
mysticism, 154–156, 175, 380. *See also*
dreams and visions

Narrenschiff vom buntschuch (Adelphus),
15 (fig.)
National Socialism, 350, 382
natural resource management, 4–5, 51,
59–63, 85–86, 90, 119, 172, 370–371
Naundorf, 80, 294
Nebuchandnezzar, King, 154
Neckargartach, 230
Neckar River, 200
Neckarsulm, 103, 201, 210
Neckartal band, 219
Necker, Ursula, 54
negotiations, 233–235, 270–271,
310–311, 334
Neuenburg, 233, 284
Neustadt, 63, 259
Niedermünster, 295

Niederorschel, 274
Niklashausen, 10, 241, 256
Nikolsburg, 351, 352
Ninety-Five Theses, 16, 78, 104, 383–384
Nordhausen, 274
Nördlingen, 373, 374
Nose Dance (Beham), 47 (fig.)
'Nun bitten wir den Heiligen Geist'
(Müntzer), 278
nuns, 23, 24, 79, 100–101, 125–126,
129, 131, 136, 148, 179, 189,
210, 223, 235, 265–266,
291–292, 294–295, 302–303,
310, 353, 367–368
Nuremberg, 16, 37, 38, 40, 84, 108–109,
132, 136, 180, 265, 267, 323–324,
325, 360–361, 372
Nützel, Caspar, 348

oath-swearing, 12, 76, 100, 138–139,
144, 183 (fig.), 183, 189, 209,
215, 272, 355
Oberholzheim, 129
Obernai, 373
Oberndorf, 111
Obhausen, 59
Ochsenfurt, 333
Ochsenhausen, 181, 184, 295
Odenwald, 38, 142, 204, 219, 226
Odenwald band, 269, 282–283, 333
Oecolampadius, 109
Öhringen, 200, 219, 301
Oldisleben, 219
On Monastic Vows (Luther), 344
On Secular Authority (Luther), 160–161
On the Babylonian Captivity (Luther),
17, 159
*On the New Transformation of the Christian
Life* (Hergot), 108–109, 172–174
Öpfingen, 51
Ordinance of the Memmingen
league, 121–122
Orlamünde, 69–70, 73, 176
Osnabrück, 373
Osterhausen, 276
Ottensass, Johann, 247, 253
Otthera, Johann von, 358
Ottobeuren, 185, 287
Otto I, 75

pacifism, 352
Palatinate, 244, 258, 263
Palm, Peter, 194 (fig.)
Passion of Christ and Antichrist
(Melanchthon), 114
Paßler, Peter, 263
Pässler, Peter, 63
Pavia, 305, 363
peace agreements, 243, 257, 314
Peasant Couple at Market, The (Dürer),
45 (fig.)
peasants
  artistic depictions of, 43–48, 279–281,
    289, 313 (fig.), 347–348, 363
  bands of, 111–112, 114–116, 138–141,
    158–159
  brotherhood with lords, 288–289,
    311–312
  clothing of, 280–281
  conceptions of distance, 39
  crops, 40–41, 48
  as defenders of the gospel, 19–20, 24,
    79–80, 94, 96, 179, 282
  demands of, 101–102
  dreams and visions of, 156–157, 172–174
  'evangelical,' 20
  as freedom fighters, 18
  grievances of, 28–29, 51, 57–65, 88–89,
    94, 100–102, 114–115, 358
  hatred of monks and nuns, 24–25
  Haufen formation, 200, 206, 209, 213,
    215–217, 225–227
  joint filing of legal complaints, 238–239
  kin relationships among, 134
  labour, 41, 48–50, 56–57
  legal rights, 365
  Leibeigenschaft system, 52–54, 56
  as lords, 212
  meanings of freedom to, 88, 89–90, 93
  mobilization of, 214–219, 244
  opposition to lords, 130–131, 145
  pose of, 281–282
  prosperity of, 50, 370
  relationships with landlords, 50–52
  restrictions on movement of, 220
  slaughter of, 243, 256, 270, 277, 312,
    320, 326–329, 334, 339, 341–342,
    347, 353, 355, 360, 363–368
  social organization, 41–43

theology of, 88–96, 160, 240–241, 371
tithes paid by, 10, 21, 25, 27–28, 31, 51,
  55–56, 91, 119
views of land, 39
visions of authority, 143–145
wealth of, 286–287
writings of, 159–165
Peasants' Fair (Beham), 48–49 (fig.)
Peasants' War
  as an antipilgrimage, 241
  Battle of Frankenhausen, 270, 271,
    275–278, 319–320
  Battle of Leipheim, 192–197, 194 (fig.)
  beginnings of, 2, 10, 22
  bloodiness of, 338–339, 355
  casualties, 1, 190, 193, 312, 320,
    327, 355
  causes of, 50–51, 65–66
  changes due to, 376–377
  chronicles of, 340–341, 354
  failure of, 371–376
  financing of, 235–238, 368
  folklore of, 28–29
  legacies of, 377–389
  as a mass movement, 4–5, 89
  monuments, 362 (fig.), 363
  punishments following, 355–359
  spread of, 1, 96, 192, 243–244
  Weinsberg atrocity, 202–204, 203 (fig.),
    205–206, 214, 219, 230,
    246, 332–333
  women's participation in, 299–302,
    303–304
Peasant War in Germany, The (Engels), 379
Pegnitz River, 61
Pelt, Hans, 326
Pencz, Georg, 108
Peringer, Diepold, 19–20, 20 (fig.), 21
  (fig.), 199, 279
Pfeddersheim, 259, 339
Pfeiffer, Heinrich, 82, 83, 108–110, 153,
  154, 272, 273, 300, 322–323, 324
Pfingsten, 299
Philip of Hesse, 126, 167, 230, 244, 248,
  249, 250–256, 268–269, 271, 277,
  308–309, 320–322, 355
Philipp of Waldeck, 132
pilgrimage, 10, 17, 34, 40, 80, 107, 182,
  206, 222, 256, 296, 376

Piper and Drummer (Dürer), 229 (fig.)
Pirckheimer, Charitas, 367
Pirckheimer, Willibald, 109
poaching, 99
political reformation, 165–174
Pond in a Wood (Dürer), 38–39
Poor Conrad movement, 13, 14, 15, 119, 196, 312–313
power, symbols of, 39–40, 221
Practica vber die grossen vnd mannigfeltigen Coniunction der Planeten...1524 (Reynmann), 26 (fig.)
Prague, 77–78
Prague Manifesto, 77–78
priests
    anticlericalism, 12, 16, 29–31, 78, 84–85, 297–298, 373
    attacks on, 68, 77
    excluded from brotherhood, 296
    Hubmaier's preaching against, 30–31
    Luther's understanding of, 20–23
    as members of military orders, 24
    role of, 70–71
    Schwabach contract of employment, 118
    in Teutonic Knights, 24, 25, 105
    tithes supporting, 27, 85
property rights, 21–22, 92, 197, 237–238, 244
Prussia, 57, 102–103, 105
Puttyger, Hans, 152–153

Quedlinburg, 75–76, 266

Rahl, Stefan, 183 (fig.), 183
rape, 309–310, 327
Rappertsweiler, 108, 180–181, 183 (fig.), 215
Rappoltstein, 284, 299
Rautenzweig, Claus, 314
Ravensburg, 292
Rebmann, Johann, 353
Reckenbacher, 238
Reformation
    as congregational, 95–99
    disorder caused by, 68, 235, 237–238
    freedom and, 70–71, 72
    influence of on peasantry, 2–3, 51, 66
    radical vision of, 5
    Swiss, 107
    See also specific Reformation leaders

reformation, political, 165–174
Reformation of Emperor Friedrich III, 167
Regensburg, 30, 296
Regnitz River, 61
Reichart, Hans, 79
Reichskammergericht, 33
Reifenstein, 274
Reinhard, Martin, 70, 71
Reinsdorf, 140
Reischach, Komtur Ludwig von, 104–105
relics, 182, 186
religion, role of, 15–16, 26, 33, 51, 89, 135–136, 196, 227–228, 252, 260, 388
    Drummer of Niklashausen revolt, 10–11, 14
    Speyer uprising, 12
    views of peasants, 19, 34
    See also Reformation
Renner, Margareta ('Schwarze/Black Hofmännin'), 204, 235, 301–302
rents, 11, 27, 31, 41, 49, 55, 57
rent strikes, 11
Rettbach, 218
Reuter, Hans, 208
revolts and uprisings
    artistic depictions of, 183 (fig.), 184 (fig.), 185 (fig.)
    banners, 15, 141, 241, 277
    boots as symbol of, 12, 15 (fig.)
    code words, 14
    miners' role in, 75, 79–80, 264–270, 273, 372
    against monastic rule, 180–186, 197
    oath-swearing, 138–139
    religion's role in, 10–11, 12, 15–16, 26, 51, 89, 135–136, 227–228
    secret signs, 14
    women's participation in, 80, 272, 286, 299–302
    See also Peasants' War; *specific towns and villages*
Revolution of 1848, 32
Reynmann, Leonhard, 26 (fig.)
Reyter, Christian, 114–115
Rhegius, Urbanus, 187, 263–264
Rheinfelden, 54–55
Rheingau, 296, 364
Rhine, 38

Rhine (Rhein) river, 37, 38
Riedliingen, 354
Ries plain, 38
Robisheaux, Tom, 52
Roda, 296
Roda, Bonifacius von, 72
Rodemann, Sebastian, 82–83
Rödern Castle, 263
Rohrbach, 296
Rohrbach, Jäcklein, 61, 106–107,
    203–205, 212, 219, 223, 295,
    301–302, 306, 333
Rothenburg ob der Tauber, 135, 175,
    198–199, 208–209, 211, 231, 233,
    296, 299, 333, 337, 344–345, 353,
    373, 374
Rott, Johann, 280
Rottweil, 357
Rückert, Nicolaus, 79
Rühel, Johann, 269, 320, 321–322,
    344, 348
rumours and gossip, spread of, 218–219
'running the gauntlet,' 202 (fig.), 202,
    205–206, 228, 230, 285
Ryhiner, Heinrich, 283

Sabbata (Kesser), 354
Sacramentarianism, 71–72, 86, 109,
    322, 345, 364
Salem, 223, 289–290
salt panning, 59–60
Salza, 273
Salzburg, 57, 264, 359
Salzungen, 159, 249
Samland, 289, 350
Sangerhausen, 227
Saverne, 260, 263, 270, 310, 327–328, 350
Saxony, 38, 42, 105, 125, 135, 136, 243,
    244, 264–265, 292, 367, 372
Saxony-Anhalt, 367
Schaffhausen, 330
Schafstädt, Sophia von, 294–295
Schappeler, Christoph, 3, 112–115,
    120–121, 160, 196, 241
Scharfenstein castle, 274
Schedel, Hartmann, 11 (fig.)
Schefflenz Valley, 211
Schellenberger, 238
Schemmerberg, 192

Scheuerberg, 206
Schid, Ulrich, 119–120
Schierkner, Hans, 286
Schilling, Hans, 84
Schillingsfürst, 218, 224
Schirmer, Uwe, 50
Schlettstadt, 12, 263
Schleusingen, 157, 247, 249
Schlick, Stefan, 269, 325, 372
Schlotheim, 274, 303, 321
Schmalkalden, 90, 140, 252, 311, 373
Schmaltznapff, Hainrich, 54
Schmid, Ulrich, 91, 100, 196, 331
Schneeberg, 73, 265, 267, 268, 325
Schöntal, 185–186, 198, 200, 210, 223
Schorlitz, Andris, 218–219
Schorndorf, 13
Schulte, Hans, 131
Schussenreid, 184
Schwabach, 23
Schwäbisch Hall, 88, 186, 231, 259,
    348, 373
Schwanenberg, 359
Schwanhauser, Johannes, 354
Schwarzach band, 234
Schwarzburg, Günther XL von, 143, 274
Schwarzburg, Heinrich, 274
Schwarzburg family, 125, 245
'Schwarze Hofmännin.' See Renner,
    Margareta ('Schwarze/Black
    Hofmännin')
'Schwarz Haufen,' 217
Schwaz, 84, 263, 267
Schweinfurt, 109, 323
Schweygker, Nikolas, 280
scripture
    authority of, 94
    dreams in, 147
    'fools of,' 14
    interpretation of by laity, 70–71, 114
    Luther's use of, 3, 5
    peasants as defenders of, 19–20, 24,
        79–80, 94, 96, 179, 282
    peasant theology and, 89–94, 115
    preaching of the gospel, 21–22, 24,
        84, 101, 106, 113, 121
    primacy of, 14
    Twelve Articles' use of, 3, 17–18,
        57, 117–118

seals, 107–108
Second Landesordnung, 171
second serfdom, 49, 56–57, 375
Second Zurich Disputation, 114
secret leagues, 12
secret signs, 14
secular authority, 160–162, 349–350
seigneurialism, 52
Seitz, Alexander, 13, 26–27, 148, 164
Seitzenweiler, Hans, 206
September (Wertinger), 7 (fig.)
serfdom, 2, 5, 24, 28, 41, 49, 51, 52–56,
    88, 90, 93, 131, 187, 244, 350
servants, 133–134
Several Main Points of Christian Teaching
    (Karlstadt), 86–87
sheep farming, 64–65
Ship of Fools, The (Brant), 14
Sickingen, Franz von, 132, 167
Sigismund of Poland, 102–103
Sippel, Hans, 319
slavery, 92–93
Small Councils, 43
smelting, 60, 61, 74, 267, 372
snails, 28–29
social distinctions, 141–143
social justice, 326
social organization, 41–43, 75
Solothurn, 143, 350
Sondershausen, 275
Sontag, Mertin, 369
Sontheim, 200, 204, 301
Sonthofen, 181
Spalatin, Georg, 69, 294, 347
Spangenberg, Cyriakus, 322
Spessart, 38
Speyer, 12, 259–260, 374
spinning parlours, 99
spirit, vs flesh, 113, 150–151, 155, 162
spring, season of, 179
Stalin, Joseph, 78
St Annaberg, 137, 265, 267
Star Inn, 82
Staufen, 181
Staupitz, Johann von, 155
St Blasien Abbey, 28, 29, 30, 357
St Blasius Abby, 29–30, 33, 237
St Blasius church, 82, 104
St Clare convent, 367

Steigerwald, 38
Stein, Philip von, 221
Steinhaim, 101
Steinmetz, Max, 382–383
St Gangolf church, 354
St Georg abbey, 184–185, 232–233
St George, 268
St Georgenberg monastery, 259
St Johannszell convent, 368
St Mary church, 82, 104, 110, 256,
    271, 272
St Nikolaus church, 83, 109–110
Stockach, 196
St Odile convent, 295
Stolberg, 74–75
Stolberg, Wolfgang von, 276
Strasbourg, 37, 240, 260–263, 284–285,
    295, 327–329, 339, 348, 361, 372
Strauss, Jakob, 84–85, 199, 263, 324
strikes, 11, 51
St Trudpert monastery, 33
Stühingen, 330
Stühlingen, 28–29, 30, 33–34, 100,
    238, 332
Stumpf, Marx, 201
Sturm, Jakob, 271
Stuttgart, 13, 191, 212, 329
Sulmingen, 100–101
Sultzdorf, 334
Sundgau, 54, 297
Swabia, 38, 62, 217, 274
Swabian League, 4, 13, 40, 94, 111,
    114, 117, 121, 182, 244, 257,
    271, 306, 332
    Black Forest revolts, 190–192
    castle destruction, 224 (fig.), 225
    functions of, 129–131
    mutinies, 308
    requests for help from, 34–35, 196, 341
    truces, 197
    Ulm headquarters, 193
    Ulrich deposed by, 124–125
    Wuzach victory, 205
Swiss Reformation, 107
Switzerland, 163, 188

Tauber, Andres, 218
Tauberbischofsheim, 142
Tauber Valley, 10, 217, 226

Tauler, Johannes, 151, 155, 176
taxes, 10, 13, 15, 25, 49–50, 52, 64, 119,
    162, 191–192, 204, 357
Teistungenburg, 274
Tennstedt, 216, 221, 283
Teuschlin, Johann, 199, 296, 353
Teutonic Knights, 24, 25, 53, 54, 56,
    82, 102–105, 110, 142, 157, 198,
    200, 204–205, 210, 229, 264,
    271, 300
Teutonic Order, 103, 207, 219
Teutscher nation notturft, 167
Textor, Johannes, 25
Thirty-One Points of Christian Doctrine
    (Lotzer), 113
Thirty Years' War, 238
Thompson, E. P., 386
Three Peasants in Conversation (Dürer),
    44 (fig.), 44
thresholds, symbolic meaning of, 216
Thunfeld, Conrad von, 10
Thuringia, 38, 40, 105, 233, 243–245,
    257, 264, 274, 292, 296, 319, 367
tithes
    condemnation of, 114, 119
    Lenten hen, 11, 28, 53, 115
    Luther on, 187
    paid by peasants, 10, 21, 25, 27–28,
        31, 51, 91, 119
    priests supported by, 27, 85
    types of, 55–56
    uses of, 85
Torgau, 292
To the Assembly of the Common Peasantry
    (*An die Versammlung*), 160, 161–165,
    164 (fig.), 174, 176, 261, 290–291,
    302, 359
To the Christian Nobility (Luther),
    16–17, 160
towns, 135–136, 211, 219–220, 233–235,
    289, 358, 373–374
treaties, 142, 253, 357–358
Trier, 132
Trithemius, Johannes, 14
Trockau, Michael Gross von, 143, 340
Truchsess Georg. *See* Waldburg, Georg von
    ('Bauernjörg')
Tübingen, 181
Tübke, Werner, 383–384

Twelve Articles, 3, 18, 57, 88, 89, 115,
    119–121, 144, 159, 170, 180, 211,
    216, 245, 246, 259, 276, 281,
    371, 388
tyranny, 162–163, 377
Tyrol, 171, 263, 264, 265, 358, 372
Tyrolean Alps, 108

Uffenheim, 337
Ulbrich, Claudia, 212
Ulm, 101, 192, 193–195, 372
Ulrich, Duke of Württemberg, 13, 15, 124,
    130, 190–192, 203, 240, 305, 368
Ulrich of Rappolstein, 127, 130
Ummendorf, 131
Underweysung der Messung, 362 (fig.)
University of Leipzig, 76
Upper Germany, 38
Upper Swabia, 62, 64, 88, 114, 134, 160,
    180, 196, 197–198, 209, 211, 365
uprisings. *See* revolts and uprisings
usury, 30, 31, 84–85, 199, 296, 297
utopianism, 156, 364, 389

Vacha, 230, 250–251, 252
Vessra, 228–229
villages, 41–43
Villingen, 125, 192, 195–196, 217,
    219, 341–342
Vindelicien, 38
Vindication and Refutation (Müntzer), 109
Virdung, Johann, 25
Virgil, 43
Virgin Mary
    excluded from Peasants' War, 241, 388
    featured on banners, 15
    icon at Mallerbach chapel, 80
    'Maria im Nesselbusch' pilgrimage
        site, 206
    Niklashausen shrine to, 10, 241, 256
    protectress of the castle, 341
    Regensburg chapel to, 30, 188, 199, 296
    visions of, 7 (fig.), 10–11
Vischer, Peter, 22 (fig.)
visions. *See* dreams and visions
Vogler, Günter, 382, 384
Vöhrenbach, 285
Volckamer, Clemens, 101, 271
Volkmaner, Conrad, 299

Vollcyr, Nicolas, 308
Vollrath, Georg, 369
Von Milterung der Fürsten (Brenz), 348 (fig.)

Wagenburg, 277, 320
Waiblingen, Rudolf von, 252
Waldburg, Georg von ('Bauernjörg'), 4,
    130–131, 182, 190–192, 195–196,
    212, 227, 236, 243–244, 283, 305,
    308, 329–332, 339, 357
Waldshut, 29–31, 33–34, 84, 100,
    107–108, 109, 125, 179, 188–190,
    299, 350–351, 353, 357
Walkenried, 275
Walpurgisnacht, 10
Waltershofen, 94
Wanbach, Heintz von, 249
Wanner, Christian, 359
warfare, 132
Wartburg, 68
water resources, 61
weapons, 306–307, 326–327, 369
weather and climate, 40
weaving industry, 63–64
Wehe, Jakob, 192–195, 298, 324, 369
Weigandt, Friedrich, 167–168, 174
Weiler, Dietrich von, 201
Weingarten, 180–182, 196, 197, 243
Weinsberg, 201–207, 203 (fig.), 214, 217,
    219, 230, 246, 286, 301, 332–333
Weissenau, 180–182, 184, 217, 263,
    292, 339
Weissenbourg, 263
Welner, Hans, 230
Wendelstein, 23
Werdenstein, Georg von, 309, 311
Werra band, 217, 245, 246, 257, 275
Wertinger, Hans
    December, 97 (fig.)
    June, 317
    March, 177 (fig.)
    September, 7 (fig.)
West Germany, 378, 384–385
Wettenhausen, 101, 116
Wettich, Johannes, 82–83
Wetzel, Johann, 183–184
Wildenburg, 211
Wilhelm of Honstein, 211
Wilpurger, Jos, 221

Wimpfen, 219
Windsheim, 300, 374
wine, 17, 18, 27, 38, 64, 182, 207, 231,
    244, 247, 363
winter, season of, 40, 99–100
witch hunts, 375
Wittenberg
    Castle Church, 16
    local government, 135
    monastery at, 23
    Reformation implementation, 68
Witzel, Georg, 324
women
    absent from images of war, 279
    clothing of, 280, 281
    dreams and visions of, 156
    excluded from brotherhood, 279, 289,
        291, 299, 386
    grievances of, 120
    humiliation of Wilhelm's wife, 254
    lack of voice in Gemeinde, 42, 174
    Leibeigenschaft system and, 52–54
    mining industry role, 74
    Müntzer and spiritual views of, 151
    nuns, 23, 24, 79, 100–101, 125–126,
        129, 131, 136, 148, 179, 189,
        210, 223, 231, 265–266, 291–292,
        294–295, 302–303, 310,
        353, 367–368
    ordered to summon men
        home, 355–356
    participation in revolts, 80, 272, 286,
        299–302, 303–304
    peace agreements, 314
    punishment of Leipheim's, 195, 299
    radicalization of, 109, 207
    rape and assault of, 309–310, 327, 328
    role of in early Reformation, 31–32
wood resources, 59–60
Worbis, 274
works, freedom and, 85–86
World War II, 378, 385
Worms, 259
Wunderer, Hans, 212, 240
Wunnenstein, 212
Württemberg
    challenges to authority in, 11
    correspondence network, 139–140
    crops, 38

landlord-peasant relations, 51
peace agreements, 243
peasant mobilization, 217
revolts, 13, 14, 15, 124, 180
secularization of monasteries, 368
Wurzach, 195, 239, 243
Würzburg
  army provisions, 233–234
  atrocities, 335, 360
  in *Chronicle of the World* woodcut,
    11 (fig.)
  correspondence network, 139
  council tree, 366
  crops, 38
  Drummer of Niklashausen's march to,
    10–11, 14, 222
  peasant mobilization, 217, 226–227,
    228, 233–235
  revolt, 10–11, 34, 319, 373
  storming of the castle in, 256–258
  support for peasants in, 209
  town council, 339–340

Zasius, Ulrich, 329
Zeiß, Hans, 79–81, 134, 226, 275,
  294–295, 326, 371
Zell, 196, 330, 332
Zell, Katharina Schütz, 364
Zell, Matthäus, 262, 364
Ziegler, Clemens, 260, 364
Ziegler, Ludwig, 260
Zimmerman, Wilhelm, 378–379
Zimmern, 105–106
Zurich, 30, 35, 114, 237, 350–351
Zweifel, Thomas, 340
Zwick, Johannes, 354
Zwickau, 25, 76–77, 140, 265, 281
Zwiefalten, 65
Zwingli, Huldrych
  Hubmaier and, 107, 351, 364
  ideas of godly justice, 118–119, 385
  influence of, 3, 30, 114, 352, 385
  understanding of peasants' grievances, 35
  views on the Eucharist, 71, 86
Zwinglianism, 72, 86, 376

LYNDAL ROPER is Regius Professor of History at the University of Oxford, the first woman to hold the post. Her previous books include *Martin Luther* and *Witch Craze*. She is a fellow of the British Academy, a fellow of the Australian Academy of the Humanities, and a fellow of the Berlin-Brandenburgische Akademie der Wissenschaften. She lives in Oxford, South Wales, and Berlin.